D0802586

Collins World Atlas

MINI EDITION

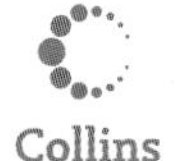

Collins

COLLINS WORLD ATLAS
MINI EDITION

Collins
An imprint of HarperCollins Publishers
77–85 Fulham Palace Road
London
W6 8JB

First Published as Collins Mini Atlas of the World 1999
Second edition 2004
Third Edition 2007

Fourth Edition 2009

Copyright © HarperCollins Publishers 2009
Maps © Collins Bartholomew Ltd 2009

Printed by Imago in Singapore

British Library Cataloguing in Publication Data.
A catalogue record for this book is available from the British Library.

ISBN 978-0-00-728906-6

All mapping in this atlas is generated from Collins
Bartholomew™ digital databases. Collins Bartholomew™,
the UK's leading independent geographical information
supplier, can provide a digital, custom, and premium
mapping service to a variety of markets.
For further information:
Tel: +44 (0) 306 3752
e-mail: collinsbartholomew@harpercollins.co.uk

We also offer a choice of books, atlases and maps that
can be customized to suit a customer's own requirements.
For further information:
Tel +44 (0) 1242 258155
e-mail: business.gifts@harpercollins.co.uk

or visit our website at: www.collinsbartholomew.com

Pages	Title	Scale

GEOGRAPHICAL INFORMATION

6–19	**COUNTRIES** of the **WORLD**	
20–21	**OCEANIA PHYSICAL** Features	
22–23	**ASIA PHYSICAL** Features	
24–25	**EUROPE PHYSICAL** Features	
26–27	**AFRICA PHYSICAL** Features	
28–29	**NORTH AMERICA** Physical Features	
30–31	**SOUTH AMERICA** Physical Features	
32–33	**OCEANS** and **POLES** Physical Features	
34–35	**CLIMATE**	
36–37	**LAND COVER**	
38–39	**POPULATION**	
40–41	**URBANIZATION**	
42–43	**SYMBOLS** and **ABBREVIATIONS**	

WORLD

44–45	**WORLD** Physical Features	1:170 000 000
46–47	**WORLD** Countries	1:170 000 000

OCEANIA — 1:70 000 000

48–49	**OCEANIA**	1:70 000 000
50–51	**AUSTRALIA**	1:25 000 000
52–53	**AUSTRALIA** Southeast	1:10 000 000
54	**NEW ZEALAND**	1:10 000 000

ANTARCTICA — 1:60 000 000

55	**ANTARCTICA**	1:60 000 000

ASIA — 1:70 000 000

56–57	**ASIA**	1:70 000 000
58–59	**SOUTHEAST ASIA**	1:30 000 000
60–61	**MALAYSIA** and **INDONESIA** West	1:15 000 000
62–63	**CONTINENTAL SOUTHEAST ASIA**	1:15 000 000
64	**PHILIPPINES**	1:15 000 000

CONTENTS

Pages	Title	Scale
65	**NORTH KOREA** AND **SOUTH KOREA**	1:9 000 000
66–67	**JAPAN**	1:10 000 000
68–69	**CHINA** AND **MONGOLIA**	1:30 000 000
70–71	**CHINA** Central	1:15 000 000
72–73	**SOUTH ASIA**	1:20 000 000
74–75	**PAKISTAN, INDIA** AND **BANGLADESH**	1:15 000 000
76–77	**CENTRAL ASIA**	1:20 000 000
78–79	**ARABIAN PENINSULA**	1:15 000 000
80–81	**EAST MEDITERRANEAN**	1:15 000 000
82–83	**RUSSIAN FEDERATION**	1:42 000 000
84–85	EUROPE	1:40 000 000
86–87	**EUROPEAN RUSSIAN FEDERATION**	1:20 000 000
88–89	**NORTHEAST EUROPE**	1:8 000 000
90–91	**UKRAINE** AND **MOLDOVA**	1:8 000 000
92–93	**SCANDINAVIA** AND **ICELAND**	1:10 000 000
94–95	**BRITISH ISLES**	1:8 000 000
96	**SCOTLAND**	1:4 000 000
97	**IRELAND**	1:4 000 000
98–99	**ENGLAND** AND **WALES**	1:4 000 000
100–101	**NORTHWEST EUROPE**	1:4 000 000
102–103	**CENTRAL EUROPE**	1:8 000 000
104–105	**FRANCE** AND **SWITZERLAND**	1:8 000 000
106–107	**SPAIN** AND **PORTUGAL**	1:8 000 000
108–109	**ITALY** AND **THE BALKANS**	1:8 000 000
110–111	**GREECE, ROMANIA** AND **BULGARIA**	1:8 000 000
112–113	AFRICA	1:60 000 000
114–115	**NORTHWEST AFRICA**	1:26 000 000

CONTENTS

Pages	Title	Scale
116–117	**NORTHEAST AFRICA**	1:26 000 000
118–119	**CENTRAL AFRICA**	1:20 000 000
120–121	**SOUTHERN AFRICA**	1:20 000 000
122–123	**REPUBLIC OF SOUTH AFRICA**	1:10 000 000
124–125	NORTH AMERICA	1:70 000 000
126–127	**CANADA**	1:30 000 000
128–129	**CANADA** West	1:15 000 000
130–131	**CANADA** East	1:15 000 000
132–133	**UNITED STATES OF AMERICA**	1:25 000 000
134–135	**USA** West	1:11 000 000
136–137	**USA** North Central	1:11 000 000
138–139	**USA** South Central	1:11 000 000
140–141	**USA** Northeast	1:11 000 000
142–143	**USA** Southeast	1:11 000 000
144–145	**MEXICO**	1:15 000 000
146–147	**CARIBBEAN**	1:20 000 000
148–149	SOUTH AMERICA	1:70 000 000
150–151	**SOUTH AMERICA** North	1:25 000 000
152–153	**SOUTH AMERICA** South	1:25 000 000
154–155	**BRAZIL** Southeast	1:10 000 000
	OCEANS	
156–157	**PACIFIC OCEAN**	1:120 000 000
158	**ATLANTIC OCEAN**	1:120 000 000
159	**INDIAN OCEAN**	1:120 000 000
160	**ARCTIC OCEAN**	1:60 000 000
161–256	INDEX	

AFGHANISTAN
Islamic State of Afghanistan
Capital Kābul

Area sq km	652 225	**Currency** Afghani
Area sq miles	251 825	**Languages** Dari, Pushtu,
Population	27 145 000	Uzbek, Turkmen

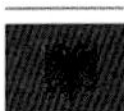

ALBANIA
Republic of Albania
Capital Tirana (Tiranë)

Area sq km	28 748	**Currency** Lek
Area sq miles	11 100	**Languages** Albanian, Greek
Population	3 190 000	

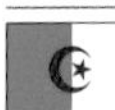

ALGERIA
People's Democratic Republic of Algeria
Capital Algiers (Alger)

Area sq km	2 381 741	**Currency** Algerian dinar
Area sq miles	919 595	**Languages** Arabic, French,
Population	33 858 000	Berber

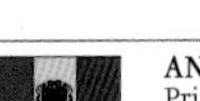

ANDORRA
Principality of Andorra
Capital Andorra la Vella

Area sq km	465	**Currency** Euro
Area sq miles	180	**Languages** Spanish,
Population	75 000	Catalan, French

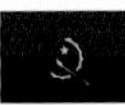

ANGOLA
Republic of Angola
Capital Luanda

Area sq km	1 246 700	**Currency** Kwanza
Area sq miles	481 354	**Languages** Portuguese,
Population	17 024 000	Bantu, local lang.

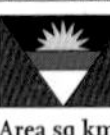

ANTIGUA AND BARBUDA
Capital St John's

Area sq km	442	**Currency** East Caribbean
Area sq miles	171	dollar
Population	85 000	**Languages** English, creole

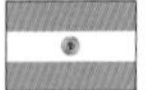

ARGENTINA
Argentine Republic
Capital Buenos Aires

Area sq km	2 766 889	**Currency** Argentinian peso
Area sq miles	1 068 302	**Languages** Spanish, Italian,
Population	39 531 000	Amerindian lang.

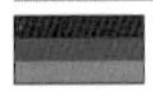

ARMENIA
Republic of Armenia
Capital Yerevan (Erevan)

Area sq km	29 800	**Currency** Dram
Area sq miles	11 506	**Languages** Armenian, Azeri
Population	3 002 000	

AUSTRALIA
Commonwealth of Australia
Capital Canberra

Area sq km	7 692 024	**Currency** Australian dolla
Area sq miles	2 969 907	**Languages** English, Italian
Population	20 743 000	Greek

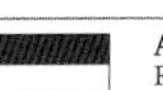

AUSTRIA
Republic of Austria
Capital Vienna (Wien)

Area sq km	83 855	**Currency** Euro
Area sq miles	32 377	**Languages** German,
Population	8 361 000	Croatian, Turkis

AZERBAIJAN
Republic of Azerbaijan
Capital Baku (Bakı)

Area sq km	86 600	**Currency** Azerbaijani mar
Area sq miles	33 436	**Languages** Azeri, Armeniar
Population	8 467 000	Russian, Lezgiar

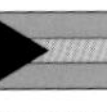

THE BAHAMAS
Commonwealth of The Bahamas
Capital Nassau

Area sq km	13 939	**Currency** Bahamian dolla
Area sq miles	5 382	**Languages** English, creole
Population	331 000	

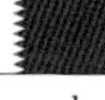

BAHRAIN
Kingdom of Bahrain
Capital Manama (Al Manāmah)

Area sq km	691	**Currency** Bahraini dinar
Area sq miles	267	**Languages** Arabic, English
Population	753 000	

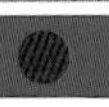

BANGLADESH
People's Republic of Bangladesh
Capital Dhaka (Dacca)

Area sq km	143 998	**Currency** Taka
Area sq miles	55 598	**Languages** Bengali, English
Population	158 665 000	

BARBADOS
Capital Bridgetown

Area sq km	430	**Currency** Barbados dollar
Area sq miles	166	**Languages** English, creole
Population	294 000	

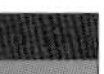

BELARUS
Republic of Belarus
Capital Minsk

Area sq km	207 600	**Currency**	Belarus rouble
Area sq miles	80 155	**Languages**	Belorussian,
Population	9 689 000		Russian

BELGIUM
Kingdom of Belgium
Capital Brussels (Bruxelles)

Area sq km	30 520	**Currency**	Euro
Area sq miles	11 784	**Languages**	Dutch (Flemish),
Population	10 457 000		French (Walloon),
			German

BELIZE
Capital Belmopan

Area sq km	22 965	**Currency**	Belize dollar
Area sq miles	8 867	**Languages**	English, Spanish,
Population	288 000		Mayan, creole

BENIN
Republic of Benin
Capital Porto-Novo

Area sq km	112 620	**Currency**	CFA franc*
Area sq miles	43 483	**Languages**	French, Fon,
Population	9 033 000		Yoruba, Adja,
			local lang.

BHUTAN
Kingdom of Bhutan
Capital Thimphu

Area sq km	46 620	**Currency**	Ngultrum,
Area sq miles	18 000		Indian rupee
Population	658 000	**Languages**	Dzongkha,
			Nepali, Assamese

BOLIVIA
Republic of Bolivia
Capital La Paz/Sucre

Area sq km	1 098 581	**Currency**	Boliviano
Area sq miles	424 164	**Languages**	Spanish, Quechua,
Population	9 525 000		Aymara

BOSNIA-HERZEGOVINA
Republic of Bosnia and Herzegovina
Capital Sarajevo

Area sq km	51 130	**Currency**	Marka
Area sq miles	19 741	**Languages**	Bosnian, Serbian,
Population	3 935 000		Croatian

BOTSWANA
Republic of Botswana
Capital Gaborone

Area sq km	581 370	**Currency**	Pula
Area sq miles	224 468	**Languages**	English, Setswana,
Population	1 882 000		Shona, local lang.

BRAZIL
Federative Republic of Brazil
Capital Brasília

Area sq km	8 514 879	**Currency**	Real
Area sq miles	3 287 613	**Languages**	Portuguese
Population	191 791 000		

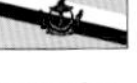

BRUNEI
State of Brunei Darussalam
Capital Bandar Seri Begawan

Area sq km	5 765	**Currency**	Brunei dollar
Area sq miles	2 226	**Languages**	Malay, English,
Population	390 000		Chinese

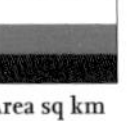

BULGARIA
Republic of Bulgaria
Capital Sofia (Sofiya)

Area sq km	110 994	**Currency**	Lev
Area sq miles	42 855	**Languages**	Bulgarian,
Population	7 639 000		Turkish, Romany,
			Macedonian

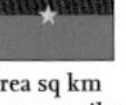

BURKINA
Democratic Republic of Burkina Faso
Capital Ouagadougou

Area sq km	274 200	**Currency**	CFA franc*
Area sq miles	105 869	**Languages**	French, Moore
Population	14 784 000		(Mossi), Fulani,
			local lang.

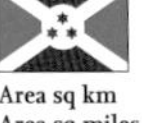

BURUNDI
Republic of Burundi
Capital Bujumbura

Area sq km	27 835	**Currency**	Burundian franc
Area sq miles	10 747	**Languages**	Kirundi (Hutu,
Population	8 508 000		Tutsi), French

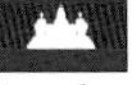

CAMBODIA
Kingdom of Cambodia
Capital Phnom Penh

Area sq km	181 035	**Currency**	Riel
Area sq miles	69 884	**Languages**	Khmer,
Population	14 444 000		Vietnamese

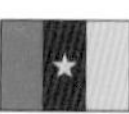

CAMEROON
Republic of Cameroon
Capital Yaoundé

Area sq km	475 442	**Currency**	CFA franc*
Area sq miles	183 569	**Languages**	French, English,
Population	18 549 000		Fang, Bamileke, local lang.

COLOMBIA
Republic of Colombia
Capital Bogotá

Area sq km	1 141 748	**Currency**	Colombian pes
Area sq miles	440 831	**Languages**	Spanish,
Population	46 156 000		Amerindian la

CANADA
Capital Ottawa

Area sq km	9 984 670	**Currency**	Canadian dollar
Area sq miles	3 855 103	**Languages**	English, French
Population	32 876 000		

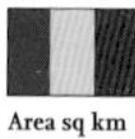

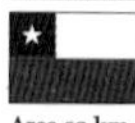

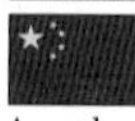

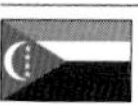

COMOROS
Union of the Comoros
Capital Moroni

Area sq km	1 862	**Currency**	Comoros franc
Area sq miles	719	**Languages**	Comorian,
Population	839 000		French, Arabic

CAPE VERDE
Republic of Cape Verde
Capital Praia

Area sq km	4 033	**Currency**	Cape Verde
Area sq miles	1 557		escudo
Population	530 000	**Languages**	Portuguese, creole

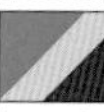

CONGO
Republic of the Congo
Capital Brazzaville

Area sq km	342 000	**Currency**	CFA franc*
Area sq miles	132 047	**Languages**	French, Kongo,
Population	3 768 000		Monokutuba, local lang.

CENTRAL AFRICAN REPUBLIC
Capital Bangui

Area sq km	622 436	**Currency**	CFA franc*
Area sq miles	240 324	**Languages**	French, Sango,
Population	4 343 000		Banda, Baya, local lang.

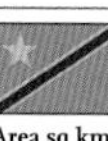

CONGO, DEMOCRATIC REPUBLIC OF THE
Capital Kinshasa

Area sq km	2 345 410	**Currency**	Congolese fran
Area sq miles	905 568	**Languages**	French, Lingala
Population	62 636 000		Swahili, Kongo, local lang.

CHAD
Republic of Chad
Capital Ndjamena

Area sq km	1 284 000	**Currency**	CFA franc*
Area sq miles	495 755	**Languages**	Arabic, French,
Population	10 781 000		Sara, local lang.

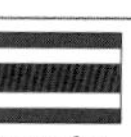

COSTA RICA
Republic of Costa Rica
Capital San José

Area sq km	51 100	**Currency**	Costa Rican col
Area sq miles	19 730	**Languages**	Spanish
Population	4 468 000		

CHILE
Republic of Chile
Capital Santiago

Area sq km	756 945	**Currency**	Chilean peso
Area sq miles	292 258	**Languages**	Spanish,
Population	16 635 000		Amerindian lang.

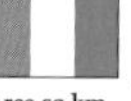

CÔTE D'IVOIRE
Republic of Côte d'Ivoire
Capital Yamoussoukro

Area sq km	322 463	**Currency**	CFA franc*
Area sq miles	124 504	**Languages**	French, creole,
Population	19 262 000		Akan, local lang

CHINA
People's Republic of China
Capital Beijing (Peking)

Area sq km	9 584 492	**Currency**	Yuan, HK dollar,
Area sq miles	3 700 593		Macao pataca
Population	1 313 437 000	**Languages**	Mandarin, Hsiang, Cantonese, Wu, regional lang.

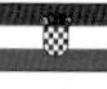

CROATIA
Republic of Croatia
Capital Zagreb

Area sq km	56 538	**Currency**	Kuna
Area sq miles	21 829	**Languages**	Croatian, Serbia
Population	4 555 000		

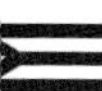

CUBA
Republic of Cuba
Capital Havana (La Habana)

Area sq km	110 860	**Currency**	Cuban peso
Area sq miles	42 803	**Languages**	Spanish
Population	11 268 000		

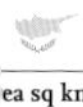

CYPRUS
Republic of Cyprus
Capital Nicosia (Lefkosia)

Area sq km	9 251	**Currency**	Euro
Area sq miles	3 572	**Languages**	Greek, Turkish,
Population	855 000		English

CZECH REPUBLIC
Capital Prague (Praha)

Area sq km	78 864	**Currency**	Czech koruna
Area sq miles	30 450	**Languages**	Czech, Moravian,
Population	10 186 000		Slovak

DENMARK
Kingdom of Denmark
Capital Copenhagen (København)

Area sq km	43 075	**Currency**	Danish krone
Area sq miles	16 631	**Languages**	Danish
Population	5 442 000		

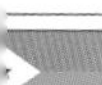

DJIBOUTI
Republic of Djibouti
Capital Djibouti

Area sq km	23 200	**Currency**	Djibouti franc
Area sq miles	8 958	**Languages**	Somali, Afar,
Population	833 000		French, Arabic

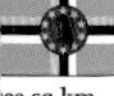

DOMINICA
Commonwealth of Dominica
Capital Roseau

Area sq km	750	**Currency**	East Caribbean
Area sq miles	290		dollar
Population	67 000	**Languages**	English, creole

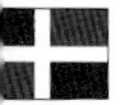

DOMINICAN REPUBLIC
Capital Santo Domingo

Area sq km	48 442	**Currency**	Dominican peso
Area sq miles	18 704	**Languages**	Spanish, creole
Population	9 760 000		

EAST TIMOR
Democratic Republic of Timor-Leste
Capital Dili

Area sq km	14 874	**Currency**	US dollar
Area sq miles	5 743	**Languages**	Portuguese, Tetun,
Population	1 155 000		English

ECUADOR
Republic of Ecuador
Capital Quito

Area sq km	272 045	**Currency**	US dollar
Area sq miles	105 037	**Languages**	Spanish, Quechua,
Population	13 341 000		and other
			Amerindian lang.

EGYPT
Arab Republic of Egypt
Capital Cairo (Al Qāhirah)

Area sq km	1 000 250	**Currency**	Egyptian pound
Area sq miles	386 199	**Languages**	Arabic
Population	75 498 000		

EL SALVADOR
Republic of El Salvador
Capital San Salvador

Area sq km	21 041	**Currency**	El Salvador colón,
Area sq miles	8 124		US dollar
Population	6 857 000	**Languages**	Spanish

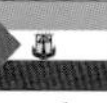

EQUATORIAL GUINEA
Republic of Equatorial Guinea
Capital Malabo

Area sq km	28 051	**Currency**	CFA franc*
Area sq miles	10 831	**Languages**	Spanish, French,
Population	507 000		Fang

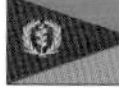

ERITREA
State of Eritrea
Capital Asmara

Area sq km	117 400	**Currency**	Nakfa
Area sq miles	45 328	**Languages**	Tigrinya, Tigre
Population	4 851 000		

ESTONIA
Republic of Estonia
Capital Tallinn

Area sq km	45 200	**Currency**	Kroon
Area sq miles	17 452	**Languages**	Estonian, Russian
Population	1 335 000		

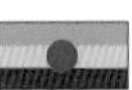

ETHIOPIA
Federal Democratic Republic of Ethiopia
Capital Addis Ababa (Ādīs Ābeba)

Area sq km	1 133 880	**Currency** Birr
Area sq miles	437 794	**Languages** Oromo, Amharic,
Population	83 099 000	Tigrinya,
		local lang.

FIJI
Sovereign Democratic Republic of Fiji
Capital Suva

Area sq km	18 330	**Currency** Fiji dollar
Area sq miles	7 077	**Languages** English, Fijian,
Population	839 000	Hindi

FINLAND
Republic of Finland
Capital Helsinki (Helsingfors)

Area sq km	338 145	**Currency** Euro
Area sq miles	130 559	**Languages** Finnish, Swedish
Population	5 277 000	

FRANCE
French Republic
Capital Paris

Area sq km	543 965	**Currency** Euro
Area sq miles	210 026	**Languages** French, Arabic
Population	61 647 000	

GABON
Gabonese Republic
Capital Libreville

Area sq km	267 667	**Currency** CFA franc*
Area sq miles	103 347	**Languages** French, Fang,
Population	1 331 000	local lang.

THE GAMBIA
Republic of The Gambia
Capital Banjul

Area sq km	11 295	**Currency** Dalasi
Area sq miles	4 361	**Languages** English, Malinke,
Population	1 709 000	Fulani, Wolof

Gaza
semi-autonomous region
Capital Gaza

Area sq km	363	**Currency** Israeli shekel
Area sq miles	140	**Languages** Arabic
Population	1 586 008	

GEORGIA
Republic of Georgia
Capital T'bilisi

Area sq km	69 700	**Currency** Lari
Area sq miles	26 911	**Languages** Georgian, Russ
Population	4 395 000	Armenian, Azer
		Ossetian, Abkh

GERMANY
Federal Republic of Germany
Capital Berlin

Area sq km	357 022	**Currency** Euro
Area sq miles	137 849	**Languages** German, Turkis
Population	82 599 000	

GHANA
Republic of Ghana
Capital Accra

Area sq km	238 537	**Currency** Cedi
Area sq miles	92 100	**Languages** English, Hausa
Population	23 478 000	Akan, local lan

GREECE
Hellenic Republic
Capital Athens (Athina)

Area sq km	131 957	**Currency** Euro
Area sq miles	50 949	**Languages** Greek
Population	11 147 000	

GRENADA
Capital St George's

Area sq km	378	**Currency** East Caribbean
Area sq miles	146	dollar
Population	106 000	**Languages** English, creole

GUATEMALA
Republic of Guatemala
Capital Guatemala City

Area sq km	108 890	**Currency** Quetzal, US do
Area sq miles	42 043	**Languages** Spanish,
Population	13 354 000	Mayan lang.

GUINEA
Republic of Guinea
Capital Conakry

Area sq km	245 857	**Currency** Guinea franc
Area sq miles	94 926	**Languages** French, Fulani,
Population	9 370 000	Malinke,
		local lang.

GUINEA-BISSAU
Republic of Guinea-Bissau
Capital Bissau

Area sq km	36 125	**Currency**	CFA franc*
Area sq miles	13 948	**Languages**	Portuguese,
Population	1 695 000		crioulo, local lang.

GUYANA
Co-operative Republic of Guyana
Capital Georgetown

Area sq km	214 969	**Currency**	Guyana dollar
Area sq miles	83 000	**Languages**	English, creole,
Population	738 000		Amerindian lang.

HAITI
Republic of Haiti
Capital Port-au-Prince

Area sq km	27 750	**Currency**	Gourde
Area sq miles	10 714	**Languages**	French, creole
Population	9 598 000		

HONDURAS
Republic of Honduras
Capital Tegucigalpa

Area sq km	112 088	**Currency**	Lempira
Area sq miles	43 277	**Languages**	Spanish,
Population	7 106 000		Amerindian lang.

HUNGARY
Republic of Hungary
Capital Budapest

Area sq km	93 030	**Currency**	Forint
Area sq miles	35 919	**Languages**	Hungarian
Population	10 030 000		

ICELAND
Republic of Iceland
Capital Reykjavík

Area sq km	102 820	**Currency**	Icelandic króna
Area sq miles	39 699	**Languages**	Icelandic
Population	301 000		

INDIA
Republic of India
Capital New Delhi

Area sq km	3 064 898	**Currency**	Indian rupee
Area sq miles	1 183 364	**Languages**	Hindi, English,
Population	1 169 016 000		many regional lang.

INDONESIA
Republic of Indonesia
Capital Jakarta

Area sq km	1 919 445	**Currency**	Rupiah
Area sq miles	741 102	**Languages**	Indonesian,
Population	231 627 000		local lang.

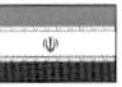

IRAN
Islamic Republic of Iran
Capital Tehrän

Area sq km	1 648 000	**Currency**	Iranian rial
Area sq miles	636 296	**Languages**	Farsi, Azeri,
Population	71 208 000		Kurdish, regional lang.

IRAQ
Republic of Iraq
Capital Baghdäd

Area sq km	438 317	**Currency**	Iraqi dinar
Area sq miles	169 235	**Languages**	Arabic, Kurdish,
Population	28 993 000		Turkmen

IRELAND
Republic of Ireland
Capital Dublin (Baile Átha Cliath)

Area sq km	70 282	**Currency**	Euro
Area sq miles	27 136	**Languages**	English, Irish
Population	4 301 000		

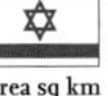

ISRAEL
State of Israel
Capital Jerusalem* (Yerushalayim) (El Quds)

Area sq km	20 770	**Currency**	Shekel
Area sq miles	8 019	**Languages**	Hebrew, Arabic
Population	6 928 000		

* De facto capital. Disputed.

ITALY
Italian Republic
Capital Rome (Roma)

Area sq km	301 245	**Currency**	Euro
Area sq miles	116 311	**Languages**	Italian
Population	58 877 000		

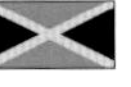

JAMAICA
Capital Kingston

Area sq km	10 991	**Currency**	Jamaican dollar
Area sq miles	4 244	**Languages**	English, creole
Population	2 714 000		

Jammu and Kashmir
Disputed territory (India/Pakistan/China)
Capital Srinagar

Area sq km	222 236	
Area sq miles	85 806	
Population	13 000 000	

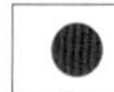

JAPAN
Capital Tōkyō

Area sq km	377 727	**Currency** Yen
Area sq miles	145 841	**Languages** Japanese
Population	127 967 000	

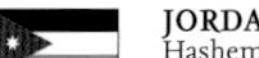

JORDAN
Hashemite Kingdom of Jordan
Capital 'Ammān

Area sq km	89 206	**Currency** Jordanian dinar
Area sq miles	34 443	**Languages** Arabic
Population	5 924 000	

KAZAKHSTAN
Republic of Kazakhstan
Capital Astana (Akmola)

Area sq km	2 717 300	**Currency** Tenge
Area sq miles	1 049 155	**Languages** Kazakh, Russian, Ukrainian, German, Uzbek, Tatar
Population	15 422 000	

KENYA
Republic of Kenya
Capital Nairobi

Area sq km	582 646	**Currency** Kenyan shilling
Area sq miles	224 961	**Languages** Swahili, English, local lang.
Population	37 538 000	

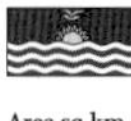

KIRIBATI
Republic of Kiribati
Capital Bairiki

Area sq km	717	**Currency** Australian dollar
Area sq miles	277	**Languages** Gilbertese, English
Population	95 000	

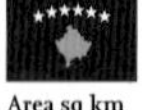

KOSOVO
Republic of Kosovo
Capital Prishtinë (Priština)

Area sq km	10 908	**Currency** Euro
Area sq miles	4 212	**Languages** Albanian, Serbian
Population	2 070 000	

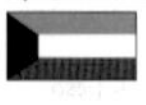

KUWAIT
State of Kuwait
Capital Kuwait (Al Kuwayt)

Area sq km	17 818	**Currency** Kuwaiti dinar
Area sq miles	6 880	**Languages** Arabic
Population	2 851 000	

KYRGYZSTAN
Kyrgyz Republic
Capital Bishkek (Frunze)

Area sq km	198 500	**Currency** Kyrgyz som
Area sq miles	76 641	**Languages** Kyrgyz, Russian, Uzbek
Population	5 317 000	

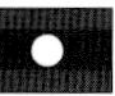

LAOS
Lao People's Democratic Republic
Capital Vientiane (Viangchan)

Area sq km	236 800	**Currency** Kip
Area sq miles	91 429	**Languages** Lao, local lang.
Population	5 859 000	

LATVIA
Republic of Latvia
Capital Rīga

Area sq km	63 700	**Currency** Lats
Area sq miles	24 595	**Languages** Latvian, Russian
Population	2 277 000	

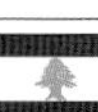

LEBANON
Republic of Lebanon
Capital Beirut (Beyrouth)

Area sq km	10 452	**Currency** Lebanese pound
Area sq miles	4 036	**Languages** Arabic, Armenian, French
Population	4 099 000	

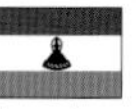

LESOTHO
Kingdom of Lesotho
Capital Maseru

Area sq km	30 355	**Currency** Loti, S. African rand
Area sq miles	11 720	**Languages** Sesotho, English, Zulu
Population	2 008 000	

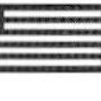

LIBERIA
Republic of Liberia
Capital Monrovia

Area sq km	111 369	**Currency** Liberian dollar
Area sq miles	43 000	**Languages** English, creole, local lang.
Population	3 750 000	

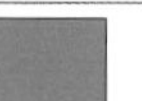

LIBYA
Great Socialist People's Libyan Arab Jamahiriya
Capital Tripoli (Ṭarābulus)

Area sq km	1 759 540	**Currency** Libyan dinar
Area sq miles	679 362	**Languages** Arabic, Berber
Population	6 160 000	

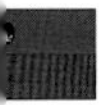

LIECHTENSTEIN
Principality of Liechtenstein
Capital Vaduz

		Currency	Swiss franc
a sq km	160	Languages	German
a sq miles	62		
ulation	35 000		

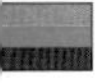

LITHUANIA
Republic of Lithuania
Capital Vilnius

		Currency	Litas
a sq km	65 200	Languages	Lithuanian,
a sq miles	25 174		Russian, Polish
ulation	3 390 000		

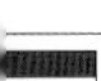

LUXEMBOURG
Grand Duchy of Luxembourg
Capital Luxembourg

		Currency	Euro
a sq km	2 586	Languages	Letzeburgish,
a sq miles	998		German, French
ulation	467 000		

MACEDONIA (F.Y.R.O.M.)
Republic of Macedonia
Capital Skopje

		Currency	Macedonian denar
a sq km	25 713	Languages	Macedonian,
a sq miles	9 928		Albanian, Turkish
ulation	2 038 000		

MADAGASCAR
Republic of Madagascar
Capital Antananarivo

		Currency	Malagasy franc
a sq km	587 041		Malagasy Ariary
a sq miles	226 658		
ulation	19 683 000	Languages	Malagasy, French

MALAWI
Republic of Malawi
Capital Lilongwe

		Currency	Malawian kwacha
a sq km	118 484	Languages	Chichewa,
a sq miles	45 747		English, local lang.
ulation	13 925 000		

MALAYSIA
Federation of Malaysia
Capital Kuala Lumpur/Putrajaya

		Currency	Ringgit
a sq km	332 965	Languages	Malay, English,
a sq miles	128 559		Chinese, Tamil,
ulation	26 572 000		local lang.

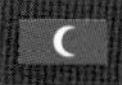

MALDIVES
Republic of the Maldives
Capital Male

		Currency	Rufiyaa
Area sq km	298	Languages	Divehi
Area sq miles	115		(Maldivian)
Population	306 000		

MALI
Republic of Mali
Capital Bamako

		Currency	CFA franc*
Area sq km	1 240 140	Languages	French, Bambara,
Area sq miles	478 821		local lang.
Population	12 337 000		

MALTA
Republic of Malta
Capital Valletta

		Currency	Euro
Area sq km	316	Languages	Maltese, English
Area sq miles	122		
Population	407 000		

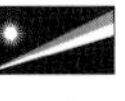

MARSHALL ISLANDS
Republic of the Marshall Islands
Capital Delap-Uliga-Djarrit

		Currency	US dollar
Area sq km	181	Languages	English,
Area sq miles	70		Marshallese
Population	59 000		

MAURITANIA
Islamic Arab and African Rep. of Mauritania
Capital Nouakchott

		Currency	Ouguiya
Area sq km	1 030 700	Languages	Arabic, French,
Area sq miles	397 955		local lang.
Population	3 124 000		

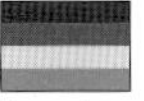

MAURITIUS
Republic of Mauritius
Capital Port Louis

		Currency	Mauritius rupee
Area sq km	2 040	Languages	English, creole,
Area sq miles	788		Hindi, Bhojpuri,
Population	1 262 000		French

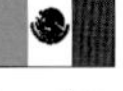

MEXICO
United Mexican States
Capital Mexico City

		Currency	Mexican peso
Area sq km	1 972 545	Languages	Spanish,
Area sq miles	761 604		Amerindian lang.
Population	106 535 000		

MICRONESIA, FEDERATED STATES OF
Capital Palikir

Area sq km	701	Currency	US dollar
Area sq miles	271	Languages	English,
Population	111 000		Chuukese,
			Pohnpeian,
			local lang.

MOLDOVA
Republic of Moldova
Capital Chişinău (Kishinev)

Area sq km	33 700	Currency	Moldovan leu
Area sq miles	13 012	Languages	Romanian,
Population	3 794 000		Ukrainian,
			Gagauz, Russian

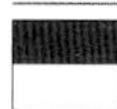

MONACO
Principality of Monaco
Capital Monaco-Ville

Area sq km	2	Currency	Euro
Area sq miles	1	Languages	French,
Population	33 000		Monégasque,
			Italian

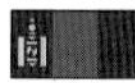

MONGOLIA
Capital Ulan Bator (Ulaanbaatar)

Area sq km	1 565 000	Currency	Tugrik (tögrög)
Area sq miles	604 250	Languages	Khalka
Population	2 629 000		(Mongolian),
			Kazakh,
			local lang.

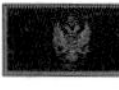

MONTENEGRO
Republic of Montenegro
Capital Podgorica

Area sq km	13 812	Currency	Euro
Area sq miles	5 333	Languages	Serbian
Population	598 000		(Montenegrin),
			Albanian

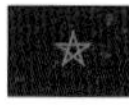

MOROCCO
Kingdom of Morocco
Capital Rabat

Area sq km	446 550	Currency	Moroccan dirham
Area sq miles	172 414	Languages	Arabic, Berber,
Population	31 224 000		French

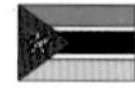

MOZAMBIQUE
Republic of Mozambique
Capital Maputo

Area sq km	799 380	Currency	Metical
Area sq miles	308 642	Languages	Portuguese,
Population	21 397 000		Makua, Tsonga,
			local lang.

MYANMAR (Burma)
Union of Myanmar
Capital Nay Pyi Taw/Rangoon (Yangôn)

Area sq km	676 577	Currency	Kyat
Area sq miles	261 228	Languages	Burmese, Sha
Population	48 798 000		Karen, local la

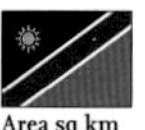

NAMIBIA
Republic of Namibia
Capital Windhoek

Area sq km	824 292	Currency	Namibian doll
Area sq miles	318 261	Languages	English, Afrika
Population	2 074 000		German, Ovan
			local lang.

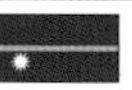

NAURU
Republic of Nauru
Capital Yaren

Area sq km	21	Currency	Australian dol
Area sq miles	8	Languages	Nauruan, Engl
Population	10 000		

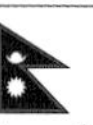

NEPAL
Capital Kathmandu

Area sq km	147 181	Currency	Nepalese rupe
Area sq miles	56 827	Languages	Nepali, Maithi
Population	28 196 000		Bhojpuri, Eng.
			local lang.

NETHERLANDS
Kingdom of the Netherlands
Capital Amsterdam/The Hague ('s-Graven

Area sq km	41 526	Currency	Euro
Area sq miles	16 033	Languages	Dutch, Frisian
Population	16 419 000		

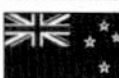

NEW ZEALAND
Capital Wellington

Area sq km	270 534	Currency	New Zealand
Area sq miles	104 454		dollar
Population	4 179 000	Languages	English, Maor

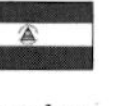

NICARAGUA
Republic of Nicaragua
Capital Managua

Area sq km	130 000	Currency	Córdoba
Area sq miles	50 193	Languages	Spanish,
Population	5 603 000		Amerindian la

NIGER
Republic of Niger
Capital Niamey

ea sq km	1 267 000	**Currency**	CFA franc*
ea sq miles	489 191	**Languages**	French, Hausa,
pulation	14 226 000		Fulani, local lang.

NIGERIA
Federal Republic of Nigeria
Capital Abuja

ea sq km	923 768	**Currency**	Naira
ea sq miles	356 669	**Languages**	English, Hausa,
pulation	148 093 000		Yoruba, Ibo,
			Fulani, local lang.

NORTH KOREA
Democratic People's Republic of Korea
Capital P'yŏngyang

ea sq km	120 538	**Currency**	North Korean won
ea sq miles	46 540	**Languages**	Korean
pulation	23 790 000		

NORWAY
Kingdom of Norway
Capital Oslo

ea sq km	323 878	**Currency**	Norwegian krone
ea sq miles	125 050	**Languages**	Norwegian
pulation	4 698 000		

OMAN
Sultanate of Oman
Capital Muscat (Masqaṭ)

ea sq km	309 500	**Currency**	Omani riyal
ea sq miles	119 499	**Languages**	Arabic, Baluchi,
pulation	2 595 000		Indian lang.

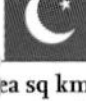

PAKISTAN
Islamic Republic of Pakistan
Capital Islamabad

ea sq km	803 940	**Currency**	Pakistani rupee
ea sq miles	310 403	**Languages**	Urdu, Punjabi,
pulation	163 902 000		Sindhi, Pushtu
			English

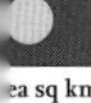

PALAU
Republic of Palau
Capital Melekeok

ea sq km	497	**Currency**	US dollar
ea sq miles	192	**Languages**	Palauan, English
pulation	20 000		

PANAMA
Republic of Panama
Capital Panama City

Area sq km	77 082	**Currency**	Balboa
Area sq miles	29 762	**Languages**	Spanish, English,
Population	3 343 000		Amerindian lang.

PAPUA NEW GUINEA
Independent State of Papua New Guinea
Capital Port Moresby

Area sq km	462 840	**Currency**	Kina
Area sq miles	178 704	**Languages**	English,
Population	6 331 000		Tok Pisin (creole),
			local lang.

PARAGUAY
Republic of Paraguay
Capital Asunción

Area sq km	406 752	**Currency**	Guaraní
Area sq miles	157 048	**Languages**	Spanish, Guaraní
Population	6 127 000		

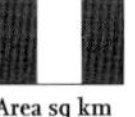

PERU
Republic of Peru
Capital Lima

Area sq km	1 285 216	**Currency**	Sol
Area sq miles	496 225	**Languages**	Spanish, Quechua,
Population	27 903 000		Aymara

PHILIPPINES
Republic of the Philippines
Capital Manila

Area sq km	300 000	**Currency**	Philippine peso
Area sq miles	115 831	**Languages**	English, Filipino,
Population	87 960 000		Tagalog, Cebuano,
			local lang.

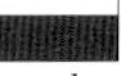

POLAND
Polish Republic
Capital Warsaw (Warszawa)

Area sq km	312 683	**Currency**	Złoty
Area sq miles	120 728	**Languages**	Polish, German
Population	38 082 000		

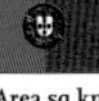

PORTUGAL
Portuguese Republic
Capital Lisbon (Lisboa)

Area sq km	88 940	**Currency**	Euro
Area sq miles	34 340	**Languages**	Portuguese
Population	10 623 000		

QATAR
State of Qatar
Capital Doha (Ad Dawḥah)

Area sq km	11 437	**Currency**	Qatari riyal
Area sq miles	4 416	**Languages**	Arabic
Population	841 000		

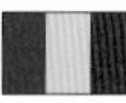

ROMANIA
Capital Bucharest (Bucureşti)

Area sq km	237 500	**Currency**	Romanian leu
Area sq miles	91 699	**Languages**	Romanian,
Population	21 438 000		Hungarian

RUSSIAN FEDERATION
Capital Moscow (Moskva)

Area sq km	17 075 400	**Currency**	Russian rouble
Area sq miles	6 592 849	**Languages**	Russian, Tatar,
Population	142 499 000		Ukrainian,
			local lang.

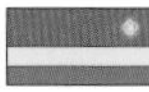

RWANDA
Republic of Rwanda
Capital Kigali

Area sq km	26 338	**Currency**	Rwandan franc
Area sq miles	10 169	**Languages**	Kinyarwanda,
Population	9 725 000		French, English

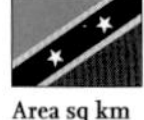

ST KITTS AND NEVIS
Federation of St Kitts and Nevis
Capital Basseterre

Area sq km	261	**Currency**	East Caribbean
Area sq miles	101		dollar
Population	50 000	**Languages**	English, creole

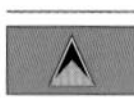

ST LUCIA
Capital Castries

Area sq km	616	**Currency**	East Caribbean
Area sq miles	238		dollar
Population	165 000	**Languages**	English, creole

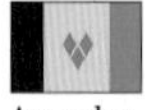

ST VINCENT AND THE GRENADINES
Capital Kingstown

Area sq km	389	**Currency**	East Caribbean
Area sq miles	150		dollar
Population	120 000	**Languages**	English, creole

SAMOA
Independent State of Samoa
Capital Apia

Area sq km	2 831	**Currency**	Tala
Area sq miles	1 093	**Languages**	Samoan, English
Population	187 000		

SAN MARINO
Republic of San Marino
Capital San Marino

Area sq km	61	**Currency**	Euro
Area sq miles	24	**Languages**	Italian
Population	31 000		

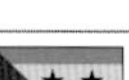

SÃO TOMÉ AND PRÍNCIPE
Democratic Rep. of São Tomé and Prín
Capital São Tomé

Area sq km	964	**Currency**	Dobra
Area sq miles	372	**Languages**	Portuguese, cre
Population	158 000		

SAUDI ARABIA
Kingdom of Saudi Arabia
Capital Riyadh (Ar Riyāḍ)

Area sq km	2 200 000	**Currency**	Saudi Arabian
Area sq miles	849 425		riyal
Population	24 735 000	**Languages**	Arabic

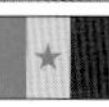

SENEGAL
Republic of Senegal
Capital Dakar

Area sq km	196 720	**Currency**	CFA franc*
Area sq miles	75 954	**Languages**	French, Wolof,
Population	12 379 000		Fulani, local lar

SERBIA
Republic of Serbia
Capital Belgrade (Beograd)

Area sq km	77 453	**Currency**	Serbian dinar,
Area sq miles	29 904	**Languages**	Serbian,
Population	7 788 000		Hungarian

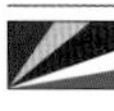

SEYCHELLES
Republic of Seychelles
Capital Victoria

Area sq km	455	**Currency**	Seychelles rupe
Area sq miles	176	**Languages**	English, French
Population	87 000		creole

SIERRA LEONE
Republic of Sierra Leone
Capital Freetown

Area sq km	71 740	**Currency**	Leone
Area sq miles	27 699	**Languages**	English, creole
Population	5 866 000		Mende, Temne
			local lang.

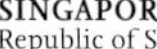

SINGAPORE
Republic of Singapore
Capital Singapore

Area sq km	639	**Currency**	Singapore dollar
Area sq miles	247	**Languages**	Chinese, English,
Population	4 436 000		Malay, Tamil

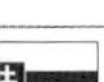

SLOVAKIA
Slovak Republic
Capital Bratislava

Area sq km	49 035	**Currency**	Euro
Area sq miles	18 933	**Languages**	Slovak,
Population	5 390 000		Hungarian, Czech

SLOVENIA
Republic of Slovenia
Capital Ljubljana

Area sq km	20 251	**Currency**	Euro
Area sq miles	7 819	**Languages**	Slovene, Croatian,
Population	2 002 000		Serbian

SOLOMON ISLANDS
Capital Honiara

Area sq km	28 370	**Currency**	Solomon Islands
Area sq miles	10 954		dollar
Population	496 000	**Languages**	English, creole,
			local lang.

SOMALIA
Somali Republic
Capital Mogadishu (Muqdisho)

Area sq km	637 657	**Currency**	Somali shilling
Area sq miles	246 201	**Languages**	Somali, Arabic
Population	8 699 000		

SOUTH AFRICA, REPUBLIC OF
Capital Pretoria (Tshwane)/Cape Town

Area sq km	1 219 090	**Currency**	Rand
Area sq miles	470 693	**Languages**	Afrikaans,
Population	48 577 000		English, nine
			official local lang.

SOUTH KOREA
Republic of Korea
Capital Seoul (Sŏul)

Area sq km	99 274	**Currency**	South Korean
Area sq miles	38 330		won
Population	48 224 000	**Languages**	Korean

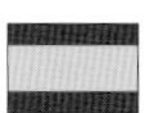

SPAIN
Kingdom of Spain
Capital Madrid

Area sq km	504 782	**Currency**	Euro
Area sq miles	194 897	**Languages**	Spanish, Castilian,
Population	44 279 000		Catalan, Galician,
			Basque

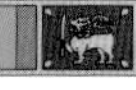

SRI LANKA
Democratic Socialist Republic of Sri Lanka
Capital Sri Jayewardenepura Kotte

Area sq km	65 610	**Currency**	Sri Lankan rupee
Area sq miles	25 332	**Languages**	Sinhalese,
Population	19 299 000		Tamil, English

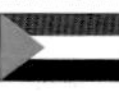

SUDAN
Republic of the Sudan
Capital Khartoum

Area sq km	2 505 813	**Currency**	Sudanese pound
Area sq miles	967 500		(Sudani)
Population	38 560 000	**Languages**	Arabic, Dinka,
			Nubian, Beja,
			Nuer, local lang.

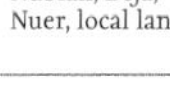

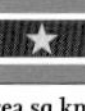

SURINAME
Republic of Suriname
Capital Paramaribo

Area sq km	163 820	**Currency**	Suriname guilder
Area sq miles	63 251	**Languages**	Dutch,
Population	458 000		Surinamese,
			English, Hindi

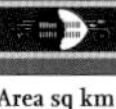

SWAZILAND
Kingdom of Swaziland
Capital Mbabane

Area sq km	17 364	**Currency**	Emalangeni,
Area sq miles	6 704		South African
Population	1 141 000		rand
		Languages	Swazi, English

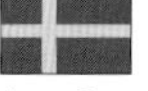

SWEDEN
Kingdom of Sweden
Capital Stockholm

Area sq km	449 964	**Currency**	Swedish krona
Area sq miles	173 732	**Languages**	Swedish
Population	9 119 000		

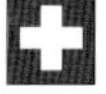

SWITZERLAND
Swiss Confederation
Capital Bern (Berne)

Area sq km	41 293	**Currency**	Swiss franc
Area sq miles	15 943	**Languages**	German, French,
Population	7 484 000		Italian, Romansch

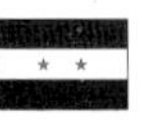

SYRIA
Syrian Arab Republic
Capital Damascus (Dimashq)

Area sq km	185 180	**Currency**	Syrian pound
Area sq miles	71 498	**Languages**	Arabic, Kurdish,
Population	19 929 000		Armenian

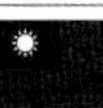

TAIWAN
Republic of China
Capital T'aipei

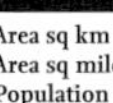

Area sq km	36 179	**Currency**	Taiwan dollar
Area sq miles	13 969	**Languages**	Mandarin, Min,
Population	22 880 000		Hakka, local lang.

The People's Republic of China claims Taiwan as its 23rd province.

TAJIKISTAN
Republic of Tajikistan
Capital Dushanbe

Area sq km	143 100	**Currency**	Somoni
Area sq miles	55 251	**Languages**	
Population	6 736 000		Tajik, Uzbek, Russian

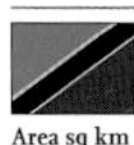

TANZANIA
United Republic of Tanzania
Capital Dodoma

Area sq km	945 087	**Currency**	Tanzanian shilling
Area sq miles	364 900	**Languages**	Swahili, English,
Population	40 454 000		Nyamwezi, local lang.

THAILAND
Kingdom of Thailand
Capital Bangkok (Krung Thep)

Area sq km	513 115	**Currency**	Baht
Area sq miles	198 115	**Languages**	Thai, Lao,
Population	63 884 000		Chinese, Malay, Mon-Khmer lang.

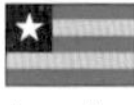

TOGO
Republic of Togo
Capital Lomé

Area sq km	56 785	**Currency**	CFA franc*
Area sq miles	21 925	**Languages**	French, Ewe,
Population	6 585 000		Kabre, local lang.

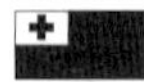

TONGA
Kingdom of Tonga
Capital Nuku'alofa

Area sq km	748	**Currency**	Pa'anga
Area sq miles	289	**Languages**	Tongan, English
Population	100 000		

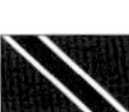

TRINIDAD AND TOBAGO
Republic of Trinidad and Tobago
Capital Port of Spain

Area sq km	5 130	**Currency**	Trinidad and
Area sq miles	1 981		Tobago dollar
Population	1 333 000	**Languages**	English, creole, Hindi

TUNISIA
Tunisian Republic
Capital Tunis

Area sq km	164 150	**Currency**	Tunisian dinar
Area sq miles	63 379	**Languages**	Arabic, French
Population	10 327 000		

TURKEY
Republic of Turkey
Capital Ankara

Area sq km	779 452	**Currency**	Lira
Area sq miles	300 948	**Languages**	Turkish, Kurdi
Population	74 877 000		

TURKMENISTAN
Republic of Turkmenistan
Capital Aşgabat (Ashkhabad)

Area sq km	488 100	**Currency**	Turkmen man
Area sq miles	188 456	**Languages**	Turkmen, Uzb
Population	4 965 000		Russian

TUVALU
Capital Vaiaku

Area sq km	25	**Currency**	Australian dol
Area sq miles	10	**Languages**	Tuvaluan, Eng
Population	11 000		

UGANDA
Republic of Uganda
Capital Kampala

Area sq km	241 038	**Currency**	Ugandan shill
Area sq miles	93 065	**Languages**	English, Swahi
Population	30 884 000		Luganda, local lang.

UKRAINE
Capital Kiev (Kyiv)

Area sq km	603 700	**Currency**	Hryvnia
Area sq miles	233 090	**Languages**	Ukrainian,
Population	46 205 000		Russian

UNITED ARAB EMIRATES
Federation of Emirates
Capital Abu Dhabi (Abū Ẓabī)

Area sq km	77 700	**Currency**	UAE dirham
Area sq miles	30 000	**Languages**	Arabic, English
Population	4 380 000		

UNITED KINGDOM
United Kingdom of Great Britain and
Northern Ireland
Capital London

Area sq km	243 609	**Currency**	Pound sterling
Area sq miles	94 058	**Languages**	English, Welsh,
Population	60 769 000		Gaelic

UNITED STATES OF AMERICA
Capital Washington D.C.

Area sq km	9 826 635	**Currency**	US dollar
Area sq miles	3 794 085	**Languages**	English, Spanish
Population	305 826 000		

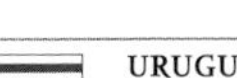

URUGUAY
Oriental Republic of Uruguay
Capital Montevideo

Area sq km	176 215	**Currency**	Uruguayan peso
Area sq miles	68 037	**Languages**	Spanish
Population	3 340 000		

UZBEKISTAN
Republic of Uzbekistan
Capital Toshkent

Area sq km	447 400	**Currency**	Uzbek som
Area sq miles	172 742	**Languages**	Uzbek, Russian,
Population	27 372 000		Tajik, Kazakh

VANUATU
Republic of Vanuatu
Capital Port Vila

Area sq km	12 190	**Currency**	Vatu
Area sq miles	4 707	**Languages**	English,
Population	226 000		Bislama (creole),
			French

VATICAN CITY
Vatican City State or Holy See
Capital Vatican City

Area sq km	0.5	**Currency**	Euro
Area sq miles	0.2	**Languages**	Italian
Population	557		

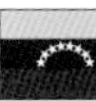

VENEZUELA
Republic of Venezuela
Capital Caracas

Area sq km	912 050	**Currency**	Bolívar fuerte
Area sq miles	352 144	**Languages**	Spanish,
Population	27 657 000		Amerindian lang.

VIETNAM
Socialist Republic of Vietnam
Capital Ha Nôi

Area sq km	329 565	**Currency**	Dong
Area sq miles	127 246	**Languages**	Vietnamese, Thai,
Population	87 375 000		Khmer, Chinese,
			local lang.

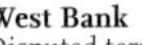

West Bank
Disputed territory

Area sq km	5 860	**Currency**	Jordanian dinar,
Area sq miles	2 263		Isreali shekel
Population	2 676 284	**Languages**	Arabic, Hebrew

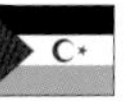

Western Sahara
Disputed territory (Morocco)
Capital Laâyoune

Area sq km	266 000	**Currency**	Moroccan dirham
Area sq miles	102 703	**Languages**	Arabic
Population	480 000		

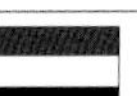

YEMEN
Republic of Yemen
Capital Şan'ā'

Area sq km	527 968	**Currency**	Yemeni riyal
Area sq miles	203 850	**Languages**	Arabic
Population	22 389 000		

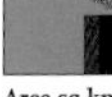

ZAMBIA
Republic of Zambia
Capital Lusaka

Area sq km	752 614	**Currency**	Zambian kwacha
Area sq miles	290 586	**Languages**	English, Bemba,
Population	11 922 000		Nyanja, Tonga,
			local lang.

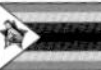

ZIMBABWE
Republic of Zimbabwe
Capital Harare

Area sq km	390 759	**Currency**	Zimbabwean
Area sq miles	150 873		dollar
Population	13 349 000	**Languages**	English, Shona,
			Ndebele

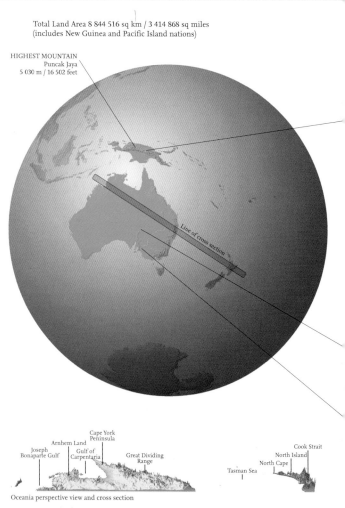

Total Land Area 8 844 516 sq km / 3 414 868 sq miles
(includes New Guinea and Pacific Island nations)

HIGHEST MOUNTAIN
Puncak Jaya
5 030 m / 16 502 feet

Line of cross section

Joseph
Bonaparte Gulf

Arnhem Land

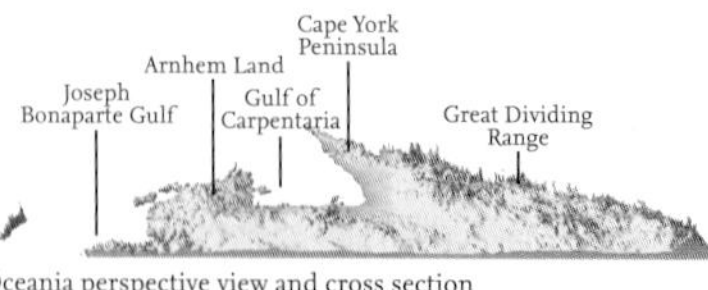

Cape York
Peninsula

Gulf of
Carpentaria

Great Dividing
Range

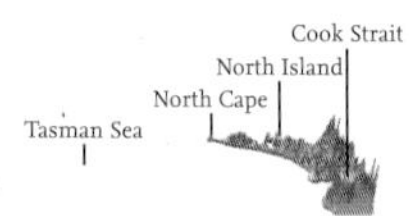

Cook Strait

North Island

North Cape

Tasman Sea

Oceania perspective view and cross section

20

HIGHEST MOUNTAINS	metres	feet	Map page
Puncak Jaya, Indonesia	5 030	16 502	59 D3
Puncak Trikora, Indonesia	4 730	15 518	59 D3
Puncak Mandala, Indonesia	4 700	15 420	59 D3
Puncak Yamin, Indonesia	4 595	15 075	—
Mt Wilhelm, Papua New Guinea	4 509	14 793	59 D3
Mt Kubor, Papua New Guinea	4 359	14 301	—

— LARGEST ISLAND
New Guinea
808 510 sq km /
312 167 sq miles

LARGEST ISLANDS	sq km	sq miles	Map page
New Guinea	808 510	312 167	59 D3
South Island, New Zealand	151 215	58 384	54 B2
North Island, New Zealand	115 777	44 701	54 B1
Tasmania	67 800	26 178	51 D4

LONGEST RIVERS	km	miles	Map page
Murray-Darling	3 750	2 330	52 B2
Darling	2 739	1 702	52 B2
Murray	2 589	1 609	52 B3
Murrumbidgee	1 690	1 050	52 B2
Lachlan	1 480	920	53 C2
Macquarie	950	590	53 C2

LARGEST LAKES	sq km	sq miles	Map page
Lake Eyre	0–8 900	0–3 436	52 A1
Lake Torrens	0–5 780	0–2 232	52 A1

LARGEST LAKE AND LOWEST POINT
Lake Eyre
0 – 8 900 sq km / 0 – 3 436 sq miles
16 m / 53 feet below sea level

LONGEST RIVER AND
LARGEST DRAINAGE BASIN
Murray-Darling
3 750 km / 2 330 miles
1 058 000 sq km / 408 000 sq miles

Total Land Area 45 036 492 sq km / 17 388 686 sq miles

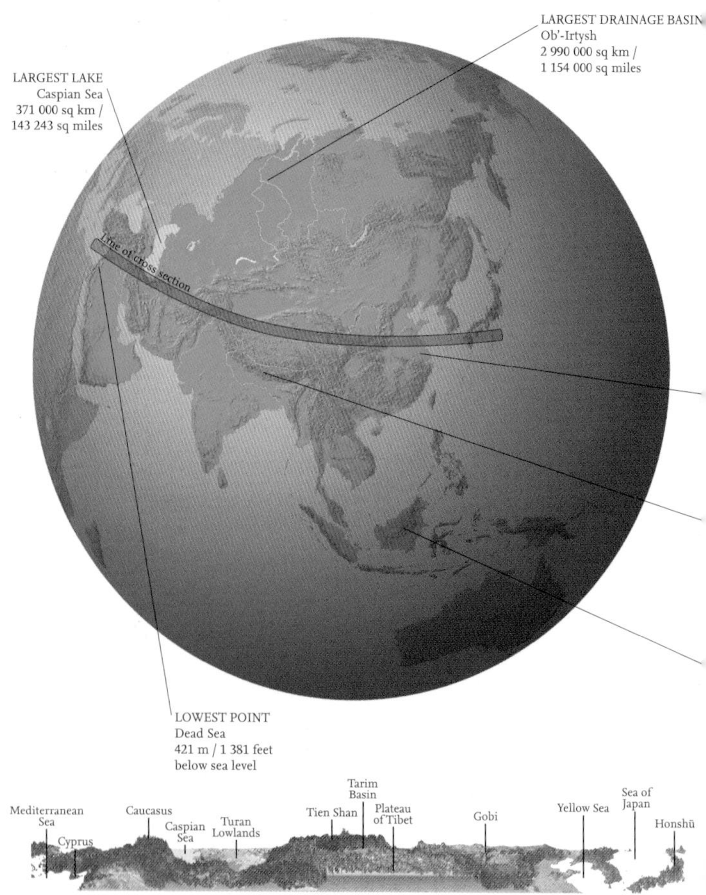

LARGEST DRAINAGE BASIN
Ob'-Irtysh
2 990 000 sq km /
1 154 000 sq miles

LARGEST LAKE
Caspian Sea
371 000 sq km /
143 243 sq miles

Line of cross section

LOWEST POINT
Dead Sea
421 m / 1 381 feet
below sea level

Mediterranean Sea · Cyprus · Caucasus · Caspian Sea · Turan Lowlands · Tien Shan · Tarim Basin · Plateau of Tibet · Gobi · Yellow Sea · Sea of Japan · Honshū

Asia perspective view and cross section

HIGHEST MOUNTAINS	metres	feet	Map page
Mt Everest (Sagarmatha/ Qomolangma Feng), China/Nepal	8 848	29 028	75 C2
K2 (Qogir Feng), China/Pakistan	8 611	28 251	74 B1
Kangchenjunga, India/Nepal	8 586	28 169	75 C2
Lhotse, China/Nepal	8 516	27 939	—
Makalu, China/Nepal	8 463	27 765	—
Cho Oyu, China/Nepal	8 201	26 906	—

LARGEST ISLANDS	sq km	sq miles	Map page
Borneo	745 561	287 861	61 C1
Sumatra (Sumatera)	473 606	182 859	60 A1
Honshū	227 414	87 805	67 B3
Celebes (Sulawesi)	189 216	73 056	58 C3
Java (Jawa)	132 188	51 038	61 B2
Luzon	104 690	40 421	64 B1

LONGEST RIVER
Yangtze (Chang Jiang)
6 380 km /
3 965 miles

LONGEST RIVERS	km	miles	Map page
Yangtze (Chang Jiang)	6 380	3 965	70 C2
Ob'-Irtysh	5 568	3 460	86 F2
Yenisey-Angara-Selenga	5 550	3 449	83 H3
Yellow (Huang He)	5 464	3 395	70 B2
Irtysh	4 440	2 759	86 F2
Mekong	4 425	2 750	63 B2

HIGHEST MOUNTAIN
Mt Everest
8 848 m / 29 028 feet

LARGEST LAKES	sq km	sq miles	Map page
Caspian Sea	371 000	143 243	81 C1
Lake Baikal (Ozero Baykal)	30 500	11 776	69 D1
Lake Balkhash (Ozero Balkhash)	17 400	6 718	77 D2
Aral Sea (Aral'skoye More)	17 158	6 625	76 B2
Ysyk-Köl	6 200	2 394	77 D2

LARGEST ISLAND
Borneo
745 561 sq km /
287 861 sq miles

Total Land Area 9 908 599 sq km / 3 825 710 sq miles

LARGEST ISLAND
Great Britain
218 476 sq km /
84 354 sq miles

Line of cross section

HIGHEST MOUNTAIN
El'brus
5 642 m / 18 510 feet

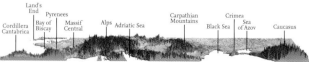

Land's
End
Cordillera   Bay of   Pyrenees   Carpathian   Crimea
Cantabrica   Biscay   Massif   Alps Adriatic Sea   Mountains   Sea
                        Central   Black Sea of Azov   Caucasus

Europe perspective view and cross section

HIGHEST MOUNTAINS	metres	feet	Map pages
El'brus, Russian Federation	5 642	18 510	87 D4
Gora Dykh-Tau, Russian Federation	5 204	17 073	—
Shkhara, Georgia/Russian Federation	5 201	17 063	—
Kazbek, Georgia/Russian Federation	5 047	16 558	76 A2
Mont Blanc, France/Italy	4 808	15 774	105 D2
Dufourspitze, Italy/Switzerland	4 634	15 203	—

LARGEST ISLANDS	sq km	sq miles	Map pages
Great Britain	218 476	84 354	95 C3
Iceland	102 820	39 699	92 A3
Novaya Zemlya	90 650	35 000	86 E1
Ireland	83 045	32 064	97 C2
Spitsbergen	37 814	14 600	82 C1
Sicily (Sicilia)	25 426	9 817	108 B3

LONGEST RIVER AND
LARGEST DRAINAGE BASIN
Volga
3 688 km / 2 292 miles
1 380 000 sq km / 533 000 sq miles

LONGEST RIVERS	km	miles	Map pages
Volga	3 688	2 292	89 F2
Danube	2 850	1 771	110 A1
Dnieper	2 285	1 420	91 C2
Kama	2 028	1 260	86 E3
Don	1 931	1 200	89 E3
Pechora	1 802	1 120	86 E2

LARGEST LAKE AND LOWEST POINT
Caspian Sea
371 000 sq km / 143 243 sq miles
28m / 92 feet below sea level

LARGEST LAKES	sq km	sq miles	Map pages
Caspian Sea	371 000	143 243	81 C1
Lake Ladoga (Ladozhskoye Ozero)	18 390	7 100	86 C2
Lake Onega (Onezhskoye Ozero)	9 600	3 707	86 C2
Vänern	5 585	2 156	93 F4
Rybinskoye Vodokhranilishche	5 180	2 000	89 E2

Total Land Area 30 343 578 sq km / 11 715 721 sq miles

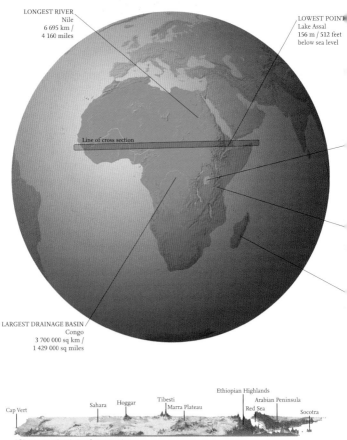

LONGEST RIVER
Nile
6 695 km /
4 160 miles

LOWEST POINT
Lake Assal
156 m / 512 feet
below sea level

Line of cross section

LARGEST DRAINAGE BASIN
Congo
3 700 000 sq km /
1 429 000 sq miles

Cap Vert   Sahara   Hoggar   Tibesti   Ethiopian Highlands
                                  Marra Plateau   Arabian Peninsula
                                                   Red Sea   Socotra

Africa perspective view and cross section

HIGHEST MOUNTAINS	metres	feet	Map page
Kilimanjaro, Tanzania	5 892	19 330	119 D3
Mt Kenya (Kirinyaga), Kenya	5 199	17 057	119 D3
Margherita Peak, Democratic Republic of the Congo/Uganda	5 110	16 765	119 C2
Meru, Tanzania	4 565	14 977	119 D3
Ras Dejen, Ethiopia	4 533	14 872	117 B3
Mt Karisimbi, Rwanda	4 510	14 796	—

LARGEST ISLANDS	sq km	sq miles	Map page
Madagascar	587 040	226 656	121 D3

LONGEST RIVERS	km	miles	Map page
Nile	6 695	4 160	116 B1
Congo	4 667	2 900	118 B3
Niger	4 184	2 600	115 C4
Zambezi	2 736	1 700	120 C2
Webi Shabeelle	2 490	1 547	117 C4
Ubangi	2 250	1 398	118 B3

LARGEST LAKES	sq km	sq miles	Map page
Lake Victoria	68 870	26 591	52 B2
Lake Tanganyika	32 600	12 587	119 C3
Lake Nyasa (Lake Malawi)	29 500	11 390	121 C1
Lake Volta	8 482	3 275	114 C4
Lake Turkana	6 500	2 510	119 D2
Lake Albert	5 600	2 162	119 D2

LARGEST LAKE
Lake Victoria
68 870 sq km /
26 591 sq miles

HIGHEST MOUNTAIN
Kilimanjaro
5 892 m / 19 330 feet

LARGEST ISLAND
Madagascar
587 040 sq km /
226 656 sq miles

Total Land Area 24 680 331 sq km / 9 529 076 sq miles
(including Hawaiian Islands)

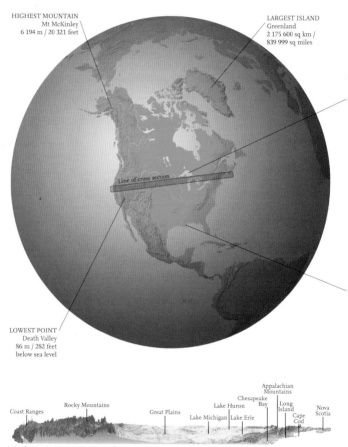

HIGHEST MOUNTAIN
Mt McKinley
6 194 m / 20 321 feet

LARGEST ISLAND
Greenland
2 175 600 sq km /
839 999 sq miles

Line of cross section

LOWEST POINT
Death Valley
86 m / 282 feet
below sea level

Coast Ranges | Rocky Mountains | Great Plains | Lake Michigan | Lake Huron | Lake Erie | Chesapeake Bay | Appalachian Mountains | Long Island | Cape Cod | Nova Scotia

North America perspective view and cross section

HIGHEST MOUNTAINS	metres	feet	Map page
Mt McKinley, USA	6 194	20 321	124 F2
Mt Logan, Canada	5 959	19 550	126 B2
Pico de Orizaba, Mexico	5 610	18 405	145 C3
Mt St Elias, USA	5 489	18 008	126 B2
Volcán Popocatépetl, Mexico	5 452	17 887	145 C3
Mt Foraker, USA	5 303	17 398	—

LARGEST LAKE
Lake Superior
82 100 sq km /
31 699 sq miles

LARGEST ISLANDS	sq km	sq miles	Map page
Greenland	2 175 600	839 999	127 I2
Baffin Island	507 451	195 927	127 G2
Victoria Island	217 291	83 896	126 D2
Ellesmere Island	196 236	75 767	127 F1
Cuba	110 860	42 803	146 B2
Newfoundland	108 860	42 031	131 E2
Hispaniola	76 192	29 418	147 C2

LONGEST RIVERS	km	miles	Map page
Mississippi-Missouri	5 969	3 709	133 D3
Mackenzie-Peace-Finlay	4 241	2 635	126 C2
Missouri	4 086	2 539	137 E3
Mississippi	3 765	2 340	142 C3
Yukon	3 185	1 979	126 A2
Rio Grande (Rio Bravo del Norte)	3 057	1 900	144 B1

LONGEST RIVER AND
LARGEST DRAINAGE BASIN
Mississippi-Missouri
5 969 km / 3 709 miles
3 250 000 sq km / 1 255 000 sq
miles

LARGEST LAKES	sq km	sq miles	Map page
Lake Superior	82 100	31 699	140 B1
Lake Huron	59 600	23 012	140 C2
Lake Michigan	57 800	22 317	140 B2
Great Bear Lake	31 328	12 096	126 C2
Great Slave Lake	28 568	11 030	128 C1
Lake Erie	25 700	9 923	140 C2
Lake Winnipeg	24 387	9 416	129 E2
Lake Ontario	18 960	7 320	141 D2

Total Land Area 17 815 420 sq km / 6 878 534 sq miles

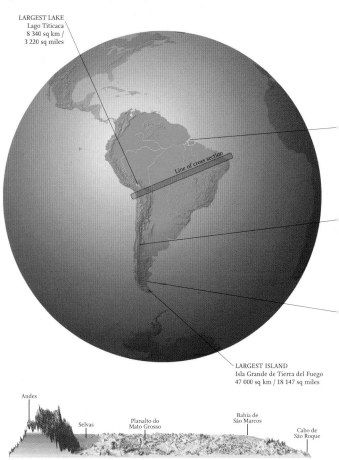

LARGEST LAKE
Lago Titicaca
8 340 sq km /
3 220 sq miles

Line of cross section

LARGEST ISLAND
Isla Grande de Tierra del Fuego
47 000 sq km / 18 147 sq miles

Andes

Selvas

Planalto do
Mato Grosso

Bahia de
São Marcos

Cabo de
São Roque

South America perspective view and cross section

HIGHEST MOUNTAINS	metres	feet	Map page
Cerro Aconcagua, Argentina	6 959	22 831	153 B4
Nevado Ojos del Salado, Argentina/Chile	6 908	22 664	152 B3
Cerro Bonete, Argentina	6 872	22 546	—
Cerro Pissis, Argentina	6 858	22 500	—
Cerro Tupungato, Argentina/Chile	6 800	22 309	—
Cerro Mercedario, Argentina	6 770	22 211	—

LARGEST ISLANDS	sq km	sq miles	Map page
Isla Grande de Tierra del Fuego	47 000	18 147	153 B6
Isla de Chiloé	8 394	3 241	153 A5
East Falkland	6 760	2 610	153 C6
West Falkland	5 413	2 090	153 B6

LONGEST RIVER AND
LARGEST DRAINAGE BASIN
Amazon
8 516 km / 4 049 miles
7 050 000 sq km / 2 722 000 sq miles

LONGEST RIVERS	km	miles	Map page
Amazon (Amazonas)	6 516	4 049	150 C1
Río de la Plata-Paraná	4 500	2 796	153 C4
Purus	3 218	2 000	150 B2
Madeira	3 200	1 988	150 C2
São Francisco	2 900	1 802	151 E3
Tocantins	2 750	1 709	151 D2

HIGHEST MOUNTAIN
Cerro Aconcagua
6 959 m / 22 831 feet

LARGEST LAKES	sq km	sq miles	Map page
Lake Titicaca	8 340	3 220	152 B2

LOWEST POINT
Laguna del Carbón
105 m / 345 feet below sea level

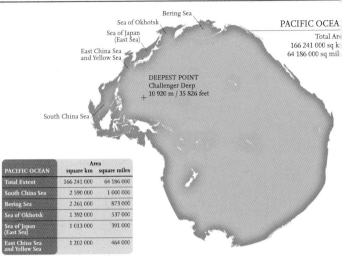

PACIFIC OCEAN

Total Area
166 241 000 sq km
64 186 000 sq miles

Bering Sea

Sea of Okhotsk

Sea of Japan
(East Sea)

East China Sea
and Yellow Sea

DEEPEST POINT
Challenger Deep
10 920 m / 35 826 feet

South China Sea

PACIFIC OCEAN	Area	
	square km	square miles
Total Extent	166 241 000	64 186 000
South China Sea	2 590 000	1 000 000
Bering Sea	2 261 000	873 000
Sea of Okhotsk	1 392 000	537 000
Sea of Japan (East Sea)	1 013 000	391 000
East China Sea and Yellow Sea	1 202 000	464 000

ANTARCTICA

Total Land Area 12 093 000 sq km /
4 669 107 sq miles (excluding ice shelves)

HIGHEST MOUNTAIN
Vinson Massif
4 897 m / 16 066 feet

HIGHEST MOUNTAINS	Height	
	metres	feet
Vinson Massif	4 897	16 066
Mt Tyree	4 852	15 918
Mt Kirkpatrick	4 528	14 855
Mt Markham	4 351	14 275
Mt Jackson	4 190	13 747
Mt Sidley	4 181	13 717

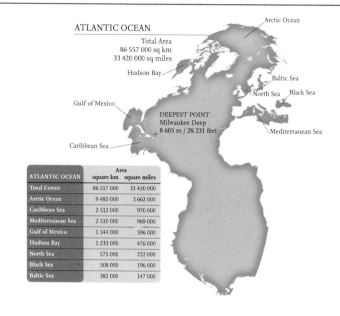

ATLANTIC OCEAN

Total Area
86 557 000 sq km
33 420 000 sq miles

Arctic Ocean

Hudson Bay

Baltic Sea

North Sea   Black Sea

Gulf of Mexico

DEEPEST POINT
Milwaukee Deep
8 605 m / 28 231 feet

Mediterranean Sea

Caribbean Sea

ATLANTIC OCEAN	Area	
	square km	square miles
Total Extent	86 557 000	33 420 000
Arctic Ocean	9 485 000	3 662 000
Caribbean Sea	2 512 000	970 000
Mediterranean Sea	2 510 000	969 000
Gulf of Mexico	1 544 000	596 000
Hudson Bay	1 233 000	476 000
North Sea	575 000	222 000
Black Sea	508 000	196 000
Baltic Sea	382 000	147 000

The Gulf

Red Sea

Bay of Bengal

DEEPEST POINT
Java Trench
7 125 m / 23 376 feet

INDIAN OCEAN	Area	
	square km	square miles
Total Extent	73 427 000	28 350 000
Bay of Bengal	2 172 000	839 000
Red Sea	453 000	175 000
The Gulf	238 000	92 000

INDIAN OCEAN

Total Area
73 427 000 sq km
28 350 000 sq miles

MAJOR CLIMATIC REGIONS AND SUB-TYPES

Köppen classification system
Winkel Tripel Projection
scale 1:200 000 000

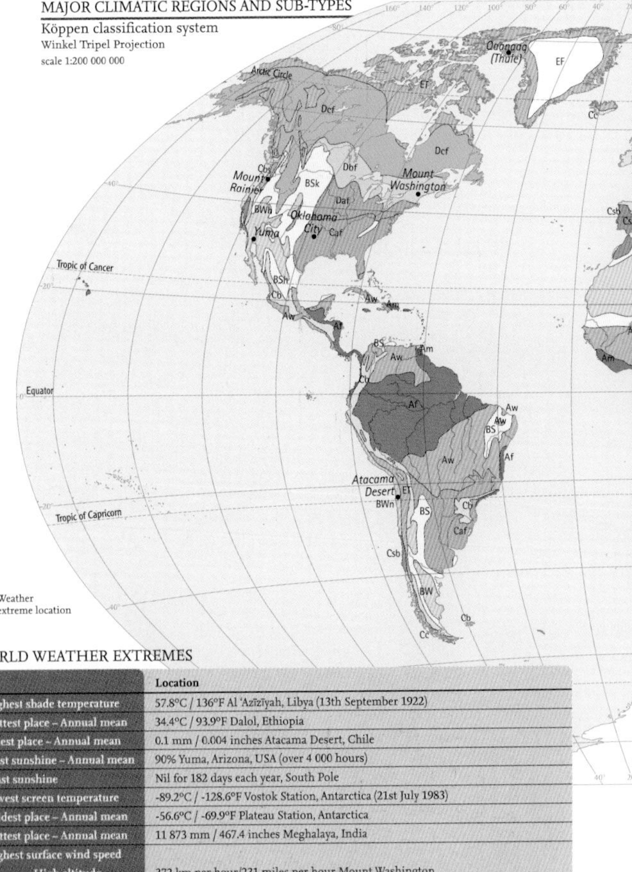

• Weather
extreme location

WORLD WEATHER EXTREMES

	Location
Highest shade temperature	57.8°C / 136°F Al 'Azīzīyah, Libya (13th September 1922)
Hottest place – Annual mean	34.4°C / 93.9°F Dalol, Ethiopia
Driest place – Annual mean	0.1 mm / 0.004 inches Atacama Desert, Chile
Most sunshine – Annual mean	90% Yuma, Arizona, USA (over 4 000 hours)
Least sunshine	Nil for 182 days each year, South Pole
Lowest screen temperature	-89.2°C / -128.6°F Vostok Station, Antarctica (21st July 1983)
Coldest place – Annual mean	-56.6°C / -69.9°F Plateau Station, Antarctica
Wettest place – Annual mean	11 873 mm / 467.4 inches Meghalaya, India
Highest surface wind speed	
- High altitude	372 km per hour/231 miles per hour Mount Washington, New Hampshire, USA, (12th April 1934)
- Low altitude	333 km per hour/207 miles per hour Qaanaaq (Thule), Greenland (8th March 1972)
- Tornado	512 km per hour / 318 miles per hour in a tornado, Oklahoma City, Oklahoma, USA (3rd May 1999)
Greatest snowfall	31 102 mm / 1 224.5 inches Mount Rainier, Washington, USA (19th February 1971 – 18th February 1972)

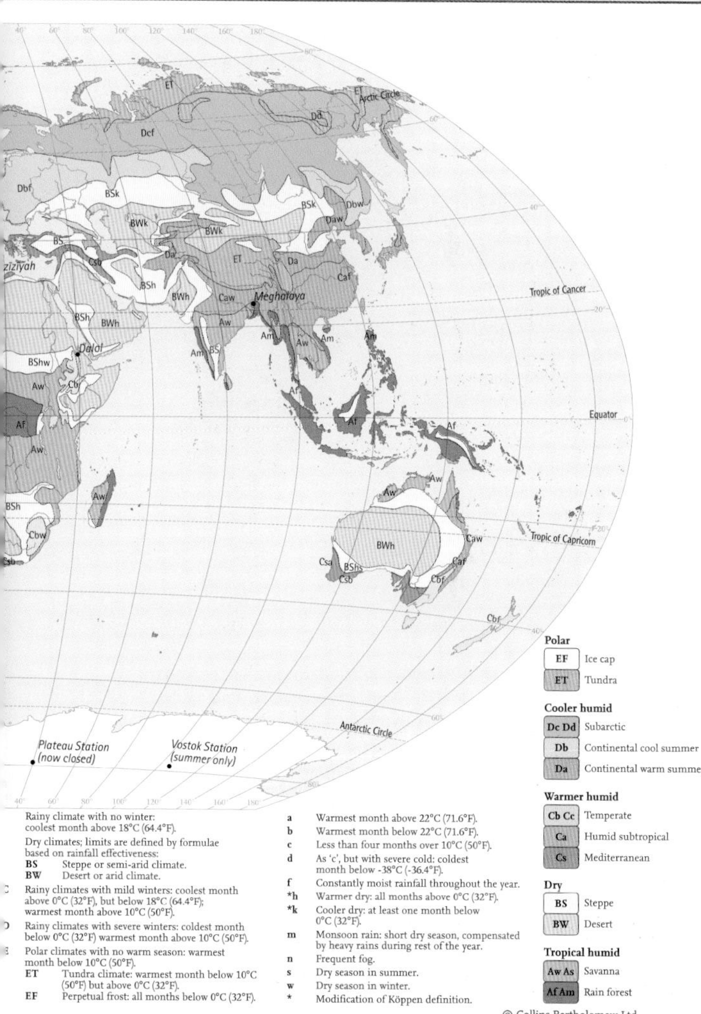

Rainy climate with no winter:
coolest month above 18°C (64.4°F).

Dry climates; limits are defined by formulae
based on rainfall effectiveness:
 BS   Steppe or semi-arid climate.
 BW Desert or arid climate.

Rainy climates with mild winters: coolest month
above 0°C (32°F), but below 18°C (64.4°F);
warmest month above 10°C (50°F).

Rainy climates with severe winters: coldest month
below 0°C (32°F) warmest month above 10°C (50°F).

Polar climates with no warm season: warmest
month below 10°C (50°F).
 ET   Tundra climate: warmest month below 10°C
      (50°F) but above 0°C (32°F).
 EF   Perpetual frost: all months below 0°C (32°F).

a	Warmest month above 22°C (71.6°F).
b	Warmest month below 22°C (71.6°F).
c	Less than four months over 10°C (50°F).
d	As 'c', but with severe cold: coldest month below -38°C (-36.4°F).
f	Constantly moist rainfall throughout the year.
*h	Warmer dry: all months above 0°C (32°F).
*k	Cooler dry: at least one month below 0°C (32°F).
m	Monsoon rain: short dry season, compensated by heavy rains during rest of the year.
n	Frequent fog.
s	Dry season in summer.
w	Dry season in winter.
*	Modification of Köppen definition.

Polar
 EF Ice cap
 ET Tundra

Cooler humid
 Dc Dd Subarctic
 Db Continental cool summer
 Da Continental warm summer

Warmer humid
 Cb Cc Temperate
 Ca Humid subtropical
 Cs Mediterranean

Dry
 BS Steppe
 BW Desert

Tropical humid
 Aw As Savanna
 Af Am Rain forest

© Collins Bartholomew Ltd

WORLD LAND COVER

Winkel Tripel Projection
scale: 1:190 000 000

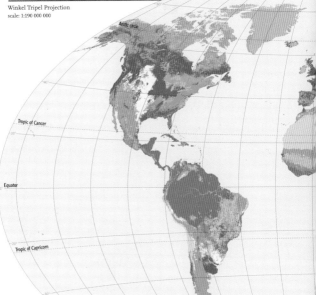

Evergreen needleleaf forest
Evergreen broadleaf forest
Deciduous needleleaf forest
Deciduous broadleaf forest
Mixed forest
Closed shrublands
Open shrublands
Woody savannas
Savannas
Grasslands
Permanent wetlands
Croplands
Urban and built-up
Cropland/Natural vegetation mosaic
Snow and Ice
Barren or sparsely vegetated
Water bodies

CONTINENTAL LAND COVER COMPOSITION

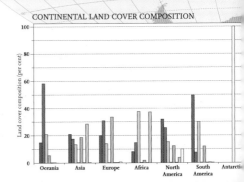

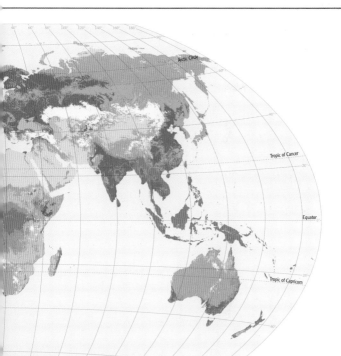

LAND COVER GRAPHS - CLASSIFICATION

Class description	Map classes
Forest/Woodland	Evergreen needleleaf forest
	Evergreen broadleaf forest
	Deciduous needleleaf forest
	Deciduous broadleaf forest
	Mixed forest
Shrubland	Closed shrublands
	Open shrublands
Grass/Savanna	Woody savannas
	Savannas
	Grasslands
Wetland	Permanent wetlands
Crops/Mosaic	Croplands
	Cropland/Natural vegetation mosaic
Urban	Urban and built-up
Snow/Ice	Snow and Ice
Barren	Barren or sparsely vegetated

GLOBAL LAND COVER COMPOSITION

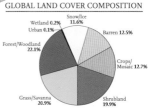

Snow/Ice 11.6%
Wetland 0.2%
Urban 0.1%
Forest/Woodland 22.1%
Barren 12.5%
Crops/Mosaic 12.7%
Grass/Savanna 20.9%
Shrubland 19.9%

© Collins Bartholomew Ltd

WORLD POPULATION DISTRIBUTION

Population Density
Winkel Tripel Projection
scale 1:190 000 000

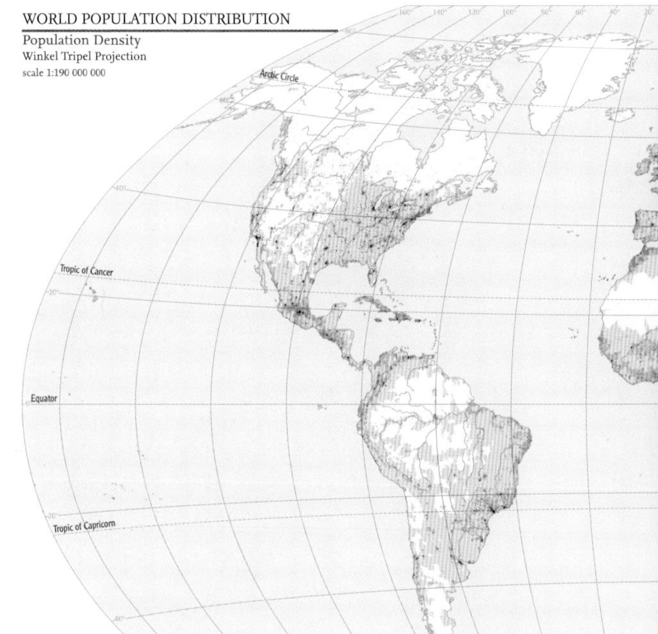

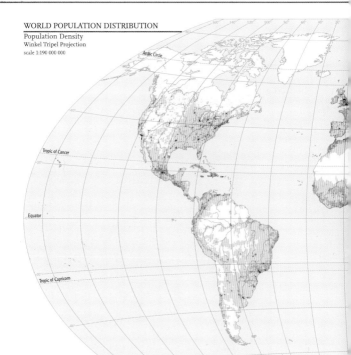

KEY POPULATION STATISTICS FOR MAJOR REGIONS

	Population 2007 (millions)	Growth (per cent)	Infant mortality rate	Total fertility rate	Life expectancy (years)
World	6 671	1.2	49	2.6	67
More developed regions[1]	1 223	0.3	7	1.6	77
Less developed regions[2]	5 448	1.4	54	2.8	65
Africa	965	2.3	87	4.7	53
Asia	4 030	1.1	43	2.3	69
Europe[3]	731	0.0	8	1.5	75
Latin America and the Caribbean[4]	572	1.2	22	2.4	73
North America	339	1.0	6	2	79
Oceania	34	1.2	26	2.3	75

1. Europe, North America, Australia, New Zealand and Japan.

2. Africa, Asia (excluding Japan), Latin America and the Caribbean and Oceania (excluding Australia and New Zealand).

3. Includes Russian Federation.

4. South America, Central America (including Mexico) and all Caribbean Islands.

Except for population (2007) the data are annual averages projected for the period 2005–2010.

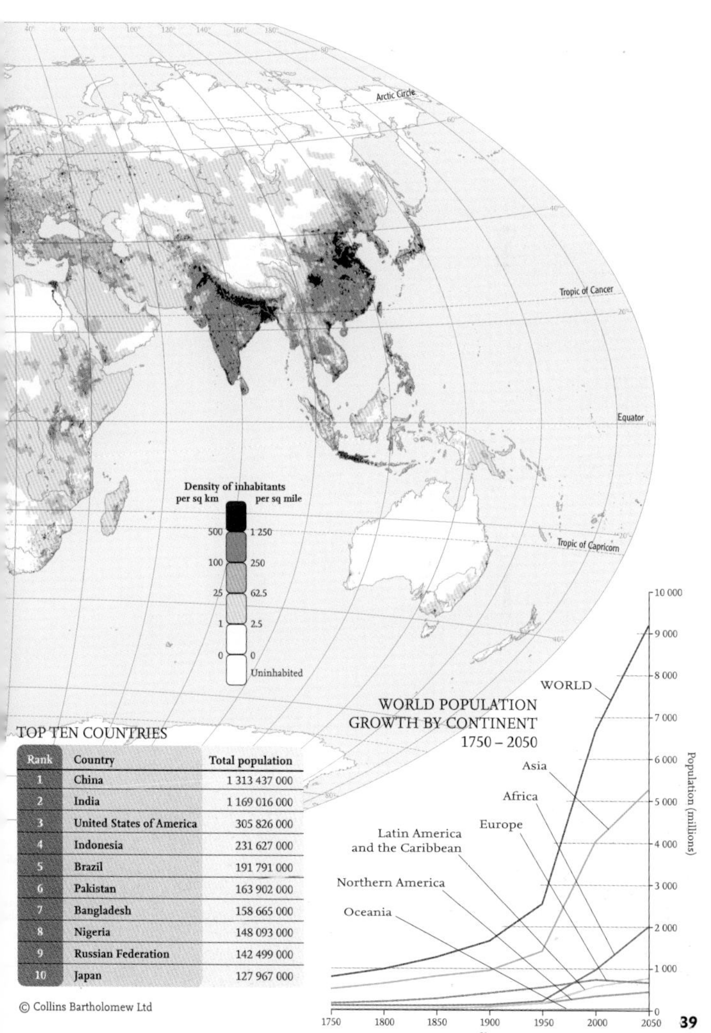

Density of inhabitants
per sq km   per sq mile

500	1 250
100	250
25	62.5
1	2.5
0	0
	Uninhabited

TOP TEN COUNTRIES

Rank	Country	Total population
1	China	1 313 437 000
2	India	1 169 016 000
3	United States of America	305 826 000
4	Indonesia	231 627 000
5	Brazil	191 791 000
6	Pakistan	163 902 000
7	Bangladesh	158 665 000
8	Nigeria	148 093 000
9	Russian Federation	142 499 000
10	Japan	127 967 000

WORLD POPULATION
GROWTH BY CONTINENT
1750 – 2050

WORLD

Asia

Africa

Europe

Latin America
and the Caribbean

Northern America

Oceania

THE WORLD'S MAJOR CITIES

Urban agglomerations with over
1 million inhabitants.
Winkel Tripel Projection
scale 1:190 000 000

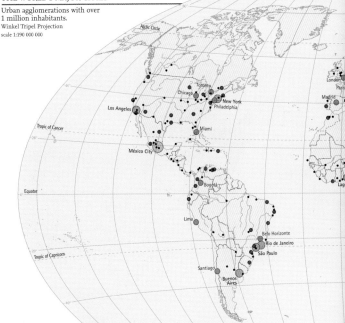

LEVEL OF URBANIZATION BY MAJOR REGION 1970–2030

Urban population as a percentage of total population

	1970	2010	2030
World	35.9	50.8	59.9
More developed regions[1]	64.6	75.2	80.8
Less developed regions[2]	25.2	45.5	56.1
Africa	23.4	40.5	50.7
Asia	22.7	42.5	54.1
Europe[3]	62.6	72.9	78.3
Latin America and the Caribbean[4]	57.2	79.1	84.3
Northern America	73.8	82.1	86.7
Oceania	70.8	71.2	73.8

1. Europe, North America, Australia,
New Zealand and Japan.
2. Africa, Asia (excluding Japan), Latin
America and the Caribbean, and
Oceania (excluding Australia and
New Zealand).
3. Includes Russian Federation.
4. South America, Central America
(including Mexico) and all Caribbean
Islands.

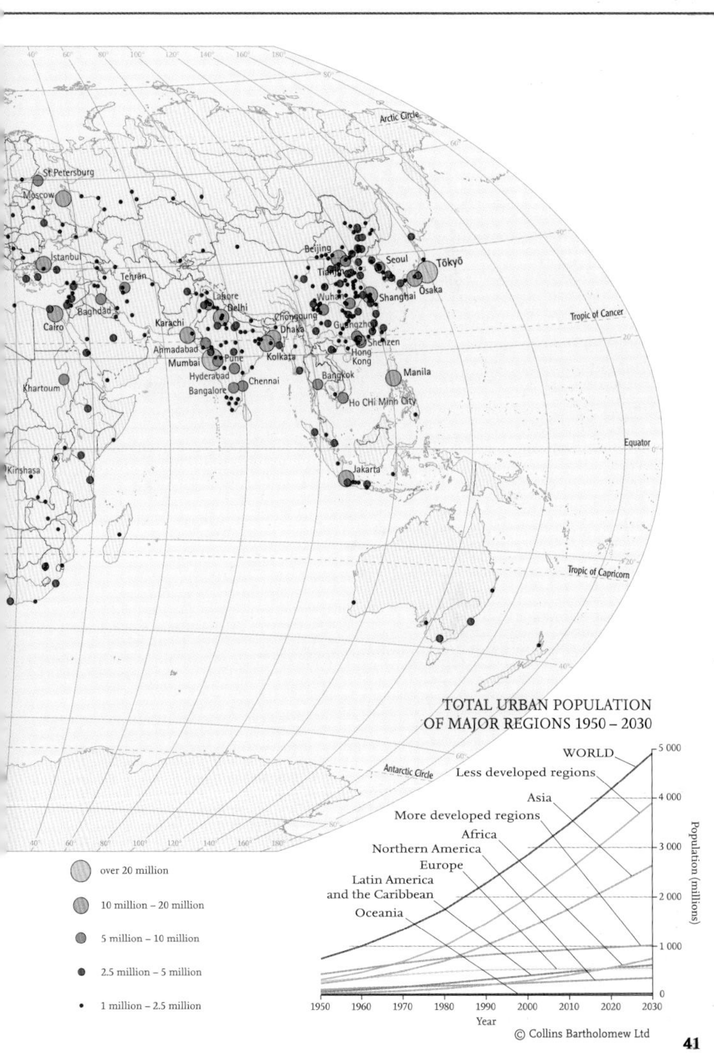

TOTAL URBAN POPULATION
OF MAJOR REGIONS 1950 – 2030

WORLD
Less developed regions
Asia
More developed regions
Africa
Northern America
Europe
Latin America
and the Caribbean
Oceania

Population (millions)

5 000
4 000
3 000
2 000
1 000

1950 1960 1970 1980 1990 2000 2010 2020 2030
Year

over 20 million
10 million – 20 million
5 million – 10 million
2.5 million – 5 million
1 million – 2.5 million

© Collins Bartholomew Ltd

SYMBOLS

Map symbols used on the map pages are explained here. The status of nations and their boundaries are shown in this atlas as they are in reality at time of going to press, as far as can be ascertained. Where international boundaries are subject of disputes the aim is to take a strictly neutral viewpoint, based on advice from expert consultants. Settlements are classified in terms of both population and administrative significance. The abbreviations listed are those used in place names on the map pages and within the index.

BOUNDARIES

International boundary

Disputed international boundary or alignment unconfirmed

Administrative boundary
Shown for selected countries only.

Ceasefire line or other boundary described on the map

TRANSPORT

Motorway

Main road

Track

Main railway

Canal

Main airport

LAND AND WATER FEATURES

Lake

Impermanent lake

Salt lake or lagoon

Impermanent salt lake

Dry salt lake or salt pan

River

Impermanent river

Ice cap / Glacier

Pass
height in metres

Summit
height in metres

Site of special interest

Wall

CITIES AND TOWNS

Population	National Capital	Administrative Capital Shown for selected countries only	Other City or Town
over 10 million	BEIJING ▣	São Paulo ◉	New York ◉
5 to 10 million	PARIS ▣	St Petersburg ◎	Chicago ◉
1 to 5 million	KUWAIT □	Sydney ○	Seattle ◉
500 000 to 1 million	BANGUI □	Winnipeg ○	Jeddah ○
100 000 to 500 000	WELLINGTON □	Edinburgh ○	Apucarana ○
50 000 to 100 000	PORT OF SPAIN □	Bismarck ○	Invercargill ○
under 50 000	MALABO ▫	Charlottetown ○	Ceres ○

STYLES OF LETTERING

Cities and towns are explained separately

Country	**FRANCE**
Overseas Territory/Dependency	**Guadeloupe**
Disputed Territory	AKSAI CHIN
Administrative name Shown for selected countries only.	**SCOTLAND**
Area name	PATAGONIA

Physical features

Island	*Gran Canaria*
Lake	*Lake Erie*
Mountain	*Mt Blanc*
River	*Thames*
Region	*LAPPLAND*

CONTINENTAL MAPS

BOUNDARIES

———— International boundary

------- Disputed international boundary

········ Ceasefire line

CITIES AND TOWNS

National capital	Other city or town
Kuwait □	Seattle ○

ABBREVIATIONS

Arch.	Archipelago				**Mts**	Mountains Monts	French	hills, mountains
B.	Bay				**N.**	North, Northern		
	Bahia, Baía	Portuguese	bay		**O.**	Ostrov	Russian	island
	Bahía	Spanish	bay		**Pt**	Point		
	Baie	French	bay		**Pta**	Punta	Italian, Spanish	cape, point
C.	Cape				**R.**	River		
	Cabo	Portuguese, Spanish	cape, headland			Rio	Portuguese	river
	Cap	French	cape, headland			Río	Spanish	river
Co	Cerro	Spanish	hill, peak, summit			Rivière	French	river
E.	East, Eastern				**Ra.**	Range		
Est.	Estrecho	Spanish	strait		**S.**	South, Southern		
						Salar, Salina, Salinas	Spanish	saltpan, saltpans
Gt	Great				**Sa**	Serra	Portuguese	mountain range
I.	Island, Isle					Sierra	Spanish	mountain range
	Ilha	Portuguese	island					
	Islas	Spanish	island		**Sd**	Sound		
Is	Islands, Isles				**S.E.**	Southeast, Southeastern		
	Islas	Spanish	islands		**St**	Saint		
Khr.	Khrebet	Russian	mountain range			Sankt	German	
						Sint	Dutch	saint
L.	Lake				**Sta**	Santa	Italian, Portuguese, Spanish	saint
	Loch	(Scotland)	lake					
	Lough	(Ireland)	lake		**Ste**	Sainte	French	saint
	Lac	French	lake		**Ste.**	Strait		
	Lago	Portuguese, Spanish	lake		**W.**	West, Western		
M.	Mys	Russian	cape, point			Wadi, Wādī	Arabic	watercourse
Mt	Mount							
	Mont	French	hill, mountain					
Mts	Mountain							

© Collins Bartholomew Ltd

43

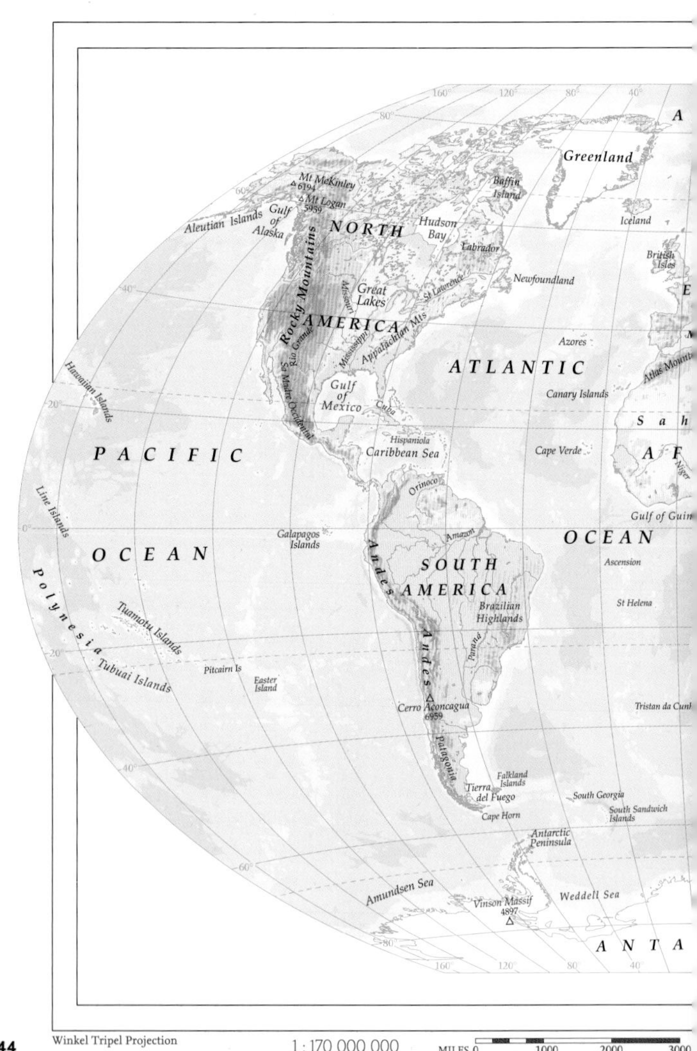

Greenland

Iceland

British Isles

Mt McKinley
6194
Mt Logan
5959

Aleutian Islands
Gulf of Alaska

Baffin Island

NORTH

Hudson Bay

Labrador

Newfoundland

Rocky Mountains

Great Lakes

St Lawrence

AMERICA

Appalachian Mts

Azores

ATLANTIC

Hawaiian Islands

Rio Grande

Gulf of Mexico

Sierra Madre

Canary Islands

Cuba

Sahara

PACIFIC

Hispaniola

Caribbean Sea

Cape Verde

AF

Line Islands

Orinoco

Gulf of Guin

OCEAN

Galapagos Islands

OCEAN

SOUTH

Amazon

Ascension

Polynesia

Andes

AMERICA

Brazilian Highlands

St Helena

Tuamotu Islands

Tubuai Islands

Pitcairn Is

Easter Island

Paraná

Cerro Aconcagua
6959

Patagonia

Tristan da Cunl

Falkland Islands

Tierra del Fuego

South Georgia

South Sandwich Islands

Cape Horn

Antarctic Peninsula

Amundsen Sea

Vinson Massif
4897

Weddell Sea

ANTA

Winkel Tripel Projection 1 : 170 000 000 MILES 0   1000   2000   3000

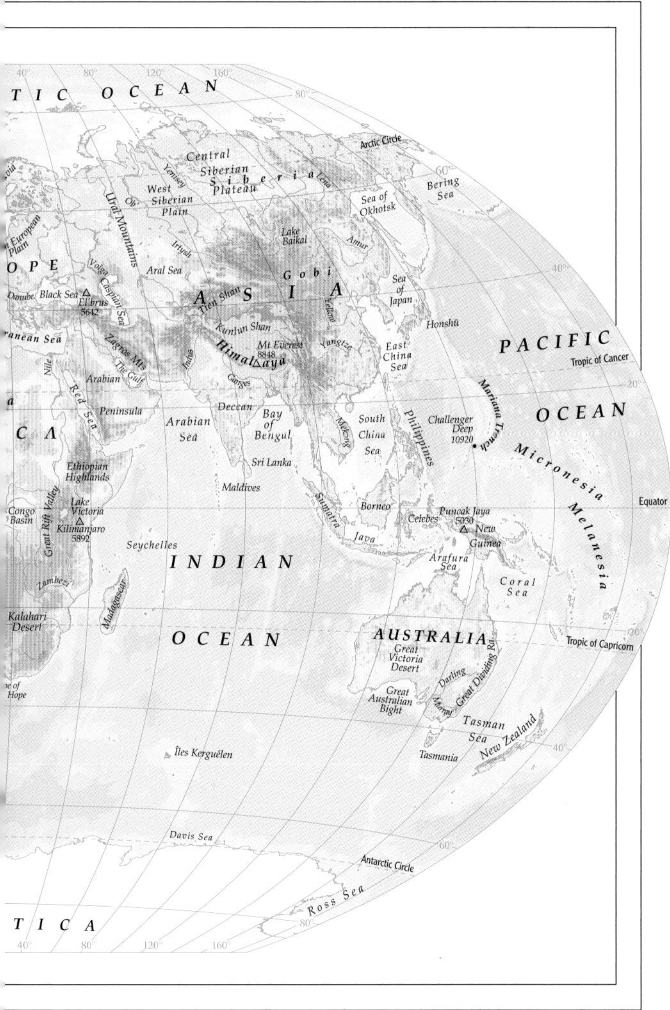

TIC OCEAN

Arctic Circle

Central
Siberian
Plateau

West
Siberian
Plain

S i b e r i a

Lena

Yenisey

Ob

Ural Mountains

Irtysh

Aral Sea

Sea of
Okhotsk

Bering
Sea

Lake
Baikal

Amur

60

OPE

European
Plain

Danube

Black Sea △
Elbrus
5642

Caspian Sea

Volga

Tien Shan

Gobi

A S I A

Sea
of
Japan

40

Mediterranean Sea

Zagros Mts

The Gulf

Kunlun Shan

Mt Everest
8848
Himalaya△ayu

Honshū

PACIFIC

Indus

Ganges

Yangtze

East
China
Sea

Tropic of Cancer

20

Nile

Arabian
Peninsula

Red Sea

Arabian
Sea

Deccan

Bay
of
Bengal

Mekong

South
China
Sea

Philippines

Challenger
Deep
10920

Mariana Trench

OCEAN

Micronesia

Ethiopian
Highlands

Sri Lanka

Maldives

Sumatra

Borneo

Celebes

Puncak Jaya
5030
△ New
Guinea

Equator

Melanesia

Congo
Basin

Great Rift Valley

Lake
Victoria

Kilimanjaro
5892

Java

Arafura
Sea

Seychelles

INDIAN

Coral
Sea

Zambezi

Madagascar

OCEAN

AUSTRALIA

Great
Victoria
Desert

Tropic of Capricorn

20

Kalahari
Desert

Darling

Great Dividing Ra.

ne of
Hope

Great
Australian
Bight

Murray

Tasman
Sea

New Zealand

40

Îles Kerguélen

Tasmania

Davis Sea

Antarctic Circle

60

TICA

Ross Sea

80

© Collins Bartholomew Ltd

0   1000   2000   3000   4000   5000 KILOMETRES

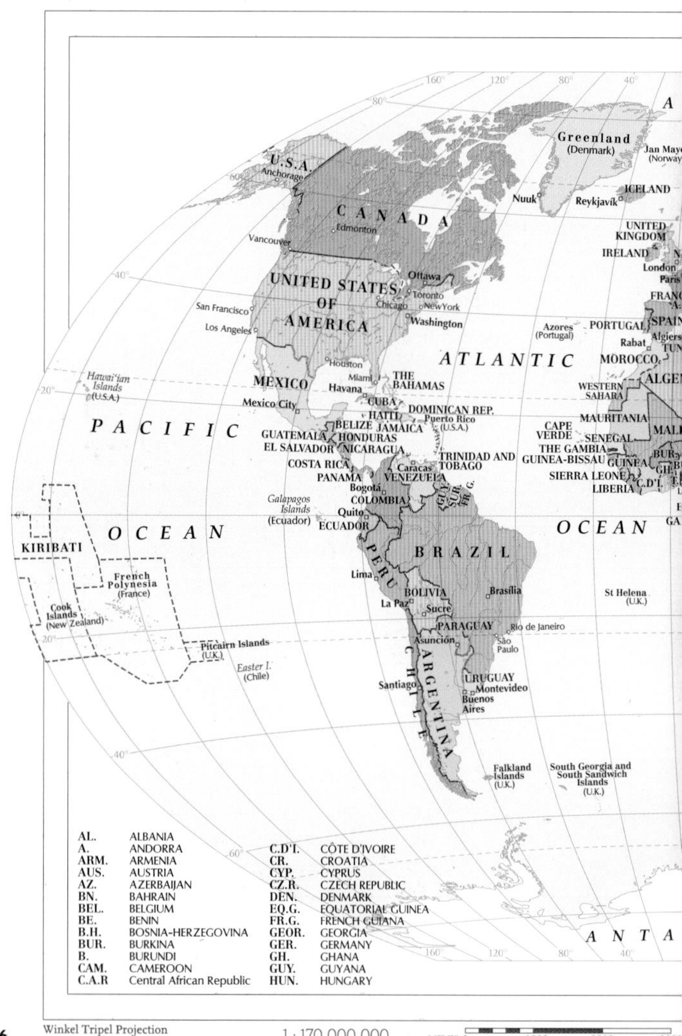

AL.   ALBANIA
A.   ANDORRA
ARM.   ARMENIA
AUS.   AUSTRIA
AZ.   AZERBAIJAN
BN.   BAHRAIN
BEL.   BELGIUM
BE.   BENIN
B.H.   BOSNIA–HERZEGOVINA
BUR.   BURKINA
B.   BURUNDI
CAM.   CAMEROON
C.A.R   Central African Republic

C.D'I.   CÔTE D'IVOIRE
CR.   CROATIA
CYP.   CYPRUS
CZ.R.   CZECH REPUBLIC
DEN.   DENMARK
EQ.G.   EQUATORIAL GUINEA
FR.G.   FRENCH GUIANA
GEOR.   GEORGIA
GER.   GERMANY
GH.   GHANA
GUY.   GUYANA
HUN.   HUNGARY

Winkel Tripel Projection   1 : 170 000 000   MILES 0   1000   2000   3000

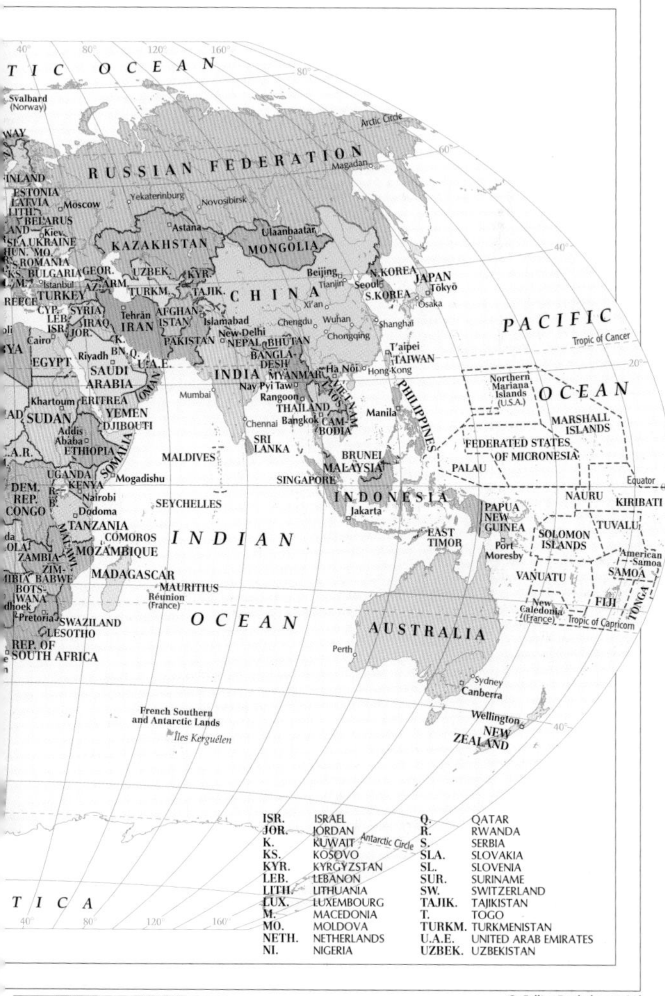

ISR.	ISRAEL	Q.	QATAR
JOR.	JORDAN	R.	RWANDA
K.	KUWAIT	S.	SERBIA
KS.	KOSOVO	SLA.	SLOVAKIA
KYR.	KYRGYZSTAN	SL.	SLOVENIA
LEB.	LEBANON	SUR.	SURINAME
LITH.	LITHUANIA	SW.	SWITZERLAND
LUX.	LUXEMBOURG	TAJIK.	TAJIKISTAN
M.	MACEDONIA	T.	TOGO
MO.	MOLDOVA	TURKM.	TURKMENISTAN
NETH.	NETHERLANDS	U.A.E.	UNITED ARAB EMIRATES
NI.	NIGERIA	UZBEK.	UZBEKISTAN

0   1000   2000   3000   4000   5000 KILOMETRES

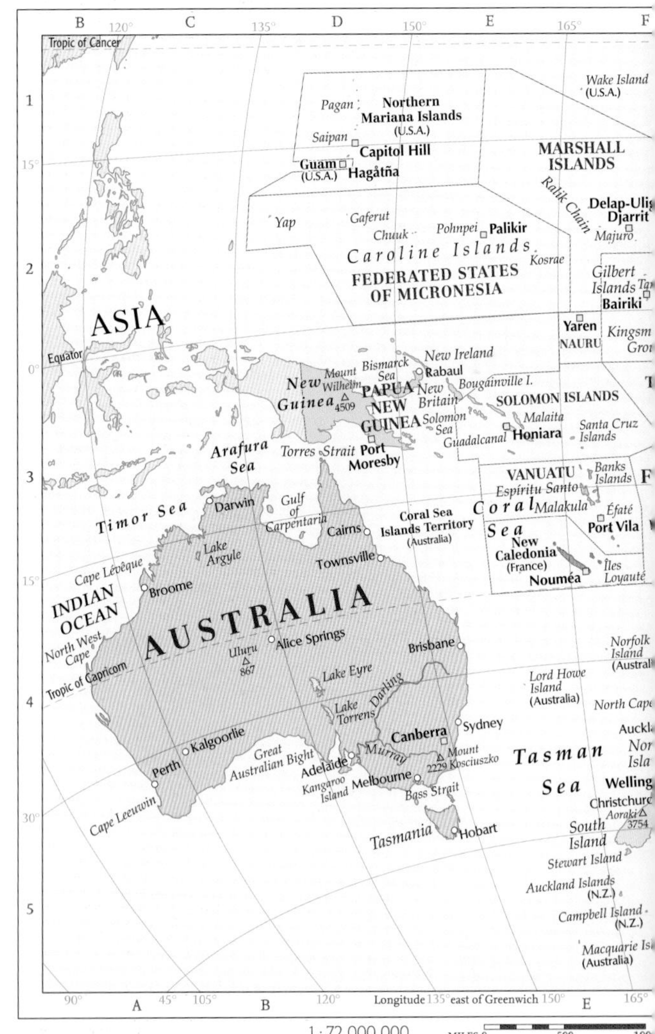

B 120° **C** 135° **D** 150° **E** 165° **F**

Tropic of Cancer

Wake Island (U.S.A.)

Pagan **Northern Mariana Islands** (U.S.A.)

Saipan **Capitol Hill**

Guam (U.S.A.) **Hagåtña**

MARSHALL ISLANDS

Gaferut **Delap-Uli Djarrit**

Yap *Chuuk* *Pohnpei* **Palikir** *Majuro*

Ca r o l i n e I s l a n d s

FEDERATED STATES OF MICRONESIA *Kosrae*

Gilbert Islands Ta

Bairiki

Yaren

NAURU *Kingsm Gro*

ASIA

Equator

Mount Wilhelm **New** *Bismarck Sea* **Rabaul** *New Ireland*

4509 **Guinea** **PAPUA** *New Bougainville I.* *Britain*

NEW GUINEA *Solomon Sea* **SOLOMON ISLANDS**

Malaita

Port *Guadalcanal* **Honiara**

Moresby *Santa Cruz Islands*

Arafura Sea *Torres Strait*

VANUATU *Banks Islands*

Espiritu Santo *C o r a l* *Éfaté*

Timor Sea **Darwin** *Malakula* *Sea* **Port Vila**

Gulf of Carpentaria **Coral Sea Islands Territory** (Australia) **New Caledonia** (France)

Cape Lévêque **Broome** *Cairns* *Îles Loyauté*

Nouméa

INDIAN OCEAN

North West Cape

AUSTRALIA

Townsville

Norfolk Island (Australia)

Lake Argyle

Uluru **Alice Springs** **Brisbane**

Tropic of Capricorn *867*

Lord Howe Island (Australia) *North Cape*

Lake Eyre *Darling*

Auckla

Perth *Kalgoorlie* *Lake Torrens* **Sydney** *Nor Isla*

T a s m a n

Adelaide *Murray* **Canberra**

Great Australian Bight *Mount 2229 Kosciuszko* **Welling**

Kangaroo Island **Melbourne** *Sea* **Christchur**

Cape Leeuwin *Bass Strait* *Aoraki 3754*

Tasmania **Hobart** *South Island*

Stewart Island

Auckland Islands (N.Z.)

Campbell Island (N.Z.)

Macquarie Isl (Australia)

90° **A** 45° 105° **B** 120° Longitude 135° east of Greenwich 150° **E**

1 : 72 000 000 MILES 0 500 100

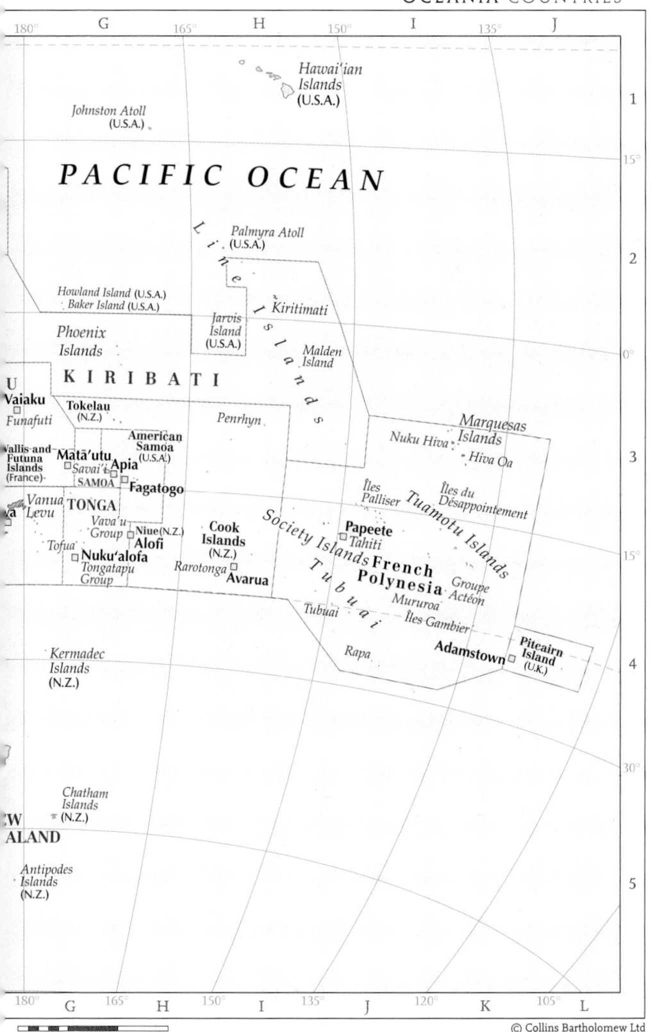

PACIFIC OCEAN

180° G 165° H 150° I 135° J

1

15°

Johnston Atoll
(U.S.A.)

2

Palmyra Atoll
(U.S.A.)

Howland Island (U.S.A.)
Baker Island (U.S.A.)

Jarvis
Island
(U.S.A.)

Kiritimati

Malden
Island

0°

Phoenix
Islands

KIRIBATI

U
Vaiaku □ **Tokelau**
Funafuti *(N.Z.)*

Penrhyn

Nuku Hiva

Marquesas
Islands
Hiva Oa

Ameriĉan
Samoa

Wallis and **Matā'utu** *(U.S.A.)*
Futuna □*Savai'i* **Apia**
Islands **SAMOA** □ **Fagatogo**
(France)

Îles
Palliser

Îles du
Désappointement

Tuamotu Islands

3

Vanua Levu
TONGA

Vava'u
Group □ **Niue** *(N.Z.)*
Tofua' □ **Alofi**
Nuku'alofa
Tongatapu
Group

Cook
Islands
(N.Z.)
Rarotonga □
Avarua

Society Islands

Papeete
Tahiti

French
Polynesia

Groupe
Actéon

15°

T u b u a i
Tubuai

Mururoa
Îles Gambier

Kermadec
Islands
(N.Z.)

Rapa

Adamstown □

Pitcairn
Island
(U.K.)

4

30°

Chatham
Islands
(N.Z.)

W
ALAND

Antipodes
Islands
(N.Z.)

5

180° G 165° H 150° I 135° J 120° K 105° L

© Collins Bartholomew Ltd

0 500 1000 1500 KILOMETRES

49

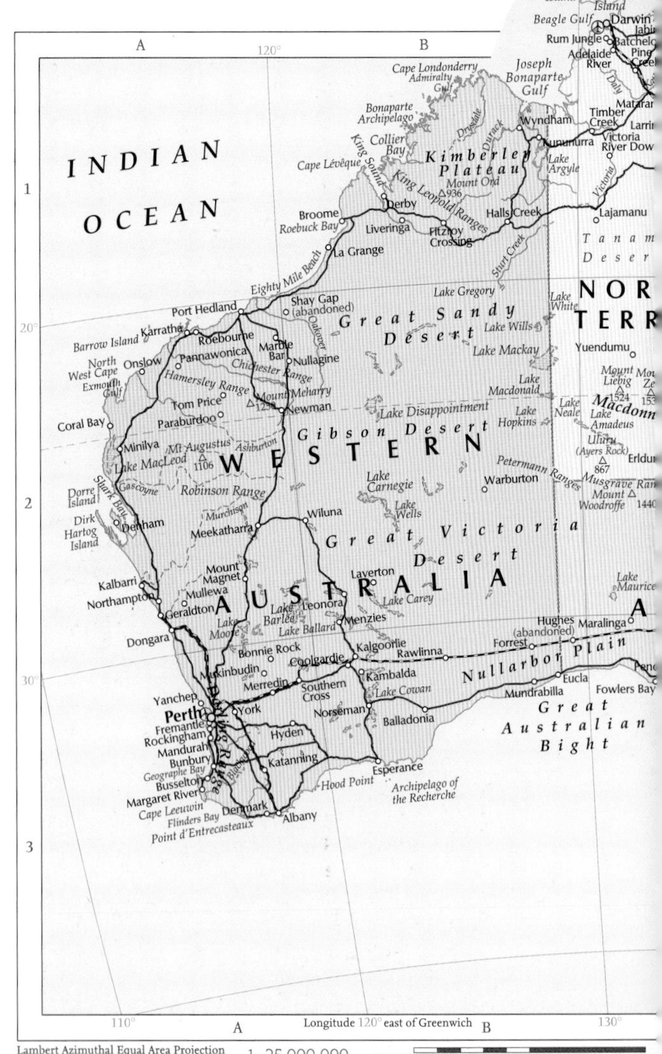

INDIAN

OCEAN

WESTERN

AUSTRALIA

Kimberley Plateau

Great Sandy Desert

Gibson Desert

Great Victoria Desert

Tanami Desert

NOR
TERR

Nullarbor Plain

Great Australian Bight

Bathurst Island
Melville Island
Cape
Beagle Gulf
Darwin
Jabi
Rum Jungle
Adelaide River
Batchel
Pin
Mataran
Timber Creek
Larri
Victoria River Dow

Cape Londonderry
Admiralty
Bonaparte Archipelago
Joseph Bonaparte Gulf
Wyndham
Kununurra
Lake Argyle
Collier Bay
King Leopold Ranges
Mount Ord 936
Halls Creek
Lajamanu

Cape Lévêque
King Sound
Derby
Liveringa
Fitzroy Crossing
Sturt Creek
Lake White

Broome
Roebuck Bay
La Grange

Eighty Mile Beach
Shay Gap (abandoned)
Lake Gregory
Yuendumu

Port Hedland
Barrow Island
Karratha
Roebourne
Marble Bar
Nullagine
Fortescue
Lake Wills
Mount Liebig
Mou
Ze

North West Cape
Exmouth Gulf
Onslow
Pannawonica
Chichester Range
Mount Meharry
Lake Mackay

Coral Bay
Tom Price
Paraburdoo
Hamersley Range
Ashburton
Newman
Lake Disappointment
Lake Macdonald
Mt
Macdonn

Minilya
Mt Augustus 1106
Robinson Range
Lake Hopkins
Lake Neale
Mount Amadeus
(Ayers Rock)
Erldur

Dorre Island
Lake MacLeod
Gascoyne
Murchison
Lake Carnegie
Warburton
Petermann Ranges
Musgrave Rang
Mount Woodroffe 1440

Dirk Hartog Island
Denham
Meekatharra
Lake Wells
Mount Woodroffe

Kalbarri
Northampton
Mullewa
Geraldton
Mount Magnet
Wiluna
Lake Carey
Laverton
Lake Maurice

Dongara
Lake Moore
Leonora
Menzies
Hughes
Maralinga
A

Bonnie Rock
Mukinbudin
Kalgoorlie
Rawlinna
Forrest
Pene

Perth
Fremantle
Rockingham
Mandurah
Bunbury
Busselton
Merredin
Coolgardie
Kambalda
Eucla
Mundrabilla
Fowlers Bay

Yanchep
York
Southern Cross
Norseman
Lake Cowan
Balladonia

Katanning
Hyden
Esperance
Hood Point

Margaret River
Geographe Bay
Denmark
Albany
Archipelago of the Recherche

Cape Leeuwin
Flinders Bay
Point d'Entrecasteaux

Lambert Azimuthal Equal Area Projection   1 : 25 000 000   MILES 0   250   500

A   120°   B

110°   A   Longitude 120° east of Greenwich   B   130°

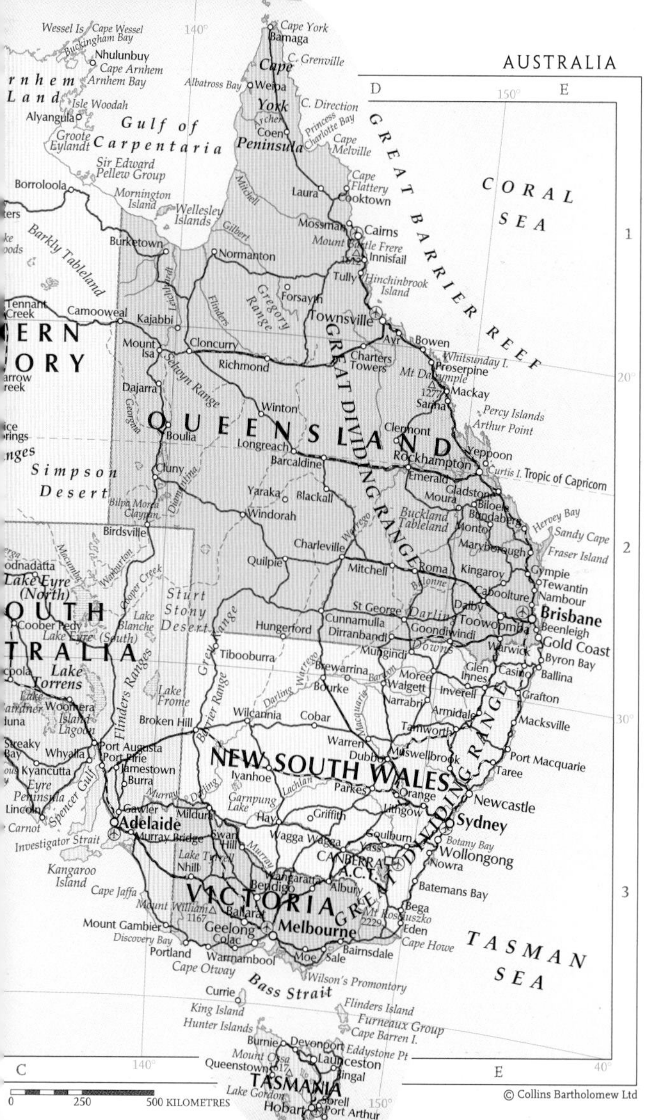

Wessel Is Cape Wessel
Bingham Bay
Nhulunbuy
Cape Arnhem
Arnhem Bay
Isle Woodah
rnhem
Land
Alyangula
Groote
Eylandt
Sir Edward
Pellew Group
Borroloola

Gulf of
Carpentaria

Mornington
Island
Wellesley
Islands

Cape York
Bamaga
C. Grenville
Cape
Yorki
ychel
Princess
Charlotte Bay
Cape
Melville

CORAL

SEA

Cape
York
Peninsula

Weipa
C. Direction

Albatross Bay

Cape Arnhem

Burketown

Normanton

Laura

Cape
Flattery
Cooktown

Mossman
Mount Bartle Frere
Cairns
Innisfail

GREAT BARRIER REEF

1

ke
oods

Barkly Tableland

Tennant
Creek

RN
ORY

arrow
reek

ice
rings

nges

Camooweal

Mount
Isa

Dajarra

Kajabbi

Cloncurry

Richmond

Forsayth

Tully
Hinchinbrook
Island

Townsville

Charters
Towers

Ayr

Bowen
Whitsunday I.
Proserpine

Mt Dalrymple

Mackay

20°

Simpson
Desert

Boulia

Cluny

Winton

Longreach

Barcaldine

Sarina

Percy Islands
Arthur Point

Clermont

Rockhampton

Yeppoon

Birdsville

Bilpa Morea
Claypan

Yaraka

Blackall

Windorah

Emerald

Moura

Curtis I. Tropic of Capricorn

Gladstone

odnadatta
Lake Eyre
(North)

Coober Pedy

opola

OUTH
TRALIA

Lake
Eyre
(South)

Sturt
Stony
Desert

Quilpie

Charleville

Mitchell

Roma

Kingaroy

Buckland
Tableland

Biloela
Monto

Maryborough

Gympie

Hervey Bay

Sandy Cape

Fraser Island

Bundaberg

2

ce
rings

nges

Lake
Blanche

Birdsville

Windorah

St George

Hungerford

Cunnamulla

Dirranbandi

Goondiwindi

Dalby
Toowoomba

Nambour
Caboolture

Brisbane
Beenleigh
Gold Coast

Tibooburra

Brewarrina

Mungindi

Warwick

Byron Bay

Casino

Ballina

Lake
Torrens

Flinders Ranges

Lake
Frome

Wilcannia

Bourke

Walgett

Moree

Inverell

Glen Innes

Grafton

Macksville

ow
nel

Broken Hill

Cobar

Narrabri

Armidale

Port Macquarie

30°

Streaky
Bay

Whyalla

Port Augusta
Port Pirie
Jamestown
Burra

Warren

Dubbo

Tamworth

Muswellbrook

Taree

NEW SOUTH WALES

arnot

Kyancutta

Eyre
Peninsula

Lincoln

Woomera
Iuna

Gawler

Iyanhoe

Carngung
Lake

Parkes

Orange

Newcastle

Gulargambone

Adelaide

Murray Bridge

Hay

Griffith

Lithgow

Sydney

Botany Bay

Wollongong

Investigator Strait

Kangaroo
Island

Cape Jaffa

Lake
Alexandrina

Nhill

Swan
Hill

Wagga Wagga

CANBERRA
A.C.T.

Kosciuszko

Nowra

Batemans Bay

3

Mount Gambier

VICTORIA

Mount William
1167

Ballarat
Bendigo

Shepparton

Bega

Eden

Cape Howe

TASMAN

Geelong
Colac

Melbourne

Moe
Sale

Bairnsdale

SEA

Portland

Warrnambool

Cape Otway

Discovery Bay

Wilson's Promontory

Bass Strait

Currie

King Island

Flinders Island

Furneaux Group

Cape Barren I.

Hunter Islands

Burnie
Mount
Queenstown

Devonport
Cleveland

Launceston

Eddystone Pt

St Helens

Lake Gordon

TASMANIA

Hobart

Sorell

Port Arthur

GREAT DIVIDING RANGE

QUEENSLAND

Gregory Range

Gilbert

Flinders

Georgina

Mulligan

Thomson

Barcoo

Cooper Creek

Warrego

Darling

Macquarie

Lachlan

Murrumbidgee

Murray

140°

D

150°

E

40°

C

140°

150°

E

0   250   500 KILOMETRES

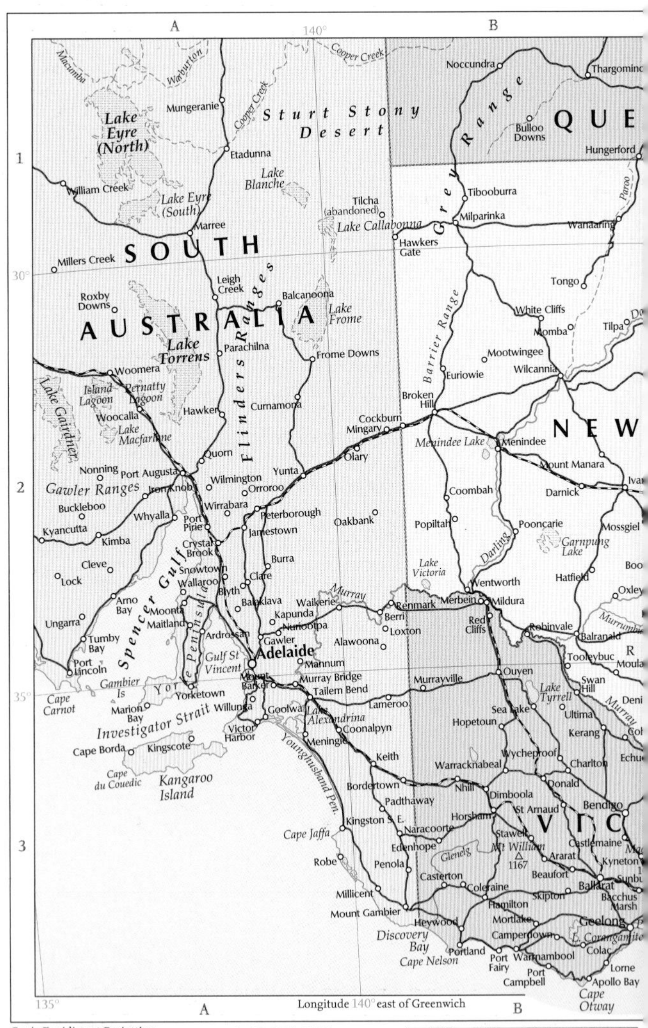

A

140°

B

Lake Eyre (North)

Macumba

Warburton

Macumba

Mungeranie

Copper Creek

Copper Creek

Noccundra

Thargomin

Sturt Stony Desert

Bulloo Downs

QUE

Hungerford

William Creek

Etadunna

Lake Blanche

Grey Range

Paroo

1

Lake Eyre (South)

Marree

Tilcha (abandoned)

Lake Callabonna

Hawkers Gate

Tibooburra

Milparinka

Wanaaring

Millers Creek

SOUTH

Leigh Creek

Roxby Downs

Balcanoona

Lake Frome

Tongo

White Cliffs

Momba

Tilpa

Do

30°

Parachilna

Frome Downs

Barrier Range

AUSTRALIA

Lake Torrens

Flinders Ranges

Curnamona

Mootwingee

Wilcannia

Euriowie

Woomera

Pernatty Lagoon

Island Lagoon

Woocalla

Hawker

Lake Macfarlane

Cockburn Mingary

Broken Hill

NEW

Lake Gairdner

Nonning

Quorn

Yunta

Olary

Menindee Lake

Menindee

Mount Manara

2

Gawler Ranges

Port Augusta

Iron Knob

Wilmington

Orroroo

Coombah

Darnick

Iva

Buckleboo

Whyalla

Wirrabara

Peterborough

Popiltah

Pooncarie

Garnpung Lake

Mossgie

Kyancutta

Port Pirie

Jamestown

Oakbank

Darling

Boo

Kimba

Crystal Brook

Burra

Lake Victoria

Hatfield

Oxley

Cleve

Snowtown

Clare

Wentworth

Lock

Wallaroo

Blyth

Balaklava

Walkerie

Murray

Renmark

Merbein

Mildura

Murrum

Ungarra

Arno Bay

Moonta

Maitland

Kapunda

Nuriootpa

Berri

Loxton

Red Cliffs

Robinvale

Balranald

R

Tumby Bay

Ardrossan

Gawler

Alawoona

Tooleybuc

Moula

Port Lincoln

Adelaide

Spencer Gulf

Yorke Peninsula

Gulf St Vincent

Murray Bridge

Tailem Bend

Murrayville

Ouyen

Lake Tyrrell

Swan Hill

Deni

35°

Gambier Is

Marion Bay

Yorketown

Willunga

Goolwa

Mannum

Lameroo

Sea Lake

Ultima

Kerang

Gol

Cape Carnot

Investigator Strait

Cape Borda

Kingscote

Victor Harbor

Meningie

Lake Alexandrina

Coonalpyn

Hopetoun

Wycheproof

Charlton

Echu

Cape du Couedic

Kangaroo Island

Keith

Warracknabeal

Nhill

Dimboola

Donald

Bendig

Coonalpyn Downs Pen.

Bordertown

Padthaway

Naracoorte

Horsham

St Arnaud

Stawell

VIC

Cape Jaffa

Edenhope

Kingston S.E.

Penola

Glenelg

Casterton

Coleraine

Mt William △ 1167

Ararat

Beaufort

Kyneton

Ballarat

Castlemaine

Sunbu

Bacchus Marsh

3

Robe

Millicent

Mount Gambier

Heywood

Hamilton

Mortlake

Kipton

Geelong

Co

Discovery Bay

Cape Nelson

Portland

Fairy

Port Warrnambool

Campervown

Colac

Corang

Port Campbell

Lorne

Apollo Bay

Cape Otway

Longitude 140° east of Greenwich

A

B

52

Conic Equidistant Projection

1:10 000 000

MILES 0

100

200

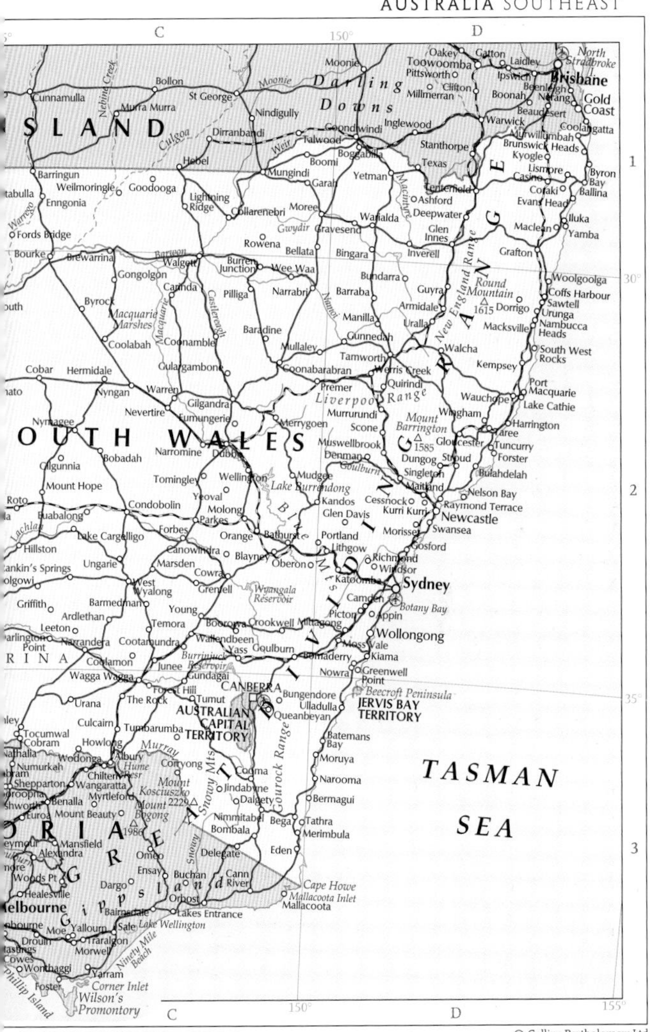
TASMAN
SEA
Sydney
Newcastle
Wollongong
Brisbane
Gold Coast
CANBERRA
AUSTRALIAN CAPITAL TERRITORY
JERVIS BAY TERRITORY
Darling Downs
Blue Mts
Snowy Mts
New England Range
Liverpool Range
Gourock Range
Mount Kosciuszko 2229
Mount Barrington 1585
Round Mountain 1615
Mount Bogong 1986
Botany Bay
Beecroft Peninsula
Cape Howe
Mallacoota Inlet
Wilson's Promontory
Corner Inlet
Phillip Island
Ninety Mile Beach
Lake Wellington
Lake Burrendong
Wyangala Reservoir
Burrinjuck Reservoir
Hume Resr
Macquarie Marshes
150°
155°
30°
35°
C
D
1
2
3
0
100
200
300 KILOMETRES
© Collins Bartholomew Ltd

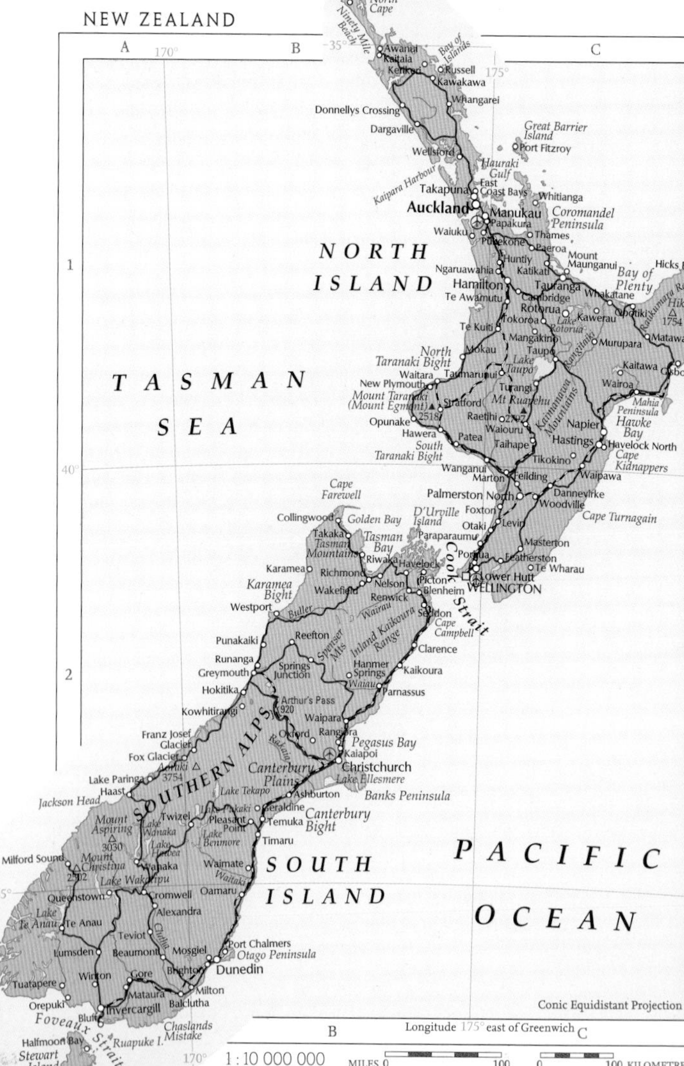

NEW ZEALAND

A B C

170° 35° 175°

Te Paki
North
Cape
Ninety Mile Beach
Awanui
Kaitaia
Kerikeri
Bay of Islands
Russell
Kawakawa
Whangarei

Donnellys Crossing
Dargaville
Wellsford
Takapuna
Kaipara Harbour
East Coast Bays
Auckland
Manukau
Papakura
Waiuku
Pukekohe
Ngaruawahia
Huntly
Te Awamutu
Hamilton
Te Kuiti

Great Barrier Island
Port Fitzroy
Hauraki Gulf
Whitianga
Coromandel Peninsula
Thames
Paeroa
Mount Maunganui
Katikati
Tauranga
Cambridge
Rotorua
Kawerau
Lake Rotorua

Hicks Bay

Bay of Plenty
Opotiki
Matawai
Gisborne
Kaitawa
Wairoa
Mahia Peninsula
Hawke Bay

NORTH
ISLAND

TASMAN
SEA

North
Taranaki Bight
Mokau
Waitara
New Plymouth
Mount Taranaki
(Mount Egmont)
Opunake
Hawera
Patea
South
Taranaki Bight

Taumarunui
Stratford
Raetihi
Mt Ruapehu
Waiouru
Taihape

Lake Taupo
Turangi
Napier
Hastings
Havelock North
Cape Kidnappers

Wanganui
Marton
Feilding
Palmerston North
Foxton
Otaki
Levin

Dannevirke
Woodville
Waipawa
Waipukurau
Cape Turnagain

40°

Cape Farewell

Collingwood
Takaka
Golden Bay
Tasman Mountains
Karamea
Karamea Bight
Westport
Punakaiki
Runanga
Greymouth
Hokitika
Kowhitirangi

Riwaka
Motueka
Tasman Bay
Nelson
Richmond
Wakefield
Renwick
Havelock
Picton
Blenheim
Buller
Reefton
Murchison
Springs Junction

D'Urville Island
Paraparaumu

Cook Strait
Lower Hutt
WELLINGTON
Masterton
Carterton
Greytown
Te Wharau
Featherston

Seddon
Cape Campbell
Clarence
Inland Kaikoura Range
Kaikoura
Hanmer Springs
Waiau
Parnassus
Waipara

2

Arthur's Pass
1020
Franz Josef Glacier
Fox Glacier
Aoraki 3754
Haast
Jackson Head

SOUTHERN ALPS

Lake Paringa
Mount Aspiring 3030
Milford Sound
Lake Te Anau
Te Anau
Tuatapere
Orepuki

Lake Coleridge
Oxford
Rangiora
Pegasus Bay
Kaiapoi
Christchurch
Lake Ellesmere
Banks Peninsula
Canterbury Plains
Darfield

Methven
Geraldine
Ashburton
Temuka
Timaru
Canterbury Bight

Lake Tekapo
Twizel
Lake Pukaki
Pleasant Point
Lake Ohau
Fairlie
Lake Benmore
Waimate
Waitaki
Oamaru

PACIFIC
OCEAN

45°

Queenstown
Lake Wanaka
Lake Hawea
Wanaka
Cromwell
Alexandra
Teviot

SOUTH
ISLAND

Lake Wakatipu
Lumsden
Winton
Gore
Mataura
Clutha
Balclutha

Mosgiel
Brighton
Dunedin
Port Chalmers
Otago Peninsula
Milton

Invercargill
Bluff
Chaslands Mistake

Foveaux Strait
Ruapuke I.

Halfmoon Bay
Stewart Island

B C
Longitude 175° east of Greenwich

170°

1 : 10 000 000

MILES 0   100
0   100 KILOMETRES

Conic Equidistant Projection

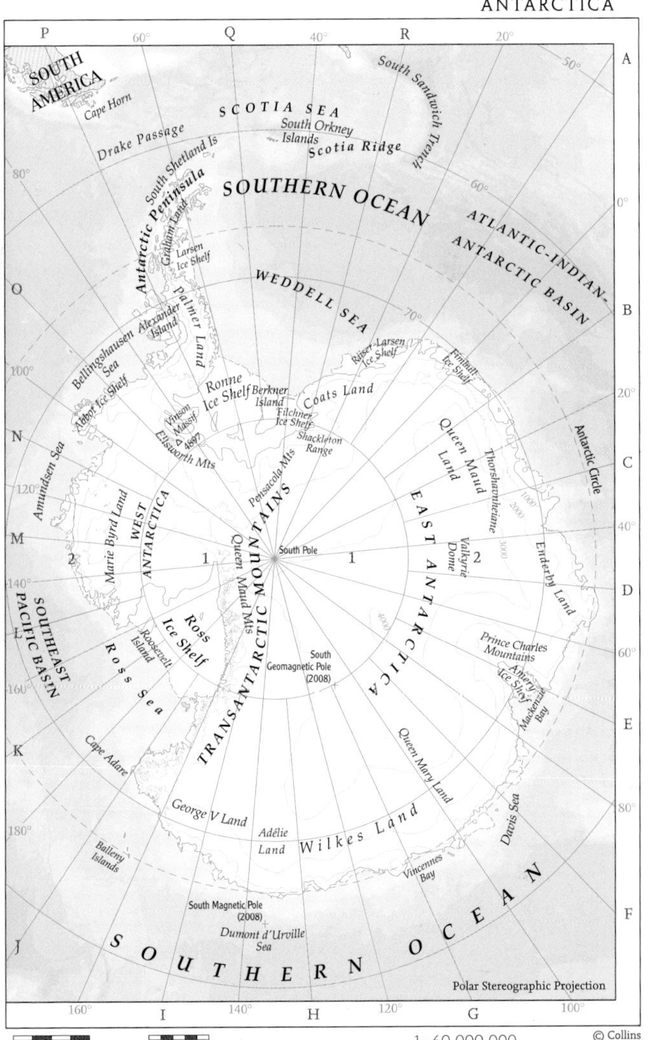

ANTARCTICA

P 60° Q 40° R 20° A

SOUTH AMERICA
Cape Horn
Drake Passage
SCOTIA SEA
South Sandwich Trench
South Orkney Islands
Scotia Ridge
South Shetland Is
Antarctic Peninsula
Graham Land
SOUTHERN OCEAN
ATLANTIC-INDIAN-
ANTARCTIC BASIN
Larsen Ice Shelf
Palmer Land
WEDDELL SEA
Bellingshausen Sea
Alexander Island
Riiser-Larsen Ice Shelf
Fimbul Ice Shelf
Abbot Ice Shelf
Ronne Ice Shelf
Berkner Island
Filchner Ice Shelf
Coats Land
Shackleton Range
Queen Maud Land
Thorshavnheiane
Antarctic Circle
Amundsen Sea
Vinson Massif △ 4897
Ellsworth Mts
Pensacola Mts
EAST ANTARCTICA
Valkyrie Dome
Enderby Land
Marie Byrd Land
WEST ANTARCTICA
Queen Maud Mts
South Pole
Ross Ice Shelf
Roosevelt Island
Ross Sea
TRANSANTARCTIC MOUNTAINS
South Geomagnetic Pole (2008)
Prince Charles Mountains
Amery Ice Shelf
Mac. Robertson Land
SOUTHEAST PACIFIC BASIN
Cape Adare
Balleny Islands
George V Land
Adélie Land
Wilkes Land
Queen Mary Land
Davis Sea
Vincennes Bay
South Magnetic Pole (2008)
Dumont d'Urville Sea
SOUTHERN OCEAN
Polar Stereographic Projection

0 400 MILES   0 500 KILOMETRES   1 : 60 000 000

© Collins Bartholomew Ltd   55

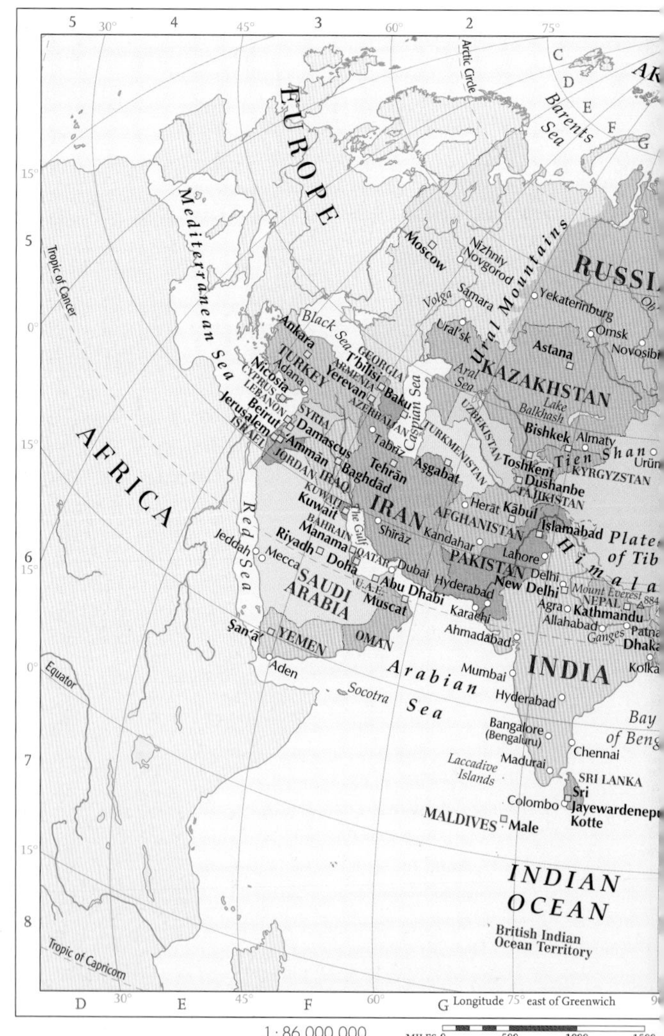
EUROPE
AFRICA
RUSSIA
KAZAKHSTAN
IRAN
INDIA
SAUDI ARABIA
Mediterranean Sea
Black Sea
Caspian Sea
Red Sea
Arabian Sea
INDIAN OCEAN
Ural Mountains
Moscow
Nizhniy Novgorod
Samara
Yekaterinburg
Omsk
Astana
Ankara
TURKEY
Nicosia
CYPRUS
Beirut
LEBANON
Jerusalem
ISRAEL
Damascus
SYRIA
'Ammān
JORDAN
Baghdād
IRAQ
Kuwait
KUWAIT
Manama
BAHRAIN
Doha
QATAR
Riyadh
Abu Dhabi
U.A.E.
Muscat
OMAN
Şan'ā'
YEMEN
Aden
Tehrān
Tabrīz
Shīrāz
T'bilisi
GEORGIA
Yerevan
ARMENIA
Baku
AZERBAIJAN
Aşgabat
TURKMENISTAN
UZBEKISTAN
Toshkent
Dushanbe
TAJIKISTAN
Bishkek
Almaty
KYRGYZSTAN
Kābul
AFGHANISTAN
Herāt
Kandahar
Islamabad
PAKISTAN
Lahore
Karachi
Hyderabad
New Delhi
Delhi
Kathmandu
NEPAL
Mumbai
Chennai
Colombo
Sri Jayewardenepura Kotte
SRI LANKA
Male
MALDIVES
British Indian Ocean Territory
Tropic of Cancer
Tropic of Capricorn
Equator
Arctic Circle
Longitude 75° east of Greenwich
1 : 86 000 000
MILES 0 500 1000 1500

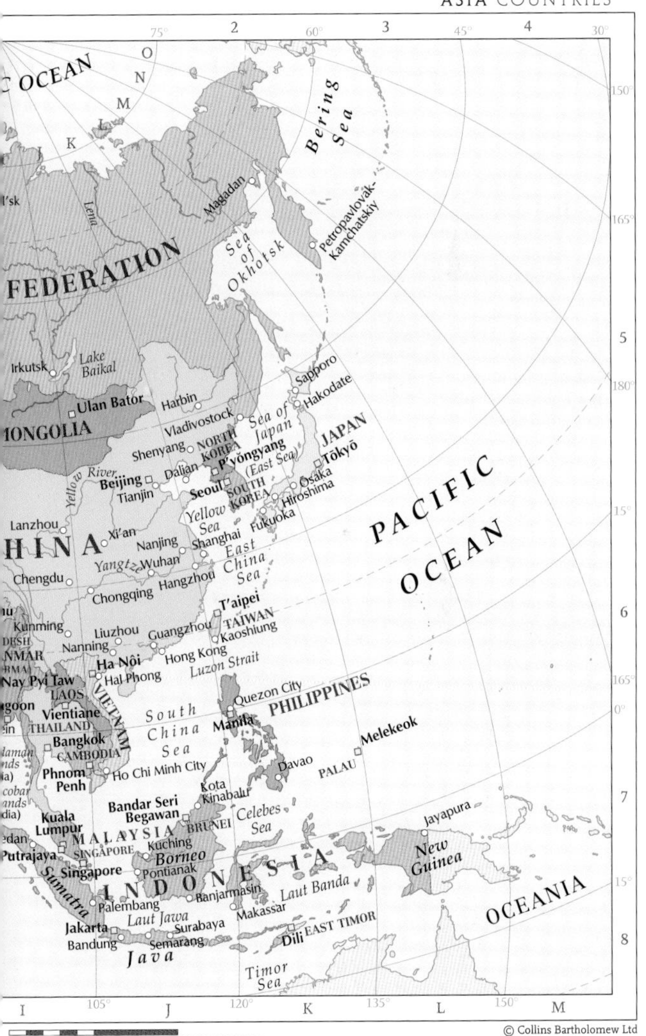

C OCEAN

FEDERATION

Bering
Sea

Lena

I'sk

Irkutsk

Lake
Baikal

Ulan Bator

MONGOLIA

Lanzhou

CHINA

Chengdu

Kunming

DISH

NMAR

Nay Pyi Taw

goon

Vientiane

THAILAND

Bangkok

Phnom
Penh

Kuala
Lumpur

Putrajaya

Singapore

Sumatra

Jakarta

Bandung

Java

Magadan

Sea
of
Okhotsk

Petropavlovsk-
Kamchatskiy

Sapporo

Hakodate

Harbin

Vladivostock

Shenyang

NORTH
KOREA

Sea of
Japan
(East Sea)

JAPAN

Beijing

Dalian

P'yongyang

Tokyo

Tianjin

Seoul

SOUTH
KOREA

Osaka

Hiroshima

Yellow River

Xi'an

Nanjing

Yellow
Sea

Shanghai

Fukuoka

Yangtze

Wuhan

East
China
Sea

Chongqing

Hangzhou

Liuzhou

Guangzhou

T'aipei

TAIWAN

Nanning

Kaoshiung

Ha Noi

Hong Kong

Hai Phong

Luzon Strait

LAOS

South
China
Sea

Quezon City

PHILIPPINES

Manila

Melekeok

CAMBODIA

Ho Chi Minh City

Davao

PALAU

Kota
Kinabalu

Bandar Seri
Begawan

Celebes
Sea

Jayapura

BRUNEI

MALAYSIA

Kuching

SINGAPORE

Borneo

Pontianak

INDONESIA

New
Guinea

Palembang

Laut Jawa

Banjarmasin

Makassar

Laut Banda

OCEANIA

Surabaya

Semarang

Dili

EAST TIMOR

Timor
Sea

PACIFIC

OCEAN

0   1000   2000 KILOMETRES

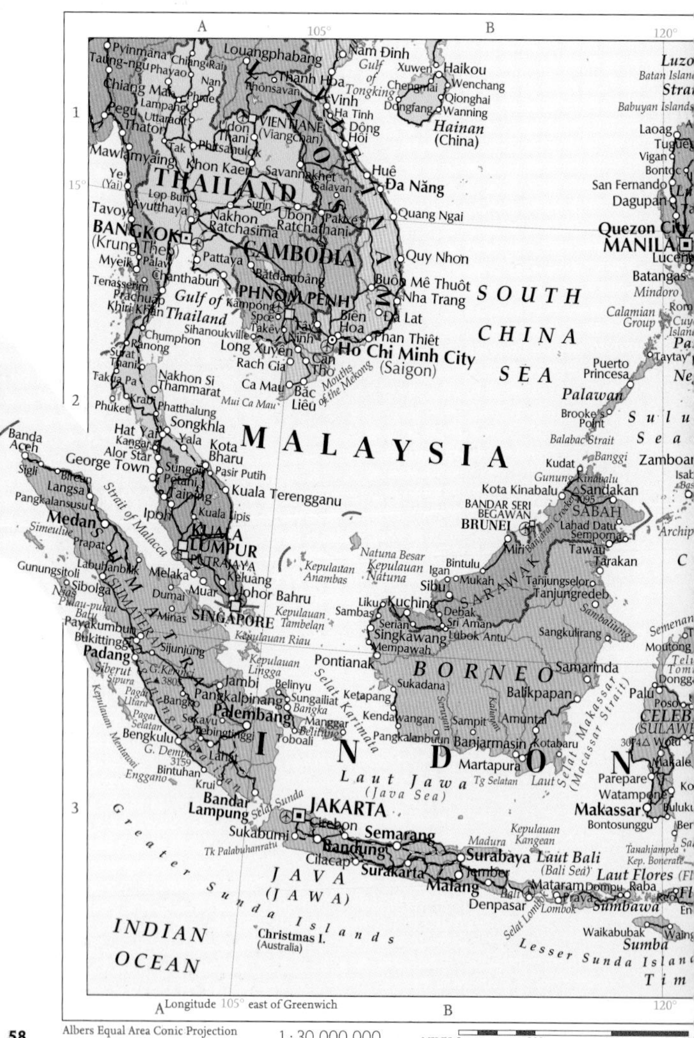

Albers Equal Area Conic Projection   1 : 30 000 000   MILES 0   200   400   60

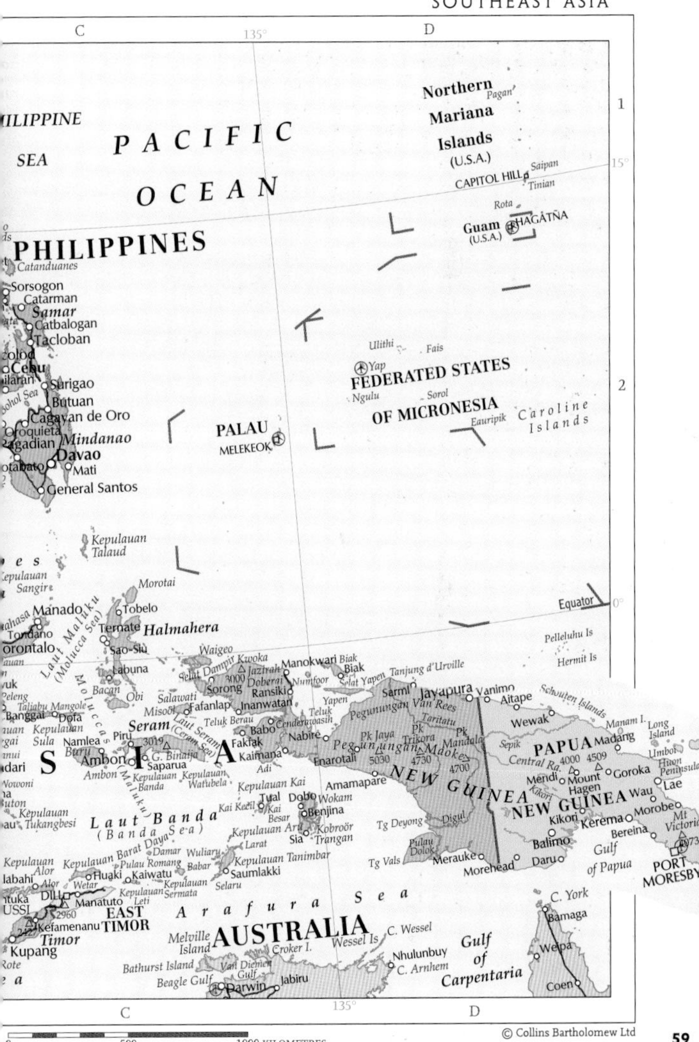

PACIFIC OCEAN

PHILIPPINE SEA

Northern Mariana Islands (U.S.A.)

CAPITOL HILL Saipan
Tinian
Rota
Guam (U.S.A.) HAGÅTÑA
Pagan

PHILIPPINES

Catanduanes
Sorsogon
Catarman
Samar Catbalogan
Tacloban
Cebu
ilaran Surigao
Butuan
Cagayan de Oro
Oroquieta
Jagadian Mindanao
Davao
General Santos
Mati

PALAU
MELEKEOK

Ulithi Fais
Ngulu Sorol
FEDERATED STATES
OF MICRONESIA
Eauripik Caroline Islands

Kepulauan Talaud

Kepulauan Sangir

Morotai
Manado
Tondano
Gorontalo
Ternate Halmahera
Sao-Siu Tobelo
Labuna
Obi Waigeo
Bacan Dampir Kwoka Manokwari Biak
Misool Sorong Doberai Numfoor Slat Yapen
Salawati Jnanwatan Yapen Tanjung d'Urville
Fakfak Nabire Sarmi Jayapura Vanimo
Adi Enarotali Pegunungan Van Rees Aitape

Equator 0°

Pelleluhu Is
Hermit Is

Schouten Islands

Wewak
Sepik
Madang Manam Long
Island

PAPUA
NEW GUINEA
Central Ra. Goroka
Mendi Mount Hagen
Kikori Wau
Kerema Moresby
Balimo Daru
Morehead Gulf
of Papua
PORT MORESBY

Seram
Piru
Ambon
Saparua
Ambon Kepulauan Banda
Malaku
Laut Banda
(Banda Sea)
Kepulauan Barat Daya
Damar Wuliaru
Pulau Romang
Kaiwatu
Kepulauan Tanimbar
Saumlakki
Wetar Leti
Kepulauan
Selaru

EAST TIMOR
DILI
Kefamenanu
Kupang

Arafura Sea

C. Wessel
Wessel Is
Melville Island C. Arnhem
Bathurst Island Van Diemen Gulf
Beagle Gulf Darwin Jabiru

AUSTRALIA

Nhulunbuy
Gulf of Carpentaria
C. York
Bamaga
Weipa
Coen

ASIA
NEW GUINEA

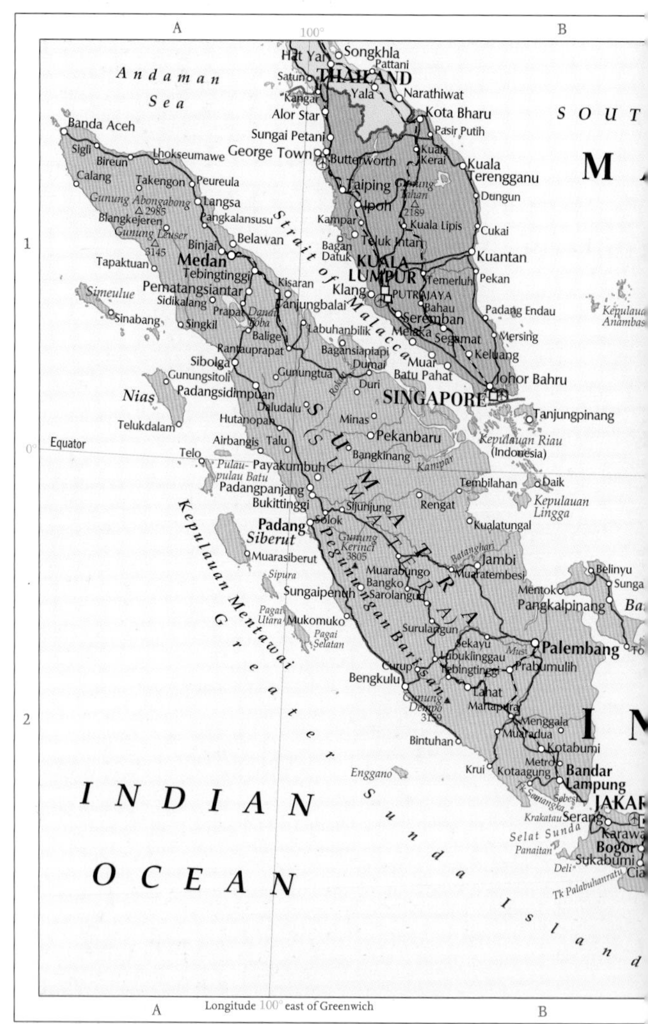

A

100°

**Andaman
Sea**

Banda Aceh

Sigli
Bireun
Calang
Lhokseumawe
Takengon Peureula
Gunung Abongabong
Blangkejeren △2985
Langsa
Gunung Leuser
Pangkalansusu
Tapaktuan △145 Belawan
Medan
Simeulue
Tebingtinggi
Pematangsiantar Kisaran
Sidikalang Prapat Danau Tanjungbalai
Sinabang Singkil Baligè Labuhanbilik
Rantauprapat
Bagansiapiapi
Sibolga
Gunungsitoli Gunungtua
Nias Padangsidimpuan Daludalu
Hutanopan
Telukdalam Airbangis Talu
Telo
Pulau Payakumbuh
pulau Batu
Padangpanjang
Bukittinggi
Padang
Siberut Solok
Muarasiberut
Sipura
Sungaipenuh
Pagai
Utara Mukomuko
Pagai
Selatan
Bengkulu

Bintuhan

Songkhla
Hat Yai Pattani
Satun **THAILAND**
Kangar Yala Narathiwat
Alor Star
Kota Bharu
Sungai Petani Pasir Putih
George Town Butterworth Kuala
Krai Kuala
Taiping Terengganu
Gunung Dungun
Ipoh *Tahan*
Kampar △2189 Kuala Lipis
Teluk Intan Cukai
Bagan
Datuk **KUALA** Kuantan
LUMPUR
Klang PUTRAJAYA Pekan
Bahau
Seremban Padang Endau *Kepulauan*
Melaka Segamat *Anambas*
Muar Mersing
Batu Pahat Keluang
Dumai Johor Bahru
Duri **SINGAPORE**
Minas Tanjungpinang
Pekanbaru *Kepulauan Riau*
Bangkinang *(Indonesia)*
Kampar
Rengat Tembilahan Daik
Kepulauan
Lingga
Gunung Sijunjung Kualatungal
Kerinci
△3805 *Batanghari*
Muarabungo Muaratembesi
Bangko Jambi
Sarolangun Mentok
Pangkalpinang *Ba*
Musi **Palembang** *To* Belinyu Sunga
Surulangun
Sekayu
Lubuklinggau
Curup Sebingtinggi Prabumulih
Lahat
Gunung Muaradua
Dempo Menggala
△31 Muaradua Kotabumi
Metro
Krui Kotaagung **Bandar
Lampung**
Gunung Serang **JAKAR**
Krakatau Karawa
Selat Sunda **Bogor**
Panaitan Sukabumi Cia
Deli
Tk Palabuhanratu

SOUT
M
Kepulauan
Anambas

Strait of Malacca

S U M A T R A

Pesisir dan Pegunungan Barisan

INDIAN

OCEAN

Kepulauan Mentawai

G r e a t e r

Enggano

S u n d a

i s l a n d

I N

Equator 0°

1

2

B

Longitude 100° east of Greenwich

A B

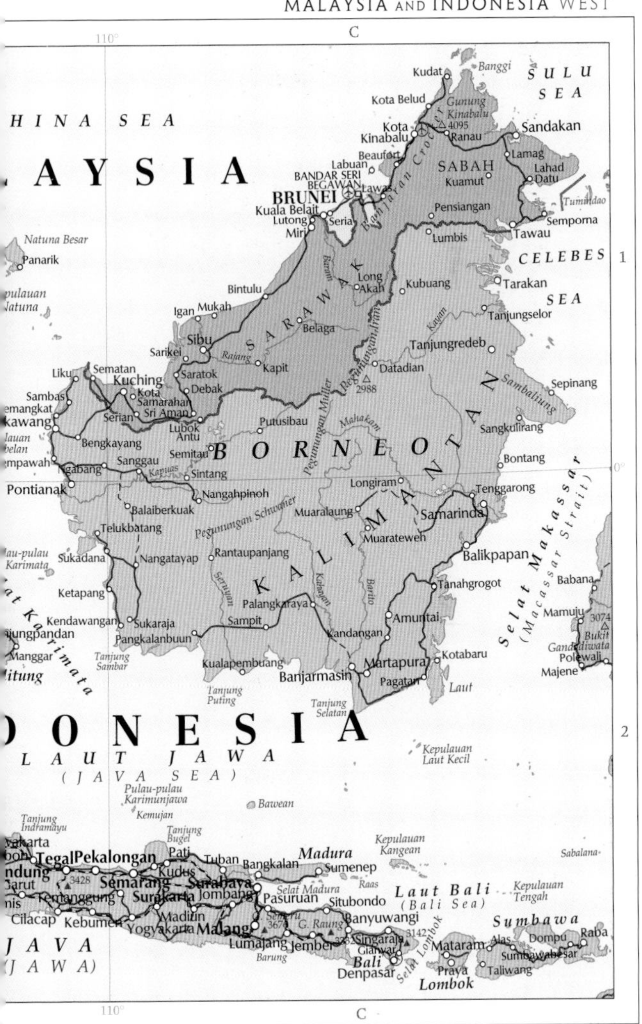
C
110°
SULU SEA
CELEBES SEA
HINA SEA
AYSIA
BRUNEI
SABAH
SARAWAK
BORNEO
KALIMANTAN
ONESIA
LAUT JAWA
(JAVA SEA)
JAVA
(JAWA)
Laut Bali
(Bali Sea)
Selat Makassar
(Macassar Strait)
Kudat
Banggi
Kota Belud
Gunung Kinabalu
4095
Kota Kinabalu
Ranau
Sandakan
Beaufort
Labuan
BANDAR SERI BEGAWAN
Lawas
Lamag
Kuamut
Lahad Datu
Tumindao
Kuala Belait
Lutong
Miri
Seria
Pensiangan
Semporna
Lumbis
Tawau
Natuna Besar
Panarik
Tarakan
Long Akah
Kubuang
Bintulu
Tanjungselor
Igan
Mukah
Belaga
Sibu
Tanjungredeb
Sarikei
Rajang
Kapit
Datadian
2988
Liku
Sematan
Kuching
Saratok
Debak
Sepinang
Sambas
Kota Samarahan
Sri Aman
Serian
Putusibau
Mahakam
Lubok Antu
Sangkulirang
Bengkayang
Semitau
Bontang
Sanggau
Kapuas
Sintang
Pontianak
Ngabang
Longiram
Tenggarong
Nangahpinoh
Balaiberkuak
Muaralaung
Samarinda
Pegunungan Schwaner
Telukbatang
Muarateweh
Rantaupanjang
Balikpapan
Sukadana
Nangatayap
Ketapang
Tanahgrogot
Babana
Palangkaraya
Mamuju
3074
Bukit Gandadiwata
Kendawangan
Sukaraja
Sampit
Amuntai
Pangkalanbuun
Kandangan
Polewali
Majene
Kotabaru
Tanjung Sambar
Kualapembuang
Martapura
Banjarmasin
Pagatan
Laut
Tanjung Puting
Tanjung Selatan
Kepulauan Laut Kecil
Pulau-pulau Karimunjawa
Kemujan
Bawean
Tanjung Indramayu
Tanjung Bugel
Kepulauan Kangean
Sabalana
TegalPekalongan
Pati
Tuban
Madura
Bangkalan
Sumenep
Kudus
3428
Semarang
Surabaya
Selat Madura
Raas
Kepulauan Tengah
Temanggung
Surakarta
Jombang
Pasuruan
Situbondo
Madiun
Semeru
3676
Banyuwangi
Cilacap
Kebumen
Yogyakarta
Malang
G. Raung
Sumbawa
3142
Lumajang
Jember
3332
Singaraja
Mataram
Alas
Dompu
Raba
Barung
Gianyar
Selat Lombok
Sumbawabesar
Bali
Denpasar
Praya
Taliwang
Lombok
Baram
Kayan
Sambaliung
Pegunungan Muller
Pegunungan Iran
Banjaran Crocker
Seruyan
Katingan
Barito
1
2
0°
500 KILOMETRES
0
250

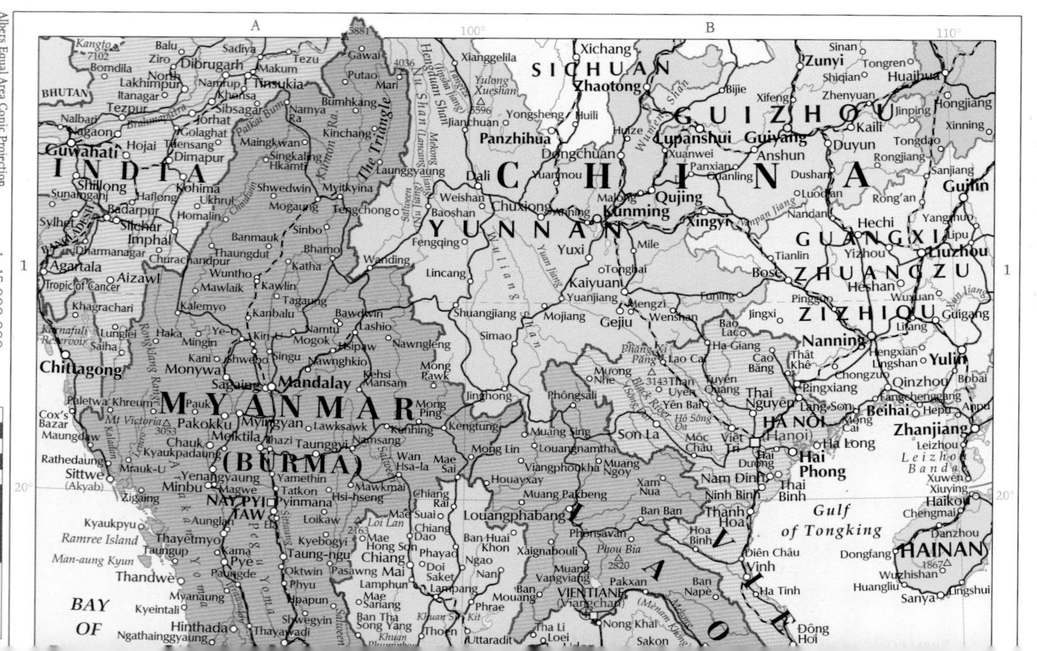

Albers Equal Area Conic Projection   1 : 15 000 000   MILES 0   100   200   300

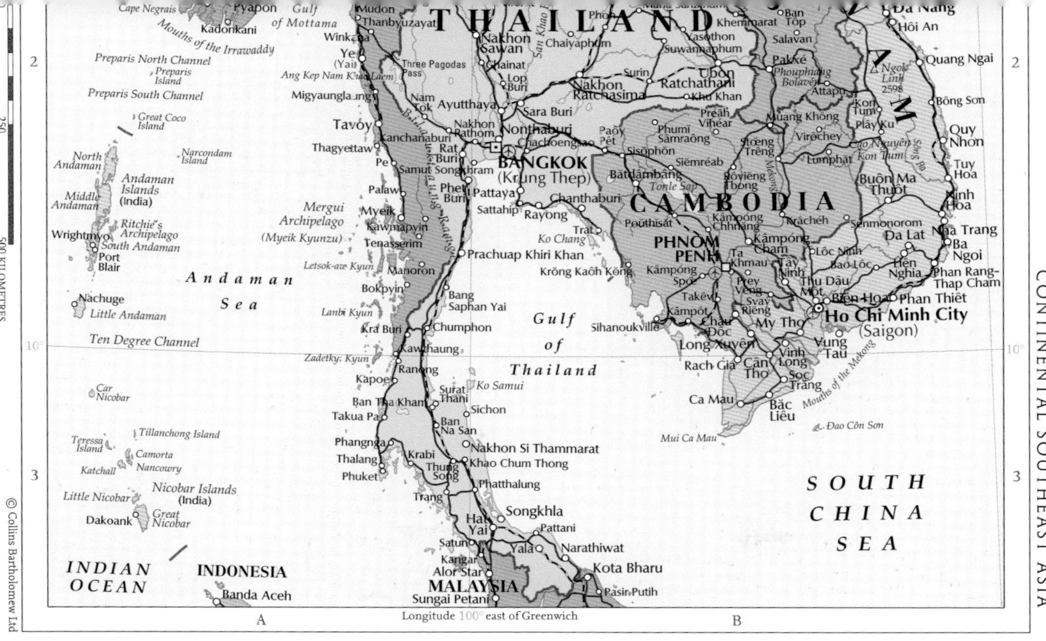

© Collins Bartholomew Ltd

250   500 KILOMETRES

THAILAND
CAMBODIA
MALAYSIA
INDONESIA
Andaman Sea
Gulf of Thailand
SOUTH CHINA SEA
INDIAN OCEAN
BANGKOK
(Krung Thep)
PHNOM PENH
Ho Chi Minh City
(Saigon)
Gulf of Mottama
Mouths of the Irrawaddy
Mouths of the Mekong
Tonle Sap
Mergui Archipelago
(Myeik Kyunzu)
Andaman Islands
(India)
Nicobar Islands
(India)
Ten Degree Channel
Preparis North Channel
Preparis Island
Preparis South Channel
Great Coco Island
Narcondam Island
North Andaman
Middle Andaman
South Andaman
Ritchie's Archipelago
Wrightmyo
Port Blair
Nachuge
Little Andaman
Car Nicobar
Tillanchong Island
Teressa Island
Camorta
Nancowry
Katchall
Little Nicobar
Great Nicobar
Dakoank
Banda Aceh
Kota Bharu
Pasir Putih
Narathiwat
Pattani
Songkhla
Hat Yai
Yala
Sungai Petani
Alor Star
Kangar
Satun
Trang
Phatthalung
Nakhon Si Thammarat
Khao Chum Thong
Thung Song
Krabi
Phuket
Phangnga
Thalang
Takua Pa
Ban Tha Kham
Surat Thani
Ko Samui
Sichon
Ban Na San
Chumphon
Bang Saphan Yai
Prachuap Khiri Khan
Ranong
Kawthaung
Zadetkyi Kyun
Kra Buri
Lanbi Kyun
Kapoe
Bokpyin
Manoron
Letsok-aw Kyun
Tenasserim
Kawmapyin
Myeik
Palaw
Pe
Thagyettaw
Tavoy
Migyaunglaung
Ang Kep Nam Kuan Laem
Ye
(Yai)
Winkana
Thanbyuzayat
Mudon
Kadonkani
Pyapon
Cape Negrais
Three Pagodas Pass
Kanchanaburi
Nam Tok
Ratchaburi
Samut Songkhram
Phetchaburi
Nakhon Pathom
Nonthaburi
Chachoengsao
Ayutthaya
Sara Buri
Lop Buri
Chainat
Nakhon Sawan
Chaiyaphum
Nakhon Ratchasima
Surin
Suwannaphum
Yasothon
Ubon Ratchathani
Khemmarat
Khu Khan
Pattaya
Sattahip
Rayong
Chanthaburi
Trat
Ko Chang
Krŏng Kaôh Kŏng
Sihanoukville
Kâmpôt
Takêv
Kâmpóng Spœ
Batdâmbâng
Poŭthĭsăt
Siĕmréab
Sisŏphŏn
Paôy Pêt
Phumĭ Sâmraông
Preăh Vihéar
Kâmpóng Chhnăng
Kâmpóng Cham
Krâchéh
Stœng Trêng
Rôviĕng Tbong
Prey Vêng
Svay Riĕng
Ta Khmau
Châu Đôc
Long Xuyên
Rach Gia
Ca Mau
Mui Ca Mau
Bac Liêu
Sóc Trăng
Cân Thơ
Vinh Long
My Tho
Vung Tau
Biên Hoa
Thu Dâu Môt
Lôc Ninh
Bao Lôc
Sênmonorom
Da Lat
Liên Nghia
Phan Thiêt
Phan Rang-Thap Cham
Nha Trang
Ba Ngoi
Ninh Hoa
Tuy Hoa
Quy Nhon
Buôn Ma Thuôt
Plây Ku
Kon Tum
Bông Son
Quang Ngai
Hôi An
Đa Nang
Ngok Linh
2598
Attapu
Pakxé
Salavan
Ban Tôp
Muang Không
Virôchey
Lumphăt
Phouphiang Bolavén
Đao Côn Son
Longitude 100° east of Greenwich
3
10°

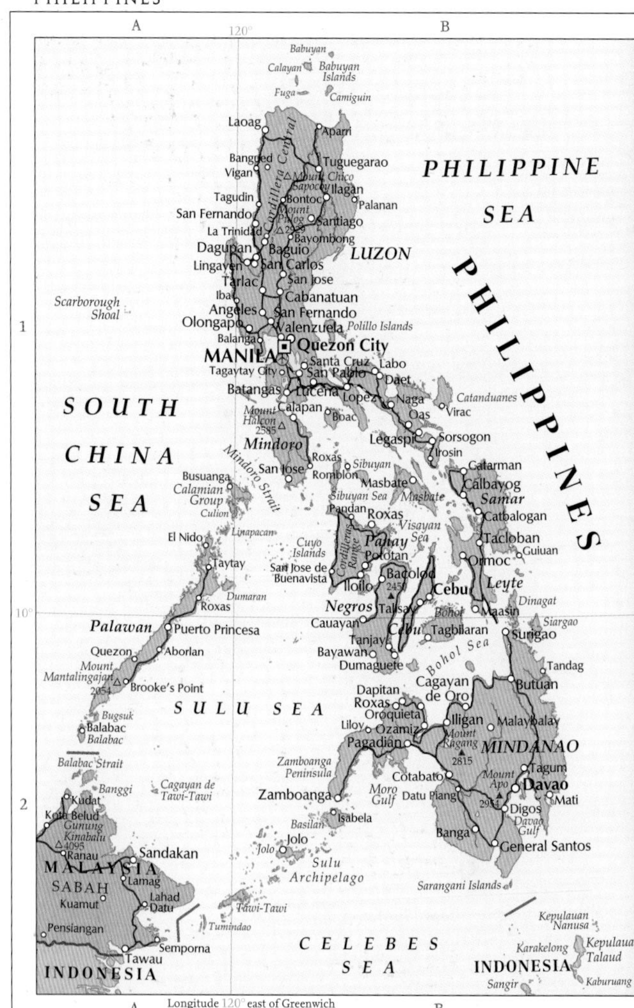

PHILIPPINE
SEA

PHILIPPINES

SOUTH
CHINA
SEA

LUZON

Scarborough
Shoal

Babuyan
Calayan Babuyan
Islands
Fuga Camiguin
Aparri

Laoag
Banguedo Tuguegarao
Vigan Mount Chico
Bapocto Ilagan
Tagudin Bontoc Palanan
San Fernando Mount Santiago
La Trinidad Alos
Dagupan Baguio Bayombong
Lingayen San Carlos Palanan
Tarlac San Jose
Ibato Cabanatuan
Angeles San Fernando Polillo Islands
Olongapo Valenzuela
Balanga Quezon City
MANILA Santa Cruz Labo
Tagaytay City San Pablo Daet Catanduanes
Batangas Lucena Lopez Naga Virac
Calapan Boac Oas
Mount Legaspi Sorsogon
Halcon Irosin
Mindoro Roxas Sibuyan Calamian
Sibuyan Sea Masbate Calbayog
Busuanga Romblon Samar
Calamian Masbate Catbalogan
Group Pandan
Culion Roxas Visayan Tacloban
El Nido Linapacan Sea Guiuan
Cuyo Panay Pototan Leyte
Calamian Islands Palompon Dinagat
San Jose de Iloilo Bacolod Cebu Siargao
Buenavista Talsay Maasin
Roxas Cebu Bohol Surigao
Palawan Puerto Princesa Negros Tagbilaran
Dumaran Cauayan Tandag
Quezon Bayawan Tanjay Bohol Sea Butuan
Aborlan Dumaguete
Mount Dapitan Cagayan Malaybalay
Mantalingajan Roxas de Oro
Brooke's Point Oroquieta Iligan
SULU SEA Liloy Ozamiz Mount MINDANAO
Bugsuk Paquliao Ragang Tagum
Balabac Zamboanga Cotabato Mount Davao
Balabac Peninsula 2815 Apo Mati
Balabac Strait Zamboanga Datu Piang Davao
Banggi Cagayan de Moro Gulf
Kudat Tawi-Tawi Isabela Banga
Kota Belud Basilan General Santos
Gunung Jolo Jolo
Kinabalu Sandakan Sulu Sarangani Islands
Ranau Archipelago
MALAYSIA Lamag
SABAH Lahad Kepulauan
Kuamut Datu Nanusa
Pensiangan Tawi-Tawi Kepulauan
Tumindao Karakelong Talaud
Balabac CELEBES Kaburuang
Semporna SEA INDONESIA
Tawau Sangir
INDONESIA

Mindoro Strait

SULU SEA

Zamboanga
Peninsula

Moro
Gulf

Cagayan de
Tawi-Tawi

Albers Equal Area Conic
Projection

Longitude 120° east of Greenwich

1 : 15 000 000   MILES 0   100   0   250 KILOMETRE

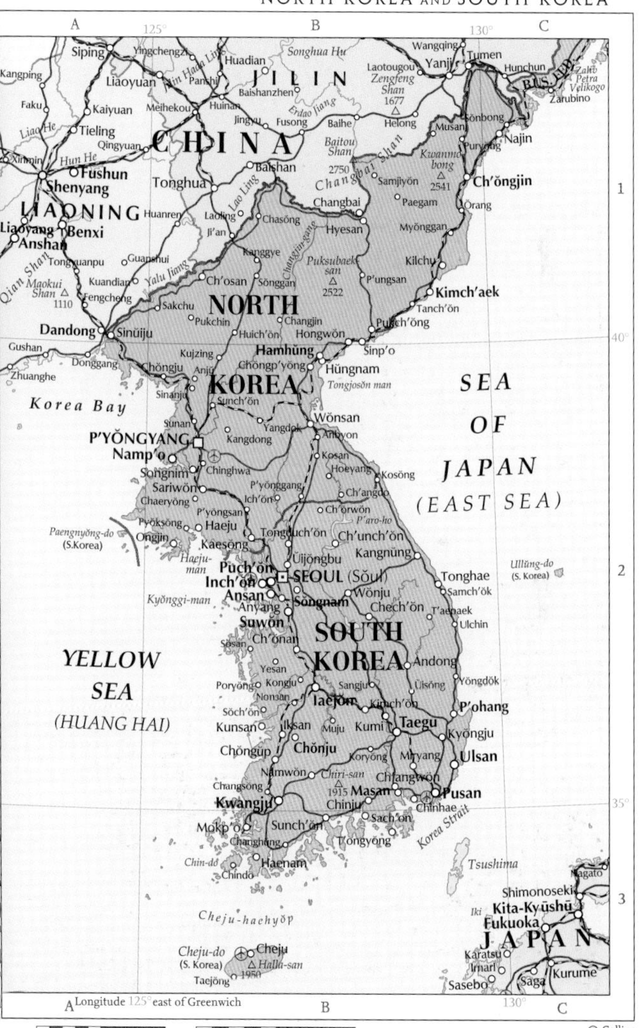

MILES 0   50   100   0   100   200 KILOMETRES   1 : 9 000 000   © Collins Bartholomew Ltd

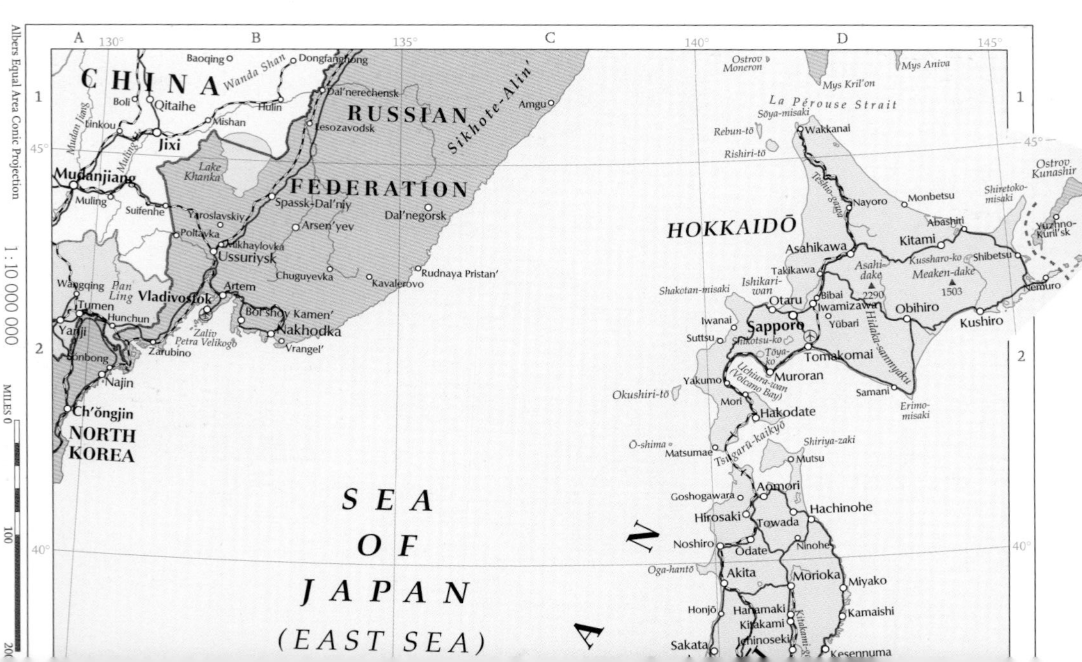

Albers Equal Area Conic Projection 1 : 10 000 000 MILES 0 100 200

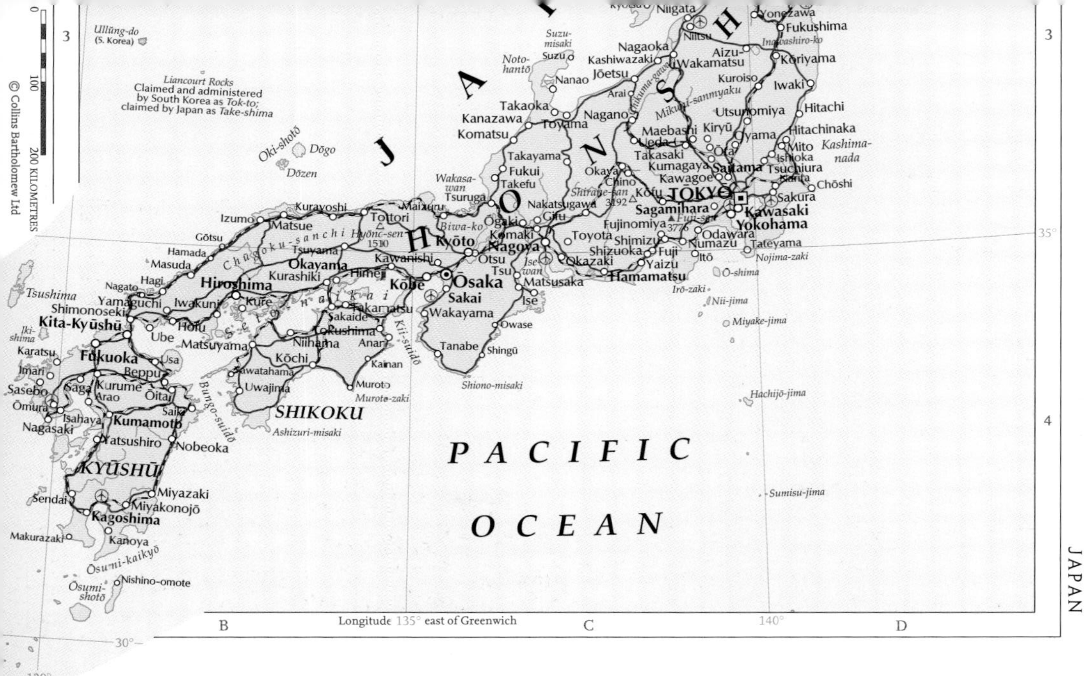

3

4

35°

D

140°

Pacific Ocean labels:
P A C I F I C

O C E A N

C

Longitude 135° east of Greenwich

B

30°

130°

Hachijō-jima

Sumisu-jima

Nijima-zaki

Shima

Ō-shima

Nii-jima

Miyake-jima

Nishino-omote
Ōsumi-shotō

Nakano-shima
Kuchino-shima
Tokara-rettō

Uturo
Toi-misaki

Tanegashima

Yaku-shima

Tsushima

Kami-agata
Shimo-agata

Iki-shima

Sasebo

Ōmuta

Saga

Karatsu

Nagasaki

Imari

Isahaya

Shimabara

Amakusa

Yatsushiro

Minamata

Hitoyoshi

Izumi

Sendai

Makurazaki

Ibusuki

Kanoya

KYŪSHŪ

Kagoshima

Kirishima

Miyakonojō

Miyazaki

Nobeoka

Ōita

Beppu

Kumamoto

Aso

Saiki

Usuki

Tsukumi

Usa

Nakatsu

Kitakyūshū
Kita-Kyūshū

Shimonoseki

Ube

Yamaguchi

Nagato

Hagi

Masuda

Fukuoka

Kurume

Tosu

Iizuka

Iki-suidō

Bungo-suidō

SHIKOKU

Uwajima

Matsuyama

Iwatajima

Imabari

Niihama

Saijō

Kōchi

Tosa

Nakamura

Ashizuri-misaki

Muroto-misaki

Muroto

Anan

Tokushima

Naruto

Takamatsu

Sakaide

Marugame

Tadotsu

Kannon-ji

Iyo-nada

Suō-nada

Hiroshima

Kure

Iwakuni

Hōfu

Tokuyama

Onomichi

Fukuyama

Mihara

Kasaoka

Kurashiki

Okayama

Izumo

Gōtsu

Hamada

Tsuwano

Masuda

Ōda

Matsue

Yonago

Kurayoshi

Tottori

H i d a k a - s a n c h i

Chūgoku-sanchi

Sandan-zan
1590

Tsuyama

Takahashi

Nakatsugawa?

Nishino-shima

Dōgo

Oki-shotō

Dōzen

Imabari

Ullŭng-do
(S. Korea)

Liancourt Rocks
Claimed and administered
by South Korea as Tok-to;
claimed by Japan as Take-shima

Shima

Wakayama

Kii-suidō

Tanabe

Owase

Shingū

Kumano

Shima

Ise

Matsusaka

Tsu

Suzuka

Yokkaichi

Kuwana

Nagoya

Ichinomiya

Gifu

Komaki

Kasugai

Toyota

Okazaki

Toyohashi

Hamamatsu

Kakegawa

Shizuoka

Shimizu

Fuji

Fujinomiya

Fukuroi

Yaizu

Irō-zaki

Numazu

Fuji-san
3776

Ōmiya

Isezaki

Ōtsu

Kōbe

Ōsaka

Sakai

Nara

Kyōto

Kōka

Tsuruga

Wakasa-wan

Maizuru

Fukuchiyama

Ōbama

Echizen-misaki

Fukui

Komatsu

Kanazawa

Takaoka

Toyama

Noto-hantō

Nanao

Suzu-misaki

Niigata

Nagaoka

Jōetsu

Kashiwazaki

Wakamatsu

Nagaoka

Nagano

Matsumoto

Ueda

Suwa

Iida

Nakatsugawa

Shiojiri

Saku

Takasaki

Maebashi

Kiryū

Ashikaga

Kumagaya

Kawagoe

Kawasaki

TŌKYŌ

Yokohama

Chiba

Kisarazu

Kazusa

Bōsō-hantō

Nojima-zaki

Tateyama

Kamogawa

Chōshi

Sakura

Mito

Kashima-nada

Hitachi

Hitachinaka

Kashima

Tsuchiura

Utsunomiya

Kōriyama

Kōfu

Odawara

Atami

Itō

Sagamihara

Hachiōji

Ōta

Aizu-
Wakamatsu

Fukushima

Iwaki

Shirakawa

Nasu-dake
1917

Nikkō

Iwaki

J A P A N

H O N S H Ū

Sadoga-shima
Niigata

Nagaoka

0   100   200 KILOMETRES

© Collins Bartholomew Ltd

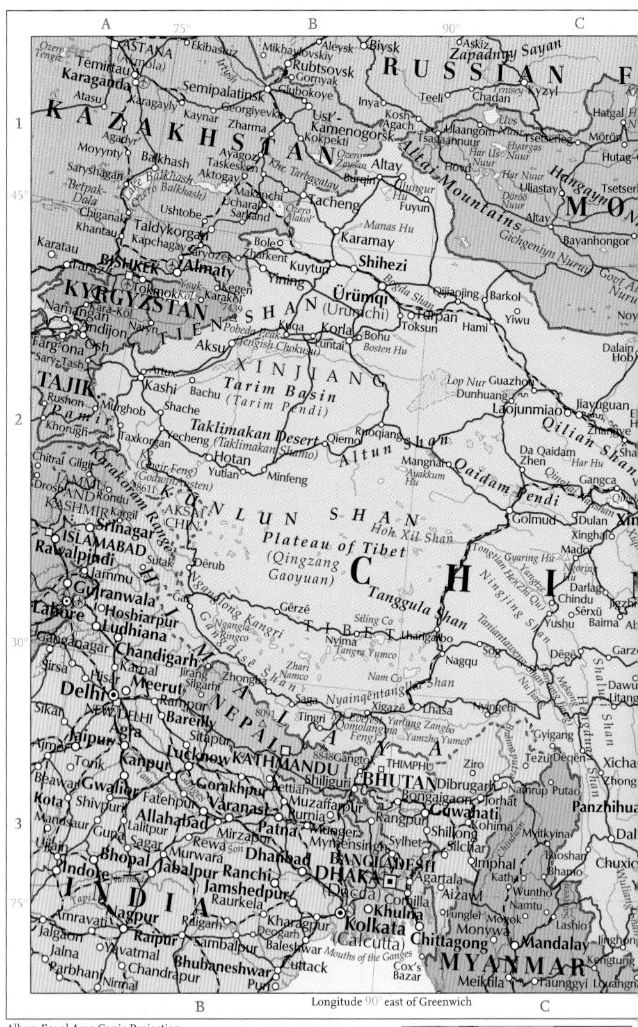

RUSSIAN F

KAZAKHSTAN

MONGOLIA

KYRGYZSTAN

TAJIK

XINJIANG

Tarim Basin
(Tarim Pendi)

Taklimakan Desert
(Taklimakan Shamo)

KUNLUN SHAN

CHINA

Plateau of Tibet
(Qingzang Gaoyuan)

Qaidam Pendi

KASHMIR

ISLAMABAD

Rawalpindi

Lahore

Ludhiana

Chandigarh

Delhi
NEW DELHI

NEPAL

KATHMANDU

THIMPHU
BHUTAN

INDIA

Kanpur

Lucknow

Varanasi

Patna

BANGLADESH

DHAKA

Kolkata
(Calcutta)

MYANMAR

Mandalay

Nagpur

Raipur

Bhubaneshwar

Mouths of the Ganges

Chittagong

Guwahati

Longitude 90 east of Greenwich

B   C

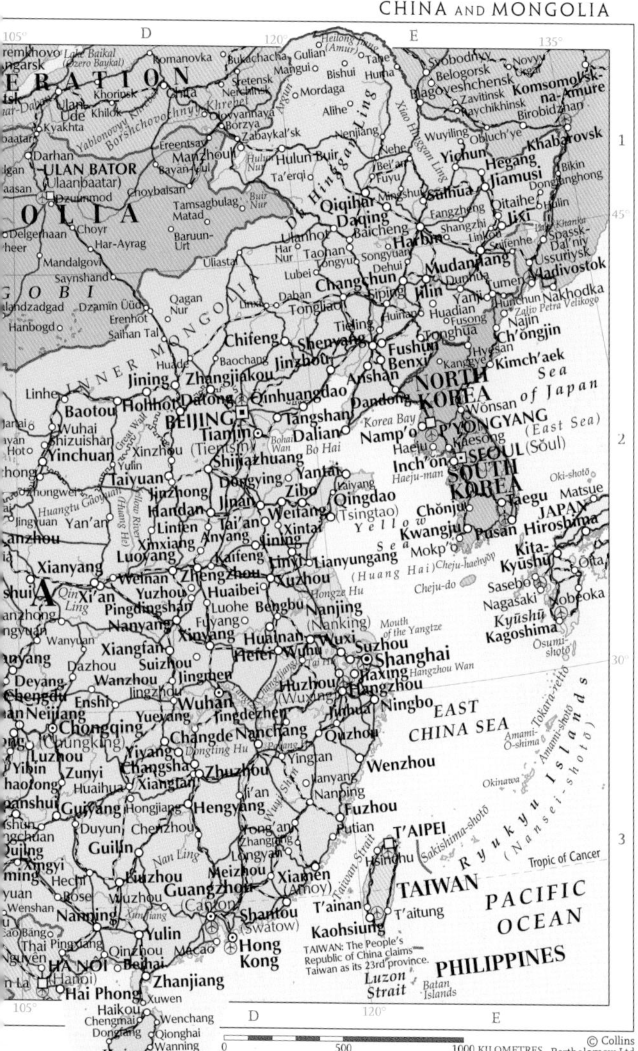
Lake Baikal
(Ozero Baykal)
Romanovka
Bukachacha
Gulian
Heilong Jiang (Amur)
Tahe
Svobodnyy
Novyy Urgal
Belogorsk
Blagoveshchensk
Komsomol'sk-na-Amure
Zavitinsk
Raychikhinsk
Birobidzhan
Sretensk
Nerchinsk
Mangui
Bishui
Huma
Mordaga
Khorinsk
Chita
Khrebet
Ulan-Ude
Khilok
Yablonovyy Khrebet
Borshchovochnyy
Kyakhta
Borzya
Zabaykal'sk
Alihe
Nenjiang
Wuyiling
Obluch'ye
Khabarovsk
Bikin
Xiao Hinggan Ling
Da Hinggan Ling
Darhan
ULAN BATOR
(Ulaanbaatar)
Ereentsav
Manzhouli
Bayan-Uul
Hulun Nur
Hulun Buir
Ta'erqi
Nehe
Bei'an
Fuyu
Yichun
Hegang
Jiamusi
Dongfanghong
Choybalsan
Dzuunmod
Tamsagbulag
Buir Nur
Matad
Qiqihar
Mingshui
Suihua
Qitaihe
Hulin
Daqing
Fangzheng
Jixi
MONGOLIA
Delgerhaan
Choyr
Har-Ayrag
Baruun-Urt
Ulanhot
Baicheng
Shangzhi
Linkou
Khanka
Spassk-Dal'niy
Harbin
Suifenhe
Ussuriysk
Mandalgovi
Uliastai
Har Nur
Taonan
Tongyu
Songyuan
Dehui
Mudanjiang
Vladivostok
Saynshand
Lubei
Changchun
Dunhua
Tumen
Nakhodka
GOBI
Dalandzadgad
Dzamïn Üüd
Qagan Nur
Linxi
Daban
Tongliao
Siping
Jilin
Yanji
Hunchun
Zaliv Petra Velikogo
Erenhot
Huinan
Huadian
Fusong
Najin
Hanbogd
Saihan Tal
Tieling
Tonghua
Ch'ŏngjin
Chifeng
Shenyang
Fushun
Hyesan
INNER MONGOLIA
Huade
Baochang
Jinzhou
Benxi
Kanggye
Kimch'aek
Sea of Japan
(East Sea)
Jining
Zhangjiakou
Anshan
NORTH KOREA
Linhe
Hohhot
Datong
Qinhuangdao
Dandong
Wŏnsan
Baotou
BEIJING
Tangshan
Korea Bay
P'YONGYANG
Wuhai
Tianjin
Dalian
Namp'o
Shizuishan
Bohai Wan
Bo Hai
Haeju
Kaesŏng
Hoto
Yinchuan
Great Wall
Xinzhou
(Tientsin)
SEOUL (Sŏul)
Yulin
Shijiazhuang
Yantai
Inch'ŏn
SOUTH KOREA
Taiyuan
Dongying
Haeju-man
Oki-shotō
Jinzhong
Zibo
Laiyang
Qingdao
Taegu
Matsue
Huangtu Gaoyuan
Yellow River (Huang He)
Handan
Jinan
Weifang
(Tsingtao)
Chŏnju
JAPAN
Jingyuan
Yan'an
Linfen
Tai'an
Xintai
Yellow Sea
(Huang Hai)
Kwangju
Pusan
Hiroshima
Lanzhou
Xinxiang
Anyang
Jining
Mokp'o
Cheju-haehyŏp
Kita-Kyūshū
Luoyang
Kaifeng
Linyi
Lianyungang
Ōita
Xianyang
Weinan
Zhengzhou
Xuzhou
Cheju-do
Sasebo
Qin Ling
Xi'an
Yuzhou
Huaibei
Hongze Hu
Nagasaki
Nobeoka
Pingdingshan
Luohe
Bengbu
Nanjing
Kyūshū
Nanyang
Fuyang
(Nanking)
Mouth of the Yangtze
Kagoshima
Wanyuan
Xinyang
Huainan
Wuxi
Ōsumi-shotō
Xiangfan
Hefei
Wuhu
Suzhou
Shanghai
Dazhou
Suizhou
Tai Hu
Jiaxing
Hangzhou Wan
Deyang
Wanzhou
Jingmen
Huzhou
Chengdu
Jingzhou
(Wuxing)
Hangzhou
Enshi
Wuhan
Neijiang
Yueyang
Jingdezhen
Jinhua
Ningbo
EAST CHINA SEA
Chongqing
(Chungking)
Changde
Nanchang
Quzhou
Amami-Ō-shima
Tokara-rettō
Amami-shotō
Luzhou
Yiyang
Dongting Hu
Poyang Hu
Yingtan
Yibin
Zunyi
Changsha
Zhuzhou
Wenzhou
Zhaotong
Huaihua
Xiangtan
Wuyi Shan
Nanping
Okinawa
Ryukyu Islands
(Nansei-shotō)
Guiyang
Hongjiang
Hengyang
Ji'an
Fuzhou
Duyun
Chenzhou
Yong'an
Putian
T'AIPEI
Sakishima-shotō
Qujing
Guilin
Zhangping
Hsinchu
Nan Ling
Longyan
Taiwan Strait
Tropic of Cancer
Gejiu
Liuzhou
Meizhou
Xiamen
(Amoy)
Hechi
TAIWAN
Wenshan
Bose
Wuzhou
Guangzhou
(Canton)
T'ainan
PACIFIC OCEAN
Nanning
Xun Jiang
Shantou
(Swatow)
T'aitung
Cao Bang
Thai Nguyen
Pingxiang
Yulin
Hong Kong
Kaohsiung
HA NOI
(Hanoi)
Qinzhou
Beihai
Macao
TAIWAN: The People's Republic of China claims Taiwan as its 23rd province.
PHILIPPINES
Hai Phong
Zhanjiang
Luzon Strait
Batan Islands
Xuwen
Haikou
Chengmai
Wenchang
Dongfang
Qionghai
Wanning
Hainan
105°
120°
135°
45°
30°
D
E
1
2
3
0
500
1000 KILOMETRES

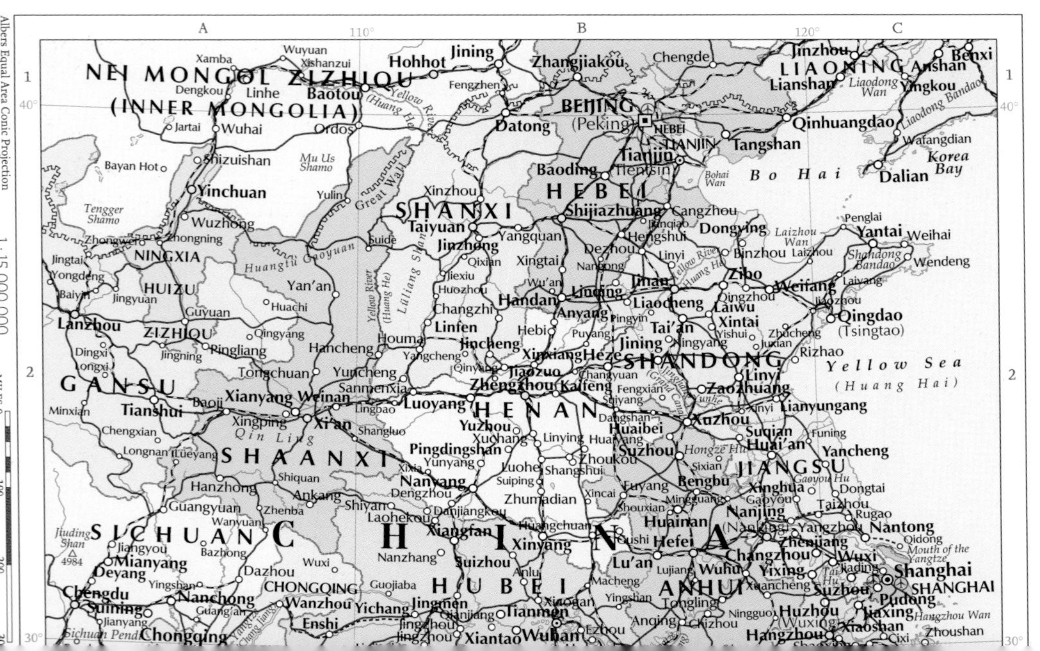

Albers Equal Area Conic Projection　　1 : 15 000 000　　MILES 0　　100　　200

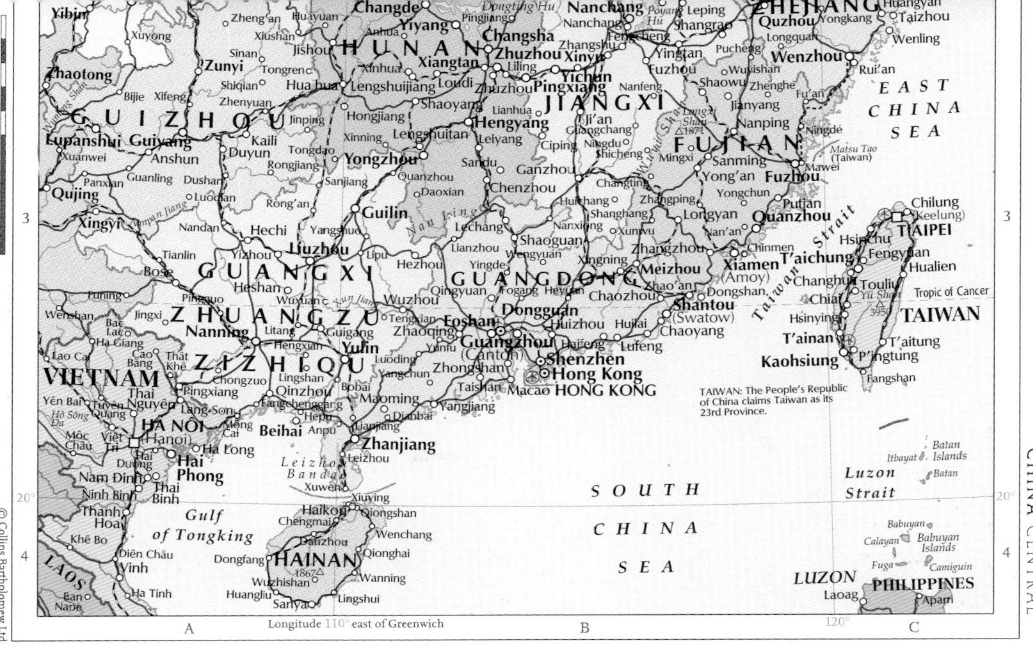
HUNAN
JIANGXI
FUJIAN
GUANGDONG
GUANGXI ZHUANGZU ZIZHIQU
GUIZHOU
ZHEJIANG
HAINAN
TAIWAN
VIETNAM
LAOS
PHILIPPINES
LUZON
HONG KONG
EAST CHINA SEA
SOUTH CHINA SEA
Gulf of Tongking
Luzon Strait
Taiwan Strait
Leizhou Bandao
Tropic of Cancer
TAIWAN: The People's Republic of China claims Taiwan as its 23rd Province.
Longitude 110° east of Greenwich
Changsha
Nanchang
Fuzhou
Guangzhou (Canton)
Guiyang
Nanning
HA NÔI (Hanoi)
T'AIPEI
Hong Kong
Macao
Shenzhen
Xiamen (Amoy)
Shantou (Swatow)
Kaohsiung
T'aichung
T'ainan
Wenzhou
Guilin
Liuzhou
Zhanjiang
Haikou
Sanya
Hai Phong
Zunyi
Hengyang
Zhuzhou
Xiangtan
Changde
Ganzhou
Shaoguan
Foshan
Dongguan
Quanzhou
Meizhou
Zhangzhou

0 250 500 KILOMETRES

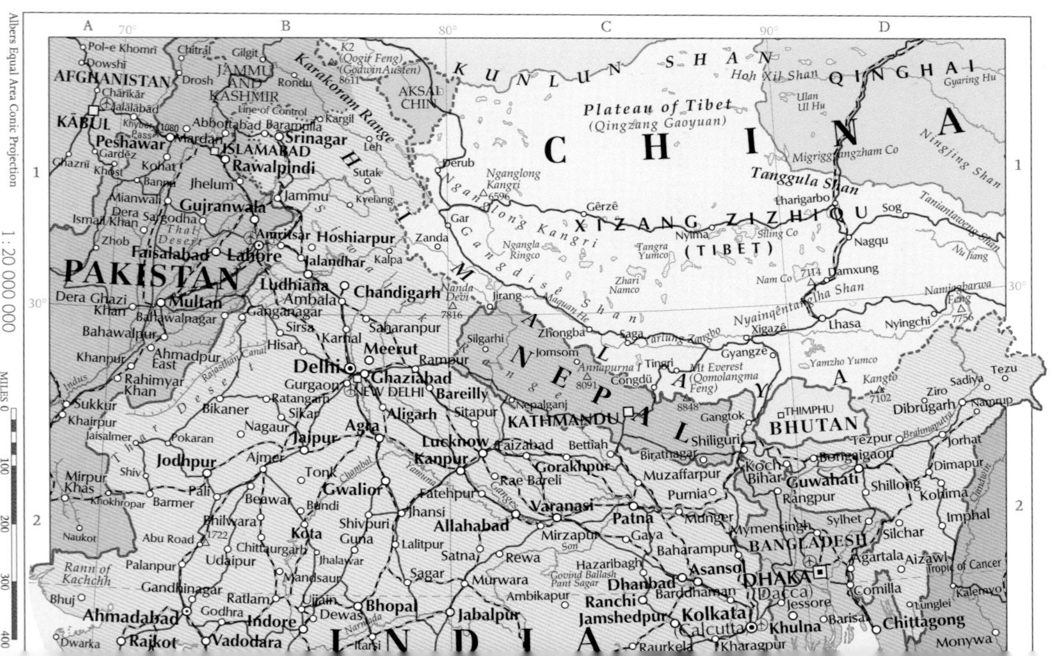

Albers Equal Area Conic Projection

1 : 20 000 000

MILES 0   100   200   300   400

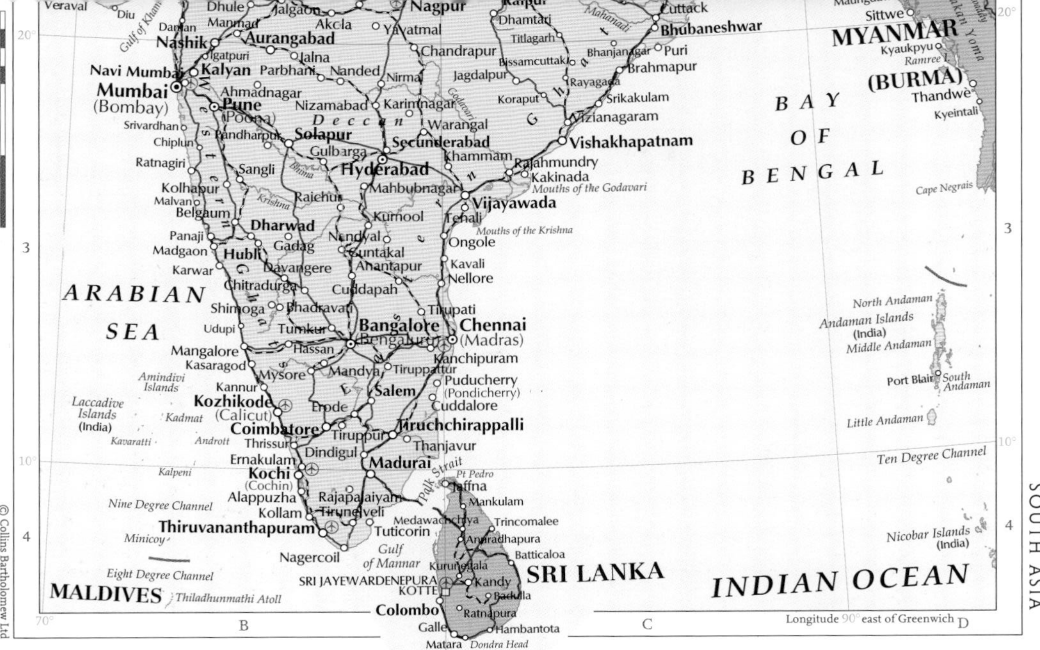

MYANMAR
(BURMA)

B A Y

O F

B E N G A L

North Andaman
Andaman Islands
(India)
Middle Andaman

Port Blair South Andaman

Little Andaman

INDIAN OCEAN

Nicobar Islands
(India)

Ten Degree Channel

Longitude 90° east of Greenwich D

Cuttack
Bhubaneshwar
Puri

Deccan

Nagpur
Yavatmal
Akola
Chandrapur
Brahmapur

Sikakulam
Vizianagaram
Vishakhapatnam

Rajahmundry
Kakinada
Mouths of the Godavari

Warangal
Secunderabad
Hyderabad
Khammam
Vijayawada

Mouths of the Krishna

Kurnool
Nalgonda
Guntur
Ongole
Kavali
Nellore

Gulbarga
Mahbubnagar

Raichur
Kurnool
Nandyal
Guntakal
Anantapur
Cuddapah

Tirupati
Chennai
(Madras)

Kanchipuram
Puducherry
(Pondicherry)
Cuddalore

SRI LANKA

Jaffna

Pt Pedro

Pk Strait

Mankulam
Trincomalee
Anuradhapura
Batticaloa

Kandy

Kurunegala

Medawachchiya

Gulf
of Mannar

Pedro
Ratnapura
Colombo
SRI JAYEWARDENEPURA
KOTTE

Matara Dondra Head
Galle
Hambantota

Bangalore
Salem
Tiruppur
Tiruchirappalli
Thanjavur
Madurai
Rajapalaiyam
Tuticorin

Coimbatore
Erode
Dindigul

Kochi
(Cochin)
Alappuzha
Kollam
Thiruvananthapuram
Nagercoil

ARABIAN
SEA

MALDIVES

Thiladhunmathi Atoll

Eight Degree Channel

Nine Degree Channel

Minicoy

Kalpeni

Androth

Kavaratti

Kadmat

Amindivi
Islands

Laccadive
Islands
(India)

Mangalore
Kasaragod
Udupi

Kannur
Kozhikode
(Calicut)
Thrissur
Ernakulam

Hassan
Mysore
Kamrup
Mandya
Dharwad
Hubli
Gadag
Davangere
Shimoga
Chitradurga

Belgaum
Panaji
Madgaon
Karwar

Kolhapur
Sangli
Miraj

Ratnagiri
Malvani
Chiplun
Srivardhan

Mumbai
(Bombay)
Navi Mumbai
Kalyan

Pune
Ahmadnagar

Sholapur
Bidar

Nanded
Parbhani
Nizamabad
Karimnagar

Nirmal
Aurangabad

Nashik
Dhule
Jalgaon
Bhusawal
Amravati

Dahanu

Veraval
Diu

Gulf of Khambhat

0   200   400   600 KILOMETRES

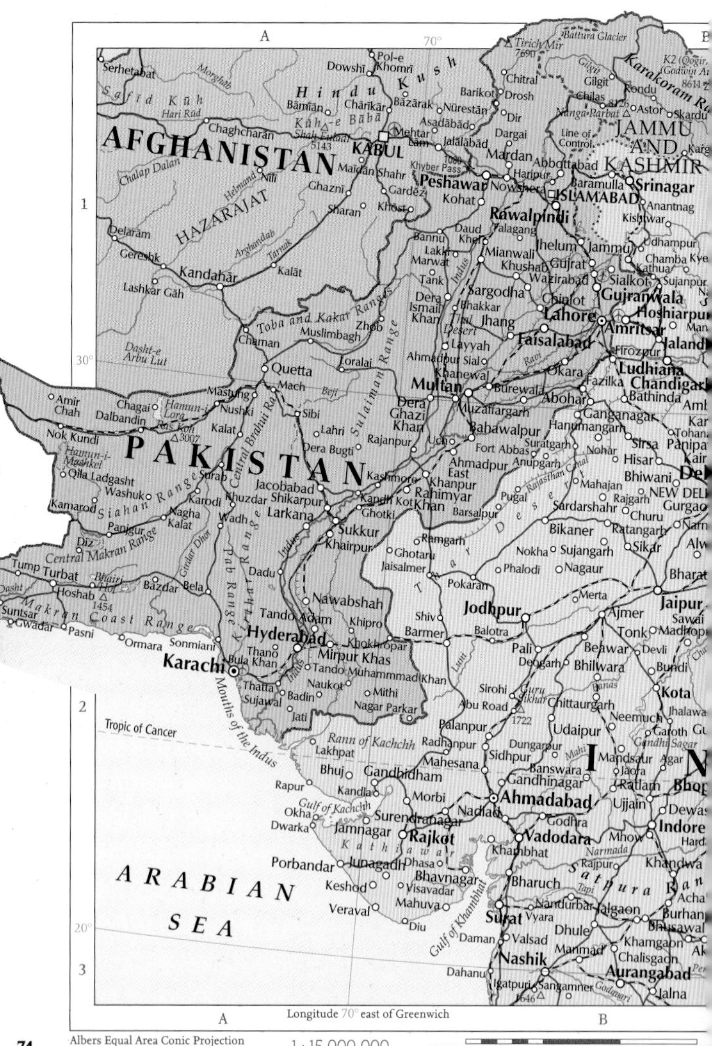

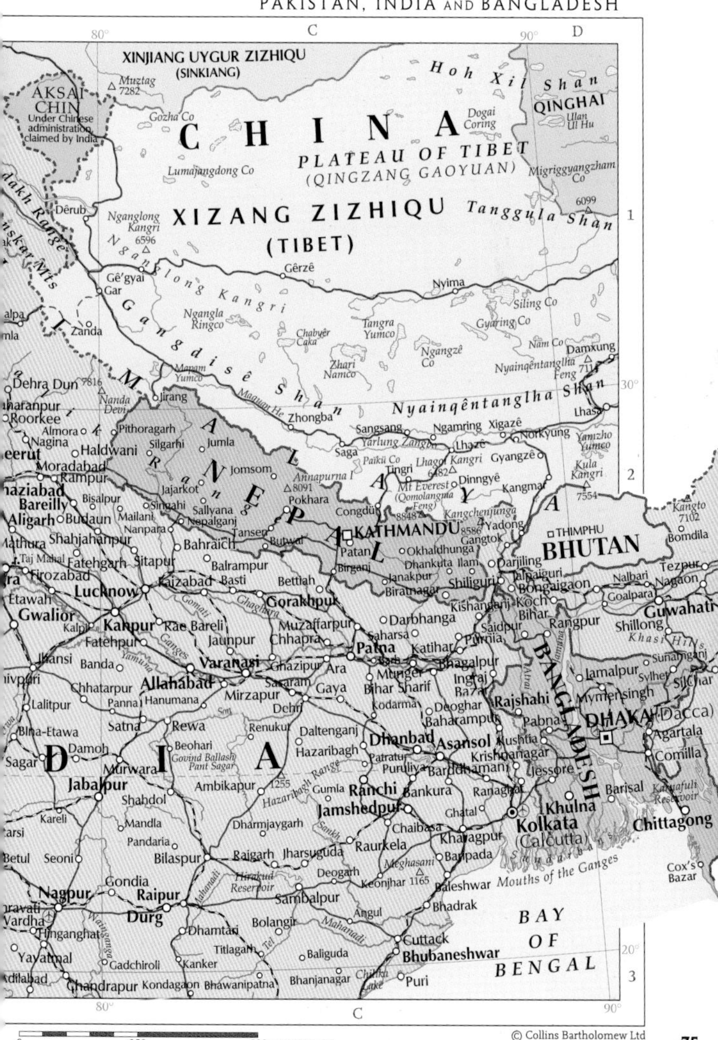
CHINA
XINJIANG UYGUR ZIZHIQU
(SINKIANG)
XIZANG ZIZHIQU
(TIBET)
PLATEAU OF TIBET
(QINGZANG GAOYUAN)
QINGHAI
AKSAI CHIN
Under Chinese administration, claimed by India
NEPAL
KATHMANDU
BHUTAN
THIMPHU
BANGLADESH
DHAKA (Dacca)
INDIA
Hoh Xil Shan
Tanggula Shan
Nganglong Kangri
Gangdisê Shan
Nyainqêntanglha Shan
HIMALAYA
Kolkata
(Calcutta)
Mouths of the Ganges
BAY OF BENGAL
Lucknow
Kanpur
Varanasi
Allahabad
Patna
Gorakhpur
Jabalpur
Nagpur
Raipur
Ranchi
Jamshedpur
Chittagong
Khulna
Guwahati
Lhasa
Mt Everest (Qomolangma Feng) 8848
Kangchenjunga 8586
Annapurna I 8091
Sundarbans
Gwalior
Jhansi
Durg
Bhubaneshwar
Cuttack
Puri
Shillong
Rajshahi
Mymensingh
Comilla
Agartala
Dhanbad
Asansol
Gaya
Bareilly
Aligarh
Moradabad
Dehra Dun
Mahanadi
Ganges
Yamuna
Ghaghara
Gomati
Son
Khasi Hills
Hazaribagh Range
80°
90°
30°
20°
C
D
1
2
3

Scale: 0 250 500 KILOMETRES

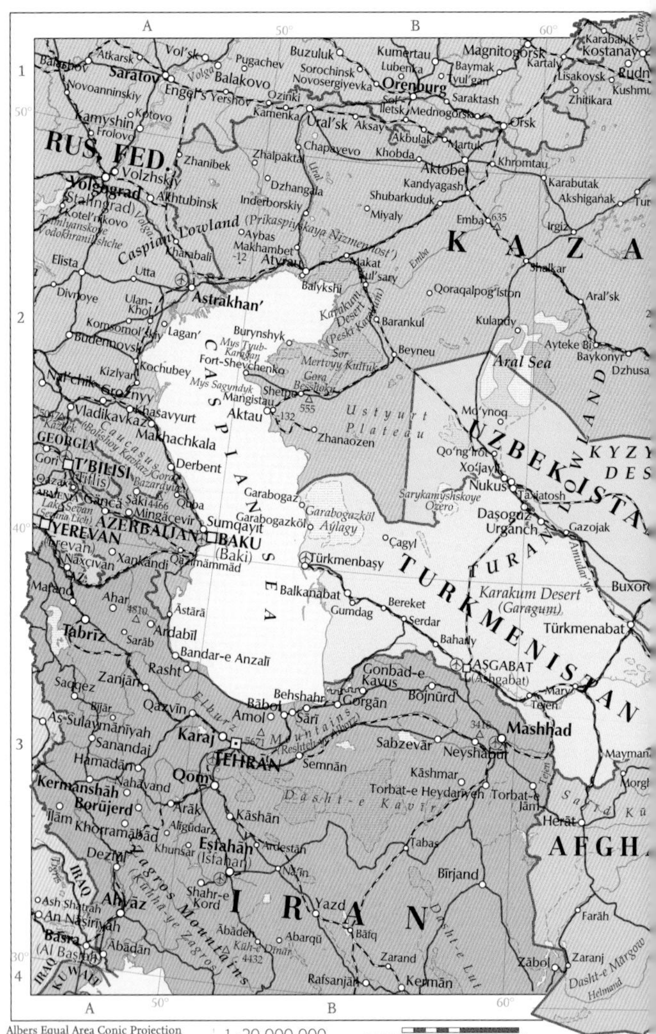

Albers Equal Area Conic Projection 1 : 20 000 000 MILES 0   100   200

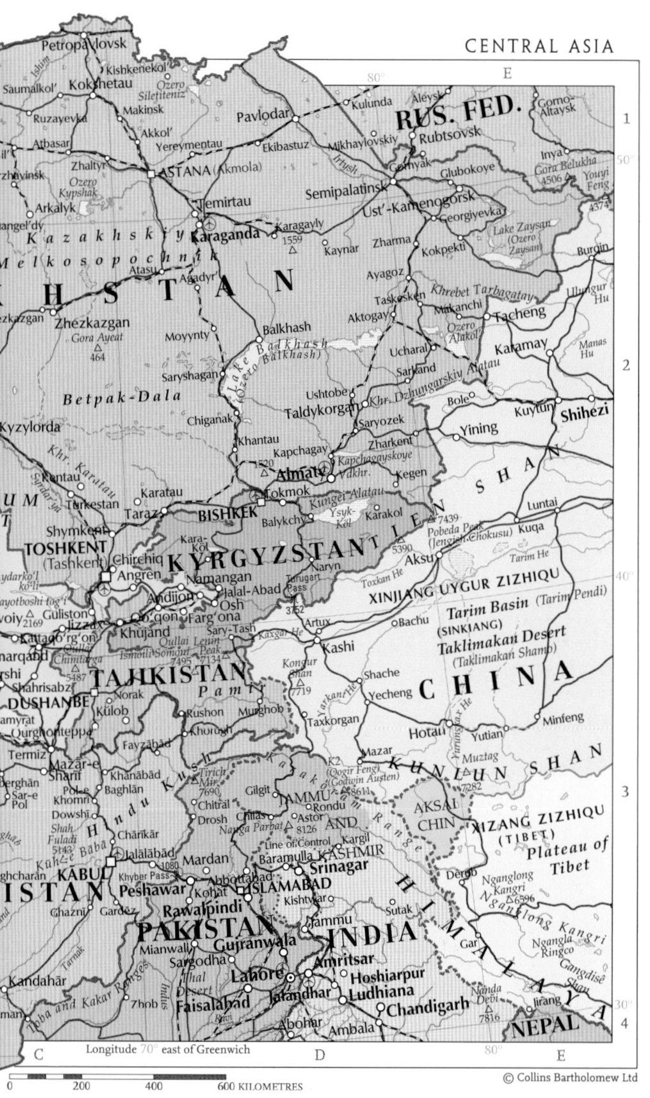

© Collins Bartholomew Ltd

Longitude 70° east of Greenwich

0   200   400   600 KILOMETRES

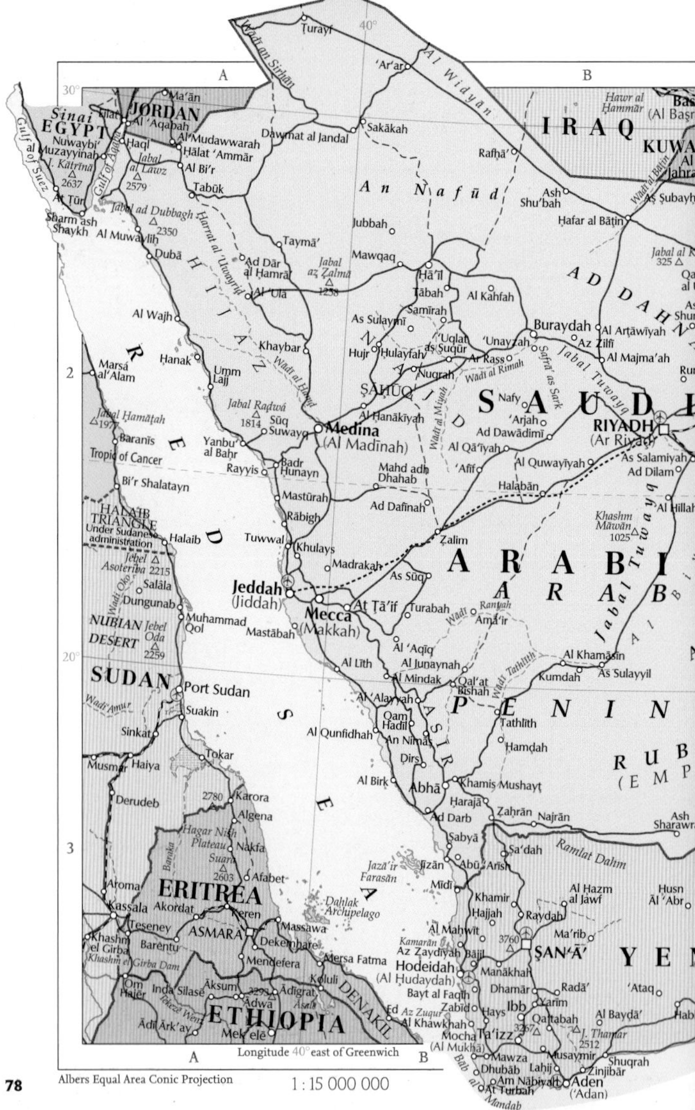
JORDAN
EGYPT
Sinai
IRAQ
KUWAIT
SAUDI ARABIA
ARABIAN PENINSULA
SUDAN
ERITREA
ETHIOPIA
RED SEA
An Nafūd
AD DAHNA
HIJAZ
NAJD
ASIR
Medina (Al Madīnah)
Mecca (Makkah)
Jeddah (Jiddah)
RIYADH (Ar Riyāḍ)
ASMARA
ṢAN'Ā'
Port Sudan
Hodeidah (Al Ḥudaydah)
Aden ('Adan)
Ta'izz
Tabūk
Ḥā'il
Buraydah
Abhā
Ṭā'if
Gulf of Suez
Gulf of Aqaba
Tropic of Cancer
HALAIB TRIANGLE Under Sudanese administration
NUBIAN DESERT
Dahlak Archipelago
DENAKIL
Ramlat Dahm
Wādī al Bāṭin
Al Widyān
Jabal Ṭuwayq
Longitude 40° east of Greenwich
A
B
2
3
30°
20°
40°

Albers Equal Area Conic Projection

1 : 15 000 000

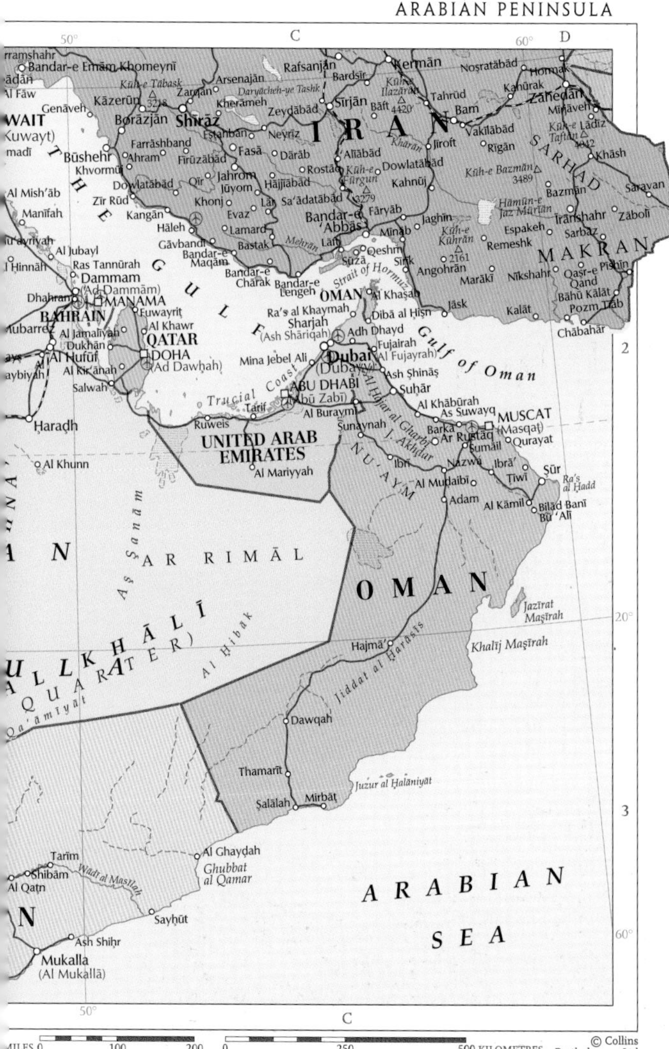

© Collins
Bartholomew Ltd

IRAN
OMAN
UNITED ARAB EMIRATES
QATAR
DOHA
(Ad Dawḩah)
MUSCAT
(Masqaţ)
ABU DHABI
(Abū Zabī)
Dubai
(Dubayy)
Sharjah
(Ash Shāriqah)
MANAMA
BAHRAIN
Shīrāz
Kermān
Zāhedān
Bandar-e 'Abbās
Şalālah
Mukalla
(Al Mukallā)
Gulf of Oman
Strait of Hormuz
ARABIAN SEA
RUB' AL KHĀLĪ
(EMPTY QUARTER)
AR RIMĀL
MAKRAN
SARHAD
Jazīrat Maşīrah
Khalīj Maşīrah
Juzur al Ḩalāniyāt
Ghubbat al Qamar

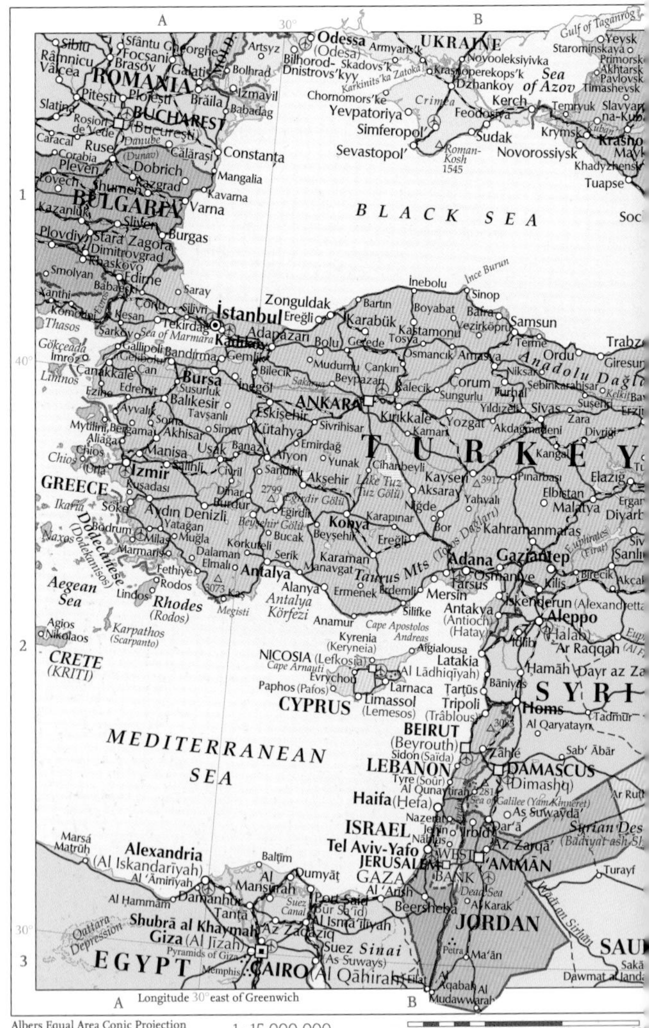

Albers Equal Area Conic Projection

1 : 15 000 000

MILES 0   100   200

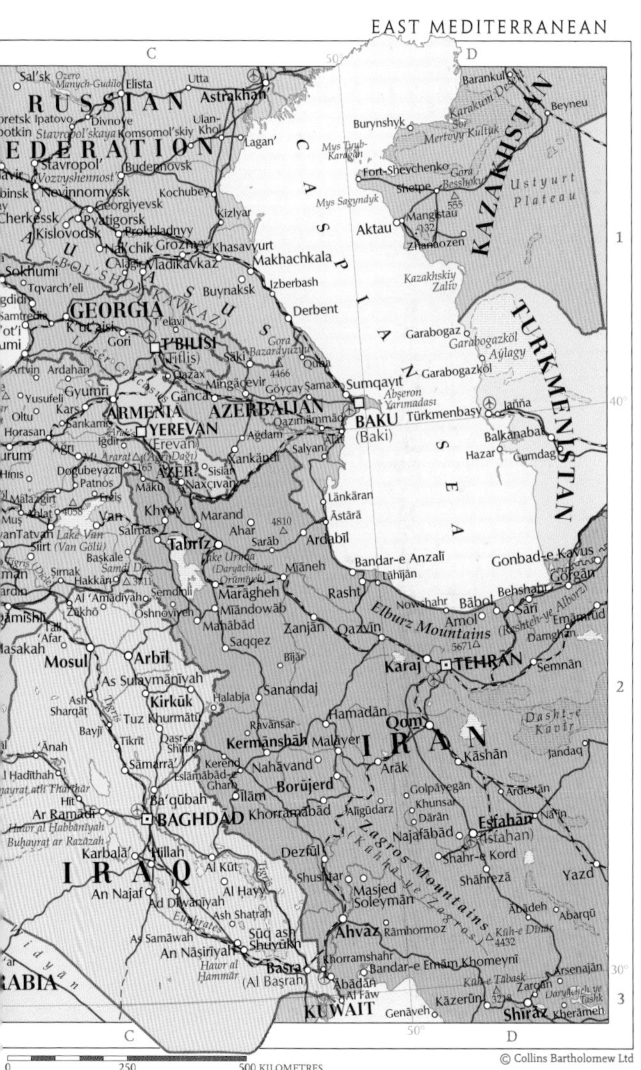
C
D
1
2
3
40°
30°
50°
Sal'sk
Ozero Manych-Gudilo
Elista
Utta
Astrakhan'
RUSSIAN FEDERATION
Ipatovo
Divnoye
Stavropol'skaya
Komsomol'skiy
Ulan-Khol
Lagan'
Stavropol'
Budennovsk
Vozvyshennost'
Nevinnomyssk
Kochubey
Georgiyevsk
Pyatigorsk
Kislovodsk
Prokhladnyy
Kizlyar
Nal'chik
Groznyy
Khasavyurt
Makhachkala
Alagir
Vladikavkaz
Sokhumi
Tqvarch'eli
Buynaksk
Izberbash
Derbent
GEORGIA
K'ut'aisi
T'elavi
Gori
T'BILISI
(Tiflis)
Artvin
Ardahan
Yusufeli
Gyumri
Kars
Oltu
Sarıkamış
Horasan
ARMENIA
YEREVAN
(Erevan)
AZERBAIJAN
Qazax
Gäncä
Mingäçevir
Göyçay
Şamaxı
Säki
Quba
Gora Bazardyuzyu
4466
Sumqayıt
Abşeron Yarımadası
BAKU
(Baki)
Qazimämmäd
Ağdam
Ələt
Salyan
Xankändi
Iğdir
Ağrı
Mt Ararat
(Ağrı Dağı)
5165
Doğubeyazıt
Patnos
Ercis
Maku
AZER.
Sisian
Naxçıvan
Malazgirt
Ahlat
4058
Muş
Tatvan
Van
Lake Van
(Van Gölü)
Khvoy
Salmas
Siirt
Baskale
Şırnak
Hakkâri
3711
Tigris (Dicle)
Marand
Ahar
4810
Sarāb
Ardabīl
Länkäran
Āstārā
Tabrīz
Lake Urmia
(Daryācheh-ye Orūmīyeh)
Mīāneh
Marāgheh
Mīāndowāb
Al 'Amādīyah
Zākhō
Oshnovīyeh
Mahābād
Saqqez
Tall 'Afar
Mosul
Arbīl
As Sulaymānīyah
Kirkūk
Halabja
Sanandaj
Bījār
Zanjān
Qazvīn
Rasht
Lāhījān
Bandar-e Anzalī
Nowshahr
Bābol
Āmol
Behshahr
Sārī
Gorgān
Gonbad-e Kāvus
Elburz Mountains
(Reshteh-ye Alborz)
5671
Emāmrūd
Damghān
Semnān
Karaj
TEHRAN
Dasht-e Kavīr
Ash Sharqāţ
Bayjī
Tuz Khurmātū
Tikrīt
Qasr-e Shīrīn
Sāmarrā'
'Ānah
Hadīthah
Kerend
Eslāmābād-e Gharb
Kermānshāh
Ravānsar
Hamadān
Malāyer
Nahāvand
Borūjerd
Arāk
Qom
IRAN
Kāshān
Jandaq
Hīt
Ar Ramādī
Buhayrat ath Tharthār
Hawr al Habbānīyah
Buhayrat ar Razāzah
Ba'qūbah
BAGHDĀD
Īlām
Khorramābād
Alīgūdarz
Golpāyegān
Khunsar
Dārān
Ardestān
Nā'īn
Esfahān
(Isfahan)
Najafābād
Shahr-e Kord
Karbalā'
Hillah
Al Kūt
IRAQ
Dezfūl
Shushtar
Zagros Mountains
(Kūhhā-ye Zagros)
Masjed Soleymān
Shāhrezā
Yazd
An Najaf
Al Hayy
Ad Dīwānīyah
Ash Shatrah
Euphrates
Tigris
As Samāwah
An Nāşirīyah
Sūq ash Shuyūkh
Ahvāz
Rāmhormoz
Ābādeh
Abarqū
Kūh-e Dīnār
4432
Hawr al Hammār
Basra
(Al Başrah)
Khorramshahr
Bandar-e Emām Khomeynī
Ābādān
Al Fāw
KUWAIT
Genāveh
Kāzerūn
Kūh-e Tābask
3218
Zargān
Arsenajān
Shīrāz
Daryācheh-ye Tashk
Kherāmeh
CASPIAN SEA
Mys Tyub-Karagan
Burynshyk
Fort-Shevchenko
Mys Sagyndyk
Aktau
Shetpe
Mangistau
-132
555
Zhanaozen
Barankul
Karakum Desert
Sor Mertvyy Kultuk
Gora Besshoky
KAZAKHSTAN
Beyneu
Ustyurt Plateau
Kazakhskiy Zaliv
TURKMENISTAN
Garabogaz
Garabogazköl
Aýlagy
Garabogazköl
Türkmenbaşy
Jaňňa
Balkanabat
Hazar
Gumdag
0
250
500 KILOMETRES

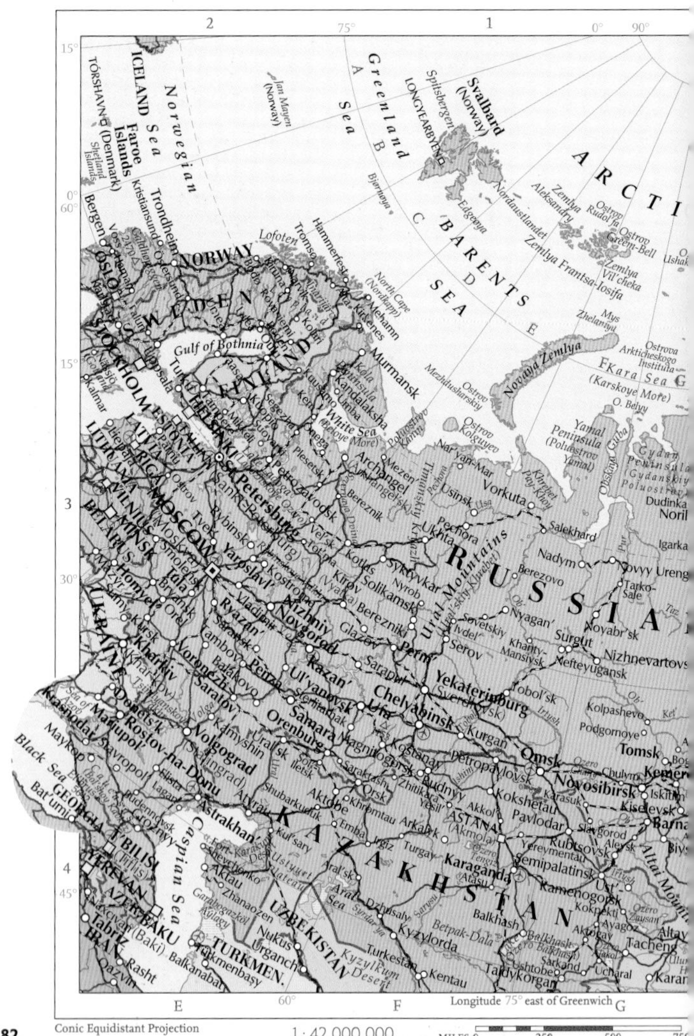

Conic Equidistant Projection

1 : 42 000 000

MILES 0   250   500   750

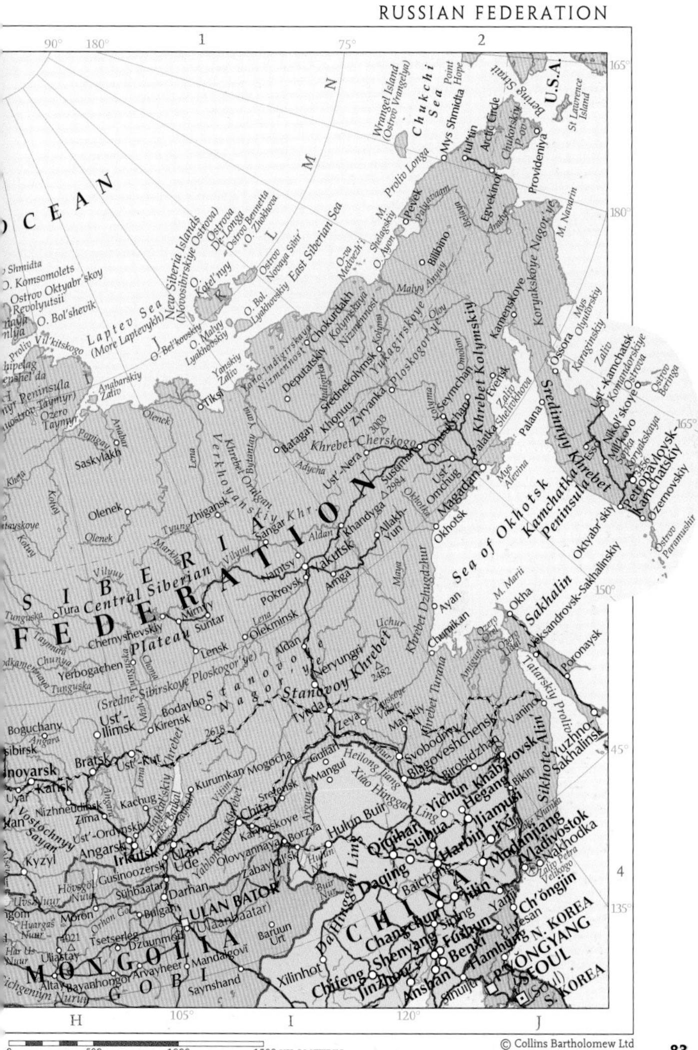

0   500   1000   1500 KILOMETRES

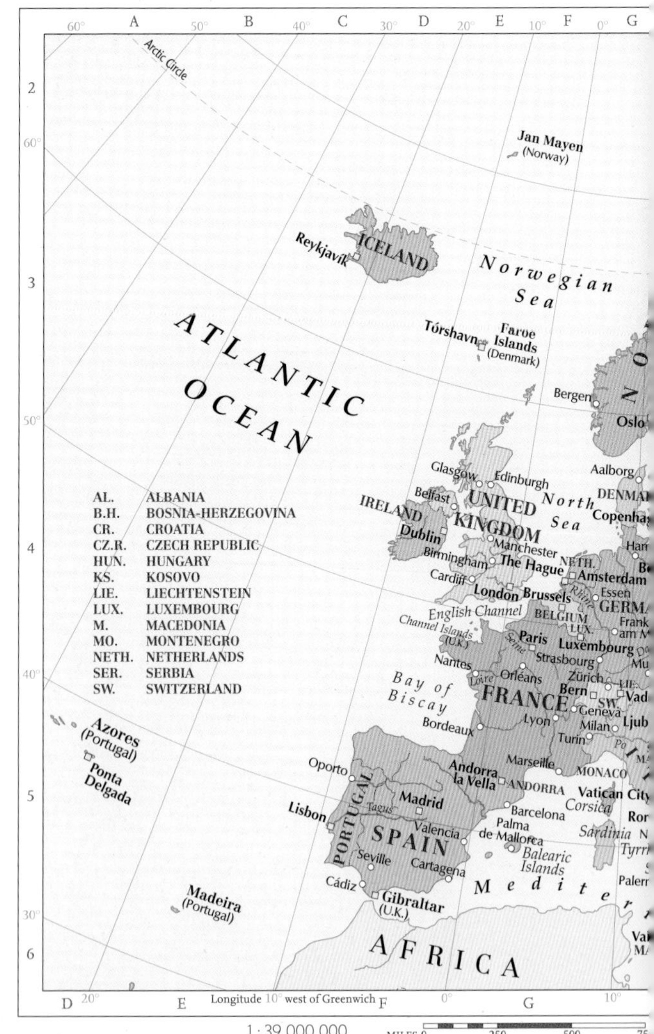

ATLANTIC OCEAN

Norwegian Sea

Jan Mayen
(Norway)

Reykjavík ICELAND

Tórshavn Faroe Islands
(Denmark)

Bergen

Oslo

Glasgow Edinburgh Aalborg

Belfast North DENMARK

IRELAND UNITED Sea Copenha

Dublin KINGDOM

Birmingham Manchester NETH. Ham

Cardiff The Hague

London Amsterdam

Brussels Essen

English Channel BELGIUM GERMA

Channel Islands Paris LUX. Frank

(U.K.) Luxembourg am M

Nantes Strasbourg Mu

Orléans Zürich LIE. Vad

Bay of FRANCE Bern SW.

Biscay Loire Geneva Ljub

Bordeaux Lyon Milan

Turin Po M

Marseille MONACO

Oporto Andorra la Vella ANDORRA Vatican City

Madrid Barcelona Corsica Ror

Lisbon Valencia Palma Sardinia Tyrr

SPAIN de Mallorca

Seville Cartagena Balearic Islands

Cádiz Gibraltar M e d i t e r

(U.K.) Palerr

Madeira Va

(Portugal) M

A F R I C A

AL. ALBANIA
B.H. BOSNIA-HERZEGOVINA
CR. CROATIA
CZ.R. CZECH REPUBLIC
HUN. HUNGARY
KS. KOSOVO
LIE. LIECHTENSTEIN
LUX. LUXEMBOURG
M. MACEDONIA
MO. MONTENEGRO
NETH. NETHERLANDS
SER. SERBIA
SW. SWITZERLAND

Azores
(Portugal)

Ponta Delgada

Arctic Circle

Longitude 10° west of Greenwich

1 : 39 000 000

MILES 0   250   500   75

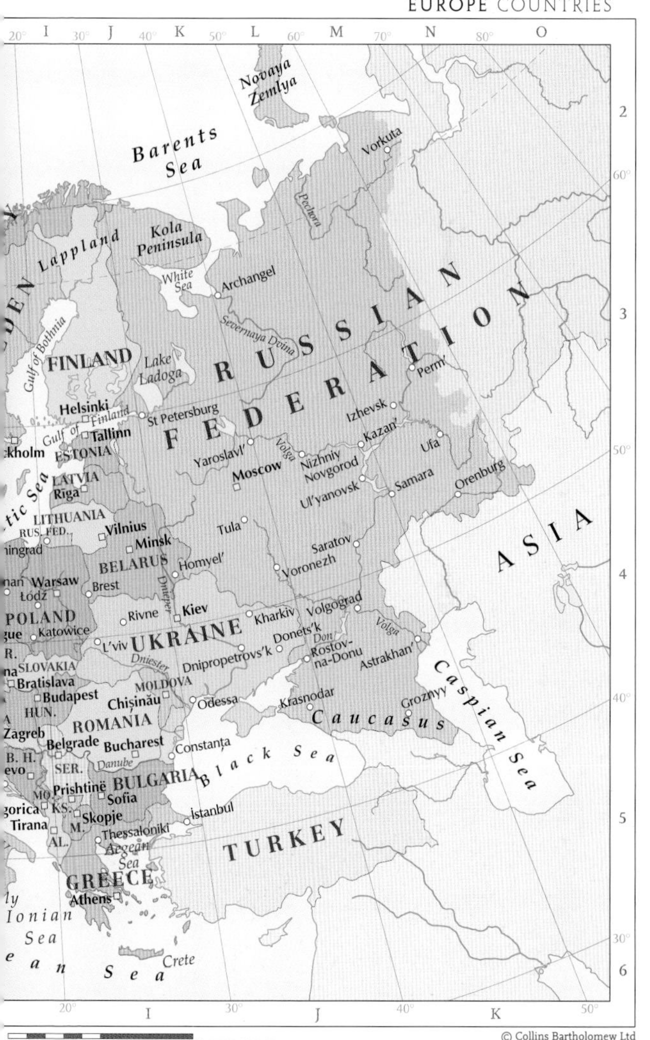

Novaya Zemlya

Barents Sea

Kola Peninsula

Vorkuta

SWEDEN Lappland

White Sea

Archangel

FINLAND

Lake Ladoga

Helsinki

RUSSIAN FEDERATION

St Petersburg

Izhevsk

Perm'

Severnaya Dvina

Pechora

ckholm

Tallinn

ESTONIA

Yaroslavl'

Nizhniy Novgorod

Kazan'

Ufa

Gulf of Finland

tic Sea

Gulf of Bothnia

LATVIA

Riga

Moscow

Volga

Ul'yanovsk

Samara

Orenburg

LITHUANIA

RUS. FED.

Vilnius

Tula

ASIA

ningrad

Minsk

Saratov

nan

Warsaw

BELARUS

Homyel'

Voronezh

Łodz

Rivne

Dnieper

Kiev

Kharkiv

Volgograd

Volga

POLAND

Brest

Katowice

L'viv

UKRAINE

Donets'k

Don

Rostov-na-Donu

Astrakhan'

R.

Dniester

Dnipropetrovs'k

Caspian Sea

SLOVAKIA

Bratislava

MOLDOVA

Chişinău

Krasnodar

Groz",

Caucasus

na

HUN.

Budapest

ROMANIA

Odessa

Zagreb

Belgrade

Bucharest

Constanţa

B. H.

SER.

Danube

Black Sea

evo

MO.

Prishtinë

BULGARIA

gorica

KS.

Sofia

İstanbul

Tirana

Skopje

AL.

M.

Thessaloniki

TURKEY

GREECE

Aegean Sea

Athens

ly

Ionian Sea

ean Sea

Crete

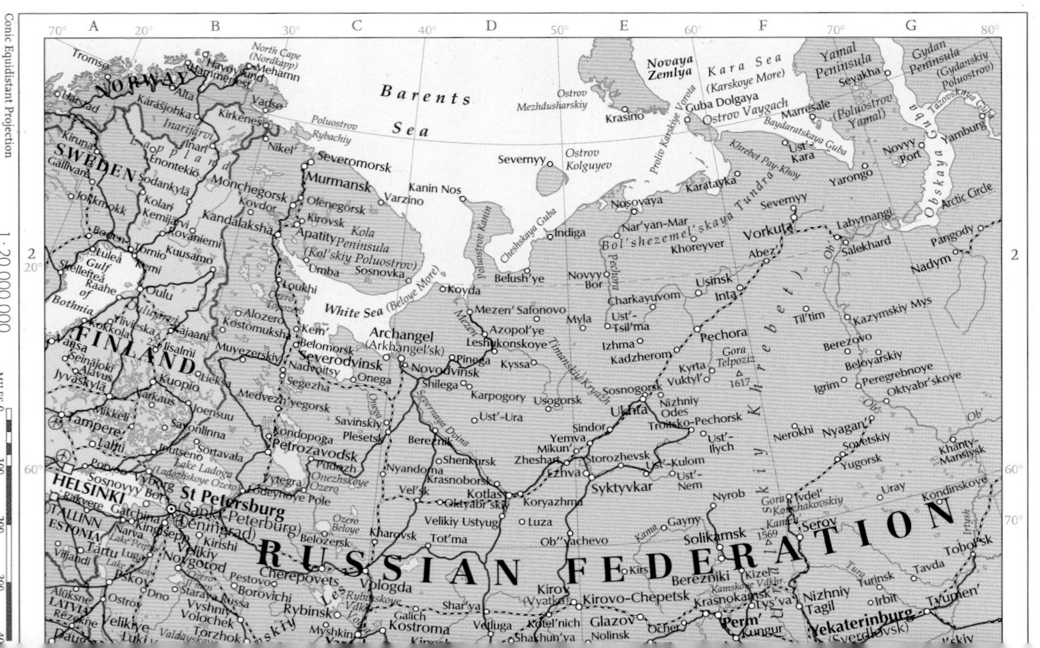

Conic Equidistant Projection

1 : 20 000 000

MILES 0   100   200   300   40

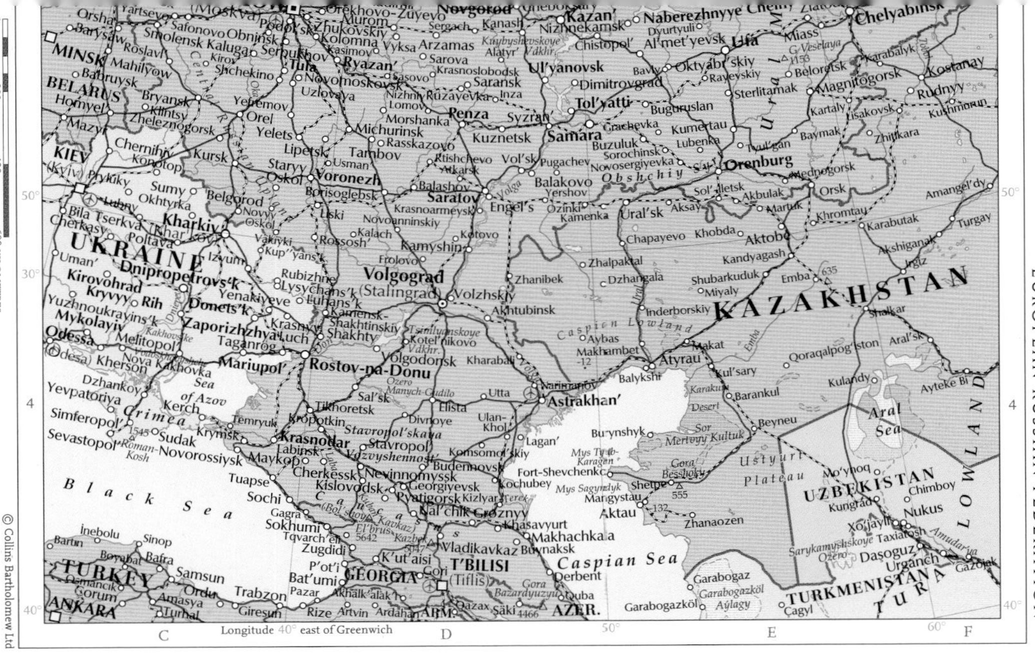
KAZAKHSTAN
UKRAINE
BELARUS
UZBEKISTAN
TURKMENISTAN
GEORGIA
TURKEY
AZER.
ARM.
Black Sea
Caspian Sea
Sea of Azov
Aral Sea
Crimea
Caspian Lowland
Ustyurt Plateau
Volgograd (Stalingrad)
Rostov-na-Donu
Astrakhan'
Samara
Saratov
Voronezh
Kharkiv
Dnipropetrovs'k
Donets'k
Zaporizhzhya
Odessa
KIEV (Kyiv)
MINSK
T'BILISI (Tiflis)
ANKARA
Orenburg
Ufa
Kazan'
Chelyabinsk
Aktobe
Atyrau
Aktau
Makhachkala
Krasnodar
Stavropol'
Sochi
Trabzon
Samsun
Longitude 40° east of Greenwich
0 200 400 600 KILOMETRES

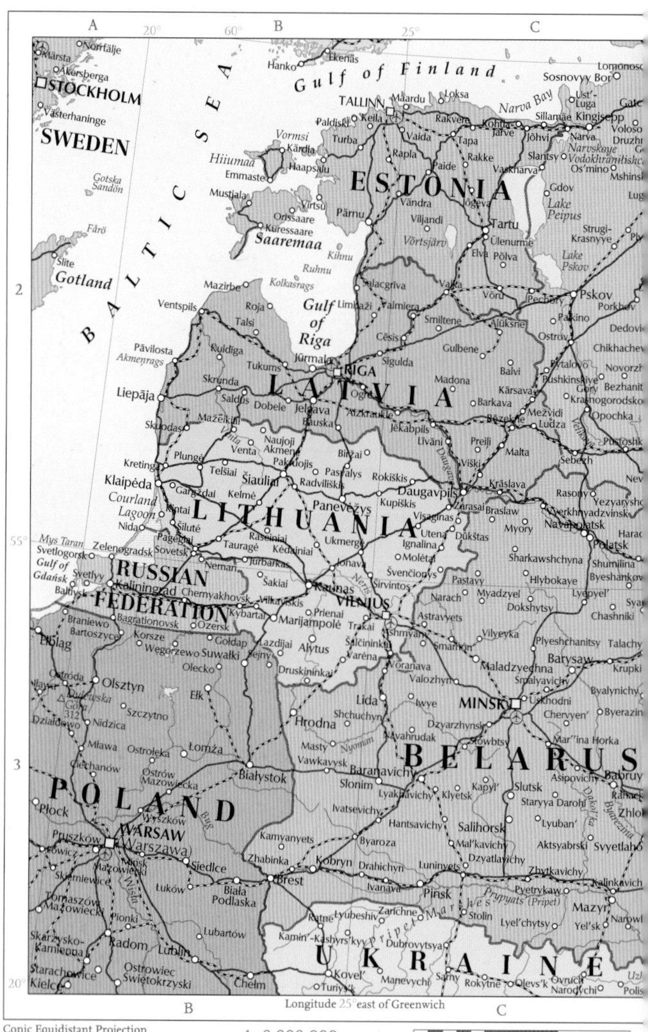

Conic Equidistant Projection

1 : 8 000 000

MILES 0   50   100   150

Longitude 25° east of Greenwich

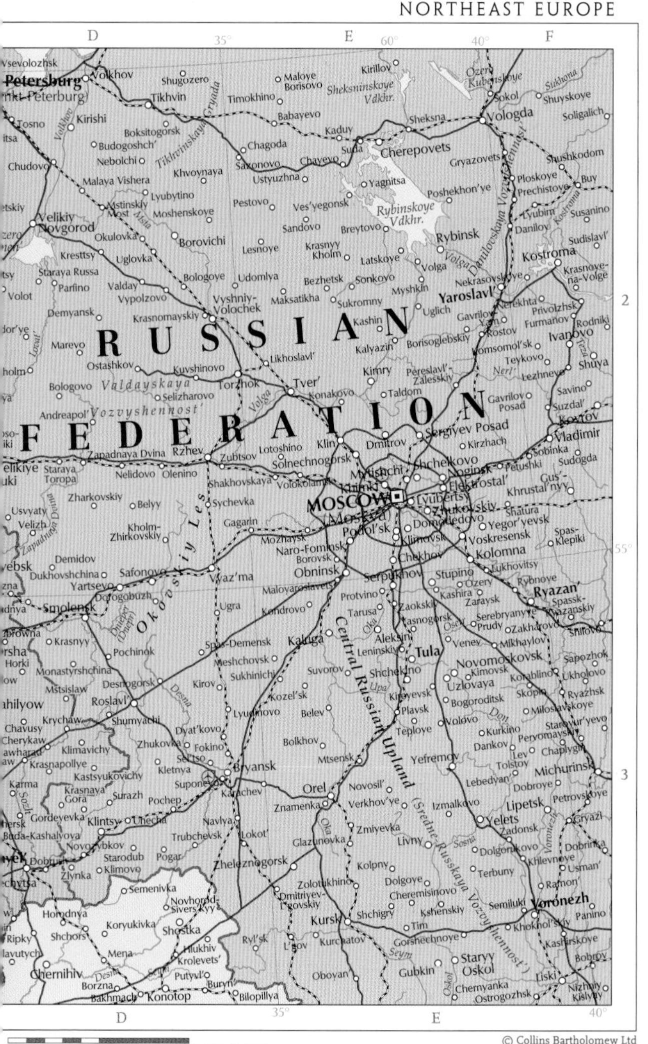

© Collins Bartholomew Ltd

0   100   200 KILOMETRES

RUSSIAN FEDERATION
MOSCOW (Moskva)
St Petersburg
Vologda
Cherepovets
Rybinskoye Vdkhr.
Yaroslavl'
Kostroma
Tver'
Vladimir
Ryazan'
Tula
Kaluga
Bryansk
Orel
Kursk
Voronezh
Lipetsk
Smolensk
Velikiy Novgorod
Central Russian Upland
Valdayskaya Vozvyshennost'

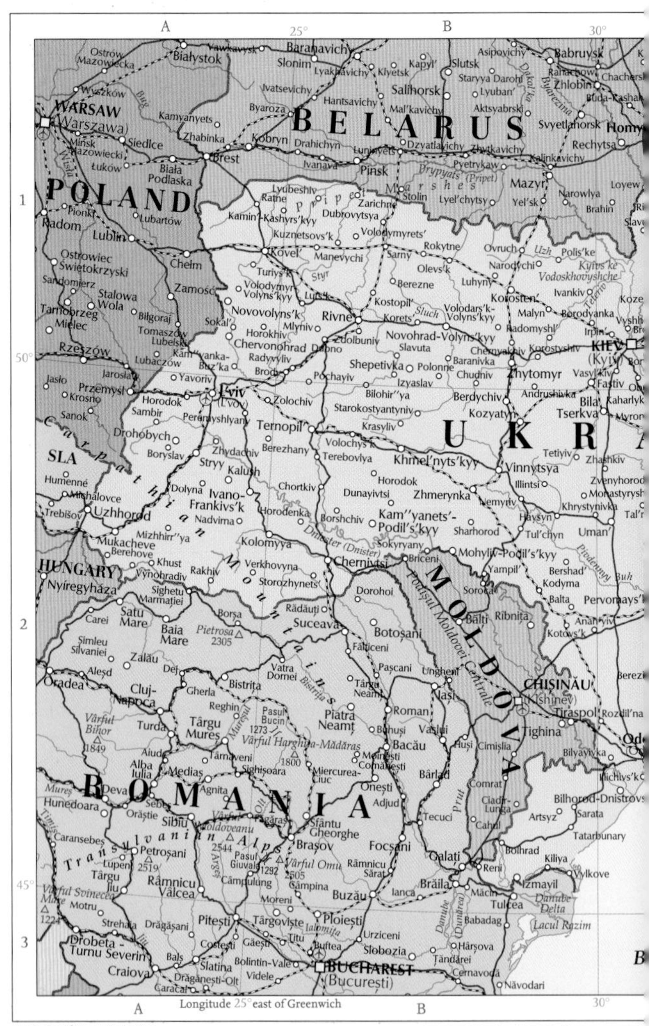

Conic Equidistant Projection   1 : 8 000 000   MILES 0   50   100   15

Longitude 25° east of Greenwich

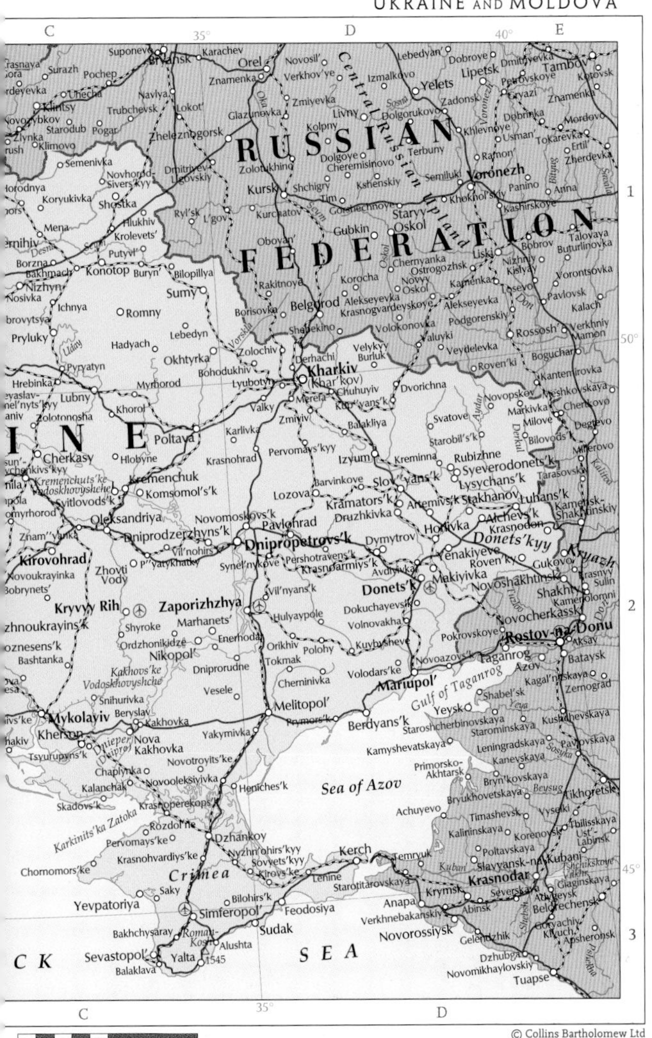
RUSSIAN FEDERATION
Central Russian Upland
Sea of Azov
Gulf of Taganrog
Crimea
SEA
Kharkiv (Khar'kov)
Dnipropetrovs'k
Donets'k
Zaporizhzhya
Rostov-na-Donu
Voronezh
Kursk
Belgorod
Poltava
Simferopol'
Sevastopol'
Krasnodar
Novorossiysk
Mariupol'
Mykolayiv
Kherson
Kryvyy Rih
Kirovohrad
Kremenchuk
Sumy
Luhans'k
Melitopol'
Kerch
Yalta
Feodosiya
Yevpatoriya
Taganrog
Bryansk
Orel
Lipetsk
Tambov
Yelets
Starvy Oskol
Lozova
Kramators'k
Horlivka
Makiyivka
Berdyans'k
Nikopol'
Karkinits'ka Zatoka
Kakhovs'ke Vodoskhovyshche
Kremenchuts'ke Vodoskhovyshche
Dnieper (Dnipro)
© Collins Bartholomew Ltd
0 100 200 KILOMETRES

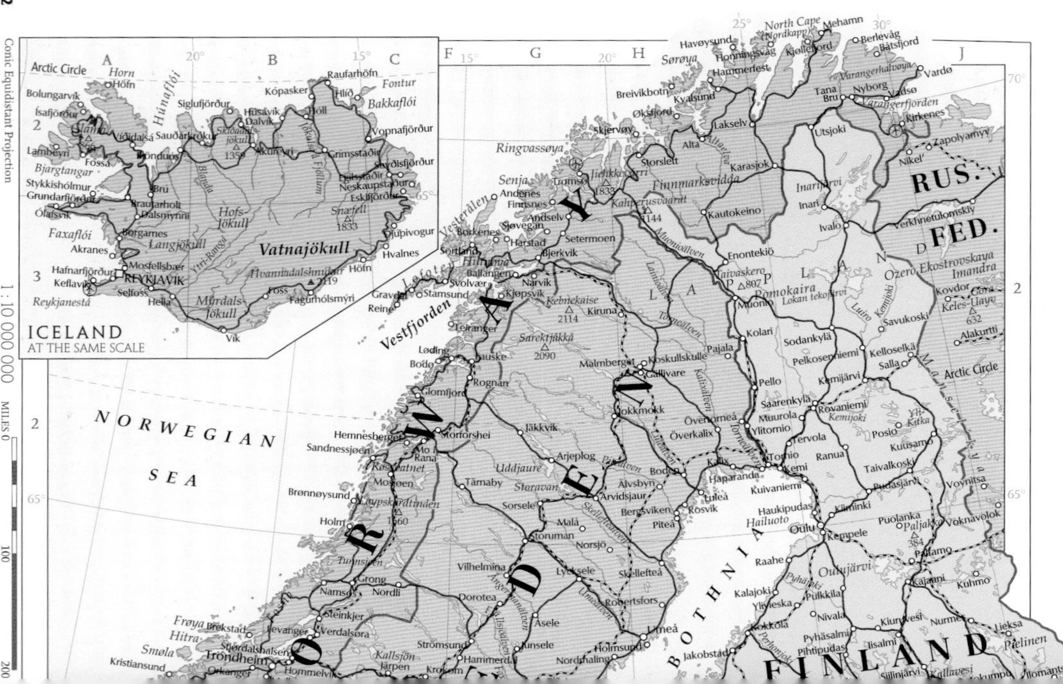

ICELAND
AT THE SAME SCALE

Conic Equidistant Projection

92

1 : 10 000 000

MILES 0   100   200

KILOMETRES 0   100   200   300

NORWEGIAN SEA

GULF OF BOTHNIA

FINLAND

RUS. FED.

SWEDEN

NORWAY

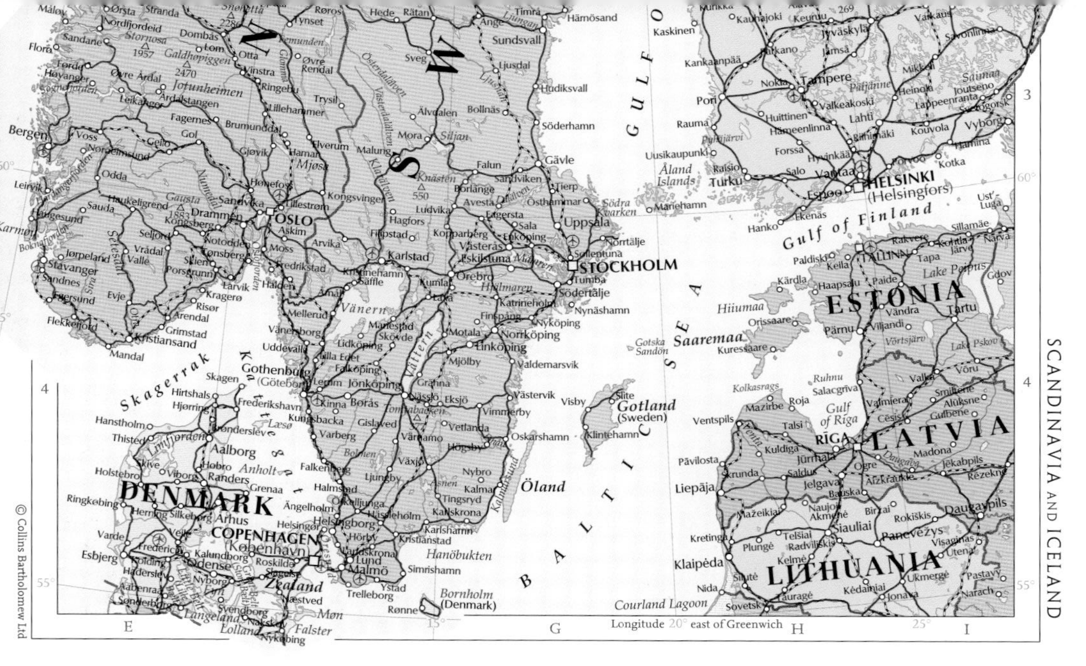

GULF OF BOTHNIA
BALTIC SEA
Gulf of Finland
Gulf of Riga
ESTONIA
LATVIA
LITHUANIA
DENMARK
Skagerrak
Kattegat
HELSINKI
(Helsingfors)
STOCKHOLM
OSLO
RĪGA
COPENHAGEN
(København)
TALLINN
Gotland
(Sweden)
Öland
Bornholm
(Denmark)
Saaremaa
Hiiumaa
Åland Islands
Zealand
Vänern
Vättern
Lake Peipus
Gothenburg
(Göteborg)
Malmö
Lund
Helsingborg
Uppsala
Västerås
Örebro
Norrköping
Linköping
Jönköping
Karlstad
Gävle
Sundsvall
Falun
Kalmar
Karlskrona
Visby
Tampere
Turku
Pori
Lahti
Vantaa
Espoo
Tartu
Pärnu
Liepāja
Ventspils
Jelgava
Daugavpils
Klaipėda
Šiauliai
Panevėžys
Bergen
Stavanger
Kristiansand
Drammen
Lillehammer
Aalborg
Århus
Odense
Esbjerg
Lolland
Falster
Møn
Courland Lagoon
Longitude 20° east of Greenwich

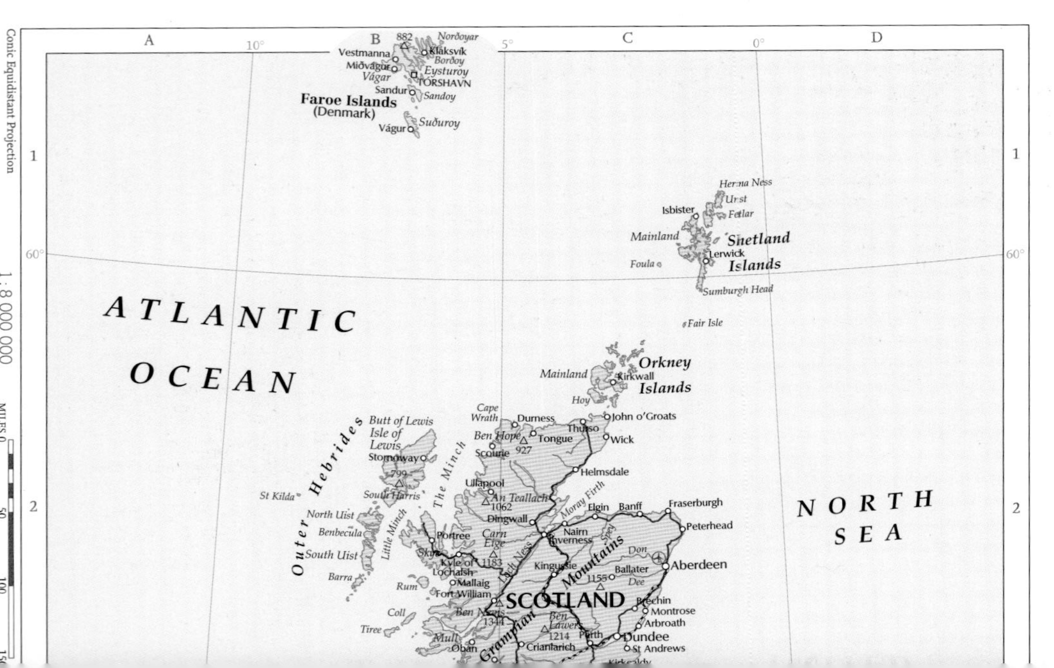

94

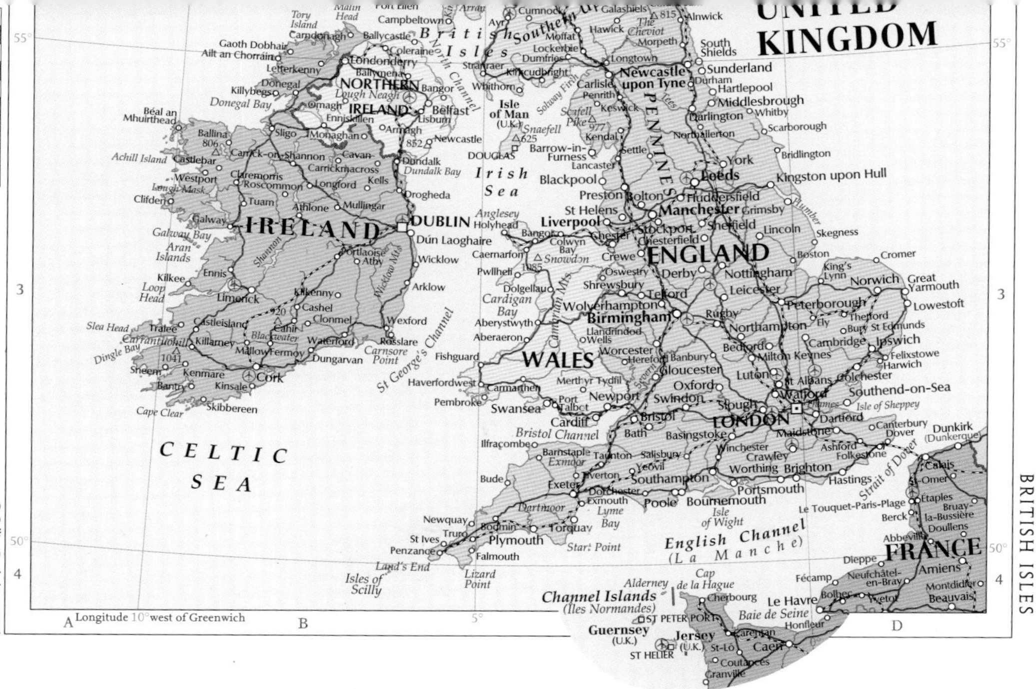

UNITED KINGDOM
IRELAND
NORTHERN IRELAND
ENGLAND
WALES
FRANCE
CELTIC SEA
Irish Sea
English Channel
(La Manche)
North Channel
St George's Channel
Bristol Channel
Strait of Dover
British Isles
PENNINES
LONDON
DUBLIN
Birmingham
Manchester
Liverpool
Leeds
Sheffield
Newcastle upon Tyne
Kingston upon Hull
Bristol
Cardiff
Swansea
Plymouth
Southampton
Portsmouth
Brighton
Norwich
Nottingham
Leicester
Belfast
Cork
Limerick
Galway
Waterford
Channel Islands
(Îles Normandes)
Guernsey
Jersey
Isle of Man
Isle of Wight
Isles of Scilly
Land's End
Lizard Point
Le Havre
Calais
Dunkirk
Amiens
Longitude 10° west of Greenwich
0
100
200 KILOMETRES

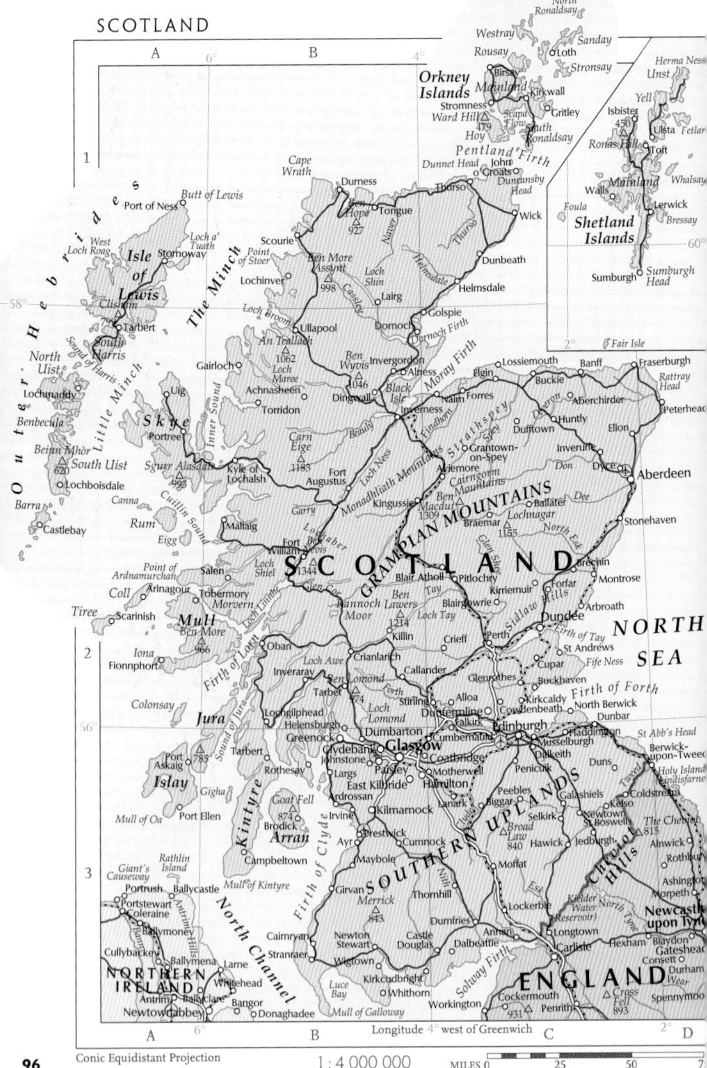

SCOTLAND

A · B · C

Orkney Islands
North Ronaldsay
Westray
Rousay · Sanday
Gritley · Stronsay
Mainland
Stromness · Kirkwall
Ward Hills · 479
Hoy · Scapa Flow
South Ronaldsay
Dunnet Head · John o'Groats
Pentland Firth
Duncansby Head

Shetland Islands
Herma Ness
Unst
Isbister · 450
Yell
Uyea · Fetlar
Ronas Hill
Mainland · Whalsay
Foula · Lerwick
Bressay
Sumburgh
Sumburgh Head
60°

Cape Wrath
Durness
Butt of Lewis
Port of Ness
Tongue
Thurso
Wick
Ben Hope · 927
West Loch Roag
Loch a' Tuath
Scourie
Dunbeath
Isle of Lewis
Stornoway
Point of Stoer
Lochinver
Ben More Assynt · 998
Loch Shin
Loch Naver
Helmsdale
The Minch
Laing
Helmsdale
58°
North Harris
Clisham
Tarbert
Ullapool
Loch Broom
Dornoch
Golspie
Dornoch Firth
An Teallach · 1062
Ben Wyvis · 1046
Invergordon
Alness
Lossiemouth
Elgin
Forres
Buckie
Banff
Fraserburgh
South Harris
Sound of Harris
Uig
Gairloch
Achnasheen
Loch Maree
Dingwall
Black Isle
Nairn
Rattray Head
Peterhead
North Uist
Lochmaddy
Little Minch
Skye
Torridon
Beauly
Strathspey
Dufftown
Huntly
Ellon
Aberchirder
Benbecula
Portree
Carn Eige · 1183
Loch Ness
Grantown-on-Spey
Inverurie
Dyce
Beinn Mhòr · 620
South Uist
Sgurr Alasdair · 993
Kyle of Lochalsh
Fort Augustus
Monadhliath Mountains
Kingussie
Cairngorm Mountains
Ballater
Aberdeen
Lochboisdale
Cuillin Hills
Garry
Macdui · 1309
Cairngorm
Braemar
Lochnagar · 1155
Dee
Barra
Canna
Rum
Eigg
Mallaig
Fort William
Ben Nevis · 1344
Blair Atholl
Pitlochry
Forfar
Stonehaven
Castlebay
Arinagour
Salen
Loch Shiel
Glen Coe
SCOTLAND
GRAMPIAN MOUNTAINS
Ben Nevis
Kirriemuir
Sidlaw Hills
Montrose
Point of Ardnamurchan
Coll
Tobermory
Morvern
Mull
Ben More · 966
Loch Linnhe
Rannoch Moor
Ben Lawers · 1214
Blairgowrie
Dundee
Firth of Tay
Arbroath
NORTH SEA
Tiree
Iona
Fionnphort
Oban
Loch Awe
Inveraray
Ben Cruachan · 1126
Crianlarich
Killin
Loch Tay
Crieff
Perth
St Andrews
Fife Ness
Colonsay
Jura
Sound of Jura
Firth of Lorn
Lochgilphead
Loch Fyne
Loch Lomond
Ben Lomond · 974
Callander
Stirling
Glenrothes
Cupar
Buckhaven
Firth of Forth
56°
Scarinish
Kintyre
Tarbert
Helensburgh
Dumbarton
Clydebank
Glasgow
Cumbernauld
Falkirk
Alloa
Dunfermline
Edinburgh
Musselburgh
North Berwick
Dunbar
St Abb's Head
Port Askaig
Islay
Gigha
Greenock
Paisley
Motherwell
Hamilton
Penicuik
Dalkeith
Duns
Berwick-upon-Tweed
Port Ellen
Mull of Oa
Rothesay
Largs
Ardrossan
East Kilbride
Kilmarnock
Lanark
Biggar
Peebles
Galashiels
Coldstream
Holy Island
Lindisfarne
Arran
Goat Fell · 874
Brodick
Irvine
Prestwick
Ayr
SOUTHERN UPLANDS
Selkirk
Hawick
Jedburgh
Cheviot Hills
The Cheviot · 815
Rothbury
Ashington
Giant's Causeway
Portrush
Rathlin Island
Ballycastle
Mull of Kintyre
Campbeltown
Maybole
Cumnock
Moffat
Broad Law · 840
Newton Stewart
Lockerbie
Annan
Liddel Water (Reservoir)
Longtown
Hexham
Newcastle upon Tyne
Gateshead
Blaydon
Consett · 580
Portstewart
Coleraine
Cullybackey
Ballymena
Larne
Cairnryan
Girvan
Merrick · 843
Thornhill
Dumfries
Dalbeattie
Carlisle
Penrith
Cross Fell · 893
Spennymoor
NORTHERN IRELAND
Antrim
Ballymoney
Whitehead
Wigtown
Kirkcudbright
Castle Douglas
Solway Firth
Workington
Cockermouth · 931
ENGLAND
Newtownabbey
Bangor
Donaghadee
Luce Bay
Whithorn
Mull of Galloway

Longitude 4° west of Greenwich

1 : 4 000 000

MILES 0 · 25 · 50

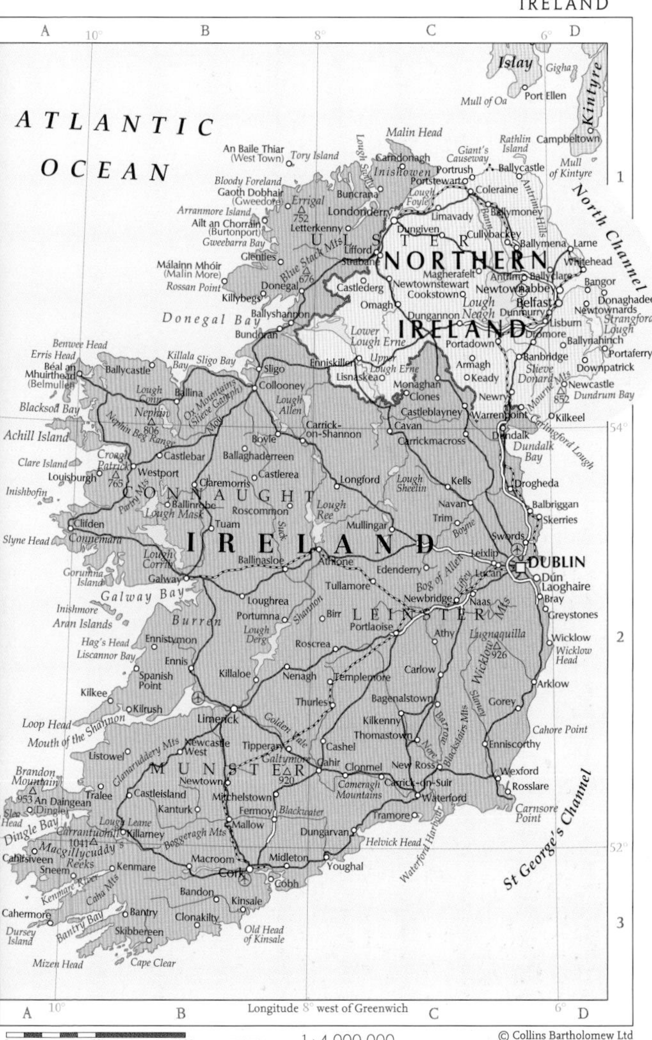

ATLANTIC
OCEAN

Islay
Mull of Oa
Port Ellen
Gigha

North Channel
Mull of Kintyre

An Baile Thiar
(West Town)
Tory Island
Malin Head
Inishowen
Campbeltown
Carndonagh
Whitehead
Giant's
Causeway
Rathlin Island
Ballycastle
Bloody Foreland
Gaoth Dobhair
(Gweedore)
Buncrana
Portstewart
Portrush
Coleraine
Ballymoney
Ballycastle
Arranmore Island
Allt an Chorráin
(Burtonport)
Gweebarra Bay
Errigal
752
Letterkenny
Londonderry
Limavady
Dungiven
Cullybackey
Ballymena
Larne

ULSTER Mts
Lifford
Strabane
Magherafelt
Antrim
Ballyclare
Larne

Málainn Mhóir
(Malin More)
Rossan Point
Killybegs
Glenties
Donegal
Castlederg
Omagh
Newtownstewart
Cookstown
Lough
Neagh
NORTHERN
Newtownabbey
Belfast
Bangor
Donaghadee
Newtownards
Strangford
Lough

Donegal Bay
Ballyshannon
Bundoran
Lower
Lough Erne
Upper
Lough Erne
Enniskillen
Lisnaskea
Clones
Monaghan
IRELAND
Portadown
Lisburn
Lurgan
Dromore
Banbridge
Slieve
Donard
852
Lisburn
Portaferry
Ardglass

Benwee Head
Erris Head
Ballycastle
Killala
Bay
Killala
Ballina
Sligo Bay
Sligo
Ox Mountains
Colloney
Lough
Gill
Carrick-
on-Shannon
Cavan
Castleblayney
Carrickmacross
Armagh
Keady
Newry
Warrenpoint
Carlingford Lough
Kilkeel
Newcastle
Dundrum Bay

Béal an
Mhuirthead
(Belmullet)
Blacksod Bay
Achill Island
Clare Island
Inishbofin
Nephin
806
Nephin Beg Range
Crossmolina
Lough
Conn
Slieve Anierin
Lough
Allen
Boyle
Ballaghaderreen
Longford
Lough
Sheelin
Kells
Navan
Trim
Dundalk
Dundalk
Bay
Drogheda
Balbriggan
Skerries
54

Croagh
Patrick
765
Westport
Castlebar
Claremorris
Castlerea
Roscommon
Lough
Ree
Mullingar
Swords
DUBLIN
Dún
Laoghaire

Louisburgh
Clew Bay
CONNAUGHT
Ballinrobe
Lough Mask
Tuam
Ballinasloe
Athlone
Edenderry
Leixlip
Naas
Bray
Greystones

Clifden
Slyne Head
Connemara
Lough
Corrib
Galway
IRELAND
Loughrea
Tullamore
Birr
LEINSTER
Portlaoise
Roscrea
Athy
Carlow
Lugnaquilla
926
Wicklow
Wicklow
Head

Gorumna
Island
Galway Bay
Inishmore
Inishmaan
Aran Islands
Hag's Head
Liscannor Bay
Burren
Ennistimon
Ennis
Lough
Derg
Nenagh
Templemore
Bagenalstown
Wicklow Mts
Arklow

Spanish
Point
Killaloe
Thurles
Kilkenny
Thomastown
Gorey
Enniscorthy

Kilkee
Kilrush
Limerick
Tipperary
Cashel
Clonmel
Carrick-on-Suir
New Ross
Wexford
Rosslare
Carnsore
Point

Loop Head
Mouth of the Shannon
Listowel
Newcastle
West
Galtymore
919
Galtee Mts
Comeragh
Mountains
Waterford
Tramore
Waterford Harbour
St George's Channel

Brandon
Mountain
953
An Daingean
(Dingle)
Dingle Bay
Tralee
MUNSTER
Newtown
Castleisland
Kanturk
Michelstown
Fermoy
Blackwater
Dungarvan
Helvick Head

Carrauntoohil
1041
Macgillycuddy's
Reeks
Cahirciveen
Sneem
Killarney
Lough
Leane
Macroom
Mallow
Midleton
Youghal

Cahermore
Kenmare
Kenmare River
Bantry
Bantry Bay
Bandon
Cork
Cobh

Dursey
Island
Skibbereen
Clonakilty
Kinsale
Old Head
of Kinsale

Mizen Head
Cape Clear

52

0   50   100 KILOMETRES   1 : 4 000 000

© Collins Bartholomew Ltd   **97**

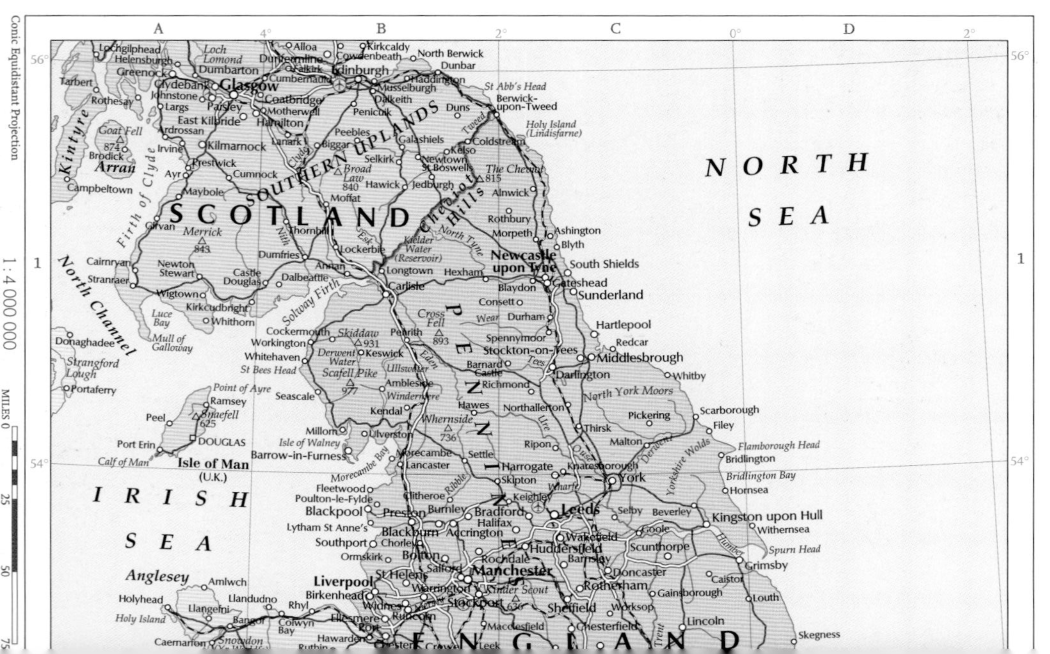

Conic Equidistant Projection

1 : 4 000 000

MILES 0   25   50   75

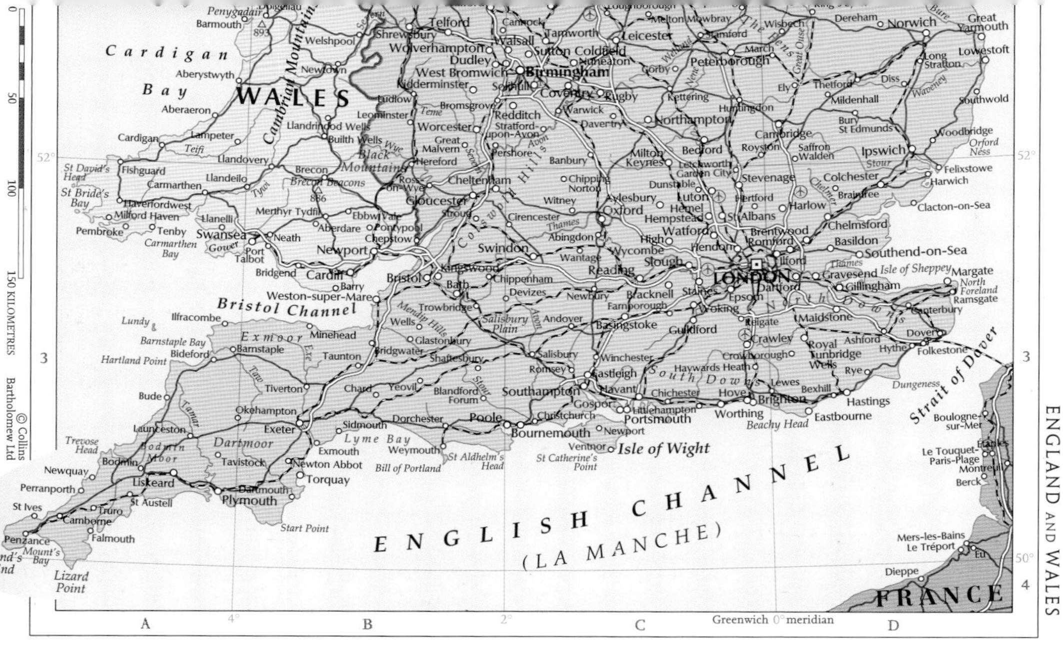
WALES
ENGLISH CHANNEL
(LA MANCHE)
FRANCE
Cardigan Bay
Bristol Channel
Strait of Dover
Cambrian Mountains
Black Mountains
Brecon Beacons
Cotswold Hills
Exmoor
Dartmoor
Bodmin Moor
Isle of Wight
Isle of Sheppey
Lyme Bay
Mendip Hills
Salisbury Plain
The Fens
North Downs
South Downs
LONDON
Birmingham
Bristol
Cardiff
Swansea
Newport
Plymouth
Exeter
Southampton
Portsmouth
Brighton
Norwich
Ipswich
Cambridge
Oxford
Reading
Leicester
Peterborough
Coventry
Northampton
Gloucester
Worcester
Hereford
Bournemouth
Poole
Canterbury
Dover
Folkestone
Hastings
Greenwich 0° meridian
0
50
100
150 KILOMETRES
© Collins Bartholomew Ltd

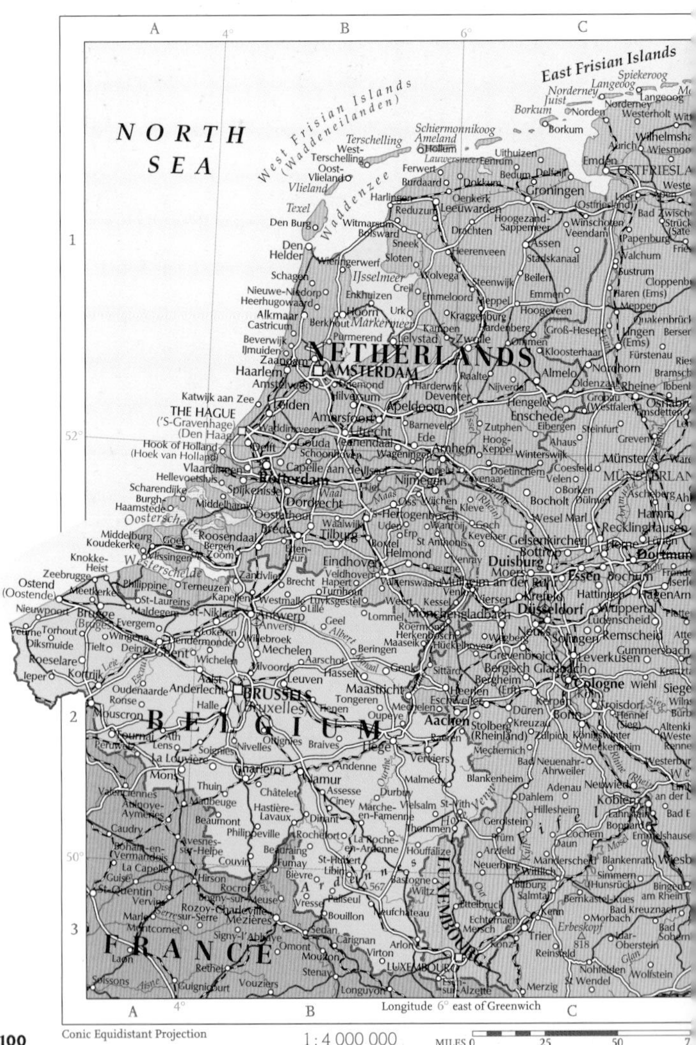
A
B
C
4°
6°
1
2
3
52°
50°
NORTH SEA
West Frisian Islands (Waddeneilanden)
East Frisian Islands
Spiekeroog
Langeoog
Norderney
Juist
Borkum
Norden
Westerholt
Wilhelmshaven
Aurich
Emden
OSTFRIESLAND
Schiermonnikoog
Ameland
Hollum
Terschelling
West-Terschelling
Oost-Vlieland
Vlieland
Texel
Den Burg
Waddenzee
Lauwersmeer
Uithuizen
Eenrum
Ferwert
Bedum
Delfzijl
Burdaard
Dokkum
Groningen
Harlingen
Oenkerk
Leeuwarden
Reduzum
Hoogezand-Sappemeer
Winschoten
Veendam
Leer
Papenburg
Witmarsum
Bolsward
Drachten
Sneek
Assen
Den Helder
Wieringerwerf
Sloten
Heerenveen
Stadskanaal
Walchum
Schagen
IJsselmeer
Wolvega
Steenwijk
Beilen
Creil
Emmeloord
Meppel
Emmen
Nieuwe-Niedorp
Heerhugowaard
Enkhuizen
Alkmaar
Castricum
Hoorn
Urk
Kraggenburg
Hoogeveen
Markermeer
Berkhout
Kampen
Hardenberg
Lelystad
Zwolle
Ommen
Purmerend
Beverwijk
IJmuiden
Zaandam
NETHERLANDS
Kloosterhaar
Nordhorn
Haarlem
AMSTERDAM
Almelo
Amstelveen
Raalte
Oldenzaal
Rheine
Hilversum
Harderwijk
Nijverdal
Katwijk aan Zee
Leiden
Deventer
Hengelo
Enschede
Gronau (Westfalen)
THE HAGUE ('S-Gravenhage) (Den Haag)
Amersfoort
Apeldoorn
Barneveld
Zutphen
Eibergen
Steinfurt
Utrecht
Ede
Greven
Hook of Holland (Hoek van Holland)
Delft
Gouda
Veenendaal
Schoonhoven
Wageningen
Arnhem
Hoog-Keppel
Ahaus
Winterswijk
Münster
Vlaardingen
Capelle aan de IJssel
Doetinchem
Coesfeld
Hellevoetsluis
Rotterdam
Nijmegen
Zevenaar
Velen
Scharendijke
Burgh-Haamstede
Spijkenisse
Waal
Maas
Borken
Middelharnis
Dordrecht
Oss
Wijchen
Kleve
Bocholt
Dülmen
Oosterschelde
Oosterhout
's-Hertogenbosch
Wesel
Marl
Hamm
Middelburg
Koudekerke
Goes
Roosendaal
Bergen op Zoom
Waalwijk
Tilburg
Uden
Erp
Goch
Kevelaer
Gelsenkirchen
Recklinghausen
Breda
Boxtel
St Anthonis
Helmond
Bottrop
Herne
Dortmund
Knokke-Heist
Vlissingen
Westerschelde
Etten-Leur
Eindhoven
Venray
Duisburg
Zeebrugge
Zandvliet
Brecht
Veldhoven
Moers
Essen
Bochum
Ostend (Oostende)
Meetkerke
Philippine
Terneuzen
Hapert
Turnhout
Valkenswaard
Mülheim an der Ruhr
Kapellen
St-Laureins
Westmalle
Lille
Lyksgestel
Weert
Kessel
Viersen
Krefeld
Hattingen
Hagen
Nieuwpoort
Maldegem
St-Niklaas
Düsseldorf
Wuppertal
Bruges (Brugge)
Evergem
Antwerp (Anvers)
Geel
Lommel
Mönchengladbach
Lüdenscheid
Veurne
Torhout
Wingene
Lokeren
Albert Kanaal
Roermond
Neuss
Remscheid
Diksmuide
Tielt
Deinze
Dendermonde
Willebroek
Herkenbosch
Maaseik
Solingen
Mechelen
Beringen
Hückelhoven
Wegberg
Gummersbach
Roeselare
Ghent (Gent)
Wichelen
Aarschot
Grevenbroich
Leverkusen
Ieper
Kortrijk
Aalst
Vilvoorde
Hasselt
Genk
Sittard
Bergisch Gladbach
Leuven
Bergheim (Erft)
Cologne (Köln)
Wiehl
Siegen
Oudenaarde
Anderlecht
BRUSSELS (Bruxelles)
Maastricht
Heerlen
Kerpen
Ronse
Halle
Tongeren
Tienen
Eschweiler
Troisdorf
Mouscron
Oupeye
Düren
Bonn
Hennef (Sieg)
BELGIUM
Aachen
Stolberg (Rheinland)
Kreuzau
Königswinter
Tournai
Ath
Ottignies
Braives
Liège
Zülpich
Peruwelz
Lens
Soignies
Nivelles
Raeren
Mechernich
Meckenheim
La Louvière
Verviers
Bad Neuenahr-Ahrweiler
Mons
Charleroi
Andenne
Malmédy
Blankenheim
Thuin
Namur
Ourthe
Valenciennes
Châtelet
Assesse
Durbuy
Adenau
Neuwied
Koblenz
Aulnoye-Aymeries
Maubeuge
Ciney
Marche-en-Famenne
Vielsalm
St-Vith
Dahlem
Hillesheim
Hastière-Lavaux
Dinant
Eifel
Beaumont
Philippeville
Gerolstein
Caudry
Thommen
Boppard
Rochefort
La Roche-en-Ardenne
Cochem
Mosel
Bohain-en-Vermandois
Avesnes-sur-Helpe
Beauraing
Houffalize
Daun
Couvin
Arzfeld
Manderscheid
Blankenrath
Fumay
St-Hubert
Neuerburg
Wittlich
La Capelle
Libin
Guise
Hirson
Bièvre
Ardennes
567
Bastogne
Simmern (Hunsrück)
Bingen am Rhein
Wiltz
Bitburg
St-Quentin
Rocroi
LUXEMBOURG
Salmtal
Bernkastel-Kues
Vervins
Bogny-sur-Meuse
Vresse
Paliseul
Ettelbruck
Bad Kreuznach
Marle
Rozoy-sur-Serre
Charleville-Mézières
Bouillon
Neufchâteau
Echternach
Kenn
Morbach
Montcornet
Mersch
Trier
Erbeskopf
818
Sedan
Idar-Oberstein
Signy-l'Abbaye
Carignan
Arlon
Konz
Reinsfeld
FRANCE
Omont
Laon
Mouzon
Virton
Rethel
Stenay
LUXEMBOURG
Nohfelden
Wolfstein
Soissons
Aisne
Guignicourt
Vouziers
Longuyon
Esch-sur-Alzette
Merzig
St Wendel
A
4°
B
Longitude 6° east of Greenwich
C
Conic Equidistant Projection
1 : 4 000 000
MILES 0
25
50

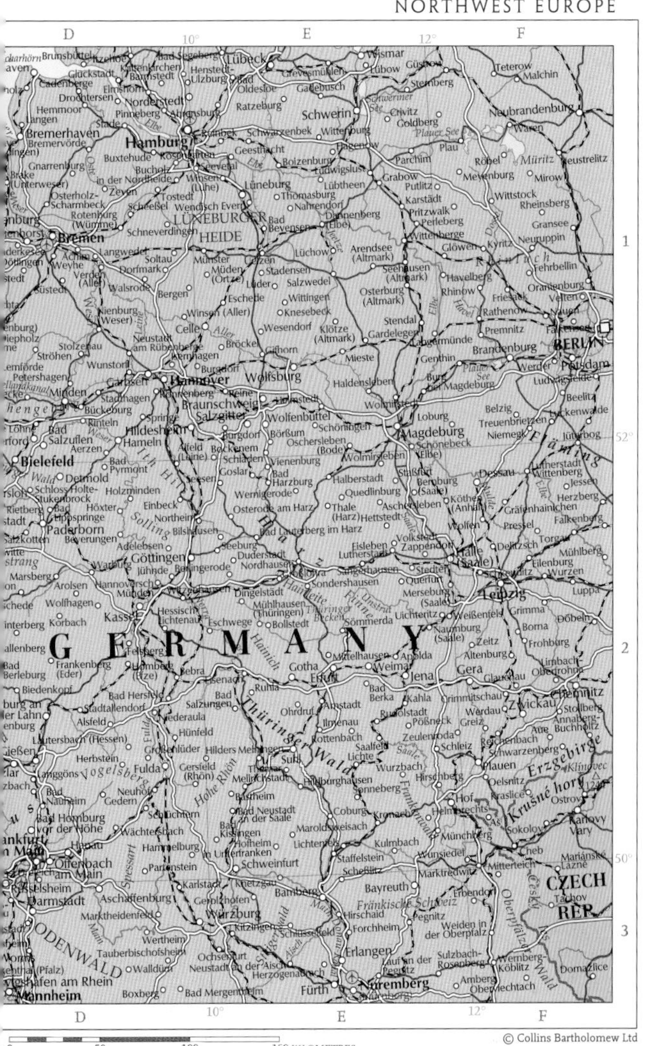
D
E
F
10°
12°
52°
50°
1
2
3
GERMANY
CZECH REP.
Hamburg
Bremen
Bremerhaven
Lübeck
Wismar
Schwerin
Neubrandenburg
Lüneburg
LÜNEBURGER HEIDE
Hannover
Braunschweig
Salzgitter
Wolfsburg
Wolfenbüttel
Hildesheim
Hameln
Bielefeld
Paderborn
Göttingen
Kassel
Magdeburg
BERLIN
Potsdam
Brandenburg
Dessau
Halle (Saale)
Leipzig
Erfurt
Weimar
Jena
Gera
Gotha
Zwickau
Chemnitz
Plauen
Hof
Bayreuth
Bamberg
Schweinfurt
Würzburg
Erlangen
Fürth
Nuremberg
Fulda
Offenbach am Main
Darmstadt
Mannheim
Cheb
Karlovy Vary
Mariánské Lázně
Tachov
Domažlice
Thüringer Wald
Erzgebirge
Krušné hory
Fränkische Schweiz
Oberpfälzer Wald
Vogelsberg
Hohe Rhön
Spessart
ODENWALD
Elbe
Saale
Müritz
Solling

0 50 100 150 KILOMETRES

Conic Equidistant Projection

NORTH SEA

GERMANY

NETHERLANDS

FRANCE

SWITZERLAND

BEL.

LUX.

LIECHTENSTEIN

ITALY

CZEC...

Helgoländer Bucht

West Frisian Islands (Waddeneilanden)

East Frisian Islands

AMSTERDAM

BERLIN

Hamburg

Bremen

Hannover

Köln (Cologne)

Frankfurt am Main

München (Munich)

Stuttgart

Zürich

Longitude 10° east of Greenwich

1 : 8 000 000

MILES 0   50   100   15

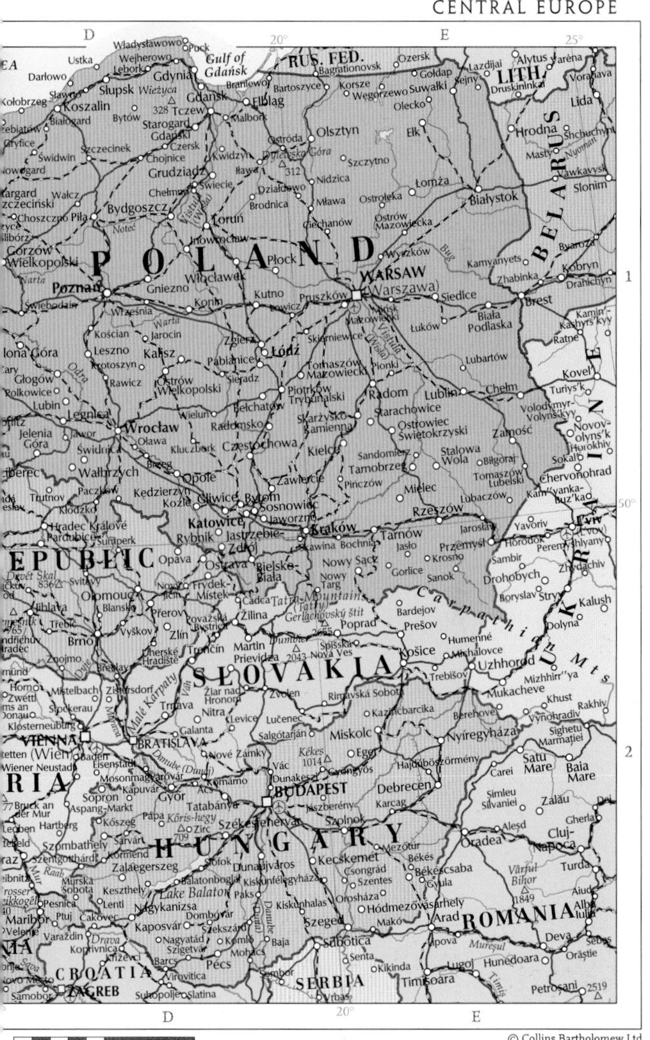
D
E
20°
25°
50°
1
2
POLAND
SLOVAKIA
HUNGARY
ROMANIA
CROATIA
SERBIA
BELARUS
UKRAINE
LITH.
RUS. FED.
REPUBLIC
Gulf of Gdańsk
Carpathian Mts
Tatra Mountains (Tatry)
WARSAW (Warszawa)
BUDAPEST
VIENNA (Wien)
BRATISLAVA
ZAGREB
Gdańsk
Gdynia
Słupsk
Koszalin
Elbląg
Olsztyn
Bydgoszcz
Toruń
Grudziądz
Płock
Włocławek
Poznań
Gniezno
Konin
Kutno
Łódź
Wrocław
Legnica
Wałbrzych
Opole
Częstochowa
Katowice
Kraków
Kielce
Radom
Lublin
Białystok
Łomża
Siedlce
Chełm
Zamość
Rzeszów
Tarnów
Przemyśl
Nowy Sącz
Brest
Hrodna
Kovel'
L'viv
Drohobych
Ostrava
Olomouc
Brno
Žilina
Poprad
Košice
Prešov
Uzhhorod
Nitra
Trnava
Zvolen
Miskolc
Eger
Debrecen
Nyíregyháza
Győr
Sopron
Székesfehérvár
Kecskemét
Szeged
Pécs
Kaposvár
Nagykanizsa
Lake Balaton
Szolnok
Oradea
Cluj-Napoca
Arad
Timișoara
Subotica
Danube
Vistula (Wisła)
Odra
Warta
Bug
Drava
Sava
Tisza
Mureșul

![scale bar] 0 100 200 KILOMETRES

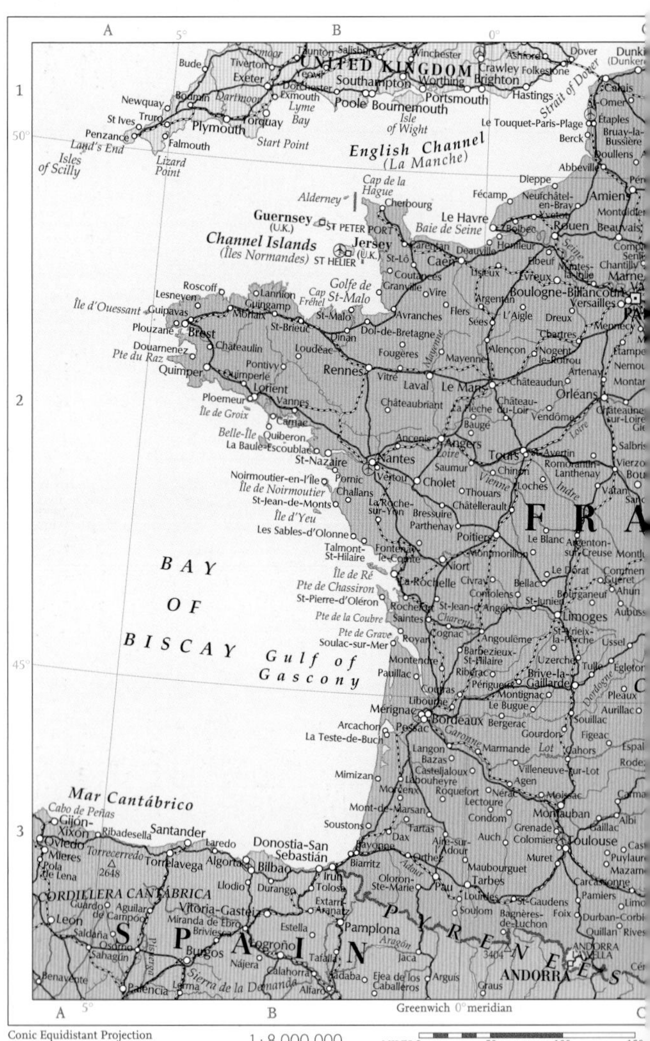

Conic Equidistant Projection

1 : 8 000 000

MILES 0   50   100   150

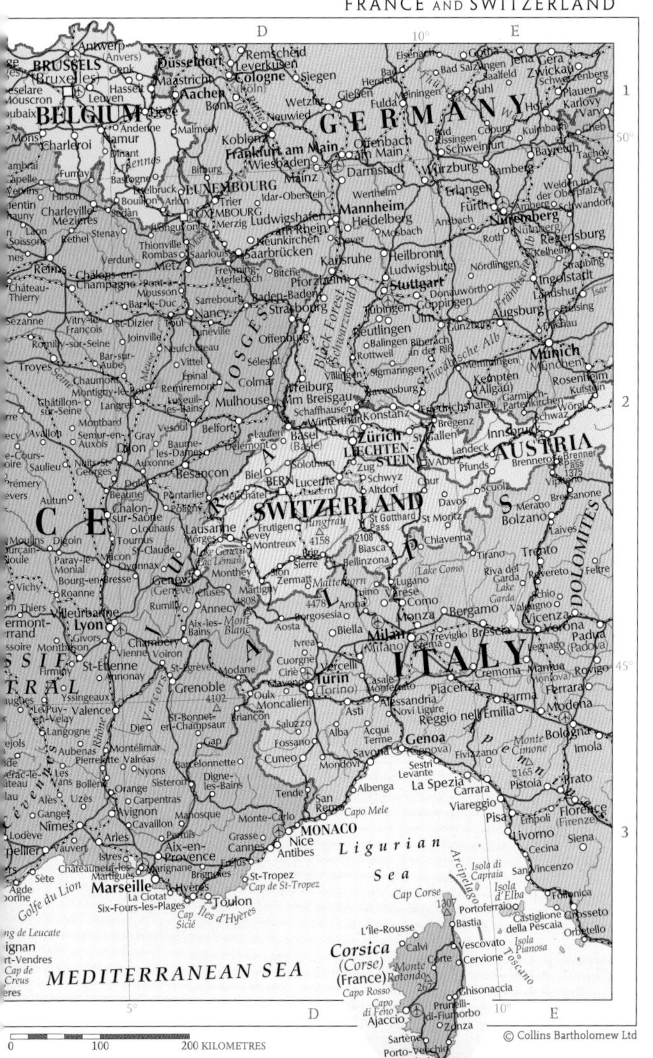

© Collins Bartholomew Ltd

0   100   200 KILOMETRES

3
50°
45°
5°
BELGIUM
BRUSSELS
(Bruxelles)
Antwerp
(Anvers)
Genk
Hasselt
Leuven
Mons
Charleroi
Namur
Dinant
Liège
Mouscron
LUXEMBOURG
GERMANY
Düsseldorf
Remscheid
Leverkusen
Cologne
(Köln)
Siegen
Aachen
Maastricht
Bonn
Koblenz
Neuwied
Wetzlar
Gießen
Frankfurt am Main
Offenbach am Main
Wiesbaden
Mainz
Darmstadt
Fulda
Meiningen
Suhl
Eisenach
Gotha
Bad Salzungen
Jena
Gera
Zwickau
Plauen
Saalfeld
Hof
Kulmbach
Coburg
Bayreuth
Bad Kissingen
Schweinfurt
Würzburg
Bamberg
Erlangen
Fürth
Nürnberg
Amberg
Schwandorf
Regensburg
Kelheim
Straubing
Ingolstadt
Landshut
Freising
Dachau
Munich
(München)
Rosenheim
Kufstein
Augsburg
Günzburg
Ulm
Göppingen
Stuttgart
Ludwigsburg
Heilbronn
Nördlingen
Donauwörth
Mannheim
Heidelberg
Mosbach
Ludwigshafen am Rhein
Speyer
Karlsruhe
Pforzheim
Baden-Baden
Tübingen
Reutlingen
Balingen
Biberach an der Riß
Rottweil
Sigmaringen
Villingen
Memmingen
Kempten
(Allgäu)
Ravensburg
Friedrichshafen
Konstanz
Freiburg im Breisgau
Offenburg
Black Forest
(Schwarzwald)
Schwäbische Alb
Fränkische Alb
Trier
Idar-Oberstein
Merzig
Saarlouis
Saarbrücken
Neunkirchen
Kaiserslautern
Wertheim
Ansbach
Roth
Karlovy Vary
Cheb
Tachov
Weiden in der Oberpfalz
Garmisch-Partenkirchen
AUSTRIA
Innsbruck
Bregenz
Landeck
Schwaz
Wörgl
Brenner Pass
1375
LIECHTENSTEIN
VADUZ
SWITZERLAND
Zürich
Winterthur
Schaffhausen
St Gallen
Basel
(Basle)
Laufen
Delémont
Solothurn
Biel
BERN
Lucerne
(Luzern)
Zug
Schwyz
Altdorf
Chur
Davos
St Moritz
St Gotthard Pass
2108
Frutigen
Jungfrau
4158
Vevey
Montreux
Lausanne
Morges
Neuchâtel
Lake Geneva
(Lac Léman)
Geneva
(Genève)
Monthey
Sion
Sierre
Brig
Zermatt
Matterhorn
4478
Martigny
Biasca
Bellinzona
Lugano
Chiavenna
FRANCE
Reims
Châlons-en-Champagne
Château-Thierry
Charleville-Mézières
Sedan
Rethel
Stenay
Verdun
Metz
Thionville
Longuyon
Nancy
Toul
Lunéville
Épinal
Vittel
Neufchâteau
Remiremont
Luxeuil-les-Bains
Vesoul
Belfort
Mulhouse
Colmar
Sélestat
Strasbourg
Sarrebourg
Saverne
Bitche
Freyming-Merlebach
Bar-le-Duc
Pont-à-Mousson
St-Dizier
Vitry-le-François
Joinville
Bar-sur-Aube
Troyes
Chaumont
Langres
Montigny-le-Roi
Châtillon-sur-Seine
Montbard
Semur-en-Auxois
Avallon
Dijon
Gray
Auxonne
Besançon
Baume-les-Dames
Pontarlier
Poligny
Dole
Beaune
Nuits-St-Georges
Saulieu
Autun
Chalon-sur-Saône
Louhans
Tournus
Mâcon
Digoin
Paray-le-Monial
Bourg-en-Bresse
Oyonnax
St-Claude
Roanne
Vichy
Thiers
Clermont-Ferrand
Villeurbanne
Lyon
Givors
Vienne
St-Étienne
Annonay
Chambéry
Voiron
Annecy
Aix-les-Bains
Rumilly
Cluses
Mont Blanc
4808
Grenoble
4102
St-Égrève
Modane
Briançon
St-Bonnet-en-Champsaur
Gap
Die
Valence
Le Puy-en-Velay
Yssingeaux
Langogne
Aubenas
Montélimar
Pierrelatte
Valréas
Nyons
Orange
Carpentras
Avignon
Cavaillon
Sisteron
Digne-les-Bains
Barcelonnette
Manosque
Pertuis
Aix-en-Provence
Marseille
Marignane
Martigues
Istres
Arles
Nîmes
Alès
Uzès
Bollène
Ganges
Lodève
Vauvert
Sète
Agde
Toulon
Hyères
La Ciotat
Six-Fours-les-Plages
Cap Sicié
Îles d'Hyères
Brignoles
Fréjus
St-Tropez
Cap de St-Tropez
Cannes
Antibes
Grasse
Nice
Tende
MONACO
Monte-Carlo
Golfe du Lion
Vosges
Jura
Alps
Vercors
Cévennes
Rhône
Meuse
Seine
Moselle
Rhine
Italy
Aosta
Ivrea
Biella
Borgosesia
Arona
Varese
Como
Lake Como
Monza
Bergamo
Brescia
Milan
(Milano)
Treviglio
Crema
Vercelli
Turin
(Torino)
Cuorgnè
Ciriè
Oulx
Moncalieri
Casale Monferrato
Asti
Alessandria
Novi Ligure
Saluzzo
Alba
Fossano
Acqui Terme
Cuneo
Mondovì
Savona
Genoa
(Genova)
Albenga
San Remo
Capo Mele
Sestri Levante
La Spezia
Carrara
Viareggio
Pisa
Livorno
Cecina
Empoli
Florence
(Firenze)
Prato
Pistoia
Siena
Piacenza
Cremona
Parma
Reggio nell'Emilia
Modena
Bologna
Imola
Ferrara
Rovigo
Mantua
(Mantova)
Legnago
Verona
Vicenza
Padua
(Padova)
Valdagno
Schio
Rovereto
Trento
Riva del Garda
Lake Garda
Tirano
Bolzano
Merano
Bressanone
Laives
Feltre
Dolomites
Fivizzano
Monte Cimone
2165
Apennines
San Vincenzo
Follonica
Grosseto
Castiglione della Pescaia
Orbetello
Isola di Capraia
Isola d'Elba
Portoferraio
Isola Pianosa
Arcipelago Toscano
Ligurian Sea
Cap Corse
1307
Bastia
L'Île-Rousse
Calvi
Corsica
(Corse)
(France)
Monte Rotondo
2622
Corte
Vescovato
Cervione
Ghisonaccia
Prunelli-di-Fiumorbo
Zonza
Capo Rosso
Capo di Feno
Ajaccio
Sartène
Porto-Vecchio
Bonifacio
MEDITERRANEAN SEA
Cap de Creus

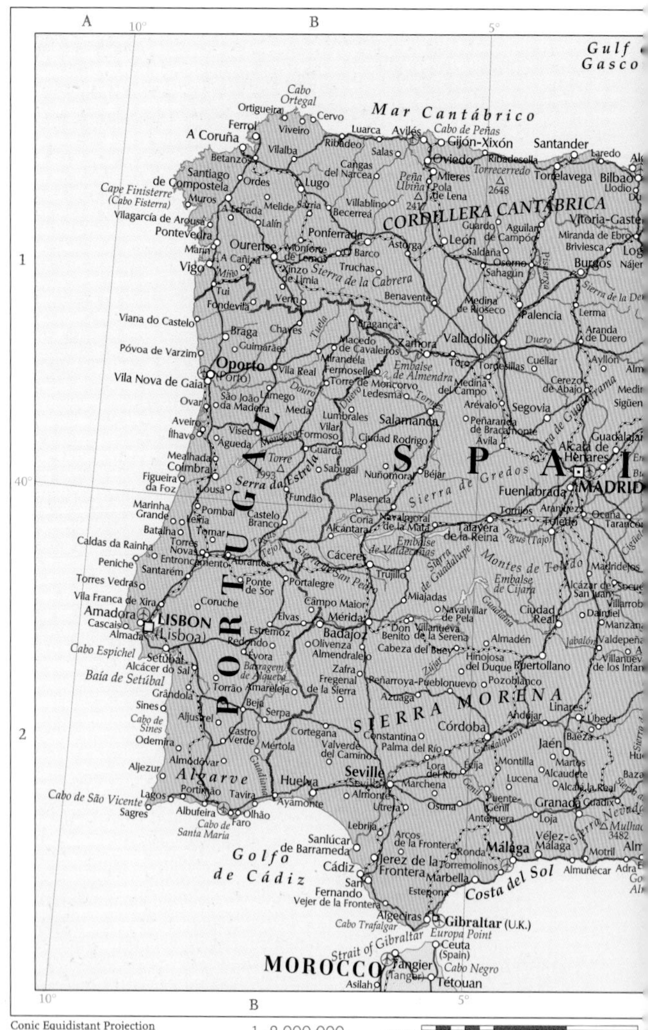

Conic Equidistant Projection

1 : 8 000 000

MILES 0   50   100   150

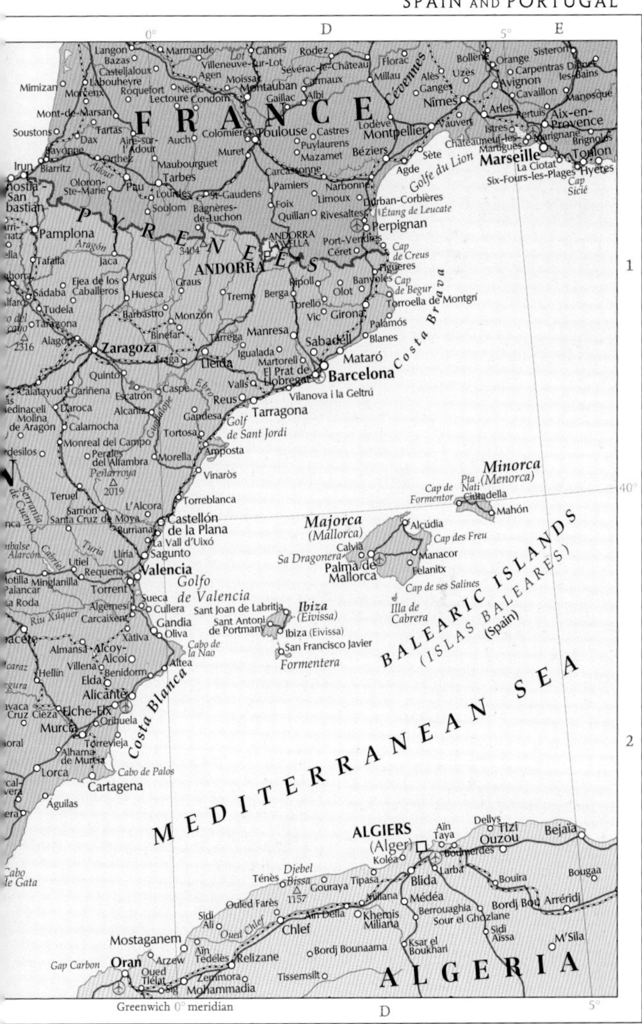

© Collins Bartholomew Ltd

0   100   200 KILOMETRES

5°
40°
FRANCE
Langon
Bazas
Marmande
Lot
Cahors
Rodez
Florac
Bollène
Orange
Sisteron
Casteljaloux
Villeneuve-sur-Lot
Sévérac-le-Château
Millau
Alès
Uzès
Carpentras
Digne-les-Bains
Mimizan
Labouheyre
Agen
Moissac
Carmaux
Cévennes
Avignon
Morcenx
Roquefort
Nérac
Montauban
Albi
Ganges
Cavaillon
Manosque
Lectoure
Condom
Gaillac
Nîmes
Mont-de-Marsan
Arles
Pertuis
Aix-en-Provence
Tartas
Lodève
Vauvert
Istres
Soustons
Dax
Aire-sur-l'Adour
Auch
Colomiers
Toulouse
Castres
Montpellier
Marignane
Brignoles
Puylaurens
Châteauneuf-les-Martigues
Bayonne
Orthez
Muret
Mazamet
Béziers
Sète
Marseille
Toulon
Irun
Biarritz
Adour
Maubourguet
Carcassonne
Agde
Golfe du Lion
La Ciotat
Hyères
Oloron-Ste-Marie
Pau
Tarbes
Pamiers
Narbonne
Six-Fours-les-Plages
Cap Sicié
Lourdes
St-Gaudens
Limoux
Durban-Corbières
Soulom
Bagnères-de-Luchon
Foix
Quillan
Rivesaltes
Étang de Leucate
PYRENEES
Perpignan
Pamplona
Aragón
ANDORRA LA VELLA
Port-Vendres
3404
Céret
Cap de Creus
Tafalla
Jaca
ANDORRA
Figueres
Ejea de los Caballeros
Arguis
Graus
Ripoll
Banyoles
Cap de Begur
Sádaba
Huesca
Tremp
Berga
Olot
Torroella de Montgrí
Tudela
Barbastro
Monzón
Torelló
Vic
Girona
Tarazona
Costa Brava
Palamós
2316
Alagón
Binéfar
Tàrrega
Manresa
Sabadell
Blanes
Zaragoza
Igualada
Lleida
Fraga
Martorell
Mataró
El Prat de Llobregat
Barcelona
Quinto
Valls
Caspe
Calatayud
Cariñena
Escatrón
Ebro
Reus
Vilanova i la Geltrú
Daroca
Alcañiz
Tarragona
Molina de Aragón
Calamocha
Gandesa
Golf de Sant Jordi
Guadalope
Tortosa
Monreal del Campo
Perales del Alfambra
Morella
Amposta
Peñarroya
Vinaròs
2019
Teruel
Minorca (Menorca)
Pta Nati
Cap de Formentor
Ciutadella
Serranía de Cuenca
Sarrión
L'Alcora
Torreblanca
Mahón
Santa Cruz de Moya
Castellón de la Plana
Majorca (Mallorca)
Alcúdia
Burriana
Cap des Freu
Turia
La Vall d'Uixó
Calvià
Cabriel
Llíria
Sagunto
Sa Dragonera
Manacor
Utiel
Requena
Valencia
Palma de Mallorca
Felanitx
BALEARIC ISLANDS (ISLAS BALEARES) (Spain)
Minglanilla
Golfo de Valencia
Torrent
Cap de ses Salines
Sueca
Algemesí
Cullera
Sant Joan de Labritja
Ibiza (Eivissa)
Illa de Cabrera
Riu Xúquer
Carcaixent
Gandia
Sant Antoni de Portmany
Oliva
Ibiza (Eivissa)
Xàtiva
Cabo de la Nao
Almansa
Alcoy-Alcoi
San Francisco Javier
Altea
Formentera
Villena
Hellín
Benidorm
Elda
Alicante
Costa Blanca
Cieza
Elche-Elx
Murcia
Orihuela
MEDITERRANEAN SEA
Torrevieja
Alhama de Murcia
Lorca
Cabo de Palos
Cartagena
Águilas
Cabo de Gata
Dellys
Aïn Taya
ALGIERS (Alger)
Tizi Ouzou
Bejaïa
Boumerdes
Koléa
Larba
Djebel Bissa
1157
Ténès
Gouraya
Tipasa
Blida
Bouira
Bougaa
Miliana
Médéa
Ouled Farès
Bordj Bou Arréridj
Berrouaghia
Sidi Ali
Aïn Defla
Khemis Miliana
Sour el Ghozlane
Oued Chlef
Chlef
Sidi Aïssa
Mostaganem
M'Sila
Ksar el Boukhari
Bordj Bounaama
Arzew
Aïn Tedelès
Relizane
ALGERIA
Gap Carbon
Oran
Oued Tlélat
Zemmora
Tissemsilt
Sig
Mohammadia
Greenwich 0° meridian
5°

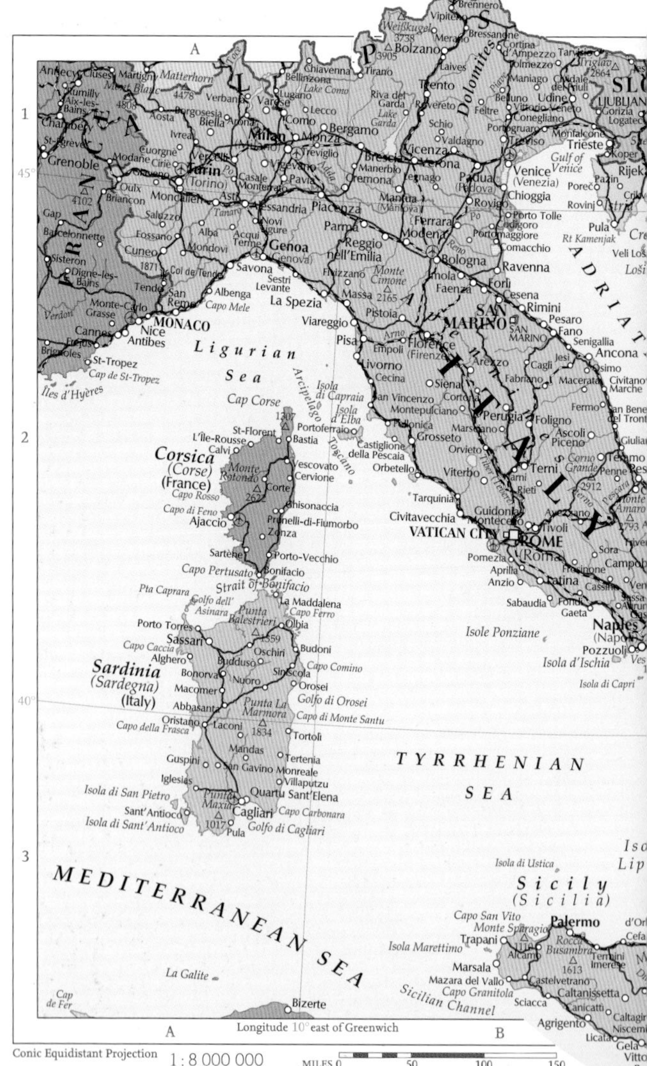

A

P S

Vipiteno
Brennero
Velikovec
2038
Meran
Bressanone
Cortina d'Ampezzo
Maniago Gavdale Tarvisio
2864
Chiavenna
Tirano
Bolzano
Trigno
SLO
Martigny Matterhorn
Lake Como
Riva del Garda
Trento
Dolomites
Belluno
Udine
LJUBLJANA
Monte Blanc
4478
Aosta
Bellinzona
Verbania
Lecco
Schio
Valdagno
Feltre
Conegliano
Pordenone
Monfalcone
Gorizia
Logatec
Annecy
Cluses
Chambéry
Aix-les-Bains
Brig
Domodossola
Varese
Como
Bergamo
Vicenza
Verona
Padua
Portogruaro
Trieste
Koper
Rijeka

Ivrea
Biella
Monza
Milan
Treviso
Brescia
Manerbio
Venice (Venezia)
Gulf of Venice
45
Grenoble
Turin (Torino)
Vercelli
Pavia
Cremona
Mantua (Mantova)
Rovigo
Chioggia
Rovinj
Pula

Dulx
Briançon
4102
Monginevro
Asti
Casale Monferrato
Alessandria
Piacenza
Parma
Modena
Ferrara
Po
Portomaggiore
Comacchio
Rt Kamenjak
Veli Losi

Gap
Saluzzo
Fossano
Acqui Terme
Novi Ligure
Reggio nell'Emilia
Bologna
Ravenna

Barcelonnette
Cuneo
Mondovi
Genoa (Genova)
Fivizzano
Monte Cimone 2165
Faenza
Forli
Cesena
ADRIAT

Sisteron
Col di Tenda
Savona
Sestri Levante
Massa
Pistoia
Rimini
Pesaro
SAN MARINO

Digne-les-Bains
Monte Grasso
San Remo
Albenga
Capo Mele
La Spezia
Viareggio
Pisa
Arno
Florence (Firenze)
SAN MARINO
Fano
Senigallia
Ancona

Verdon
Monaco
Nice
Antibes
Capo Corse
Empoli
Arezzo
Cagli
Fabriano
Macerata
Civitano Marche

Brignoles
Cannes
St-Tropez
Îles d'Hyères

Ligurian Sea

Cap Corse

Arcipelago Toscano

Isola di Capraia

Isola d'Elba

Portoferraio

San Vincenzo

Cecina

Siena

Montepulciano

Grosseto

Orbetello

Viterbo

Cortona

Perugia

Foligno

Terni

Nera

Corno Grande 2912

Monte Amaro

Ascoli Piceno

Fermo

Teramo

Giulian

Pes

2

Corsica (Corse) (France)

Capo Rosso

Ajaccio

Sartène

Capo di Feno

Monte Rotondo

Corte

Ghisonaccia

Zonza

Prunelli-di-Fiumorbo

Porto-Vecchio

Bonifacio

Strait of Bonifacio

L'Île-Rousse

St-Florent

Calvi

Bastia

Vescovato

Cervione

Tarquinia

Civitavecchia

Montefiascone

VATICAN CITY

Guidonia

Rieti

Tivoli

ROME (Roma)

Pomezia

Aprilia

Anzio

Latina

Sabaudia

Fondi

Gaeta

Cassi

Campo

Napl

Naples (Napoli)

ITALY

Pta Caprara

Golfo dell'Asinara

La Maddalena

Capo Ferro

Olbia

Golfo di Aranci

Porto Torres

Asinara

Punta Palestrieri 1359

Sassari

Alghero

Oschiri

Buddusò

Budoni

Capo Comino

Isole Ponziane

Pozzuoli

Isola d'Ischia

Isola di Capri

Ves

40

Sardinia (Sardegna) (Italy)

Capo Caccia

Bonorva

Macomer

Nuoro

Siniscola

Orosei

Golfo di Orosei

Abbasanta

Oristano

Punta La Marmora 1834

Laconi

Monte di Monte Santu

Capo della Frasca

Guspini

Mandas

Tertenia

Tortoli

TYRRHENIAN SEA

Iglesias

Isola di San Pietro

Sant'Antioco

Isola di Sant'Antioco

Gavino Monreale

Villaputzu

Punta Maxia 1017

Quartu Sant'Elena

Cagliari

Capo Carbonara

Pula

Golfo di Cagliari

3

MEDITERRANEAN SEA

Isola di Ustica

Iso Lip

Sicily (Sicilia)

Capo San Vito

Monte Sparagio

Trapani

Palermo

d'Orl

Rocco

Fe

Isola Marettimo

Alcamo

Monte Busambra 1613

Termini Imerese

La Galite

Marsala

Mazara del Vallo

Capo Granitola

Castelvetrano

Sciacca

Caltanissetta

Ra

Cap de Fer

Bizerte

Sicilian Channel

Agrigento

Caltag

Nisceme

Lica

A

Longitude 10° east of Greenwich

B

Conic Equidistant Projection

1 : 8 000 000

MILES 0   50   100   150

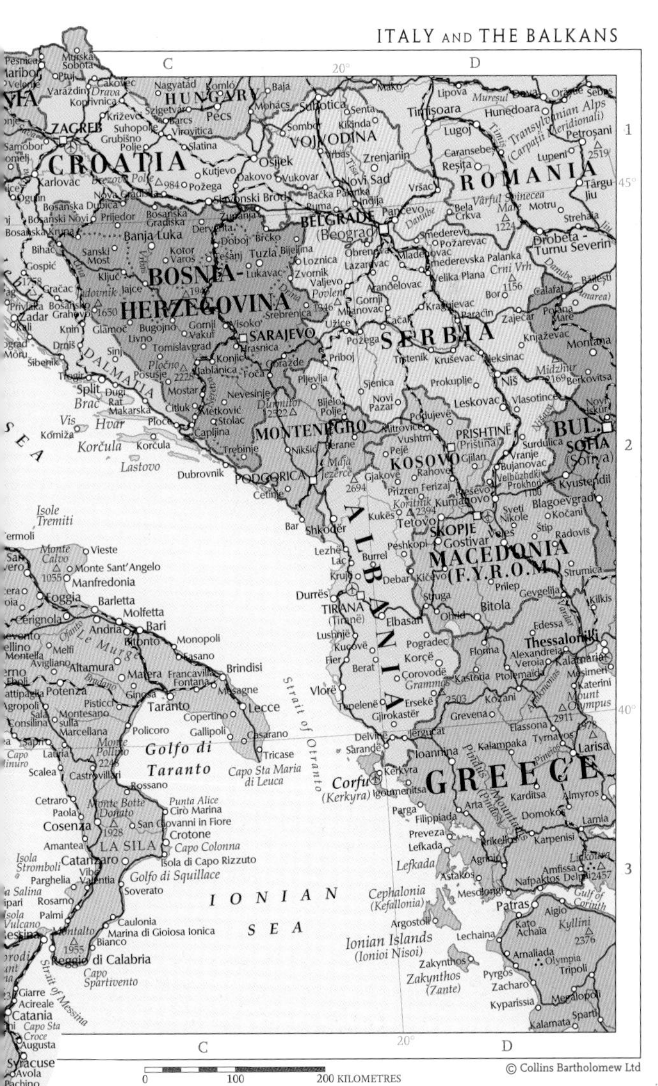
C
D
20°
1
2
3
45°
40°
HUNGARY
Pecs
Nagyatád
Kaposvár
Szigetvár
Barcs
Baja
Mohács
Subotica
Senta
Kikinda
Sombor
VOJVODINA
Zrenjanin
Novi Sad
Vršac
Timișoara
Lipova
Mureșul
Hunedoara
Lugoj
Caransebeș
Reșița
Petroșani
Lupeni
Târgu Jiu
ROMANIA
Transylvanian Alps (Carpații Meridionali)
Vârful Svinecea Mare
Motru
Strehaia
Bela Crkva
Drobeta - Turnu Severin
Danube
Băilești
Calafat
ZAGREB
Varaždin
Koprivnica
Križevci
Čakovec
Murska Sobota
Ptuj
Maribor
Samobor
Karlovac
CROATIA
Virovitica
Slatina
Suhopolje
Grubišno Polje
Osijek
Kutjevo
Požega
Đakovo
Vukovar
Slavonski Brod
Bačka Palanka
Inđija
Ruma
BELGRADE (Beograd)
Pančevo
Smederevo
Požarevac
Smederevska Palanka
Velika Plana
Crni Vrh
Bor
Zaječar
Knjaževac
Montana
Berkovitsa
Midzhur
Bosanska Dubica
Bosanski Novi
Prijedor
Bosanska Gradiška
Bosanska Krupa
Banja Luka
Derventa
Doboj
Brčko
Bihać
Sanski Most
Kotor Varoš
Tešanj
Tuzla
Bijeljina
Loznica
Zvornik
Lukavac
BOSNIA-HERZEGOVINA
Gospić
Gračac
Ključ
Jajce
Srebrenica
Valjevo
Povlen
Gornji Milanovac
Aranđelovac
Lazarevac
Obrenovac
Mladenovac
Kragujevac
Paraćin
Zadar
Glamoč
Bugojno
Gornji Vakuf
Livno
Tomislavgrad
Visoko
SARAJEVO
Hrasnica
Užice
Požega
Čačak
SERBIA
Trstenik
Kruševac
Aleksinac
Niš
Prokuplje
Leskovac
Vlasotince
Knin
Drniš
Šibenik
Sinj
Trogir
Split
DALMATIA
Konjic
Jablanica
Goražde
Foča
Priboj
Pljevlja
Sjenica
Novi Pazar
Posušje
Mostar
Čitluk
Nevesinje
Brač
Makarska
Ploče
Metković
Stolac
Čapljina
Hvar
Vis
Komiža
Korčula
Lastovo
Dubrovnik
Trebinje
Bijelo Polje
Durmitor
MONTENEGRO
Nikšić
Berane
PODGORICA
Cetinje
Bar
Maja Jezercë
Podujevë
Mitrovicë
Vushtrri
PRISHTINË (Priština)
KOSOVO
Pejë
Gjakovë
Rahovec
Prizren
Ferizaj
Gjilan
Surdulica
Vranje
Bujanovac
Preševo
Velbŭzhdki Prokhod
BUL.
SOFIA (Sofiya)
Kyustendil
Blagoevgrad
Kočani
Sveti Nikole
Kumanovo
SKOPJE
Veles
Štip
Radoviš
Tetovo
Gostivar
Korab
MACEDONIA (F.Y.R.O.M.)
Kičevo
Prilep
Strumica
Gevgelija
Kilkis
Bitola
Ohrid
Struga
Debar
ALBANIA
Shkodër
Lezhë
Lac
Krujë
Burrel
Peshkopi
Kukës
Durrës
TIRANA (Tiranë)
Elbasan
Lushnjë
Kuçovë
Fier
Berat
Pogradec
Korçë
Çorovodë
Grammos
Ersekë
Vlorë
Tepelenë
Gjirokastër
Delvinë
Sarandë
Florina
Edessa
Thessaloniki
Alexandreia
Veroia
Kalamaria
Kastoria
Ptolemaida
Kozani
Katerini
Mount Olympus
Grevena
Elassona
Tyrnavos
Larisa
Ioannina
Kalampaka
GREECE
Pindus Mountains (Pindos)
Corfu (Kerkyra)
Kerkyra
Igoumenitsa
Parga
Arta
Filippiada
Preveza
Lefkada
Karditsa
Almyros
Domokos
Lamia
Karpenisi
Agrinio
Astakos
Mesolongi
Nafpaktos
Amfissa
Delphi
Gulf of Corinth
Patras
Aigio
Kato Achaïa
Kyllini
Cephalonia (Kefallonia)
Argostoli
Ionian Islands (Ionioi Nisoi)
Lechaina
Amaliada
Olympia
Tripoli
Zakynthos
Zakynthos (Zante)
Pyrgos
Zacharo
Kyparissia
Megalopoli
Kalamata
Sparti
Isole Tremiti
Termoli
Vieste
Monte Calvo
Monte Sant'Angelo
Manfredonia
Foggia
Barletta
Molfetta
Cerignola
Andria
Bari
Bitonto
Monopoli
Fasano
Le Murge
Melfi
Altamura
Matera
Francavilla Fontana
Brindisi
Mesagne
Lecce
Potenza
Ginosa
Taranto
Pisticci
Montesano sulla Marcellana
Copertino
Gallipoli
Casarano
Tricase
Policoro
Monte Pollino
Golfo di Taranto
Capo Sta Maria di Leuca
Strait of Otranto
Scalea
Castrovillari
Rossano
Cetraro
Paola
Monte Botte Donato
Punta Alice
Cirò Marina
Cosenza
San Giovanni in Fiore
Crotone
Capo Colonna
Amantea
LA SILA
Isola di Capo Rizzuto
Catanzaro
Vibo Valentia
Golfo di Squillace
Soverato
IONIAN SEA
Caulonia
Marina di Gioiosa Ionica
Bianco
Reggio di Calabria
Capo Spartivento
Strait of Messina
Giarre
Acireale
Catania
Capo Sta Croce
Augusta
Syracuse
Avola
Pachino
Isola Stromboli
Palmi
Rosarno
Parghelia
0
100
200 KILOMETRES

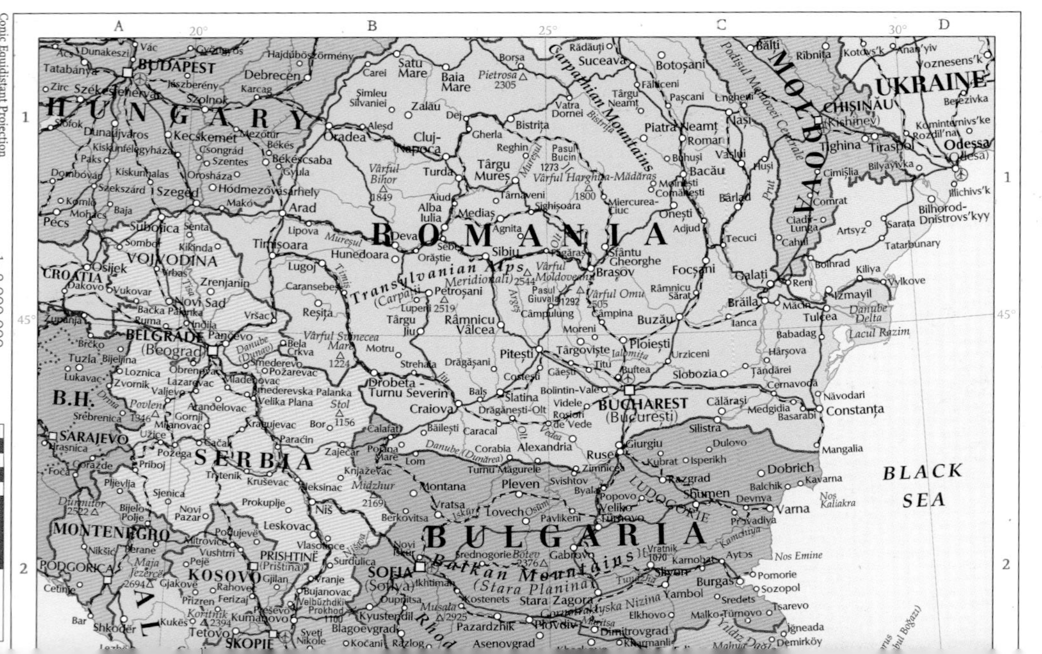

Conic Equidistant Projection

1 : 8 000 000

MILES 0   50   100   150

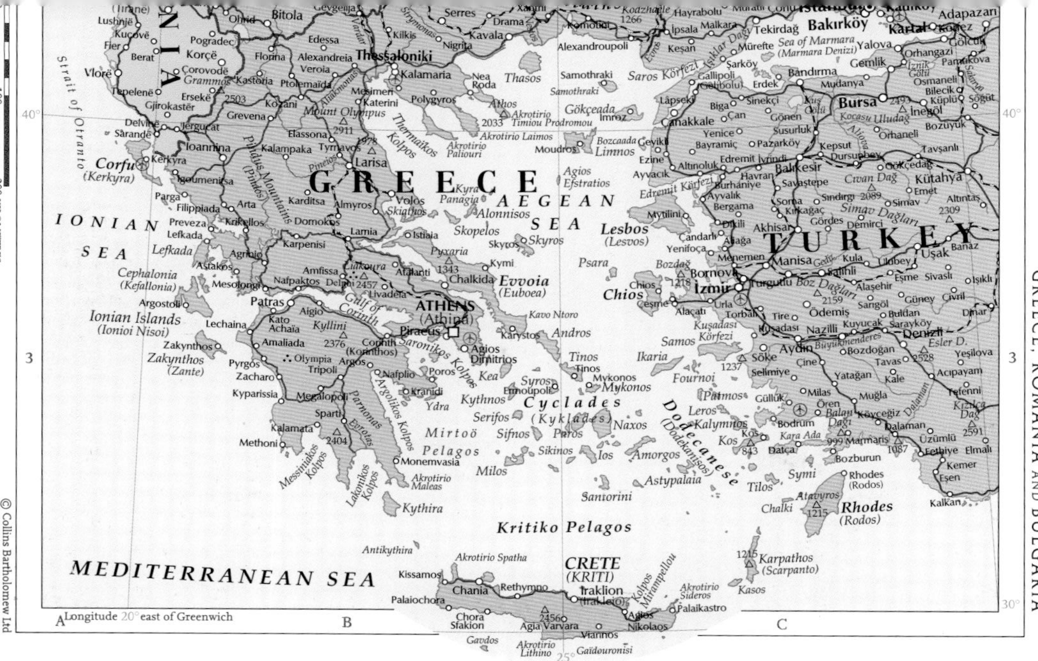

MEDITERRANEAN SEA

IONIAN SEA

AEGEAN SEA

Kritiko Pelagos

Strait of Otranto

© Collins Bartholomew Ltd

A Longitude 20° east of Greenwich

100   200 KILOMETRES

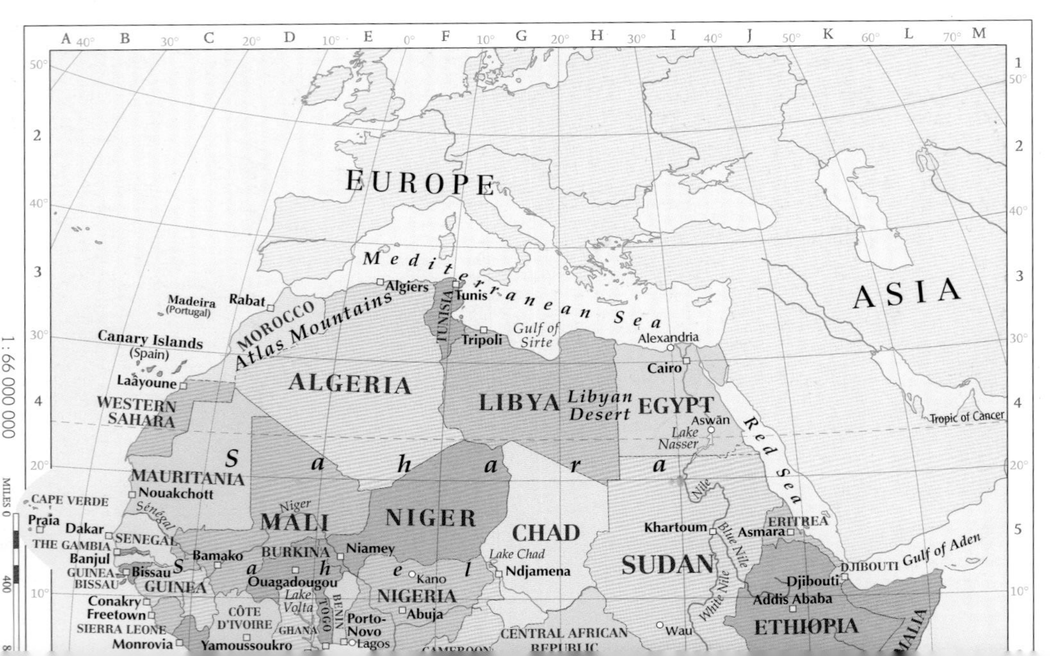
EUROPE
ASIA
Mediterranean Sea
Red Sea
Gulf of Aden
Gulf of Sirte
Tropic of Cancer
Sahara
Sahel
Atlas Mountains
Libyan Desert
Madeira (Portugal)
Canary Islands (Spain)
Rabat
MOROCCO
Laâyoune
WESTERN SAHARA
ALGERIA
Algiers
TUNISIA
Tunis
Tripoli
LIBYA
EGYPT
Alexandria
Cairo
Aswān
Lake Nasser
Nile
MAURITANIA
Nouakchott
Sénégal
CAPE VERDE
Praia
Dakar
SENEGAL
THE GAMBIA
Banjul
GUINEA-BISSAU
Bissau
GUINEA
Conakry
Freetown
SIERRA LEONE
Monrovia
Bamako
MALI
Niger
BURKINA
Ouagadougou
Lake Volta
CÔTE D'IVOIRE
Yamoussoukro
GHANA
TOGO
BENIN
Porto-Novo
Lagos
NIGER
Niamey
NIGERIA
Kano
Abuja
CHAD
Lake Chad
Ndjamena
SUDAN
Khartoum
Blue Nile
White Nile
Wau
CENTRAL AFRICAN REPUBLIC
ERITREA
Asmara
DJIBOUTI
Djibouti
Addis Ababa
ETHIOPIA

1 : 66 000 000

MILES 0 400

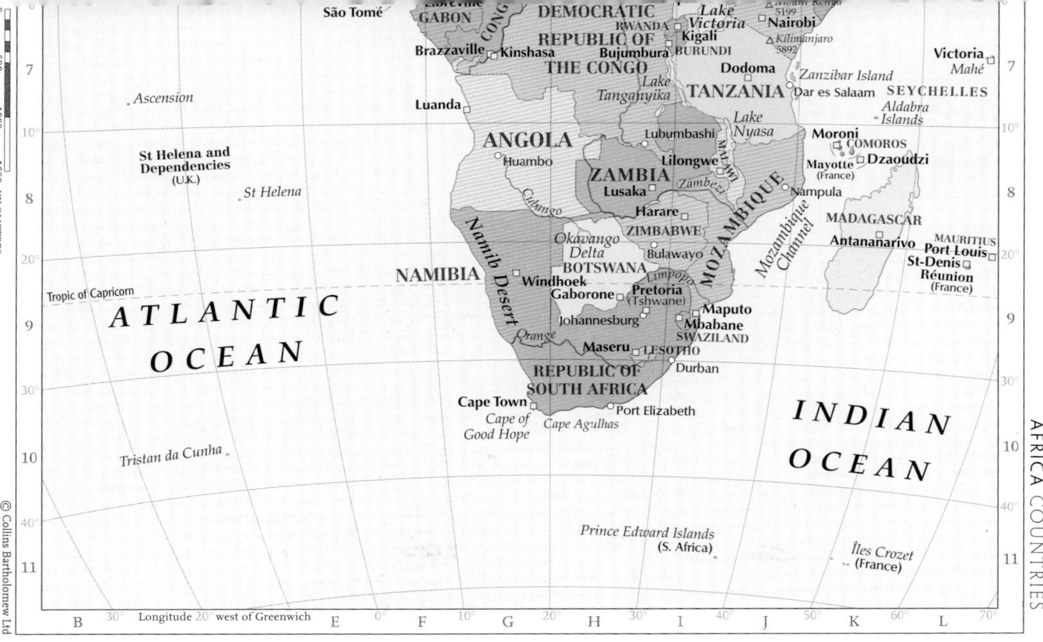

ATLANTIC OCEAN

INDIAN OCEAN

SEYCHELLES
Victoria □
Mahé

MAURITIUS
Port Louis □
St-Denis □
Réunion
(France)

MADAGASCAR
Antananarivo □

COMOROS
Moroni □
Mayotte □ Dzaoudzi
(France)
Aldabra
Islands
Zanzibar Island

Îles Crozet
~ (France)

KENYA
Nairobi □
Kilimanjaro
5895

Dar es Salaam
Dodoma
Lake
Nyasa
TANZANIA

Kampala

RWANDA
Kigali □
BURUNDI
Bujumbura □
Lake
Tanganyika

DEMOCRATIC
REPUBLIC OF
THE CONGO
Kinshasa □

Lubumbashi □

MALAWI
Lilongwe □
Zambezi

MOZAMBIQUE
Maputo □
SWAZILAND
Mbabane □

Mozambique
Channel

ZAMBIA
Lusaka □

ZIMBABWE
Harare □
Bulawayo □

BOTSWANA
Gaborone □

Pretoria □Tshwane
Johannesburg □
Maseru □ LESOTHO
Durban

Okavango
Delta

Cuando

ANGOLA
Luanda □
Huambo □
Cubango

NAMIBIA
Windhoek □
Namib Desert

REPUBLIC OF
SOUTH AFRICA
Orange
Cape Town □
Cape of
Good Hope
Cape Agulhas
Port Elizabeth

GABON

CONGO
Brazzaville □

São Tomé □

Ascension

St Helena and
Dependencies
(U.K.)
. St Helena

Tropic of Capricorn

Tristan da Cunha

Prince Edward Islands
(S. Africa)

Longitude 20° west of Greenwich

© Collins Bartholomew Ltd

0   500   1000   1500 KILOMETRES

113

ATLANTIC OCEAN
Madeira (Portugal)
FUNCHAL
SANTA CRUZ DE TENERIFE
La Palma
Tenerife
La Gomera
El Hierro
Gran Canaria
Lanzarote
Fuerteventura
LAS PALMAS DE GRAN CANARIA
Canary Islands (Islas Canarias) (Spain)
SPAIN
Gibraltar (U.K.)
Strait of Gibraltar
Málaga
Almeria
Tangier (Tanger)
Ceuta (Spain)
Tétouan
Melilla (Spain)
Larache
Mostaganem
Oran
Kenitra
Ksar el Kebir
Oujda
Tlemcen
RABAT
Casablanca
Meknès
Fès (Fez)
Taza
El Jadida
Settat
MOROCCO
Safi
Beni Mellal
Marrakech
Essaouira
Haut Atlas (High Atlas)
ATLAS MOUNTAINS
Hauts Plateaux
Bouârfa
Aïn Sefra
Figuig
Er Rachidia
Toubkal 4167
Taroudannt
Agadir
Ouarzazate
Béchar
Abadla
Beni Abbès
Grand Erg Occidental
Tiznit
Anti-Atlas
Sidi Ifni
Guelmine
Hamada du Drâa
Tabelbala
El Homr
Timimoun
Ksabi
Adrar
Sbaa
LAÂYOUNE
Tindouf
Es Semara
ALGERIA
Boujdour
El Eglab
Reggane
Sebkha Mekerrhane
Sebkha Azzel Matti
Chenachane
Gallat Zemmour
Aïn Ben Tili
Bir Mogreïn
Chegga
WESTERN SAHARA
Tropic of Cancer
Ad Dakhla
El Hammâmi
ERG CHECH
Tanezrouft
Zouérat
Fdérik
Taoudenni
Tichla
Nouâdhibou
Choûm
OUARÂNE
Atâr
Akjoujt
Nouâmghâr
MAURITANIA
NOUAKCHOTT
Tidjikja
Tîchît
Araouane
Adrar des Iforas
Kidal
Boutilimit
Magta' Lahjar
HÔD
MALI
Anéfis
Rosso
Aleg
Ayoûn el Atroûs
Oualâta
IRÎGUI
Sénégal
St-Louis
Dagana
Kaédi
Kiffa
Néma
Lac Faguibine
Gourma-Rharous
Bourem
Louga
Linguère
Mbout
Timbedgha
Bassikounou
Goundam
Niger
Timbuktu (Tombouctou)
Gao
Ménaka
DAKAR
Matam
Sélibabi
Yélimané
Nioro
Ballé
Nara
Youvarou
Lac Niangay
Ansongo
Diourbel
Bakel
Kayes
Diéma
Nampala
Mopti
Douentza
Hombori
SENEGAL
Mbour
Kaolack
Kaffrine
Goudiri
Kidira
Ténenkou
Niono
Bandiagara
Gorom Gorom
Tillabéri
BANJUL
Tambacounda
Georgetown
Bafoulabé
Kolokani
Ségou
Macina
Koro
Djibo
THE GAMBIA
Ziguinchor
Kolda
Kédougou
Lac de Manantali
Kita
Kati
Koulikoro
Djenné
San
Ouahigouya
Dori
Niger
Cacheu
Bafatá
Gabú
Koundara
Satadougou
Tougan
Yako
Kaya
Bogandé
NIAMEY
GUINEA-BISSAU
Bissau
Gaoual
Mali
BAMAKO
Bla
Koutiala
Nouna
BURKINA
Bolama
Buba
Fouta Djallon
Koudougou
OUAGADOUGOU
Fada-N'Gourma
Kantchari
Arquipélago dos Bijagós
Cacine
Labé
Bafing
Siguiri
Kangaba
Lac de Sélingué
Bougouni
Tenkodogo
Diapaga
Boké
Fria
GUINEA
Dabola
Kouroussa
Sikasso
Bobo-Dioulasso
Manga
Léo
Pô
Bawku
Mandiana
Orodara
Banfora
Lawra
Bolgatanga
Dapaong
Dubréka
Mamou
Kankan
Kadiolo
Black Volta
White Volta
BENIN
Natitingou
Djougou
CONAKRY
Kindia
Faranah
Odienné
Ferkessédougou
Téhini
Wa
Port Loko
Lungi
Makeni
Kissidougou
Boundiali
Bouna
Yendi
Kara
Bassar
FREETOWN
Sefadu
Beyla
Korhogo
Damongo
Tamale
Salaga
Sokodé
Kailahun
Touba
Dianra
CÔTE D'IVOIRE
SIERRA LEONE
Lunsar
Bo
Kenema
Nzérékoré
Mankono
Séguéla
Lac de Kossou
Bondoukou
Bouaké
GHANA
Kintampo
Techiman
Wenchi
Sunyani
TOGO
Zimmi
Zorzor
Danané
Man
Atakpamé
Abeokuta
Gbarnga
Lake Volta
Robertsport
LIBERIA
Tapeta
Daloa
Abengourou
Kumasi
Abomey
MONROVIA
YAMOUSSOUKRO
Bongouanou
Koforidua
PORTO-NOVO
Ho
Buchanan
Gagnoa
Divo
Obuasi
Adzopé
Zwedru
Abidjan
Winneba
LOMÉ
ACCRA
Sassandra
Tarkwa
Cape Coast
Slave Coast
Greenville
Grand-Lahou
Axim
Sekondi
Harper
San-Pédro
Cape Palmas
Tabou
Three Points
Gold Coast
Bight of Benin
GULF OF GUINEA
A
20°
10°
0°
30°
20°
10°
1
2
3
4

Lambert Azimuthal Equal Area Projection

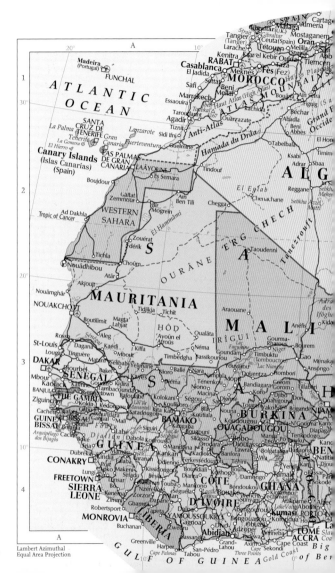

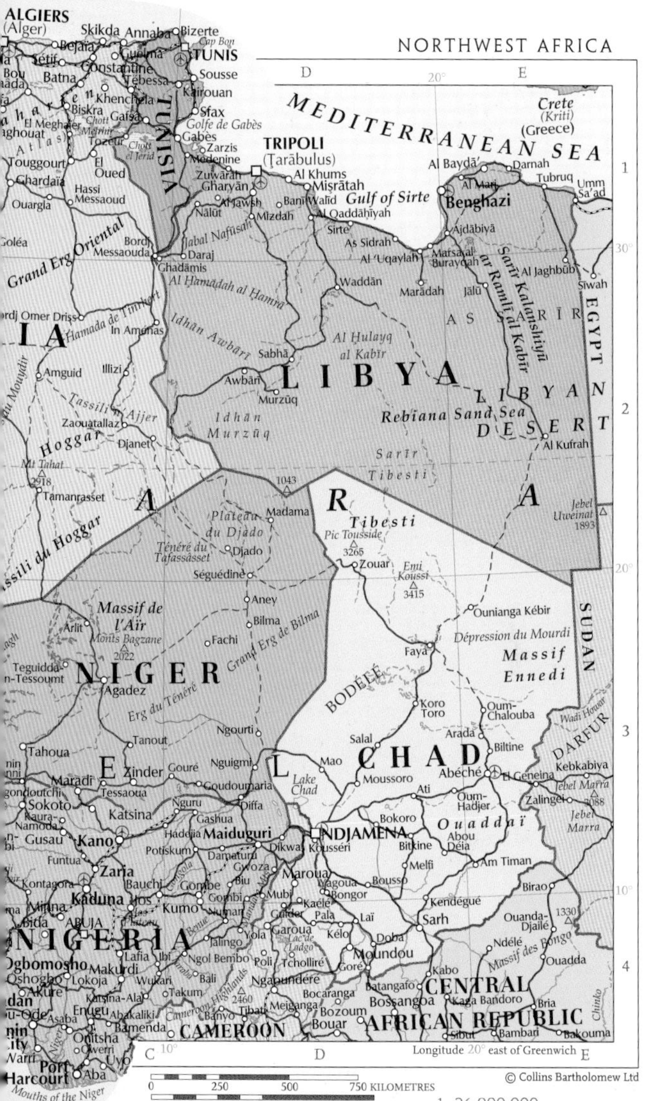

ALGIERS
(Alger)
Skikda Annaba
Bejaïa Guelma Bizerte Cap Bon
Sétif Constantine Tébessa TUNIS
Bou Batna Khenchela Sousse
aada Biskra Gafsa Kairouan
El Meghaïer Chott el Sfax
ghouat El Oued Jerid Golfe de Gabès
Touggourt Hassi Médenine Gabès
Messaoud Zarzis
Chardaïa Ouargla Zuwārah TRIPOLI
(Ṭarābulus)
Goléa Bordj Ghary'ān Al Khums
Messaouda Banī Walīd Al Qaddāḥīyah
Grand Erg Oriental Daraj Mizdah Sirte
Ghadāmis Al Ḥamādah al Ḥamrā Waddān
rdj Omer Driss Jabal Nafūsah Marādah
A In Amenas Idhān Awbārī Sabhā
Amguid Illizi Awbārī Al Ḥulayq al Kabīr
Tassili n'Ajjer Murzūq
Zaouatallaz Djanet Idhān Rebiana Sand
Hoggar Murzūq
Tamanrasset Madama
Plateau Pic Toussidé
du Djado 3265
Ténéré du Djado
Tafassasset Zouar

D 20° E

MEDITERRANEAN SEA

Crete
(Kriti)
(Greece)

Al Baydā' Darnah
Tubruq Umm
Benghazi Sa'ad
Ajdābiyā
Maṣṣad Būrayqah
Al 'Uqaylah Jālū Al Jaghbūb Siwah
Jabal Buraydah
AS Ramī al Kabīr EGYPT
SIRĪR

LIBYA
LIBYAN
Rebiana Sand Sea DESERT
Sarīr
Tibesti Al Kufrah
Jebel
Uweinat
1893

SUDAN

1

30°

2

20°

Massif de
l'Aïr
Monts Bagzane Bilma
2022 Fachi
Arlit
Teguidda-
n-Tessoum Agadez Erg du Ténéré
Tahoua Tanout Ngourti
E Zinder Goudoumaria
Maradi Go600 Nguigmi
ngodoutchi Tessaoua Nguru Diffa
Koura- Katsina Gashua
Namoda Hadejia Maiduguri
Gusau Kano Potiskum Damaturu Dikwa
Funtua Gwoza
Kontagora Zaria Gombe Biu Mubi
Minna Kaduna Jos Gombi Kaélé
bida ABUJA Kumo Garkida Garoua
Lafia Ngol Bembo Yola
Ogbomosho Lokoja Jalingo Tcholliré
Oshogbo Wukari Bali Takum
dan Enugu Abakaliki Tibati
ty Onitsha Bamenda
Warri Oweri
Port Uyo
Harcourt CAMEROON
Mouths of the Niger

Aney
Koro
Toro
Ngourti Salal
Lake Mao Moussoro Abéché
Chad Ati Oum-
Bol Hadjer Abou
Bokoro Déia
NDJAMENA Bitkine
Kousséri Melfi Am Timan
Bougou Bousso
Maroua Bongor Kendégué
Garoua Pala Sarh
Laï Doba
Moundou Gore Batangafo
Bocaranga Bossangoa
Bozoum Bouar

NIGER

Ténéré du
Tafassasset
Séguédine

Grand Erg de Bilma

BODÉLÉ

CHAD

Tibesti
Emi
Koussi
3415

Ounianga Kébir

Dépression du Mourdi
Massif
Ennedi

DARFUR
Wadi Howar
Kebkabiya
Geneina Jebel
Zalingei Marra
3088
Jebel
Marra
Birao 10°
Ouanda-
Djallé 1330
Ndélé
Massif des Bongo
Ouadda
Bria Chinko
Bambari Bakouma

CENTRAL
AFRICAN REPUBLIC

C 10° D Longitude 20° east of Greenwich E

0 250 500 750 KILOMETRES
0 250 500 MILES 1 : 26 000 000

© Collins Bartholomew Ltd

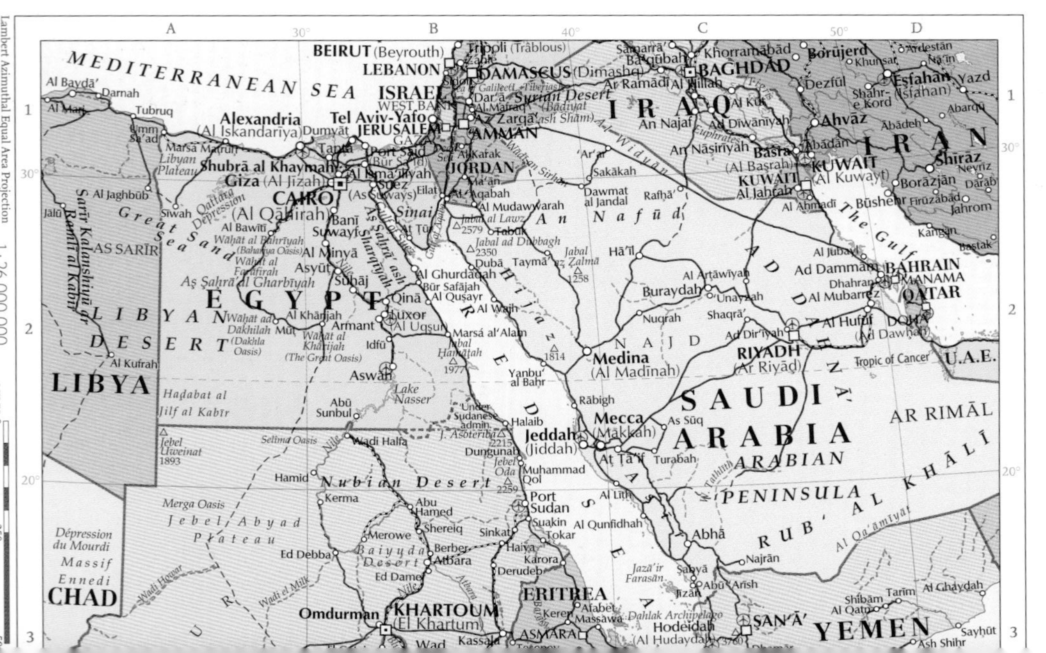

Lambert Azimuthal Equal Area Projection   1 : 26 000 000   MILES 0   250   50

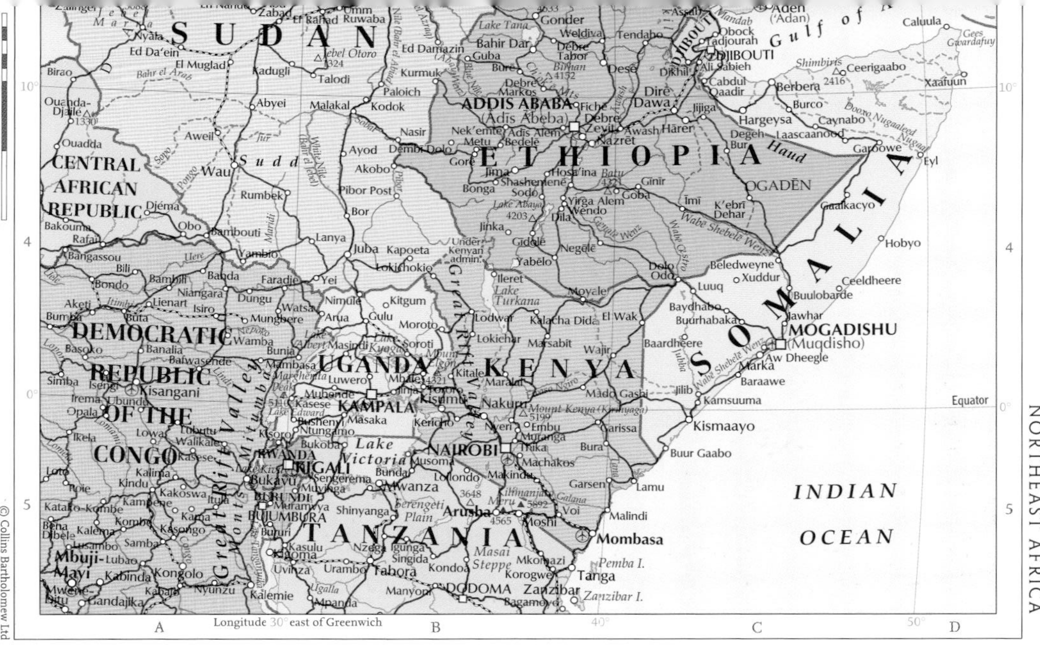

© Collins Bartholomew Ltd

0   250   500   750 KILOMETRES

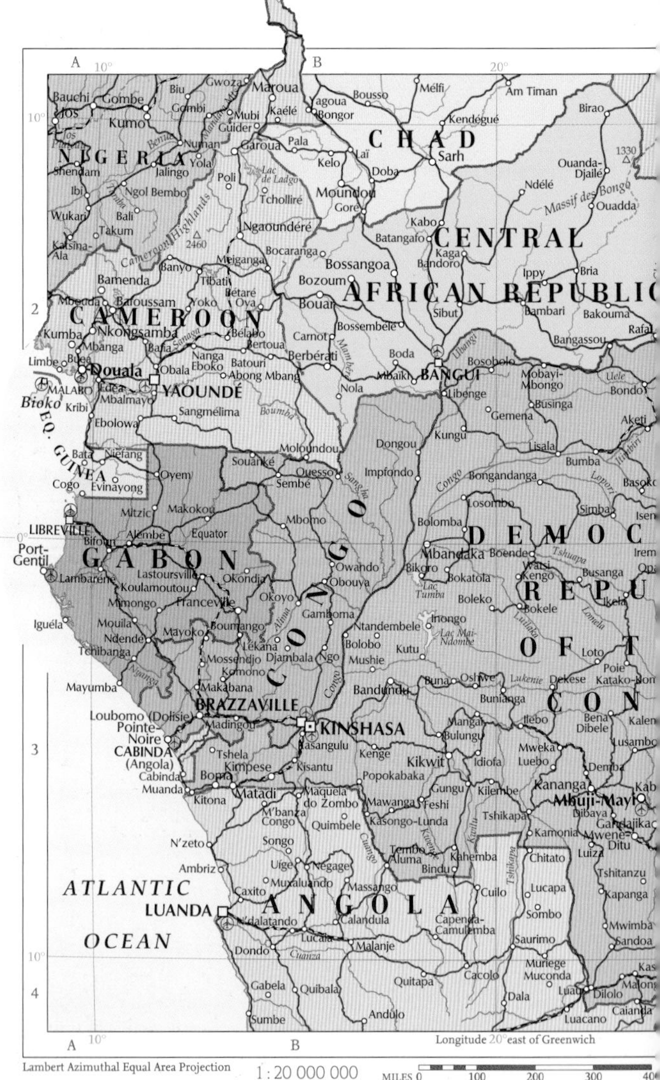

Lambert Azimuthal Equal Area Projection   1 : 20 000 000   MILES 0   100   200   300   40

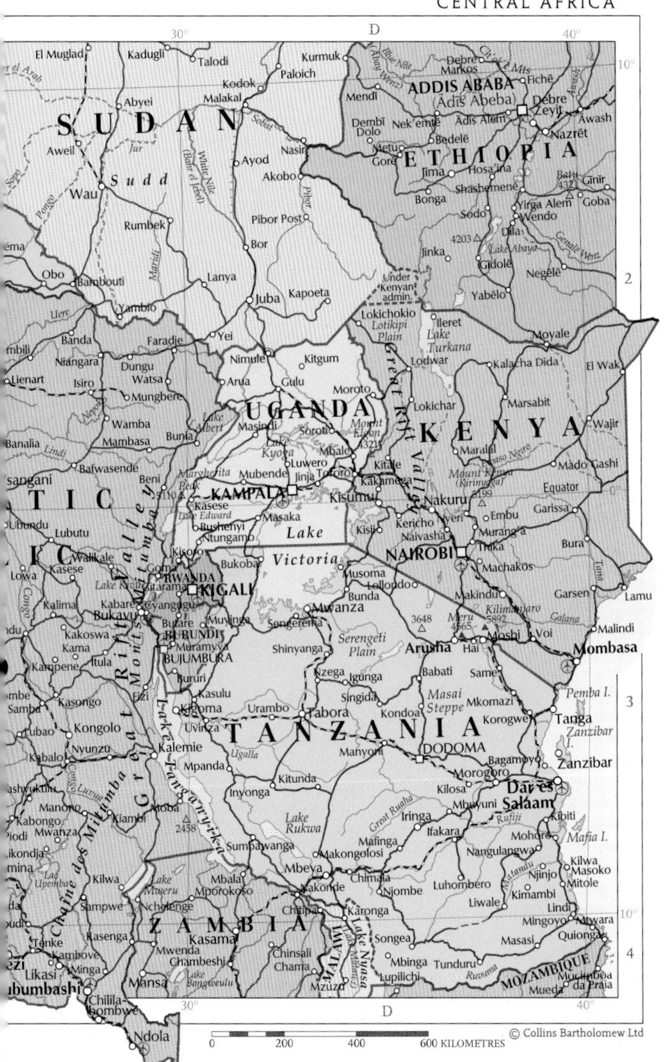

© Collins Bartholomew Ltd

SUDAN
ETHIOPIA
ADDIS ABABA
(Ādīs Ābeba)
UGANDA
KENYA
KAMPALA
NAIROBI
RWANDA
KIGALI
BURUNDI
BUJUMBURA
TANZANIA
DODOMA
Dar es Salaam
ZAMBIA
MALAWI
MOZAMBIQUE
Lake Victoria
Lake Turkana
Lake Tanganyika
Lake Rukwa
Lake Nyasa
Great Rift Valley
Mombasa
Zanzibar
Juba
Mwanza
Arusha
Kisumu
Nakuru
Tabora
Kigoma
Mbeya
Kasama
Lubumbashi
Ndola
0 200 400 600 KILOMETRES

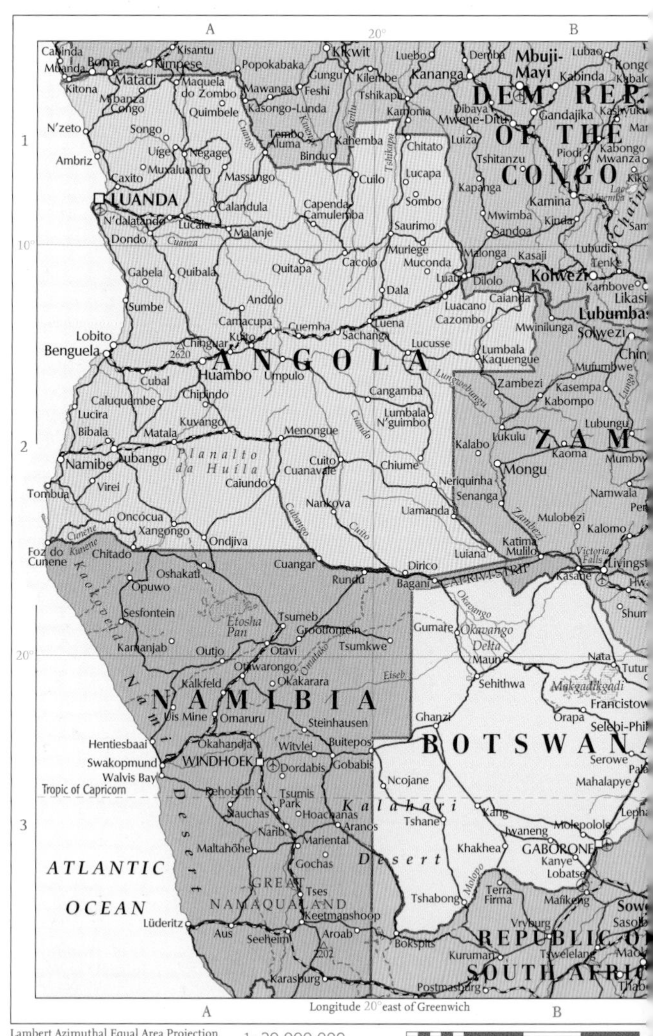

A

20°

B

1

10°

2

20°

3

Cabinda
Mbanda
Kitona
N'zeto
Ambriz
LUANDA
N'dalatando
Dondo
Gabela
Sumbe
Lobito
Benguela
Cubal
Caluquembe
Lucira
Bibala
Namibe
Tombua
Virei
Oncócua
Xangongo
Foz do Cunene
Chitado
Opuwo
Sesfontein
Kamanjab
Henties baai
Swakopmund
Walvis Bay
Tropic of Capricorn
Karibib
Usakos
Maltahöhe
Lüderitz
Aus
Seeheim

Boma
Matadi
Mbanza Congo
Songo
Uige
Muxaluando
Negage
Massango
Calandula
Lucala
Malanje
Quibala
Anddio
Camacupa
Chinguar
Huambo
Chipindo
Kuvango
Caiundo
Ondjiva
Cuangar

Kisantu
Kimpese
Popokabaka
Maquela do Zombo
Quimbele
Kasongo-Lunda
Tembo Aluma
Bindu
Capenda Camulemba
Quitapa
Cacolo
Quemba
Kuito
2620
Umpulo
Menongue
Cuito
Cuanavale
Nankova
Rundu

Mawanga
Feshi
Kahemba
Cuilo
Sombo
Saurimo
Dala
Luena
Sachanga
Cangamba
Chiume
Uamanda
Dirico
Bagani

Lkwit
Luebo
Gungu
Kilembe
Tshikapa
Kamonia
Chitato
Lucapa
Muriege
Muconda
Luau
Lumbala
Lucusse
Lumbala N'guimbo
Neriquinha
Senanga
Luiana
Katima Mulilo

Demba
Kananga
Mwene-Ditu
Luiza
Kapanga
Mwimba
Sandoa
Dilolo
Caianda
Cazombo
Mwinilunga
Kaquengue
Zambezi
Kalabo
Mongo
Mulobezi
Kalomo

Mbuji-Mayi
Lubao
Kabinda
Piodi
Kamina
Lubudi
Kolwezi
Luacano
Lumbala
Kasempa
Kabompo
Lukulu
Kaoma
Namwala

Lubao
Gandajika
Mwanza
Kinda
Kambove
Caianda
Mufumbwe
Kabompo
Lubungu
Mumbwe

Kongo
Kabinda
Kabongo
Kamina
Lubudi
Tenke
Lubumbashi
Solwezi
ZA
Kaoma

DEM. REP. OF THE CONGO

ANGOLA

Planalto da Huíla

Etosha Pan

Tsumeb
Grootfontein
Gumare
Okavango Delta
Maun
Sehithwa

Z A M
Kasanga
Livingston
Victoria Falls

3

Oshakati
Tsumkwe
Otavi
Otjiwarongo
Okakarara
Kalkfeld
Omaruru
Steinhausen
Okahandja
WINDHOEK
Witvlei
Buitepos
Dordabis
Gobabis
Rehoboth
Tsumis Park
Hoachanas
Nauchas
Narib
Gochas
Mariental
Tses
Keetmanshoop
Bokspits
Aroab

Ghanzi
Ncojane
Kang
Iwaneng
Tshane
Khakhea

Nata
Orapa
Serowe
Mahalapye
Molepolole
GABORONE
Kanye
Lobatse
Tshabong
Terra Firma

Tutur
Francistown
Selebi-Phik
Palap
Lepha

BOTSWANA

Outjo

NAMIBIA

Makgadikgadi

Kalahari Desert

GREAT NAMAQUALAND

ATLANTIC OCEAN

Vryburg
Kuruman
Postmasburg

REPUBLIC OF SOUTH AFRIC
Mafikeng
Sows
Sasol
Twelelang

Karasburg

Longitude 20° east of Greenwich

A

B

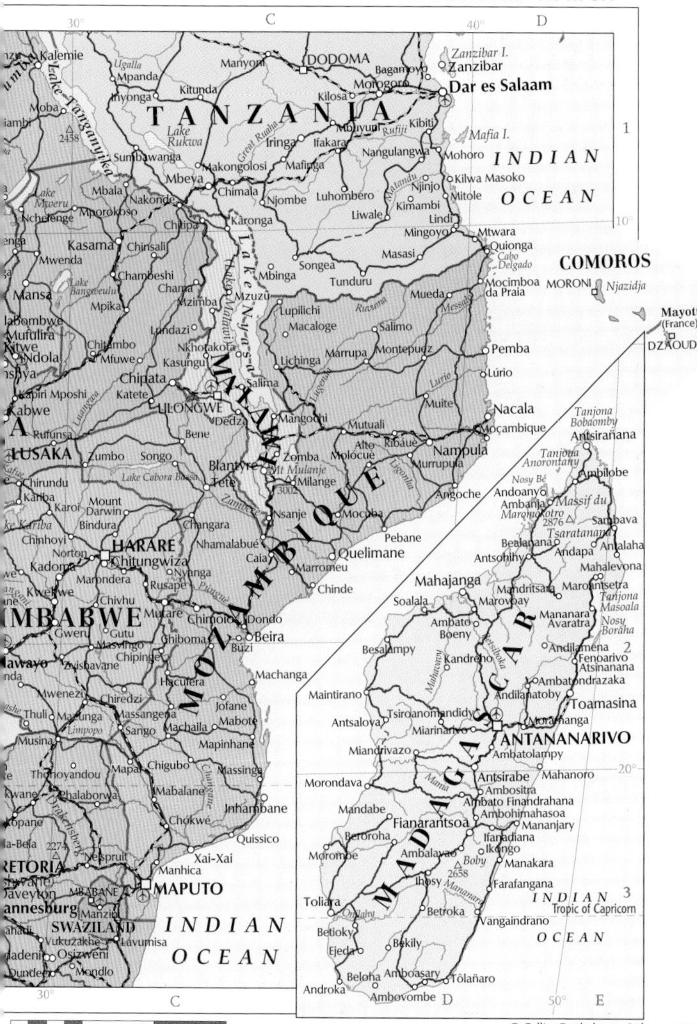
TANZANIA
DODOMA
Zanzibar
Dar es Salaam
INDIAN OCEAN
COMOROS
MORONI
Mayotte (France)
DZAOUDZI
MALAWI
LILONGWE
MOZAMBIQUE
MAPUTO
LUSAKA
HARARE
SWAZILAND
MBABANE
MADAGASCAR
ANTANANARIVO
Lake Tanganyika
Lake Nyasa (Lake Malawi)
Lake Cabora Bassa
Beira
Nampula
Quelimane
Toamasina
Mahajanga
Toliara
Fianarantsoa
Antsiranana
Tropic of Capricorn
0 200 400 600 KILOMETRES

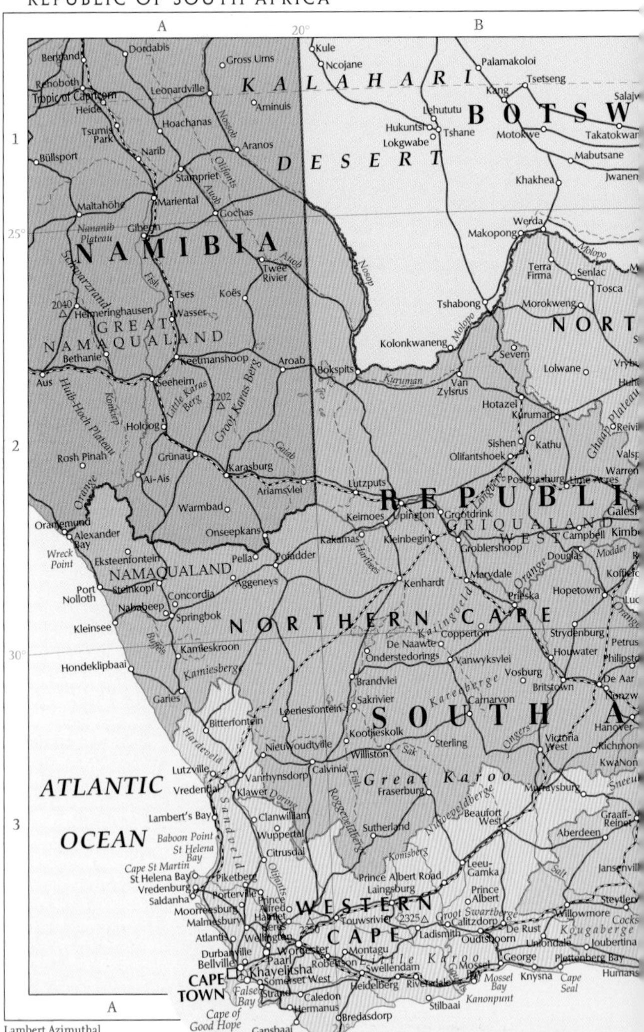

A
B
20°
25°
30°
1
2
3
KALAHARI DESERT
BOTSW
NAMIBIA
GREAT NAMAQUALAND
NAMAQUALAND
NORTHERN CAPE
REPUBLI
SOUTH A
WESTERN CAPE
GRIQUALAND WEST
ATLANTIC OCEAN
Great Karoo
Little Karoo
Windhoek
Rehoboth
Tropic of Capricorn
Dordabis
Gross Ums
Leonardville
Aminuis
Kule
Ncojane
Palamakoloi
Tsetseng
Kang
Lehututu
Hukuntsi
Tshane
Lokgwabe
Motokwe
Takatokwane
Mabutsane
Khakhea
Jwaneng
Werda
Makopong
Heide
Tsumis Park
Hoachanas
Aranos
Nossob
Narib
Büllsport
Stampriet
Olifants
Auob
Mariental
Maltahöhe
Gochas
Gibeon
Nananib Plateau
Schwarzrand
Fish
Twee Rivier
Tses
Koës
Wasser
2040
Helmeringhausen
Bethanie
Keetmanshoop
Aroab
Aus
Seeheim
Huib-Hoch Plateau
Konkiep
Little Karas Berg
Groot Karas Berg
2202
Holoog
Rosh Pinah
Grünau
Gaib
Karasburg
Ai-Ais
Orange
Ariamsvlei
Warmbad
Oranjemund
Alexander Bay
Onseepkans
Wreck Point
Eksteenfontein
Pella
Pofadder
Port Nolloth
Steinkopf
Aggeneys
Concordia
Nababeep
Springbok
Kleinsee
Buffels
Kamieskroon
Kamiesberge
Hondeklipbaai
Garies
Bitterfontein
Hardeveld
Lutzville
Vredendal
Vanrhynsdorp
Klawer
Doring
Sandveld
Lambert's Bay
Clanwilliam
Wuppertal
Baboon Point
St Helena Bay
Citrusdal
Cape St Martin
St Helena Bay
Piketberg
Vredenburg
Saldanha
Porterville
Moorreesburg
Malmesbury
Prince Alfred Hamlet
Ceres
Atlantis
Wellington
Durbanville
Bellville
Paarl
Worcester
CAPE TOWN
Khayelitsha
Somerset West
Strand
False Bay
Caledon
Hermanus
Cape of Good Hope
Gansbaai
Bredasdorp
Struis Bay
Cape Agulhas
Nosop
Molopo
Tshabong
Kolonkwaneng
Bokspits
Kuruman
Van Zylsrus
Terra Firma
Senlac
Tosca
Morokweng
Severn
Lolwane
Vryburg
Hotazel
Kuruman
Ghaap Plateau
Reivilo
Sishen
Kathu
Olifantshoek
Langberg
Postmasburg
Lime Acres
Warrenton
Lutzputs
Upington
Groblershoop
Keimoes
Kakamas
Kleinbegin
Hartbees
Groblershoop
Campbell
Kimberley
Douglas
Modder
Marydale
Kenhardt
Prieska
Hopetown
Kaaingveld
Copperton
De Naawte
Onderstedorings
Vanwyksvlei
Strydenburg
Houwater
Petrusville
Philipstown
Vosburg
Britstown
De Aar
Brandvlei
Sakrivier
Carnarvon
Kareeberge
Loeriesfontein
Kootjieskolk
Sterling
Ongers
Victoria West
Hanover
Richmond
Nieuwoudtville
Williston
Sak
Calvinia
Fish
Fraserburg
Roggeveldberge
Nuweveldberge
Murraysburg
Beaufort West
Sutherland
Aberdeen
Graaff-Reinet
Komsberg
Leeu-Gamka
Salt
Prince Albert Road
Laingsburg
Prince Albert
Groot Swartberge
Touwsrivier
2325
2250
Calitzdorp
Ladismith
Oudtshoorn
De Rust
Willowmore
Kougaberge
Uniondale
Joubertina
Montagu
Robertson
Swellendam
Mossel Bay
George
Plettenberg Bay
Knysna
Cape Seal
Heidelberg
Riversdale
Stilbaai
Kanonpunt
Gouritz
Jansenville
Steytlerville

A

Lambert Azimuthal
Equal Area Projection

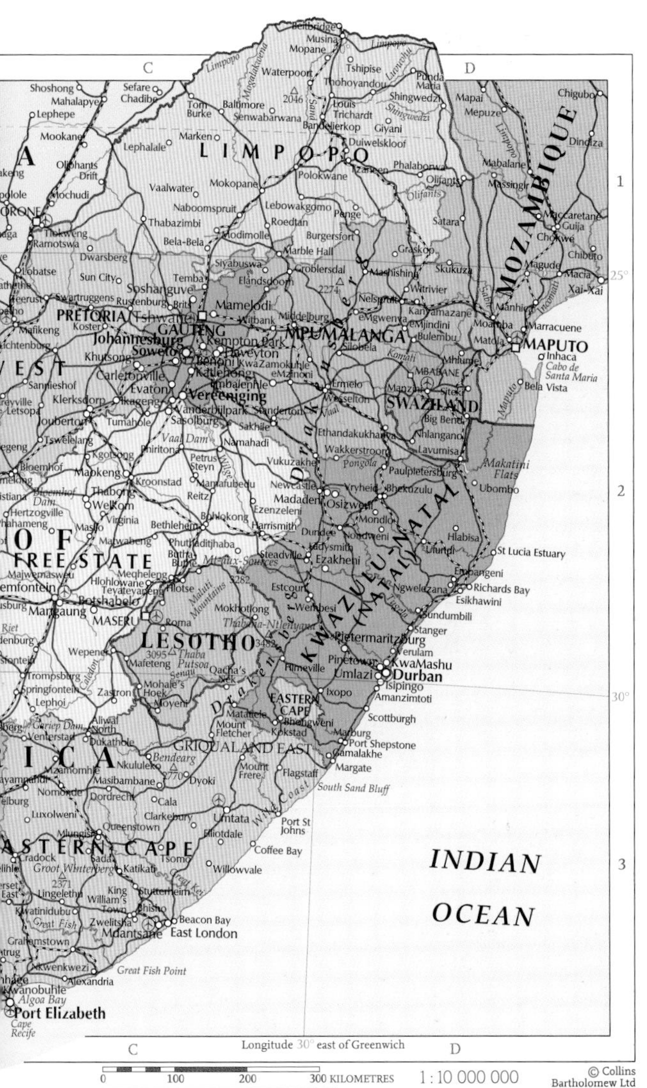

INDIAN

OCEAN

© Collins
Bartholomew Ltd

1 : 10 000 000

Longitude 30° east of Greenwich

| 0 | 100 | 200 | 300 KILOMETRES |

| 0 | 100 | 200 MILES |

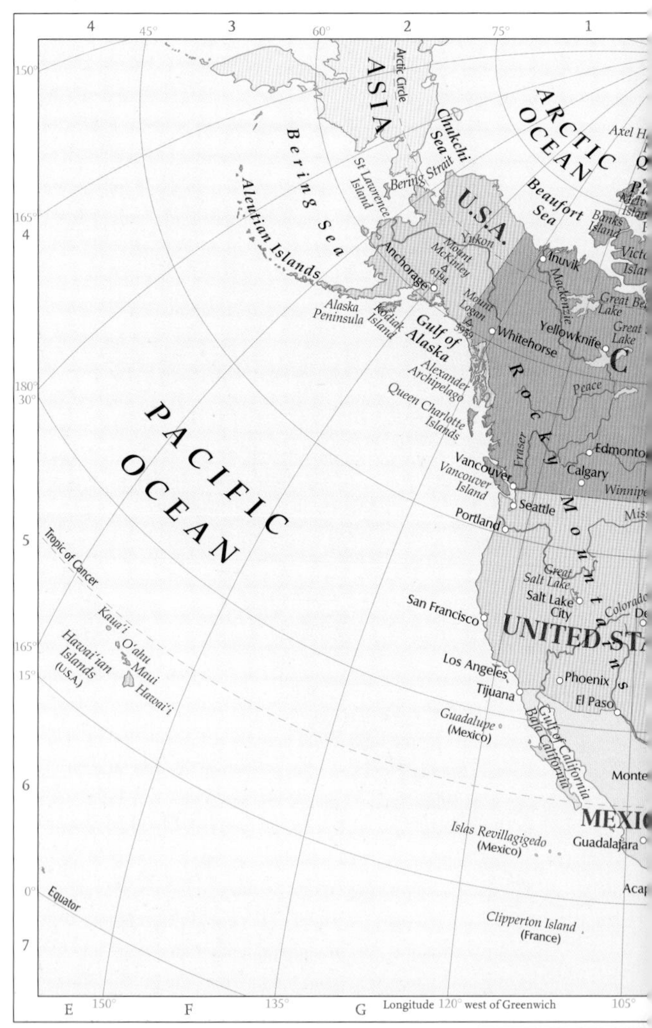

ASIA
Arctic Circle
Chukchi Sea
Bering Strait
St Lawrence Island
Bering Sea
Aleutian Islands
ARCTIC OCEAN
Beaufort Sea
Banks Island
U.S.A.
Yukon
Mount McKinley
6194
Anchorage
Alaska Peninsula
Kodiak Island
Gulf of Alaska
Mount Logan
5959
Inuvik
Mackenzie
Whitehorse
Yellowknife
Great Slave Lake
Great Bear Lake
Alexander Archipelago
Queen Charlotte Islands
Peace
Rocky Mountains
Fraser
Edmonton
Calgary
Vancouver
Vancouver Island
Seattle
Portland
PACIFIC OCEAN
Tropic of Cancer
Great Salt Lake
Salt Lake City
San Francisco
UNITED STATES
Kaua'i
O'ahu
Maui
Hawai'i
Hawai'ian Islands (U.S.A.)
Los Angeles
Tijuana
Phoenix
El Paso
Guadalupe (Mexico)
Gulf of California
Baja California
MEXICO
Islas Revillagigedo (Mexico)
Guadalajara
Equator
Clipperton Island (France)
Longitude 120° west of Greenwich
1 : 72 000 000
MILES 0 500 100

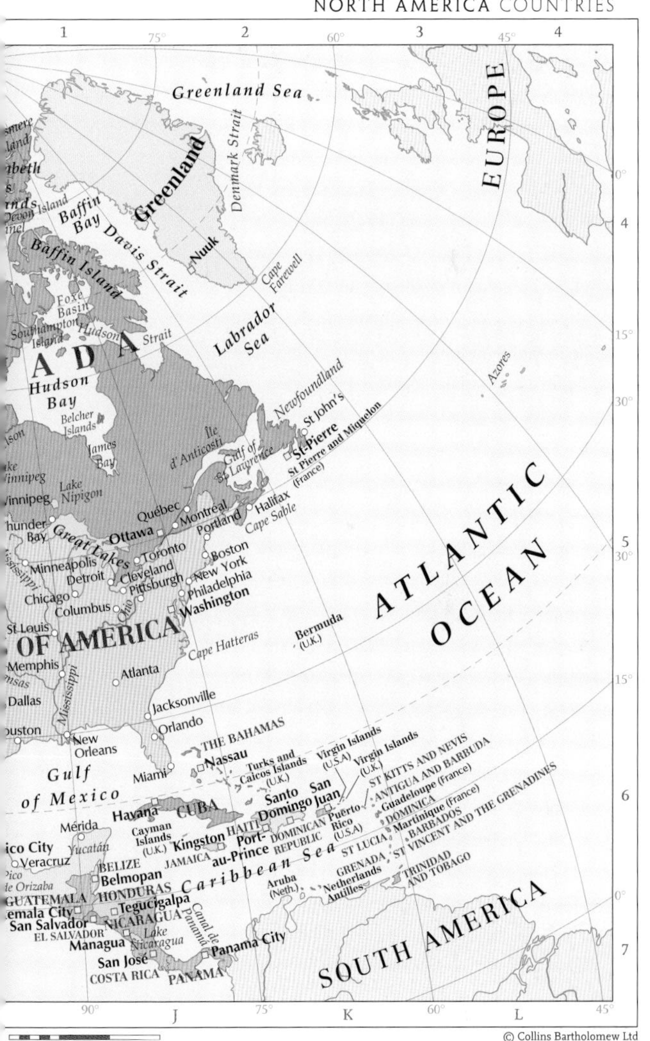

NORTH AMERICA COUNTRIES

Greenland Sea

Greenland

Baffin
Bay

Davis Strait

Denmark Strait

Nuuk

Cape
Farewell

EUROPE

Baffin Island

Foxe
Basin

Southampton
Island

Hudson
Strait

Labrador
Sea

A D A

Hudson
Bay

Belcher
Islands

James
Bay

Île
d'Anticosti

Newfoundland

St John's

Labrador Sea

St Pierre
St Pierre and Miquelon
(France)

Lake
Winnipeg

Lake
Nipigon

Great Lakes

Ottawa

Québec

Montréal

Gulf of
St Lawrence

Thunder
Bay

Minneapolis

Toronto

Portland

Halifax

Cape Sable

Detroit

Cleveland

Boston

Chicago

Pittsburgh

New York

Columbus

Philadelphia

Washington

St Louis

OF AMERICA

Memphis

Atlanta

Cape Hatteras

Bermuda
(U.K.)

ATLANTIC

Dallas

Jacksonville

OCEAN

Houston

Orlando

New
Orleans

Gulf
of Mexico

Miami

THE BAHAMAS

Nassau

Turks and
Caicos Islands
(U.K.)

Virgin Islands
(U.S.A)

Virgin Islands
(U.K.)

ST KITTS AND NEVIS

ANTIGUA AND BARBUDA

Mexico City

Mérida

Havana

CUBA

Santo
Domingo

San
Juan

Puerto
Rico
(U.S.A.)

Guadeloupe (France)

DOMINICA

Veracruz

Yucatán

Cayman
Islands
(U.K.)

Kingston

HAITI

Port-
au-Prince

DOMINICAN
REPUBLIC

Martinique (France)

Pico de
Orizaba

BELIZE

Belmopan

JAMAICA

Caribbean Sea

ST LUCIA

BARBADOS

GUATEMALA

HONDURAS

GRENADA

ST VINCENT AND THE GRENADINES

Guatemala City

Tegucigalpa

NICARAGUA

Aruba
(Neth.)

Netherlands
Antilles

TRINIDAD
AND TOBAGO

San Salvador

EL SALVADOR

Managua

Lake
Nicaragua

San José

COSTA RICA

Canal de
Panamá

Panama City

PANAMA

SOUTH AMERICA

© Collins Bartholomew Ltd

0   500   1000   1500 KILOMETRES

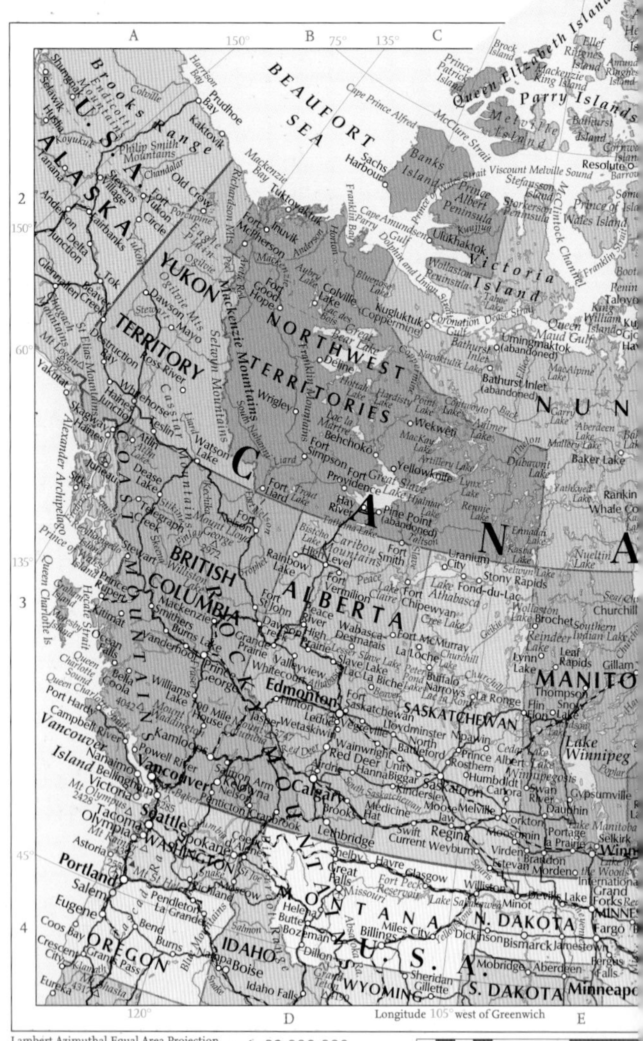

Lambert Azimuthal Equal Area Projection   1 : 30 000 000   MILES 0   200   400

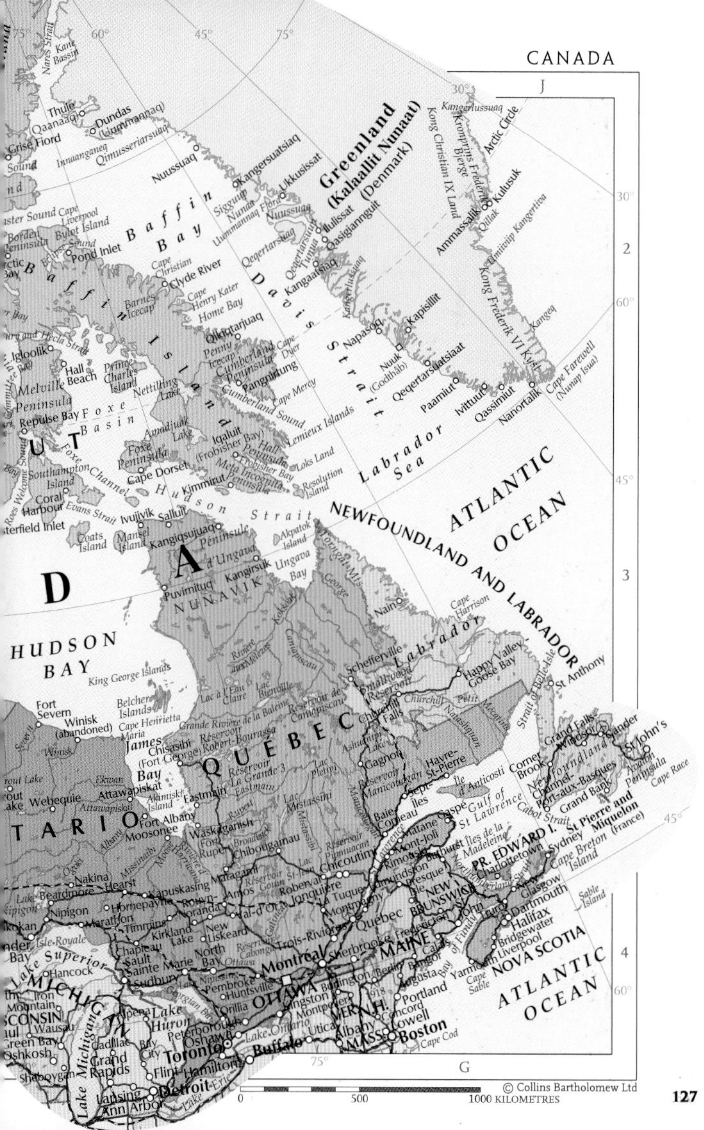
Nares Strait
Kane Bassin
Thule (Qaanaaq)
Dundas (Uummannaq)
Grise Fiord
Innaanganeq
Qimusseriarsuaq
Nuussuaq
Kangersuatsiaq
Upernavik
Ukkusissat
Sigguup Nunaa
Uummannaq Fjord
Nuussuaq
Greenland (Kalaallit Nunaat) (Denmark)
Ilulissat
Qasigiannguit
Qeqertarsuaq
Qeqertarsuup Tunua
Kangaatsiaq
Kangerlussuaq
Kong Christian IX Land
Kronprins Frederik Bjerge
Kangerlussuaq
Arctic Circle
Kulusuk
Ammassalik
Qillak
Umiiviip Kangertiva
Kong Frederik VI Kyst
Kangeq
Cape Farewell (Nunap Isua)
Nanortalik
Qassimiut
Ivittuut
Paamiut
Qeqertarsuatsiaat
Nuuk (Godthåb)
Kapisillit
Napasoq
Baffin Bay
Lancaster Sound
Cape Liverpool
Bylot Island
Borden Peninsula
Eclipse Sound
Pond Inlet
Arctic Bay
Baffin Island
Cape Christian
Clyde River
Barnes Icecap
Cape Henry Kater
Home Bay
Davis Strait
Qikiqtarjuaq
Penny Icecap
Cumberland Peninsula
Cape Dyer
Pangnirtung
Cape Mercy
Cumberland Sound
Lemieux Islands
Fury and Hecla Strait
Igloolik
Hall Beach
Prince Charles Island
Melville Peninsula
Committee Bay
Nettilling Lake
Repulse Bay
Foxe Basin
Amadjuak Lake
Iqaluit (Frobisher Bay)
Hall Peninsula
Frobisher Bay
Foxe Peninsula
Cape Dorset
Meta Incognita Peninsula
Loks Land
Resolution Island
Kimmirut
Labrador Sea
Foxe Channel
Southampton Island
Roes Welcome Sound
Coral Harbour
Evans Strait
Hudson Strait
Chesterfield Inlet
Ivujivik
Salluit
Coats Island
Mansel Island
Kangiqsujuaq
Péninsule d'Ungava
Akpatok Island
Kangirsuk
Ungava Bay
Torngat Mts
ATLANTIC OCEAN
NEWFOUNDLAND AND LABRADOR
Puvirnituq
NUNAVIK
George
Koksoak
Nain
Cape Harrison
Labrador
HUDSON BAY
King George Islands
Caniapiscau
Rivière aux Mélèzes
Lac à l'Eau Claire
Lac Bienville
Schefferville
Smallwood Reservoir
Réservoir de Caniapiscau
Churchill
Churchill Falls
Happy Valley-Goose Bay
Petit Mécatina
Natashquan
Strait of Belle Isle
St Anthony
Fort Severn
Belcher Islands
Winisk (abandoned)
Cape Henrietta Maria
Grande Rivière de la Baleine
Réservoir Robert-Bourassa
Chisasibi (Fort George)
QUÉBEC
James Bay
Réservoir La Grande 3
Eastmain
Ashuanipi Lake
Gagnon
Lac Plétipi
Réservoir Manicouagan
Havre-St-Pierre
Île d'Anticosti
Sept-Îles
Grand Falls-Windsor
Gander
St John's
Corner Brook
Newfoundland
Channel-Port-aux-Basques
Avalon Peninsula
Cape Race
Grand Bank
Gulf of St Lawrence
Cabot Strait
St Pierre and Miquelon (France)
Ekwan
Attawapiskat
Akimiski Island
Webequie
Lac Mistassini
Baie-Comeau
Gaspé
Matane
Mont-Joli
Îles de la Madeleine
PR. EDWARD I.
Charlottetown
Sydney
Cape Breton Island
Fort Albany
Moosonee
Waskaganish (Fort Rupert)
Chibougamau
Réservoir Pipmuacan
Chicoutimi
Rimouski
Bathurst
Miramichi
Northumberland Strait
New Glasgow
Sable Island
Nakina
Hearst
Kapuskasing
Matagami
Amos
Roberval
Jonquière
La Tuque
Edmundston
Presque Isle
NEW BRUNSWICK
Lake Nipigon
Beardmore
Nipigon
Hornepayne
Rouyn-Noranda
Val-d'Or
Shawinigan
Québec
Fredericton
Saint John
Truro
Dartmouth
Halifax
Bridgewater
Liverpool
Marathon
Timmins
Kirkland Lake
New Liskeard
Trois-Rivières
Sherbrooke
MAINE
Bay of Fundy
Yarmouth
Cape Sable
NOVA SCOTIA
Lake Superior
Chapleau
Sault Sainte Marie
North Bay
Montréal
Calais
Bangor
Isle Royale
Hancock
MICHIGAN
Sudbury
Nipissing
Pembroke
Huntsville
OTTAWA
Burlington
Berlin
Augusta
Portland
Iron Mountain
WISCONSIN
Wausau
Green Bay
Oshkosh
Sheboygan
Lake Michigan
Alpena
Lake Huron
Georgian Bay
Orillia
Peterborough
Oshawa
Kingston
Montpelier
VERMONT
N.H.
Concord
Lowell
Boston
Cape Cod
Cadillac
Bay City
Grand Rapids
Flint
Toronto
Hamilton
Lake Ontario
Buffalo
Utica
Albany
MASS.
Lansing
Ann Arbor
Detroit
Lake Erie
ONTARIO
1000 KILOMETRES

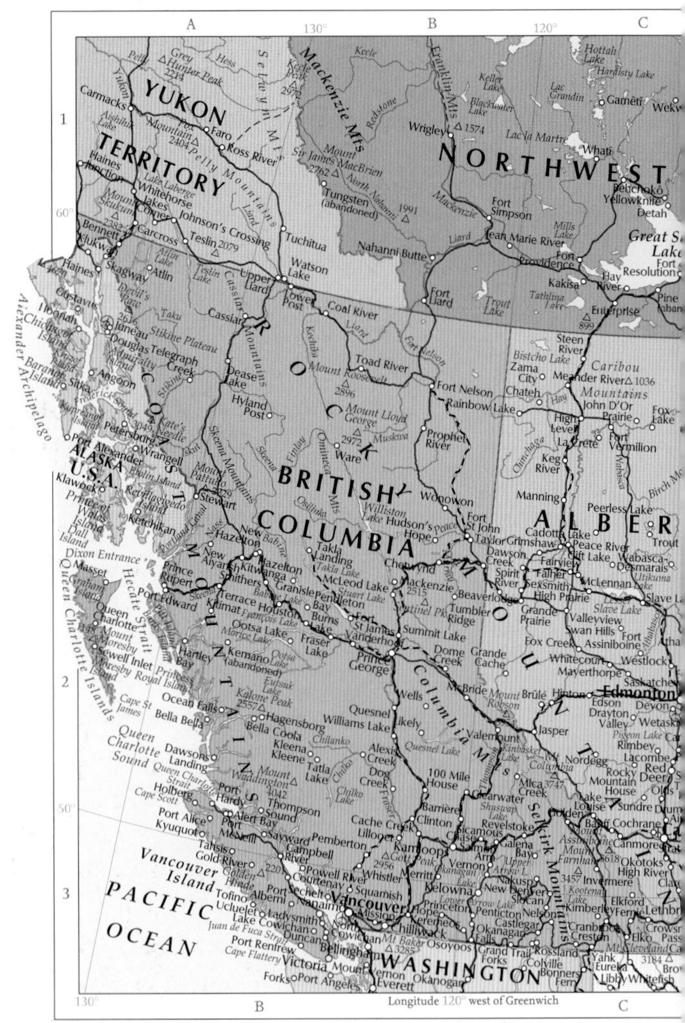

Lambert Azimuthal Equal Area Projection   1 : 15 000 000   MILES 0   100   200   30

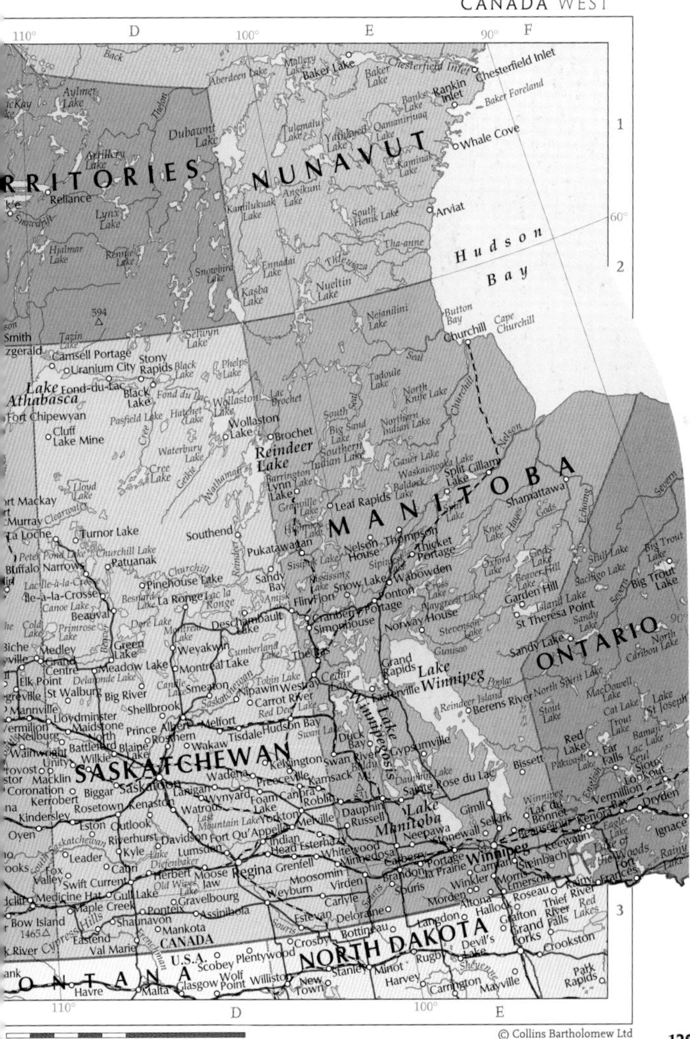

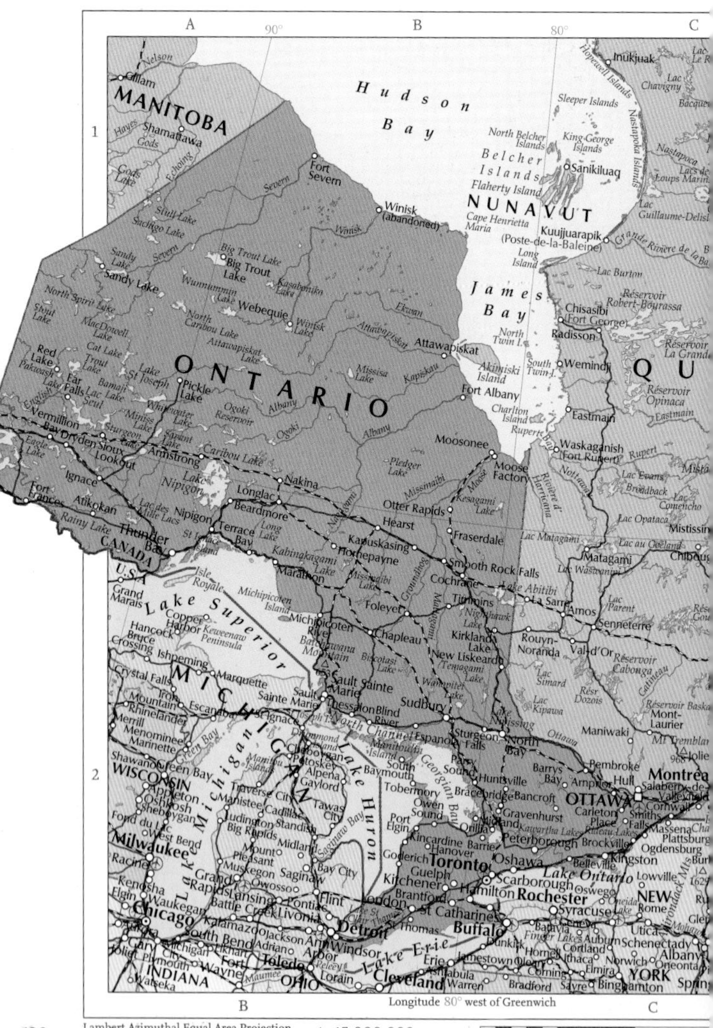

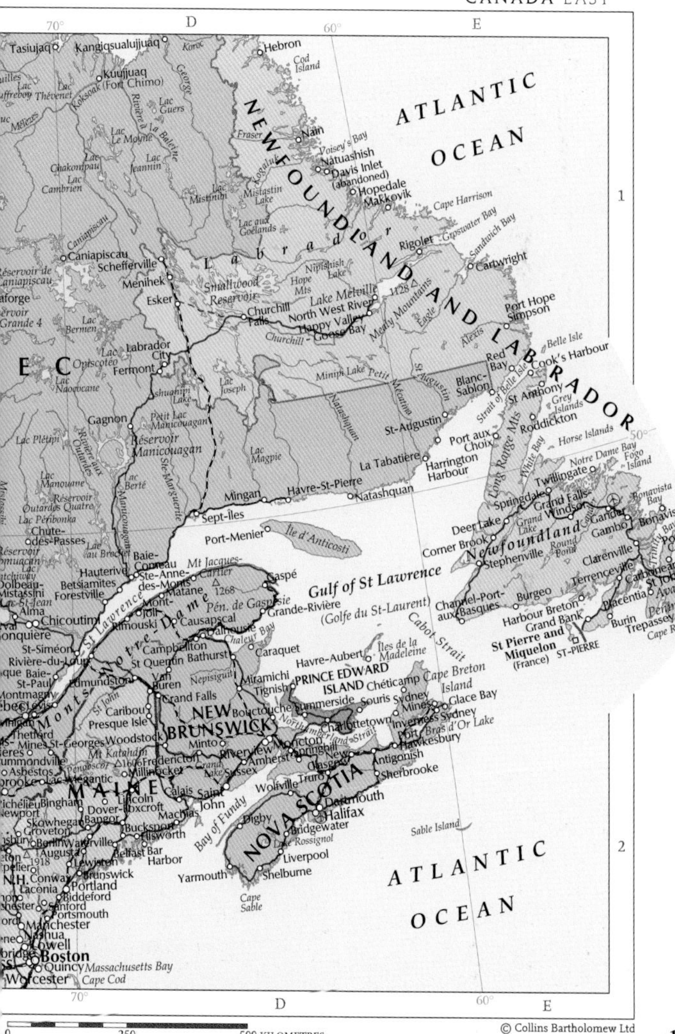

ATLANTIC OCEAN

NEWFOUNDLAND AND LABRADOR

Tasiujaq   Kangiqsualujjuaq   Kuujjuaq (Fort Chimo)   Hebron   Cod Island

Lac Thévenet   Rivière George   Kuujjuaq   Nain   Voisey's Bay   Natuashish   Davis Inlet (abandoned)   Hopedale   Makkovik   Cape Harrison

Chakonipau   Lac Cambrien   Lac Jeannin   Mistinibi   Rigolet   Goose Bay   Sandwich Bay   Cartwright

Caniapiscau   Caniapiscau   Scheffervile   Menihek   Esker   Smallwood Reservoir   Churchill Falls   North West River   Happy Valley-Goose Bay   Mealy Mountains   Port Hope Simpson

Reservoir de Caniapiscau   Laforge   Réservoir Grande 4   Lac Bermen   Labrador City   Fermont   Fermont   Wabush   Lac Joseph   Alexis   Blanc-Sablon   Crook's Harbour   Belle Isle

E C   Lac Naocane   Gagnon   Onistagane   Minia Lake   Petit   Port aux Choix   St Anthony   Roddickton   Grey Islands

Lac Pletin   Réservoir Manicouagan   Lac Magpie   St-Augustin   Harrington Harbour   Horse Islands   Notre Dame Bay   Fogo Island

Lac Manouane   Berté   Mingan   Havre-St-Pierre   Natashquan   La Tabatière   Twillingate   Grand Falls-Windsor   Bonavista

Réservoir Outardes Quatre   Chute-des-Passes   Baie-Comeau   Port-Menier   Île d'Anticosti   Springdale   Gander   Gambo   Bonavista

Mistassini   Forestville   Hauterive   Mt Jacques   Gaspé   Deer Lake   Newfoundland   Clarenville   Pouch Cove

St-Jean   Chicoutimi   Ste-Anne-des-Monts   Pén. de Gaspésie   Grande-Rivière   Corner Brook   Stephenville   Gander   Carbonear   St John's

Jonquiere   St-Siméon   Rimouski   Matane   Causapscal   Channel-Port-aux-Basques   Burgeo   Harbour Breton   Grand Bank   Burin   Placentia   Avalon Peninsula

Rivière-du-Loup   Campbellton   Bathurst   Havre-Aubert   Îles de la Madeleine   St Pierre and Miquelon (France)   ST-PIERRE   Trepassey   Cape Race

Edmundston   St Quentin   Caraquet   Miramichi   Tignish   PRINCE EDWARD ISLAND   Chéticamp   Cape Breton

Caribou   Presque Isle   Grand Falls   Nepisiguit   Bouctouche   Summerside   Souris   Cape Breton Island   Sydney   Glace Bay

MAINE   Woodstock   Minto   Riverview   Moncton   Charlottetown   Inverness   Bras D'Or Lake   New Waterford

Millinocket   Fredericton   NEW BRUNSWICK   Sussex   Amherst   Antigonish   Hawkesbury

Calais   Saint John   Wolfville   Truro   NOVA SCOTIA   Sherbrooke

Bangor   Dover-Foxcroft   Machias   Digby   Bridgewater   Dartmouth   Halifax   Sable Island

NH   Skowhegan   Augusta   Belfast   Lincoln   Bath   Yarmouth   Liverpool   Shelburne

Portland   Biddeford   Portsmouth   Manchester   Cape Sable

ATLANTIC OCEAN

Boston   Quincy   Massachusetts Bay   Cape Cod   Worcester   Lowell

Labrador   Labrador Sea   Strait of Belle Isle   Gulf of St Lawrence (Golfe du St-Laurent)   Cabot Strait   Bay of Fundy

St-Laurent   Fleuve Saint-Laurent

0   250   500 KILOMETRES

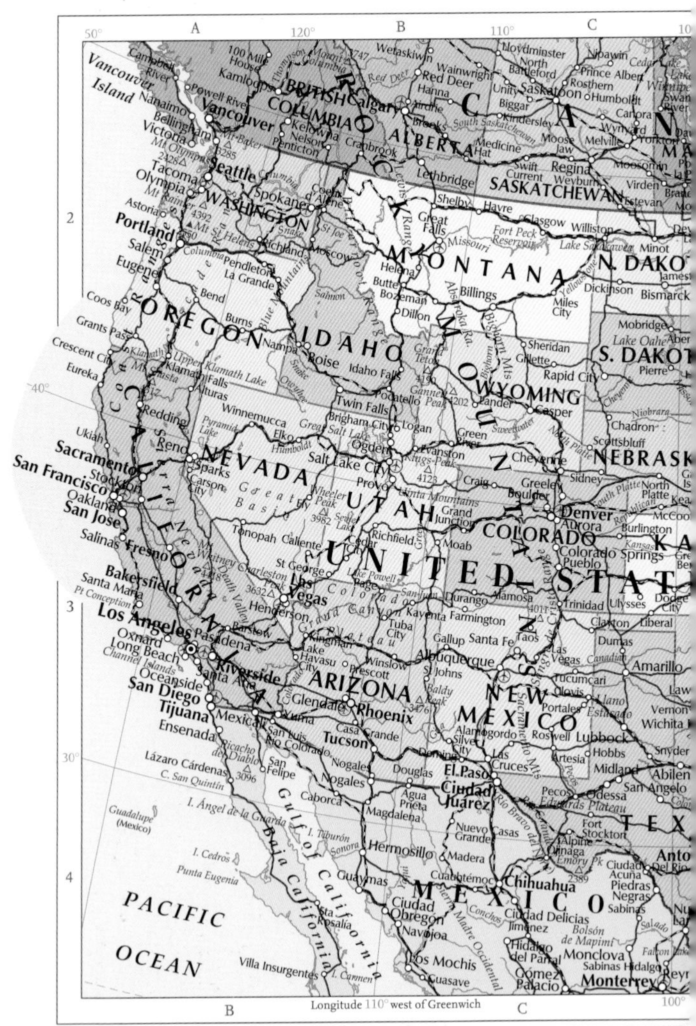

Lambert Azimuthal Equal Area Projection   1 : 25 000 000   MILES 0   250   50

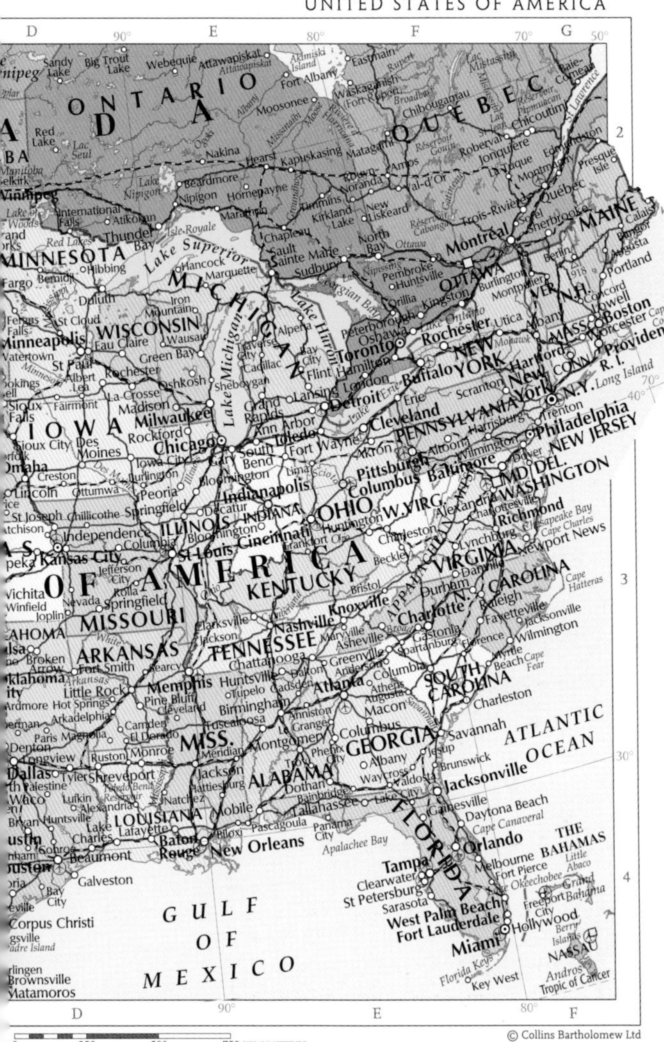

© Collins Bartholomew Ltd

0   250   500   750 KILOMETRES

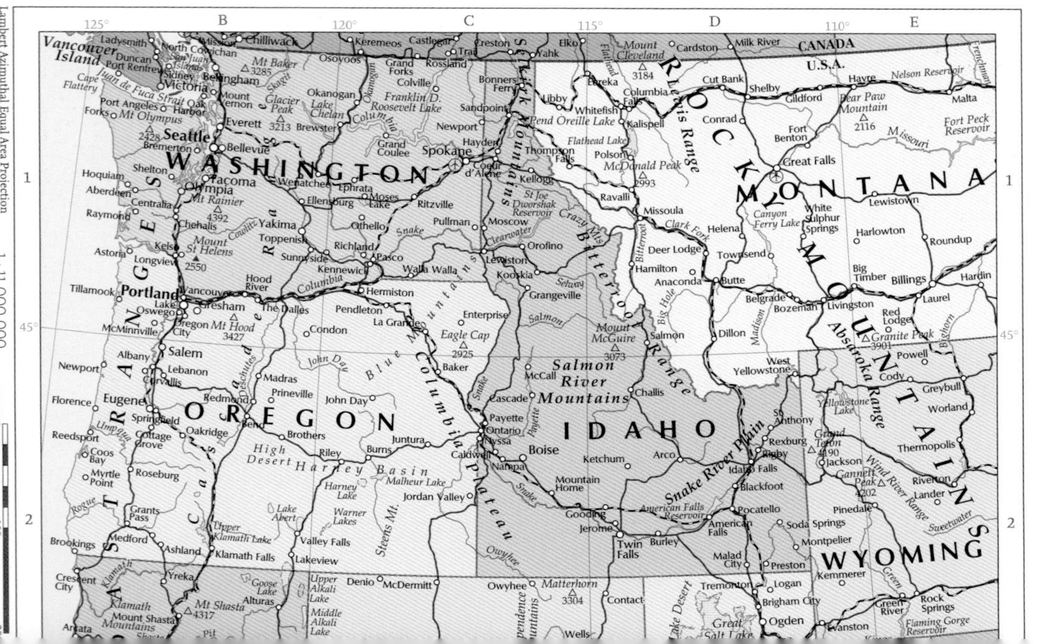

Lambert Azimuthal Equal Area Projection   1 : 11 000 000   MILES 0   100   200

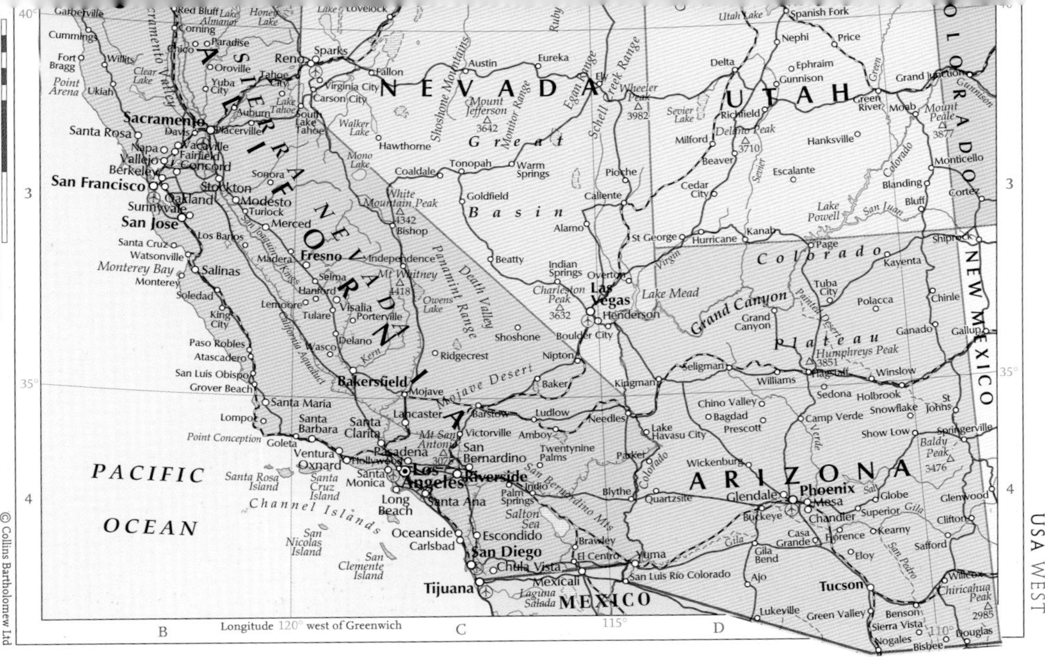

© Collins Bartholomew Ltd

0   100   200   300 KILOMETRES

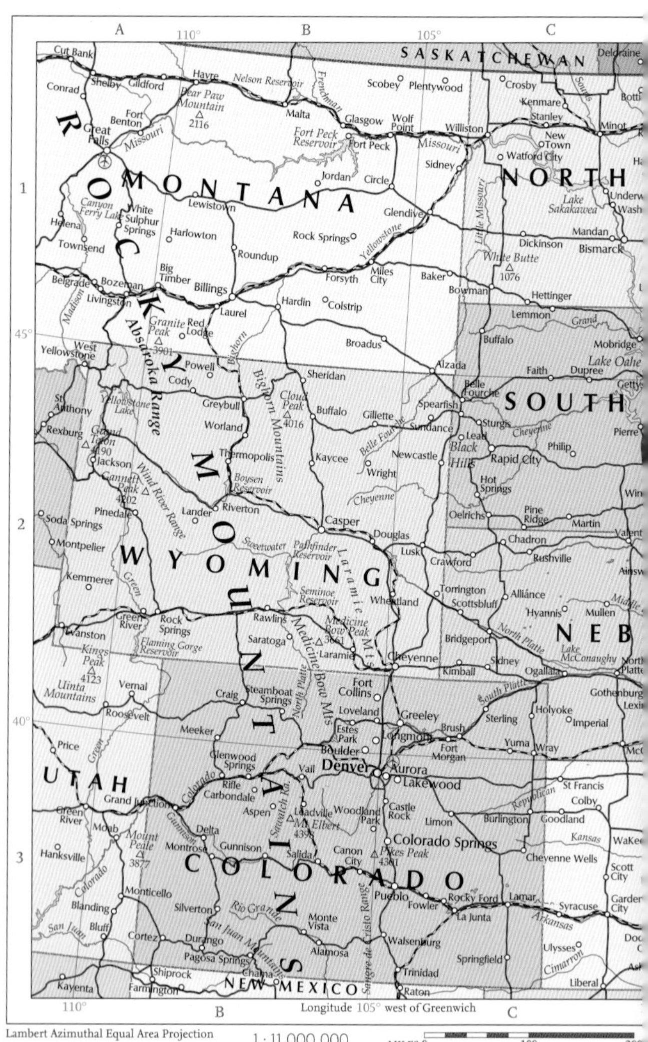

Lambert Azimuthal Equal Area Projection   1 : 11 000 000   MILES 0   100   200

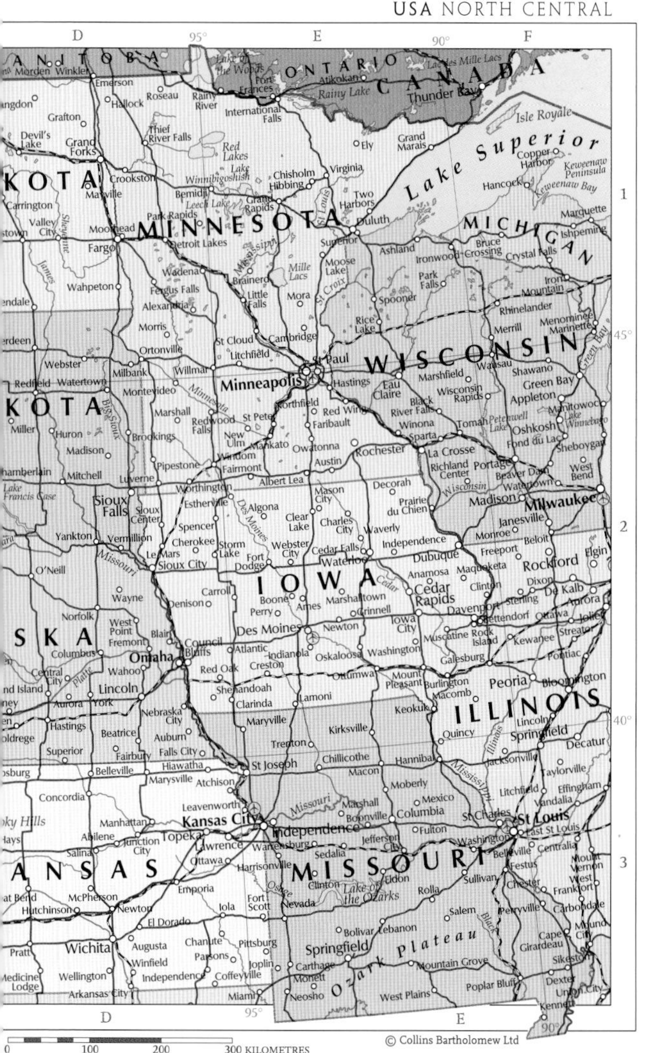
D
95°
E
90°
F
1
2
3
45°
40°
CANADA
ONTARIO
Lake of the Woods
Lac des Mille Lacs
Morden
Winkler
Emerson
Hallock
Roseau
Rainy River
Fort Frances
International Falls
Atikokan
Rainy Lake
Thunder Bay
Isle Royale
Lake Superior
Copper Harbor
Keweenaw Peninsula
Keweenaw Bay
Hancock
Grafton
Devil's Lake
Grand Forks
Thief River Falls
Red Lakes
Lake Winnibigoshish
Chisholm
Hibbing
Virginia
Ely
Grand Marais
Crookston
Mayville
Bemidji
Leech Lake
Grand Rapids
St Louis
Two Harbors
Duluth
Carrington
Valley City
Sheyenne
Park Rapids
MINNESOTA
Moorhead
Fargo
Detroit Lakes
Mississippi
Superior
Ashland
Ironwood
Bruce Crossing
Crystal Falls
Marquette
Ishpeming
MICHIGAN
James
Wahpeton
Wadena
Brainerd
Mille Lacs
Moose Lake
St Croix
Park Falls
Iron Mountain
Fergus Falls
Alexandria
Little Falls
Mora
Spooner
Rhinelander
Rice Lake
Menominee
Marinette
Green Bay
Morris
Merrill
St Cloud
Cambridge
Ortonville
Litchfield
WISCONSIN
Webster
St Paul
Wausau
Shawano
Milbank
Willmar
Minneapolis
Hastings
Marshfield
Redfield
Watertown
Montevideo
Eau Claire
Wisconsin Rapids
Appleton
Minnesota
Northfield
Black River Falls
Manitowoc
Lake Winnebago
Marshall
Red Wing
Petenwell Lake
Oshkosh
Big Sioux
Redwood Falls
St Peter
Faribault
Winona
Tomah
Miller
Huron
Brookings
New Ulm
Mankato
Owatonna
Rochester
Sparta
La Crosse
Fond du Lac
Sheboygan
Madison
Windom
Austin
Pipestone
Fairmont
Richland Center
Portage
Chamberlain
Mitchell
Luverne
Worthington
Albert Lea
Decorah
Beaver Dam
West Bend
Lake Francis Case
Estherville
Mason City
Wisconsin
Watertown
Milwaukee
Sioux Falls
Sioux Center
Algona
Des Moines
Clear Lake
Charles City
Prairie du Chien
Janesville
Spencer
Waverly
Yankton
Vermillion
Cherokee
Storm Lake
Webster City
Cedar Falls
Independence
Monroe
Beloit
Le Mars
Fort Dodge
Waterloo
Dubuque
Freeport
Missouri
Sioux City
Rockford
Elgin
O'Neill
IOWA
Cedar
Anamosa
Maquoketa
Cedar Rapids
Clinton
Dixon
De Kalb
Carroll
Sterling
Aurora
Wayne
Boone
Ames
Marshalltown
Denison
Perry
Grinnell
Davenport
Bettendorf
Ottawa
Joliet
Norfolk
West Point
Iowa City
Des Moines
Newton
Muscatine
Rock Island
Kewanee
Streator
Blair
Fremont
Council Bluffs
Columbus
Omaha
Atlantic
Indianola
Oskaloosa
Washington
Pontiac
Galesburg
Wahoo
Red Oak
Creston
Central City
Platte
Ottumwa
Mount Pleasant
Burlington
Peoria
Bloomington
Grand Island
Lincoln
Shenandoah
Macomb
Aurora
York
Clarinda
Lamoni
Keokuk
ILLINOIS
Nebraska City
Maryville
Lincoln
Hastings
Kirksville
Beatrice
Auburn
Springfield
Holdrege
Quincy
Decatur
Illinois
Superior
Fairbury
Falls City
Trenton
Hiawatha
Chillicothe
Hannibal
Jacksonville
Belleville
St Joseph
Marysville
Atchison
Macon
Taylorville
Moberly
Mississippi
Concordia
Litchfield
Effingham
Missouri
Marshall
Mexico
Vandalia
Leavenworth
Manhattan
Kansas City
Boonville
Columbia
St Charles
St Louis
Abilene
Junction City
Topeka
Independence
Fulton
East St Louis
Hays
Lawrence
Jefferson City
Washington
Salina
Warrensburg
Sedalia
Belleville
Centralia
Ottawa
Harrisonville
MISSOURI
Festus
Mount Vernon
Eldon
Sullivan
Emporia
Osage
Clinton
Lake of the Ozarks
Chester
West Frankfort
Great Bend
McPherson
Rolla
Hutchinson
Newton
Iola
Fort Scott
Nevada
Salem
Perryville
Carbondale
El Dorado
Bolivar
Lebanon
Black
Mound City
Pratt
Wichita
Augusta
Chanute
Pittsburg
Ozark Plateau
Cape Girardeau
Parsons
Springfield
Winfield
Joplin
Carthage
Mountain Grove
Sikeston
Medicine Lodge
Wellington
Independence
Coffeyville
Monett
Dexter
Poplar Bluff
Union City
Arkansas City
Miami
Neosho
West Plains
Kennett
D
95°
E
90°
0
100
200
300 KILOMETRES

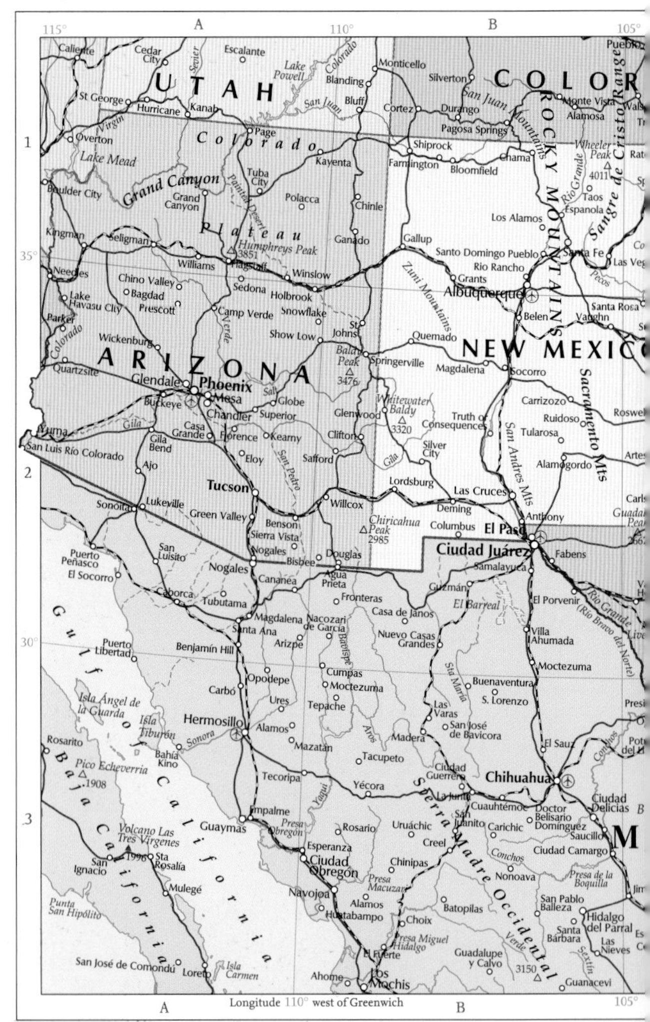

1 : 11 000 000   MILES 0   100

Longitude 110° west of Greenwich

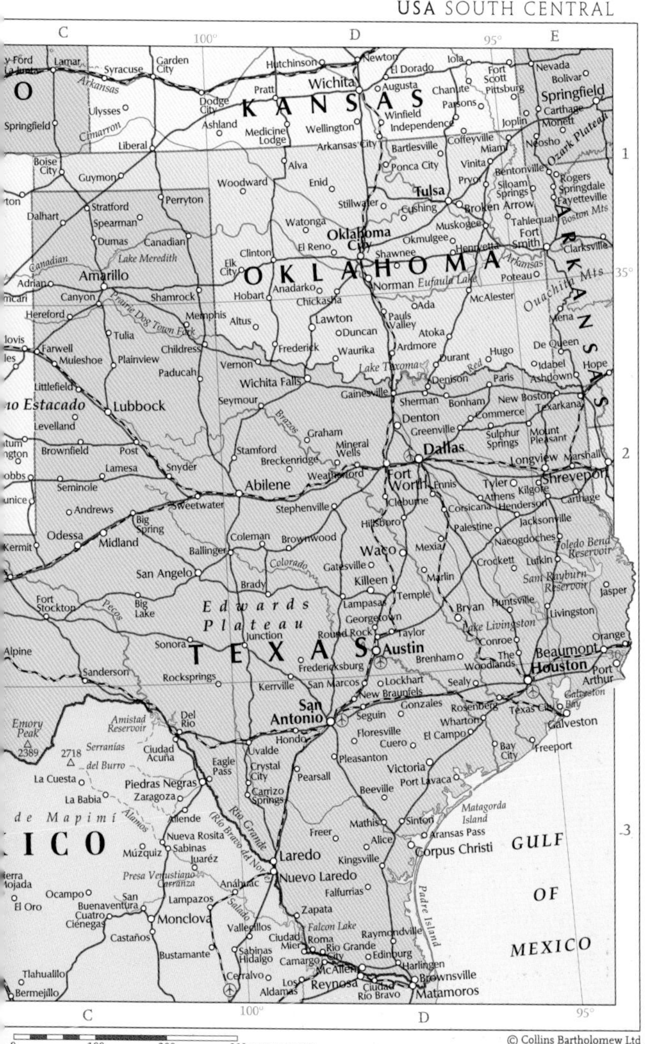

0   100   200   300 KILOMETRES

© Collins Bartholomew Ltd

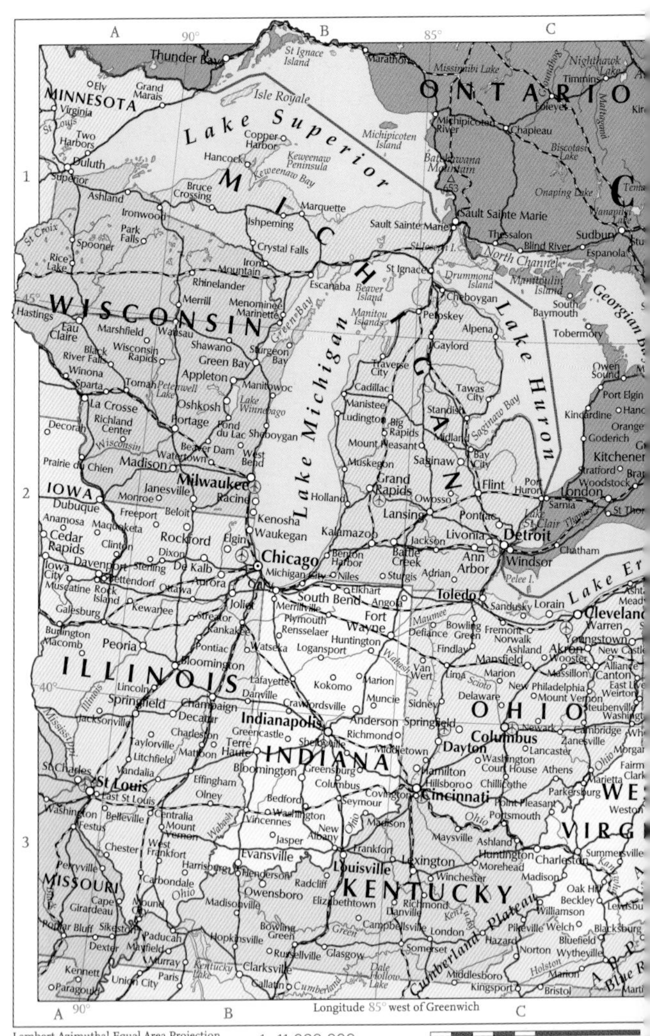

Lambert Azimuthal Equal Area Projection   1 : 11 000 000   MILES 0   100   20

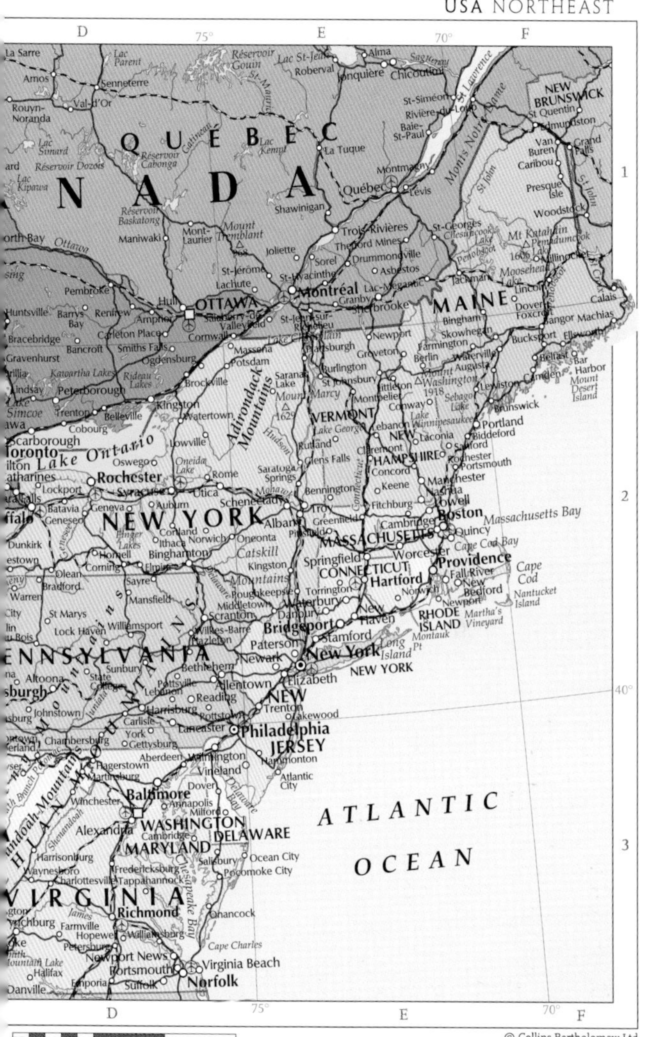
D
75°
E
70°
F
1
2
3
40°
La Sarre
Amos
Senneterre
Rouyn-Noranda
Val-d'Or
Lac Parent
Réservoir Gouin
Lac St-Jean
Roberval
Jonquière
Alma
Chicoutimi
Saguenay
St Lawrence
St-Siméon
Rivière-du-Loup
Baie-St-Paul
Monts Notre Dame
NEW BRUNSWICK
St Quentin
Edmundston
Grand Falls
Van Buren
Caribou
Presque Isle
Woodstock
St John
QUÉBEC
CANADA
Lac Simard
Réservoir Dozois
Lac Kipawa
Réservoir Cabonga
Gatineau
Lac Kempt
La Tuque
Montmagny
Québec
Lévis
Shawinigan
Réservoir Baskatong
Maniwaki
Mont-Laurier
Mount Tremblant
968
Joliette
Trois-Rivières
Thetford Mines
Drummondville
Sorel
Asbestos
St-Georges
Chesuncook Lake
Penobscot
Mt Katahdin
1606
Pemadumcook Lake
Millinocket
Moosehead Lake
Jackman
Lincoln
Calais
St-Jérôme
Lachute
St-Hyacinthe
Montréal
Lac-Mégantic
Granby
Sherbrooke
MAINE
Dover-Foxcroft
Bangor
Machias
Ottawa
Pembroke
Hull
OTTAWA
Huntsville
Barrys Bay
Renfrew
Arnprior
Salaberry-de-Valleyfield
St-Jean-sur-Richelieu
Bingham
Skowhegan
Bucksport
Ellsworth
Bracebridge
Carleton Place
Cornwall
Newport
Farmington
Bancroft
Smiths Falls
Massena
Plattsburgh
Groveton
Berlin
Waterville
Belfast
Bar Harbor
Gravenhurst
Ogdensburg
Potsdam
Burlington
Augusta
Camden
Mount Desert Island
Kawartha Lakes
Rideau Lakes
Brockville
Saranac Lake
St Johnsbury
Mount Washington
1918
Lewiston
Peterborough
Adirondack Mountains
Mount Marcy
1629
Montpelier
Littleton
Sebago Lake
Brunswick
Lake Simcoe
Trenton
Belleville
Kingston
Watertown
VERMONT
Conway
Lake Winnipesaukee
Portland
Cobourg
Lake George
Lebanon
NEW HAMPSHIRE
Laconia
Biddeford
Scarborough
Toronto
Lake Ontario
Lowville
Hudson
Rutland
Claremont
Sanford
Rochester
Portsmouth
Oswego
Oneida Lake
Glens Falls
Connecticut
Concord
Rochester
Rome
Saratoga Springs
Manchester
Lockport
Syracuse
Utica
Mohawk
Bennington
Keene
Nashua
Lowell
Batavia
Geneva
Auburn
Schenectady
Troy
Fitchburg
Boston
Massachusetts Bay
Geneseo
NEW YORK
Albany
Greenfield
Cambridge
Quincy
Dunkirk
Finger Lakes
Cortland
Ithaca
Norwich
Oneonta
Pittsfield
MASSACHUSETTS
Cape Cod Bay
Hornell
Binghamton
Catskill
Worcester
Providence
Cape Cod
Corning
Elmira
Kingston
Springfield
CONNECTICUT
Fall River
Olean
Bradford
Sayre
Mountains
Hartford
New Bedford
Nantucket Island
Warren
Mansfield
Poughkeepsie
Torrington
Waterbury
Norwich
Newport
St Marys
Middletown
Danbury
New Haven
RHODE ISLAND
Martha's Vineyard
Lock Haven
Williamsport
Scranton
Wilkes-Barre
Bridgeport
Stamford
Montauk Pt
Hazleton
Paterson
Long Island
PENNSYLVANIA
Newark
New York
Sunbury
Bethlehem
Elizabeth
NEW YORK
Altoona
State College
Pottsville
Allentown
Lebanon
Reading
NEW
Johnstown
Harrisburg
Pottstown
Trenton
Lakewood
Carlisle
York
Lancaster
Philadelphia
Chambersburg
Gettysburg
JERSEY
Aberdeen
Wilmington
Hammonton
Hagerstown
Martinsburg
Vineland
Atlantic City
Dover
Delaware Bay
Baltimore
Winchester
Annapolis
Milford
ATLANTIC
Alexandria
WASHINGTON
Cambridge
DELAWARE
MARYLAND
Harrisonburg
Salisbury
Ocean City
OCEAN
Waynesboro
Fredericksburg
Pocomoke City
Charlottesville
Tappahannock
Chesapeake Bay
VIRGINIA
Richmond
Onancock
Lynchburg
James
Farmville
Hopewell
Williamsburg
Petersburg
Cape Charles
Newport News
Virginia Beach
Halifax
Portsmouth
Norfolk
Danville
Emporia
Suffolk
0
100
200
300 KILOMETRES

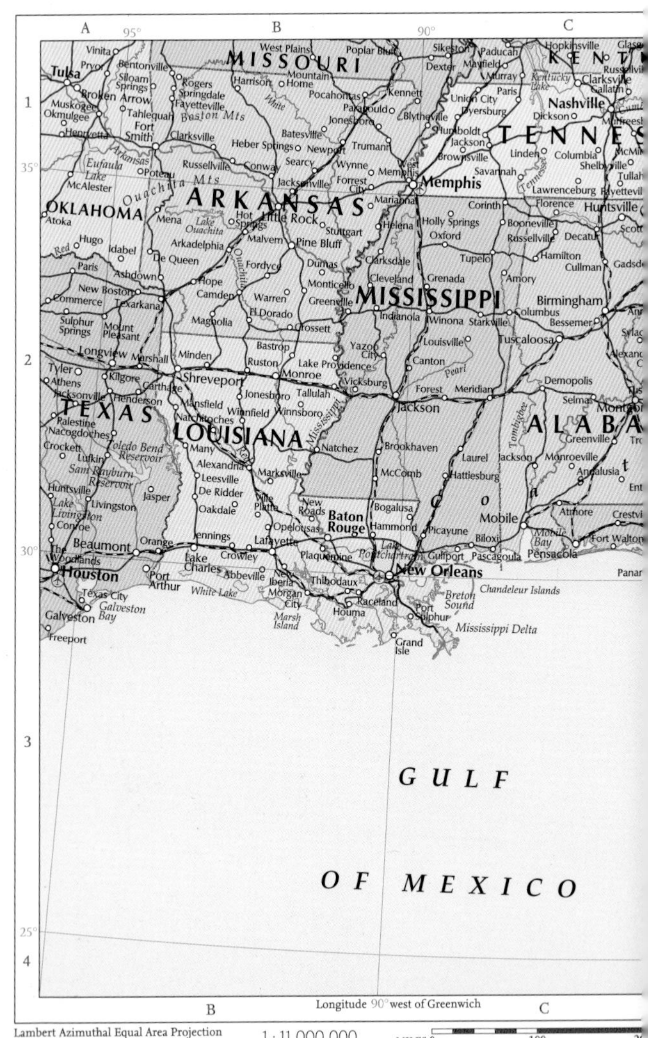

A   95°   B   90°   C

MISSOURI

KENT

Vinita
Tulsa   Pryor
Bentonville
Siloam Springs   Rogers   Fayetteville
Muskogee   Fort Smith
Okmulgee   Tahlequah
Henryetta

West Plains   Poplar Bluff
Harrison   Mountain Home
Pocahontas   Dexter   Sikeston   Paducah
Springdale   White   Paragould   Kennett   Union City   Paris   Dyersburg
Boston Mts.   Jonesboro   Blytheville
Clarksville   Batesville   Newport   Trumann   Humboldt   Jackson
Russellville   Searcy   Wynne   Forrest City   Brownsville
Heber Springs   Jacksonville   Conway   Memphis   Savannah

Hopkinsville
Clarksville   Gallatin
Dickson   **Nashville**

TENNE

Russellv
Murfrees
Columbia   McMi
Shelbyville   Tullah
Lawrenceburg   Fayetteville

OKLAHOMA

Atoka
Eufaula Lake
McAlester

ARKANSAS

Ouachita Mts.
Hot Springs   Little Rock
Lake Ouachita
Mena   Malvern   Stuttgart
Arkadelphia   Pine Bluff
De Queen

OKLAHOMA

Hugo   Idabel
Paris
New Boston
Commerce
Sulphur Springs   Mount Pleasant

Red
Ashdown
Hope
Camden
Magnolia
El Dorado

Fordyce
Warren
Monticello
Dumas
Rosston
Greenville

Clarksdale
Cleveland
Grenada

Corinth
Holly Springs
Oxford
Booneville
Tupelo
Amory

Florence   Huntsville
Decatur
Hamilton
Cullman
Birmingham
Columbus   Bessemer
Starkville   Tuscaloosa

Rossville
Decatur
Scott
Gadsde

Sylac

TEXAS

Tyler
Athens   Kilgore
Henderson
Palestine
Nacogdoches
Crockett
Lufkin   Toledo Bend Reservoir
Huntsville
Sam Rayburn Reservoir

Longview   Marshall
Minden
Carthage
Mansfield   Winnfield
Natchitoches
Many
Jasper
Livingston

Shreveport
LOUISIANA
Alexandria
Leesville
De Ridder
Oakdale

Ruston   Monroe
Jonesboro
Tallulah
Vicksburg
MISSISSIPPI
Indianola   Winona
Louisville
Yazoo City
Canton
Jackson
Forest   Meridian
Brookhaven

Demopolis
Selma   Monto
ALABA
t   Tr
Monroeville
Andalusia

Ent

Lake Livingston
Conroe
Beaumont
The Woodlands
Houston
Texas City
Galveston
Galveston Bay
Freeport

Orange
Port Arthur
White Lake

Jennings
Lake Charles
Crowley
Abbeville
New Iberia
Morgan City
Marsh Island

Opelousas
Lafayette
Baton Rouge
Plaquemine
Thibodaux
Raceland
Houma
Grand Isle

Natchez
Bogalusa
Hammond
Picayune
Pontchartrain
New Orleans
Port Sulphur
Mississippi Delta

Laurel
Hattiesburg
Jackson
Mobile Bay
Biloxi
Gulfport
Pascagoula
Mobile
Pensacola

Monroeville
Atmore
Crestvi
Fort Walton
Panar

Bretons Sound
Chandeleur Islands

G U L F

O F M E X I C O

25°

B   Longitude 90° west of Greenwich   C

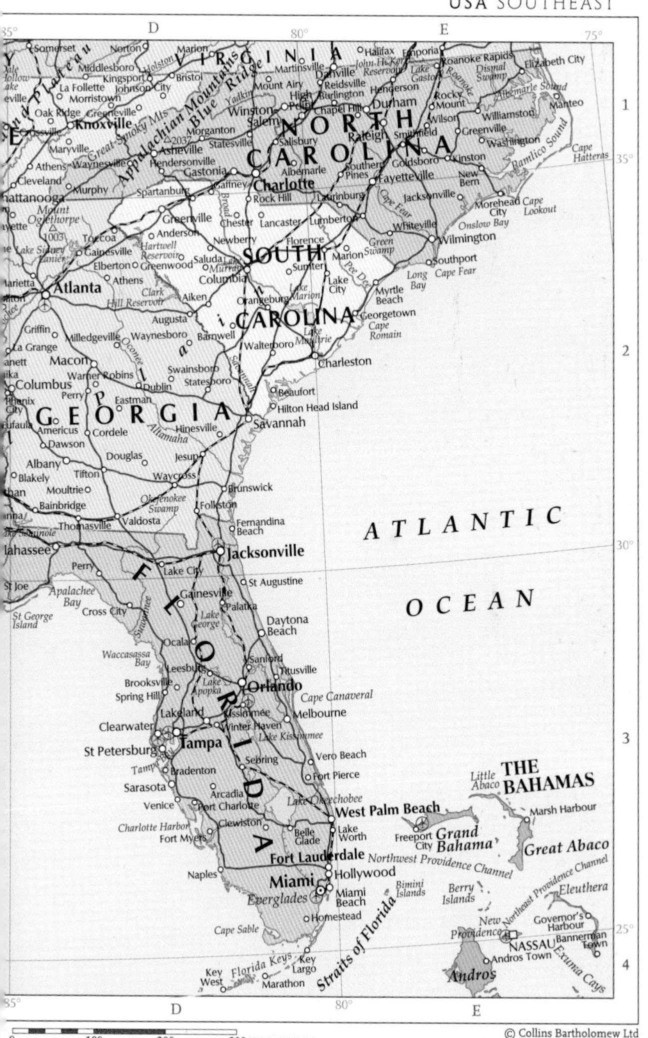

VIRGINIA
NORTH CAROLINA
SOUTH CAROLINA
GEORGIA
FLORIDA
ATLANTIC
OCEAN
THE BAHAMAS
Knoxville
Charlotte
Atlanta
Jacksonville
Orlando
Tampa
Miami
Savannah
Charleston
Durham
Raleigh
Fayetteville
Wilmington
Columbia
Augusta
Macon
Columbus
Tallahassee
Gainesville
Daytona Beach
St Petersburg
West Palm Beach
Fort Lauderdale
Hollywood
Miami Beach
Key West
Key Largo
Marathon
Grand Bahama
Great Abaco
Eleuthera
Andros
NASSAU
Straits of Florida
Northwest Providence Channel
Cape Hatteras
Cape Canaveral
Everglades
Florida Keys
Lake Okeechobee
300 KILOMETRES

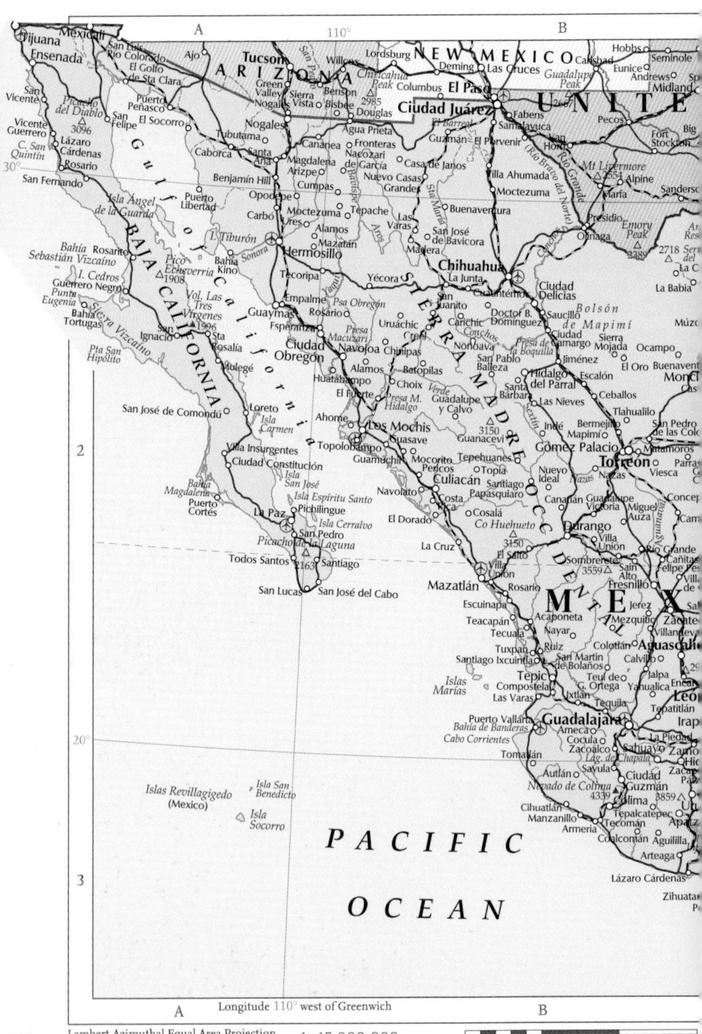

A 110° B

NEW MEXICO

Tijuana Mexicali | San Luis Río Colorado | Ajo | Tucson | Lordsburg | Deming | Las Cruces | Hobbs | Seminole
Ensenada | El Golfo de Sta Clara | Sierra Vista | Benson | Willcox | Chiricahua | Columbus | El Paso | Fabens | Guadalupe Peak | Carlsbad | Eunice | Andrews | Seminole
San Vicente | Puerto Peñasco | Green Valley | 2995 | | Ciudad Juárez | | Samalayuca | Pecos | | Midland

ARIZONA
UNITE

Vicente Guerrero | I. San Felipe | Nogales | Magdalena de Kino | Agua Prieta | Guzmán | El Porvenir | | Mt Livermore | St Pton
San Quintín | Cárdenas | Rosario | San Fernando | Benjamin Hill | Arizpe | Casa de Janos | Nuevo Casas Grandes | Villa Ahumada | Moctezuma | Marfa | Alpine | Sanderso

Isla Ángel de la Guarda | Puerto Libertad | Tiburón | Moctezuma | Tepache | San José de Bavícora | Buenaventura | Ojinaga | Presidio | Emory Peak | Ar Re

Bahía Rosario Sebastián Vizcaíno | Guerrero Negro | Punta Eugenia | Bahía Tortugas | Pta Eugenia | Pta San Hipólito

BAJA CALIFORNIA
Gulf of California

Picos Echeverría 1908 | Vol. Las Tres Vírgenes | Bahía Kino | Hermosillo | Ures | Mazatán | Tecoripa | Yécora | Chihuahua | La Junta | Cuauhtémoc | Ciudad Delicias | Bolsón de Mapimí | La Babia | Múz

Santa Rosalía | Mulegé | Guaymas | Empalme | Rosario | Cd. Obregón | Navojoa | Chínipas | Creel | San Juanito | Carichí | Naboa | Hidalgo del Parral | Santa Bárbara | Las Nieves | El Oro Buenavent | Monc

2
San José de Comondú | Loreto | Isla del Carmen | Huatabampo | Álamos | Batopilas | Guadalupe y Calvo | 3150 | Inde | Tepehuanes | Mapimí | Gómez Palacio | Torreón | Matamoros | Parra

Isla Magdalena | Ciudad Constitución | Isla Santa Margarita | Puerto Cortés | La Paz | Isla San José | Isla Espíritu Santo | Isla San Pedro | Pichilingue | Ahome | Los Mochis | Guasave | Guamúchil | Mocorito | Tepehuanes | Peñoles | Topia | Nuevo Ideal | Canatlán | Durango | Guadalupe Victoria | Villa Unión | Río Grande | Viesca | Canitas

Pta Conejo | Bahía Magdalena | Picacho La Laguna | San Cerralvo | El Dorado | Navolato | Culiacán | Costa Rica | Cosalá | Co Huehueto 3150 | Sombrerete | Alto Felipe | Fresnillo

San José del Cabo | Todos Santos | Santiago | San Lucas | La Cruz | Rosario | Villa Unión | Mazatlán

MEX

Escuinapa | Acaponeta | Mezquital | Zacate | Jerez | Villanev | Aguascali

Islas Marías | Teacapán | Nayar | Tecuala | Ruiz | San Martín de Bolaños | Colotlán | Calvillo | Jalpa | León

Islas Revillagigedo (Mexico) | Isla San Benedicto | Tuxpan | Santiago Ixcuintla | Tepic | Teúl de Ortega | Yahualica | Encar | Irap

Isla Socorro | Compostela | Las Varas | Puerto Vallarta | Bahía de Banderas | Cabo Corrientes | Ameca | Cocula | Zacoalco | Lag. de Chapala | Guadalajara | Santiago | La Piedad | Zamo

20°
Tomatlán | Autlán | Sayula | Ciudad Guzmán | Colima 3859 | Apaze

PACIFIC
Nevado de Colima 4339 | Cihuatlán | Manzanillo | Tecomán | Coalcomán | Aguililla

OCEAN
Armería | Arteaga | Lázaro Cárdenas | Zihua

144 Lambert Azimuthal Equal Area Projection

A Longitude 110° west of Greenwich B

1 : 15 000 000   MILES 0   100   200   30

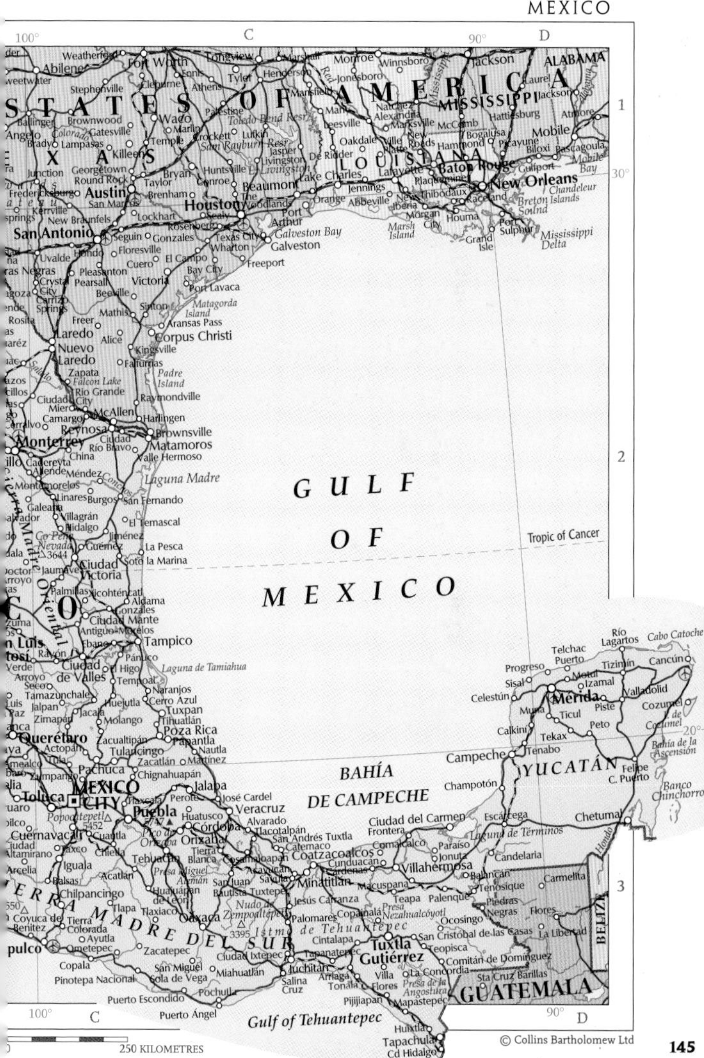

UNITED STATES OF AMERICA

TEXAS

LOUISIANA

MISSISSIPPI

ALABAMA

GULF

OF

MEXICO

Tropic of Cancer

BAHÍA
DE CAMPECHE

YUCATÁN

TIERRA MADRE DEL SUR

GUATEMALA

BELIZE

Gulf of Tehuantepec

© Collins Bartholomew Ltd

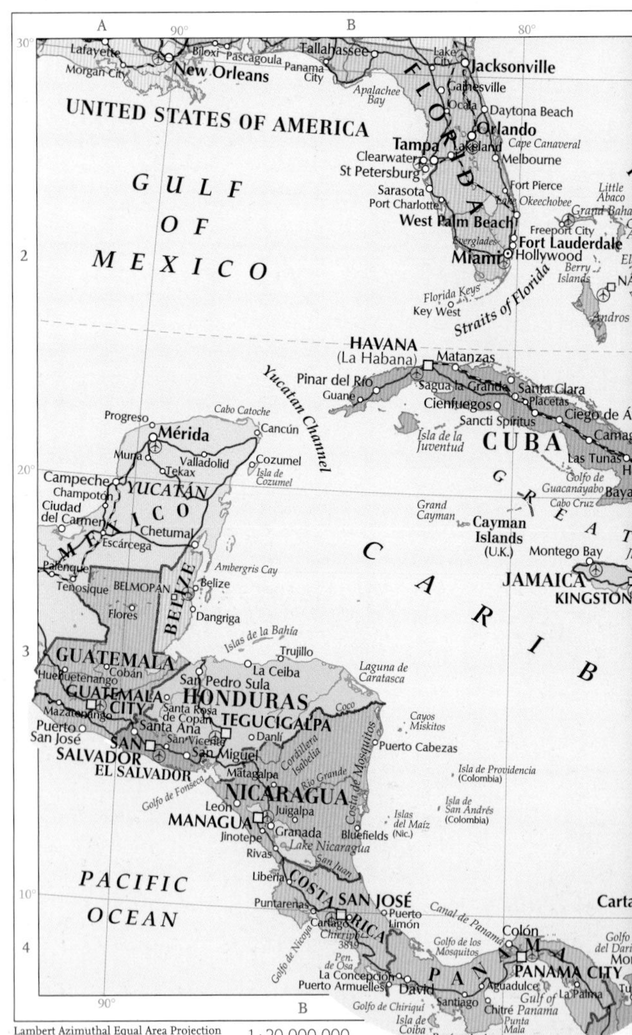

A

90°

B

80°

30°

Lafayette
Morgan City
New Orleans
Biloxi Pascagoula
Panama
City
Tallahassee
Lake
City
Jacksonville
Gainesville

UNITED STATES OF AMERICA

Apalachee
Bay
Ocala
Daytona Beach

Orlando
Melbourne
Cape Canaveral

Tampa
Lakeland

Clearwater
St Petersburg
Sarasota
Port Charlotte
Fort Pierce
Lake
Okeechobee

West Palm Beach
Fort Lauderdale
Hollywood

Little
Abaco
Grand Baha

Freeport City

GULF

OF

MEXICO

Miami

Everglades

Berry
Islands

El

Florida Keys
Key West

Andros

Straits of Florida

HAVANA
(La Habana)
Matanzas

Pinar del Río
Guane

Sagua la Grande
Santa Clara
Placetas

Cienfuegos
Sancti Spíritus

Ciego de Á

Camag

Progreso
Cabo Catoche

Mérida
Cancún

Isla de la
Juventud

CUBA

GREAT

Las Tunas

Ho

Campeche
Muna
Valladolid
Tekax

Golfo de
Guacanayabo
Baya

Champotón
Ciudad
del Carmen

YUCATÁN

Cozumel
Isla de
Cozumel

Grand
Cayman

Cruz

CARIB

Escárcega

Chetumal

Cayman
Islands
(U.K.)

Montego Bay

JAMAICA
KINGSTON

Palenque
Tenosique

BELMOPAN

Ambergris Cay

Belize

Flores
Dangriga

Islas de la Bahía

Trujillo

GUATEMALA

Cobán

La Ceiba

Laguna de
Caratasca

Huehuetenango

San Pedro Sula

GUATEMALA
CITY

Santa Rosa
de Copán

HONDURAS

TEGUCIGALPA

Cayos
Miskitos

Mazatenango

Santa Ana

Danlí

Puerto
San José

San Vicente

San Miguel

Puerto Cabezas

SAN
SALVADOR

EL SALVADOR

Matagalpa

Isla de Providencia
(Colombia)

Cordillera
Isabelia

Golfo de Fonseca

NICARAGUA

Costa de Mosquitos

León

Juigalpa

Isla de
San Andrés
(Colombia)

MANAGUA

Granada
Bluefields

Jinotepe
Rivas

Islas
del Maíz
(Nic.)

Lake Nicaragua

PACIFIC

Liberia

Río San Juan

COSTA

Canal de Panamá

Colón

Carta

OCEAN

Puntarenas

SAN JOSÉ
RICA
Puerto
Limón

Golfo de los
Mosquitos

Golfo
del Darié

PAN

PANAMA CITY

Chirripó
3810

Pen. de
Osa

La Concepción

David

Santiago

Aguadulce

La Patria

Puerto Armuelles

Chitré
Panamá

Golfo de Nicoya

Golfo de
Chiriquí

Isla de
Coiba

Peninsula de
Azuero

Punta
Mala

10°

4

90°

B

80°

Lambert Azimuthal Equal Area Projection   1 : 20 000 000

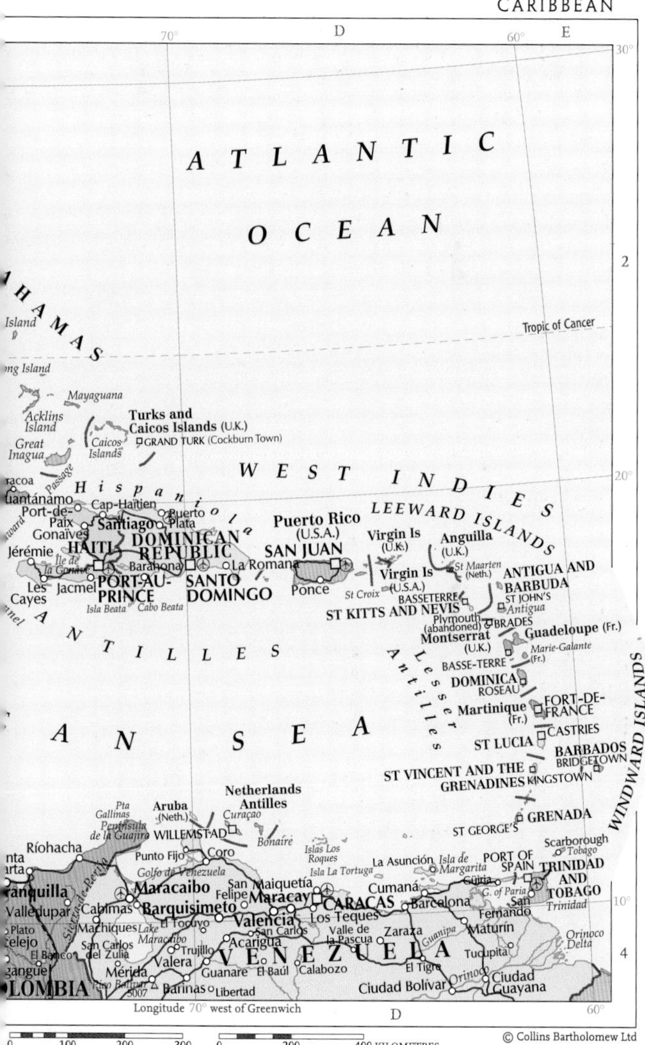

A T L A N T I C

O C E A N

Tropic of Cancer

W E S T   I N D I E S

Turks and Caicos Islands (U.K.)
○GRAND TURK (Cockburn Town)

LEEWARD ISLANDS

Mayaguana
Acklins Island
Caicos Islands
Great Inagua

Puerto Rico (U.S.A.)

Virgin Is (U.K.)
Virgin Is (U.S.A.)

Anguilla (U.K.)
St Maarten (Neth.)

ANTIGUA AND BARBUDA
ST JOHN'S Antigua

BASSETERRE
ST KITTS AND NEVIS
Montserrat (abandoned) ○BRADES (U.K.)

Guadeloupe (Fr.)
Marie-Galante (Fr.)

BASSE-TERRE
DOMINICA
ROSEAU

Martinique (Fr.)
FORT-DE-FRANCE

CASTRIES
ST LUCIA

BARBADOS
BRIDGETOWN

ST VINCENT AND THE GRENADINES KINGSTOWN

ST GEORGE'S **GRENADA**

H i s p a n i o l a

Guantánamo
Cap-Haïtien
Port-de-Paix ○Santiago ○Puerto Plata
Gonaïves
Jérémie **HAÏTI** **DOMINICAN REPUBLIC**
Les ○La Romana
Cayes Jacmel **PORT-AU-PRINCE** **SANTO DOMINGO**
Isla Beata Cabo Beata
Ile de la Gonâve

SAN JUAN
Ponce St Croix (U.S.A.)

G. of Paria

L e s s e r   A n t i l l e s

C A R I B B E A N   S E A

G R E A T E R   A N T I L L E S

Netherlands Antilles (Neth.)
Curaçao
Aruba (Neth.)
Bonaire

WINDWARD ISLANDS

Scarborough
○Tobago
TRINIDAD AND TOBAGO
PORT OF SPAIN
Trinidad

Pta Gallinas
Península de la Guajira

Ríohacha
Punta Fijo○ Coro
Islas Los Roques
Isla La Tortuga
La Asunción Isla de Margarita
○Cumaná
Güiria

○anguilla
alledupar

El Toroyo
G. de Venezuela
Maracaibo
Cabimas
Maiquetía
CARACAS
Barcelona
Maturín
Orinoco Delta

Machiques Lake Maracaibo
San Felipe
Barquisimeto
Valencia
Maracay
Los Teques
San Fernando
Zaraza

El Banco de Zulia
San Carlos del Zulia
Valera
Acarigua
San Carlos
Valle de la Pascua
El Tigre
Tucupita

○elejo
Trujillo○
Mérida
○5007
Guanare El Baúl
Calabozo
Zaraza
Ciudad Guayana

LOMBIA
Barinas
Libertad
VENEZUELA
Ciudad Bolívar
Orinoco

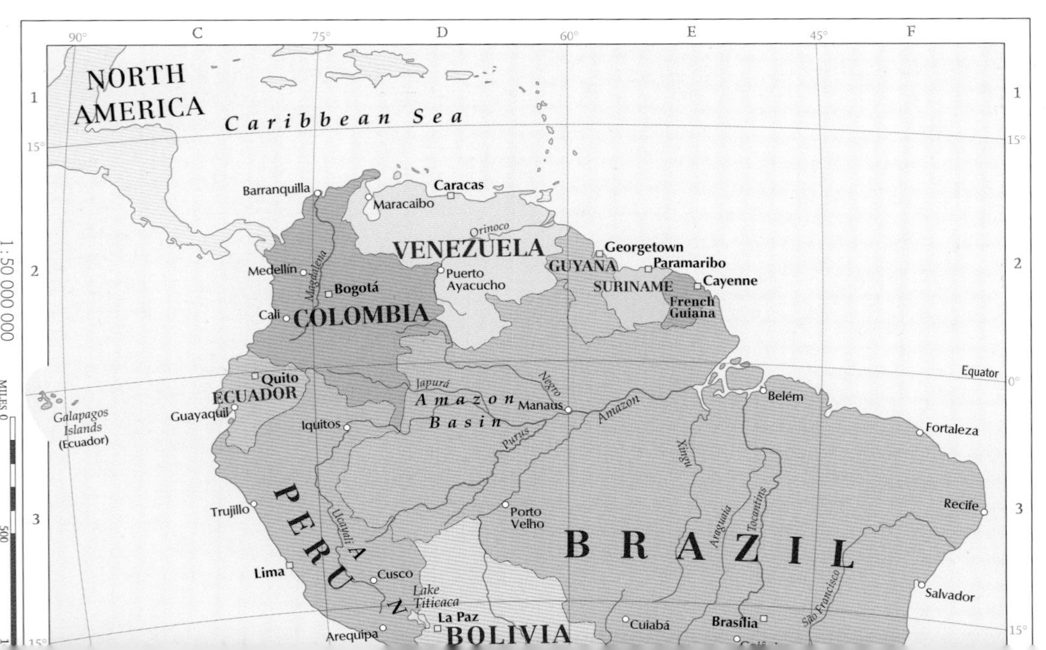
NORTH AMERICA
Caribbean Sea
Galapagos Islands (Ecuador)
Barranquilla
Maracaibo
Caracas
Orinoco
VENEZUELA
Puerto Ayacucho
Georgetown
GUYANA
Paramaribo
SURINAME
Cayenne
French Guiana
Medellín
Magdalena
Bogotá
Cali
COLOMBIA
Quito
ECUADOR
Guayaquil
Iquitos
Japurá
Negro
Amazon Basin
Manaus
Amazon
Purus
Equator
Belém
Fortaleza
Xingu
Trujillo
PERU
Ucayali
Porto Velho
BRAZIL
Araguaia
Tocantins
Recife
Lima
Cusco
Lake Titicaca
La Paz
BOLIVIA
Arequipa
Cuiabá
Brasília
São Francisco
Salvador
C
D
E
F
1
2
3
90°
75°
60°
45°
15°
0°

1 : 50 000 000

MILES 0 500 1

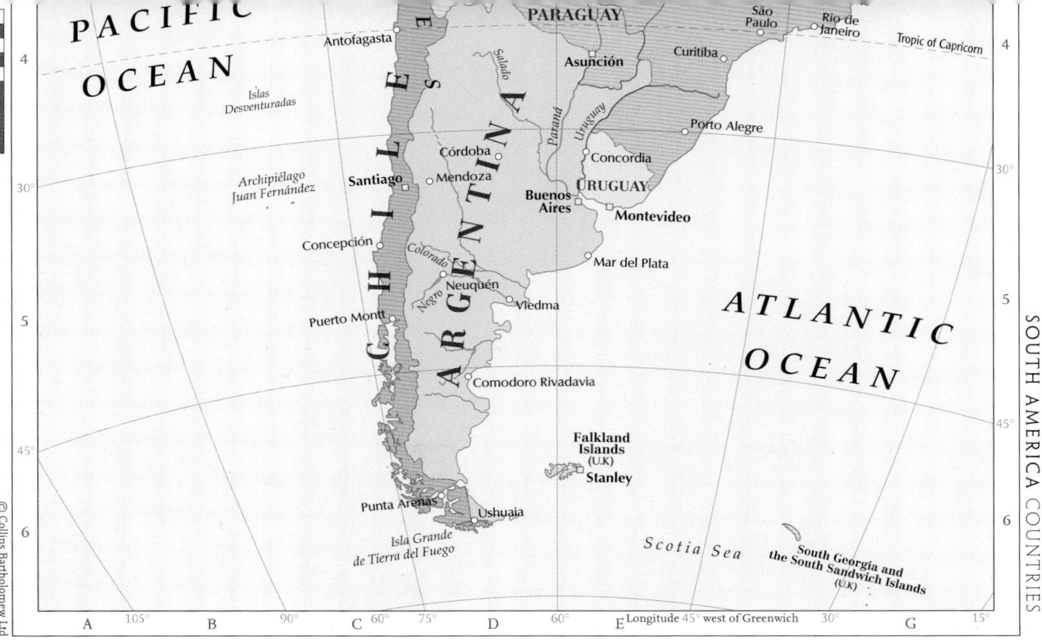

ATLANTIC OCEAN

PACIFIC OCEAN

Scotia Sea

Tropic of Capricorn

Rio de Janeiro

São Paulo

Curitiba

Porto Alegre

PARAGUAY

Asunción

Concordia

URUGUAY

Montevideo

Mar del Plata

Buenos Aires

ARGENTINA

Salado

Córdoba

Mendoza

Santiago

Neuquén

Viedma

Comodoro Rivadavia

CHILE

Concepción

Puerto Montt

Punta Arenas

Ushuaia

Isla Grande de Tierra del Fuego

Falkland Islands (U.K.)

Stanley

South Georgia and the South Sandwich Islands (U.K.)

Antofagasta

Islas Desventuradas

Archipiélago Juan Fernández

E Longitude 45° west of Greenwich

Paraná

Uruguay

Colorado

Negro

E Longitude 45° west of Greenwich

0   500   1000 KILOMETRES

© Collins Bartholomew Ltd

149

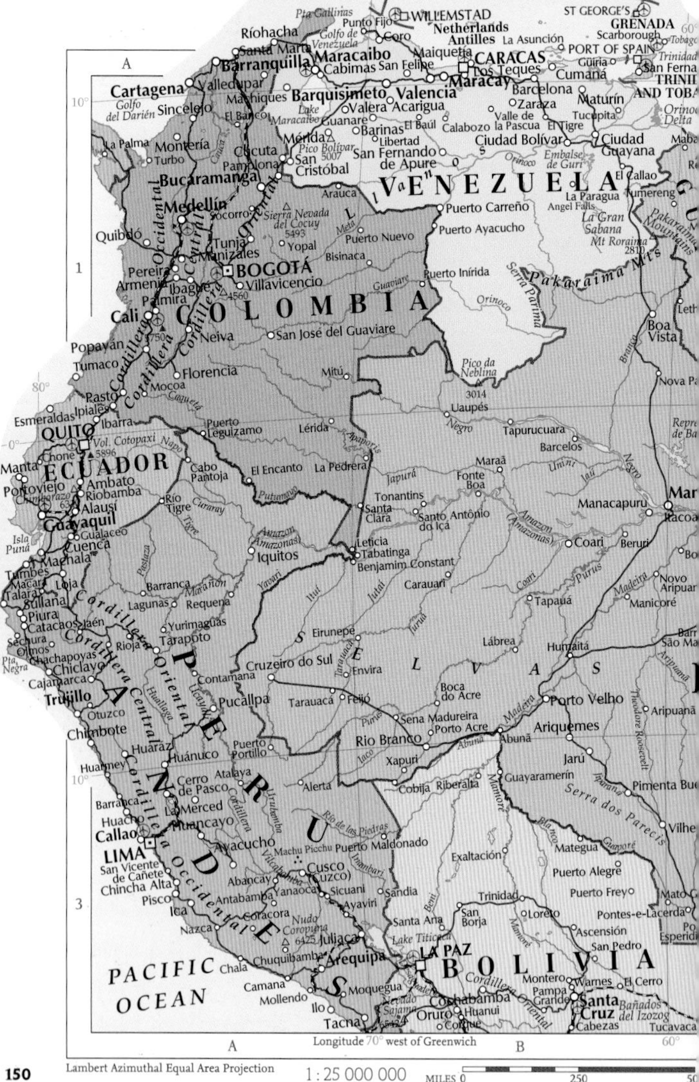

PACIFIC OCEAN

Lambert Azimuthal Equal Area Projection   1 : 25 000 000   MILES 0   250   500

Longitude 70° west of Greenwich

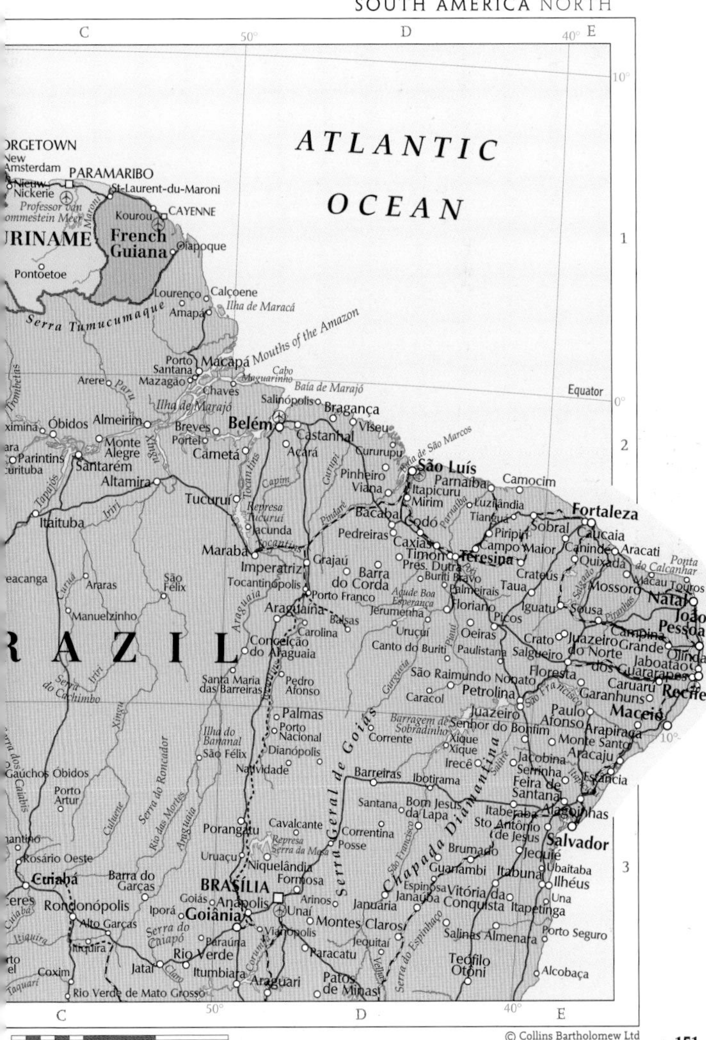

ATLANTIC

OCEAN

ORGETOWN
New
Amsterdam
Nieuw PARAMARIBO
Nickerie St-Laurent-du-Maroni
Professor van
ommessten Merr Kourou CAYENNE
URINAME French
Guiana
Pontoetoe Oiapoque

Serra Tumucumaque

Lourenço Calçoene
Amapá Ilha de Maracá

Porto Macapá Mouths of the Amazon
Santana
Mazagão Chaves Cabo
Norte
Ilha de Marajó Baía de Marajó Salinópolis
ximina Óbidos Almeirim Bragança
Breves Belém Castanhal Viseu
ara Monte Portel
Parintins Alegre Cametá Acará Pinheiro Gurupí Camocim
Curitiba Santarém Altamira Vidal São Luís
Tucuruí Parnaíba Teresina Itapicuru Tianguá Sobral Fortaleza
Itaituba Represa Mirim Piripiri Caucaia
Tucuruí Bacabal Codó Luziânia Caninde Aracati
Marabá Caxias Timon Campo Maior Quixadá Ponta
Araras Grajaú Pres. Dutra Burití Bravo Tauá do Calcanhar
Manuelzinho São Barra Franca Floriano Piçós Crateús Iguatu Mossoró Macau Touros
Félix do Corda Balsas Jerumenha Oeiras Sousa Natal
eacanga Imperatriz Porto Franco Uruçuí Picos Juazeiro Campina João
Tocantinópolis Paulistana do Norte Grande Pessoa
RAZIL Conceição Carolina Canto do Burití São Raimundo Nonato Salgueiro Jaboatão
do Araguaia Santa Maria Pedro Crato Floresta Caruaru Recife
das Barreiras Afonso Petrolina Garanhuns
Serra Araguaína Palmas Juazeiro Maceió
do Cachimbo Porto Senhor Monte Santo Arapiraca
Gaúchos Óbidos Nacional Corrente do Bonfim Paulo
Porto Dianópolis Jacobina Afonso Aracaju
Artur São Félix Natividade Barreiras Xique- Senhora Estância
Cuiabá Ibotirama Xique Irecê Feira de Itabaiana
eres Porangatu Santana Bom Jesus Santa Santo Salvador
Rosário Oeste Uruaçu Correntina da Lapa Brumado Antônio Jaguaripe
Porangatu Posse Itaberaba de Jesus
Coxim Cuiabá Represa Cavalcante Jequié Ubaitaba Ilhéus
Rondonópolis de Mara Formosa Itabuna Una
BRASÍLIA Januária Vitória da Itapetinga
el Alto Garças Goiás Anápolis Unaí Montes Claros Conquista
Jatai Iporá Goiânia Janaúba Porto Seguro
Rio Verde Paraúna Salinas Almenara
Coxim Itumbiara Jequitaí Teófilo Alcobaça
Rio Verde de Mato Grosso Araguari Patos Paracatu Otoni
de Minas

0   250   500   750 KILOMETRES

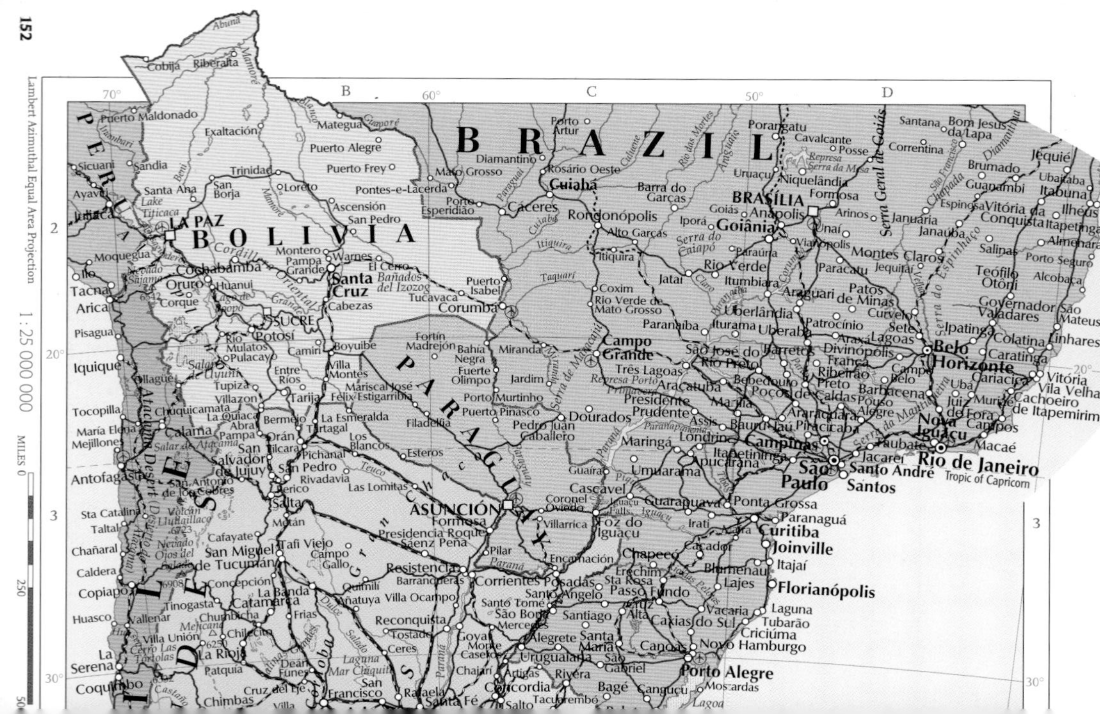

152 Lambert Azimuthal Equal Area Projection   1 : 25 000 000   MILES 0   250   500

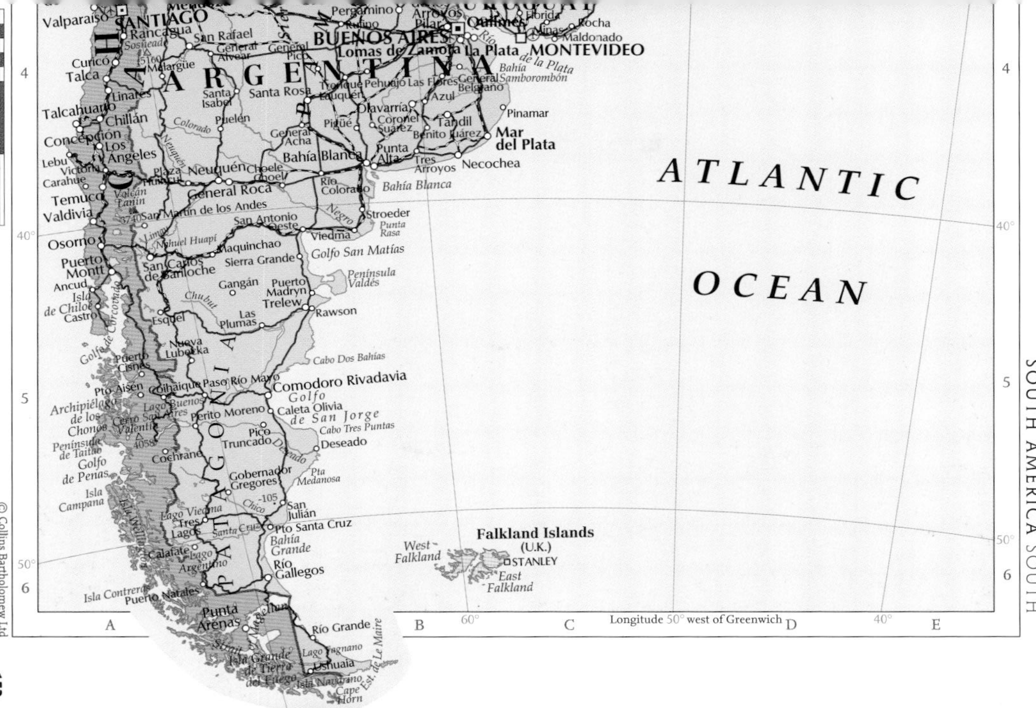

ATLANTIC
OCEAN
ARGENTINA
PATAGONIA
Falkland Islands
(U.K.)
STANLEY
East Falkland
West Falkland
SANTIAGO
Valparaíso
BUENOS AIRES
MONTEVIDEO
Lomas de Zamora
La Plata
Mar del Plata
Bahía Blanca
Neuquén
General Roca
Comodoro Rivadavia
Río Gallegos
Punta Arenas
Ushuaia
Río Grande
Puerto Montt
Osorno
Valdivia
Temuco
Concepción
Talcahuano
Talca
Chillán
Los Angeles
Viedma
Rawson
Trelew
Puerto Madryn
Esquel
Coihaique
Golfo San Matías
Golfo de San Jorge
Bahía Blanca
Isla de Chiloé
Archipiélago de los Chonos
Golfo de Penas
Isla Wellington
Isla Grande de Tierra del Fuego
Cape Horn
Santa Rosa
Tandil
Azul
Olavarría
Necochea
Pinamar
Tres Arroyos
Deseado
San Julián
Pto Santa Cruz
Puerto Natales
Calafate
Longitude 50° west of Greenwich
40°
50°
60°
A
B
C
D
E
4
5
6
0
250
500
750 KILOMETRES

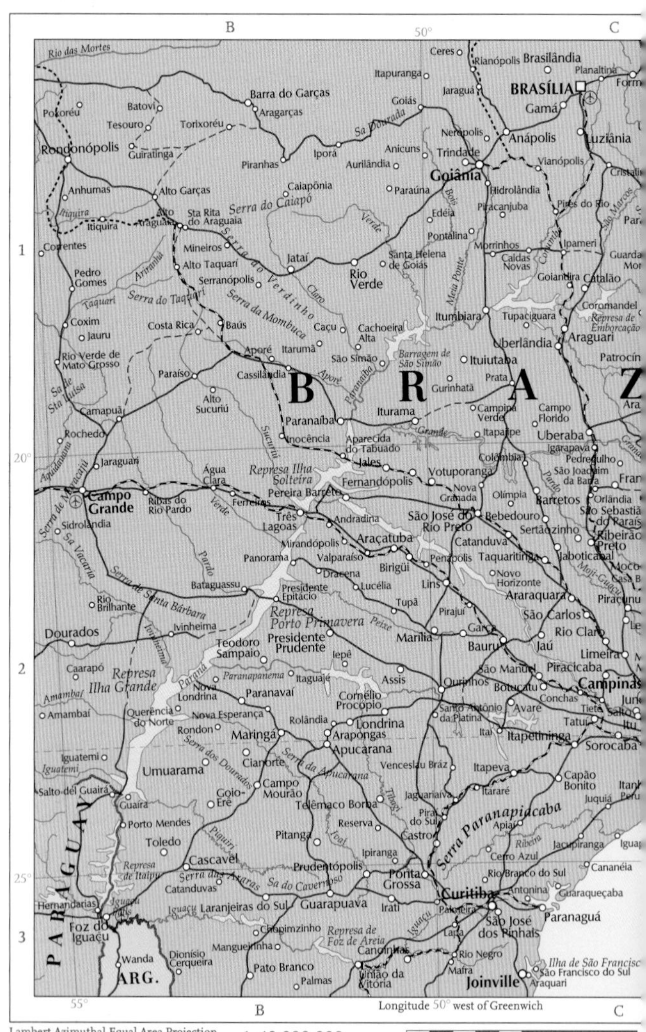

Lambert Azimuthal Equal Area Projection

1 : 10 000 000

MILES 0   100   200

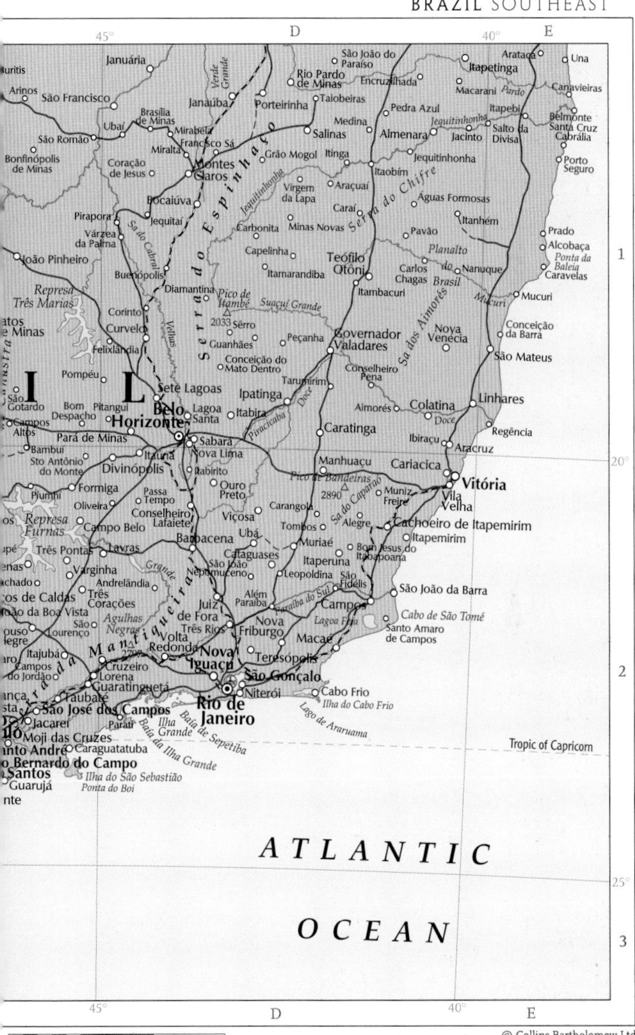

ATLANTIC

OCEAN

Tropic of Capricorn

0   100   200   300 KILOMETRES

© Collins Bartholomew Ltd

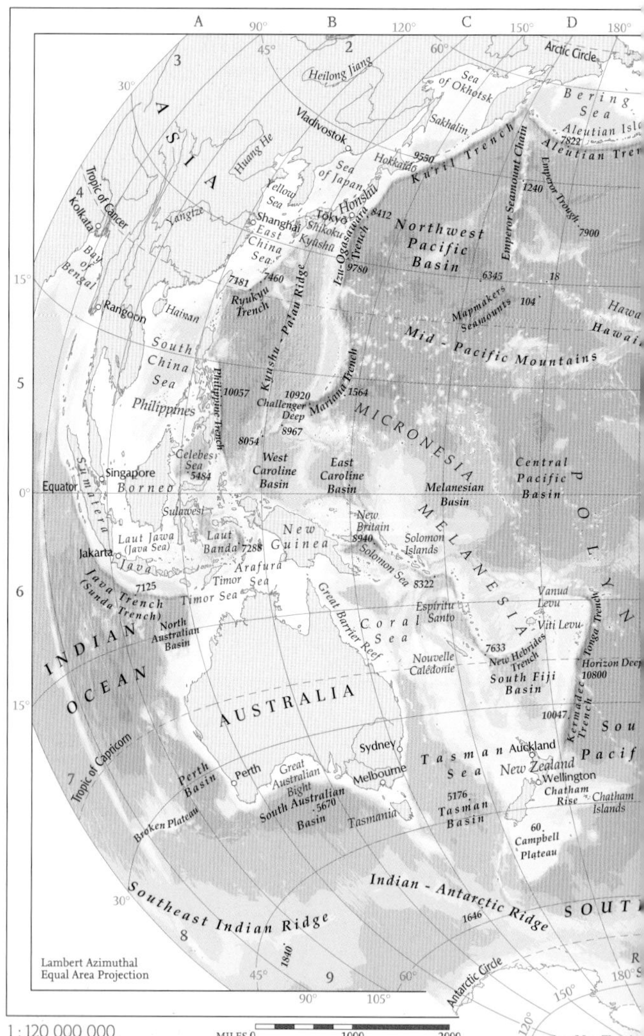

A 90° B 120° C 150° D 180°

3

Heilong Jiang

45°

30°

A S I A

Sea of Okhotsk

Arctic Circle

Vladivostok

Sakhalin

Bering Sea

Tropic of Cancer

Huang He

Sea of Japan

Hokkaido

Aleutian Isle

9550

7823

Aleutian Trenc

Kuril Trench

Emperor Seamount Chain

Yangtze

Yellow Sea

Honshu

Tokyo

8412

1240

Emperor Trench

7900

Shanghai

East China Sea

Shikoku

Kyushu

9780

Izu-Ogasawara Trench

Northwest Pacific Basin

6345

18

Kolkata

Bay of Bengal

7181

7460

Ryukyu Trench

Mapmakers Seamounts

104

Hawa

Rangoon

Hainan

Kyushu – Palau Ridge

Mid – Pacific Mountains

Hawai

South China Sea

10057

Philippine Trench

10920

Challenger Deep

8967

1564

Mariana Trench

MICRONESIA

Philippines

8054

West Caroline Basin

East Caroline Basin

Central Pacific Basin

P O L Y N

Celebes Sea

5454

Singapore

Borneo

Equator

Sulawesi

Melanesian Basin

M E L A N E S I A

Sumatera

Jakarta

Laut Jawa (Java Sea)

Java

Laut Banda

7288

New Guinea

Arafura Sea

New Britain

5940

Solomon Islands

Solomon Sea

8322

Java Trench (Sunda Trench)

7125

Timor Sea

Timor

Great Barrier Reef

Vanua Levu

Viti Levu

INDIAN

North Australian Basin

Coral Sea

Espiritu Santo

7633

New Hebrides Trench

Tonga Trench

Horizon Deep

10800

OCEAN

Nouvelle Calédonie

South Fiji Basin

10047

Sou

Kermadec Trench

AUSTRALIA

Tasman Sea

Pacif

Sydney

Auckland

New Zealand

15°

Tropic of Capricorn

Perth Basin

Great Australian Bight

Perth

Melbourne

Wellington

Chatham Rise

Chatham Islands

Broken Plateau

South Australian Basin

5670

Tasmania

Tasman Basin

5176

60

Campbell Plateau

30°

Southeast Indian Ridge

1646

Indian – Antarctic Ridge

S O U T

1580

Antarctic Circle

R

150°

120°

A N T A

Lambert Azimuthal
Equal Area Projection

156 1 : 120 000 000

MILES 0 1000 2000

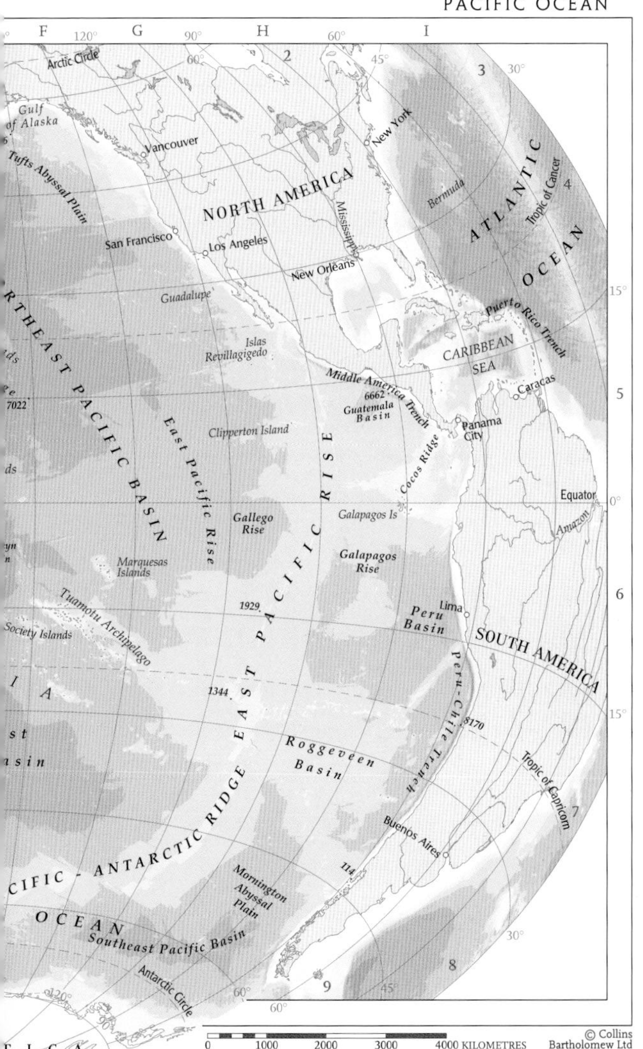

F 120° G 90° H 60° I

Arctic Circle
60°
2
45°
3
30°

Gulf of Alaska

Vancouver
New York

Tufts Abyssal Plain

NORTH AMERICA
Bermuda

ATLANTIC

Tropic of Cancer

San Francisco
Los Angeles
Mississippi

New Orleans
OCEAN

Guadalupe
15°

RTHEAST PACIFIC
Islas Revillagigedo
CARIBBEAN SEA

ds
e
7022
Middle America Trench
6662
Guatemala Basin
Caracas

Clipperton Island
East Pacific Rise
Panama City

Cocos Ridge

Equator
0°

Amazon

yn
n
Gallego Rise
Galapagos Is

Marquesas Islands
Galapagos Rise

Tuamotu Archipelago
Lima
6

Society Islands
1929
Peru Basin

SOUTH AMERICA

I A
1344

s t
Peru-Chile Trench
15°

a s i n
8170

Tropic of Capricorn

Roggeveen Basin

PACIFIC – ANTARCTIC RIDGE
EAST PACIFIC RISE

CIFIC
Buenos Aires

OCEAN
Mornington Abyssal Plain
114
30°

Southeast Pacific Basin

Antarctic Circle
60°
45°

120°
8

T I C A
9

0 1000 2000 3000 4000 KILOMETRES

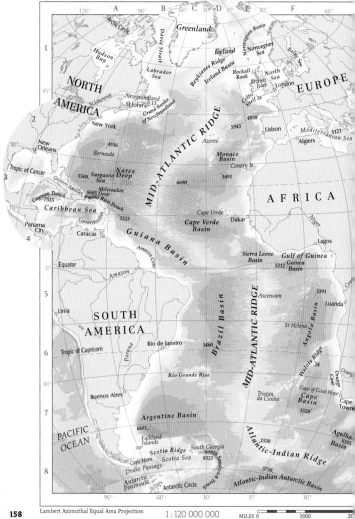

Lambert Azimuthal Equal Area Projection

1 : 120 000 000

MILES 0   1000   20

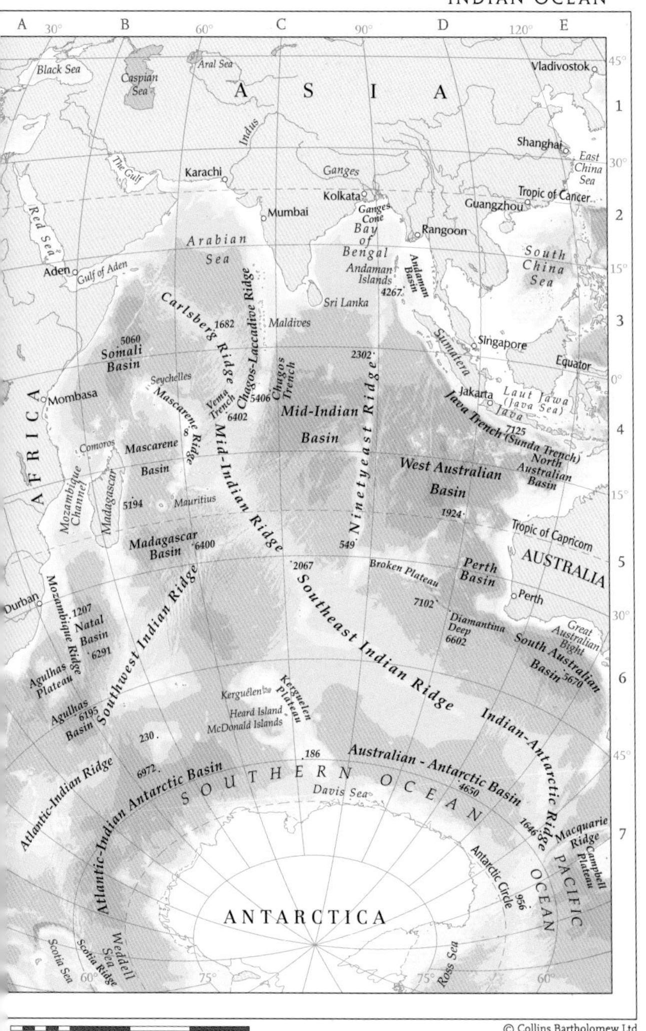

A 30° B 60° C 90° D 120° E

Black Sea
Caspian Sea
Aral Sea
Vladivostok
A S I A
1
Indus
The Gulf
Karachi
Shanghai
East China Sea
Ganges
Tropic of Cancer
Guangzhou
Red Sea
Kolkata
Aden
Gulf of Aden
Mumbai
Rangoon
2
Arabian Sea
Bay of Bengal
Ganges Cone
South China Sea
Andaman Islands
Andaman Basin
4267
Carlsberg Ridge
1682
Maldives
Sri Lanka
3
5060
Somali Basin
2302
Sumatra
Singapore
Equator
Seychelles
Chagos-Laccadive Ridge
Laut (Jawa) (Java Sea)
Mombasa
Yema Trench
5406
Jakarta
Java Trench (Sunda Trench)
7125
North Australian Basin
Mascarene Ridge
Mid-Indian Basin
Nineteast Ridge
4
AFRICA
Comoros
Mascarene Basin
West Australian Basin
5194
Mauritius
Mid-Indian Ridge
Mozambique Channel
Madagascar
1924
Tropic of Capricorn
Madagascar Basin
·6400
2067
Broken Plateau
Perth Basin
AUSTRALIA
5
549
7102
Perth
Durban
1207
Natal Basin
Southeast Indian Ridge
Diamantina Deep
6602
Great Australian Bight
Agulhas Plateau
·6291
South Australian Basin
3670
Agulhas Basin
6195
Kerguélen
Kerguelen Plateau
6
Southwest Indian Ridge
230
Heard Island
McDonald Islands
186
Indian-Antarctic Ridge
Macquarie Ridge
Atlantic-Indian Ridge
6972
Antarctic Basin
Australian - Antarctic Basin
4650
1646
Campbell Plateau
Atlantic-Indian Antarctic Basin
S O U T H E R N   O C E A N
Davis Sea
PACIFIC
956
Scotia Sea
Weddell Sea
Ross Sea
Antarctic Circle
OCEAN
7
Scotia Ridge
A N T A R C T I C A
60°
75°
60°

45° 1
30° 2
15°
0°
15°
30°
45° 6
7

0   1000   2000   3000   4000 KILOMETRES

© Collins Bartholomew Ltd

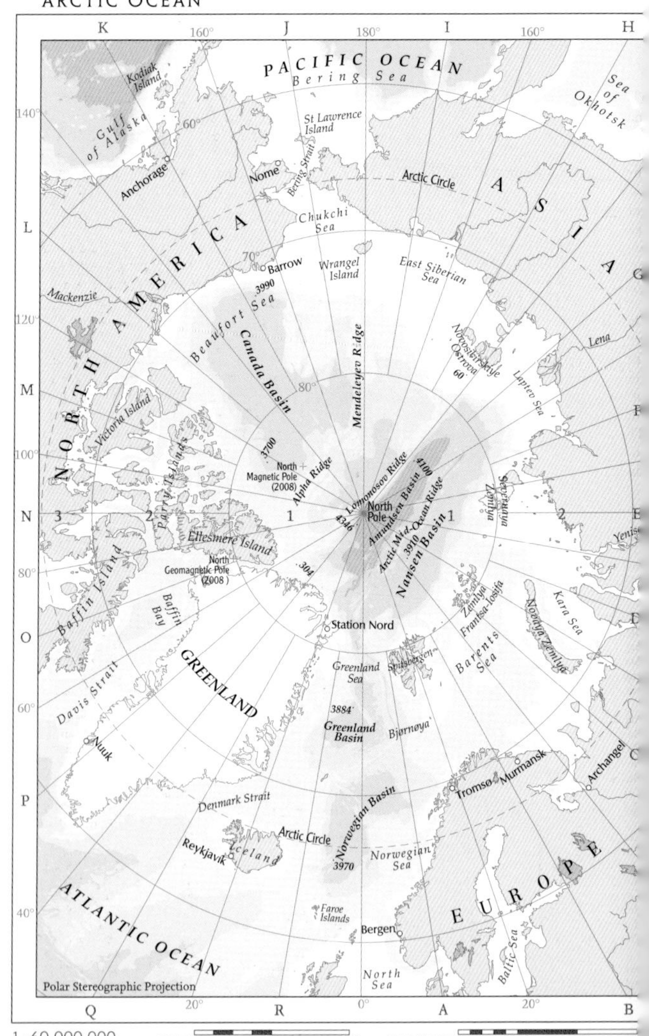

ARCTIC OCEAN

K   160°   J   180°   I   160°   H

PACIFIC OCEAN
Bering Sea

Kodiak Island
Gulf of Alaska
140°   60°
Anchorage
St Lawrence Island
Nome
Bering Strait
Arctic Circle

ASIA

Chukchi Sea

L
70°   Barrow
3990
Wrangel Island
East Siberian Sea

Mackenzie
Beaufort Sea
Canada Basin
Novosibirskiye Ostrova
60
Lena
Laptev Sea

G

M
80°
3700
North Magnetic Pole (2008)
Alpha Ridge
Mendeleyev Ridge
Severnaya Zemlya
120°
100°
Victoria Island

Parry Islands

F

N
3
2
1
Lomonosov Ridge
North Pole
4344
Amundsen Basin
Arctic Mid-Ocean Ridge
3910
Nansen Basin
1
2
Zemlya Frantsa-Iosifa
Kara Sea
Novaya Zemlya
Yenisey
E

North Geomagnetic Pole (2008)
Ellesmere Island
304
4100

Baffin Island
Baffin Bay

O
Station Nord
Greenland Sea
Spitsbergen
Barents Sea

Davis Strait
GREENLAND
60°
Nuuk
3884
Greenland Basin
Bjørnøya
Tromsø   Murmansk   Archangel

C

P
Denmark Strait
Arctic Circle
Reykjavik   Iceland
Norwegian Basin
3970
Norwegian Sea
Bergen

40°
Faroe Islands
North Sea

EUROPE
Baltic Sea

B

ATLANTIC OCEAN

Polar Stereographic Projection

Q   20°   R   0°   A   20°   B

160   1 : 60 000 000   MILES 0   400   800   KILOMETRES 0   500   1000   15

INTRODUCTION TO THE INDEX

The index includes all names shown on the maps in the Atlas of the World. Names are referenced by page number and by a grid reference. The grid reference correlates to the alphanumeric values which appear within each map frame. Each entry also includes the country or geographical area in which the feature is located. Entries relating to names appearing on insets are indicated by a small box symbol: □, followed by a grid reference if the inset has its own alphanumeric values.

Name forms are as they appear on the maps, with additional alternative names or name forms included as cross-references which refer the user to the entry for the map form of the name. Names beginning with Mc or Mac are alphabetized exactly as they appear. The terms Saint, Sainte, etc, are abbreviated to St, Ste, etc, but alphabetized as if in the full form.

Names of physical features beginning with generic, geographical terms are permuted – the descriptive term is placed after the main part of the name. For example, Lake Superior is indexed as Superior, Lake; Mount Everest as Everest, Mount. This policy is applied to all languages.

Entries, other than those for towns and cities, include a descriptor indicating the type of geographical feature. Descriptors are not included where the type of feature is implicit in the name itself.

Administrative divisions are included to differentiate entries of the same name and feature type within the one country. In such cases, duplicate names are alphabetized in order of administrative division. Additional qualifiers are also included for names within selected geographical areas.

INDEX ABBREVIATIONS

admin. div.	administrative division	Fin.	Finland		Guinea
Afgh.	Afghanistan	for.	forest	Pol.	Poland
Alg.	Algeria	g.	gulf	Port.	Portugal
Arg.	Argentina	Ger.	Germany	prov.	province
Austr.	Australia	Guat.	Guatemala	reg.	region
aut. reg.	autonomous region	hd	headland	Rep.	Republic
aut. rep.	autonomous republic	Hond.	Honduras	Rus. Fed.	Russian Federation
		imp. l.	impermanent lake		
Azer.	Azerbaijan	Indon.	Indonesia	S.	South
Bangl.	Bangladesh	isth.	isthmus	Switz.	Switzerland
Bol.	Bolivia	Kazakh.	Kazakhstan	Tajik.	Tajikistan
Bos.-Herz.	Bosnia Herzegovina	Kyrg.	Kyrgyzstan	Tanz.	Tanzania
Bulg.	Bulgaria	lag.	lagoon	terr.	territory
Can.	Canada	Lith.	Lithuania	Thai.	Thailand
C.A.R.	Central African Republic	Lux.	Luxembourg	Trin. and Tob.	Trinidad and Tobago
		Madag.	Madagascar		
Col.	Colombia	Maur.	Mauritania	Turkm.	Turkmenistan
Czech Rep.	Czech Republic	Mex.	Mexico	U.A.E.	United Arab Emirates
Dem. Rep. Congo	Democratic Republic of the Congo	Moz.	Mozambique	U.K.	United Kingdom
		mun.	municipality	Ukr.	Ukraine
		N.	North	Uru.	Uruguay
depr.	depression	Neth.	Netherlands	U.S.A.	United States of America
des.	desert	Nic.	Nicaragua		
Dom. Rep.	Dominican Republic	N.Z.	New Zealand	Uzbek.	Uzbekistan
		Pak.	Pakistan	val.	valley
esc.	escarpment	Para.	Paraguay	Venez.	Venezuela
est.	estuary	Phil.	Philippines		
Eth.	Ethiopia	plat.	plateau		
		P.N.G.	Papua New		

1

128 B2 **100 Mile House** Can.

A

93 E4 **Aabenraa** Denmark
100 C2 **Aachen** Ger.
93 E4 **Aalborg** Denmark
100 B2 **Aalst** Belgium
100 B2 **Aarschot** Belgium
68 C2 **Aba** China
115 C4 **Aba** Nigeria
81 C2 **Ābādān** Iran
81 D2 **Ābādeh** Iran
114 B1 **Abadla** Alg.
115 C4 **Abakaliki** Nigeria
83 H3 **Abakan** Rus. Fed.
150 A3 **Abancay** Peru
81 D2 **Abarqū** Iran
66 D2 **Abashiri** Japan
117 B4 **Abaya, Lake** Eth.
Ābay Wenz *r.* Eth./Sudan *see* **Blue Nile**
82 G3 **Abaza** Rus. Fed.
108 A2 **Abbasanta** *Sardegna* Italy
104 C1 **Abbeville** France
142 B3 **Abbeville** U.S.A.
55 O2 **Abbot Ice Shelf** Antarctica
74 B1 **Abbottabad** Pak.
115 E3 **Abéché** Chad
114 B4 **Abengourou** Côte d'Ivoire
114 C4 **Abeokuta** Nigeria
99 A2 **Aberaeron** U.K.
96 C2 **Aberchirder** U.K.
99 B3 **Aberdare** U.K.
99 A2 **Aberdaron** U.K.
122 B3 **Aberdeen** S. Africa
96 C2 **Aberdeen** U.K.
141 D3 **Aberdeen** *MD* U.S.A.
137 D1 **Aberdeen** *SD* U.S.A.
134 B1 **Aberdeen** *WA* U.S.A.
129 E1 **Aberdeen Lake** Can.
119 D2 **Abert, Lake** Dem. Rep. Congo/Uganda
134 B2 **Abert, Lake** U.S.A.
99 A2 **Aberystwyth** U.K.
86 F2 **Abez'** Rus. Fed.
78 B3 **Abhā** Saudi Arabia
Abiad, Bahr el *r.* Sudan/Uganda *see* **White Nile**
114 B4 **Abidjan** Côte d'Ivoire
137 D3 **Abilene** *KS* U.S.A.
139 D2 **Abilene** *TX* U.S.A.
99 C3 **Abingdon** U.K.
91 D3 **Abinsk** Rus. Fed.
130 B2 **Abitibi, Lake** Can.
Åbo Fin. *see* **Turku**
74 B1 **Abohar** India
114 C4 **Abomey** Benin
60 A1 **Abongabong, Gunung** *mt.* Indon.
118 B2 **Abong Mbang** Cameroon
64 A2 **Aborlan** Phil.
115 D3 **Abou Déia** Chad
106 B2 **Abrantes** Port.
152 B3 **Abra Pampa** Arg.
136 A2 **Absaroka Range** *mts* U.S.A.
81 C1 **Abşeron Yarımadası** *pen.* Azer.
78 B3 **Abū 'Arīsh** Saudi Arabia
79 C2 **Abu Dhabi** U.A.E.
116 B3 **Abu Hamed** Sudan
115 C4 **Abuja** Nigeria
81 C2 **Abū Kamāl** Syria
152 B1 **Abunã** *r.* Bol./Brazil
150 B2 **Abunã** Brazil
74 B2 **Abu Road** India
116 B2 **Abū Sunbul** Egypt
117 A3 **Abu Zabad** Sudan
Abū Zabī U.A.E. *see* **Abu Dhabi**
117 A4 **Abyei** Sudan
145 B2 **Acambaro** Mex.
106 B1 **A Cañiza** Spain
144 B2 **Acaponeta** Mex.
145 C3 **Acapulco** Mex.
151 D2 **Acará** Brazil
150 B1 **Acarigua** Venez.
145 C3 **Acatlán** Mex.
145 C3 **Acayucán** Mex.
114 B4 **Accra** Ghana
98 B2 **Accrington** U.K.
74 B2 **Achalpur** India
97 A2 **Achill Island** Ireland
101 D1 **Achim** Ger.
96 B2 **Achnasheen** U.K.
91 D2 **Achuyevo** Rus. Fed.
111 C3 **Acıpayam** Turkey
109 C3 **Acireale** *Sicilia* Italy
147 C2 **Acklins Island** Bahamas
153 B4 **Aconcagua, Cerro** *mt.* Arg.
106 B1 **A Coruña** Spain
108 A2 **Acqui Terme** Italy
103 D2 **Ács** Hungary
145 C2 **Actopán** Mex.
139 D2 **Ada** U.S.A.
79 C2 **Adam** Oman
49 J4 **Adamstown** Pitcairn Is
'Adan Yemen *see* **Aden**
80 B2 **Adana** Turkey
111 D2 **Adapazarı** Turkey
Adapazari Turkey *see* **Adapazarı**
108 A1 **Adda** *r.* Italy
78 B2 **Ad Dafīnah** Saudi Arabia
78 B2 **Ad Dahnā'** *des.* Saudi Arabia
78 B2 **Ad Dahnā'** *des.* Saudi Arabia
114 A2 **Ad Dakhla** Western Sahara
Ad Dammām Saudi Arabia *see* **Dammam**
78 A2 **Ad Dār al Ḩamrā'** Saudi Arabia
78 B3 **Ad Darb** Saudi Arabia
78 B2 **Ad Dawādimī** Saudi Arabia
Ad Dawḩah Qatar *see* **Doha**
78 B2 **Ad Dilam** Saudi Arabia
116 C2 **Ad Dir'īyah** Saudi Arabia
117 B4 **Addis Ababa** Eth.
81 C2 **Ad Dīwānīyah** Iraq
52 A2 **Adelaide** Austr.
50 C1 **Adelaide River** Austr.
101 D2 **Adelebsen** Ger.
55 J2 **Adélie Land** Antarctica
78 B3 **Aden** Yemen
117 C3 **Aden, Gulf of** Somalia/Yemen
100 C2 **Adenau** Ger.
79 C2 **Adh Dhayd** U.A.E.
59 C3 **Adi** *i.* Indon.
78 A3 **Ādī Ārk'ay** Eth.
116 B3 **Ādīgrat** Eth.
75 B3 **Adilabad** India
141 E2 **Adirondack Mountains** U.S.A.
Ādīs Ābeba Eth. *see* **Addis Ababa**
117 B4 **Ādīs Alem** Eth.
110 C1 **Adjud** Romania
50 B1 **Admiralty Gulf** Austr.
128 A2 **Admiralty Island** U.S.A.
104 B3 **Adour** *r.* France
106 C2 **Adra** Spain
114 B2 **Adrar** Alg.
140 C2 **Adrian** *MI* U.S.A.
139 C1 **Adrian** *TX* U.S.A.
108 B2 **Adriatic Sea** Europe
116 B3 **Ādwa** Eth.
83 K2 **Adycha** *r.* Rus. Fed.
91 D3 **Adygeysk** Rus. Fed.
114 B4 **Adzopé** Côte d'Ivoire
111 B3 **Aegean Sea** Greece/Turke
101 D1 **Aerzen** Ger.
106 B1 **A Estrada** Spain
116 B3 **Afabet** Eritrea
76 C3 **Afghanistan** *country* Asia
78 B2 **'Afīf** Saudi Arabia
80 B2 **Afyon** Turkey
115 C3 **Agadez** Niger
114 B1 **Agadir** Morocco
77 D2 **Agadyr'** Kazakh.
74 B2 **Agar** India
75 D2 **Agartala** India
81 C2 **Ağdam** Azer.
105 C3 **Agde** France
104 C3 **Agen** France
122 A2 **Aggeneys** S. Africa
111 C3 **Agia Varvara** Greece
111 B3 **Agios Dimitrios** Greece
111 C3 **Agios Efstratios** *i.* Greece
111 C3 **Agios Nikolaos** Greece
110 B1 **Agnita** Romania
75 B2 **Agra** India
81 C2 **Ağrı** Turkey
Ağrı Dağı *mt.* Turkey *see* **Ararat, Mount**
108 B3 **Agrigento** *Sicilia* Italy
111 B3 **Agrinio** Greece
109 B2 **Agropoli** Italy
154 B2 **Água Clara** Brazil
146 B4 **Aguadulce** Panama
144 B2 **Aguanaval** *r.* Mex.
144 B1 **Agua Prieta** Mex.
144 B2 **Aguascalientes** Mex.
155 D1 **Águas Formosas** Brazil
106 B1 **Águeda** Port.
106 C1 **Aguilar de Campóo** Spain
107 C2 **Águilas** Spain
144 B3 **Aguililla** Mex.
122 B3 **Agulhas, Cape** S. Africa
155 D2 **Agulhas Negras** *mt.* Brazil
111 C2 **Ağva** Turkey
81 C2 **Ahar** Iran
100 C1 **Ahaus** Ger.
81 C2 **Ahlat** Turkey
100 C2 **Ahlen** Ger.
74 B2 **Ahmadabad** India
73 B3 **Ahmadnagar** India
74 B2 **Ahmadpur East** Pak.
74 B1 **Ahmadpur Sial** Pak.
144 B2 **Ahome** Mex.
79 C2 **Ahram** Iran
101 E1 **Ahrensburg** Ger.
104 C2 **Ahun** France
81 C2 **Ahvāz** Iran
122 A2 **Ai-Ais** Namibia
80 B2 **Aigialousa** Cyprus
111 B3 **Aigio** Greece
143 D2 **Aiken** U.S.A.
97 B1 **Ailt an Chorráin** Ireland
155 D1 **Aimorés** Brazil
155 D1 **Aimorés, Serra dos** *hills* B
114 B2 **'Aïn Ben Tili** Maur.
107 D2 **Aïn Defla** Alg.
114 B1 **Aïn Sefra** Alg.
136 D2 **Ainsworth** U.S.A.
Aintab Turkey *see* **Gaziant**
107 D2 **Aïn Taya** Alg.
107 D2 **Aïn Tédélès** Alg.
115 C3 **Aïr, Massif de l'** *mts* Nige
60 A1 **Airbangis** Indon.

8 C2 **Airdrie** Can.
4 B3 **Aire-sur-l'Adour** France
1 E3 **Aisch** *r.* Ger.
8 A1 **Aishihik Lake** Can.
0 A3 **Aisne** *r.* France
9 D3 **Aitape** P.N.G.
0 B1 **Aiud** Romania
5 D3 **Aix-en-Provence** France
5 D2 **Aix-les-Bains** France
2 A1 **Aizawl** India
8 C2 **Aizkraukle** Latvia
7 C3 **Aizu-Wakamatsu** Japan
5 D3 **Ajaccio** *Corse* France
5 E1 **Ajdābiyā** Libya
4 B2 **Ajmer** India
8 A2 **Ajo** U.S.A.
7 E3 **Akbulak** Rus. Fed.
0 B2 **Akçakale** Turkey
0 B2 **Akdağmadeni** Turkey
8 A2 **Åkersberga** Sweden
8 C2 **Aketi** Dem. Rep. Congo
7 D4 **Akhalk'alak'i** Georgia
9 C2 **Akhḑar, Jabal** *mts* Oman
1 C3 **Akhisar** Turkey
7 D4 **Akhtubinsk** Rus. Fed.
0 B1 **Akimiski Island** Can.
6 D3 **Akita** Japan
4 A3 **Akjoujt** Maur.
7 D1 **Akkol'** Kazakh.
8 B2 **Akmeņrags** *pt* Latvia
Akmola Kazakh. *see* **Astana**
7 B4 **Akobo** Sudan
4 B2 **Akola** India
8 A3 **Akordat** Eritrea
7 G2 **Akpatok Island** Can.
2 A3 **Akranes** Iceland
0 C2 **Akron** U.S.A.
5 B1 **Aksai Chin** *terr.* Asia
0 B2 **Aksaray** Turkey
6 B1 **Aksay** Kazakh.
1 D2 **Aksay** Rus. Fed.
0 B2 **Akşehir** Turkey
6 C2 **Akshiganak** Kazakh.
7 E2 **Aksu** China
8 A3 **Āksum** Eth.
6 B2 **Aktau** Kazakh.
6 B1 **Aktobe** Kazakh.
7 D2 **Aktogay** Kazakh.
8 C3 **Aktsyabrski** Belarus
5 C4 **Akure** Nigeria
2 B2 **Akureyri** Iceland
2 C2 **Alabama** *r.* U.S.A.
2 C2 **Alabama** *state* U.S.A.
1 C3 **Alaçatı** Turkey
1 C1 **Alagir** Rus. Fed.
1 E3 **Alagoinhas** Brazil
7 C1 **Alagón** Spain
9 B2 **Al Aḩmadī** Kuwait
7 E2 **Alakol', Ozero** *salt l.* Kazakh.
2 J2 **Alakurtti** Rus. Fed.
8 B3 **Al 'Alayyah** Saudi Arabia
1 C2 **Al 'Amādīyah** Iraq
0 A2 **Al 'Āmirīyah** Egypt
5 C3 **Alamo** U.S.A.
8 B2 **Alamogordo** U.S.A.
4 A2 **Alamos** *Sonora* Mex.
4 B2 **Alamos** *Sonora* Mex.
4 B2 **Alamos** *r.* Mex.
6 B3 **Alamosa** U.S.A.
3 G3 **Åland Islands** Fin.
0 B2 **Alanya** Turkey
3 B4 **Alappuzha** India
0 B3 **Al 'Aqabah** Jordan
8 B2 **Al 'Aqīq** Saudi Arabia
7 C2 **Alarcón, Embalse de** *resr* Spain
0 B2 **Al 'Arīsh** Egypt

78 B2 **Al Arţāwīyah** Saudi Arabia
61 C2 **Alas** Indon.
111 C3 **Alaşehir** Turkey
128 A2 **Alaska** *state* U.S.A.
124 F3 **Alaska, Gulf of** U.S.A.
81 C2 **Älät** Azer.
87 D3 **Alatyr'** Rus. Fed.
150 A2 **Alausí** Ecuador
93 H3 **Alavus** Fin.
52 B2 **Alawoona** Austr.
108 A2 **Alba** Italy
107 C2 **Albacete** Spain
110 B1 **Alba Iulia** Romania
109 C2 **Albania** *country* Europe
50 A3 **Albany** Austr.
130 B1 **Albany** *r.* Can.
143 D2 **Albany** *GA* U.S.A.
141 E2 **Albany** *NY* U.S.A.
134 B2 **Albany** *OR* U.S.A.
Al Başrah Iraq *see* **Basra**
51 D1 **Albatross Bay** Austr.
116 A2 **Al Bawītī** Egypt
115 E1 **Al Bayḑā'** Libya
78 B3 **Al Bayḑā'** Yemen
143 D1 **Albemarle** U.S.A.
143 E1 **Albemarle Sound** *sea chan.* U.S.A.
108 A2 **Albenga** Italy
51 C2 **Alberga** *watercourse* Austr.
128 C2 **Alberta** *prov.* Can.
100 B2 **Albert Kanaal** *canal* Belgium
119 D2 **Albert, Lake** Dem. Rep. Congo/Uganda
137 E2 **Albert Lea** U.S.A.
104 C3 **Albi** France
78 A2 **Al Bi'r** Saudi Arabia
78 B3 **Al Birk** Saudi Arabia
78 B2 **Al Biyāḑh** *reg.* Saudi Arabia
Alborz, Reshteh-ye *mts* Iran *see* **Elburz Mountains**
106 B2 **Albufeira** Port.
138 B1 **Albuquerque** U.S.A.
79 C2 **Al Buraymī** Oman
53 C3 **Albury** Austr.
106 B2 **Alcácer do Sal** Port.
106 C1 **Alcalá de Henares** Spain
106 C2 **Alcalá la Real** Spain
108 B3 **Alcamo** *Sicilia* Italy
107 C1 **Alcañiz** Spain
106 B2 **Alcántara** Spain
106 C2 **Alcaraz** Spain
106 C2 **Alcaraz, Sierra de** *mts* Spain
106 C2 **Alcaudete** Spain
106 C2 **Alcázar de San Juan** Spain
91 D2 **Alchevs'k** Ukr.
155 E1 **Alcobaça** Brazil
107 C2 **Alcoy-Alcoi** Spain
107 D2 **Alcúdia** Spain
145 C2 **Aldama** Mex.
83 J3 **Aldan** Rus. Fed.
83 J2 **Aldan** *r.* Rus. Fed.
95 C4 **Alderney** *i.* Channel Is
114 A3 **Aleg** Maur.
155 D2 **Alegre** Brazil
152 C3 **Alegrete** Brazil
83 K3 **Aleksandrovsk-Sakhalinskiy** Rus. Fed.
91 D1 **Alekseyevka** *Belgorodskaya Oblast'* Rus. Fed.
91 D1 **Alekseyevka** *Belgorodskaya Oblast'* Rus. Fed.
89 E3 **Aleksin** Rus. Fed.
109 D2 **Aleksinac** Serbia
118 B3 **Alèmbé** Gabon
155 D2 **Além Paraíba** Brazil
93 F3 **Ålen** Norway
104 C2 **Alençon** France

80 B2 **Aleppo** Syria
150 A3 **Alerta** Peru
128 B2 **Alert Bay** Can.
105 C3 **Alès** France
110 B1 **Aleşd** Romania
108 A2 **Alessandria** Italy
93 E3 **Ålesund** Norway
124 C3 **Aleutian Islands** U.S.A.
83 L3 **Alevina, Mys** *c.* Rus. Fed.
128 A2 **Alexander Archipelago** *is* U.S.A.
122 A2 **Alexander Bay** S. Africa
142 C2 **Alexander City** U.S.A.
55 O2 **Alexander Island** Antarctica
53 C3 **Alexandra** Austr.
54 A3 **Alexandra** N.Z.
111 B2 **Alexandreia** Greece
Alexandretta Turkey *see* **İskenderun**
116 A1 **Alexandria** Egypt
110 C2 **Alexandria** Romania
123 C3 **Alexandria** S. Africa
142 B2 **Alexandria** *LA* U.S.A.
137 D1 **Alexandria** *MN* U.S.A.
141 D3 **Alexandria** *VA* U.S.A.
52 A3 **Alexandrina, Lake** Austr.
111 C2 **Alexandroupoli** Greece
131 E1 **Alexis** *r.* Can.
128 B2 **Alexis Creek** Can.
77 E1 **Aleysk** Rus. Fed.
107 C1 **Alfaro** Spain
81 C3 **Al Fāw** Iraq
101 D2 **Alfeld (Leine)** Ger.
155 C2 **Alfenas** Brazil
Al Fujayrah U.A.E. *see* **Fujairah**
Al Furāt *r.* Iraq/Syria *see* **Euphrates**
106 B2 **Algeciras** Spain
107 C2 **Algemesí** Spain
78 A3 **Algena** Eritrea
Alger Alg. *see* **Algiers**
114 C2 **Algeria** *country* Africa
79 C3 **Al Ghayḑah** Yemen
108 A2 **Alghero** *Sardegna* Italy
116 B2 **Al Ghurdaqah** Egypt
79 B2 **Al Ghwaybiyah** Saudi Arabia
115 C1 **Algiers** Alg.
123 C3 **Algoa Bay** S. Africa
137 E2 **Algona** U.S.A.
106 C1 **Algorta** Spain
81 C2 **Al Ḩadīthah** Iraq
79 C2 **Al Ḩajar al Gharbī** *mts* Oman
107 C2 **Alhama de Murcia** Spain
80 A2 **Al Ḩammām** Egypt
78 B2 **Al Ḩanākīyah** Saudi Arabia
81 C2 **Al Ḩasakah** Syria
81 C2 **Al Ḩayy** Iraq
78 B3 **Al Ḩazm al Jawf** Yemen
79 C3 **Al Ḩibāk** *des.* Saudi Arabia
78 B2 **Al Ḩillah** Saudi Arabia
79 B2 **Al Ḩinnāh** Saudi Arabia
Al Ḩudaydah Yemen *see* **Hodeidah**
79 B2 **Al Hufūf** Saudi Arabia
115 D2 **Al Ḩulayq al Kabīr** *hills* Libya
79 C2 **'Alīābād** Iran
111 C3 **Aliağa** Turkey
111 B2 **Aliakmonas** *r.* Greece
107 C2 **Alicante** Spain
139 D3 **Alice** U.S.A.
109 C3 **Alice, Punta** *pt* Italy
51 C2 **Alice Springs** Austr.
75 B2 **Aligarh** India
81 C2 **Alīgūdarz** Iran
69 E1 **Alihe** China
118 B3 **Alima** *r.* Congo

111 C3 **Aliova** *r.* Turkey
117 C3 **Ali Sabieh** Djibouti
Al Iskandarīyah Egypt *see* **Alexandria**
116 B1 **Al Ismā'īlīyah** Egypt
123 C3 **Aliwal North** S. Africa
115 E2 **Al Jaghbūb** Libya
78 B2 **Al Jahrah** Kuwait
79 C2 **Al Jamalīyah** Qatar
115 D1 **Al Jawsh** Libya
106 B2 **Aljezur** Port.
Al Jīzah Egypt *see* **Giza**
79 B2 **Al Jubayl** Saudi Arabia
78 B2 **Al Junaynah** Saudi Arabia
106 B2 **Aljustrel** Port.
78 B2 **Al Kahfah** Saudi Arabia
79 C2 **Al Kāmil** Oman
80 B2 **Al Karak** Jordan
79 C2 **Al Khābūrah** Oman
78 B2 **Al Khamāsīn** Saudi Arabia
116 B2 **Al Khārijah** Egypt
79 C2 **Al Khaṣab** Oman
78 B3 **Al Khawkhah** Yemen
79 C2 **Al Khawr** Qatar
115 D1 **Al Khums** Libya
79 B2 **Al Khunn** Saudi Arabia
79 C2 **Al Kir'ānah** Qatar
100 B1 **Alkmaar** Neth.
115 E2 **Al Kufrah** Libya
81 C2 **Al Kūt** Iraq
Al Kuwayt Kuwait *see* **Kuwait**
Al Lādhiqīyah Syria *see* **Latakia**
75 C2 **Allahabad** India
83 K2 **Allakh-Yun'** Rus. Fed.
141 D2 **Allegheny** *r.* U.S.A.
140 C3 **Allegheny Mountains** U.S.A.
97 B1 **Allen, Lough** *l.* Ireland
145 B2 **Allende** *Coahuila* Mex.
145 B2 **Allende** *Nuevo León* Mex.
141 D2 **Allentown** U.S.A.
101 D1 **Aller** *r.* Ger.
136 C2 **Alliance** *NE* U.S.A.
140 C2 **Alliance** *OH* U.S.A.
78 B2 **Al Līth** Saudi Arabia
96 C2 **Alloa** U.K.
131 C2 **Alma** Can.
Alma-Ata Kazakh. *see* **Almaty**
106 B2 **Almada** Port.
106 C2 **Almadén** Spain
Al Madīnah Saudi Arabia *see* **Medina**
116 B1 **Al Mafraq** Jordan
78 B3 **Al Maḥwīt** Yemen
78 B2 **Al Majma'ah** Saudi Arabia
135 B2 **Almanor, Lake** U.S.A.
107 C2 **Almansa** Spain
80 B2 **Al Manṣūrah** Egypt
79 C2 **Al Mariyyah** U.A.E.
115 E1 **Al Marj** Libya
77 D2 **Almaty** Kazakh.
106 C1 **Almazán** Spain
151 C2 **Almeirim** Brazil
100 C1 **Almelo** Neth.
155 D1 **Almenara** Brazil
106 B1 **Almendra, Embalse de** *resr* Spain
106 B2 **Almendralejo** Spain
106 C2 **Almería** Spain
106 C2 **Almería, Golfo de** *b.* Spain
87 E3 **Al'met'yevsk** Rus. Fed.
78 B2 **Al Mindak** Saudi Arabia
116 B2 **Al Minyā** Egypt
79 B2 **Al Mish'āb** Saudi Arabia
106 B2 **Almodôvar** Port.
106 B2 **Almonte** Spain
75 B2 **Almora** India
79 B2 **Al Mubarrez** Saudi Arabia
79 C2 **Al Muḍaibī** Oman
80 B3 **Al Mudawwarah** Jordan
Al Mukallā Yemen *see* **Mukalla**
Al Mukhā Yemen *see* **Mocha**
106 C2 **Almuñécar** Spain
78 A2 **Al Muwayliḥ** Saudi Arabia
111 B3 **Almyros** Greece
96 B2 **Alness** U.K.
98 C1 **Alnwick** U.K.
49 G4 **Alofi** Niue
111 B3 **Alonnisos** *i.* Greece
59 C3 **Alor** *i.* Indon.
59 C3 **Alor, Kepulauan** *is* Indon.
60 B1 **Alor Star** Malaysia
Alost Belgium *see* **Aalst**
86 C2 **Alozero** Rus. Fed.
140 C1 **Alpena** U.S.A.
139 C2 **Alpine** U.S.A.
105 D2 **Alps** *mts* Europe
79 B3 **Al Qa'āmīyāt** *reg.* Saudi Arabia
115 D1 **Al Qaddāḥīyah** Libya
Al Qāhirah Egypt *see* **Cairo**
78 B2 **Al Qā'īyah** Saudi Arabia
81 C2 **Al Qāmishlī** Syria
80 B2 **Al Qaryatayn** Syria
79 B3 **Al Qaṭn** Yemen
106 B2 **Alqueva, Barragem de** *resr* Port.
80 B2 **Al Qunayṭirah** Syria
78 B3 **Al Qunfidhah** Saudi Arabia
116 B2 **Al Quṣayr** Egypt
78 B2 **Al Quwayīyah** Saudi Arabia
101 D2 **Alsfeld** Ger.
92 H2 **Alta** Norway
92 H2 **Altaelva** *r.* Norway
68 B1 **Altai Mountains** Asia
143 D2 **Altamaha** *r.* U.S.A.
151 C2 **Altamira** Brazil
109 C2 **Altamura** Italy
68 B1 **Altay** China
68 C1 **Altay** Mongolia
105 D2 **Altdorf** Switz.
107 C2 **Altea** Spain
101 F2 **Altenburg** Ger.
100 C2 **Altenkirchen (Westerwald)** Ger.
111 C3 **Altınoluk** Turkey
111 D3 **Altıntaş** Turkey
152 B2 **Altiplano** *plain* Bol.
154 B1 **Alto Araguaia** Brazil
107 C1 **Alto del Moncayo** *mt.* Spain
154 B1 **Alto Garças** Brazil
121 C2 **Alto Molócuè** Moz.
129 E3 **Altona** Can.
141 D2 **Altoona** U.S.A.
154 B1 **Alto Sucuriú** Brazil
154 B1 **Alto Taquarí** Brazil
102 C2 **Altötting** Ger.
68 B2 **Altun Shan** *mts* China
134 B2 **Alturas** U.S.A.
139 D2 **Altus** U.S.A.
88 C2 **Alūksne** Latvia
78 A2 **Al 'Ulā** Saudi Arabia
115 D1 **Al 'Uqaylah** Libya
Al Uqṣur Egypt *see* **Luxor**
91 C3 **Alushta** Ukr.
139 D1 **Alva** U.S.A.
145 C3 **Alvarado** Mex.
93 F3 **Älvdalen** Sweden
93 F3 **Alvdalen** *val.* Sweden
92 H2 **Älvsbyn** Sweden
78 A2 **Al Wajh** Saudi Arabia
74 B2 **Alwar** India
81 C2 **Al Widyān** *plat.* Iraq/Saudi Arabia
Alxa Youqi China *see* **Ehen Hudag**
Alxa Zuoqi China *see* **Bayan Hot**
51 C1 **Alyangula** Austr.
88 B3 **Alytus** Lith.
136 C1 **Alzada** U.S.A.
100 D3 **Alzey** Ger.
50 C2 **Amadeus, Lake** *imp. l.* Aust
127 G2 **Amadjuak Lake** Can.
106 B2 **Amadora** Port.
78 B2 **Amā'ir** Saudi Arabia
93 F4 **Åmål** Sweden
111 B3 **Amaliada** Greece
59 D3 **Amamapare** Indon.
154 A2 **Amambaí** Brazil
154 B2 **Amambaí** *r.* Brazil
69 E3 **Amami-Ō-shima** *i.* Japan
69 E3 **Amami-shotō** *is* Japan
77 C1 **Amangel'dy** Kazakh.
109 C3 **Amantea** Italy
123 D3 **Amanzimtoti** S. Africa
151 C1 **Amapá** Brazil
106 B2 **Amareleja** Port.
139 C1 **Amarillo** U.S.A.
108 B2 **Amaro, Monte** *mt.* Italy
80 B1 **Amasya** Turkey
150 C1 **Amazon** *r.* S. America
151 D1 **Amazon, Mouths of the** Br
Amazonas *r.* S. America *see* **Amazon**
74 B1 **Ambala** India
121 D3 **Ambalavao** Madag.
121 D2 **Ambanja** Madag.
150 A2 **Ambato** Ecuador
121 D2 **Ambato Boeny** Madag.
121 D3 **Ambato Finandrahana** Ma
121 D2 **Ambatolampy** Madag.
121 D2 **Ambatondrazaka** Madag.
101 E3 **Amberg** Ger.
146 B3 **Ambergris Cay** *i.* Belize
75 C2 **Ambikapur** India
121 D2 **Ambilobe** Madag.
98 B1 **Ambleside** U.K.
121 D3 **Amboasary** Madag.
121 D3 **Ambohimahasoa** Madag.
59 C3 **Ambon** Indon.
59 C3 **Ambon** *i.* Indon.
121 D3 **Ambositra** Madag.
121 D3 **Ambovombe** Madag.
135 C4 **Amboy** U.S.A.
120 A1 **Ambriz** Angola
145 B2 **Amealco** Mex.
144 B2 **Ameca** Mex.
100 B1 **Ameland** *i.* Neth.
134 D2 **American Falls** U.S.A.
134 D2 **American Falls Reservoir** U.S.A.
135 D2 **American Fork** U.S.A.
49 G3 **American Samoa** *terr.* S. Pacific Ocean
143 D2 **Americus** U.S.A.
100 B1 **Amersfoort** Neth.
55 F2 **Amery Ice Shelf** Antarctica
137 E2 **Ames** U.S.A.
111 B3 **Amfissa** Greece
83 J2 **Amga** Rus. Fed.
66 C1 **Amgu** Rus. Fed.
115 C2 **Amguid** Alg.
83 K3 **Amgun'** *r.* Rus. Fed.
131 D2 **Amherst** Can.
104 C2 **Amiens** France
73 B3 **Amindivi Islands** India
122 A1 **Aminuis** Namibia
74 A2 **Amir Chah** Pak.
129 D2 **Amisk Lake** Can.
139 C3 **Amistad Reservoir** Mex./U.
98 A2 **Amlwch** U.K.
80 B2 **'Ammān** Jordan

7 I2 **Ammassalik** Greenland
8 B3 **Am Nābiyah** Yemen
1 D2 **Amol** Iran
1 C3 **Amorgos** *i.* Greece
2 C2 **Amory** U.S.A.
0 C2 **Amos** Can.
Amoy China *see* **Xiamen**
5 C2 **Amparo** Brazil
7 D1 **Amposta** Spain
5 B2 **Amravati** India
4 B1 **Amritsar** India
0 B1 **Amstelveen** Neth.
0 B1 **Amsterdam** Neth.
3 C2 **Amstetten** Austria
5 E3 **Am Timan** Chad
6 B2 **Amudar'ya** *r.* Asia
6 E1 **Amund Ringnes Island** Can.
6 C2 **Amundsen Gulf** Can.
5 M2 **Amundsen Sea** Antarctica
1 C2 **Amuntai** Indon.
Amur *r.* China *see* **Heilong Jiang**
8 A3 **'Amur, Wadi** *watercourse* Sudan
3 I2 **Anabar** *r.* Rus. Fed.
3 I2 **Anabarskiy Zaliv** *b.* Rus. Fed.
4 D1 **Anaconda** U.S.A.
9 D1 **Anadarko** U.S.A.
0 B1 **Anadolu Dağları** *mts* Turkey
3 M2 **Anadyr'** *r.* Rus. Fed.
1 C2 **'Ānah** Iraq
5 B2 **Anáhuac** Mex.
0 B1 **Anambas, Kepulauan** *is* Indon.
7 E2 **Anamosa** U.S.A.
0 B2 **Anamur** Turkey
7 B4 **Anan** Japan
3 B3 **Anantapur** India
4 B1 **Anantnag** India
0 B2 **Anan'yiv** Ukr.
1 D3 **Anapa** Rus. Fed.
4 C1 **Anápolis** Brazil
2 B3 **Añatuya** Arg.
7 B1 **An Baile Thiar** Ireland
5 B2 **Anbyon** N. Korea
4 B2 **Ancenis** France
8 B2 **Ancona** Italy
3 A5 **Ancud** Chile
Anda China *see* **Daqing**
7 A2 **An Daingean** Ireland
3 E3 **Åndalsnes** Norway
2 C2 **Andalusia** U.S.A.
3 D3 **Andaman Islands** India
3 A2 **Andaman Sea** Indian Ocean
1 D2 **Andapa** Madag.
0 B2 **Andelst** Neth.
2 G2 **Andenes** Norway
0 B2 **Andenne** Belgium
0 B2 **Anderlecht** Belgium
6 C2 **Anderson** *r.* Can.
6 B2 **Anderson** *AK* U.S.A.
0 B2 **Anderson** *IN* U.S.A.
3 D2 **Anderson** *SC* U.S.A.
8 D3 **Andes** *mts* S. America
7 D2 **Andijon** Uzbek.
1 D2 **Andilamena** Madag.
1 D2 **Andilanatoby** Madag.
1 D2 **Andoany** Madag.
Andong China *see* **Dandong**
5 B2 **Andong** S. Korea
7 D1 **Andorra** *country* Europe
7 D1 **Andorra la Vella** Andorra
9 C3 **Andover** U.K.
4 B2 **Andradina** Brazil
9 D2 **Andreapol'** Rus. Fed.
5 D2 **Andrelândia** Brazil
9 C2 **Andrews** U.S.A.
9 C2 **Andria** Italy
1 D3 **Androka** Madag.
146 C2 **Andros** *i.* Bahamas
111 B3 **Andros** *i.* Greece
143 E4 **Andros Town** Bahamas
73 B3 **Andrott** *i.* India
90 B1 **Andrushivka** Ukr.
92 G2 **Andselv** Norway
106 C2 **Andújar** Spain
120 A2 **Andulo** Angola
114 C3 **Anéfis** Mali
115 D3 **Aney** Niger
83 H3 **Angara** *r.* Rus. Fed.
69 C1 **Angarsk** Rus. Fed.
93 G3 **Ånge** Sweden
144 A2 **Ángel de la Guarda, Isla** *i.* Mex.
64 B1 **Angeles** Phil.
150 B1 **Angel Falls** Venez.
93 F4 **Ängelholm** Sweden
92 G3 **Ångermanälven** *r.* Sweden
104 B2 **Angers** France
129 E1 **Angikuni Lake** Can.
98 A2 **Anglesey** *i.* U.K.
121 C2 **Angoche** Moz.
79 C2 **Angohrān** Iran
120 A2 **Angola** *country* Africa
140 C2 **Angola** U.S.A.
128 A2 **Angoon** U.S.A.
104 C2 **Angoulême** France
77 D2 **Angren** Uzbek.
147 D3 **Anguilla** *terr.* West Indies
75 C2 **Angul** India
93 F4 **Anholt** *i.* Denmark
71 B3 **Anhua** China
70 B2 **Anhui** *prov.* China
154 B1 **Anhumas** Brazil
154 C1 **Anicuns** Brazil
66 D1 **Aniva, Mys** *c.* Rus. Fed.
65 B2 **Anjŭ** N. Korea
70 A2 **Ankang** China
80 B2 **Ankara** Turkey
70 B2 **Anlu** China
91 E1 **Anna** Rus. Fed.
115 C1 **Annaba** Alg.
101 F2 **Annaberg-Buchholtz** Ger.
78 B2 **An Nafūd** *des.* Saudi Arabia
81 C2 **An Najaf** Iraq
96 C3 **Annan** U.K.
141 D3 **Annapolis** U.S.A.
75 C2 **Annapurna I** *mt.* Nepal
140 C2 **Ann Arbor** U.S.A.
150 C1 **Anna Regina** Guyana
81 C2 **An Nāşirīyah** Iraq
105 D2 **Annecy** France
78 B3 **An Nimāş** Saudi Arabia
62 B1 **Anning** China
142 C2 **Anniston** U.S.A.
105 C2 **Annonay** France
79 B2 **An Nu'ayrīyah** Saudi Arabia
121 D2 **Anorontany, Tanjona** *hd* Madag.
71 B3 **Anpu** China
70 B2 **Anqing** China
102 C2 **Ansbach** Ger.
70 C1 **Anshan** China
71 A3 **Anshun** China
114 C3 **Ansongo** Mali
150 A3 **Antabamba** Peru
80 B2 **Antakya** Turkey
121 E2 **Antalaha** Madag.
80 B2 **Antalya** Turkey
80 B2 **Antalya Körfezi** *g.* Turkey
121 D2 **Antananarivo** Madag.
55 Q3 **Antarctic Peninsula** Antarctica
96 B2 **An Teallach** *mt.* U.K.
106 C2 **Antequera** Spain
138 B2 **Anthony** U.S.A.
114 B2 **Anti-Atlas** *mts* Morocco
105 D3 **Antibes** France
131 D2 **Anticosti, Île d'** *i.* Can.
131 D2 **Antigonish** Can.
147 D3 **Antigua** *i.* Antigua
147 D3 **Antigua and Barbuda** *country* West Indies
145 C2 **Antiguo-Morelos** Mex.
111 B3 **Antikythira** *i.* Greece
Antioch Turkey *see* **Antakya**
49 F6 **Antipodes Islands** N.Z.
152 A3 **Antofagasta** Chile
154 C3 **Antonina** Brazil
97 C1 **Antrim** U.K.
97 C1 **Antrim Hills** U.K.
121 D2 **Antsalova** Madag.
121 D2 **Antsirabe** Madag.
121 D2 **Antsirañana** Madag.
121 D2 **Antsohihy** Madag.
100 B2 **Antwerp** Belgium
An Uaimh Ireland *see* **Navan**
74 B2 **Anupgarh** India
73 C4 **Anuradhapura** Sri Lanka
Anvers Belgium *see* **Antwerp**
51 C3 **Anxious Bay** Austr.
70 B2 **Anyang** China
65 B2 **Anyang** S. Korea
108 B2 **Anzio** Italy
66 D2 **Aomori** Japan
54 B2 **Aoraki** *mt.* N.Z.
108 A1 **Aosta** Italy
143 D3 **Apalachee Bay** U.S.A.
150 B2 **Apaporis** *r.* Col.
154 B2 **Aparecida do Tabuado** Brazil
64 B1 **Aparri** Phil.
86 C2 **Apatity** Rus. Fed.
144 B3 **Apatzingán** Mex.
100 B1 **Apeldoorn** Neth.
100 C1 **Apen** Ger.
108 A2 **Apennines** *mts* Italy
49 G3 **Apia** Samoa
154 C2 **Apiaí** Brazil
64 B2 **Apo, Mount** *vol.* Phil.
101 E2 **Apolda** Ger.
52 B3 **Apollo Bay** Austr.
143 D3 **Apopka, Lake** U.S.A.
154 B1 **Aporé** Brazil
154 B1 **Aporé** *r.* Brazil
80 B2 **Apostolos Andreas, Cape** Cyprus
133 E3 **Appalachian Mountains** U.S.A.
53 D2 **Appin** Austr.
140 B2 **Appleton** U.S.A.
108 B2 **Aprilia** Italy
91 D3 **Apsheronsk** Rus. Fed.
154 B2 **Apucarana** Brazil
154 B2 **Apucarana, Serra da** *hills* Brazil
78 A2 **Aqaba, Gulf of** Asia
154 A1 **Aquidauana** *r.* Brazil
75 C2 **Ara** India
117 A4 **Arab, Bahr el** *watercourse* Sudan
Arabian Gulf Asia *see* **The Gulf**
78 B2 **Arabian Peninsula** Asia
56 G5 **Arabian Sea** Indian Ocean
151 E3 **Aracaju** Brazil
151 E2 **Aracati** Brazil
154 B2 **Araçatuba** Brazil
155 D1 **Aracruz** Brazil
155 D1 **Araçuaí** Brazil
110 B1 **Arad** Romania
115 E3 **Arada** Chad
156 C6 **Arafura Sea** Austr./Indon.
154 B1 **Aragarças** Brazil
107 C1 **Aragón** *r.* Spain
151 D2 **Araguaia** *r.* Brazil
151 D2 **Araguaína** Brazil

154 C1 **Araguari** Brazil
67 C3 **Arai** Japan
115 C2 **Arak** Alg.
81 C2 **Arāk** Iran
62 A1 **Arakan Yoma** *mts* Myanmar
81 C1 **Arak's** *r.* Armenia
76 C2 **Aral Sea** *salt l.* Kazakh./Uzbek.
76 C2 **Aral'sk** Kazakh.
Aral'skoye More *salt l.* Kazakh./Uzbek. *see* **Aral Sea**
106 C1 **Aranda de Duero** Spain
109 D2 **Arandelovac** Serbia
97 B2 **Aran Islands** Ireland
106 C1 **Aranjuez** Spain
122 A1 **Aranos** Namibia
139 D3 **Aransas Pass** U.S.A.
67 B4 **Arao** Japan
114 B3 **Araouane** Mali
151 E2 **Arapiraca** Brazil
154 B2 **Arapongas** Brazil
154 C3 **Araquari** Brazil
78 B1 **'Ar'ar** Saudi Arabia
154 C2 **Araraquara** Brazil
151 C2 **Araras** Brazil
154 B3 **Araras, Serra das** *mts* Brazil
52 B3 **Ararat** Austr.
81 C2 **Ararat, Mount** Turkey
155 D2 **Araruama, Lago de** *lag.* Brazil
155 E1 **Arataca** Brazil
Aratürük China *see* **Yiwu**
150 A1 **Arauca** Col.
154 C1 **Araxá** Brazil
81 C2 **Arbīl** Iraq
96 C2 **Arbroath** U.K.
74 A2 **Arbu Lut, Dasht-e** *des.* Afgh.
104 B3 **Arcachon** France
143 D3 **Arcadia** U.S.A.
134 B2 **Arcata** U.S.A.
145 B3 **Arcelia** Mex.
86 D2 **Archangel** Rus. Fed.
51 D1 **Archer** *r.* Austr.
134 D2 **Arco** U.S.A.
106 B2 **Arcos de la Frontera** Spain
127 F2 **Arctic Bay** Can.
160 **Arctic Ocean**
126 C2 **Arctic Red** *r.* Can.
81 C2 **Ardabīl** Iran
81 C1 **Ardahan** Turkey
93 E3 **Årdalstangen** Norway
100 B3 **Ardennes** *plat.* Belgium
81 D2 **Ardestān** Iran
53 C2 **Ardlethan** Austr.
139 D2 **Ardmore** U.S.A.
96 A2 **Ardnamurchan, Point of** U.K.
52 A2 **Ardrossan** Austr.
96 B3 **Ardrossan** U.K.
135 B3 **Arena, Point** U.S.A.
93 E4 **Arendal** Norway
101 E1 **Arendsee (Altmark)** Ger.
150 A3 **Arequipa** Peru
151 C2 **Arere** Brazil
106 C1 **Arévalo** Spain
108 B2 **Arezzo** Italy
104 B2 **Argentan** France
153 B4 **Argentina** *country* S. America
153 A6 **Argentino, Lago** *l.* Arg.
104 C2 **Argenton-sur-Creuse** France
110 C2 **Argeș** *r.* Romania
74 A1 **Arghandab** *r.* Afgh.
111 B3 **Argolikos Kolpos** *b.* Greece
111 B3 **Argos** Greece
111 B3 **Argostoli** Greece
107 C1 **Arguís** Spain
69 E1 **Argun'** *r.* China/Rus. Fed.
50 B1 **Argyle, Lake** Austr.
93 F4 **Århus** Denmark
122 A2 **Ariamsvlei** Namibia
152 A2 **Arica** Chile
96 A2 **Arinagour** U.K.
155 C1 **Arinos** Brazil
150 C3 **Aripuanã** Brazil
150 B2 **Aripuanã** *r.* Brazil
150 B2 **Ariquemes** Brazil
154 B1 **Ariranhá** *r.* Brazil
138 A2 **Arizona** *state* U.S.A.
144 A1 **Arizpe** Mex.
78 B2 **'Arjah** Saudi Arabia
92 G2 **Arjeplog** Sweden
142 B2 **Arkadelphia** U.S.A.
77 C1 **Arkalyk** Kazakh.
142 B2 **Arkansas** *r.* U.S.A.
142 B1 **Arkansas** *state* U.S.A.
137 D3 **Arkansas City** U.S.A.
Arkhangel'sk Rus. Fed. *see* **Archangel**
97 C2 **Arklow** Ireland
102 C1 **Arkona, Kap** *c.* Ger.
82 G1 **Arkticheskogo Instituta, Ostrova** *is* Rus. Fed.
105 C3 **Arles** France
115 C3 **Arlit** Niger
100 B3 **Arlon** Belgium
97 C1 **Armagh** U.K.
116 B2 **Armant** Egypt
81 C1 **Armavir** Rus. Fed.
81 C1 **Armenia** *country* Asia
150 A1 **Armenia** Col.
144 B3 **Armeria** Mex.
53 D2 **Armidale** Austr.
130 B1 **Armstrong** Can.
80 B1 **Armyans'k** Ukr.
80 B2 **Arnauti, Cape** Cyprus
100 B2 **Arnhem** Neth.
51 C1 **Arnhem, Cape** Austr.
51 C1 **Arnhem Bay** Austr.
51 C1 **Arnhem Land** *reg.* Austr.
108 B2 **Arno** *r.* Italy
52 A2 **Arno Bay** Austr.
130 C2 **Arnprior** Can.
100 D2 **Arnsberg** Ger.
101 E2 **Arnstadt** Ger.
122 A2 **Aroab** Namibia
101 D2 **Arolsen** Ger.
78 A3 **Aroma** Sudan
108 A1 **Arona** Italy
144 B2 **Aros** *r.* Mex.
81 C2 **Ar Ramādī** Iraq
96 B3 **Arran** *i.* U.K.
97 B1 **Arranmore Island** Ireland
80 B2 **Ar Raqqah** Syria
104 C1 **Arras** France
78 B2 **Ar Rass** Saudi Arabia
145 C3 **Arriagá** Mex.
79 C2 **Ar Rimāl** *reg.* Saudi Arabia
Ar Riyāḍ Saudi Arabia *see* **Riyadh**
145 C2 **Arroyo Seco** Mex.
79 C2 **Ar Rustāq** Oman
80 C2 **Ar Ruṭbah** Iraq
81 D3 **Arsenajān** Iran
66 B2 **Arsen'yev** Rus. Fed.
111 B3 **Arta** Greece
144 B3 **Arteaga** Mex.
66 B2 **Artem** Rus. Fed.
91 D2 **Artemivs'k** Ukr.
104 C2 **Artenay** France
138 C2 **Artesia** U.S.A.
51 E2 **Arthur Point** Austr.
54 B2 **Arthur's Pass** N.Z.
152 C4 **Artigas** Uru.
129 D1 **Artillery Lake** Can.
90 B2 **Artsyz** Ukr.
77 D3 **Artux** China
81 C1 **Artvin** Turkey
59 C3 **Aru, Kepulauan** *is* Indon.
119 D2 **Arua** Uganda
147 D3 **Aruba** *terr.* West Indies
119 D3 **Arusha** Tanz.
69 C1 **Arvayheer** Mongolia
129 E1 **Arviat** Can.
92 G2 **Arvidsjaur** Sweden
93 F4 **Arvika** Sweden
87 D3 **Arzamas** Rus. Fed.
107 C2 **Arzew** Alg.
100 C2 **Arzfeld** Ger.
101 F2 **Aš** Czech Rep.
115 C4 **Asaba** Nigeria
74 B1 **Asadābād** Afgh.
66 D2 **Asahi-dake** *vol.* Japan
66 D2 **Asahikawa** Japan
78 B3 **Āsalē** *l.* Eth.
75 C2 **Asansol** India
131 C2 **Asbestos** Can.
109 C2 **Ascea** Italy
152 B2 **Ascensión** Bol.
113 D7 **Ascension** *i.* S. Atlantic Oce
145 D3 **Ascensión, Bahía de la** *b.* M
101 D3 **Aschaffenburg** Ger.
100 C2 **Ascheberg** Ger.
101 E2 **Aschersleben** Ger.
108 B2 **Ascoli Piceno** Italy
92 G3 **Åsele** Sweden
110 B2 **Asenovgrad** Bulg.
76 B3 **Aşgabat** Turkm.
50 A2 **Ashburton** *watercourse* Aust
54 B2 **Ashburton** N.Z.
142 B2 **Ashdown** U.S.A.
143 D1 **Asheville** U.S.A.
53 D1 **Ashford** Austr.
99 D3 **Ashford** U.K.
Ashgabat Turkm. *see* **Aşgab**
98 C1 **Ashington** U.K.
67 B4 **Ashizuri-misaki** *pt* Japan
136 D3 **Ashland** *KS* U.S.A.
140 C3 **Ashland** *KY* U.S.A.
140 C2 **Ashland** *OH* U.S.A.
134 B2 **Ashland** *OR* U.S.A.
140 A1 **Ashland** *WI* U.S.A.
88 C3 **Ashmyany** Belarus
78 B3 **Ash Sharawrah** Saudi Arabi
Ash Shāriqah U.A.E. *see* **Sharjah**
81 C2 **Ash Sharqāṭ** Iraq
81 C2 **Ash Shaṭrah** Iraq
79 B3 **Ash Shiḥr** Yemen
79 C2 **Ash Şhināş** Oman
78 B2 **Ash Shu'bah** Saudi Arabia
78 B2 **Ash Shumlūl** Saudi Arabia
140 C2 **Ashtabula** U.S.A.
131 D1 **Ashuanipi Lake** Can.
106 B2 **Asilah** Morocco
108 A2 **Asinara, Golfo dell'** *b. Sardegna* Italy
82 G3 **Asino** Rus. Fed.
88 C3 **Asipovichy** Belarus
78 B2 **'Asīr** *reg.* Saudi Arabia
93 F4 **Askim** Norway
68 C1 **Askiz** Rus. Fed.
116 B3 **Asmara** Eritrea
93 F4 **Åsnen** *l.* Sweden
116 B2 **Asoteriba, Jebel** *mt.* Sudan
103 D2 **Aspang-Markt** Austria
136 B3 **Aspen** U.S.A.
54 A2 **Aspiring, Mount** N.Z.
117 C3 **Assab** Eritrea
Aş Şaḥrā' al Gharbīyah *des.* Egypt *see* **Western Desert**
Aş Şaḥrā' ash Sharqīyah *de* Egypt *see* **Eastern Desert**
78 B2 **As Salamiyah** Saudi Arabia
81 C2 **As Samāwah** Iraq

C2 **Aş Şanām** *reg.* Saudi Arabia
E2 **As Sarīr** *reg.* Libya
C1 **Assen** Neth.
B2 **Assesse** Belgium
D1 **As Sidrah** Libya
D3 **Assiniboia** Can.
C2 **Assiniboine, Mount** Can.
B2 **Assis** Brazil
B2 **Aş Şubayḩīyah** Kuwait
C2 **As Sulaymānīyah** Iraq
B2 **As Sulaymī** Saudi Arabia
B2 **As Sulayyil** Saudi Arabia
B2 **As Sūq** Saudi Arabia
B2 **As Suwaydā'** Syria
C2 **As Suwayq** Oman
As Suways Egypt *see* **Suez**
B3 **Astakos** Greece
D1 **Astana** Kazakh.
C2 **Āstārā** Iran
A2 **Asti** Italy
B1 **Astor** Pak.
B1 **Astorga** Spain
B1 **Astoria** U.S.A.
D4 **Astrakhan'** Rus. Fed.
C3 **Astravyets** Belarus
C3 **Astypalaia** *i.* Greece
2 C3 **Asunción** Para.
6 B2 **Aswān** Egypt
6 B2 **Asyūţ** Egypt
Atacama, Desierto de *des.* Chile *see* **Atacama Desert**
2 B3 **Atacama, Salar de** *salt flat* Chile
2 B3 **Atacama Desert** *des.* Chile
4 C4 **Atakpamé** Togo
B3 **Atalanti** Greece
0 A3 **Atalaya** Peru
7 C3 **Atamyrat** Turkm.
8 B3 **'Ataq** Yemen
4 A2 **Atâr** Maur.
5 B3 **Atascadero** U.S.A.
7 D2 **Atasu** Kazakh.
1 C3 **Atavyros** *mt.* Greece
6 B3 **Atbara** Sudan
6 B3 **Atbara** *r.* Sudan
7 C1 **Atbasar** Kazakh.
7 D3 **Atchison** U.S.A.
8 B2 **Aterno** *r.* Italy
8 B2 **Atessa** Italy
0 A2 **Ath** Belgium
8 C2 **Athabasca** Can.
9 C2 **Athabasca** *r.* Can.
9 D2 **Athabasca, Lake** Can.
1 B3 **Athens** Greece
3 D2 **Athens** *GA* U.S.A.
0 C3 **Athens** *OH* U.S.A.
3 D1 **Athens** *TN* U.S.A.
9 D2 **Athens** *TX* U.S.A.
Athina Greece *see* **Athens**
7 C2 **Athlone** Ireland
1 B2 **Athos** *mt.* Greece
7 C2 **Athy** Ireland
5 D3 **Ati** Chad
0 A2 **Atikokan** Can.
7 D3 **Atkarsk** Rus. Fed.
3 D2 **Atlanta** U.S.A.
7 D2 **Atlantic** U.S.A.
1 E3 **Atlantic City** U.S.A.
8 **Atlantic Ocean**
2 A3 **Atlantis** S. Africa
4 B1 **Atlas Mountains** Africa
4 C1 **Atlas Saharien** *mts* Alg.
8 A2 **Atlin** Can.
8 A2 **Atlin Lake** Can.
2 C2 **Atmore** U.S.A.
9 D2 **Atoka** U.S.A.
5 C2 **Atrai** *r.* India

78 B2 **Aţ Ţā'if** Saudi Arabia
63 B2 **Attapu** Laos
130 B1 **Attawapiskat** Can.
130 B1 **Attawapiskat** *r.* Can.
130 B1 **Attawapiskat Lake** Can.
100 C2 **Attendorn** Ger.
116 B2 **Aţ Ţūr** Egypt
78 B3 **At Turbah** Yemen
76 B2 **Atyrau** Kazakh.
105 C3 **Aubenas** France
126 C2 **Aubry Lake** Can.
142 C2 **Auburn** *AL* U.S.A.
135 B3 **Auburn** *CA* U.S.A.
137 D2 **Auburn** *NE* U.S.A.
141 D2 **Auburn** *NY* U.S.A.
104 C2 **Aubusson** France
104 C3 **Auch** France
54 B1 **Auckland** N.Z.
48 F6 **Auckland Islands** *is* N.Z.
101 F2 **Aue** Ger.
102 C2 **Augsburg** Ger.
109 C3 **Augusta** *Sicilia* Italy
143 D2 **Augusta** *GA* U.S.A.
137 D3 **Augusta** *KS* U.S.A.
141 F2 **Augusta** *ME* U.S.A.
50 A2 **Augustus, Mount** Austr.
100 A2 **Aulnoye-Aymeries** France
62 A2 **Aunglan** Myanmar
122 B2 **Auob** *watercourse* Namibia/S. Africa
74 B3 **Aurangabad** India
100 C1 **Aurich** Ger.
154 B1 **Aurilândia** Brazil
104 C3 **Aurillac** France
136 C3 **Aurora** *CO* U.S.A.
140 B2 **Aurora** *IL* U.S.A.
137 D2 **Aurora** *NE* U.S.A.
122 A2 **Aus** Namibia
137 E2 **Austin** *MN* U.S.A.
135 C3 **Austin** *NV* U.S.A.
139 D2 **Austin** *TX* U.S.A.
50 B2 **Australia** *country* Oceania
159 D7 **Australian-Antarctic Basin** Southern Ocean
53 C3 **Australian Capital Territory** *admin. div.* Austr.
102 C2 **Austria** *country* Europe
144 B3 **Autlán** Mex.
105 C2 **Autun** France
105 C2 **Auxerre** France
105 D2 **Auxonne** France
105 C2 **Avallon** France
131 E2 **Avalon Peninsula** Can.
154 C2 **Avaré** Brazil
49 H4 **Avarua** Cook Is
91 D2 **Avdiyivka** Ukr.
106 B1 **Aveiro** Port.
109 B2 **Avellino** Italy
100 A2 **Avesnes-sur-Helpe** France
93 G3 **Avesta** Sweden
108 B2 **Avezzano** Italy
96 C2 **Aviemore** U.K.
109 C2 **Avigliano** Italy
105 C3 **Avignon** France
106 C1 **Ávila** Spain
106 B1 **Avilés** Spain
109 C3 **Avola** *Sicilia* Italy
99 B2 **Avon** *r. England* U.K.
99 C3 **Avon** *r. England* U.K.
104 B2 **Avranches** France
54 B1 **Awanui** N.Z.
117 C4 **Āwash** Eth.
117 C3 **Āwash** *r.* Eth.
115 D2 **Awbārī** Libya
115 D2 **Awbārī, Idhān** *des.* Libya
117 C4 **Aw Dheegle** Somalia
96 B2 **Awe, Loch** *l.* U.K.

117 A4 **Aweil** Sudan
126 E1 **Axel Heiberg Island** Can.
114 B4 **Axim** Ghana
150 A3 **Ayacucho** Peru
77 E2 **Ayagoz** Kazakh.
68 B2 **Ayakkum Hu** *salt l.* China
106 B2 **Ayamonte** Spain
83 K3 **Ayan** Rus. Fed.
150 A3 **Ayaviri** Peru
76 A2 **Aybas** Kazakh.
91 D2 **Aydar** *r.* Ukr.
77 C2 **Aydarko'l ko'li** *l.* Uzbek.
111 C3 **Aydın** Turkey
77 C2 **Ayeat, Gora** *h.* Kazakh.
Ayers Rock *h.* Austr. *see* **Uluru**
99 C3 **Aylesbury** U.K.
106 C1 **Ayllón** Spain
129 D1 **Aylmer Lake** Can.
117 B4 **Ayod** Sudan
83 M2 **Ayon, Ostrov** *i.* Rus. Fed.
114 B3 **'Ayoûn el 'Atroûs** Maur.
51 D1 **Ayr** Austr.
96 B3 **Ayr** U.K.
98 A1 **Ayre, Point of** Isle of Man
76 C2 **Ayteke Bi** Kazakh.
110 C2 **Aytos** Bulg.
145 C3 **Ayutla** Mex.
63 B2 **Ayutthaya** Thai.
111 C3 **Ayvacık** Turkey
111 C3 **Ayvalık** Turkey
114 C3 **Azaouagh, Vallée de** *watercourse* Mali/Niger
Azbine *mts* Niger *see* **Aïr, Massif de l'**
81 C1 **Azerbaijan** *country* Asia
86 D2 **Azopol'ye** Rus. Fed.
84 D5 **Azores** *aut. reg.* Port.
91 D2 **Azov** Rus. Fed.
91 D2 **Azov, Sea of** Rus. Fed./Ukr.
Azraq, Bahr el *r.* Eth./Sudan *see* **Blue Nile**
106 B2 **Azuaga** Spain
146 B4 **Azuero, Península de** *pen.* Panama
153 C4 **Azul** Arg.
80 B2 **Az Zaqāzīq** Egypt
80 B2 **Az Zarqā'** Jordan
78 B3 **Az Zaydīyah** Yemen
114 C2 **Azzel Matti, Sebkha** *salt pan* Alg.
78 B2 **Az Zilfī** Saudi Arabia
78 B3 **Az Zuqur** *i.* Yemen

B

63 B2 **Ba, Sông** *r.* Vietnam
117 C4 **Baardheere** Somalia
77 C3 **Bābā, Kūh-e** *mts* Afgh.
110 C2 **Babadag** Romania
111 C2 **Babaeski** Turkey
117 C3 **Bāb al Mandab** *str.* Africa/Asia
61 C2 **Babana** Indon.
59 C3 **Babar** *i.* Indon.
119 D3 **Babati** Tanz.
89 E2 **Babayevo** Rus. Fed.
128 B2 **Babine** *r.* Can.
128 B2 **Babine Lake** Can.
59 C3 **Babo** Indon.
81 D2 **Bābol** Iran
122 A3 **Baboon Point** S. Africa
88 C3 **Babruysk** Belarus
64 B1 **Babuyan** *i.* Phil.
64 B1 **Babuyan Islands** Phil.
151 D2 **Bacabal** Brazil
59 C3 **Bacan** *i.* Indon.

110 C1 **Bacău** Romania
52 B3 **Bacchus Marsh** Austr.
77 D3 **Bachu** China
129 E1 **Back** *r.* Can.
109 C1 **Bačka Palanka** Serbia
63 B3 **Bạc Liêu** Vietnam
64 B1 **Bacolod** Phil.
130 C1 **Bacqueville, Lac** *l.* Can.
106 B2 **Badajoz** Spain
62 A1 **Badarpur** India
101 E2 **Bad Berka** Ger.
101 D2 **Bad Berleburg** Ger.
101 E1 **Bad Bevensen** Ger.
100 C2 **Bad Ems** Ger.
103 D2 **Baden** Austria
102 B2 **Baden-Baden** Ger.
101 E2 **Bad Harzburg** Ger.
101 D2 **Bad Hersfeld** Ger.
102 C2 **Bad Hofgastein** Austria
101 D2 **Bad Homburg vor der Höhe** Ger.
74 A2 **Badin** Pak.
Bādiyat ash Shām *des.* Asia *see* **Syrian Desert**
101 E2 **Bad Kissingen** Ger.
100 C3 **Bad Kreuznach** Ger.
101 E2 **Bad Lauterberg im Harz** Ger.
101 D2 **Bad Lippspringe** Ger.
101 D3 **Bad Mergentheim** Ger.
101 D2 **Bad Nauheim** Ger.
100 C2 **Bad Neuenahr-Ahrweiler** Ger.
101 E2 **Bad Neustadt an der Saale** Ger.
101 E1 **Bad Oldesloe** Ger.
101 D2 **Bad Pyrmont** Ger.
78 A2 **Badr Ḥunayn** Saudi Arabia
101 D1 **Bad Salzuflen** Ger.
101 E2 **Bad Salzungen** Ger.
102 C1 **Bad Schwartau** Ger.
101 E1 **Bad Segeberg** Ger.
100 C3 **Bad Sobernheim** Ger.
73 C4 **Badulla** Sri Lanka
100 D1 **Bad Zwischenahn** Ger.
106 C2 **Baeza** Spain
114 A3 **Bafatá** Guinea-Bissau
160 O2 **Baffin Bay** *sea* Can./Greenland
127 G2 **Baffin Island** Can.
118 B2 **Bafia** Cameroon
114 A3 **Bafing** *r.* Africa
114 A3 **Bafoulabé** Mali
118 B2 **Bafoussam** Cameroon
76 B3 **Bāfq** Iran
80 B1 **Bafra** Turkey
79 C2 **Bāft** Iran
119 C2 **Bafwasende** Dem. Rep. Congo
119 D3 **Bagamoyo** Tanz.
60 B1 **Bagan Datuk** Malaysia
120 B2 **Bagani** Namibia
60 B1 **Bagansiapiapi** Indon.
138 A2 **Bagdad** U.S.A.
152 C4 **Bagé** Brazil
97 C2 **Bagenalstown** Ireland
81 C2 **Baghdād** Iraq
77 C3 **Baghlān** Afgh.
104 C3 **Bagnères-de-Luchon** France
88 B3 **Bagrationovsk** Rus. Fed.
Bagrax China *see* **Bohu**
64 B1 **Baguio** Phil.
115 C3 **Bagzane, Monts** *mts* Niger
Bahamas *country* West Indies *see* **The Bahamas**
146 C2 **Bahamas, The** *country* West Indies
75 C2 **Baharampur** India
Bahariya Oasis Egypt *see* **Bahrīyah, Wāḥāt al**
76 B3 **Baharly** Turkm.
60 B1 **Bahau** Malaysia
72 B2 **Bahawalnagar** Pak.
74 B2 **Bahawalpur** Pak.
153 B4 **Bahía Blanca** Arg.
144 A2 **Bahía Kino** Mex.
152 C3 **Bahía Negra** Para.
144 A2 **Bahía Tortugas** Mex.
117 B3 **Bahir Dar** Eth.
75 C2 **Bahraich** India
79 C2 **Bahrain** *country* Asia
116 A2 **Bahrīyah, Wāḥāt al** *oasis* Egypt
79 D2 **Bāhū Kālāt** Iran
110 B1 **Baia Mare** Romania
69 E1 **Baicheng** China
131 D2 **Baie-Comeau** Can.
Baie-du-Poste Can. *see* **Mistissini**
131 C2 **Baie-St-Paul** Can.
65 B1 **Baihe** China
69 D1 **Baikal, Lake** Rus. Fed.
110 B2 **Băilești** Romania
68 C2 **Baima** China
143 D2 **Bainbridge** U.S.A.
48 F2 **Bairiki** Kiribati
Bairin Youqi China *see* **Daban**
53 C3 **Bairnsdale** Austr.
65 B1 **Baishan** *Jilin* China
65 B1 **Baishanzhen** *Jilin* China
65 B1 **Baitou Shan** *mt.* China/N. Korea
70 A2 **Baiyin** China
116 B3 **Baiyuda Desert** Sudan
103 D2 **Baja** Hungary
144 A1 **Baja California** *pen.* Mex.
78 B3 **Bājil** Yemen
114 A3 **Bakel** Senegal
135 C3 **Baker** *CA* U.S.A.
136 C1 **Baker** *MT* U.S.A.
134 C2 **Baker** *OR* U.S.A.
134 B1 **Baker, Mount** *vol.* U.S.A.
129 E1 **Baker Foreland** *hd* Can.
49 G2 **Baker Island** N. Pacific Ocean
129 E1 **Baker Lake** Can.
129 E1 **Baker Lake** Can.
135 C3 **Bakersfield** U.S.A.
91 C3 **Bakhchysaray** Ukr.
91 C1 **Bakhmach** Ukr.
Bākhtarān Iran *see* **Kermānshāh**
Bakı Azer. *see* **Baku**
111 C2 **Bakırköy** Turkey
92 C2 **Bakkaflói** *b.* Iceland
118 C2 **Bakouma** C.A.R.
81 C1 **Baku** Azer.
64 A2 **Balabac** Phil.
64 A2 **Balabac** *i.* Phil.
64 A2 **Balabac Strait** Malaysia/Phil.
61 C2 **Balaiberkuak** Indon.
52 A2 **Balaklava** Austr.
91 C3 **Balaklava** Ukr.
91 D2 **Balakliya** Ukr.
87 D3 **Balakovo** Rus. Fed.
145 C3 **Balancán** Mex.
111 C3 **Balan Dağı** *h.* Turkey
64 B1 **Balanga** Phil.
87 D3 **Balashov** Rus. Fed.
103 D2 **Balaton, Lake** Hungary
103 D2 **Balatonboglár** Hungary
150 C2 **Balbina, Represa de** *resr* Brazil
97 C2 **Balbriggan** Ireland
52 A2 **Balcanoona** Austr.
110 C2 **Balchik** Bulg.
54 A3 **Balclutha** N.Z.
129 E2 **Baldock Lake** Can.
129 D2 **Baldy Mountain** *h.* Can.
138 B2 **Baldy Peak** U.S.A.
Baleares, Islas *is* Spain *see* **Balearic Islands**
107 D2 **Balearic Islands** *is* Spain
155 E1 **Baleia, Ponta da** *pt* Brazil
130 C1 **Baleine, Grande Rivière de** *r.* Can.
131 D1 **Baleine, Rivière à la** *r.* Can.
75 C2 **Baleshwar** India
108 A2 **Balestrieri, Punta** *mt.* *Sardegna* Italy
61 C2 **Bali** *i.* Indon.
115 D4 **Bali** Nigeria
60 A1 **Balige** Indon.
75 C2 **Baliguda** India
111 C3 **Balıkesir** Turkey
61 C2 **Balikpapan** Indon.
59 D3 **Balimo** P.N.G.
102 B2 **Balingen** Ger.
Bali Sea Indon. *see* **Laut Ba**
76 B3 **Balkanabat** Turkm.
110 B2 **Balkan Mountains** Bulg./Serbia
77 D2 **Balkhash** Kazakh.
77 D2 **Balkhash, Lake** Kazakh.
Balkhash, Ozero *l.* Kazakh. *see* **Balkhash, Lake**
50 B3 **Balladonia** Austr.
97 B2 **Ballaghaderreen** Ireland
92 G2 **Ballangen** Norway
52 B3 **Ballarat** Austr.
50 B2 **Ballard, Lake** *imp. l.* Austr.
96 C2 **Ballater** U.K.
114 B3 **Ballé** Mali
53 D1 **Ballina** Austr.
97 B1 **Ballina** Ireland
97 B2 **Ballinasloe** Ireland
139 D2 **Ballinger** U.S.A.
97 B2 **Ballinrobe** Ireland
97 B1 **Ballycastle** Ireland
97 C1 **Ballycastle** U.K.
97 D1 **Ballyclare** U.K.
97 C1 **Ballymena** U.K.
97 C1 **Ballymoney** U.K.
97 D1 **Ballynahinch** U.K.
97 B1 **Ballyshannon** Ireland
95 B2 **Ballyvoy** U.K.
51 D2 **Balonne** *r.* Austr.
74 B2 **Balotra** India
75 C2 **Balrampur** India
52 B2 **Balranald** Austr.
110 B2 **Balș** Romania
151 D2 **Balsas** Brazil
145 C3 **Balsas** Mex.
90 B2 **Balta** Ukr.
90 B2 **Bălți** Moldova
93 G4 **Baltic Sea** *g.* Europe
80 B2 **Balṭīm** Egypt
123 C1 **Baltimore** S. Africa
141 D3 **Baltimore** U.S.A.
88 A3 **Baltiysk** Rus. Fed.
62 A1 **Balu** India
88 C2 **Balvi** Latvia
77 D2 **Balykchy** Kyrg.
87 E4 **Balykshi** Kazakh.
79 C2 **Bam** Iran
51 D1 **Bamaga** Austr.
130 A1 **Bamaji Lake** Can.
114 B3 **Bamako** Mali
118 C2 **Bambari** C.A.R.
101 E3 **Bamberg** Ger.
119 C2 **Bambili** Dem. Rep. Congo
119 C2 **Bambouti** C.A.R.
155 C2 **Bambuí** Brazil
118 B2 **Bamenda** Cameroon
74 A1 **Bāmīān** Afgh.
119 C2 **Banalia** Dem. Rep. Congo
151 C3 **Bananal, Ilha do** *i.* Brazil

4 B2 **Banas** *r.* India
1 C3 **Banaz** Turkey
2 B2 **Ban Ban** Laos
7 C1 **Banbridge** U.K.
9 C2 **Banbury** U.K.
0 C2 **Bancroft** Can.
9 C2 **Banda** Dem. Rep. Congo
5 C2 **Banda** India
9 C3 **Banda, Kepulauan** *is* Indon.
9 C3 **Banda, Laut** *sea* Indon.
0 A1 **Banda Aceh** Indon.
9 C2 **Bandar-e 'Abbās** Iran
1 C2 **Bandar-e Anzalī** Iran
9 C2 **Bandar-e Chārak** Iran
1 C2 **Bandar-e Emām Khomeynī** Iran
9 C2 **Bandar-e Lengeh** Iran
9 C2 **Bandar-e Maqām** Iran
0 B2 **Bandar Lampung** Indon.
1 C1 **Bandar Seri Begawan** Brunei
Banda Sea Indon. *see* **Banda, Laut**
5 D2 **Bandeiras, Pico de** *mt.* Brazil
3 C1 **Bandelierkop** S. Africa
4 B2 **Banderas, Bahía de** *b.* Mex.
4 B3 **Bandiagara** Mali
1 C2 **Bandırma** Turkey
7 B3 **Bandon** Ireland
8 B3 **Bandundu** Dem. Rep. Congo
1 B2 **Bandung** Indon.
8 C2 **Banff** Can.
6 C2 **Banff** U.K.
4 B3 **Banfora** Burkina
4 B2 **Banga** Phil.
3 B3 **Bangalore** India
8 C2 **Bangassou** C.A.R.
9 C3 **Banggai** Indon.
9 C3 **Banggai, Kepulauan** *is* Indon.
1 C1 **Banggi** *i. Sabah* Malaysia
0 B2 **Bangka** *i.* Indon.
1 C2 **Bangkalan** Indon.
0 B1 **Bangkinang** Indon.
0 B2 **Bangko** Indon.
3 B2 **Bangkok** Thai.
5 C2 **Bangladesh** *country* Asia
3 B2 **Ba Ngoi** Vietnam
7 D1 **Bangor** *Northern Ireland* U.K.
8 A2 **Bangor** *Wales* U.K.
1 F2 **Bangor** U.S.A.
3 A2 **Bang Saphan Yai** Thai.
4 B1 **Bangued** Phil.
8 B2 **Bangui** C.A.R.
1 B2 **Bangweulu, Lake** Zambia
2 B2 **Ban Huai Khon** Thai.
6 B2 **Banī Suwayf** Egypt
5 D1 **Banī Walīd** Libya
0 B2 **Bāniyās** Syria
9 C2 **Banja Luka** Bos.-Herz.
1 C2 **Banjarmasin** Indon.
4 A3 **Banjul** Gambia
8 A2 **Banks Island** *B.C.* Can.
6 C2 **Banks Island** *N.W.T.* Can.
8 F3 **Banks Islands** Vanuatu
9 E1 **Banks Lake** Can.
4 B2 **Banks Peninsula** N.Z.
5 C2 **Bankura** India
2 A1 **Banmauk** Myanmar
2 B2 **Ban Mouang** Laos
7 C1 **Bann** *r.* U.K.
2 B2 **Ban Napè** Laos
3 A3 **Ban Na San** Thai.
3 E4 **Bannerman Town** Bahamas
4 B1 **Bannu** Pak.
4 B2 **Banswara** India
3 A3 **Ban Tha Kham** Thai.
2 A2 **Ban Tha Song Yang** Thai.
3 B2 **Ban Tôp** Laos

97 B3 **Bantry** Ireland
97 B3 **Bantry Bay** Ireland
118 B2 **Banyo** Cameroon
107 D1 **Banyoles** Spain
61 C2 **Banyuwangi** Indon.
Bao'an China *see* **Shenzhen**
69 D2 **Baochang** China
70 B2 **Baoding** China
70 A2 **Baoji** China
62 B1 **Bao Lac** Vietnam
63 B2 **Bao Lôc** Vietnam
66 B1 **Baoqing** China
62 A1 **Baoshan** China
70 B1 **Baotou** China
81 C2 **Ba'qūbah** Iraq
109 C2 **Bar** Montenegro
117 C4 **Baraawe** Somalia
147 C2 **Baracoa** Cuba
53 C2 **Baradine** Austr.
147 C3 **Barahona** Dom. Rep.
116 B3 **Baraka** *watercourse* Eritrea/Sudan
61 C1 **Baram** *r. Sarawak* Malaysia
74 B1 **Baramulla** India
88 C3 **Baranavichy** Belarus
78 A2 **Baranīs** Egypt
90 B1 **Baranivka** Ukr.
76 B2 **Barankul** Kazakh.
128 A2 **Baranof Island** U.S.A.
59 C3 **Barat Daya, Kepulauan** *is* Indon.
155 D2 **Barbacena** Brazil
147 E3 **Barbados** *country* West Indies
107 D1 **Barbastro** Spain
104 B2 **Barbezieux-St-Hilaire** France
51 D2 **Barcaldine** Austr.
107 D1 **Barcelona** Spain
150 B1 **Barcelona** Venez.
105 D3 **Barcelonnette** France
150 B2 **Barcelos** Brazil
Barcoo Creek *watercourse* Austr. *see* **Cooper Creek**
103 D2 **Barcs** Hungary
75 C2 **Barddhaman** India
103 E2 **Bardejov** Slovakia
79 C2 **Bardsīr** Iran
75 B2 **Bareilly** India
160 B2 **Barents Sea** Arctic Ocean
78 A3 **Barentu** Eritrea
75 C2 **Barh** India
141 F2 **Bar Harbor** U.S.A.
109 C2 **Bari** Italy
74 B1 **Barikot** Afgh.
150 A1 **Barinas** Venez.
75 C2 **Baripada** India
75 D2 **Barisal** Bangl.
60 B2 **Barisan, Pegunungan** *mts* Indon.
61 C2 **Barito** *r.* Indon.
79 C2 **Barkā** Oman
88 C2 **Barkava** Latvia
51 C1 **Barkly Tableland** *reg.* Austr.
68 C2 **Barkol** China
110 C1 **Bârlad** Romania
105 D2 **Bar-le-Duc** France
50 A2 **Barlee, Lake** *imp. l.* Austr.
109 C2 **Barletta** Italy
53 C2 **Barmedman** Austr.
74 B2 **Barmer** India
99 A2 **Barmouth** U.K.
101 D1 **Barmstedt** Ger.
98 C1 **Barnard Castle** U.K.
53 B2 **Barnato** Austr.
82 G3 **Barnaul** Rus. Fed.
127 G2 **Barnes Icecap** Can.
100 B1 **Barneveld** Neth.
98 C2 **Barnsley** U.K.

99 A3 **Barnstaple** U.K.
99 A3 **Barnstaple Bay** U.K.
143 D2 **Barnwell** U.S.A.
Baroda India *see* **Vadodara**
150 B1 **Barquisimeto** Venez.
96 A2 **Barra** *i.* U.K.
53 D2 **Barraba** Austr.
151 D2 **Barra do Corda** Brazil
154 B1 **Barra do Garças** Brazil
150 C2 **Barra do São Manuel** Brazil
150 A3 **Barranca** *Lima* Peru
150 A2 **Barranca** *Loreto* Peru
152 C3 **Barranqueras** Arg.
150 A1 **Barranquilla** Col.
151 D3 **Barreiras** Brazil
154 C2 **Barretos** Brazil
130 C2 **Barrie** Can.
128 B2 **Barrière** Can.
52 B2 **Barrier Range** *hills* Austr.
53 D2 **Barrington, Mount** Austr.
129 D2 **Barrington Lake** Can.
53 C1 **Barringun** Austr.
97 C2 **Barrow** *r.* Ireland
51 C2 **Barrow Creek** Austr.
98 B1 **Barrow-in-Furness** U.K.
50 A2 **Barrow Island** Austr.
126 E2 **Barrow Strait** Can.
99 B3 **Barry** U.K.
130 C2 **Barrys Bay** Can.
74 B2 **Barsalpur** India
135 C4 **Barstow** U.S.A.
105 C2 **Bar-sur-Aube** France
80 B1 **Bartın** Turkey
51 D1 **Bartle Frere, Mount** Austr.
139 D1 **Bartlesville** U.S.A.
103 E1 **Bartoszyce** Pol.
61 C2 **Barung** *i.* Indon.
69 D1 **Baruun-Urt** Mongolia
91 D2 **Barvinkove** Ukr.
53 C2 **Barwon** *r.* Austr.
88 C3 **Barysaw** Belarus
110 C2 **Basarabi** Romania
105 D2 **Basel** Switz.
91 C2 **Bashtanka** Ukr.
64 B2 **Basilan** *i.* Phil.
99 D3 **Basildon** U.K.
99 C3 **Basingstoke** U.K.
81 C2 **Başkale** Turkey
130 C2 **Baskatong, Réservoir** *resr* Can.
Basle Switz. *see* **Basel**
118 C2 **Basoko** Dem. Rep. Congo
81 C2 **Basra** Iraq
128 C2 **Bassano** Can.
114 C4 **Bassar** Togo
63 A2 **Bassein** Myanmar
147 D3 **Basse-Terre** Guadeloupe
147 D3 **Basseterre** St Kitts and Nevis
114 B3 **Bassikounou** Maur.
51 D3 **Bass Strait** Austr.
79 C2 **Bastak** Iran
101 E2 **Bastheim** Ger.
75 C2 **Basti** India
105 D3 **Bastia** *Corse* France
100 B2 **Bastogne** Belgium
142 B2 **Bastrop** U.S.A.
Basuo China *see* **Dongfang**
118 A2 **Bata** Equat. Guinea
83 J2 **Batagay** Rus. Fed.
154 B2 **Bataguassu** Brazil
106 B2 **Batalha** Port.
71 C3 **Batan** *i.* Phil.
118 B2 **Batangafo** C.A.R.
64 B1 **Batangas** Phil.
60 B2 **Batanghari** *r.* Indon.
71 C3 **Batan Islands** Phil.
141 D2 **Batavia** U.S.A.
91 D2 **Bataysk** Rus. Fed.

130 B2 **Batchawana Mountain** *h.* Can.
50 C1 **Batchelor** Austr.
63 B2 **Bătdâmbâng** Cambodia
53 D3 **Batemans Bay** Austr.
142 B1 **Batesville** U.S.A.
89 D2 **Batetskiy** Rus. Fed.
99 B3 **Bath** U.K.
74 B1 **Bathinda** India
53 C2 **Bathurst** Austr.
131 D2 **Bathurst** Can.
126 D2 **Bathurst Inlet** Can.
126 D2 **Bathurst Inlet (abandoned)** Can.
50 C1 **Bathurst Island** Austr.
126 E1 **Bathurst Island** Can.
78 B1 **Bāţin, Wādī al** *watercourse* Asia
81 C2 **Batman** Turkey
115 C1 **Batna** Alg.
142 B2 **Baton Rouge** U.S.A.
144 B2 **Batopilas** Mex.
118 B2 **Batouri** Cameroon
154 B1 **Batovi** Brazil
92 I1 **Båtsfjord** Norway
73 C4 **Batticaloa** Sri Lanka
109 B2 **Battipaglia** Italy
129 D2 **Battle** *r.* Can.
140 B2 **Battle Creek** U.S.A.
135 C2 **Battle Mountain** U.S.A.
74 B1 **Battura Glacier** Pak.
117 B4 **Batu** *mt.* Eth.
60 A2 **Batu, Pulau-pulau** *is* Indon.
81 C1 **Bat'umi** Georgia
60 B1 **Batu Pahat** Malaysia
59 C3 **Baubau** Indon.
115 C3 **Bauchi** Nigeria
104 B2 **Baugé** France
105 D2 **Baume-les-Dames** France
154 C2 **Bauru** Brazil
154 B1 **Baús** Brazil
88 B2 **Bauska** Latvia
102 C1 **Bautzen** Ger.
144 B2 **Bavispe** *r.* Mex.
87 E3 **Bavly** Rus. Fed.
62 A1 **Bawdwin** Myanmar
61 C2 **Bawean** *i.* Indon.
114 B3 **Bawku** Ghana
146 C2 **Bayamo** Cuba
Bayan Gol China *see* **Dengkou**
68 C1 **Bayanhongor** Mongolia
70 A2 **Bayan Hot** China
69 D1 **Bayan-Uul** Mongolia
64 B2 **Bayawan** Phil.
80 C1 **Bayburt** Turkey
140 C2 **Bay City** *MI* U.S.A.
139 D3 **Bay City** *TX* U.S.A.
86 F2 **Baydaratskaya Guba** Rus. Fed.
117 C4 **Baydhabo** Somalia
81 C2 **Bayjī** Iraq
Baykal, Ozero *l.* Rus. Fed. *see* **Baikal, Lake**
83 I3 **Baykal'skiy Khrebet** *mts* Rus. Fed.
76 C2 **Baykonyr** Kazakh.
87 E3 **Baymak** Rus. Fed.
64 B1 **Bayombong** Phil.
104 B3 **Bayonne** France
111 C3 **Bayramiç** Turkey
101 E3 **Bayreuth** Ger.
78 B3 **Bayt al Faqīh** Yemen
106 C2 **Baza** Spain
106 C2 **Baza, Sierra de** *mts* Spain
74 A1 **Bāzārak** Afgh.
76 A2 **Bazardyuzyu, Gora** *mt.* Azer./Rus. Fed.
104 B3 **Bazas** France
74 A2 **Bazdar** Pak.
70 A2 **Bazhong** China
79 D2 **Bazmān** Iran
79 D2 **Bazmān, Kūh-e** *mt.* Iran
121 D2 **Bé, Nosy** *i.* Madag.
99 D3 **Beachy Head** U.K.
123 C3 **Beacon Bay** S. Africa
50 B1 **Beagle Gulf** Austr.
121 D2 **Bealanana** Madag.
97 B1 **Béal an Mhuirthead** Ireland
130 B2 **Beardmore** Can.
Bear Island Arctic Ocean *see* **Bjørnøya**
134 E1 **Bear Paw Mountain** U.S.A.
147 C3 **Beata, Cabo** *c.* Dom. Rep.
147 C3 **Beata, Isla** *i.* Dom. Rep.
137 D2 **Beatrice** U.S.A.
135 C3 **Beatty** U.S.A.
53 D1 **Beaudesert** Austr.
52 B3 **Beaufort** Austr.
61 C1 **Beaufort** *Sabah* Malaysia
143 D2 **Beaufort** U.S.A.
160 L2 **Beaufort Sea** Can./U.S.A.
122 B3 **Beaufort West** S. Africa
96 B2 **Beauly** *r.* U.K.
100 B2 **Beaumont** Belgium
54 A3 **Beaumont** N.Z.
139 E2 **Beaumont** U.S.A.
105 C2 **Beaune** France
100 B2 **Beauraing** Belgium
129 E2 **Beauséjour** Can.
104 C2 **Beauvais** France
129 D2 **Beauval** Can.
129 D2 **Beaver** *r.* Can.
135 D3 **Beaver** U.S.A.
126 B2 **Beaver Creek** Can.
140 B2 **Beaver Dam** U.S.A.
129 E2 **Beaver Hill Lake** Can.
140 B1 **Beaver Island** U.S.A.
128 C2 **Beaverlodge** Can.
74 B2 **Beawar** India
154 C2 **Bebedouro** Brazil
101 D2 **Bebra** Ger.
106 B1 **Becerreá** Spain
114 B1 **Béchar** Alg.
140 C3 **Beckley** U.S.A.
117 B4 **Bedelē** Eth.
99 C2 **Bedford** U.K.
140 B3 **Bedford** U.S.A.
100 C1 **Bedum** Neth.
53 D2 **Beecroft Peninsula** Austr.
101 F1 **Beelitz** Ger.
53 D1 **Beenleigh** Austr.
80 B2 **Beersheba** Israel
139 D3 **Beeville** U.S.A.
53 C3 **Bega** Austr.
107 D1 **Begur, Cap de** *c.* Spain
128 C1 **Behchokô** Can.
81 D2 **Behshahr** Iran
69 E1 **Bei'an** China
71 A3 **Beihai** China
70 B2 **Beijing** China
100 C1 **Beilen** Neth.
96 A2 **Beinn Mhòr** *h.* U.K.
121 C2 **Beira** Moz.
80 B2 **Beirut** Lebanon
123 C1 **Beitbridge** Zimbabwe
106 B2 **Beja** Port.
115 C1 **Bejaïa** Alg.
106 B1 **Béjar** Spain
74 A2 **Beji** *r.* Pak.
103 E2 **Békés** Hungary
103 E2 **Békéscsaba** Hungary
121 D3 **Bekily** Madag.
74 A2 **Bela** Pak.
123 C1 **Bela-Bela** S. Africa
118 B2 **Bélabo** Cameroon
109 D2 **Bela Crkva** Serbia
61 C1 **Belaga** *Sarawak* Malaysia
88 C3 **Belarus** *country* Europe
Belau *country* N. Pacific Oc *see* **Palau**
123 D2 **Bela Vista** Moz.
60 A1 **Belawan** Indon.
83 M2 **Belaya** *r.* Rus. Fed.
103 D1 **Bełchatów** Pol.
130 C1 **Belcher Islands** Can.
117 C4 **Beledweyne** Somalia
151 D2 **Belém** Brazil
138 B2 **Belen** U.S.A.
89 E3 **Belev** Rus. Fed.
97 D1 **Belfast** U.K.
141 F2 **Belfast** U.S.A.
105 D2 **Belfort** France
73 B3 **Belgaum** India
100 B2 **Belgium** *country* Europe
91 D1 **Belgorod** Rus. Fed.
109 D2 **Belgrade** Serbia
134 D1 **Belgrade** U.S.A.
60 B2 **Belinyu** Indon.
61 B2 **Belitung** *i.* Indon.
146 B3 **Belize** Belize
146 B3 **Belize** *country* Central Ame
83 K1 **Bel'kovskiy, Ostrov** *i.* Rus.
128 B2 **Bella Bella** Can.
104 C2 **Bellac** France
128 B2 **Bella Coola** Can.
53 C1 **Bellata** Austr.
136 C2 **Belle Fourche** U.S.A.
136 C2 **Belle Fourche** *r.* U.S.A.
143 D3 **Belle Glade** U.S.A.
104 B2 **Belle-Île** *i.* France
131 E1 **Belle Isle** *i.* Can.
131 E1 **Belle Isle, Strait of** Can.
130 C2 **Belleville** Can.
140 B3 **Belleville** *IL* U.S.A.
137 D3 **Belleville** *KS* U.S.A.
134 B1 **Bellevue** U.S.A.
134 B1 **Bellingham** U.S.A.
55 O2 **Bellingshausen Sea** Antarc
105 D2 **Bellinzona** Switz.
108 B1 **Belluno** Italy
122 A3 **Bellville** S. Africa
155 E1 **Belmonte** Brazil
146 B3 **Belmopan** Belize
69 E1 **Belogorsk** Rus. Fed.
121 D3 **Beloha** Madag.
155 D1 **Belo Horizonte** Brazil
140 B2 **Beloit** U.S.A.
86 C2 **Belomorsk** Rus. Fed.
91 D3 **Belorechensk** Rus. Fed.
87 E3 **Beloretsk** Rus. Fed.
Belorussia *country* Europe **Belarus**
86 F2 **Beloyarskiy** Rus. Fed.
86 C2 **Beloye, Ozero** *l.* Rus. Fed.
Beloye More *sea* Rus. Fed. **White Sea**
86 C2 **Belozersk** Rus. Fed.
77 E2 **Belukha, Gora** *mt.* Kazakh./Rus. Fed.
86 D2 **Belush'ye** Rus. Fed.
89 D2 **Belyy** Rus. Fed.
82 F2 **Belyy, Ostrov** *i.* Rus. Fed.
101 F1 **Belzig** Ger.
137 E1 **Bemidji** U.S.A.
118 C3 **Bena Dibele** Dem. Rep. Congo
53 C3 **Benalla** Austr.
106 B1 **Benavente** Spain
96 A2 **Benbecula** *i.* U.K.
134 B2 **Bend** U.S.A.
123 C3 **Bendearg** *mt.* S. Africa
52 B3 **Bendigo** Austr.
121 C2 **Bene** Moz.
102 C2 **Benešov** Czech Rep.

B2 Benevento Italy
C2 Bengal, Bay of sea Indian Ocean
 Bengaluru India see Bangalore
B2 Bengbu China
E1 Benghazi Libya
B1 Bengkayang Indon.
B1 Bengkulu Indon.
A2 Benguela Angola
B1 Ben Hope h. U.K.
B1 Beni r. Bol.
B1 Beni Dem. Rep. Congo
B1 Beni Abbès Alg.
C2 Benidorm Spain
C4 Beni Mellal Morocco
C4 Benin country Africa
C4 Benin, Bight of g. Africa
C4 Benin City Nigeria
B2 Benito Juárez Arg.
B2 Benjamim Constant Brazil
A1 Benjamín Hill Mex.
A2 Benjina Indon.
B2 Ben Lawers mt. U.K.
B2 Ben Lomond h. U.K.
B2 Ben Macdui mt. U.K.
A2 Ben More mt. U.K.
A2 Benmore, Lake N.Z.
B1 Ben More Assynt h. U.K.
A2 Bennett La.
B1 Bennetta, Ostrov i. Rus. Fed.
B2 Ben Nevis mt. U.K.
C2 Bennington U.S.A.
B2 Benoni S. Africa
D3 Bensheim Ger.
C3 Benson U.S.A.
C2 Benteng Indon.
C4 Benton Harbor U.S.A.
C4 Bentonville U.S.A.
C4 Benue r. Nigeria
B1 Benwee Head Ireland
B1 Ben Wyvis mt. U.K.
C1 Benxi China
 Beograd Serbia see Belgrade
D2 Beohari India
B4 Beppu Japan
A2 Berane Montenegro
C2 Berat Albania
C2 Berau, Teluk b. Indon.
B3 Berber Sudan
B3 Berbera Somalia
A2 Berbérati C.A.R.
C1 Berck France
D2 Berdyans'k Ukr.
D2 Berdychiv Ukr.
A2 Berehove Ukr.
B2 Bereina P.N.G.
B3 Bereket Turkm.
E2 Berens River Can.
A2 Berezhany Ukr.
A2 Berezivka Ukr.
B1 Berezne Ukr.
E3 Bereznik Rus. Fed.
E3 Berezniki Rus. Fed.
F2 Berezovo Rus. Fed.
A2 Berga Spain
A1 Bergama Turkey
A1 Bergamo Italy
C1 Bergen Mecklenburg-Vorpommern Ger.
D1 Bergen Niedersachsen Ger.
D1 Bergen Norway
D2 Bergen op Zoom Neth.
C2 Bergerac France
C2 Bergheim (Erft) Ger.
C2 Bergisch Gladbach Ger.
A1 Bergland Namibia
H2 Bergsviken Sweden

83 M3 Beringa, Ostrov i. Rus. Fed.
100 B3 Beringen Belgium
124 C3 Bering Sea N. Pacific Ocean
83 N2 Bering Strait Rus. Fed./U.S.A.
135 M3 Berkeley U.S.A.
100 B1 Berkhout Neth.
55 Q2 Berkner Island Antarctica
110 B2 Berkovitsa Bulg.
92 I1 Berlevåg Norway
101 F1 Berlin Ger.
141 E2 Berlin U.S.A.
101 E2 Berlingerode Ger.
53 D3 Bermagui Austr.
144 B2 Bermejillo Mex.
152 B3 Bermejo Bol.
131 D1 Bermen, Lac l. Can.
125 K4 Bermuda terr. N. Atlantic Ocean
105 D2 Bern Switz.
101 E2 Bernburg (Saale) Ger.
127 F2 Berne Bay Can.
100 C3 Bernkastel-Kues Ger.
121 D3 Beroroha Madag.
52 B2 Berri Austr.
107 D2 Berrouaghia Alg.
146 C2 Berry Islands Bahamas
100 C1 Bersenbrück Ger.
90 Bershad' Ukr.
131 D1 Berté, Lac l. Can.
118 B2 Bertoua Cameroon
150 B2 Beruri Brazil
98 B1 Berwick-upon-Tweed U.K.
91 C2 Beryslav Ukr.
121 D2 Besalampy Madag.
105 D2 Besançon France
129 D2 Besnard Lake Can.
142 C2 Bessemer U.S.A.
76 B2 Besshoky, Gora h. Kazakh.
106 B1 Betanzos Spain
118 B2 Bétaré Oya Cameroon
122 A2 Bethanie Namibia
123 C3 Bethlehem S. Africa
141 D2 Bethlehem U.S.A.
121 D3 Betioky Madag.
77 D2 Betpak-Dala plain Kazakh.
121 D3 Betroka Madag.
131 D2 Betsiamites Can.
121 D2 Betsiboka r. Madag.
137 E2 Bettendorf U.S.A.
75 C2 Bettiah India
75 B2 Betul India
75 B2 Betwa r. India
98 B2 Betws-y-coed U.K.
98 C2 Beverley U.K.
101 D2 Beverungen Ger.
100 B1 Beverwijk Neth.
99 D3 Bexhill U.K.
111 C2 Beykoz Turkey
114 B4 Beyla Guinea
76 B2 Beyneu Kazakh.
80 B1 Beypazarı Turkey
 Beyrouth Lebanon see Beirut
80 B2 Beyşehir Turkey
80 B2 Beyşehir Gölü l. Turkey
91 D2 Beysug r. Rus. Fed.
88 C2 Bezhanitsy Rus. Fed.
89 E2 Bezhetsk Rus. Fed.
105 C3 Béziers France
73 B3 Bhadrak India
75 C2 Bhadravati India
74 A2 Bhagalpur India
74 B1 Bhairi Hol mt. Pak.
74 B2 Bhakkar Pak.
62 A1 Bhamo Myanmar
75 C3 Bhanjanagar India
74 B2 Bharatpur India
74 B2 Bharuch India

74 B2 Bhavnagar India
75 C3 Bhawanipatna India
123 D2 Bhekuzulu S. Africa
74 B2 Bhilwara India
73 B3 Bhima r. India
123 C3 Bhisho S. Africa
74 B2 Bhiwani India
123 C3 Bhongweni S. Africa
74 B2 Bhopal India
75 C2 Bhubaneshwar India
74 A2 Bhuj India
74 B2 Bhusawal India
75 D2 Bhutan country Asia
62 B2 Bia, Phou mt. Laos
59 D3 Biak Indon.
59 D3 Biak i. Indon.
103 E1 Biała Podlaska Pol.
103 D1 Białogard Pol.
103 E1 Białystok Pol.
109 C3 Bianco Italy
104 B3 Biarritz France
105 D2 Biasca Switz.
66 D2 Bibai Japan
120 A2 Bibala Angola
102 B2 Biberach an der Riß Ger.
115 C4 Bida Nigeria
141 E2 Biddeford U.S.A.
99 A3 Bideford U.K.
101 D2 Biedenkopf Ger.
105 D2 Biel Switz.
101 D1 Bielefeld Ger.
108 A1 Biella Italy
103 D1 Bielsko-Biała Pol.
63 B2 Biên Hoa Vietnam
130 C1 Bienville, Lac l. Can.
100 B3 Bièvre Belgium
118 B3 Bifoun Gabon
111 C2 Biga Turkey
123 D2 Big Bend Swaziland
129 D2 Biggar Can.
96 C3 Biggar U.K.
134 D1 Big Hole r. U.S.A.
136 B1 Bighorn r. U.S.A.
136 B2 Bighorn Mountains U.S.A.
139 C2 Big Lake U.S.A.
140 B2 Big Rapids U.S.A.
129 D2 Big River Can.
129 E2 Big Sand Lake Can.
137 D2 Big Sioux r. U.S.A.
139 C2 Big Spring U.S.A.
134 E1 Big Timber U.S.A.
130 B1 Big Trout Lake Can.
130 A1 Big Trout Lake Can.
109 C2 Bihać Bos.-Herz.
75 C2 Bihar Sharif India
110 B1 Bihor, Vârful mt. Romania
114 A3 Bijagós, Arquipélago dos is Guinea-Bissau
81 C2 Bījār Iran
109 C2 Bijeljina Bos.-Herz.
109 C2 Bijelo Polje Montenegro
71 A3 Bijie China
74 B2 Bikaner India
69 E1 Bikin Rus. Fed.
118 B3 Bikoro Dem. Rep. Congo
79 C2 Bilād Banī Bū 'Alī Oman
75 C2 Bilaspur India
90 C2 Bila Tserkva Ukr.
63 A2 Bilauktaung Range mts Myanmar/Thai.
106 B1 Bilbao Spain
111 C2 Bilecik Turkey
103 E1 Biłgoraj Pol.
90 C2 Bilhorod-Dnistrovs'kyy Ukr.
119 C2 Bili Dem. Rep. Congo
83 M2 Bilibino Rus. Fed.
134 E1 Billings U.S.A.

99 B3 **Bill of Portland** *hd* U.K.
115 D3 **Bilma** Niger
115 D3 **Bilma, Grand Erg de** *des.* Niger
51 E2 **Biloela** Austr.
91 C2 **Bilohirs'k** Ukr.
90 B1 **Bilohir"ya** Ukr.
91 C1 **Bilopillya** Ukr.
91 D2 **Bilovods'k** Ukr.
142 C2 **Biloxi** U.S.A.
51 C2 **Bilpa Morea Claypan** *salt flat* Austr.
101 E2 **Bilshausen** Ger.
115 E3 **Biltine** Chad
90 C2 **Bilyayivka** Ukr.
143 E3 **Bimini Islands** Bahamas
75 B2 **Bina-Etawa** India
59 C3 **Binaija, Gunung** *mt.* Indon.
118 B3 **Bindu** Dem. Rep. Congo
121 C2 **Bindura** Zimbabwe
107 D1 **Binefar** Spain
53 D1 **Bingara** Austr.
100 C3 **Bingen am Rhein** Ger.
141 F1 **Bingham** U.S.A.
141 D2 **Binghamton** U.S.A.
81 C2 **Bingöl** Turkey
60 A1 **Binjai** Indon.
60 B2 **Bintuhan** Indon.
61 C1 **Bintulu** *Sarawak* Malaysia
70 B2 **Binzhou** China
109 C2 **Biograd na Moru** Croatia
118 A2 **Bioko** *i.* Equat. Guinea
118 C1 **Birao** C.A.R.
75 C2 **Biratnagar** Nepal
128 C2 **Birch Mountains** Can.
51 C2 **Birdsville** Austr.
80 B2 **Birecik** Turkey
60 A1 **Bireun** Indon.
75 C2 **Birganj** Nepal
117 B3 **Birhan** *mt.* Eth.
154 B2 **Birigüi** Brazil
76 B3 **Bīrjand** Iran
98 B2 **Birkenhead** U.K.
99 C2 **Birmingham** U.K.
142 C2 **Birmingham** U.S.A.
114 A2 **Bîr Mogreïn** Maur.
115 C3 **Birnin-Kebbi** Nigeria
115 C3 **Birnin Konni** Niger
69 E1 **Birobidzhan** Rus. Fed.
97 C2 **Birr** Ireland
96 C1 **Birsay** U.K.
78 A2 **Bi'r Shalatayn** Egypt
88 B2 **Biržai** Lith.
75 B2 **Bisalpur** India
138 B2 **Bisbee** U.S.A.
104 A2 **Biscay, Bay of** *sea* France/Spain
102 C2 **Bischofshofen** Austria
130 B2 **Biscotasi Lake** Can.
77 D2 **Bishkek** Kyrg.
135 C3 **Bishop** U.S.A.
69 E1 **Bishui** China
150 B1 **Bisinaca** Col.
115 C1 **Biskra** Alg.
136 C1 **Bismarck** U.S.A.
48 D3 **Bismarck Sea** *sea* P.N.G.
107 D2 **Bissa, Djebel** *mt.* Alg.
114 A3 **Bissau** Guinea-Bissau
129 E2 **Bissett** Can.
128 C2 **Bistcho Lake** Can.
110 B1 **Bistrița** Romania
110 C1 **Bistrița** *r.* Romania
100 C3 **Bitburg** Ger.
105 D2 **Bitche** France
115 D3 **Bitkine** Chad
109 D2 **Bitola** Macedonia
109 C2 **Bitonto** Italy
122 A3 **Bitterfontein** S. Africa
134 D1 **Bitterroot** *r.* U.S.A.
134 C1 **Bitterroot Range** *mts* U.S.A.
91 D1 **Bityug** *r.* Rus. Fed.
115 D3 **Biu** Nigeria
67 C3 **Biwa-ko** *l.* Japan
68 B1 **Biysk** Rus. Fed.
115 C1 **Bizerte** Tunisia
92 A2 **Bjargtangar** *hd* Iceland
92 G3 **Bjästa** Sweden
92 G2 **Bjerkvik** Norway
82 C2 **Bjørnøya** *i.* Arctic Ocean
114 B3 **Bla** Mali
137 E3 **Black** *r.* U.S.A.
51 D2 **Blackall** Austr.
98 B2 **Blackburn** U.K.
134 D2 **Blackfoot** U.S.A.
102 B2 **Black Forest** *mts* Ger.
136 C2 **Black Hills** U.S.A.
96 B2 **Black Isle** *pen.* U.K.
129 D2 **Black Lake** Can.
129 D2 **Black Lake** Can.
99 B3 **Black Mountains** *hills* U.K.
98 B2 **Blackpool** U.K.
62 B1 **Black River** *r.* Vietnam
140 A2 **Black River Falls** U.S.A.
140 C3 **Blacksburg** U.S.A.
80 B1 **Black Sea** Asia/Europe
97 A1 **Blacksod Bay** Ireland
97 C2 **Blackstairs Mountains** *hills* Ireland
114 B4 **Black Volta** *r.* Africa
97 C2 **Blackwater** *r.* Ireland
128 B1 **Blackwater Lake** Can.
50 A3 **Blackwood** *r.* Austr.
76 A2 **Blagodarnyy** Rus. Fed.
110 B2 **Blagoevgrad** Bulg.
69 E1 **Blagoveshchensk** Rus. Fed.
129 D2 **Blaine Lake** Can.
137 D2 **Blair** U.S.A.
96 C2 **Blair Atholl** U.K.
96 C2 **Blairgowrie** U.K.
143 D2 **Blakely** U.S.A.
105 D2 **Blanc, Mont** *mt.* France/Italy
153 B4 **Blanca, Bahía** *b.* Arg.
52 A1 **Blanche, Lake** *imp. l.* Austr.
152 B2 **Blanco** *r.* Bol.
131 E1 **Blanc-Sablon** Can.
92 A2 **Blanda** *r.* Iceland
99 B3 **Blandford Forum** U.K.
135 E3 **Blanding** U.S.A.
107 D1 **Blanes** Spain
60 A1 **Blangkejeren** Indon.
100 C2 **Blankenheim** Ger.
100 C2 **Blankenrath** Ger.
103 D2 **Blansko** Czech Rep.
121 C2 **Blantyre** Malawi
98 C1 **Blaydon** U.K.
53 C2 **Blayney** Austr.
54 B2 **Blenheim** N.Z.
115 C1 **Blida** Alg.
130 B2 **Blind River** Can.
123 C2 **Bloemfontein** S. Africa
123 C2 **Bloemhof** S. Africa
123 C2 **Bloemhof Dam** S. Africa
92 A2 **Blönduós** Iceland
97 B1 **Bloody Foreland** *pt* Ireland
138 B1 **Bloomfield** U.S.A.
140 B2 **Bloomington** *IL* U.S.A.
140 B3 **Bloomington** *IN* U.S.A.
140 C3 **Bluefield** U.S.A.
146 B3 **Bluefields** Nic.
53 C2 **Blue Mountains** Austr.
134 C1 **Blue Mountains** U.S.A.
116 B3 **Blue Nile** *r.* Eth./Sudan
126 D2 **Bluenose Lake** Can.
140 C3 **Blue Ridge** *mts* U.S.A.
97 B1 **Blue Stack Mountains** *hill* Ireland
54 A3 **Bluff** N.Z.
135 E3 **Bluff** U.S.A.
152 D3 **Blumenau** Brazil
52 A2 **Blyth** Austr.
98 C1 **Blyth** U.K.
135 D4 **Blythe** U.S.A.
142 C1 **Blytheville** U.S.A.
114 A4 **Bo** Sierra Leone
64 B1 **Boac** Phil.
151 D2 **Boa Esperança, Açude** *res* Brazil
150 B1 **Boa Vista** Brazil
53 C2 **Bobadah** Austr.
71 B3 **Bobai** China
121 D2 **Bobaomby, Tanjona** *c.* Ma
114 B3 **Bobo-Dioulasso** Burkina
89 F3 **Bobrov** Rus. Fed.
91 C1 **Bobrovytsya** Ukr.
91 C2 **Bobrynets'** Ukr.
121 D3 **Boby** *mt.* Madag.
150 B2 **Boca do Acre** Brazil
155 D1 **Bocaiúva** Brazil
118 B2 **Bocaranga** C.A.R.
103 E2 **Bochnia** Pol.
100 C2 **Bocholt** Ger.
100 C2 **Bochum** Ger.
101 E1 **Bockenem** Ger.
118 B2 **Boda** C.A.R.
83 I3 **Bodaybo** Rus. Fed.
115 D3 **Bodélé** *reg.* Chad
92 H2 **Boden** Sweden
99 A3 **Bodmin** U.K.
99 A3 **Bodmin Moor** *moorland* U
92 F2 **Bodø** Norway
111 C3 **Bodrum** Turkey
118 C3 **Boende** Dem. Rep. Congo
142 C2 **Bogalusa** U.S.A.
114 B3 **Bogandé** Burkina
68 B2 **Bogda Shan** *mts* China
53 D1 **Boggabilla** Austr.
97 B2 **Boggeragh Mountains** *hil* Ireland
100 B3 **Bogny-sur-Meuse** France
97 C2 **Bog of Allen** *reg.* Ireland
53 C3 **Bogong, Mount** Austr.
60 B2 **Bogor** Indon.
89 E3 **Bogoroditsk** Rus. Fed.
150 A1 **Bogotá** Col.
82 G3 **Bogotol** Rus. Fed.
83 H3 **Boguchany** Rus. Fed.
91 E2 **Boguchar** Rus. Fed.
70 B2 **Bo Hai** *g.* China
100 A3 **Bohain-en-Vermandois** France
70 B2 **Bohai Wan** *b.* China
123 C2 **Bohlokong** S. Africa
102 C2 **Böhmer Wald** *mts* Ger.
91 D1 **Bohodukhiv** Ukr.
64 B2 **Bohol** *i.* Phil.
64 B2 **Bohol Sea** Phil.
68 B2 **Bohu** China
155 C2 **Boi, Ponta do** *pt* Brazil
154 B1 **Bois** *r.* Brazil
126 C2 **Bois, Lac des** *l.* Can.
134 C2 **Boise** U.S.A.
139 C1 **Boise City** U.S.A.
123 C2 **Boitumelong** S. Africa
101 E1 **Boizenburg** Ger.
76 B3 **Bojnūrd** Iran
118 B3 **Bokatola** Dem. Rep. Cong
114 A3 **Boké** Guinea
118 C3 **Bokele** Dem. Rep. Congo
93 E4 **Boknafjorden** *sea chan.* Norway
115 D3 **Bokoro** Chad

A2 **Bokpyin** Myanmar
D2 **Boksitogorsk** Rus. Fed.
B2 **Bokspits** Botswana
A3 **Bolama** Guinea-Bissau
C2 **Bolangir** India
B2 **Bolavén, Phouphiang** *plat.* Laos
C2 **Bolbec** France
E2 **Bole** China
B3 **Boleko** Dem. Rep. Congo
B3 **Bolgatanga** Ghana
B2 **Bolhrad** Ukr.
B1 **Boli** China
C2 **Bolintin-Vale** Romania
E3 **Bolivar** U.S.A.
A1 **Bolívar, Pico** *mt.* Venez.
B2 **Bolivia** *country* S. America
E3 **Bolkhov** Rus. Fed.
C3 **Bollène** France
G3 **Bollnäs** Sweden
C1 **Bollon** Austr.
E2 **Bollstedt** Ger.
F4 **Bolmen** *l.* Sweden
B3 **Bolobo** Dem. Rep. Congo
B2 **Bologna** Italy
D2 **Bologovo** Rus. Fed.
D2 **Bologoye** Rus. Fed.
B2 **Bolomba** Dem. Rep. Congo
H1 **Bol'shevik, Ostrov** *i.* Rus. Fed.
E2 **Bol'shezemel'skaya Tundra** *lowland* Rus. Fed.
B2 **Bol'shoy Kamen'** Rus. Fed.
Bol'shoy Kavkaz *mts* Asia/Europe *see* **Caucasus**
K2 **Bol'shoy Lyakhovskiy, Ostrov** *i.* Rus. Fed.
B2 **Bolsón de Mapimí** *des.* Mex.
B1 **Bolsward** Neth.
B2 **Bolton** U.K.
B1 **Bolu** Turkey
A2 **Bolungarvík** Iceland
B1 **Bolzano** Italy
B3 **Boma** Dem. Rep. Congo
D2 **Bomaderry** Austr.
C3 **Bombala** Austr.
Bombay India *see* **Mumbai**
C1 **Bom Despacho** Brazil
D2 **Bomdila** India
D3 **Bom Jesus da Lapa** Brazil
D2 **Bom Jesus do Itabapoana** Brazil
D1 **Bon, Cap** *c.* Tunisia
D3 **Bonaire** *i.* Neth. Antilles
B1 **Bonaparte Archipelago** *is* Austr.
E2 **Bonavista** Can.
E2 **Bonavista Bay** Can.
C2 **Bondo** Dem. Rep. Congo
B4 **Bondoukou** Côte d'Ivoire
C3 **Bonerate, Kepulauan** *is* Indon.
C1 **Bonfinópolis de Minas** Brazil
B4 **Bonga** Eth.
D2 **Bongaigaon** India
C2 **Bongandanga** Dem. Rep. Congo
C2 **Bongo, Massif des** *mts* C.A.R.
D3 **Bongor** Chad
B4 **Bongouanou** Côte d'Ivoire
B2 **Bông Sơn** Vietnam
D2 **Bonham** U.S.A.
D3 **Bonifacio** *Corse* France
A2 **Bonifacio, Strait of** France/Italy
C2 **Bonn** Ger.
C1 **Bonners Ferry** U.S.A.
A3 **Bonnie Rock** Austr.
C2 **Bonnyville** Can.
108 A2 **Bonorva** *Sardegna* Italy
61 C1 **Bontang** Indon.
64 B1 **Bontoc** Phil.
58 B3 **Bontosunggu** Indon.
123 C3 **Bontrug** S. Africa
52 B2 **Booligal** Austr.
53 C1 **Boomi** Austr.
53 D1 **Boonah** Austr.
137 E2 **Boone** U.S.A.
142 C2 **Booneville** U.S.A.
137 E3 **Boonville** U.S.A.
53 C2 **Boorowa** Austr.
126 F2 **Boothia, Gulf of** Can.
126 E2 **Boothia Peninsula** Can.
100 C2 **Boppard** Ger.
144 B2 **Boquilla, Presa de la** *resr* Mex.
109 D2 **Bor** Serbia
117 B4 **Bor** Sudan
80 B2 **Bor** Turkey
121 E2 **Boraha, Nosy** *i.* Madag.
93 F4 **Borås** Sweden
79 C2 **Borāzjān** Iran
150 C2 **Borba** Brazil
104 B3 **Bordeaux** France
127 F2 **Borden Peninsula** Can.
52 B3 **Bordertown** Austr.
107 D2 **Bordj Bou Arréridj** Alg.
107 D2 **Bordj Bounaama** Alg.
115 C1 **Bordj Messaouda** Alg.
115 C2 **Bordj Omer Driss** Alg.
94 B1 **Borðoy** *i.* Faroe Is
92 A3 **Borgarnes** Iceland
108 A1 **Borgosesia** Italy
87 D3 **Borisoglebsk** Rus. Fed.
89 E2 **Borisoglebskiy** Rus. Fed.
91 D1 **Borisovka** Rus. Fed.
100 C2 **Borken** Ger.
92 G2 **Borkenes** Norway
100 C1 **Borkum** Ger.
100 C1 **Borkum** *i.* Ger.
93 G3 **Borlänge** Sweden
101 F2 **Borna** Ger.
61 C1 **Borneo** *i.* Asia
93 F4 **Bornholm** *i.* Denmark
111 C3 **Bornova** Turkey
90 B1 **Borodyanka** Ukr.
89 D2 **Borovichi** Rus. Fed.
89 E2 **Borovsk** Rus. Fed.
51 C1 **Borroloola** Austr.
110 B1 **Borșa** Romania
90 B2 **Borshchiv** Ukr.
69 D1 **Borshchovochnyy Khrebet** *mts* Rus. Fed.
101 E1 **Börßum** Ger.
Bortala China *see* **Bole**
81 C2 **Borūjerd** Iran
90 A2 **Boryslav** Ukr.
90 C1 **Boryspil'** Ukr.
91 C1 **Borzna** Ukr.
69 D1 **Borzya** Rus. Fed.
109 C1 **Bosanska Dubica** Bos.-Herz.
109 C1 **Bosanska Gradiška** Bos.-Herz.
109 C2 **Bosanska Krupa** Bos.-Herz.
109 C1 **Bosanski Novi** Bos.-Herz.
109 C2 **Bosansko Grahovo** Bos.-Herz.
71 A3 **Bose** China
123 C2 **Boshof** S. Africa
109 C2 **Bosnia-Herzegovina** *country* Europe
118 B2 **Bosobolo** Dem. Rep. Congo
110 C2 **Bosporus** *str.* Turkey
118 B2 **Bossangoa** C.A.R.
118 B2 **Bossembélé** C.A.R.
68 B2 **Bosten Hu** *l.* China
98 C2 **Boston** U.K.
141 E2 **Boston** U.S.A.
142 B1 **Boston Mountains** U.S.A.
53 D2 **Botany Bay** Austr.
110 B2 **Botev** *mt.* Bulg.
93 G3 **Bothnia, Gulf of** Fin./Sweden
110 C1 **Botoșani** Romania
123 C2 **Botshabelo** S. Africa
120 B3 **Botswana** *country* Africa
109 C3 **Botte Donato, Monte** *mt.* Italy
136 C1 **Bottineau** U.S.A.
100 C2 **Bottrop** Ger.
154 C2 **Botucatu** Brazil
114 B4 **Bouaké** Côte d'Ivoire
118 B2 **Bouar** C.A.R.
114 B1 **Bouârfa** Morocco
131 D2 **Bouctouche** Can.
107 E2 **Bougaa** Alg.
114 B3 **Bougouni** Mali
100 B3 **Bouillon** Belgium
107 D2 **Bouira** Alg.
114 A2 **Boujdour** Western Sahara
136 B2 **Boulder** U.S.A.
135 D3 **Boulder City** U.S.A.
51 C2 **Boulia** Austr.
104 C2 **Boulogne-Billancourt** France
99 D3 **Boulogne-sur-Mer** France
118 B3 **Boumango** Gabon
118 B2 **Boumba** *r.* Cameroon
107 D2 **Boumerdes** Alg.
114 B4 **Bouna** Côte d'Ivoire
114 B4 **Boundiali** Côte d'Ivoire
134 D2 **Bountiful** U.S.A.
114 B3 **Bourem** Mali
104 C2 **Bourganeuf** France
105 D2 **Bourg-en-Bresse** France
104 C2 **Bourges** France
53 C2 **Bourke** Austr.
99 C3 **Bournemouth** U.K.
115 C1 **Bou Saâda** Alg.
115 D3 **Bousso** Chad
114 A3 **Boutilimit** Maur.
129 C3 **Bow** *r.* Can.
51 D2 **Bowen** Austr.
129 C3 **Bow Island** Can.
140 B3 **Bowling Green** *KY* U.S.A.
140 C2 **Bowling Green** *OH* U.S.A.
136 C1 **Bowman** U.S.A.
101 D3 **Boxberg** Ger.
100 B2 **Boxtel** Neth.
80 B1 **Boyabat** Turkey
Boyang China *see* **Poyang**
97 B2 **Boyle** Ireland
97 C2 **Boyne** *r.* Ireland
136 B2 **Boysen Reservoir** U.S.A.
152 B3 **Boyuibe** Bol.
111 C3 **Bozburun** Turkey
111 C3 **Bozcaada** *i.* Turkey
111 C3 **Bozdağ** *mt.* Turkey
111 C3 **Boz Dağları** *mts* Turkey
111 C3 **Bozdoğan** Turkey
134 D1 **Bozeman** U.S.A.
118 B2 **Bozoum** C.A.R.
111 D3 **Bozüyük** Turkey
109 C2 **Brač** *i.* Croatia
130 C2 **Bracebridge** Can.
99 C3 **Bracknell** U.K.
109 C2 **Bradano** *r.* Italy
143 D3 **Bradenton** U.S.A.
98 C2 **Bradford** U.K.
141 D2 **Bradford** U.S.A.
139 D2 **Brady** U.S.A.
96 C2 **Braemar** U.K.
106 B1 **Braga** Port.
151 D2 **Bragança** Brazil
106 B1 **Bragança** Port.
155 C2 **Bragança Paulista** Brazil
89 D3 **Brahin** Belarus
73 C3 **Brahmapur** India
62 A1 **Brahmaputra** *r.* China/India

110 C1 **Brăila** Romania
137 E1 **Brainerd** U.S.A.
99 D3 **Braintree** U.K.
100 B2 **Braives** Belgium
101 D1 **Brake (Unterweser)** Ger.
100 D1 **Bramsche** Ger.
150 B2 **Branco** *r.* Brazil
101 F1 **Brandenburg** Ger.
129 E3 **Brandon** Can.
97 A2 **Brandon Mountain** *h.* Ireland
122 B3 **Brandvlei** S. Africa
103 D1 **Braniewo** Pol.
130 B2 **Brantford** Can.
131 D2 **Bras d'Or Lake** Can.
155 D1 **Brasil, Planalto do** *plat.* Brazil
154 C1 **Brasilândia** Brazil
154 C1 **Brasília** Brazil
155 D1 **Brasília de Minas** Brazil
88 C2 **Braslaw** Belarus
110 C1 **Braşov** Romania
103 D2 **Bratislava** Slovakia
83 H3 **Bratsk** Rus. Fed.
102 C2 **Braunau am Inn** Austria
101 E1 **Braunschweig** Ger.
92 A2 **Brautarholt** Iceland
Bravo del Norte, Río *r.* Mex./U.S.A. *see* **Rio Grande**
135 C4 **Brawley** U.S.A.
97 C2 **Bray** Ireland
150 C2 **Brazil** *country* S. America
139 D3 **Brazos** *r.* U.S.A.
118 B3 **Brazzaville** Congo
109 C2 **Brčko** Bos.-Herz.
96 C2 **Brechin** U.K.
100 B2 **Brecht** Belgium
139 D2 **Breckenridge** U.S.A.
103 D2 **Břeclav** Czech Rep.
99 B3 **Brecon** U.K.
99 B3 **Brecon Beacons** *reg.* U.K.
100 B2 **Breda** Neth.
122 B3 **Bredasdorp** S. Africa
102 B2 **Bregenz** Austria
92 H1 **Breivikbotn** Norway
92 E3 **Brekstad** Norway
101 D1 **Bremen** Ger.
101 D1 **Bremerhaven** Ger.
134 B1 **Bremerton** U.S.A.
101 D1 **Bremervörde** Ger.
139 D2 **Brenham** U.S.A.
108 B1 **Brennero** Italy
102 C2 **Brenner Pass** Austria/Italy
99 D3 **Brentwood** U.K.
108 B1 **Brescia** Italy
108 B1 **Bressanone** Italy
96 □ **Bressay** *i.* U.K.
104 B2 **Bressuire** France
88 B3 **Brest** Belarus
104 B2 **Brest** France
142 C3 **Breton Sound** *b.* U.S.A.
151 C2 **Breves** Brazil
53 C1 **Brewarrina** Austr.
134 C1 **Brewster** U.S.A.
89 E2 **Breytovo** Rus. Fed.
109 C1 **Brezovo Polje** *plain* Croatia
118 C2 **Bria** C.A.R.
105 D3 **Briançon** France
90 B2 **Briceni** Moldova
99 B3 **Bridgend** U.K.
141 E2 **Bridgeport** *CT* U.S.A.
136 C2 **Bridgeport** *NE* U.S.A.
147 E3 **Bridgetown** Barbados
131 D2 **Bridgewater** Can.
99 B3 **Bridgwater** U.K.
98 C1 **Bridlington** U.K.
98 C1 **Bridlington Bay** U.K.
105 D2 **Brig** Switz.
134 D2 **Brigham City** U.S.A.
54 B3 **Brighton** N.Z.
99 C3 **Brighton** U.K.
105 D3 **Brignoles** France
101 D2 **Brilon** Ger.
109 C2 **Brindisi** Italy
53 D1 **Brisbane** Austr.
99 B3 **Bristol** U.K.
143 D1 **Bristol** U.S.A.
99 A3 **Bristol Channel** *est.* U.K.
128 B2 **British Columbia** *prov.* Can.
56 G7 **British Indian Ocean Territory** *terr.* Indian Ocean
95 B2 **British Isles** *is* Europe
123 C2 **Brits** S. Africa
122 B3 **Britstown** S. Africa
104 C2 **Brive-la-Gaillarde** France
106 C1 **Briviesca** Spain
103 D2 **Brno** Czech Rep.
143 D2 **Broad** *r.* U.S.A.
130 C1 **Broadback** *r.* Can.
96 C3 **Broad Law** *h.* U.K.
136 B1 **Broadus** U.S.A.
129 D2 **Brochet** Can.
129 D2 **Brochet, Lac** *l.* Can.
131 D2 **Brochet, Lac au** *l.* Can.
101 E1 **Bröckel** Ger.
126 D1 **Brock Island** Can.
130 C2 **Brockville** Can.
127 F2 **Brodeur Peninsula** Can.
96 B3 **Brodick** U.K.
103 D1 **Brodnica** Pol.
90 B1 **Brody** Ukr.
139 D1 **Broken Arrow** U.S.A.
137 D2 **Broken Bow** U.S.A.
52 B2 **Broken Hill** Austr.
99 B2 **Bromsgrove** U.K.
93 E4 **Brønderslev** Denmark
92 F2 **Brønnøysund** Norway
64 A2 **Brooke's Point** Phil.
142 B2 **Brookhaven** U.S.A.
134 B2 **Brookings** *OR* U.S.A.
137 D2 **Brookings** *SD* U.S.A.
129 C2 **Brooks** Can.
126 B2 **Brooks Range** *mts* U.S.A.
143 D3 **Brooksville** U.S.A.
96 B2 **Broom, Loch** *inlet* U.K.
50 B1 **Broome** Austr.
134 B2 **Brothers** U.S.A.
Broughton Island Can. *see* **Qikiqtarjuaq**
90 C1 **Brovary** Ukr.
139 C2 **Brownfield** U.S.A.
128 C3 **Browning** U.S.A.
142 C1 **Brownsville** *TN* U.S.A.
139 D3 **Brownsville** *TX* U.S.A.
139 D2 **Brownwood** U.S.A.
92 A2 **Brú** Iceland
104 C1 **Bruay-la-Bussière** France
140 B1 **Bruce Crossing** U.S.A.
103 D2 **Bruck an der Mur** Austria
Bruges Belgium *see* **Brugge**
100 A2 **Brugge** Belgium
128 C2 **Brûlé** Can.
151 D3 **Brumado** Brazil
93 F3 **Brumunddal** Norway
61 C1 **Brunei** *country* Asia
102 C2 **Brunico** Italy
101 D1 **Brunsbüttel** Ger.
143 D2 **Brunswick** *GA* U.S.A.
141 F2 **Brunswick** *ME* U.S.A.
53 D1 **Brunswick Heads** Austr.
136 C2 **Brush** U.S.A.
100 B2 **Brussels** Belgium
Bruxelles Belgium *see* **Brussels**
139 D2 **Bryan** U.S.A.
89 D3 **Bryansk** Rus. Fed.
91 D2 **Bryn'kovskaya** Rus. Fed.
91 D2 **Bryukhovetskaya** Rus. Fed
103 D1 **Brzeg** Pol.
114 A3 **Buba** Guinea-Bissau
80 B2 **Bucak** Turkey
150 A1 **Bucaramanga** Col.
53 C3 **Buchan** Austr.
114 A4 **Buchanan** Liberia
110 C2 **Bucharest** Romania
101 D1 **Bucholz in der Nordheid** Ger.
110 C1 **Bucin, Pasul** *pass* Romani
101 D1 **Bückeburg** Ger.
138 A2 **Buckeye** U.S.A.
96 C2 **Buckhaven** U.K.
96 C2 **Buckie** U.K.
51 C1 **Buckingham Bay** Austr.
51 D2 **Buckland Tableland** *reg.* A
52 A2 **Buckleboo** Austr.
141 F2 **Bucksport** U.S.A.
Bucureşti Romania *see* **Bucharest**
89 D3 **Buda-Kashalyova** Belarus
103 D2 **Budapest** Hungary
75 B2 **Budaun** India
108 A2 **Buddusò** *Sardegna* Italy
99 A3 **Bude** U.K.
87 D4 **Budennovsk** Rus. Fed.
89 D2 **Budogoshch'** Rus. Fed.
108 A2 **Budoni** *Sardegna* Italy
118 A2 **Buea** Cameroon
144 B2 **Buenaventura** Mex.
106 C1 **Buendia, Embalse de** *resr* Spain
155 D1 **Buenópolis** Brazil
153 C4 **Buenos Aires** Arg.
153 A5 **Buenos Aires, Lago** *l.* Arg./Chile
141 D2 **Buffalo** *NY* U.S.A.
136 C1 **Buffalo** *SD* U.S.A.
136 B2 **Buffalo** *WY* U.S.A.
129 D2 **Buffalo Narrows** Can.
122 A2 **Buffels** *watercourse* S. Afri
110 C2 **Buftea** Romania
103 E1 **Bug** *r.* Pol.
61 C2 **Bugel, Tanjung** *pt* Indon.
109 C2 **Bugojno** Bos.-Herz.
64 A2 **Bugsuk** *i.* Phil.
87 E3 **Buguruslan** Rus. Fed.
110 C1 **Buhuşi** Romania
99 B2 **Builth Wells** U.K.
69 D1 **Buir Nur** *l.* Mongolia
120 A3 **Buitepos** Namibia
109 D2 **Bujanovac** Serbia
119 C3 **Bujumbura** Burundi
69 D1 **Bukachacha** Rus. Fed.
119 C3 **Bukavu** Dem. Rep. Congo
60 B2 **Bukittinggi** Indon.
119 D3 **Bukoba** Tanz.
53 D2 **Bulahdelah** Austr.
121 B3 **Bulawayo** Zimbabwe
111 C3 **Buldan** Turkey
123 D2 **Bulembu** Swaziland
69 C1 **Bulgan** Mongolia
110 C2 **Bulgaria** *country* Europe
54 B2 **Buller** *r.* N.Z.
52 B1 **Bulloo Downs** Austr.
122 A1 **Büllsport** Namibia
58 C3 **Bulukumba** Indon.
118 B3 **Bulungu** Dem. Rep. Cong
118 C2 **Bumba** Dem. Rep. Congo
62 A1 **Bumhkang** Myanmar
118 B3 **Buna** Dem. Rep. Congo
50 A3 **Bunbury** Austr.
97 C1 **Buncrana** Ireland
119 D3 **Bunda** Tanz.
51 E2 **Bundaberg** Austr.

D2 **Bundarra** Austr.
B2 **Bundi** India
B1 **Bundoran** Ireland
C3 **Bungendore** Austr.
B4 **Bungo-suidō** *sea chan.* Japan
D2 **Bunia** Dem. Rep. Congo
C3 **Bunianga** Dem. Rep. Congo
B2 **Buôn Ma Thuột** Vietnam
D3 **Bura** Kenya
B2 **Buraydah** Saudi Arabia
D2 **Burbach** Ger.
C4 **Burco** Somalia
B1 **Burdaard** Neth.
B2 **Burdur** Turkey
B3 **Burē** Eth.
D2 **Bure** *r.* U.K.
B1 **Burewala** Pak.
C2 **Burgas** Bulg.
E1 **Burg bei Magdeburg** Ger.
E1 **Burgdorf** *Niedersachsen* Ger.
E1 **Burgdorf** *Niedersachsen* Ger.
E2 **Burgeo** Can.
D1 **Burgersfort** S. Africa
A2 **Burgh-Haamstede** Neth.
C2 **Burgos** Mex.
C1 **Burgos** Spain
C3 **Burhaniye** Turkey
B2 **Burhanpur** India
D1 **Burhave (Butjadingen)** Ger.
E2 **Burin** Can.
D2 **Buriti Bravo** Brazil
C1 **Buritis** Brazil
C1 **Burketown** Austr.
B3 **Burkina** *country* Africa
D2 **Burley** U.S.A.
C3 **Burlington** *CO* U.S.A.
E2 **Burlington** *IA* U.S.A.
E1 **Burlington** *NC* U.S.A.
E2 **Burlington** *VT* U.S.A.
Burma *country* Asia *see* **Myanmar**
B2 **Burney** U.S.A.
D4 **Burnie** Austr.
B2 **Burnley** U.K.
C2 **Burns** U.S.A.
B2 **Burns Lake** Can.
E2 **Burqin** China
A2 **Burra** Austr.
D2 **Burrel** Albania
B2 **Burren** *reg.* Ireland
C2 **Burrendong, Lake** *resr* Austr.
C2 **Burren Junction** Austr.
C2 **Burriana** Spain
C2 **Burrinjuck Reservoir** Austr.
B2 **Burro, Serranías del** *mts* Mex.
C2 **Bursa** Turkey
B2 **Būr Safājah** Egypt
Būr Sa'īd Egypt *see* **Port Said**
C1 **Burton, Lac** *l.* Can.
C2 **Burton upon Trent** U.K.
C3 **Buru** *i.* Indon.
C3 **Burundi** *country* Africa
C3 **Bururi** Burundi
C1 **Buryn'** Ukr.
B2 **Burynshyk** Kazakh.
D2 **Bury St Edmunds** U.K.
C3 **Busanga** Dem. Rep. Congo
C2 **Būshehr** Iran
D3 **Bushenyi** Uganda
C2 **Businga** Dem. Rep. Congo
A3 **Busselton** Austr.
C3 **Bustamante** Mex.
A1 **Busuanga** Phil.
C2 **Buta** Dem. Rep. Congo
C3 **Butare** Rwanda
C2 **Butha-Buthe** Lesotho
D2 **Butler** U.S.A.
59 C3 **Buton** *i.* Indon.
134 D1 **Butte** U.S.A.
60 B1 **Butterworth** Malaysia
96 A1 **Butt of Lewis** *hd* U.K.
129 E2 **Button Bay** Can.
64 B2 **Butuan** Phil.
91 E1 **Buturlinovka** Rus. Fed.
75 C2 **Butwal** Nepal
101 D2 **Butzbach** Ger.
117 C4 **Buulobarde** Somalia
117 C5 **Buur Gaabo** Somalia
117 C4 **Buurhabaka** Somalia
76 C3 **Buxoro** Uzbek.
101 D1 **Buxtehude** Ger.
89 F2 **Buy** Rus. Fed.
87 D4 **Buynaksk** Rus. Fed.
111 C3 **Büyükmenderes** *r.* Turkey
110 C1 **Buzău** Romania
121 C2 **Búzi** Moz.
87 E3 **Buzuluk** Rus. Fed.
110 C2 **Byala** Bulg.
88 C3 **Byalynichy** Belarus
88 D3 **Byarezina** *r.* Belarus
88 B3 **Byaroza** Belarus
103 D1 **Bydgoszcz** Pol.
88 C3 **Byerazino** Belarus
88 C2 **Byeshankovichy** Belarus
89 D3 **Bykhaw** Belarus
127 F2 **Bylot Island** Can.
53 C2 **Byrock** Austr.
53 D1 **Byron Bay** Austr.
83 J2 **Bytantay** *r.* Rus. Fed.
103 D1 **Bytom** Pol.
103 D1 **Bytów** Pol.

C

154 B2 **Caarapó** Brazil
64 B1 **Cabanatuan** Phil.
117 C3 **Cabdul Qaadir** Somalia
106 B2 **Cabeza del Buey** Spain
152 B2 **Cabezas** Bol.
150 A1 **Cabimas** Venez.
120 A1 **Cabinda** Angola
118 B3 **Cabinda** *prov.* Angola
155 D2 **Cabo Frio** Brazil
155 D2 **Cabo Frio, Ilha do** *i.* Brazil
130 C2 **Cabonga, Réservoir** *resr* Can.
51 E2 **Caboolture** Austr.
150 A2 **Cabo Pantoja** Peru
144 A1 **Caborca** Mex.
131 D2 **Cabot Strait** Can.
155 D1 **Cabral, Serra do** *mts* Brazil
107 D2 **Cabrera, Illa de** *i.* Spain
106 B1 **Cabrera, Sierra de la** *mts* Spain
129 D2 **Cabri** Can.
107 C2 **Cabriel** *r.* Spain
152 C3 **Caçador** Brazil
109 D2 **Čačak** Serbia
108 A2 **Caccia, Capo** *c. Sardegna* Italy
151 C3 **Cáceres** Brazil
106 B2 **Cáceres** Spain
128 B2 **Cache Creek** Can.
114 A3 **Cacheu** Guinea-Bissau
151 C2 **Cachimbo, Serra do** *hills* Brazil
154 B1 **Cachoeira Alta** Brazil
155 D2 **Cachoeiro de Itapemirim** Brazil
114 A3 **Cacine** Guinea-Bissau
120 A2 **Cacolo** Angola
154 B1 **Caçu** Brazil
103 D2 **Čadca** Slovakia
101 D1 **Cadenberge** Ger.
145 B2 **Cadereyta** Mex.
140 B2 **Cadillac** U.S.A.
106 B2 **Cádiz** Spain
106 B2 **Cádiz, Golfo de** *g.* Spain
128 C2 **Cadotte Lake** Can.
104 B2 **Caen** France
98 A2 **Caernarfon** U.K.
98 A2 **Caernarfon Bay** U.K.
152 B3 **Cafayate** Arg.
64 B2 **Cagayan de Oro** Phil.
64 A2 **Cagayan de Tawi-Tawi** *i.* Phil.
108 B2 **Cagli** Italy
108 A3 **Cagliari** *Sardegna* Italy
108 A3 **Cagliari, Golfo di** *b. Sardegna* Italy
76 B2 **Çagyl** Turkm.
97 B3 **Caha Mountains** *hills* Ireland
97 A3 **Cahermore** Ireland
97 C2 **Cahir** Ireland
97 A3 **Cahirsiveen** Ireland
97 C2 **Cahore Point** Ireland
104 C3 **Cahors** France
90 B2 **Cahul** Moldova
121 C2 **Caia** Moz.
151 C3 **Caiabis, Serra dos** *hills* Brazil
120 B2 **Caianda** Angola
154 B1 **Caiapó, Serra do** *mts* Brazil
154 B1 **Caiapônia** Brazil
147 C2 **Caicos Islands** Turks and Caicos Is
96 C2 **Cairngorm Mountains** U.K.
98 A1 **Cairnryan** U.K.
51 D1 **Cairns** Austr.
116 B1 **Cairo** Egypt
98 C2 **Caistor** U.K.
120 A2 **Caiundo** Angola
150 A2 **Cajamarca** Peru
109 C1 **Čakovec** Croatia
123 C3 **Cala** S. Africa
150 B1 **Calabozo** Venez.
110 B2 **Calafat** Romania
153 A6 **Calafate** Arg.
107 C1 **Calahorra** Spain
104 C1 **Calais** France
141 F1 **Calais** U.S.A.
152 B3 **Calama** Chile
64 A1 **Calamian Group** *is* Phil.
107 C1 **Calamocha** Spain
120 A1 **Calandula** Angola
60 A1 **Calang** Indon.
64 B1 **Calapan** Phil.
110 C2 **Călărași** Romania
107 C1 **Calatayud** Spain
64 B1 **Calayan** *i.* Phil.
64 B1 **Calbayog** Phil.
151 E2 **Calcanhar, Ponta do** *pt* Brazil
151 C1 **Calçoene** Brazil
Calcutta India *see* **Kolkata**
106 B2 **Caldas da Rainha** Port.
154 C1 **Caldas Novas** Brazil
152 A3 **Caldera** Chile
134 C2 **Caldwell** U.S.A.
123 C3 **Caledon** *r.* Lesotho/S. Africa
122 A3 **Caledon** S. Africa
153 B5 **Caleta Olivia** Arg.
98 A1 **Calf of Man** *i.* Isle of Man
128 C2 **Calgary** Can.
150 A1 **Cali** Col.
Calicut India *see* **Kozhikode**
135 D3 **Caliente** U.S.A.
135 B2 **California** *state* U.S.A.
144 A1 **California, Gulf of** Mex.
135 B3 **California Aqueduct** *canal* U.S.A.
122 B3 **Calitzdorp** S. Africa
145 C2 **Calkiní** Mex.
52 B1 **Callabonna, Lake** *imp. l.* Austr.

96 B2 **Callander** U.K.
150 A3 **Callao** Peru
108 B3 **Caltagirone** *Sicilia* Italy
108 B3 **Caltanissetta** *Sicilia* Italy
120 A2 **Caluquembe** Angola
117 D3 **Caluula** Somalia
105 D3 **Calvi** *Corse* France
107 D2 **Calvià** Spain
144 B2 **Calvillo** Mex.
122 A3 **Calvinia** S. Africa
109 C2 **Calvo, Monte** *mt.* Italy
144 B2 **Camacho** Mex.
120 A2 **Camacupa** Angola
146 C2 **Camagüey** Cuba
150 A3 **Camana** Peru
154 B1 **Camapuã** Brazil
145 C2 **Camargo** Mex.
63 B3 **Ca Mau** Vietnam
63 B3 **Ca Mau, Mui** *c.* Vietnam
63 B2 **Cambodia** *country* Asia
99 A3 **Camborne** U.K.
105 C1 **Cambrai** France
99 B2 **Cambrian Mountains** *hills* U.K.
54 C1 **Cambridge** N.Z.
99 D2 **Cambridge** U.K.
141 E2 **Cambridge** *MA* U.S.A.
141 D3 **Cambridge** *MD* U.S.A.
137 E1 **Cambridge** *MN* U.S.A.
140 C2 **Cambridge** *OH* U.S.A.
131 D1 **Cambrien, Lac** *l.* Can.
53 D2 **Camden** Austr.
142 B2 **Camden** *AR* U.S.A.
141 F2 **Camden** *ME* U.S.A.
118 B2 **Cameroon** *country* Africa
118 B2 **Cameroon Highlands** *slope* Cameroon/Nigeria
151 D2 **Cametá** Brazil
64 B1 **Camiguin** *i.* Phil.
152 B3 **Camiri** Bol.
151 D2 **Camocim** Brazil
51 C1 **Camooweal** Austr.
63 A3 **Camorta** *i.* India
153 A5 **Campana, Isla** *i.* Chile
122 B2 **Campbell** S. Africa
54 B2 **Campbell, Cape** N.Z.
48 F6 **Campbell Island** N.Z.
128 B2 **Campbell River** Can.
140 B3 **Campbellsville** U.S.A.
131 D2 **Campbellton** Can.
96 B3 **Campbeltown** U.K.
145 C3 **Campeche** Mex.
145 C3 **Campeche, Bahía de** *g.* Mex.
52 B3 **Camperdown** Austr.
110 C1 **Câmpina** Romania
151 E2 **Campina Grande** Brazil
154 C2 **Campinas** Brazil
154 C1 **Campina Verde** Brazil
108 B2 **Campobasso** Italy
155 C2 **Campo Belo** Brazil
154 C1 **Campo Florido** Brazil
152 B3 **Campo Gallo** Arg.
154 B2 **Campo Grande** Brazil
151 D2 **Campo Maior** Brazil
106 B2 **Campo Maior** Port.
154 B2 **Campo Mourão** Brazil
155 D2 **Campos** Brazil
155 C1 **Campos Altos** Brazil
155 C2 **Campos do Jordão** Brazil
110 C1 **Câmpulung** Romania
138 A2 **Camp Verde** U.S.A.
128 C2 **Camrose** Can.
129 D2 **Camsell Portage** Can.
111 C2 **Çan** Turkey
126 F2 **Canada** *country* N. America
139 C1 **Canadian** U.S.A.
139 D1 **Canadian** *r.* U.S.A.
111 C2 **Çanakkale** Turkey
144 A1 **Cananea** Mex.
154 C2 **Cananéia** Brazil
Canarias, Islas *terr.* N. Atlantic Ocean *see* **Canary Islands**
114 A2 **Canary Islands** *terr.* N. Atlantic Ocean
155 C1 **Canastra, Serra da** *mts* Brazil
144 B2 **Canatlán** Mex.
143 D3 **Canaveral, Cape** U.S.A.
155 E1 **Canavieiras** Brazil
53 C3 **Canberra** Austr.
145 D2 **Cancún** Mex.
111 C3 **Çandarlı** Turkey
145 C3 **Candelaria** Mex.
129 D2 **Candle Lake** Can.
120 A2 **Cangamba** Angola
106 B1 **Cangas del Narcea** Spain
152 C4 **Canguçu** Brazil
70 B2 **Cangzhou** China
131 D1 **Caniapiscau** Can.
131 D1 **Caniapiscau** *r.* Can.
131 C1 **Caniapiscau, Réservoir de** *resr* Can.
108 B3 **Canicattì** *Sicilia* Italy
151 E2 **Canindé** Brazil
144 B2 **Cañitas de Felipe Pescador** Mex.
80 B1 **Çankırı** Turkey
128 C2 **Canmore** Can.
96 A2 **Canna** *i.* U.K.
105 D3 **Cannes** France
99 B2 **Cannock** U.K.
53 C3 **Cann River** Austr.
Cannanore India *see* **Kannur**
152 C3 **Canoas** Brazil
129 D2 **Canoe Lake** Can.
154 B3 **Canoinhas** Brazil
136 B3 **Canon City** U.S.A.
129 D2 **Canora** Can.
53 C2 **Canowindra** Austr.
106 C1 **Cantábrica, Cordillera** *mts* Spain
106 B1 **Cantábrico, Mar** *sea* Spain
99 D3 **Canterbury** U.K.
54 B2 **Canterbury Bight** *b.* N.Z.
54 B2 **Canterbury Plains** N.Z.
63 B2 **Cân Thơ** Vietnam
151 D2 **Canto do Buriti** Brazil
Canton China *see* **Guangzhou**
142 C2 **Canton** *MS* U.S.A.
140 C2 **Canton** *OH* U.S.A.
139 C1 **Canyon** U.S.A.
134 D1 **Canyon Ferry Lake** U.S.A.
62 B1 **Cao Băng** Vietnam
154 C2 **Capão Bonito** Brazil
155 D2 **Caparaó, Serra do** *mts* Brazil
51 D4 **Cape Barren Island** Austr.
52 A3 **Cape Borda** Austr.
131 D2 **Cape Breton Island** Can.
114 B4 **Cape Coast** Ghana
141 E2 **Cape Cod Bay** U.S.A.
127 F2 **Cape Dorset** Can.
143 E2 **Cape Fear** *r.* U.S.A.
137 F3 **Cape Girardeau** U.S.A.
155 D1 **Capelinha** Brazil
100 B2 **Capelle aan de IJssel** Neth.
120 A1 **Capenda-Camulemba** Angola
122 A3 **Cape Town** S. Africa
112 C5 **Cape Verde** *country* N. Atlantic Ocean
51 D1 **Cape York Peninsula** Austr.
147 C3 **Cap-Haïtien** Haiti
151 D2 **Capim** *r.* Brazil
58 D1 **Capitol Hill** N. Mariana Is
109 C2 **Čapljina** Bos.-Herz.
109 B3 **Capo d'Orlando** *Sicilia* Italy
108 A2 **Capraia, Isola di** *i.* Italy
108 A2 **Caprara, Punta** *pt Sardegn* Italy
108 B2 **Capri, Isola di** *i.* Italy
120 B2 **Caprivi Strip** *reg.* Namibia
150 B2 **Caquetá** *r.* Col.
110 B2 **Caracal** Romania
150 B1 **Caracas** Venez.
151 D2 **Caracol** Brazil
155 C2 **Caraguatatuba** Brazil
153 A4 **Carahue** Chile
155 D1 **Caraí** Brazil
155 D2 **Carangola** Brazil
110 B1 **Caransebeş** Romania
131 D2 **Caraquet** Can.
146 B3 **Caratasca, Laguna de** *lag.* Hond.
155 D1 **Caratinga** Brazil
150 B2 **Carauari** Brazil
107 C2 **Caravaca de la Cruz** Spain
155 E1 **Caravelas** Brazil
129 E3 **Carberry** Can.
144 A2 **Carbó** Mex.
107 C2 **Carbon, Cap** *c.* Alg.
153 B5 **Carbón, Laguna del** *l.* Arg
108 A3 **Carbonara, Capo** *c. Sardeg* Italy
136 B3 **Carbondale** *CO* U.S.A.
140 B3 **Carbondale** *IL* U.S.A.
131 E2 **Carbonear** Can.
155 D1 **Carbonita** Brazil
107 C2 **Carcaixent** Spain
104 C3 **Carcassonne** France
128 A1 **Carcross** Can.
145 C3 **Cárdenas** Mex.
99 B3 **Cardiff** U.K.
99 A2 **Cardigan** U.K.
99 A2 **Cardigan Bay** U.K.
128 C3 **Cardston** Can.
110 B1 **Carei** Romania
104 B2 **Carentan** France
50 B2 **Carey, Lake** *imp. l.* Austr.
155 D2 **Cariacica** Brazil
146 B3 **Caribbean Sea** N. Atlantic Ocean
141 F1 **Caribou** U.S.A.
130 B1 **Caribou Lake** Can.
128 C2 **Caribou Mountains** Can.
144 B2 **Carichic** Mex.
100 B3 **Carignan** France
53 C2 **Carinda** Austr.
107 C1 **Cariñena** Spain
130 C2 **Carleton Place** Can.
123 C2 **Carletonville** S. Africa
97 C1 **Carlingford Lough** *inlet* Ireland/U.K.
98 B1 **Carlisle** U.K.
141 D2 **Carlisle** U.S.A.
155 D1 **Carlos Chagas** Brazil
97 C2 **Carlow** Ireland
135 C4 **Carlsbad** *CA* U.S.A.
138 C2 **Carlsbad** *NM* U.S.A.
129 D3 **Carlyle** Can.
128 A1 **Carmacks** Can.
129 E3 **Carman** Can.
99 A3 **Carmarthen** U.K.
99 A3 **Carmarthen Bay** U.K.
104 C3 **Carmaux** France
145 C3 **Carmelita** Guat.
144 A2 **Carmen, Isla** *i.* Mex.
104 B2 **Carnac** France
122 B3 **Carnarvon** S. Africa
97 C1 **Carndonagh** Ireland
50 B2 **Carnegie, Lake** *imp. l.* Aus
96 B2 **Carn Eige** *mt.* U.K.
63 A3 **Car Nicobar** *i.* India
118 B2 **Carnot** C.A.R.

A2 **Carnot, Cape** Austr.
C2 **Carnsore Point** Ireland
D2 **Carolina** Brazil
D2 **Caroline Islands** *is* N. Pacific Ocean
D2 **Caroline Islands** N. Pacific Ocean
D2 **Carpathian Mountains** Europe
Carpații Meridionali *mts* Romania *see* **Transylvanian Alps**
C1 **Carpentaria, Gulf of** Austr.
D3 **Carpentras** France
B3 **Carrantuohill** *mt.* Ireland
E3 **Carrara** Italy
C2 **Carrickmacross** Ireland
B2 **Carrick-on-Shannon** Ireland
C2 **Carrick-on-Suir** Ireland
D1 **Carrington** U.S.A.
D3 **Carrizo Springs** U.S.A.
B2 **Carrizozo** U.S.A.
E2 **Carroll** U.S.A.
C2 **Carrollton** U.S.A.
D2 **Carrot River** Can.
C3 **Carson City** U.S.A.
A1 **Cartagena** Col.
C2 **Cartagena** Spain
B4 **Cartago** Costa Rica
E3 **Carthage** *MO* U.S.A.
E2 **Carthage** *TX* U.S.A.
E1 **Cartwright** Can.
E2 **Caruarú** Brazil
B1 **Casablanca** Morocco
C2 **Casa Branca** Brazil
B1 **Casa de Janos** Mex.
A2 **Casa Grande** U.S.A.
A1 **Casale Monferrato** Italy
C2 **Casarano** Italy
C2 **Cascade** U.S.A.
B2 **Cascade Range** *mts* Can./U.S.A.
B2 **Cascais** Port.
B2 **Cascavel** Brazil
B2 **Caserta** Italy
C2 **Cashel** Ireland
D1 **Casino** Austr.
C1 **Caspe** Spain
B2 **Casper** U.S.A.
A2 **Caspian Lowland** Kazakh./Rus. Fed.
C1 **Caspian Sea** Asia/Europe
C2 **Cássia** Brazil
B2 **Cassiar** Can.
A2 **Cassiar Mountains** Can.
B1 **Cassilândia** Brazil
B2 **Cassino** Italy
B2 **Cassley** *r.* U.K.
D2 **Castanhal** Brazil
B4 **Castaño** *r.* Arg.
B2 **Castaños** Mex.
C3 **Casteljaloux** France
C2 **Castellón de la Plana** Spain
B2 **Castelo Branco** Port.
B3 **Castelvetrano** *Sicilia* Italy
B3 **Casterton** Austr.
B2 **Castiglione della Pescaia** Italy
B2 **Castlebar** Ireland
A2 **Castlebay** U.K.
C1 **Castleblayney** Ireland
C1 **Castlederg** U.K.
C3 **Castle Douglas** U.K.
C3 **Castlegar** Can.
B2 **Castleisland** Ireland
B3 **Castlemaine** Austr.
B2 **Castlerea** Ireland
C2 **Castlereagh** *r.* Austr.
C3 **Castle Rock** U.S.A.
129 C2 **Castor** Can.
104 C3 **Castres** France
100 B1 **Castricum** Neth.
147 D3 **Castries** St Lucia
154 C2 **Castro** Brazil
153 A5 **Castro** Chile
106 B2 **Castro Verde** Port.
109 C3 **Castrovillari** Italy
150 A2 **Catacaos** Peru
155 D2 **Cataguases** Brazil
154 C1 **Catalão** Brazil
152 B3 **Catamarca** Arg.
64 B1 **Catanduanes** *i.* Phil.
154 C2 **Catanduva** Brazil
154 B3 **Catanduvas** Brazil
109 C3 **Catania** *Sicilia* Italy
109 C3 **Catanzaro** Italy
64 B1 **Catarman** Phil.
64 B1 **Catbalogan** Phil.
145 C3 **Catemaco** Mex.
147 C2 **Cat Island** Bahamas
130 A1 **Cat Lake** Can.
145 D2 **Catoche, Cabo** *c.* Mex.
141 E2 **Catskill Mountains** U.S.A.
64 B2 **Cauayan** Phil.
150 A1 **Cauca** *r.* Col.
151 E2 **Caucaia** Brazil
81 C1 **Caucasus** *mts* Asia/Europe
100 A2 **Caudry** France
109 C3 **Caulonia** Italy
131 D2 **Causapscal** Can.
105 D3 **Cavaillon** France
151 D3 **Cavalcante** Brazil
97 C2 **Cavan** Ireland
154 B3 **Cavernoso, Serra do** *mts* Brazil
151 D2 **Caxias** Brazil
152 C3 **Caxias do Sul** Brazil
120 A1 **Caxito** Angola
151 C1 **Cayenne** Fr. Guiana
146 B3 **Cayman Islands** *terr.* West Indies
117 C4 **Caynabo** Somalia
120 B2 **Cazombo** Angola
144 B2 **Ceballos** Mex.
64 B1 **Cebu** Phil.
64 B1 **Cebu** *i.* Phil.
108 B2 **Cecina** Italy
137 F2 **Cedar** *r.* U.S.A.
135 D3 **Cedar City** U.S.A.
137 E2 **Cedar Falls** U.S.A.
129 D2 **Cedar Lake** Can.
137 E2 **Cedar Rapids** U.S.A.
144 A2 **Cedros, Isla** *i.* Mex.
51 C3 **Ceduna** Austr.
117 C4 **Ceeldheere** Somalia
117 C3 **Ceerigaabo** Somalia
108 B3 **Cefalù** *Sicilia* Italy
145 B2 **Celaya** Mex.
58 C3 **Celebes** *i.* Indon.
156 B5 **Celebes Sea** Indon./Phil.
145 C2 **Celestún** Mex.
101 E1 **Celle** Ger.
95 B3 **Celtic Sea** Ireland/U.K.
59 D3 **Cenderawasih, Teluk** *b.* Indon.
150 A1 **Central, Cordillera** *mts* Col.
150 A3 **Central, Cordillera** *mts* Peru
64 B1 **Central, Cordillera** *mts* Phil.
118 C2 **Central African Republic** *country* Africa
74 A2 **Central Brahui Range** *mts* Pak.
137 D2 **Central City** U.S.A.
140 B3 **Centralia** *IL* U.S.A.
134 B1 **Centralia** *WA* U.S.A.
74 A2 **Central Makran Range** *mts* Pak.
59 D3 **Central Range** *mts* P.N.G.
89 E3 **Central Russian Upland** *hills* Rus. Fed.
83 I2 **Central Siberian Plateau** Rus. Fed.
111 B3 **Cephalonia** *i.* Greece
Ceram Sea Indon. *see* **Seram, Laut**
152 B3 **Ceres** Arg.
154 C1 **Ceres** Brazil
122 A3 **Ceres** S. Africa
104 C3 **Céret** France
106 C1 **Cerezo de Abajo** Spain
109 C2 **Cerignola** Italy
110 C2 **Cernavodă** Romania
145 C2 **Cerralvo** Mex.
144 B2 **Cerralvo, Isla** *i.* Mex.
145 B2 **Cerritos** Mex.
154 C2 **Cerro Azul** Brazil
145 C2 **Cerro Azul** Mex.
150 A3 **Cerro de Pasco** Peru
105 D3 **Cervione** *Corse* France
106 B1 **Cervo** Spain
108 B2 **Cesena** Italy
88 C2 **Cēsis** Latvia
102 C2 **České Budějovice** Czech Rep.
101 F3 **Český les** *mts* Czech Rep.
111 C3 **Çeşme** Turkey
53 D2 **Cessnock** Austr.
109 C2 **Cetinje** Montenegro
109 C3 **Cetraro** Italy
106 B2 **Ceuta** N. Africa
105 C3 **Cévennes** *mts* France
Ceylon *country* Asia *see* **Sri Lanka**
79 D2 **Chābahār** Iran
75 C1 **Chabyêr Caka** *salt l.* China
150 A2 **Chachapoyas** Peru
89 D3 **Chachersk** Belarus
63 B2 **Chachoengsao** Thai.
115 D3 **Chad** *country* Africa
115 D3 **Chad, Lake** Africa
69 C1 **Chadaasan** Mongolia
68 C1 **Chadan** Rus. Fed.
123 C1 **Chadibe** Botswana
136 C2 **Chadron** U.S.A.
65 B2 **Chaeryŏng** N. Korea
74 A2 **Chagai** Pak.
77 C3 **Chaghcharān** Afgh.
89 E2 **Chagoda** Rus. Fed.
75 C2 **Chaibasa** India
63 B2 **Chainat** Thai.
63 B2 **Chaiyaphum** Thai.
152 C4 **Chajarí** Arg.
131 D1 **Chakonipau, Lac** *l.* Can.
150 A3 **Chala** Peru
74 A1 **Chalap Dalan** *mts* Afgh.
131 D2 **Chaleur Bay** *inlet* Can.
74 B2 **Chalisgaon** India
111 C3 **Chalki** *i.* Greece
111 B3 **Chalkida** Greece
104 B2 **Challans** France
134 D2 **Challis** U.S.A.
105 C2 **Châlons-en-Champagne** France
105 C2 **Chalon-sur-Saône** France
138 B1 **Chama** U.S.A.
121 C2 **Chama** Zambia
74 A1 **Chaman** Pak.
74 B1 **Chamba** India
74 B2 **Chambal** *r.* India
137 D2 **Chamberlain** U.S.A.
141 D3 **Chambersburg** U.S.A.
105 D2 **Chambéry** France
121 C2 **Chambeshi** Zambia
140 B2 **Champaign** U.S.A.
141 E2 **Champlain, Lake** Can./U.S.A.

145 C3 **Champotón** Mex.
152 A3 **Chañaral** Chile
126 B2 **Chandalar** *r.* U.S.A.
142 C3 **Chandeleur Islands** U.S.A.
74 B1 **Chandigarh** India
138 A2 **Chandler** U.S.A.
75 B3 **Chandrapur** India
63 B2 **Chang, Ko** *i.* Thai.
Chang'an China *see* **Rong'an**
121 C3 **Changane** *r.* Moz.
121 C2 **Changara** Moz.
65 B1 **Changbai** China
65 B1 **Changbai Shan** *mts* China/ N. Korea
69 E2 **Changchun** China
71 B3 **Changde** China
65 B2 **Ch'angdo** N. Korea
71 C3 **Changhua** Taiwan
65 B3 **Changhŭng** S. Korea
Chang Jiang *r.* China *see* **Yangtze**
65 B1 **Changjin** N. Korea
65 B1 **Changjin-gang** *r.* N. Korea
71 B3 **Changsha** China
65 B2 **Changsŏng** S. Korea
71 B3 **Changting** China
65 B2 **Ch'angwŏn** S. Korea
70 B2 **Changyuan** China
70 B2 **Changzhi** China
70 B2 **Changzhou** China
111 B3 **Chania** Greece
95 C4 **Channel Islands** English Chan.
135 C4 **Channel Islands** U.S.A.
131 E2 **Channel-Port-aux-Basques** Can.
63 B2 **Chanthaburi** Thai.
104 C2 **Chantilly** France
137 D3 **Chanute** U.S.A.
82 G3 **Chany, Ozero** *salt l.* Rus. Fed.
71 B3 **Chaoyang** China
Chaoyang China *see* **Huinan**
71 B3 **Chaozhou** China
144 B2 **Chapala, Laguna de** *l.* Mex.
76 B1 **Chapayevo** Kazakh.
152 C3 **Chapecó** Brazil
143 E1 **Chapel Hill** U.S.A.
130 B2 **Chapleau** Can.
89 E3 **Chaplygin** Rus. Fed.
91 C2 **Chaplynka** Ukr.
145 B2 **Charcas** Mex.
99 B3 **Chard** U.K.
104 B2 **Charente** *r.* France
77 C3 **Chārīkār** Afgh.
86 E2 **Charkayuvom** Rus. Fed.
100 B2 **Charleroi** Belgium
141 D3 **Charles, Cape** U.S.A.
137 E2 **Charles City** U.S.A.
140 B3 **Charleston** *IL* U.S.A.
143 E2 **Charleston** *SC* U.S.A.
140 C3 **Charleston** *WV* U.S.A.
135 C3 **Charleston Peak** U.S.A.
51 D2 **Charleville** Austr.
105 C2 **Charleville-Mézières** France
143 D1 **Charlotte** U.S.A.
143 D3 **Charlotte Harbor** *b.* U.S.A.
141 D3 **Charlottesville** U.S.A.
131 D2 **Charlottetown** Can.
52 B3 **Charlton** Austr.
130 C1 **Charlton Island** Can.
51 D2 **Charters Towers** Austr.
104 C2 **Chartres** France
128 C2 **Chase** Can.
88 C3 **Chashniki** Belarus
54 A3 **Chaslands Mistake** *c.* N.Z.
65 B1 **Chasŏng** N. Korea
104 B2 **Chassiron, Pointe de** *pt* France
104 B2 **Châteaubriant** France
104 C2 **Château-du-Loir** France
104 C2 **Châteaudun** France
104 B2 **Châteaulin** France
105 D3 **Châteauneuf-les-Martigues** France
104 C2 **Châteauneuf-sur-Loire** France
105 C2 **Château-Thierry** France
128 C2 **Chateh** Can.
100 B2 **Châtelet** Belgium
104 C2 **Châtellerault** France
140 C2 **Chatham** *Ont.* Can.
49 G5 **Chatham Islands** *is* N.Z.
105 C2 **Châtillon-sur-Seine** France
143 D2 **Chattahoochee** *r.* U.S.A.
143 C1 **Chattanooga** U.S.A.
63 B2 **Châu Đôc** Vietnam
62 A1 **Chauk** Myanmar
105 D2 **Chaumont** France
105 C2 **Chauny** France
151 D2 **Chaves** Brazil
106 B1 **Chaves** Port.
130 C1 **Chavigny, Lac** *l.* Can.
89 D3 **Chavusy** Belarus
89 E2 **Chayevo** Rus. Fed.
86 E3 **Chaykovskiy** Rus. Fed.
102 C1 **Cheb** Czech Rep.
87 D3 **Cheboksary** Rus. Fed.
140 C1 **Cheboygan** U.S.A.
65 B2 **Chech'ŏn** S. Korea
114 B2 **Chegga** Maur.
134 B1 **Chehalis** U.S.A.
65 B3 **Cheju** S. Korea
65 B3 **Cheju-do** *i.* S. Korea
65 B3 **Cheju-haehyŏp** *sea chan.* S. Korea
89 E2 **Chekhov** Rus. Fed.
134 B1 **Chelan, Lake** U.S.A.
103 E1 **Chełm** Pol.
99 D3 **Chelmer** *r.* U.K.
103 D1 **Chełmno** Pol.
99 D3 **Chelmsford** U.K.
99 B3 **Cheltenham** U.K.
87 F3 **Chelyabinsk** Rus. Fed.
101 F2 **Chemnitz** Ger.
114 B2 **Chenachane** Alg.
70 B1 **Chengde** China
70 A2 **Chengdu** China
71 B4 **Chengmai** China
Chengshou China *see* **Yingshan**
70 A2 **Chengxian** China
Chengyang China *see* **Juxian**
73 C3 **Chennai** India
71 B3 **Chenzhou** China
99 B3 **Chepstow** U.K.
104 B2 **Cherbourg** France
89 E3 **Cheremisinovo** Rus. Fed.
69 C1 **Cheremkhovo** Rus. Fed.
89 E2 **Cherepovets** Rus. Fed.
91 C2 **Cherkasy** Ukr.
87 D4 **Cherkessk** Rus. Fed.
91 C1 **Chernihiv** Ukr.
91 D2 **Cherninivka** Ukr.
90 B2 **Chernivtsi** Ukr.
90 B1 **Chernyakhiv** Ukr.
88 B3 **Chernyakhovsk** Rus. Fed.
89 E3 **Chernyanka** Rus. Fed.
83 I2 **Chernyshevskiy** Rus. Fed.
137 D2 **Cherokee** U.S.A.
83 K2 **Cherskogo, Khrebet** *mts* Rus. Fed.
91 E2 **Chertkovo** Rus. Fed.
90 A1 **Chervonohrad** Ukr.
88 C3 **Chervyen'** Belarus
89 D3 **Cherykaw** Belarus
141 D3 **Chesapeake Bay** U.S.A.
86 D2 **Cheshskaya Guba** *b.* Rus.
98 B2 **Chester** U.K.
140 B3 **Chester** *IL* U.S.A.
143 D2 **Chester** *SC* U.S.A.
98 C2 **Chesterfield** U.K.
129 E1 **Chesterfield Inlet** Can.
129 E1 **Chesterfield Inlet** Can.
141 F1 **Chesuncook Lake** U.S.A.
131 D2 **Chéticamp** Can.
145 D3 **Chetumal** Mex.
128 B2 **Chetwynd** Can.
98 B1 **Cheviot Hills** U.K.
136 C2 **Cheyenne** U.S.A.
136 C2 **Cheyenne** *r.* U.S.A.
136 C3 **Cheyenne Wells** U.S.A.
75 C2 **Chhapra** India
75 B2 **Chhatarpur** India
71 C3 **Chiai** Taiwan
62 A2 **Chiang Dao** Thai.
62 A2 **Chiang Mai** Thai.
62 A2 **Chiang Rai** Thai.
108 A1 **Chiavenna** Italy
70 B3 **Chibi** China
121 C3 **Chiboma** Moz.
130 C2 **Chibougamau** Can.
123 D1 **Chibuto** Moz.
140 B2 **Chicago** U.S.A.
128 A2 **Chichagof Island** U.S.A.
99 C3 **Chichester** U.K.
50 A2 **Chichester Range** *mts* Aus
139 D1 **Chickasha** U.S.A.
150 A2 **Chiclayo** Peru
153 B5 **Chico** *r.* Arg.
135 B3 **Chico** U.S.A.
131 C2 **Chicoutimi** Can.
108 B2 **Chieti** Italy
145 C3 **Chietla** Mex.
69 D2 **Chifeng** China
155 D1 **Chifre, Serra do** *mts* Brazi
77 D2 **Chiganak** Kazakh.
145 C3 **Chignahuapán** Mex.
121 C3 **Chigubo** Moz.
144 B2 **Chihuahua** Mex.
88 C2 **Chikhachevo** Rus. Fed.
67 C3 **Chikuma-gawa** *r.* Japan
128 B2 **Chilanko** *r.* Can.
74 B1 **Chilas** Pak.
139 C2 **Childress** U.S.A.
153 A4 **Chile** *country* S. America
152 B3 **Chilecito** Arg.
75 C3 **Chilika Lake** India
121 B2 **Chililabombwe** Zambia
128 B2 **Chilko** *r.* Can.
128 B2 **Chilko Lake** Can.
153 A4 **Chillán** Chile
137 E3 **Chillicothe** *MO* U.S.A.
140 C3 **Chillicothe** *OH* U.S.A.
128 B3 **Chilliwack** Can.
153 A5 **Chiloé, Isla de** *i.* Chile
145 C3 **Chilpancingo** Mex.
53 C3 **Chiltern** Austr.
71 C3 **Chilung** Taiwan
119 D3 **Chimala** Tanz.
152 B4 **Chimbas** Arg.
150 A2 **Chimborazo** *mt.* Ecuador
150 A2 **Chimbote** Peru
87 E4 **Chimboy** Uzbek.
Chimkent Kazakh. *see* **Shymkent**
121 C2 **Chimoio** Moz.
77 C3 **Chimtargha, Qullai** *mt.* Ta
68 C2 **China** *country* Asia
145 C2 **China** Mex.
150 A3 **Chincha Alta** Peru
128 C2 **Chinchaga** *r.* Can.

D3	Chinchorro, Banco Mex.	
C2	Chinde Moz.	
B3	Chindo S. Korea	
B3	Chin-do i. S. Korea	
C1	Chindu China	
A1	Chindwin r. Myanmar	
B2	Chinghwa N. Korea	
A2	Chingola Zambia	
A2	Chinguar Angola	
C2	Chinhae S. Korea	
C2	Chinhoyi Zimbabwe	
B1	Chiniot Pak.	
C2	Chinipas Mex.	
B2	Chinju S. Korea	
C3	Chinko r. C.A.R.	
B1	Chinle U.S.A.	
C3	Chinmen Taiwan	
C3	Chino Japan	
C3	Chinon France	
A2	Chino Valley U.S.A.	
B1	Chinsali Zambia	
C3	Chioggia Italy	
C3	Chios Greece	
C3	Chios i. Greece	
A2	Chipata Zambia	
A2	Chipindo Angola	
A2	Chipinge Zimbabwe	
B1	Chiplun India	
B3	Chippenham U.K.	
C2	Chipping Norton U.K.	
C3	Chirchiq Uzbek.	
B4	Chiredzi Zimbabwe	
B4	Chiricahua Peak U.S.A.	
B4	Chiriquí, Golfo de b. Panama	
B2	Chiri-san mt. S. Korea	
B4	Chirripó mt. Costa Rica	
B2	Chirundu Zimbabwe	
C1	Chisasibi Can.	
E1	Chisholm U.S.A.	
C3	Chişinău Moldova	
E3	Chistopol' Rus. Fed.	
C4	Chita Rus. Fed.	
A2	Chitado Angola	
C2	Chitambo Zambia	
A2	Chitato Angola	
C1	Chitipa Malawi	
B1	Chitradurga India	
B1	Chitral Pak.	
D2	Chitré Panama	
B2	Chittagong Bangl.	
C2	Chittaurgarh India	
B1	Chitungwiza Zimbabwe	
C2	Chiume Angola	
C2	Chivhu Zimbabwe	
C2	Chizhou China	
C3	Chlef Alg.	
D2	Chlef, Oued r. Alg.	
B4	Choele Choel Arg.	
C3	Choix Mex.	
B3	Chojnice Pol.	
B3	Ch'ok'e Mountains Eth.	
K2	Chokurdakh Rus. Fed.	
C3	Chókwé Moz.	
C2	Cholet France	
C1	Chomutov Czech Rep.	
I2	Chona r. Rus. Fed.	
C3	Ch'ŏnan S. Korea	
A2	Chone Ecuador	
B2	Ch'ŏngjin N. Korea	
B2	Ch'ŏngju N. Korea	
B2	Chŏngju N. Korea	
B2	Chŏngp'yŏng N. Korea	
A3	Chongqing China	
A3	Chongqing mun. China	
A3	Chongzuo China	
B3	Chŏnju S. Korea	
A5	Chonos, Archipiélago de los is Chile	
154 B3	Chopimzinho Brazil	
111 B3	Chora Sfakion Greece	
98 B2	Chorley U.K.	
91 C2	Chornomors'ke Ukr.	
90 D2	Chortkiv Ukr.	
65 B2	Ch'ŏrwŏn S. Korea	
67 D3	Chōshi Japan	
103 D1	Choszczno Pol.	
114 A2	Choûm Maur.	
69 D1	Choybalsan Mongolia	
69 D1	Choyr Mongolia	
54 B2	Christchurch N.Z.	
99 C3	Christchurch U.K.	
127 G2	Christian, Cape Can.	
123 C2	Christiana S. Africa	
54 A2	Christina, Mount N.Z.	
153 B5	Chubut r. Arg.	
90 B1	Chudniv Ukr.	
89 D2	Chudovo Rus. Fed.	
	Chudskoye Ozero l. Estonia/Rus. Fed. see Peipus, Lake	
126 B2	Chugach Mountains U.S.A.	
67 B4	Chūgoku-sanchi mts Japan	
66 B2	Chuguyevka Rus. Fed.	
91 D2	Chuhuyiv Ukr.	
160 J3	Chukchi Sea Rus. Fed./U.S.A.	
83 N2	Chukotskiy Poluostrov pen. Rus. Fed.	
135 C4	Chula Vista U.S.A.	
82 G3	Chulym Rus. Fed.	
152 B3	Chumbicha Arg.	
83 K3	Chumikan Rus. Fed.	
63 A2	Chumphon Thai.	
65 B2	Ch'unch'ŏn S. Korea	
	Chungking China see Chongqing	
83 H2	Chunya r. Rus. Fed.	
150 A3	Chuquibamba Peru	
152 B3	Chuquicamata Chile	
105 D2	Chur Switz.	
62 A1	Churachandpur India	
129 E2	Churchill Can.	
129 E2	Churchill r. Man. Can.	
131 D1	Churchill r. Nfld. and Lab. Can.	
129 E2	Churchill, Cape Can.	
131 D1	Churchill Falls Can.	
129 D2	Churchill Lake Can.	
74 B2	Churu India	
131 C2	Chute-des-Passes Can.	
62 B1	Chuxiong China	
90 B2	Ciadîr-Lunga Moldova	
61 B2	Ciamis Indon.	
60 B2	Cianjur Indon.	
154 B2	Cianorte Brazil	
103 E1	Ciechanów Pol.	
146 C2	Ciego de Ávila Cuba	
146 B2	Cienfuegos Cuba	
107 C2	Cieza Spain	
106 C2	Cigüela r. Spain	
80 B2	Cihanbeyli Turkey	
144 B3	Cihuatlán Mex.	
106 B2	Cijara, Embalse de resr Spain	
61 B2	Cilacap Indon.	
139 C1	Cimarron r. U.S.A.	
90 B2	Cimişlia Moldova	
108 B2	Cimone, Monte mt. Italy	
140 C3	Cincinnati U.S.A.	
111 C3	Çine Turkey	
100 B2	Ciney Belgium	
145 C3	Cintalapa Mex.	
71 B3	Ciping China	
126 B2	Circle AK U.S.A.	
136 B1	Circle MT U.S.A.	
58 B3	Cirebon Indon.	
99 C3	Cirencester U.K.	
108 A1	Cirié Italy	
109 C3	Cirò Marina Italy	
109 C2	Čitluk Bos.-Herz.	
122 A3	Citrusdal S. Africa	
145 B2	Ciudad Acuña Mex.	
145 B3	Ciudad Altamirano Mex.	
150 B1	Ciudad Bolívar Venez.	
144 B2	Ciudad Camargo Mex.	
144 A2	Ciudad Constitución Mex.	
145 C3	Ciudad del Carmen Mex.	
144 B2	Ciudad Delicias Mex.	
145 C2	Ciudad de Valles Mex.	
150 B1	Ciudad Guayana Venez.	
138 B3	Ciudad Guerrero Mex.	
144 B3	Ciudad Guzmán Mex.	
145 C3	Ciudad Hidalgo Mex.	
145 C3	Ciudad Ixtepec Mex.	
144 B1	Ciudad Juárez Mex.	
145 C2	Ciudad Mante Mex.	
145 C2	Ciudad Mier Mex.	
144 B2	Ciudad Obregón Mex.	
106 C2	Ciudad Real Spain	
145 C2	Ciudad Río Bravo Mex.	
106 B1	Ciudad Rodrigo Spain	
145 C2	Ciudad Victoria Mex.	
107 D1	Ciutadella Spain	
111 C3	Cıvan Dağ mt. Turkey	
108 B1	Cividale del Friuli Italy	
108 B2	Civitanova Marche Italy	
108 B2	Civitavecchia Italy	
104 C2	Civray France	
111 C3	Çivril Turkey	
70 C2	Cixi China	
99 D3	Clacton-on-Sea U.K.	
128 C2	Claire, Lake Can.	
105 C2	Clamecy France	
122 A3	Clanwilliam S. Africa	
52 A2	Clare Austr.	
97 A2	Clare Island Ireland	
141 E2	Claremont U.S.A.	
97 B2	Claremorris Ireland	
54 B2	Clarence N.Z.	
131 E2	Clarenville Can.	
128 C2	Claresholm Can.	
137 D2	Clarinda U.S.A.	
123 C3	Clarkebury S. Africa	
134 C1	Clark Fork r. U.S.A.	
143 D2	Clark Hill Reservoir U.S.A.	
140 C3	Clarksburg U.S.A.	
142 B2	Clarksdale U.S.A.	
142 B1	Clarksville AR U.S.A.	
142 C1	Clarksville TN U.S.A.	
154 B1	Claro r. Brazil	
139 C1	Clayton U.S.A.	
97 B3	Clear, Cape Ireland	
137 E2	Clear Lake U.S.A.	
135 B3	Clear Lake U.S.A.	
129 C2	Clearwater r. Can.	
143 D3	Clearwater U.S.A.	
134 C1	Clearwater r. U.S.A.	
139 D2	Cleburne U.S.A.	
51 D2	Clermont Austr.	
105 C2	Clermont-Ferrand France	
52 A2	Cleve Austr.	
142 B2	Cleveland MS U.S.A.	
140 C2	Cleveland OH U.S.A.	
143 D1	Cleveland TN U.S.A.	
134 D1	Cleveland, Mount U.S.A.	
143 D3	Clewiston U.S.A.	
97 A2	Clifden Ireland	
53 D1	Clifton Austr.	
138 B2	Clifton U.S.A.	
128 B2	Clinton Can.	
137 E2	Clinton IA U.S.A.	
137 E3	Clinton MO U.S.A.	

139 D1 **Clinton** *OK* U.S.A.
96 A2 **Clisham** *h.* U.K.
98 B2 **Clitheroe** U.K.
97 B3 **Clonakilty** Ireland
51 D2 **Cloncurry** Austr.
97 C1 **Clones** Ireland
97 C2 **Clonmel** Ireland
100 D1 **Cloppenburg** Ger.
136 B2 **Cloud Peak** U.S.A.
139 C2 **Clovis** U.S.A.
129 D2 **Cluff Lake Mine** Can.
110 B1 **Cluj-Napoca** Romania
51 C2 **Cluny** Austr.
105 D2 **Cluses** France
54 A3 **Clutha** *r.* N.Z.
96 B3 **Clyde** *r.* U.K.
96 B3 **Clyde, Firth of** *est.* U.K.
96 B3 **Clydebank** U.K.
127 G2 **Clyde River** Can.
144 B3 **Coalcomán** Mex.
135 C3 **Coaldale** U.S.A.
128 B2 **Coal River** Can.
150 B2 **Coari** Brazil
150 D2 **Coari** *r.* Brazil
142 B2 **Coastal Plain** U.S.A.
128 B2 **Coast Mountains** Can.
135 B2 **Coast Ranges** *mts* U.S.A.
96 B3 **Coatbridge** U.K.
127 F2 **Coats Island** Can.
55 R2 **Coats Land** *reg.* Antarctica
145 C3 **Coatzacoalcos** Mex.
146 A3 **Cobán** Guat.
53 C2 **Cobar** Austr.
97 B3 **Cobh** Ireland
152 B2 **Cobija** Bol.
141 D2 **Cobourg** Can.
50 C1 **Cobourg Peninsula** Austr.
53 C3 **Cobram** Austr.
101 E2 **Coburg** Ger.
152 B2 **Cochabamba** Bol.
100 C2 **Cochem** Ger.
Cochin India *see* **Kochi**
128 C2 **Cochrane** *Alta* Can.
130 B2 **Cochrane** *Ont.* Can.
153 A5 **Cochrane** Chile
52 B2 **Cockburn** Austr.
Cockburn Town Turks and Caicos Is *see* **Grand Turk**
98 B1 **Cockermouth** U.K.
122 B3 **Cockscomb** *mt.* S. Africa
146 B3 **Coco** *r.* Hond./Nic.
144 B2 **Cocula** Mex.
150 A1 **Cocuy, Sierra Nevada del** *mt.* Col.
141 E2 **Cod, Cape** U.S.A.
108 B2 **Codigoro** Italy
131 D1 **Cod Island** Can.
151 D2 **Codó** Brazil
136 B2 **Cody** U.S.A.
51 D1 **Coen** Austr.
100 C2 **Coesfeld** Ger.
134 C1 **Coeur d'Alene** U.S.A.
123 C3 **Coffee Bay** S. Africa
137 D3 **Coffeyville** U.S.A.
53 D2 **Coffs Harbour** Austr.
104 B2 **Cognac** France
118 A2 **Cogo** Equat. Guinea
52 B3 **Cohuna** Austr.
146 B4 **Coiba, Isla de** *i.* Panama
153 A5 **Coihaique** Chile
73 B3 **Coimbatore** India
106 B1 **Coimbra** Port.
52 B3 **Colac** Austr.
155 D1 **Colatina** Brazil
136 C3 **Colby** U.S.A.
99 D3 **Colchester** U.K.
129 C2 **Cold Lake** Can.
96 C3 **Coldstream** U.K.
139 D2 **Coleman** U.S.A.
52 B3 **Coleraine** Austr.
97 C1 **Coleraine** U.K.
123 C3 **Colesberg** S. Africa
144 B3 **Colima** Mex.
144 B3 **Colima, Nevado de** *vol.* Mex.
96 A2 **Coll** *i.* U.K.
53 C1 **Collarenebri** Austr.
50 B1 **Collier Bay** Austr.
54 B2 **Collingwood** N.Z.
97 B1 **Collooney** Ireland
105 D2 **Colmar** France
100 C2 **Cologne** Ger.
154 C2 **Colômbia** Brazil
150 A1 **Colombia** *country* S. America
73 B4 **Colombo** Sri Lanka
104 C3 **Colomiers** France
152 C4 **Colón** Arg.
146 C4 **Colón** Panama
109 C3 **Colonna, Capo** *c.* Italy
96 A2 **Colonsay** *i.* U.K.
153 B4 **Colorado** *r.* Arg.
138 A2 **Colorado** *r.* Mex./U.S.A.
139 D3 **Colorado** *r.* U.S.A.
136 B3 **Colorado** *state* U.S.A.
135 E3 **Colorado Plateau** U.S.A.
136 C3 **Colorado Springs** U.S.A.
144 B2 **Colotlán** Mex.
136 B1 **Colstrip** U.S.A.
137 E3 **Columbia** *MO* U.S.A.
143 D2 **Columbia** *SC* U.S.A.
142 C1 **Columbia** *TN* U.S.A.
134 B1 **Columbia** *r.* U.S.A.
128 C2 **Columbia, Mount** Can.
134 D1 **Columbia Falls** U.S.A.
128 B2 **Columbia Mountains** Can.
134 C1 **Columbia Plateau** U.S.A.
143 D2 **Columbus** *GA* U.S.A.
140 B3 **Columbus** *IN* U.S.A.
142 C2 **Columbus** *MS* U.S.A.
137 D2 **Columbus** *NE* U.S.A.
138 B2 **Columbus** *NM* U.S.A.
140 C3 **Columbus** *OH* U.S.A.
134 C1 **Colville** U.S.A.
126 A2 **Colville** *r.* U.S.A.
126 C2 **Colville Lake** Can.
98 B2 **Colwyn Bay** U.K.
108 B2 **Comacchio** Italy
145 C3 **Comalcalco** Mex.
110 C1 **Comănești** Romania
130 C1 **Comencho, Lac** *l.* Can.
97 C2 **Comeragh Mountains** *hills* Ireland
75 D2 **Comilla** Bangl.
108 A2 **Comino, Capo** *c. Sardegna* Italy
145 C3 **Comitán de Domínguez** Mex.
104 C2 **Commentry** France
139 D2 **Commerce** U.S.A.
127 F2 **Committee Bay** Can.
108 A1 **Como** Italy
153 B5 **Comodoro Rivadavia** Arg.
121 D2 **Comoros** *country* Africa
104 C2 **Compiègne** France
144 B2 **Compostela** Mex.
90 B2 **Comrat** Moldova
114 A4 **Conakry** Guinea
155 E1 **Conceição da Barra** Brazil
151 D2 **Conceição do Araguaia** Brazil
155 D1 **Conceição do Mato Dentro** Brazil
152 B3 **Concepción** Arg.
153 A4 **Concepción** Chile
144 B2 **Concepción** Mex.
135 B4 **Conception, Point** U.S.A.
154 C2 **Conchas** Brazil
138 C1 **Conchas Lake** U.S.A.
144 B2 **Conchos** *r. Chihuahua* Me
145 C2 **Conchos** *r. Nuevo León/Tamaulipas* Mex.
135 B3 **Concord** *CA* U.S.A.
141 E2 **Concord** *NH* U.S.A.
152 C4 **Concordia** Arg.
122 A2 **Concordia** S. Africa
137 D3 **Concordia** U.S.A.
53 C2 **Condobolin** Austr.
104 C3 **Condom** France
134 B1 **Condon** U.S.A.
108 B1 **Conegliano** Italy
104 C2 **Confolens** France
75 C2 **Congdü** China
118 B3 **Congo** *country* Africa
118 B3 **Congo** *r.* Congo/Dem. Rep Congo
118 C3 **Congo, Democratic Repub of the** *country* Africa
129 C2 **Conklin** Can.
97 B1 **Conn, Lough** *l.* Ireland
97 B2 **Connaught** *reg.* Ireland
141 E2 **Connecticut** *r.* U.S.A.
141 E2 **Connecticut** *state* U.S.A.
97 B2 **Connemara** *reg.* Ireland
134 D1 **Conrad** U.S.A.
139 D2 **Conroe** U.S.A.
155 D2 **Conselheiro Lafaiete** Braz
155 D1 **Conselheiro Pena** Brazil
98 C1 **Consett** U.K.
63 B3 **Côn Sơn, Đao** *i.* Vietnam
110 C2 **Constanța** Romania
106 B2 **Constantina** Spain
115 C1 **Constantine** Alg.
134 D2 **Contact** U.S.A.
150 A2 **Contamana** Peru
153 A6 **Contreras, Isla** *i.* Chile
126 D2 **Contwoyto Lake** Can.
142 B1 **Conway** *AR* U.S.A.
141 E2 **Conway** *NH* U.S.A.
51 C2 **Coober Pedy** Austr.
Cook, Mount *mt.* N.Z. *see* **Aoraki**
143 C1 **Cookeville** U.S.A.
49 H4 **Cook Islands** S. Pacific Oc
131 E1 **Cook's Harbour** Can.
97 C1 **Cookstown** U.K.
54 B2 **Cook Strait** N.Z.
51 D1 **Cooktown** Austr.
53 C2 **Coolabah** Austr.
53 C2 **Coolamon** Austr.
53 D1 **Coolangatta** Austr.
50 B3 **Coolgardie** Austr.
53 C3 **Cooma** Austr.
52 B2 **Coombah** Austr.
53 C2 **Coonabarabran** Austr.
52 A3 **Coonalpyn** Austr.
53 C2 **Coonamble** Austr.
52 A1 **Cooper Creek** *watercourse* Austr.
134 B2 **Coos Bay** U.S.A.
53 C2 **Cootamundra** Austr.
145 C3 **Copainalá** Mex.
145 C3 **Copala** Mex.
93 F4 **Copenhagen** Denmark
109 C2 **Copertino** Italy
152 A3 **Copiapó** Chile
140 B1 **Copper Harbor** U.S.A.
Coppermine Can. *see* **Kugluktuk**
126 D2 **Coppermine** *r.* Can.
122 B2 **Copperton** S. Africa
152 A3 **Coquimbo** Chile
110 B2 **Corabia** Romania
155 D1 **Coração de Jesus** Brazil
150 A3 **Coracora** Peru

D1	Coraki Austr.	
A2	Coral Bay Austr.	
F2	Coral Harbour Can.	
D7	Coral Sea S. Pacific Ocean	
D4	Coral Sea Islands Territory Austr.	
B3	Corangamite, Lake Austr.	
B2	Corby U.K.	
A5	Corcovado, Golfo de sea chan. Chile	
D2	Cordele U.S.A.	
B2	Cordilleras Range mts Phil.	
B4	Córdoba Arg.	
C3	Córdoba Mex.	
C2	Córdoba Spain	
B4	Córdoba, Sierras de mts Arg.	
A3	Corfu i. Greece	
C2	Coria Spain	
C2	Corinth Greece	
C2	Corinth U.S.A.	
D1	Corinto Brazil	
C3	Cork Ireland	
B2	Çorlu Turkey	
B2	Cornélio Procópio Brazil	
E2	Corner Brook Can.	
C2	Corner Inlet b. Austr.	
C1	Corning CA U.S.A.	
D2	Corning NY U.S.A.	
	Corn Islands is Nic. see Maíz, Islas del	
B2	Corno, Grande mt. Italy	
D2	Cornwall Can.	
E1	Cornwallis Island Can.	
B1	Coro Venez.	
C1	Coromandel Brazil	
C1	Coromandel Peninsula N.Z.	
D2	Coronation Can.	
D2	Coronation Gulf Can.	
B4	Coronel Oviedo Para.	
B4	Coronel Suárez Arg.	
D3	Çorovodë Albania	
D3	Corpus Christi U.S.A.	
D2	Corque Bol.	
D3	Corrente Brazil	
B1	Correntes Brazil	
D2	Correntina Brazil	
B2	Corrib, Lough l. Ireland	
B3	Corrientes Arg.	
B2	Corrientes, Cabo c. Mex.	
C3	Corryong Austr.	
	Corse i. France see Corsica	
D3	Corse, Cap c. Corse France	
D3	Corsica i. France	
D3	Corsicana U.S.A.	
D3	Corte Corse France	
B2	Cortegana Spain	
D3	Cortez U.S.A.	
B1	Cortina d'Ampezzo Italy	
D2	Cortland U.S.A.	
D1	Cortona Italy	
B2	Coruche Port.	
	Çoruh Turkey see Artvin	
B1	Çorum Turkey	
C2	Corumbá Brazil	
C1	Corumbá r. Brazil	
B2	Corvallis U.S.A.	
B2	Corwen U.K.	
C3	Cosalá Mex.	
C3	Cosamaloapan Mex.	
C3	Cosenza Italy	
C2	Cosne-Cours-sur-Loire France	
F7	Costa Blanca coastal area Spain	
D1	Costa Brava coastal area Spain	
B2	Costa del Sol coastal area Spain	

146	B3	Costa de Mosquitos coastal area Nic.
154	B1	Costa Rica Brazil
146	B3	Costa Rica country Central America
144	B2	Costa Rica Mex.
110	B2	Costeşti Romania
64	B2	Cotabato Phil.
114	B4	Côte d'Ivoire country Africa
150	A2	Cotopaxi, Volcán vol. Ecuador
99	B3	Cotswold Hills U.K.
134	B2	Cottage Grove U.S.A.
102	C1	Cottbus Ger.
52	A3	Coubre, Pointe de la pt France
137	D2	Couedic, Cape du Austr.
88	B2	Council Bluffs U.S.A.
		Courland Lagoon b. Lith./Rus. Fed.
128	B3	Courtenay Can.
104	B3	Coutances France
104	B2	Coutras France
100	B2	Couvin Belgium
99	C2	Coventry U.K.
140	C3	Covington U.S.A.
50	B3	Cowan, Lake imp. l. Austr.
96	C2	Cowdenbeath U.K.
53	C2	Cowes Austr.
134	B1	Cowlitz r. U.S.A.
53	C2	Cowra Austr.
154	B1	Coxim Brazil
75	D2	Cox's Bazar Bangl.
145	B3	Coyuca de Benítez Mex.
145	D2	Cozumel Mex.
145	D2	Cozumel, Isla de i. Mex.
123	C3	Cradock S. Africa
136	B2	Craig U.S.A.
102	C2	Crailsheim Ger.
110	B2	Craiova Romania
129	D2	Cranberry Portage Can.
53	C3	Cranbourne Austr.
128	C3	Cranbrook Can.
151	D2	Crateús Brazil
151	E2	Crato Brazil
136	C2	Crawford U.S.A.
140	B2	Crawfordsville U.S.A.
99	C3	Crawley U.K.
134	D1	Crazy Mountains U.S.A.
129	D2	Cree r. Can.
144	B2	Creel Mex.
129	D2	Cree Lake Can.
100	B1	Creil Neth.
108	B1	Crema Italy
108	B1	Cremona Italy
108	B1	Cres i. Croatia
134	B2	Crescent City U.S.A.
128	C3	Creston Can.
137	E2	Creston U.S.A.
142	C2	Crestview U.S.A.
111	B3	Crete i. Greece
107	D1	Creus, Cap de c. Spain
98	B2	Crewe U.K.
96	B2	Crianlarich U.K.
152	D3	Criciúma Brazil
96	C2	Crieff U.K.
108	B1	Crikvenica Croatia
91	C2	Crimea pen. Ukr.
101	F2	Crimmitschau Ger.
154	C1	Cristalina Brazil
101	E1	Crivitz Ger.
		Crna Gora country Europe see Montenegro
109	D3	Crni Vrh h. Serbia
109	C1	Črnomelj Slovenia
97	B2	Croagh Patrick h. Ireland
109	C1	Croatia country Europe
61	C1	Crocker, Banjaran mts Malaysia

139	D2	Crockett U.S.A.
59	C3	Croker Island Austr.
99	C2	Cromer U.K.
54	A3	Cromwell N.Z.
137	D1	Crookston U.S.A.
53	C2	Crookwell Austr.
136	C1	Crosby U.S.A.
143	D3	Cross City U.S.A.
142	B2	Crossett U.S.A.
98	B1	Cross Fell h. U.K.
129	E2	Cross Lake Can.
143	C2	Crossville U.S.A.
109	C3	Crotone Italy
99	D3	Crowborough U.K.
142	B2	Crowley U.S.A.
128	C2	Crowsnest Pass Can.
146	C2	Cruz, Cabo c. Cuba
152	C3	Cruz Alta Brazil
152	B4	Cruz del Eje Arg.
155	D2	Cruzeiro Brazil
150	A2	Cruzeiro do Sul Brazil
52	A2	Crystal Brook Austr.
139	D3	Crystal City U.S.A.
140	B1	Crystal Falls U.S.A.
103	E2	Csongrád Hungary
120	B1	Cuando r. Angola/Zambia
120	A2	Cuangar Angola
118	B3	Cuango r. Angola/Dem. Rep. Congo
120	A1	Cuanza r. Angola
139	C3	Cuatro Ciénegas Mex.
144	B2	Cuauhtémoc Mex.
145	C3	Cuautla Mex.
146	B2	Cuba country West Indies
120	A2	Cubal Angola
120	B2	Cubango r. Angola/Namibia
150	A1	Cúcuta Col.
73	B3	Cuddalore India
73	B3	Cuddapah India
106	C1	Cuéllar Spain
120	A2	Cuemba Angola
150	A2	Cuenca Ecuador
107	C1	Cuenca Spain
107	C1	Cuenca, Serranía de mts Spain
145	C3	Cuernavaca Mex.
139	D3	Cuero U.S.A.
151	C3	Cuiabá Brazil
151	C3	Cuiabá r. Brazil
96	A2	Cuillin Sound sea chan. U.K.
120	A1	Cuilo Angola
120	B2	Cuito r. Angola
120	A2	Cuito Cuanavale Angola
60	B1	Cukai Malaysia
53	C3	Culcairn Austr.
53	C1	Culgoa r. Austr.
144	B2	Culiacán Mex.
64	A1	Culion i. Phil.
107	C2	Cullera Spain
142	C2	Cullman U.S.A.
97	C1	Cullybackey U.K.
151	C3	Cunene r. Angola
150	B1	Cumaná Venez.
141	D3	Cumberland U.S.A.
140	B3	Cumberland r. U.S.A.
129	D2	Cumberland Lake Can.
127	G2	Cumberland Peninsula Can.
142	C1	Cumberland Plateau U.S.A.
127	G2	Cumberland Sound sea chan. Can.
96	C3	Cumbernauld U.K.
135	D3	Cummings U.S.A.
96	B3	Cumnock U.K.
144	B1	Cumpas Mex.
145	C3	Cunduacán Mex.
120	A2	Cunene r. Angola
108	A2	Cuneo Italy
53	C1	Cunnamulla Austr.

108 A1 Cuorgnè Italy
96 C2 Cupar U.K.
147 D3 Curaçao i. Neth. Antilles
150 A2 Curaray r. Ecuador
153 A4 Curicó Chile
154 C3 Curitiba Brazil
52 A2 Curnamona Austr.
51 D3 Currie Austr.
51 E2 Curtis Island Austr.
151 C2 Curuá r. Brazil
60 B2 Curup Indon.
151 D2 Cururupu Brazil
155 D1 Curvelo Brazil
150 A3 Cusco Peru
139 D1 Cushing U.S.A.
134 D1 Cut Bank U.S.A.
75 C2 Cuttack India
101 D1 Cuxhaven Ger.
64 B1 Cuyo Islands Phil.
Cuzco Peru see Cusco
119 C3 Cyangugu Rwanda
111 B3 Cyclades is Greece
129 C3 Cypress Hills Can.
80 B2 Cyprus country Asia
102 C2 Czech Republic country Europe
103 D1 Czersk Pol.
103 D1 Częstochowa Pol.

D

Đa, Sông r. Vietnam see Black River
69 D2 Daban China
114 A3 Dabola Guinea
Dacca Bangl. see Dhaka
102 C2 Dachau Ger.
74 A2 Dadu Pak.
64 B1 Daet Phil.
114 A3 Dagana Senegal
64 B1 Dagupan Phil.
74 B3 Dahanu India
69 D2 Da Hinggan Ling mts China
116 C3 Dahlak Archipelago is Eritrea
100 C2 Dahlem Ger.
78 B3 Dahm, Ramlat des. Saudi Arabia/Yemen
60 B2 Daik Indon.
106 C2 Daimiel Spain
51 C2 Dajarra Austr.
114 A3 Dakar Senegal
116 A2 Dākhilah, Wāḩāt ad oasis Egypt
Dakhla Oasis Egypt see Dākhilah, Wāḩāt ad
63 A3 Dakoank India
88 C3 Dakol'ka r. Belarus
Đakovica Kosovo see Gjakovë
109 C1 Đakovo Croatia
120 B2 Dala Angola
68 C2 Dalain Hob China
93 G3 Dalälven r. Sweden
111 C3 Dalaman Turkey
111 C3 Dalaman r. Turkey
69 C2 Dalandzadgad Mongolia
63 B2 Đa Lat Vietnam
74 A2 Dalbandin Pak.
96 C3 Dalbeattie U.K.
51 E2 Dalby Austr.
143 C1 Dale Hollow Lake U.S.A.
53 C3 Dalgety Austr.
139 C1 Dalhart U.S.A.
131 D2 Dalhousie Can.
62 B1 Dali China
70 C2 Dalian China
96 C3 Dalkeith U.K.
139 D2 Dallas U.S.A.
128 A2 Dall Island U.S.A.
109 C2 Dalmatia reg. Bos.-Herz./Croatia
66 C2 Dal'negorsk Rus. Fed.
66 B1 Dal'nerechensk Rus. Fed.
114 B4 Daloa Côte d'Ivoire
51 D2 Dalrymple, Mount Austr.
92 A3 Dalsmynni Iceland
75 C2 Daltenganj India
143 D2 Dalton U.S.A.
60 B1 Daludalu Indon.
92 B2 Dalvík Iceland
50 C1 Daly r. Austr.
51 C1 Daly Waters Austr.
74 B2 Daman India
80 B2 Damanhūr Egypt
59 C3 Damar i. Indon.
80 B2 Damascus Syria
115 D3 Damaturu Nigeria
76 B3 Damāvand, Qolleh-ye mt. Iran
81 D2 Damghan Iran
79 C2 Dammam Saudi Arabia
101 D1 Damme Ger.
75 B2 Damoh India
114 B4 Damongo Ghana
59 C3 Dampir, Selat sea chan. Indon.
75 D1 Damxung China
114 B4 Danané Côte d'Ivoire
63 B2 Đa Năng Vietnam
141 E2 Danbury U.S.A.
65 A1 Dandong China
146 B3 Dangriga Belize
70 B2 Dangshan China
89 F2 Danilov Rus. Fed.
89 E2 Danilovskaya Vozvyshennost' hills Rus. Fed.
70 B2 Danjiangkou China
89 E3 Dankov Rus. Fed.
146 B3 Danlí Hond.
101 E1 Dannenberg (Elbe) Ger.
54 C2 Dannevirke N.Z.
62 B2 Dan Sai Thai.
Dantu China see Zhenjiang
110 A1 Danube r. Europe
110 C1 Danube Delta Romania/Ukr.
140 B2 Danville IL U.S.A.
140 C3 Danville KY U.S.A.
141 D3 Danville VA U.S.A.
71 A4 Danzhou China
71 B3 Daoxian China
114 C3 Dapaong Togo
64 B2 Dapitan Phil.
68 C2 Da Qaidam Zhen China
69 E1 Daqing China
80 B2 Dar'ā Syria
79 C2 Dārāb Iran
115 D1 Daraj Libya
81 D2 Dārān Iran
75 C2 Darbhanga India
119 D3 Dar es Salaam Tanz.
117 A3 Darfur reg. Sudan
74 B1 Dargai Pak.
54 B1 Dargaville N.Z.
53 C3 Dargo Austr.
69 D1 Darhan Mongolia
150 A1 Darién, Golfo del g. Col.
75 C2 Darjiling India
68 C2 Darlag China
52 B2 Darling r. Austr.
53 C1 Darling Downs hills Austr.
50 A3 Darling Range hills Austr.
98 C1 Darlington U.K.
53 C2 Darlington Point Austr.
103 D1 Darłowo Pol.
101 D3 Darmstadt Ger.
115 E1 Darnah Libya
52 B2 Darnick Austr.
107 C1 Daroca Spain
99 D3 Dartford U.K.
99 A3 Dartmoor hills U.K.
131 D2 Dartmouth Can.
99 B3 Dartmouth U.K.
59 D3 Daru P.N.G.
50 C1 Darwin Austr.
74 A2 Dasht r. Pak.
76 B2 Daşoguz Turkm.
61 C1 Datadian Indon.
111 C3 Datça Turkey
70 B1 Datong China
64 B2 Datu Piang Phil.
74 B1 Daud Khel Pak.
88 B2 Daugava r. Latvia
88 C2 Daugavpils Latvia
100 C2 Daun Ger.
129 D2 Dauphin Can.
129 E2 Dauphin Lake Can.
73 B3 Davangere India
64 B2 Davao Phil.
64 B2 Davao Gulf Phil.
137 E2 Davenport U.S.A.
99 C2 Daventry U.K.
123 C2 Daveyton S. Africa
146 B4 David Panama
129 D2 Davidson Can.
126 E3 Davidson Lake Can.
135 B3 Davis U.S.A.
131 D1 Davis Inlet (abandoned) C
159 F3 Davis Sea Antarctica
160 P3 Davis Strait Can./Greenlar
105 D2 Davos Switz.
78 A2 Dawmat al Jandal Saudi Arabia
79 C3 Dawqah Oman
126 B2 Dawson Can.
143 D2 Dawson U.S.A.
128 B2 Dawson Creek Can.
128 B2 Dawsons Landing Can.
68 C2 Dawu China
Dawukou China see Shizuishan
104 B3 Dax France
68 C2 Da Xueshan mts China
80 C2 Dayr az Zawr Syria
140 C3 Dayton U.S.A.
143 D3 Daytona Beach U.S.A.
70 A2 Dazhou China
122 B3 De Aar S. Africa
80 B2 Dead Sea salt l. Asia
71 B3 De'an China
152 B4 Deán Funes Arg.
128 B2 Dease Lake Can.
126 D2 Dease Strait Can.
135 C3 Death Valley depr. U.S.A.
104 C2 Deauville France
61 C1 Debak Sarawak Malaysia
109 D2 Debar Macedonia
103 E2 Debrecen Hungary
117 B3 Debre Markos Eth.
117 B3 Debre Tabor Eth.
117 B4 Debre Zeyit Eth.
142 C2 Decatur AL U.S.A.
140 B3 Decatur IL U.S.A.
73 B3 Deccan plat. India
102 C1 Děčín Czech Rep.
137 E2 Decorah U.S.A.
88 C2 Dedovichi Rus. Fed.
121 C2 Dedza Malawi
98 B2 Dee r. England/Wales U.K.
96 C2 Dee r. Scotland U.K.
53 D1 Deepwater Austr.
131 E2 Deer Lake Can.
134 D1 Deer Lodge U.S.A.

0 C2 **Defiance** U.S.A.
8 C2 **Dêgê** China
7 C4 **Degeh Bur** Eth.
2 C2 **Deggendorf** Ger.
1 E2 **Degtevo** Rus. Fed.
5 B1 **Dehra Dun** India
5 C2 **Dehri** India
9 E2 **Dehui** China
0 A2 **Deinze** Belgium
0 B1 **Dej** Romania
0 B2 **De Kalb** U.S.A.
8 A3 **Dekemhare** Eritrea
8 C3 **Dekese** Dem. Rep. Congo
5 C3 **Delano** U.S.A.
5 D3 **Delano Peak** U.S.A.
4 A1 **Delārām** Afgh.
3 C2 **Delareyville** S. Africa
9 D2 **Delaronde Lake** Can.
0 C2 **Delaware** U.S.A.
1 D3 **Delaware** *r.* U.S.A.
1 D3 **Delaware** *state* U.S.A.
1 D3 **Delaware Bay** U.S.A.
3 C3 **Delegate** Austr.
5 D2 **Delémont** Switz.
0 B1 **Delft** Neth.
0 C1 **Delfzijl** Neth.
1 D2 **Delgado, Cabo** *c.* Moz.
9 C1 **Delgerhaan** Mongolia
5 B2 **Delhi** India
0 B2 **Deli** *i.* Indon.
6 C2 **Délįne** Can.
1 F2 **Delitzsch** Ger.
7 D2 **Dellys** Alg.
1 D1 **Delmenhorst** Ger.
9 B1 **Delnice** Croatia
3 L1 **De-Longa, Ostrova** *is* Rus. Fed.
9 D3 **Deloraine** Can.
1 B3 **Delphi** *tourist site* Greece
9 C3 **Del Rio** U.S.A.
6 B3 **Delta** *CO* U.S.A.
5 D3 **Delta** *UT* U.S.A.
6 B2 **Delta Junction** U.S.A.
9 D3 **Delvinë** Albania
6 C1 **Demanda, Sierra de la** *mts* Spain
8 C3 **Demba** Dem. Rep. Congo
7 B4 **Dembī Dolo** Eth.
9 D2 **Demidov** Rus. Fed.
8 B2 **Deming** U.S.A.
1 C3 **Demirci** Turkey
0 C2 **Demirköy** Turkey
2 C1 **Demmin** Ger.
2 C2 **Demopolis** U.S.A.
0 B2 **Dempo, Gunung** *vol.* Indon.
9 D2 **Demyansk** Rus. Fed.
2 B3 **De Naawte** S. Africa
7 C3 **Denakil** *reg.* Africa
0 B1 **Den Burg** Neth.
0 B2 **Dendermonde** Belgium
0 A1 **Dengkou** China
0 B2 **Dengzhou** China
Den Haag Neth. *see* **The Hague**
0 A2 **Denham** Austr.
0 B1 **Den Helder** Neth.
2 B3 **Deniliquin** Austr.
4 C2 **Denio** U.S.A.
7 D2 **Denison** *IA* U.S.A.
9 D2 **Denison** *TX* U.S.A.
1 C3 **Denizli** Turkey
3 D2 **Denman** Austr.
0 A3 **Denmark** Austr.
3 E4 **Denmark** *country* Europe
0 Q3 **Denmark Strait** Greenland/Iceland
1 C2 **Denpasar** Indon.
139 D2 **Denton** U.S.A.
50 A3 **D'Entrecasteaux, Point** Austr.
136 B3 **Denver** U.S.A.
75 C2 **Deogarh** *Orissa* India
74 B2 **Deogarh** *Rajasthan* India
75 C2 **Deoghar** India
83 K2 **Deputatskiy** Rus. Fed.
68 C3 **Dêqên** China
142 B2 **De Queen** U.S.A.
74 A2 **Dera Bugti** Pak.
74 B1 **Dera Ghazi Khan** Pak.
74 B1 **Dera Ismail Khan** Pak.
87 D4 **Derbent** Rus. Fed.
50 B1 **Derby** Austr.
99 C2 **Derby** U.K.
99 D2 **Dereham** U.K.
97 B2 **Derg, Lough** *l.* Ireland
91 D1 **Derhachi** Ukr.
142 B2 **De Ridder** U.S.A.
91 D2 **Derkul** *r.* Rus. Fed./Ukr.
75 B1 **Dêrub** China
116 B3 **Derudeb** Sudan
122 B3 **De Rust** S. Africa
109 C2 **Derventa** Bos.-Herz.
98 C2 **Derwent** *r.* U.K.
98 B1 **Derwent Water** *l.* U.K.
77 C1 **Derzhavinsk** Kazakh.
152 B2 **Desaguadero** *r.* Bol.
129 D2 **Deschambault Lake** Can.
134 B1 **Deschutes** *r.* U.S.A.
117 B3 **Desē** Eth.
153 B5 **Deseado** Arg.
153 B5 **Deseado** *r.* Arg.
137 E2 **Des Moines** U.S.A.
137 E2 **Des Moines** *r.* U.S.A.
91 C1 **Desna** *r.* Rus. Fed./Ukr.
89 D3 **Desnogorsk** Rus. Fed.
101 F2 **Dessau** Ger.
126 B2 **Destruction Bay** Can.
149 C3 **Desventuradas, Islas** *is* S. Pacific Ocean
128 C1 **Detah** Can.
101 D2 **Detmold** Ger.
140 C2 **Detroit** U.S.A.
137 D1 **Detroit Lakes** U.S.A.
100 B2 **Deurne** Neth.
110 B1 **Deva** Romania
100 C1 **Deventer** Neth.
96 C2 **Deveron** *r.* U.K.
103 D2 **Devét Skal** *h.* Czech Rep.
137 D1 **Devil's Lake** U.S.A.
128 A2 **Devil's Paw** *mt.* U.S.A.
99 C3 **Devizes** U.K.
74 B2 **Devli** India
110 C2 **Devnya** Bulg.
128 C2 **Devon** Can.
126 E1 **Devon Island** Can.
51 D4 **Devonport** Austr.
74 B2 **Dewas** India
137 F3 **Dexter** U.S.A.
70 A2 **Deyang** China
59 D3 **Deyong, Tanjung** *pt* Indon.
81 C2 **Dezfūl** Iran
70 B2 **Dezhou** China
79 C2 **Dhahran** Saudi Arabia
75 D2 **Dhaka** Bangl.
78 B3 **Dhamār** Yemen
75 C2 **Dhamtari** India
75 C2 **Dhanbad** India
75 C2 **Dhankuta** Nepal
62 A1 **Dharmanagar** India
75 C2 **Dharmjaygarh** India
73 B3 **Dharwad** India
74 B2 **Dhasa** India
78 B3 **Dhubāb** Yemen
74 B2 **Dhule** India
144 A1 **Diablo, Picacho del** *mt.* Mex.
51 C2 **Diamantina** *watercourse* Austr.
155 D1 **Diamantina** Brazil
151 D3 **Diamantina, Chapada** *plat.* Brazil
151 C3 **Diamantino** Brazil
71 B3 **Dianbai** China
151 D3 **Dianópolis** Brazil
114 B4 **Dianra** Côte d'Ivoire
114 C3 **Diapaga** Burkina
79 C2 **Dibā al Ḥiṣn** U.A.E.
118 C3 **Dibaya** Dem. Rep. Congo
62 A1 **Dibrugarh** India
136 C1 **Dickinson** U.S.A.
142 C1 **Dickson** U.S.A.
Dicle *r.* Turkey *see* **Tigris**
105 D3 **Die** France
129 D2 **Diefenbaker, Lake** Can.
114 B3 **Diéma** Mali
62 B2 **Diên Châu** Vietnam
101 D1 **Diepholz** Ger.
104 C2 **Dieppe** France
115 D3 **Diffa** Niger
131 D2 **Digby** Can.
105 D3 **Digne-les-Bains** France
105 C2 **Digoin** France
64 B2 **Digos** Phil.
59 D3 **Digul** *r.* Indon.
Dihang *r.* China/India *see* **Yarlung Zangbo**
Dihang *r.* China/India *see* **Brahmaputra**
105 D2 **Dijon** France
117 C3 **Dikhil** Djibouti
111 C3 **Dikili** Turkey
100 A2 **Diksmuide** Belgium
115 D3 **Dikwa** Nigeria
117 B4 **Dīla** Eth.
59 C3 **Dili** East Timor
101 D2 **Dillenburg** Ger.
134 D1 **Dillon** U.S.A.
118 C4 **Dilolo** Dem. Rep. Congo
62 A1 **Dimapur** India
Dimashq Syria *see* **Damascus**
52 B3 **Dimboola** Austr.
110 C2 **Dimitrovgrad** Bulg.
87 D3 **Dimitrovgrad** Rus. Fed.
64 B1 **Dinagat** *i.* Phil.
104 B2 **Dinan** France
100 B2 **Dinant** Belgium
111 D3 **Dinar** Turkey
81 D2 **Dīnār, Kūh-e** *mt.* Iran
73 B3 **Dindigul** India
123 D1 **Dindiza** Moz.
101 E2 **Dingelstädt** Ger.
97 A2 **Dingle Bay** Ireland
96 B2 **Dingwall** U.K.
70 A2 **Dingxi** China
75 C2 **Dinngyê** China
154 B3 **Dionísio Cerqueira** Brazil
114 A3 **Diourbel** Senegal
74 B1 **Dir** Pak.
51 D1 **Direction, Cape** Austr.
117 C4 **Dirē Dawa** Eth.
120 B2 **Dirico** Angola
50 A2 **Dirk Hartog Island** Austr.
53 C1 **Dirranbandi** Austr.
78 B3 **Ḍirs** Saudi Arabia
50 B2 **Disappointment, Lake** *imp. l.* Austr.
52 B3 **Discovery Bay** Austr.
143 E1 **Dismal Swamp** U.S.A.
99 D2 **Diss** U.K.
108 B3 **Dittaino** *r. Sicilia* Italy
74 B2 **Diu** India
155 D2 **Divinópolis** Brazil
87 D4 **Divnoye** Rus. Fed.
114 B4 **Divo** Côte d'Ivoire

80 B2 **Divriği** Turkey
140 B2 **Dixon** U.S.A.
128 A2 **Dixon Entrance** *sea chan.* Can./U.S.A.
80 C2 **Diyarbakır** Turkey
74 A2 **Diz** Pak.
115 D2 **Djado** Niger
115 D2 **Djado, Plateau du** Niger
118 B3 **Djambala** Congo
115 C2 **Djanet** Alg.
115 C1 **Djelfa** Alg.
119 C2 **Djéma** C.A.R.
114 B3 **Djenné** Mali
114 B3 **Djibo** Burkina
117 C3 **Djibouti** *country* Africa
117 C3 **Djibouti** Djibouti
114 C4 **Djougou** Benin
92 C3 **Djúpivogur** Iceland
91 E1 **Dmitriyevka** Rus. Fed.
89 E3 **Dmitriyev-L'govskiy** Rus. Fed.
89 E2 **Dmitrov** Rus. Fed.
Dnepr *r.* Ukr. *see* **Dnieper**
91 C2 **Dnieper** *r.* Ukr.
90 B2 **Dniester** *r.* Ukr.
Dnipro *r.* Ukr. *see* **Dnieper**
91 C2 **Dniprodzerzhyns'k** Ukr.
91 D2 **Dnipropetrovs'k** Ukr.
91 C2 **Dniprorudne** Ukr.
Dnister *r.* Ukr. *see* **Dniester**
88 C2 **Dno** Rus. Fed.
115 D4 **Doba** Chad
88 B2 **Dobele** Latvia
101 F2 **Döbeln** Ger.
59 C3 **Doberai, Jazirah** *pen.* Indon.
59 C3 **Dobo** Indon.
109 C2 **Doboj** Bos.-Herz.
110 C2 **Dobrich** Bulg.
89 F3 **Dobrinka** Rus. Fed.
89 E3 **Dobroye** Rus. Fed.
89 D3 **Dobrush** Belarus
155 E1 **Doce** *r.* Brazil
145 B2 **Doctor Arroyo** Mex.
144 B2 **Doctor Belisario Domínguez** Mex.
111 C3 **Dodecanese** *is* Greece
Dodekanisos *is* Greece *see* **Dodecanese**
136 C3 **Dodge City** U.S.A.
119 D3 **Dodoma** Tanz.
100 C2 **Doetinchem** Neth.
59 C3 **Dofa** Indon.
75 C1 **Dogai Coring** *salt l.* China
128 B2 **Dog Creek** Can.
67 B3 **Dōgo** *i.* Japan
115 C3 **Dogondoutchi** Niger
81 C2 **Doğubeyazıt** Turkey
79 C2 **Doha** Qatar
62 A2 **Doi Saket** Thai.
100 B1 **Dokkum** Neth.
88 C3 **Dokshytsy** Belarus
91 D2 **Dokuchayevs'k** Ukr.
131 C2 **Dolbeau-Mistassini** Can.
104 B2 **Dol-de-Bretagne** France
105 D2 **Dole** France
99 B2 **Dolgellau** U.K.
89 E3 **Dolgorukovo** Rus. Fed.
89 E3 **Dolgoye** Rus. Fed.
Dolisie Congo *see* **Loubomo**
59 D3 **Dolok, Pulau** *i.* Indon.
108 B1 **Dolomites** *mts* Italy
117 C4 **Dolo Odo** Eth.
126 D2 **Dolphin and Union Strait** Can.
90 A2 **Dolyna** Ukr.
102 C2 **Domažlice** Czech Rep.
93 E3 **Dombås** Norway
103 D2 **Dombóvár** Hungary
128 B2 **Dome Creek** Can.
147 D3 **Dominica** *country* West Indies
147 C3 **Dominican Republic** *country* West Indies
89 E2 **Domodedovo** Rus. Fed.
111 B3 **Domokos** Greece
61 C2 **Dompu** Indon.
89 E3 **Don** *r.* Rus. Fed.
96 C2 **Don** *r.* U.K.
97 D1 **Donaghadee** U.K.
52 B3 **Donald** Austr.
Donau *r.* Austria/Ger. *see* **Danube**
102 C2 **Donauwörth** Ger.
106 B2 **Don Benito** Spain
98 C2 **Doncaster** U.K.
120 A1 **Dondo** Angola
121 C2 **Dondo** Moz.
73 C4 **Dondra Head** Sri Lanka
97 B1 **Donegal** Ireland
97 B1 **Donegal Bay** Ireland
91 D2 **Donets'k** Ukr.
91 D2 **Donets'kyy Kryazh** *hills* Rus. Fed./Ukr.
50 A2 **Dongara** Austr.
62 B1 **Dongchuan** China
71 A4 **Dongfang** China
66 B1 **Dongfanghong** China
58 B3 **Donggala** Indon.
65 A2 **Donggang** China
71 B3 **Dongguan** China
62 B2 **Đông Ha** Vietnam
Dong Hai *sea* N. Pacific Ocean *see* **East China Sea**
62 B2 **Đông Hơi** Vietnam
118 B2 **Dongou** Congo
71 B3 **Dongshan** China
70 C2 **Dongtai** China
71 B3 **Dongting Hu** *l.* China
Dong Ujimqin Qi China *see* **Uliastai**
70 B2 **Dongying** China
54 B1 **Donnellys Crossing** N.Z.
107 C1 **Donostia-San Sebastián** Spain
117 C4 **Dooxo Nugaaleed** *val.* Somalia
99 B3 **Dorchester** U.K.
122 A1 **Dordabis** Namibia
104 B2 **Dordogne** *r.* France
100 B2 **Dordrecht** Neth.
123 C3 **Dordrecht** S. Africa
129 D2 **Doré Lake** Can.
101 D1 **Dorfmark** Ger.
114 B3 **Dori** Burkina
122 A3 **Doring** *r.* S. Africa
96 B2 **Dornoch** U.K.
96 B2 **Dornoch Firth** *est.* U.K.
89 D3 **Dorogobuzh** Rus. Fed.
90 B2 **Dorohoi** Romania
68 C1 **Döröö Nuur** *salt l.* Mongolia
92 G3 **Dorotea** Sweden
50 A2 **Dorre Island** Austr.
53 D2 **Dorrigo** Austr.
100 C2 **Dortmund** Ger.
100 C2 **Dortmund-Ems-Kanal** *canal* Ger.
153 B5 **Dos Bahías, Cabo** *c.* Arg.
101 F1 **Dosse** *r.* Ger.
114 C3 **Dosso** Niger
143 C2 **Dothan** U.S.A.
101 D1 **Dötlingen** Ger.
105 C1 **Douai** France
118 A2 **Douala** Cameroon
104 B2 **Douarnenez** France
114 B3 **Douentza** Mali
98 A1 **Douglas** Isle of Man
122 B2 **Douglas** S. Africa
128 A2 **Douglas** *AK* U.S.A.
138 B2 **Douglas** *AZ* U.S.A.
143 D2 **Douglas** *GA* U.S.A.
136 B2 **Douglas** *WY* U.S.A.
104 C1 **Doullens** France
154 B1 **Dourada, Serra** *hills* Brazil
154 B2 **Dourados** Brazil
154 B2 **Dourados, Serra dos** *hills* Brazil
106 B1 **Douro** *r.* Port.
99 D3 **Dover** U.K.
141 D3 **Dover** U.S.A.
95 D3 **Dover, Strait of** France/U.K.
141 F1 **Dover-Foxcroft** U.S.A.
79 C2 **Dowlatābād** *Būshehr* Iran
79 C2 **Dowlatābād** *Kermān* Iran
97 D1 **Downpatrick** U.K.
77 C3 **Dowshī** Afgh.
67 B3 **Dōzen** *is* Japan
130 C2 **Dozois, Réservoir** *resr* Can.
114 B2 **Drâa, Hamada du** *plat.* Alg.
154 B2 **Dracena** Brazil
100 C1 **Drachten** Neth.
110 B2 **Drăgănești-Olt** Romania
110 B2 **Drăgășani** Romania
88 C3 **Drahichyn** Belarus
123 C2 **Drakensberg** *mts* Lesotho/S. Africa
123 C2 **Drakensberg** *mts* S. Africa
158 B8 **Drake Passage** S. Atlantic Ocean
111 B2 **Drama** Greece
93 F4 **Drammen** Norway
109 C1 **Drava** *r.* Europe
128 C2 **Drayton Valley** Can.
101 D2 **Dreieich** Ger.
102 C1 **Dresden** Ger.
104 C2 **Dreux** France
100 B1 **Driemond** Neth.
109 C2 **Drina** *r.* Bos.-Herz./Serbia
109 C2 **Drniš** Croatia
110 B2 **Drobeta-Turnu Severin** Romania
101 D1 **Drochtersen** Ger.
97 C2 **Drogheda** Ireland
90 A2 **Drohobych** Ukr.
97 C1 **Dromore** U.K.
74 B1 **Drosh** Pak.
53 C3 **Drouin** Austr.
128 C2 **Drumheller** Can.
140 C1 **Drummond Island** U.S.A.
131 C2 **Drummondville** Can.
88 B3 **Druskininkai** Lith.
91 D2 **Druzhkivka** Ukr.
88 D2 **Druzhnaya Gorka** Rus. Fed.
130 A2 **Dryden** Can.
50 B1 **Drysdale** *r.* Austr.
78 A2 **Ḑubā** Saudi Arabia
79 C2 **Dubai** U.A.E.
129 D1 **Dubawnt Lake** Can.
Dubayy U.A.E. *see* **Dubai**
78 A2 **Dubbagh, Jabal ad** *mt.* Saudi Arabia
53 C2 **Dubbo** Austr.
97 C2 **Dublin** Ireland
143 D2 **Dublin** U.S.A.
90 B1 **Dubno** Ukr.
141 D2 **Du Bois** U.S.A.
114 A4 **Dubréka** Guinea
109 C2 **Dubrovnik** Croatia
90 B1 **Dubrovytsya** Ukr.
89 D3 **Dubrowna** Belarus
137 E2 **Dubuque** U.S.A.
129 D2 **Duck Bay** Can.
101 E2 **Duderstadt** Ger.
82 G2 **Dudinka** Rus. Fed.
99 B2 **Dudley** U.K.
106 B1 **Duero** *r.* Spain

1 C1 **Duffreboy, Lac** *l.* Can.
6 C2 **Dufftown** U.K.
9 C2 **Dugi Rat** Croatia
0 C2 **Duisburg** Ger.
3 D1 **Duiwelskloof** S. Africa
3 C3 **Dukathole** S. Africa
9 C2 **Dukhān** Qatar
9 D2 **Dukhovshchina** Rus. Fed.
Dukou China *see* **Panzhihua**
8 C2 **Dūkštas** Lith.
8 C2 **Dulan** China
2 B4 **Dulce** *r.* Arg.
0 C2 **Dülmen** Ger.
0 C2 **Dulovo** Bulg.
7 E1 **Duluth** U.S.A.
4 B2 **Dumaguete** Phil.
0 B1 **Dumai** Indon.
4 B1 **Dumaran** *i.* Phil.
2 B2 **Dumas** *AR* U.S.A.
9 C1 **Dumas** *TX* U.S.A.
6 B3 **Dumbarton** U.K.
3 D2 **Ďumbier** *mt.* Slovakia
6 C3 **Dumfries** U.K.
5 J3 **Dumont d'Urville Sea** Antarctica
6 B1 **Dumyāţ** Egypt
Duna *r.* Hungary *see* **Danube**
Dunaj *r.* Slovakia *see* **Danube**
3 D2 **Dunakeszi** Hungary
Dunărea *r.* Romania *see* **Danube**
3 D2 **Dunaújváros** Hungary
Dunav *r.* Serbia *see* **Danube**
0 B2 **Dunayivtsi** Ukr.
6 C2 **Dunbar** U.K.
6 C1 **Dunbeath** U.K.
8 B3 **Duncan** Can.
9 D2 **Duncan** U.S.A.
6 C1 **Duncansby Head** U.K.
7 C1 **Dundalk** Ireland
7 C2 **Dundalk Bay** Ireland
7 G1 **Dundas** Greenland
3 D2 **Dundee** S. Africa
6 C2 **Dundee** U.K.
7 D1 **Dundrum Bay** U.K.
4 B3 **Dunedin** N.Z.
6 C2 **Dunfermline** U.K.
7 C1 **Dungannon** U.K.
4 B2 **Dungarpur** India
7 C2 **Dungarvan** Ireland
9 D3 **Dungeness** *hd* U.K.
7 C1 **Dungiven** U.K.
3 D2 **Dungog** Austr.
9 C2 **Dungu** Dem. Rep. Congo
0 B1 **Dungun** Malaysia
6 B2 **Dungunab** Sudan
9 E2 **Dunhua** China
8 C2 **Dunhuang** China
Dunkerque France *see* **Dunkirk**
4 C1 **Dunkirk** France
1 D2 **Dunkirk** U.S.A.
7 C2 **Dún Laoghaire** Ireland
7 D1 **Dunmurry** U.K.
6 C1 **Dunnet Head** U.K.
6 C3 **Duns** U.K.
9 C3 **Dunstable** U.K.
0 B2 **Dupnitsa** Bulg.
6 C1 **Dupree** U.S.A.
0 B1 **Durack** *r.* Austr.
4 B2 **Durango** Mex.
6 C1 **Durango** Spain
6 B3 **Durango** U.S.A.
9 D2 **Durant** U.S.A.
3 C4 **Durazno** Uru.
3 D2 **Durban** S. Africa
4 C3 **Durban-Corbières** France
122 A3 **Durbanville** S. Africa
100 B2 **Durbuy** Belgium
100 C2 **Düren** Ger.
73 C2 **Durg** India
98 C1 **Durham** U.K.
143 E1 **Durham** U.S.A.
60 B1 **Duri** Indon.
109 C2 **Durmitor** *mt.* Montenegro
96 B1 **Durness** U.K.
109 C2 **Durrës** Albania
97 A3 **Dursey Island** Ireland
111 C3 **Dursunbey** Turkey
59 D3 **D'Urville, Tanjung** *pt* Indon.
54 B2 **D'Urville Island** N.Z.
71 A3 **Dushan** China
77 C3 **Dushanbe** Tajik.
100 C2 **Düsseldorf** Ger.
71 A3 **Duyun** China
91 D2 **Dvorichna** Ukr.
74 A2 **Dwarka** India
123 C1 **Dwarsberg** S. Africa
134 C1 **Dworshak Reservoir** U.S.A.
89 D3 **Dyat'kovo** Rus. Fed.
96 C2 **Dyce** U.K.
127 G2 **Dyer, Cape** Can.
142 C1 **Dyersburg** U.S.A.
103 D2 **Dyje** *r.* Austria/Czech Rep.
103 D1 **Dylewska Góra** *h.* Pol.
91 D2 **Dymytrov** Ukr.
123 C3 **Dyoki** S. Africa
87 E3 **Dyurtyuli** Rus. Fed.
69 D2 **Dzamïn Üüd** Mongolia
120 D2 **Dzaoudzi** Mayotte
Dzhambul Kazakh. *see* **Taraz**
76 B2 **Dzhangala** Kazakh.
91 C2 **Dzhankoy** Ukr.
91 D3 **Dzhubga** Rus. Fed.
83 K3 **Dzhugdzhur, Khrebet** *mts* Rus. Fed.
77 D2 **Dzhungarskiy Alatau, Khrebet** *mts* China/Kazakh.
76 C2 **Dzhusaly** Kazakh.
103 E1 **Działdowo** Pol.
69 D1 **Dzuunmod** Mongolia
88 C3 **Dzyarzhynsk** Belarus
88 C3 **Dzyatlavichy** Belarus

E

131 E1 **Eagle** *r.* Can.
134 C1 **Eagle Cap** *mt.* U.S.A.
130 A2 **Eagle Lake** Can.
134 B2 **Eagle Lake** U.S.A.
139 C3 **Eagle Pass** U.S.A.
126 B2 **Eagle Plain** Can.
130 A1 **Ear Falls** Can.
99 D3 **Eastbourne** U.K.
156 C3 **East China Sea** N. Pacific Ocean
54 B1 **East Coast Bays** N.Z.
129 D3 **Eastend** Can.
123 C3 **Eastern Cape** *prov.* S. Africa
116 B2 **Eastern Desert** Egypt
73 B3 **Eastern Ghats** *mts* India
129 E2 **Easterville** Can.
153 C6 **East Falkland** *i.* Falkland Is
100 C1 **East Frisian Islands** Ger.
96 B3 **East Kilbride** U.K.
99 C3 **Eastleigh** U.K.
140 C2 **East Liverpool** U.S.A.
123 C3 **East London** S. Africa
130 C1 **Eastmain** Can.
130 C1 **Eastmain** *r.* Can.
143 D2 **Eastman** U.S.A.
140 A3 **East St Louis** U.S.A.
East Sea N. Pacific Ocean *see* **Japan, Sea of**
83 K2 **East Siberian Sea** Rus. Fed.
59 C3 **East Timor** *country* Asia
140 A2 **Eau Claire** U.S.A.
130 C1 **Eau Claire, Lac à l'** *l.* Can.
59 D2 **Eauripik** *atoll* Micronesia
145 C2 **Ebano** Mex.
99 B3 **Ebbw Vale** U.K.
102 C1 **Eberswalde-Finow** Ger.
109 C2 **Eboli** Italy
118 B2 **Ebolowa** Cameroon
107 D1 **Ebro** *r.* Spain
144 A2 **Echeverria, Pico** *mt.* Mex.
129 E2 **Echoing** *r.* Can.
100 C3 **Echternach** Lux.
52 B3 **Echuca** Austr.
106 B2 **Écija** Spain
102 B1 **Eckernförde** Ger.
127 F2 **Eclipse Sound** *sea chan.* Can.
150 A2 **Ecuador** *country* S. America
116 C3 **Ed** Eritrea
117 A3 **Ed Da'ein** Sudan
117 B3 **Ed Damazin** Sudan
116 B3 **Ed Damer** Sudan
116 B3 **Ed Debba** Sudan
116 B3 **Ed Dueim** Sudan
51 D4 **Eddystone Point** Austr.
100 B1 **Ede** Neth.
118 B2 **Edéa** Cameroon
154 C1 **Edéia** Brazil
53 C3 **Eden** Austr.
98 B1 **Eden** *r.* U.K.
123 C2 **Edenburg** S. Africa
97 C2 **Edenderry** Ireland
52 B3 **Edenhope** Austr.
111 B2 **Edessa** Greece
82 C1 **Edgeøya** *i.* Svalbard
139 D3 **Edinburg** U.S.A.
96 C3 **Edinburgh** U.K.
110 C2 **Edirne** Turkey
128 C2 **Edmonton** Can.
131 D2 **Edmundston** Can.
111 C3 **Edremit** Turkey
111 C3 **Edremit Körfezi** *b.* Turkey
128 C2 **Edson** Can.
119 C3 **Edward, Lake** Dem. Rep. Congo/Uganda
139 C2 **Edwards Plateau** *TX* U.S.A.
100 C1 **Eenrum** Neth.
48 F4 **Éfaté** *i.* Vanuatu
140 B3 **Effingham** U.S.A.
135 C3 **Egan Range** *mts* U.S.A.
103 E2 **Eger** Hungary
93 E4 **Egersund** Norway
92 C2 **Egilsstaðir** Iceland
80 B2 **Eğirdir** Turkey
80 B2 **Eğirdir Gölü** *l.* Turkey
104 C2 **Égletons** France
Egmont, Mount *vol.* N.Z. *see* **Taranaki, Mount**
83 M2 **Egvekinot** Rus. Fed.
116 A2 **Egypt** *country* Africa
68 C2 **Ehen Hudag** China
100 C1 **Eibergen** Neth.
100 C2 **Eifel** *hills* Ger.
96 A2 **Eigg** *i.* U.K.
73 B4 **Eight Degree Channel** India/Maldives
50 B1 **Eighty Mile Beach** Austr.
80 B3 **Eilat** Israel
101 F2 **Eilenburg** Ger.
101 D2 **Einbeck** Ger.
100 B2 **Eindhoven** Neth.
150 B2 **Eirunepé** Brazil
120 B2 **Eiseb** *watercourse* Namibia
101 E2 **Eisenach** Ger.

102 C1 **Eisenhüttenstadt** Ger.
103 D2 **Eisenstadt** Austria
101 E2 **Eisleben Lutherstadt** Ger.
Eivissa Spain *see* **Ibiza**
Eivissa *i.* Spain *see* **Ibiza**
107 C1 **Ejea de los Caballeros** Spain
121 D3 **Ejeda** Madag.
Ejin Qi China *see* **Dalain Hob**
93 H4 **Ekenäs** Fin.
77 D1 **Ekibastuz** Kazakh.
92 J2 **Ekostrovskaya Imandra, Ozero** *l.* Rus. Fed.
93 F4 **Eksjö** Sweden
122 A2 **Eksteenfontein** S. Africa
130 B1 **Ekwan** *r.* Can.
62 A2 **Ela** Myanmar
123 C2 **Elandsdoorn** S. Africa
111 B3 **Elassona** Greece
80 B2 **Elazığ** Turkey
108 B2 **Elba, Isola d'** *i.* Italy
150 A1 **El Banco** Col.
138 B2 **El Barreal** *salt l.* Mex.
109 D2 **Elbasan** Albania
150 B1 **El Baúl** Venez.
114 C1 **El Bayadh** Alg.
101 D1 **Elbe** *r.* Ger.
136 B3 **Elbert, Mount** U.S.A.
143 D2 **Elberton** U.S.A.
104 C2 **Elbeuf** France
80 B2 **Elbistan** Turkey
103 D1 **Elbląg** Pol.
87 D4 **El'brus** *mt.* Rus. Fed.
81 C2 **Elburz Mountains** Iran
150 B1 **El Callao** Venez.
139 D3 **El Campo** U.S.A.
135 C4 **El Centro** U.S.A.
152 B2 **El Cerro** Bol.
107 C2 **Elche-Elx** Spain
107 C2 **Elda** Spain
137 E3 **Eldon** U.S.A.
144 B2 **El Dorado** Mex.
142 B2 **El Dorado** *AR* U.S.A.
137 D3 **El Dorado** *KS* U.S.A.
114 B2 **El Eglab** *plat.* Alg.
106 C2 **El Ejido** Spain
89 E2 **Elektrostal'** Rus. Fed.
150 A2 **El Encanto** Col.
146 C2 **Eleuthera** *i.* Bahamas
117 A3 **El Fasher** Sudan
144 B2 **El Fuerte** Mex.
117 A3 **El Geneina** Sudan
116 B3 **El Geteina** Sudan
96 C2 **Elgin** U.K.
140 B2 **Elgin** U.S.A.
115 C1 **El Goléa** Alg.
144 A1 **El Golfo de Santa Clara** Mex.
119 D2 **Elgon, Mount** Kenya/Uganda
114 A2 **El Ḥammâmi** *reg.* Maur.
114 A2 **El Hierro** *i.* Islas Canarias
145 C2 **El Higo** Mex.
114 C2 **El Homr** Alg.
87 D4 **Elista** Rus. Fed.
141 E2 **Elizabeth** U.S.A.
143 E1 **Elizabeth City** U.S.A.
140 B3 **Elizabethtown** U.S.A.
114 B1 **El Jadida** Morocco
103 E1 **Ełk** Pol.
139 D1 **Elk City** U.S.A.
128 C2 **Elkford** Can.
140 B2 **Elkhart** U.S.A.
El Khartum Sudan *see* **Khartoum**
110 C2 **Elkhovo** Bulg.
140 D3 **Elkins** U.S.A.
128 C3 **Elko** Can.
134 C2 **Elko** U.S.A.
129 C2 **Elk Point** Can.
126 E1 **Ellef Ringnes Island** Can.
137 D1 **Ellendale** U.S.A.
134 B1 **Ellensburg** U.S.A.
54 B2 **Ellesmere, Lake** N.Z.
127 F1 **Ellesmere Island** Can.
98 B2 **Ellesmere Port** U.K.
126 E2 **Ellice** *r.* Can.
Ellice Islands *country* S. Pacific Ocean *see* **Tuvalu**
123 C3 **Elliotdale** S. Africa
96 C2 **Ellon** U.K.
141 F2 **Ellsworth** U.S.A.
55 O2 **Ellsworth Mountains** Antarctica
111 C3 **Elmalı** Turkey
115 C1 **El Meghaïer** Alg.
141 D2 **Elmira** U.S.A.
107 C2 **El Moral** Spain
101 D1 **Elmshorn** Ger.
117 A3 **El Muglad** Sudan
64 A1 **El Nido** Phil.
117 B3 **El Obeid** Sudan
144 B2 **El Oro** Mex.
115 C1 **El Oued** Alg.
138 A2 **Eloy** U.S.A.
138 B2 **El Paso** U.S.A.
144 B1 **El Porvenir** Mex.
107 D1 **El Prat de Llobregat** Spain
139 D1 **El Reno** U.S.A.
145 B2 **El Salado** Mex.
144 B2 **El Salto** Mex.
146 B3 **El Salvador** *country* Central America
145 B2 **El Salvador** Mex.
138 B3 **El Sauz** Mex.
144 A1 **El Socorro** Mex.
145 C2 **El Temascal** Mex.
150 B1 **El Tigre** Venez.
147 D4 **El Tocuyo** Venez.
88 C2 **Elva** Estonia
106 B2 **Elvas** Port.
93 F3 **Elverum** Norway
119 E2 **El Wak** Kenya
99 D2 **Ely** U.K.
137 E1 **Ely** *MN* U.S.A.
135 D3 **Ely** *NV* U.S.A.
81 D2 **Emāmrūd** Iran
93 G4 **Emån** *r.* Sweden
76 B2 **Emba** Kazakh.
76 B2 **Emba** *r.* Kazakh.
123 C2 **Embalenhle** S. Africa
154 C1 **Emborcação, Represa de** *resr* Brazil
119 D3 **Embu** Kenya
100 C1 **Emden** Ger.
51 D2 **Emerald** Austr.
129 E3 **Emerson** Can.
111 C3 **Emet** Turkey
123 D2 **eMgwenya** S. Africa
115 D3 **Emi Koussi** *mt.* Chad
110 C2 **Emine, Nos** *pt* Bulg.
80 B2 **Emirdağ** Turkey
123 D2 **eMjindini** S. Africa
88 B2 **Emmaste** Estonia
100 B1 **Emmeloord** Neth.
100 C2 **Emmelshausen** Ger.
100 C1 **Emmen** Neth.
139 C3 **Emory Peak** U.S.A.
144 A2 **Empalme** Mex.
123 D2 **Empangeni** S. Africa
108 B2 **Empoli** Italy
137 D3 **Emporia** *KS* U.S.A.
141 D3 **Emporia** *VA* U.S.A.
Empty Quarter *des.* Saudi Arabia *see* **Rub' al Khālī**
100 C1 **Ems** *r.* Ger.
100 C1 **Emsdetten** Ger.
123 C2 **eMzinoni** S. Africa
59 D3 **Enarotali** Indon.
144 B2 **Encarnación** Mex.
152 C3 **Encarnación** Para.
155 D1 **Encruzilhada** Brazil
58 C3 **Ende** Indon.
126 A2 **Endicott Mountains** U.S.A.
91 C2 **Enerhodar** Ukr.
87 D3 **Engel's** Rus. Fed.
60 B2 **Enggano** *i.* Indon.
98 C2 **England** *admin. div.* U.K.
130 A1 **English** *r.* Can.
95 C4 **English Channel** France/U
139 D1 **Enid** U.S.A.
100 B1 **Enkhuizen** Neth.
93 G4 **Enköping** Sweden
108 B3 **Enna** *Sicilia* Italy
129 D1 **Ennadai Lake** Can.
117 A3 **En Nahud** Sudan
115 E3 **Ennedi, Massif** *mts* Chad
53 C1 **Enngonia** Austr.
97 B2 **Ennis** Ireland
139 D2 **Ennis** U.S.A.
97 C2 **Enniscorthy** Ireland
97 C1 **Enniskillen** U.K.
97 B2 **Ennistymon** Ireland
102 C2 **Enns** *r.* Austria
92 H2 **Enontekiö** Fin.
53 C3 **Ensay** Austr.
100 C1 **Enschede** Neth.
144 A1 **Ensenada** Mex.
70 A2 **Enshi** China
128 C1 **Enterprise** Can.
142 C2 **Enterprise** *AL* U.S.A.
134 C1 **Enterprise** *OR* U.S.A.
152 B3 **Entre Ríos** Bol.
106 B2 **Entroncamento** Port.
115 C4 **Enugu** Nigeria
150 A2 **Envira** Brazil
135 D3 **Ephraim** U.S.A.
134 C1 **Ephrata** U.S.A.
105 D2 **Épinal** France
99 C3 **Epsom** U.K.
118 A2 **Equatorial Guinea** *country* Africa
101 F3 **Erbendorf** Ger.
100 C3 **Erbeskopf** *h.* Ger.
81 C2 **Erciş** Turkey
65 B1 **Erdao Jiang** *r.* China
111 C2 **Erdek** Turkey
80 B2 **Erdemli** Turkey
152 C3 **Erechim** Brazil
69 D1 **Ereentsav** Mongolia
80 B2 **Ereğli** *Konya* Turkey
80 B1 **Ereğli** *Zonguldak* Turkey
69 D2 **Erenhot** China
Erevan Armenia *see* **Yerevar**
101 E2 **Erfurt** Ger.
80 B2 **Ergani** Turkey
114 B2 **'Erg Chech** *des.* Alg./Mali
111 C2 **Ergene** *r.* Turkey
140 C2 **Erie** U.S.A.
140 C2 **Erie, Lake** Can./U.S.A.
66 D2 **Erimo-misaki** *c.* Japan
116 B3 **Eritrea** *country* Africa
101 E3 **Erlangen** Ger.
50 C2 **Erldunda** Austr.
123 C2 **Ermelo** S. Africa
80 B2 **Ermenek** Turkey
111 B3 **Ermoupoli** Greece
73 B4 **Ernakulam** India
73 B3 **Erode** India
100 B2 **Erp** Neth.
114 B1 **Er Rachidia** Morocco
117 B3 **Er Rahad** Sudan
97 B1 **Errigal** *h.* Ireland
97 A1 **Erris Head** Ireland

9 D2 **Ersekë** Albania
1 E1 **Ertil'** Rus. Fed.
1 D2 **Erwitte** Ger.
2 C1 **Erzgebirge** *mts* Czech Rep./Ger.
0 B2 **Erzincan** Turkey
1 C2 **Erzurum** Turkey
3 E4 **Esbjerg** Denmark
5 D3 **Escalante** U.S.A.
4 B2 **Escalón** Mex.
0 B1 **Escanaba** U.S.A.
5 C3 **Escárcega** Mex.
7 C1 **Escatrón** Spain
0 A2 **Escaut** *r.* Belgium/France
1 E1 **Eschede** Ger.
0 B3 **Esch-sur-Alzette** Lux.
1 E2 **Eschwege** Ger.
0 C2 **Eschweiler** Ger.
5 C4 **Escondido** U.S.A.
4 B2 **Escuinapa** Mex.
1 C3 **Eşen** Turkey
1 D2 **Eşfahān** Iran
3 D2 **Esikhawini** S. Africa
8 B1 **Esk** *r.* U.K.
1 D1 **Esker** Can.
2 C2 **Eskifjörður** Iceland
3 G4 **Eskilstuna** Sweden
Eskimo Point Can. *see* **Arviat**
0 B2 **Eskişehir** Turkey
1 C2 **Eslāmābād-e Gharb** Iran
1 C3 **Esler Dağı** *mt.* Turkey
1 C3 **Eşme** Turkey
0 A1 **Esmeraldas** Ecuador
9 D2 **Espakeh** Iran
4 C3 **Espalion** France
0 B2 **Espanola** Can.
8 B1 **Espanola** U.S.A.
0 B3 **Esperance** Austr.
4 B2 **Esperanza** Mex.
6 B2 **Espichel, Cabo** *c.* Port.
5 D1 **Espinhaço, Serra do** *mts* Brazil
1 D3 **Espinosa** Brazil
8 F4 **Espíritu Santo** *i.* Vanuatu
4 A2 **Espíritu Santo, Isla** *i.* Mex.
3 H3 **Espoo** Fin.
3 A5 **Esquel** Arg.
4 B1 **Essaouira** Morocco
4 A2 **Es Semara** Western Sahara
0 C2 **Essen** Ger.
0 C1 **Essequibo** *r.* Guyana
3 L3 **Esso** Rus. Fed.
9 C2 **Eşţahbān** Iran
1 E3 **Estância** Brazil
3 C2 **Estcourt** S. Africa
7 C1 **Estella** Spain
6 B2 **Estepona** Spain
6 C1 **Esteras de Medinaceli** Spain
9 D2 **Esterhazy** Can.
2 B3 **Esteros** Para.
6 B2 **Estes Park** U.S.A.
9 D3 **Estevan** Can.
7 E2 **Estherville** U.S.A.
9 D2 **Eston** Can.
8 C2 **Estonia** *country* Europe
6 B1 **Estrela, Serra da** *mts* Port.
6 B2 **Estremoz** Port.
2 A1 **Etadunna** Austr.
4 C2 **Étampes** France
4 C1 **Étaples** France
5 B2 **Etawah** India
3 D2 **Ethandakukhanya** S. Africa
7 B4 **Ethiopia** *country* Africa
9 C3 **Etna, Mount** *vol. Sicilia* Italy
8 A2 **Etolin Island** U.S.A.
0 A2 **Etosha Pan** *salt pan* Namibia
0 C3 **Ettelbruck** Lux.
0 B2 **Etten-Leur** Neth.

107 C1 **Etxarri-Aranatz** Spain
99 D3 **Eu** France
53 C2 **Euabalong** Austr.
Euboea *i.* Greece *see* **Evvoia**
50 B3 **Eucla** Austr.
143 C2 **Eufaula** U.S.A.
139 D1 **Eufaula Lake** *resr* U.S.A.
134 B2 **Eugene** U.S.A.
144 A2 **Eugenia, Punta** *pt* Mex.
53 C1 **Eulo** Austr.
53 C2 **Eumungerie** Austr.
139 C2 **Eunice** U.S.A.
80 C2 **Euphrates** *r.* Asia
134 B2 **Eureka** *CA* U.S.A.
134 C1 **Eureka** *MT* U.S.A.
135 C3 **Eureka** *NV* U.S.A.
52 B2 **Euriowie** Austr.
53 C3 **Euroa** Austr.
106 B2 **Europa Point** Gibraltar
128 B2 **Eutsuk Lake** Can.
130 C1 **Evans, Lac** *l.* Can.
53 D1 **Evans Head** Austr.
127 F2 **Evans Strait** Can.
136 A2 **Evanston** U.S.A.
140 B3 **Evansville** U.S.A.
123 C2 **Evaton** S. Africa
79 C2 **Evaz** Iran
83 L2 **Evensk** Rus. Fed.
50 C2 **Everard Range** *hills* Austr.
75 C2 **Everest, Mount** China/Nepal
134 B1 **Everett** U.S.A.
100 A2 **Evergem** Belgium
143 D3 **Everglades** *swamp* U.S.A.
118 B2 **Evinayong** Equat. Guinea
93 E4 **Evje** Norway
106 B2 **Évora** Port.
104 C2 **Évreux** France
111 C2 **Evros** *r.* Greece/Turkey
111 B3 **Evrotas** *r.* Greece
80 B2 **Evrychou** Cyprus
111 B3 **Evvoia** *i.* Greece
119 E2 **Ewaso Ngiro** *r.* Kenya
152 B2 **Exaltación** Bol.
99 B3 **Exe** *r.* U.K.
99 B3 **Exeter** U.K.
99 B3 **Exmoor** *hills* U.K.
99 B3 **Exmouth** U.K.
50 A2 **Exmouth Gulf** Austr.
146 C2 **Exuma Cays** *is* Bahamas
117 C4 **Eyl** Somalia
52 A1 **Eyre (North), Lake** *imp. l.* Austr.
51 C3 **Eyre Peninsula** Austr.
94 B1 **Eysturoy** *i.* Faroe Is
123 D2 **Ezakheni** S. Africa
123 C2 **Ezenzeleni** S. Africa
70 B2 **Ezhou** China
86 E2 **Ezhva** Rus. Fed.
111 C3 **Ezine** Turkey

F

138 B2 **Fabens** U.S.A.
108 B2 **Fabriano** Italy
115 D3 **Fachi** Niger
114 C3 **Fada-N'Gourma** Burkina
108 B2 **Faenza** Italy
59 C3 **Fafanlap** Indon.
110 B1 **Făgăraş** Romania
49 G3 **Fagatogo** American Samoa
93 E3 **Fagernes** Norway
93 G4 **Fagersta** Sweden
153 B6 **Fagnano, Lago** *l.* Arg./Chile
114 B3 **Faguibine, Lac** *l.* Mali
92 B3 **Fagurhólsmýri** Iceland

126 B2 **Fairbanks** U.S.A.
137 D2 **Fairbury** U.S.A.
135 B3 **Fairfield** U.S.A.
96 □ **Fair Isle** *i.* U.K.
137 E2 **Fairmont** *MN* U.S.A.
140 C3 **Fairmont** *WV* U.S.A.
128 C2 **Fairview** Can.
59 D2 **Fais** *i.* Micronesia
74 B1 **Faisalabad** Pak.
136 C1 **Faith** U.S.A.
75 C2 **Faizabad** India
59 C3 **Fakfak** Indon.
65 A1 **Faku** China
114 A4 **Falaba** Sierra Leone
139 D3 **Falcon Lake** Mex./U.S.A.
139 D3 **Falfurrias** U.S.A.
128 C2 **Falher** Can.
101 F2 **Falkenberg** Ger.
93 F4 **Falkenberg** Sweden
101 F1 **Falkensee** Ger.
96 C3 **Falkirk** U.K.
153 C6 **Falkland Islands** *terr.* S. Atlantic Ocean
93 F4 **Falköping** Sweden
135 C3 **Fallon** U.S.A.
141 E2 **Fall River** U.S.A.
137 D2 **Falls City** U.S.A.
99 A3 **Falmouth** U.K.
122 A3 **False Bay** S. Africa
93 F4 **Falster** *i.* Denmark
110 C1 **Fălticeni** Romania
93 G3 **Falun** Sweden
71 A3 **Fangchenggang** China
71 C3 **Fangshan** Taiwan
69 E1 **Fangzheng** China
108 B2 **Fano** Italy
119 C2 **Faradje** Dem. Rep. Congo
121 D3 **Farafangana** Madag.
116 A2 **Farāfirah, Wāḩāt al** *oasis* Egypt
76 C3 **Farāh** Afgh.
114 A3 **Faranah** Guinea
78 B3 **Farasān, Jazā'ir** *is* Saudi Arabia
127 J3 **Farewell, Cape** Greenland
54 B2 **Farewell, Cape** N.Z.
137 D1 **Fargo** U.S.A.
77 D2 **Farg'ona** Uzbek.
137 E2 **Faribault** U.S.A.
141 E2 **Farmington** *ME* U.S.A.
138 B1 **Farmington** *NM* U.S.A.
141 D3 **Farmville** U.S.A.
99 C3 **Farnborough** U.K.
128 C2 **Farnham, Mount** Can.
128 A1 **Faro** Can.
106 B2 **Faro** Port.
88 A2 **Fårö** *i.* Sweden
94 B1 **Faroe Islands** *terr.* N. Atlantic Ocean
79 C2 **Farrāshband** Iran
139 C2 **Farwell** U.S.A.
79 C2 **Fāryāb** Iran
79 C2 **Fasā** Iran
109 C2 **Fasano** Italy
90 B1 **Fastiv** Ukr.
75 B2 **Fatehgarh** India
75 C2 **Fatehpur** India
92 G2 **Fauske** Norway
92 A3 **Faxaflói** *b.* Iceland
92 G3 **Faxälven** *r.* Sweden
115 D3 **Faya** Chad
142 B1 **Fayetteville** *AR* U.S.A.
143 E1 **Fayetteville** *NC* U.S.A.
142 C1 **Fayetteville** *TN* U.S.A.
77 D3 **Fayẕābād** Afgh.
74 B1 **Fazilka** India
114 A2 **Fdérik** Maur.
143 E2 **Fear, Cape** U.S.A.

54 C2 **Featherston** N.Z.
104 C2 **Fécamp** France
102 C1 **Fehmarn** *i.* Ger.
101 F1 **Fehrbellin** Ger.
155 D2 **Feia, Lagoa** *lag.* Brazil
150 A2 **Feijó** Brazil
54 C2 **Feilding** N.Z.
151 E3 **Feira de Santana** Brazil
107 D2 **Felanitx** Spain
145 D3 **Felipe C. Puerto** Mex.
155 D1 **Felixlândia** Brazil
99 D3 **Felixstowe** U.K.
101 D2 **Felsberg** Ger.
108 B1 **Feltre** Italy
93 F3 **Femunden** *l.* Norway
71 B3 **Fengcheng** *Jiangxi* China
65 A1 **Fengcheng** *Liaoning* China
62 A1 **Fengqing** China
70 B2 **Fengxian** China
Fengxiang China *see* **Lincang**
71 C3 **Fengyüan** Taiwan
70 B1 **Fengzhen** China
105 D3 **Feno, Capo di** *c. Corse* France
121 D2 **Fenoarivo Atsinanana** Madag.
91 D2 **Feodosiya** Ukr.
108 A3 **Fer, Cap de** *c.* Alg.
137 D1 **Fergus Falls** U.S.A.
109 D2 **Ferizaj** Kosovo
114 B4 **Ferkessédougou** Côte d'Ivoire
108 B2 **Fermo** Italy
131 D1 **Fermont** Can.
106 B1 **Fermoselle** Spain
97 B2 **Fermoy** Ireland
143 D2 **Fernandina Beach** U.S.A.
154 B2 **Fernandópolis** Brazil
128 C3 **Fernie** Can.
108 B2 **Ferrara** Italy
154 B2 **Ferreiros** Brazil
108 A2 **Ferro, Capo** *c. Sardegna* Italy
106 B1 **Ferrol** Spain
100 B1 **Ferwert** Neth.
114 B1 **Fès** Morocco
118 B3 **Feshi** Dem. Rep. Congo
137 E3 **Festus** U.S.A.
111 C3 **Fethiye** Turkey
96 □ **Fetlar** *i.* U.K.
130 C1 **Feuilles, Rivière aux** *r.* Can.
Fez Morocco *see* **Fès**
121 D3 **Fianarantsoa** Madag.
117 B4 **Fichē** Eth.
109 C2 **Fier** Albania
96 C2 **Fife Ness** *pt* U.K.
104 C3 **Figeac** France
106 B1 **Figueira da Foz** Port.
107 D1 **Figueres** Spain
114 B1 **Figuig** Morocco
48 F3 **Fiji** *country* S. Pacific Ocean
152 B3 **Filadelfia** Para.
55 Q2 **Filchner Ice Shelf** Antarctica
98 C1 **Filey** U.K.
111 B3 **Filippiada** Greece
93 F4 **Filipstad** Sweden
96 C2 **Findhorn** *r.* U.K.
140 C2 **Findlay** U.S.A.
51 D4 **Fingal** Austr.
141 D2 **Finger Lakes** U.S.A.
106 B1 **Finisterre, Cape** Spain
92 I3 **Finland** *country* Europe
93 H4 **Finland, Gulf of** Europe
128 B2 **Finlay** *r.* Can.
53 C3 **Finley** Austr.
101 E2 **Finne** *ridge* Ger.
92 H2 **Finnmarksvidda** *reg.* Norway
92 G2 **Finnsnes** Norway
93 G4 **Finspång** Sweden
96 A2 **Fionnphort** U.K.
Fırat *r.* Turkey *see* **Euphrates**
Firenze Italy *see* **Florence**
105 C2 **Firminy** France
75 B2 **Firozabad** India
74 B1 **Firozpur** India
79 C2 **Fīrūzābād** Iran
122 A2 **Fish** *watercourse* Namibia
122 B3 **Fish** *r.* S. Africa
99 A3 **Fishguard** U.K.
105 C2 **Fismes** France
Fisterra, Cabo *c.* Spain *see* **Finisterre, Cape**
141 E2 **Fitchburg** U.S.A.
129 C2 **Fitzgerald** Can.
50 B1 **Fitzroy Crossing** Austr.
108 B2 **Fivizzano** Italy
119 C3 **Fizi** Dem. Rep. Congo
92 G3 **Fjällsjöälven** *r.* Sweden
123 C3 **Flagstaff** S. Africa
138 A1 **Flagstaff** U.S.A.
130 C1 **Flaherty Island** Can.
98 C1 **Flamborough Head** U.K.
101 F1 **Fläming** *hills* Ger.
136 B2 **Flaming Gorge Reservoir** U.S.A.
134 D1 **Flathead** *r.* U.S.A.
134 D1 **Flathead Lake** U.S.A.
51 D1 **Flattery, Cape** Austr.
134 B1 **Flattery, Cape** U.S.A.
98 B2 **Fleetwood** U.K.
93 E4 **Flekkefjord** Norway
102 B1 **Flensburg** Ger.
104 B2 **Flers** France
51 D1 **Flinders** *r.* Austr.
50 A3 **Flinders Bay** Austr.
51 D3 **Flinders Island** Austr.
52 A2 **Flinders Ranges** *mts* Austr.
129 D2 **Flin Flon** Can.
140 C2 **Flint** U.S.A.
107 D1 **Florac** France
108 B2 **Florence** Italy
142 C2 **Florence** *AL* U.S.A.
138 A2 **Florence** *AZ* U.S.A.
134 B2 **Florence** *OR* U.S.A.
143 E2 **Florence** *SC* U.S.A.
150 A1 **Florencia** Col.
146 B3 **Flores** Guat.
58 C3 **Flores** *i.* Indon.
58 B3 **Flores, Laut** *sea* Indon.
Flores Sea Indon. *see* **Flores, Laut**
151 E2 **Floresta** Brazil
139 D3 **Floresville** U.S.A.
151 D2 **Floriano** Brazil
152 D3 **Florianópolis** Brazil
153 C4 **Florida** Uru.
143 D2 **Florida** *state* U.S.A.
143 D4 **Florida, Straits of** N. Atlantic Ocean
143 D4 **Florida Keys** *is* U.S.A.
111 B2 **Florina** Greece
93 E3 **Florø** Norway
129 D2 **Foam Lake** Can.
109 C2 **Foča** Bos.-Herz.
110 C1 **Focşani** Romania
71 B3 **Fogang** China
109 C2 **Foggia** Italy
131 E2 **Fogo Island** Can.
104 C3 **Foix** France
89 D3 **Fokino** Rus. Fed.
130 B2 **Foleyet** Can.
108 B2 **Foligno** Italy
99 D3 **Folkestone** U.K.
143 D2 **Folkston** U.S.A.
108 B2 **Follonica** Italy
129 D2 **Fond-du-Lac** Can.
129 D2 **Fond du Lac** *r.* Can.
140 B2 **Fond du Lac** U.S.A.
106 B1 **Fondevila** Spain
108 B2 **Fondi** Italy
146 B3 **Fonseca, Golfo do** *b.* Central America
150 B2 **Fonte Boa** Brazil
104 B2 **Fontenay-le-Comte** France
92 C2 **Fontur** *pt* Iceland
53 C2 **Forbes** Austr.
101 E3 **Forchheim** Ger.
93 E3 **Førde** Norway
53 C1 **Fords Bridge** Austr.
142 B2 **Fordyce** U.S.A.
142 C2 **Forest** U.S.A.
53 C3 **Forest Hill** Austr.
131 D2 **Forestville** Can.
96 C2 **Forfar** U.K.
134 B1 **Forks** U.S.A.
108 B2 **Forlì** Italy
107 D2 **Formentera** *i.* Spain
107 D2 **Formentor, Cap de** *c.* Spain
155 C2 **Formiga** Brazil
152 C3 **Formosa** Arg.
Formosa *country* Asia *see* **Taiwan**
154 C1 **Formosa** Brazil
96 C2 **Forres** U.K.
50 B3 **Forrest** Austr.
142 B1 **Forrest City** U.S.A.
51 D1 **Forsayth** Austr.
93 H3 **Forssa** Fin.
53 D2 **Forster** Austr.
136 B1 **Forsyth** U.S.A.
74 B2 **Fort Abbas** Pak.
130 B1 **Fort Albany** Can.
151 E2 **Fortaleza** Brazil
128 C2 **Fort Assiniboine** Can.
96 B2 **Fort Augustus** U.K.
134 D1 **Fort Benton** U.S.A.
135 B3 **Fort Bragg** U.S.A.
Fort Chimo Can. *see* **Kuujj**
129 C2 **Fort Chipewyan** Can.
136 B2 **Fort Collins** U.S.A.
147 D3 **Fort-de-France** Martinique
137 E2 **Fort Dodge** U.S.A.
130 A2 **Fort Frances** Can.
Fort Franklin Can. *see* **Délį**
Fort George Can. *see* **Chisa**
126 C2 **Fort Good Hope** Can.
96 C2 **Forth** *r.* U.K.
96 C2 **Forth, Firth of** *est.* U.K.
152 C3 **Fortín Madrejón** Para.
143 D3 **Fort Lauderdale** U.S.A.
128 B1 **Fort Liard** Can.
129 C2 **Fort Mackay** Can.
129 C2 **Fort McMurray** Can.
126 C2 **Fort McPherson** Can.
136 C2 **Fort Morgan** U.S.A.
143 D3 **Fort Myers** U.S.A.
128 B2 **Fort Nelson** Can.
128 B2 **Fort Nelson** *r.* Can.
142 C2 **Fort Payne** U.S.A.
136 B1 **Fort Peck** U.S.A.
136 B1 **Fort Peck Reservoir** U.S.A.
143 D3 **Fort Pierce** U.S.A.
128 C1 **Fort Providence** Can.
129 D2 **Fort Qu'Appelle** Can.
128 C1 **Fort Resolution** Can.
Fort Rupert Can. *see* **Waskaganish**
128 B2 **Fort St James** Can.
128 B2 **Fort St John** Can.
128 C2 **Fort Saskatchewan** Can.
137 E3 **Fort Scott** U.S.A.
130 B1 **Fort Severn** Can.
76 B2 **Fort-Shevchenko** Kazakh.
128 B1 **Fort Simpson** Can.
129 C1 **Fort Smith** Can.

B1 **Fort Smith** U.S.A.
C2 **Fort Stockton** U.S.A.
C2 **Fort Sumner** U.S.A.
C2 **Fort Vermilion** Can.
C2 **Fort Walton Beach** U.S.A.
B2 **Fort Wayne** U.S.A.
B2 **Fort William** U.K.
D2 **Fort Worth** U.S.A.
B2 **Fort Yukon** U.S.A.
B3 **Foshan** China
F3 **Fosna** *pen.* Norway
E3 **Fosnavåg** Norway
B3 **Foss** Iceland
A2 **Fossá** Iceland
A2 **Fossano** Italy
C3 **Foster** Austr.
B2 **Fougères** France
□ **Foula** *i.* U.K.
C3 **Fournoi** *i.* Greece
A3 **Fouta Djallon** *reg.* Guinea
A3 **Foveaux Strait** N.Z.
C3 **Fowler** U.S.A.
C3 **Fowlers Bay** Austr.
C2 **Fox Creek** Can.
F2 **Foxe Basin** *g.* Can.
F2 **Foxe Channel** Can.
F2 **Foxe Peninsula** Can.
B2 **Fox Glacier** N.Z.
C2 **Fox Lake** Can.
A1 **Fox Mountain** Can.
C2 **Foxton** N.Z.
D2 **Fox Valley** Can.
C1 **Foyle, Lough** *b.* Ireland/U.K.
B3 **Foz de Areia, Represa de** *resr* Brazil
A2 **Foz do Cunene** Angola
B3 **Foz do Iguaçu** Brazil
D1 **Fraga** Spain
C2 **Franca** Brazil
C2 **Francavilla Fontana** Italy
C2 **France** *country* Europe
B3 **Franceville** Gabon
D2 **Francis Case, Lake** U.S.A.
D1 **Francisco Sá** Brazil
B3 **Francistown** Botswana
B2 **François Lake** Can.
D2 **Frankenberg (Eder)** Ger.
D3 **Frankenthal (Pfalz)** Ger.
E2 **Frankenwald** *mts* Ger.
C3 **Frankfort** U.S.A.
D2 **Frankfurt am Main** Ger.
C1 **Frankfurt an der Oder** Ger.
C2 **Fränkische Alb** *hills* Ger.
E3 **Fränkische Schweiz** *reg.* Ger.
D2 **Franklin** U.S.A.
C2 **Franklin Bay** Can.
C1 **Franklin D. Roosevelt Lake** U.S.A.
B1 **Franklin Mountains** Can.
E2 **Franklin Strait** Can.
E1 **Frantsa-Iosifa, Zemlya** *is* Rus. Fed.
B2 **Franz Josef Glacier** N.Z.
Franz Josef Land *is* Rus. Fed. *see* **Frantsa-Iosifa, Zemlya**
A3 **Frasca, Capo della** *c. Sardegna* Italy
B3 **Fraser** *r. B.C.* Can.
D1 **Fraser** *r. Nfld. and Lab.* Can.
B3 **Fraserburg** S. Africa
C2 **Fraserburgh** U.K.
B2 **Fraserdale** Can.
E2 **Fraser Island** Austr.
B2 **Fraser Lake** Can.
C4 **Fray Bentos** Uru.
E4 **Fredericia** Denmark
D2 **Frederick** U.S.A.
139 D2 **Fredericksburg** *TX* U.S.A.
141 D3 **Fredericksburg** *VA* U.S.A.
128 A2 **Frederick Sound** *sea chan.* U.S.A.
131 D2 **Fredericton** Can.
93 F4 **Frederikshavn** Denmark
Fredrikshamn Fin. *see* **Hamina**
93 F4 **Fredrikstad** Norway
140 B2 **Freeport** *IL* U.S.A.
139 D3 **Freeport** *TX* U.S.A.
146 C2 **Freeport City** Bahamas
139 D3 **Freer** U.S.A.
123 C2 **Free State** *prov.* S. Africa
114 A4 **Freetown** Sierra Leone
106 B2 **Fregenal de la Sierra** Spain
104 B2 **Fréhel, Cap** *c.* France
102 B2 **Freiburg im Breisgau** Ger.
102 C2 **Freising** Ger.
102 C2 **Freistadt** Austria
105 D3 **Fréjus** France
50 A3 **Fremantle** Austr.
137 D2 **Fremont** *NE* U.S.A.
140 C2 **Fremont** *OH* U.S.A.
151 C1 **French Guiana** *terr.* S. America
134 E1 **Frenchman** *r.* U.S.A.
49 I4 **French Polynesia** *terr.* S. Pacific Ocean
144 B2 **Fresnillo** Mex.
135 C3 **Fresno** U.S.A.
107 D2 **Freu, Cap des** *c.* Spain
105 D2 **Freyming-Merlebach** France
114 A3 **Fria** Guinea
152 B3 **Frias** Arg.
102 B2 **Friedrichshafen** Ger.
101 F1 **Friesack** Ger.
100 C1 **Friesoythe** Ger.
Frobisher Bay Can. *see* **Iqaluit**
127 G2 **Frobisher Bay** Can.
101 F2 **Frohburg** Ger.
87 D4 **Frolovo** Rus. Fed.
52 A2 **Frome, Lake** *imp. l.* Austr.
52 A2 **Frome Downs** Austr.
100 C2 **Fröndenberg** Ger.
145 C3 **Frontera** Mex.
144 B1 **Fronteras** Mex.
108 B2 **Frosinone** Italy
92 E3 **Frøya** *i.* Norway
Frunze Kyrg. *see* **Bishkek**
105 D2 **Frutigen** Switz.
103 D2 **Frýdek-Místek** Czech Rep.
71 B3 **Fu'an** China
106 C1 **Fuenlabrada** Spain
152 C3 **Fuerte Olimpo** Para.
114 A2 **Fuerteventura** *i.* Islas Canarias
64 B1 **Fuga** *i.* Phil.
79 C2 **Fujairah** U.A.E.
67 C3 **Fuji** Japan
71 B3 **Fujian** *prov.* China
67 C3 **Fujinomiya** Japan
67 C3 **Fuji-san** *vol.* Japan
67 C3 **Fukui** Japan
67 B4 **Fukuoka** Japan
67 D3 **Fukushima** Japan
101 D2 **Fulda** Ger.
101 D2 **Fulda** *r.* Ger.
70 A3 **Fuling** China
137 E3 **Fulton** U.S.A.
105 C2 **Fumay** France
49 F3 **Funafuti** *atoll* Tuvalu
114 A1 **Funchal** Arquipélago da Madeira
106 B1 **Fundão** Port.
131 D2 **Fundy, Bay of** *g.* Can.
70 B2 **Funing** *Jiangsu* China
71 A3 **Funing** *Yunnan* China
115 C3 **Funtua** Nigeria
79 C2 **Fürgun, Kūh-e** *mt.* Iran
89 F2 **Furmanov** Rus. Fed.
155 C2 **Furnas, Represa** *resr* Brazil
51 D4 **Furneaux Group** *is* Austr.
100 C1 **Fürstenau** Ger.
101 E3 **Fürth** Ger.
66 D3 **Furukawa** Japan
127 F2 **Fury and Hecla Strait** Can.
65 A1 **Fushun** China
65 B1 **Fusong** China
79 C2 **Fuwayriț** Qatar
70 B2 **Fuyang** China
69 E1 **Fuyu** China
68 B1 **Fuyun** China
71 B3 **Fuzhou** *Fujian* China
71 B3 **Fuzhou** *Jiangxi* China
93 F4 **Fyn** *i.* Denmark
F.Y.R.O.M. *country* Europe *see* **Macedonia**

G

117 C4 **Gaalkacyo** Somalia
120 A2 **Gabela** Angola
115 D1 **Gabès** Tunisia
115 D1 **Gabès, Golfe de** *g.* Tunisia
118 B3 **Gabon** *country* Africa
123 C1 **Gaborone** Botswana
110 C2 **Gabrovo** Bulg.
114 A3 **Gabú** Guinea-Bissau
73 B3 **Gadag** India
75 C2 **Gadchiroli** India
101 E1 **Gadebusch** Ger.
142 C2 **Gadsden** U.S.A.
110 C2 **Găești** Romania
108 B2 **Gaeta** Italy
143 D1 **Gaffney** U.S.A.
115 C1 **Gafsa** Tunisia
89 E2 **Gagarin** Rus. Fed.
114 B4 **Gagnoa** Côte d'Ivoire
131 D1 **Gagnon** Can.
81 C1 **Gagra** Georgia
122 A2 **Gaiab** *watercourse* Namibia
111 C3 **Gaïdouronisi** *i.* Greece
104 C3 **Gaillac** France
143 D3 **Gainesville** *FL* U.S.A.
143 D2 **Gainesville** *GA* U.S.A.
139 D2 **Gainesville** *TX* U.S.A.
98 C2 **Gainsborough** U.K.
52 A2 **Gairdner, Lake** *imp. l.* Austr.
96 B2 **Gairloch** U.K.
119 E3 **Galana** *r.* Kenya
103 D2 **Galanta** Slovakia
148 B3 **Galapagos Islands** Ecuador
96 C3 **Galashiels** U.K.
110 C1 **Galați** Romania
93 E3 **Galdhøpiggen** *mt.* Norway
145 B2 **Galeana** Mex.
128 C2 **Galena Bay** Can.
140 A2 **Galesburg** U.S.A.
122 B2 **Galeshewe** S. Africa
86 D3 **Galich** Rus. Fed.
116 B1 **Galilee, Sea of** *l.* Israel
142 C1 **Gallatin** U.S.A.
73 C4 **Galle** Sri Lanka
150 A1 **Gallinas, Punta** *pt* Col.
109 C2 **Gallipoli** Italy
111 C2 **Gallipoli** Turkey
92 H2 **Gällivare** Sweden
138 B1 **Gallup** U.S.A.
114 A2 **Galtat Zemmour** Western Sahara
97 B2 **Galtymore** *h.* Ireland
139 E3 **Galveston** U.S.A.
139 E3 **Galveston Bay** U.S.A.

97 B2 **Galway** Ireland
97 B2 **Galway Bay** Ireland
154 C1 **Gamá** Brazil
123 D3 **Gamalakhe** S. Africa
114 A3 **Gambia, The** *country* Africa
52 A3 **Gambier Islands** Austr.
131 E2 **Gambo** Can.
118 B3 **Gamboma** Congo
128 C1 **Gamêtî** Can.
138 B1 **Ganado** U.S.A.
81 C1 **Gäncä** Azer.
Gand Belgium *see* **Ghent**
61 C2 **Gandadiwata, Bukit** *mt.* Indon.
118 C3 **Gandajika** Dem. Rep. Congo
131 E2 **Gander** Can.
131 E2 **Gander** *r.* Can.
101 D1 **Ganderkesee** Ger.
107 D1 **Gandesa** Spain
74 B2 **Gandhidham** India
74 B2 **Gandhinagar** India
74 B2 **Gandhi Sagar** *resr* India
107 C2 **Gandia** Spain
Ganga *r.* Bangl./India *see* **Ganges**
153 B5 **Gangán** Arg.
74 B2 **Ganganagar** India
68 C2 **Gangca** China
75 C1 **Gangdisê Shan** *mts* China
75 D2 **Ganges** *r.* Bangl./India
105 C3 **Ganges** France
75 C2 **Ganges, Mouths of the** Bangl./India
75 C2 **Gangtok** India
105 C2 **Gannat** France
136 B2 **Gannett Peak** U.S.A.
122 A3 **Gansbaai** S. Africa
70 A1 **Gansu** *prov.* China
71 B3 **Ganzhou** China
114 B3 **Gao** Mali
97 B1 **Gaoth Dobhair** Ireland
114 A3 **Gaoual** Guinea
70 B2 **Gaoyou** China
70 B2 **Gaoyou Hu** *l.* China
105 D3 **Gap** France
75 C1 **Gar** China
76 B2 **Garabogaz** Turkm.
76 B2 **Garabogazköl** Turkm.
76 B2 **Garabogazköl Aýlagy** *b.* Turkm.
53 C1 **Garah** Austr.
151 E2 **Garanhuns** Brazil
135 B2 **Garberville** U.S.A.
101 D1 **Garbsen** Ger.
154 C2 **Garça** Brazil
101 E1 **Gardelegen** Ger.
136 C3 **Garden City** U.S.A.
129 E2 **Garden Hill** Can.
77 C3 **Gardēz** Afgh.
88 B2 **Gargždai** Lith.
123 C3 **Gariep Dam** *dam* S. Africa
122 A3 **Garies** S. Africa
119 D3 **Garissa** Kenya
102 C2 **Garmisch-Partenkirchen** Ger.
52 B2 **Garnpung Lake** *imp. l.* Austr.
104 B3 **Garonne** *r.* France
117 C4 **Garoowe** Somalia
74 B2 **Garoth** India
118 B2 **Garoua** Cameroon
96 B2 **Garry** *r.* U.K.
126 E2 **Garry Lake** Can.
119 E3 **Garsen** Kenya
61 B2 **Garut** Indon.
140 B2 **Gary** U.S.A.
145 B2 **Garza García** Mex.
68 C2 **Garzê** China
104 B2 **Gascony, Gulf of** France
50 A2 **Gascoyne** *r.* Austr.
115 D3 **Gashua** Nigeria
131 D2 **Gaspé** Can.
131 D2 **Gaspésie, Péninsule de la** *pen.* Can.
143 E1 **Gaston, Lake** U.S.A.
143 D1 **Gastonia** U.S.A.
107 C2 **Gata, Cabo de** *c.* Spain
88 D2 **Gatchina** Rus. Fed.
98 C1 **Gateshead** U.K.
139 D2 **Gatesville** U.S.A.
130 C2 **Gatineau** *r.* Can.
53 D1 **Gatton** Austr.
129 E2 **Gauer Lake** Can.
93 E4 **Gausta** *mt.* Norway
123 C2 **Gauteng** *prov.* S. Africa
79 C2 **Gāvbandī** Iran
111 B3 **Gavdos** *i.* Greece
93 G3 **Gävle** Sweden
89 F2 **Gavrilov Posad** Rus. Fed.
89 E2 **Gavrilov-Yam** Rus. Fed.
62 A1 **Gawai** Myanmar
52 A2 **Gawler** Austr.
52 A2 **Gawler Ranges** *hills* Austr.
75 C2 **Gaya** India
114 C3 **Gaya** Niger
140 C1 **Gaylord** U.S.A.
86 E2 **Gayny** Rus. Fed.
80 B2 **Gaza** *terr.* Asia
80 B2 **Gaziantep** Turkey
76 C2 **Gazojak** Turkm.
114 B4 **Gbarnga** Liberia
103 D1 **Gdańsk** Pol.
88 A3 **Gdańsk, Gulf of** Pol./Rus. Fed.
88 C2 **Gdov** Rus. Fed.
103 D1 **Gdynia** Pol.
116 B3 **Gedaref** Sudan
101 D2 **Gedern** Ger.
111 C3 **Gediz** *r.* Turkey
102 C1 **Gedser** Denmark
100 B2 **Geel** Belgium
52 B3 **Geelong** Austr.
101 E1 **Geesthacht** Ger.
75 C1 **Gê'gyai** China
129 D2 **Geikie** *r.* Can.
93 E3 **Geilo** Norway
62 B1 **Gejiu** China
108 B3 **Gela** *Sicilia* Italy
91 D3 **Gelendzhik** Rus. Fed.
Gelibolu Turkey *see* **Gallipoli**
100 C2 **Gelsenkirchen** Ger.
118 B2 **Gemena** Dem. Rep. Congo
111 C2 **Gemlik** Turkey
117 C4 **Genalē Wenz** *r.* Eth.
81 D3 **Genāveh** Iran
153 B4 **General Acha** Arg.
153 B4 **General Alvear** Arg.
153 C4 **General Belgrano** Arg.
144 B2 **General Cepeda** Mex.
153 B4 **General Pico** Arg.
153 B4 **General Roca** Arg.
64 B2 **General Santos** Phil.
141 D2 **Genesee** *r.* U.S.A.
141 D2 **Geneseo** U.S.A.
105 D2 **Geneva** Switz.
141 D2 **Geneva** U.S.A.
105 D2 **Geneva, Lake** France/Switz.
Genève Switz. *see* **Geneva**
106 B2 **Genil** *r.* Spain
100 B2 **Genk** Belgium
108 A2 **Genoa** Italy
Genova Italy *see* **Genoa**
101 F1 **Genthin** Ger.
50 A3 **Geographe Bay** Austr.
131 D1 **George** *r.* Can.
122 B3 **George** S. Africa
143 D3 **George, Lake** *FL* U.S.A.
141 E2 **George, Lake** *NY* U.S.A.
114 A3 **Georgetown** Gambia
151 C1 **Georgetown** Guyana
60 B1 **George Town** Malaysia
143 E2 **Georgetown** *SC* U.S.A.
139 D2 **Georgetown** *TX* U.S.A.
55 I2 **George V Land** *reg.* Antarc
81 C1 **Georgia** *country* Asia
143 D2 **Georgia** *state* U.S.A.
130 B2 **Georgian Bay** Can.
51 C2 **Georgina** *watercourse* Austr
77 E2 **Georgiyevka** Kazakh.
87 D4 **Georgiyevsk** Rus. Fed.
101 F2 **Gera** Ger.
151 D3 **Geral de Goiás, Serra** *hills* Brazil
54 B2 **Geraldine** N.Z.
50 A2 **Geraldton** Austr.
80 B1 **Gerede** Turkey
74 A1 **Gereshk** Afgh.
135 C2 **Gerlach** U.S.A.
103 E2 **Gerlachovský štít** *mt.* Slov
102 C1 **Germany** *country* Europe
100 C2 **Gerolstein** Ger.
101 E3 **Gerolzhofen** Ger.
101 D2 **Gersfeld (Rhön)** Ger.
75 C1 **Gêrzê** China
117 C4 **Gestro, Wabē** *r.* Eth.
141 D3 **Gettysburg** *PA* U.S.A.
136 D1 **Gettysburg** *SD* U.S.A.
109 D2 **Gevgelija** Macedonia
111 C3 **Geyikli** Turkey
122 B2 **Ghaap Plateau** S. Africa
115 C1 **Ghadāmis** Libya
75 C2 **Ghaghara** *r.* India
114 B4 **Ghana** *country* Africa
120 B3 **Ghanzi** Botswana
115 C1 **Ghardaïa** Alg.
115 D1 **Gharyān** Libya
75 C2 **Ghatal** India
75 B2 **Ghaziabad** India
75 C2 **Ghazipur** India
77 C3 **Ghaznī** Afgh.
100 A2 **Ghent** Belgium
110 B1 **Gherla** Romania
105 D3 **Ghisonaccia** *Corse* France
74 B2 **Ghotaru** India
74 A2 **Ghotki** Pak.
91 E3 **Giaginskaya** Rus. Fed.
97 C1 **Giant's Causeway** *lava field* U.K.
61 C2 **Gianyar** Indon.
109 C3 **Giarre** *Sicilia* Italy
108 A1 **Giaveno** Italy
122 A2 **Gibeon** Namibia
106 B2 **Gibraltar** Gibraltar
106 B2 **Gibraltar, Strait of** Morocco/Spain
50 B2 **Gibson Desert** Austr.
68 C1 **Gichgeniyn Nuruu** *mts* Mongolia
117 B4 **Gīdolē** Eth.
104 C2 **Gien** France
101 D2 **Gießen** Ger.
101 E1 **Gifhorn** Ger.
128 C2 **Gift Lake** Can.
67 C3 **Gifu** Japan
96 B3 **Gigha** *i.* U.K.
106 B1 **Gijón-Xixón** Spain
138 A2 **Gila** *r.* U.S.A.
138 A2 **Gila Bend** U.S.A.
51 D1 **Gilbert** *r.* Austr.
49 F2 **Gilbert Islands** *is* Kiribati
134 D1 **Gildford** U.S.A.
53 C2 **Gilgandra** Austr.
74 B1 **Gilgit** Pak.

B1 **Gilgit** *r.* Pak.
C2 **Gilgunnia** Austr.
E2 **Gillam** Can.
B2 **Gillette** U.S.A.
D3 **Gillingham** U.K.
E2 **Gimli** Can.
C4 **Gīnīr** Eth.
C2 **Ginosa** Italy
C3 **Gippsland** *reg.* Austr.
A2 **Girdar Dhor** *r.* Pak.
B1 **Giresun** Turkey
D1 **Girona** Spain
B3 **Girvan** U.K.
C1 **Gisborne** N.Z.
F4 **Gislaved** Sweden
C3 **Gitarama** Rwanda
B2 **Giulianova** Italy
C2 **Giurgiu** Romania
C1 **Giuvala, Pasul** *pass* Romania
C2 **Givors** France
D1 **Giyani** S. Africa
B2 **Giza** Egypt
D2 **Gjakovë** Kosovo
D2 **Gjilan** Kosovo
D2 **Gjirokastër** Albania
E2 **Gjoa Haven** Can.
F3 **Gjøvik** Norway
E2 **Glace Bay** Can.
B1 **Glacier Peak** *vol.* U.S.A.
E2 **Gladstone** Austr.
A2 **Gláma** *mts* Iceland
C2 **Glamoč** Bos.-Herz.
C3 **Glan** *r.* Ger.
B2 **Glanaruddery Mountains** *hills* Ireland
B3 **Glasgow** U.K.
B3 **Glasgow** *KY* U.S.A.
B1 **Glasgow** *MT* U.S.A.
B3 **Glastonbury** U.K.
F2 **Glauchau** Ger.
E3 **Glazov** Rus. Fed.
E3 **Glazunovka** Rus. Fed.
B2 **Glen Coe** *val.* U.K.
A2 **Glendale** U.S.A.
D2 **Glen Davis** Austr.
C1 **Glendive** U.S.A.
B3 **Glenelg** *r.* Austr.
D1 **Glen Innes** Austr.
B2 **Glennallen** U.S.A.
C2 **Glenrothes** U.K.
E2 **Glens Falls** U.S.A.
C2 **Glen Shee** *val.* U.K.
B1 **Glenties** Ireland
B2 **Glenwood** U.S.A.
B3 **Glenwood Springs** U.S.A.
D1 **Gliwice** Pol.
A2 **Globe** U.S.A.
D1 **Głogów** Pol.
F2 **Glomfjord** Norway
F4 **Glomma** *r.* Norway
D2 **Gloucester** Austr.
B3 **Gloucester** U.K.
F1 **Glöwen** Ger.
E1 **Glubokoye** Kazakh.
D1 **Glückstadt** Ger.
C2 **Gmünd** Austria
C2 **Gmunden** Austria
D1 **Gnarrenburg** Ger.
D1 **Gniezno** Pol.
Gnjilane Kosovo *see* **Gjilan**
D2 **Goalpara** India
B3 **Goat Fell** *h.* U.K.
C4 **Goba** Eth.
A3 **Gobabis** Namibia
A5 **Gobernador Gregores** Arg.
D2 **Gobi** *des.* China/Mongolia
C2 **Goch** Ger.
122 A1 **Gochas** Namibia
74 B3 **Godavari** *r.* India
73 C3 **Godavari, Mouths of the** India
130 B2 **Goderich** Can.
74 B2 **Godhra** India
129 E2 **Gods** *r.* Can.
129 E2 **Gods Lake** Can.
Godthåb Greenland *see* **Nuuk**
Godwin-Austen, Mount China/Pakistan *see* **K2**
130 C2 **Goéland, Lac au** *l.* Can.
131 D1 **Goélands, Lac aux** *l.* Can.
100 A2 **Goes** Neth.
154 C1 **Goiandira** Brazil
154 C1 **Goiânia** Brazil
154 B1 **Goiás** Brazil
154 B2 **Goio-Erê** Brazil
111 C2 **Gökçeada** *i.* Turkey
111 C3 **Gökçedağ** Turkey
121 B2 **Gokwe** Zimbabwe
93 E3 **Gol** Norway
62 A1 **Golaghat** India
111 C2 **Gölcük** Turkey
103 E1 **Gołdap** Pol.
101 F1 **Goldberg** Ger.
53 D1 **Gold Coast** Austr.
114 B4 **Gold Coast** Ghana
128 C2 **Golden** Can.
54 B2 **Golden Bay** N.Z.
128 B3 **Golden Hinde** *mt.* Can.
97 B2 **Golden Vale** *lowland* Ireland
135 C3 **Goldfield** U.S.A.
128 B3 **Gold River** Can.
143 E1 **Goldsboro** U.S.A.
135 C4 **Goleta** U.S.A.
68 C2 **Golmud** China
81 D2 **Golpāyegān** Iran
96 C2 **Golspie** U.K.
119 C3 **Goma** Dem. Rep. Congo
75 C2 **Gomati** *r.* India
115 D3 **Gombe** Nigeria
115 D3 **Gombi** Nigeria
Gomel' Belarus *see* **Homyel'**
144 B2 **Gómez Palacio** Mex.
147 C3 **Gonaïves** Haiti
147 C3 **Gonâve, Île de la** *i.* Haiti
81 D2 **Gonbad-e Kavus** Iran
117 B3 **Gonder** Eth.
75 C2 **Gondia** India
111 C2 **Gönen** Turkey
115 D4 **Gongola** *r.* Nigeria
53 C2 **Gongolgon** Austr.
145 C2 **Gonzáles** Mex.
139 D3 **Gonzales** U.S.A.
122 A3 **Good Hope, Cape of** S. Africa
134 D2 **Gooding** U.S.A.
136 C3 **Goodland** U.S.A.
53 C1 **Goodooga** Austr.
98 C2 **Goole** U.K.
53 C2 **Goolgowi** Austr.
52 A3 **Goolwa** Austr.
53 D1 **Goondiwindi** Austr.
134 B2 **Goose Lake** U.S.A.
102 B2 **Göppingen** Ger.
75 C2 **Gorakhpur** India
109 C2 **Goražde** Bos.-Herz.
111 C3 **Gördes** Turkey
89 D3 **Gordeyevka** Rus. Fed.
51 D4 **Gordon, Lake** Austr.
115 D4 **Goré** Chad
117 B4 **Gorē** Eth.
54 A3 **Gore** N.Z.
97 C2 **Gorey** Ireland
81 D2 **Gorgān** Iran
81 C1 **Gori** Georgia
108 B1 **Gorizia** Italy
Gor'kiy Rus. Fed. *see* **Nizhniy Novgorod**
103 E2 **Gorlice** Pol.
103 C1 **Görlitz** Ger.
109 D2 **Gornji Milanovac** Serbia
109 C2 **Gornji Vakuf** Bos.-Herz.
77 E1 **Gorno-Altaysk** Rus. Fed.
110 C2 **Gornotrakiyska Nizina** *lowland* Bulg.
77 E1 **Gornyak** Rus. Fed.
59 D3 **Goroka** P.N.G.
114 B3 **Gorom Gorom** Burkina
59 C2 **Gorontalo** Indon.
89 E3 **Gorshechnoye** Rus. Fed.
97 B2 **Gorumna Island** Ireland
91 D3 **Goryachiy Klyuch** Rus. Fed.
103 D1 **Gorzów Wielkopolski** Pol.
53 D2 **Gosford** Austr.
66 D2 **Goshogawara** Japan
101 E2 **Goslar** Ger.
109 C2 **Gospić** Croatia
99 C3 **Gosport** U.K.
109 D2 **Gostivar** Macedonia
Göteborg Sweden *see* **Gothenburg**
101 E2 **Gotha** Ger.
93 F4 **Gothenburg** Sweden
136 C2 **Gothenburg** U.S.A.
93 G4 **Gotland** *i.* Sweden
111 B2 **Gotse Delchev** Bulg.
93 G4 **Gotska Sandön** *i.* Sweden
67 B4 **Gōtsu** Japan
101 D2 **Göttingen** Ger.
128 B2 **Gott Peak** Can.
100 B1 **Gouda** Neth.
114 A3 **Goudiri** Senegal
115 D3 **Goudoumaria** Niger
130 C2 **Gouin, Réservoir** *resr* Can.
53 C2 **Goulburn** Austr.
53 B3 **Goulburn** *r. N.S.W.* Austr.
53 B3 **Goulburn** *r. Vic.* Austr.
114 B3 **Goundam** Mali
107 D2 **Gouraya** Alg.
104 C3 **Gourdon** France
115 D3 **Gouré** Niger
122 B3 **Gourits** *r.* S. Africa
114 B3 **Gourma-Rharous** Mali
53 C3 **Gourock Range** *mts* Austr.
155 D1 **Governador Valadares** Brazil
143 E3 **Governor's Harbour** Bahamas
68 C2 **Govĭ Altayn Nuruu** *mts* Mongolia
75 C2 **Govind Ballash Pant Sagar** *resr* India
99 A3 **Gower** *pen.* U.K.
152 C3 **Goya** Arg.
81 C1 **Göyçay** Azer.
75 C1 **Gozha Co** *salt l.* China
122 B3 **Graaff-Reinet** S. Africa
101 E1 **Grabow** Ger.
109 C2 **Gračac** Croatia
87 E3 **Grachevka** Rus. Fed.
101 F2 **Gräfenhainichen** Ger.
53 D1 **Grafton** Austr.
137 D1 **Grafton** U.S.A.
139 D2 **Graham** U.S.A.
128 A2 **Graham Island** Can.
55 P3 **Graham Land** *pen.* Antarctica
123 C3 **Grahamstown** S. Africa
151 D2 **Grajaú** Brazil
111 B2 **Grammos** *mt.* Greece
96 B2 **Grampian Mountains** U.K.
146 B3 **Granada** Nic.
106 C2 **Granada** Spain
141 E1 **Granby** Can.
114 A2 **Gran Canaria** *i.* Islas Canarias
152 B3 **Gran Chaco** *reg.* Arg./Para.

136 C1 **Grand** *r.* U.S.A.
146 C2 **Grand Bahama** *i.* Bahamas
131 E2 **Grand Bank** Can.
158 C2 **Grand Banks of Newfoundland** N. Atlantic Ocean
138 A1 **Grand Canyon** U.S.A.
138 A1 **Grand Canyon** *gorge* U.S.A.
146 B3 **Grand Cayman** *i.* Cayman Is
129 C2 **Grand Centre** Can.
134 C1 **Grand Coulee** U.S.A.
152 B2 **Grande** *r.* Bol.
154 B2 **Grande** *r.* Brazil
153 B6 **Grande, Bahía** *b.* Arg.
155 D2 **Grande, Ilha** *i.* Brazil
128 C2 **Grande Cache** Can.
Grand Canal *canal* China *see* **Jinghang Yunhe**
128 C2 **Grande Prairie** Can.
114 B1 **Grand Erg Occidental** *des.* Alg.
115 C2 **Grand Erg Oriental** *des.* Alg.
131 D2 **Grande-Rivière** Can.
152 B4 **Grandes, Salinas** *salt flat* Arg.
131 D2 **Grand Falls** *N.B.* Can.
131 E2 **Grand Falls-Windsor** *Nfld. and Lab.* Can.
128 C3 **Grand Forks** Can.
137 D1 **Grand Forks** U.S.A.
128 C1 **Grandin, Lac** *l.* Can.
137 D2 **Grand Island** U.S.A.
142 B3 **Grand Isle** U.S.A.
136 B3 **Grand Junction** U.S.A.
114 B4 **Grand-Lahou** Côte d'Ivoire
131 D2 **Grand Lake** *N.B.* Can.
131 E2 **Grand Lake** *Nfld. and Lab.* Can.
137 E1 **Grand Marais** U.S.A.
106 B2 **Grândola** Port.
129 E2 **Grand Rapids** Can.
140 B2 **Grand Rapids** *MI* U.S.A.
137 E1 **Grand Rapids** *MN* U.S.A.
136 A2 **Grand Teton** *mt.* U.S.A.
147 C2 **Grand Turk** Turks and Caicos Is
134 C1 **Grangeville** U.S.A.
128 B2 **Granisle** Can.
134 E1 **Granite Peak** U.S.A.
108 B3 **Granitola, Capo** *c. Sicilia* Italy
93 F4 **Gränna** Sweden
101 F1 **Gransee** Ger.
99 C2 **Grantham** U.K.
96 C2 **Grantown-on-Spey** U.K.
138 B1 **Grants** U.S.A.
134 B2 **Grants Pass** U.S.A.
104 B2 **Granville** France
129 D2 **Granville Lake** Can.
155 D1 **Grão Mogol** Brazil
123 D1 **Graskop** S. Africa
105 D3 **Grasse** France
107 D1 **Graus** Spain
92 F2 **Gravdal** Norway
104 B2 **Grave, Pointe de** *pt* France
129 D3 **Gravelbourg** Can.
130 C2 **Gravenhurst** Can.
53 D1 **Gravesend** Austr.
99 D3 **Gravesend** U.K.
105 D2 **Gray** France
103 D2 **Graz** Austria
146 C2 **Great Abaco** *i.* Bahamas
50 B3 **Great Australian Bight** *g.* Austr.
54 C1 **Great Barrier Island** N.Z.
51 D1 **Great Barrier Reef** Austr.
135 C3 **Great Basin** U.S.A.
126 D2 **Great Bear Lake** Can.
93 F4 **Great Belt** *sea chan.* Denmark
137 D3 **Great Bend** U.S.A.
63 A2 **Great Coco Island** Cocos Is
53 B3 **Great Dividing Range** *mts* Austr.
146 B2 **Greater Antilles** *is* Caribbean Sea
60 A3 **Greater Sunda Islands** *is* Indon.
134 D1 **Great Falls** U.S.A.
123 C3 **Great Fish** *r.* S. Africa
123 C3 **Great Fish Point** S. Africa
147 C2 **Great Inagua** *i.* Bahamas
122 B3 **Great Karoo** *plat.* S. Africa
123 C3 **Great Kei** *r.* S. Africa
99 B2 **Great Malvern** U.K.
122 A2 **Great Namaqualand** *reg.* Namibia
63 A3 **Great Nicobar** *i.* India
99 D2 **Great Ouse** *r.* U.K.
119 D3 **Great Rift Valley** Africa
119 D3 **Great Ruaha** *r.* Tanz.
134 D2 **Great Salt Lake** U.S.A.
135 D2 **Great Salt Lake Desert** U.S.A.
116 A2 **Great Sand Sea** *des.* Egypt/Libya
50 B2 **Great Sandy Desert** Austr.
128 C1 **Great Slave Lake** Can.
143 D1 **Great Smoky Mountains** U.S.A.
50 B2 **Great Victoria Desert** Austr.
70 B1 **Great Wall** *tourist site* China
99 D2 **Great Yarmouth** U.K.
106 B1 **Gredos, Sierra de** *mts* Spain
111 B3 **Greece** *country* Europe
136 C2 **Greeley** U.S.A.
82 F1 **Greem-Bell, Ostrov** *i.* Rus. Fed.
140 B3 **Green** *r. KY* U.S.A.
136 B3 **Green** *r. WY* U.S.A.
140 B2 **Green Bay** U.S.A.
140 B1 **Green Bay** U.S.A.
140 C3 **Greenbrier** *r.* U.S.A.
140 B3 **Greencastle** U.S.A.
143 D1 **Greeneville** U.S.A.
141 E2 **Greenfield** U.S.A.
129 D2 **Green Lake** Can.
127 I2 **Greenland** *terr.* N. America
160 R2 **Greenland Sea** Greenland/Svalbard
96 B3 **Greenock** U.K.
135 D3 **Green River** *UT* U.S.A.
136 B2 **Green River** *WY* U.S.A.
140 B3 **Greensburg** *IN* U.S.A.
141 D2 **Greensburg** *PA* U.S.A.
143 E2 **Green Swamp** U.S.A.
138 A2 **Green Valley** U.S.A.
114 B4 **Greenville** Liberia
142 C2 **Greenville** *AL* U.S.A.
142 B2 **Greenville** *MS* U.S.A.
143 E1 **Greenville** *NC* U.S.A.
143 D2 **Greenville** *SC* U.S.A.
139 D2 **Greenville** *TX* U.S.A.
53 D2 **Greenwell Point** Austr.
143 D2 **Greenwood** U.S.A.
50 B2 **Gregory, Lake** *imp. l.* Austr.
51 D1 **Gregory Range** *hills* Austr.
102 C1 **Greifswald** Ger.
101 F2 **Greiz** Ger.
93 F4 **Grenaa** Denmark
142 C2 **Grenada** U.S.A.
147 D3 **Grenada** *country* West Indies
104 C3 **Grenade** France
53 C2 **Grenfell** Austr.
129 D2 **Grenfell** Can.
105 D2 **Grenoble** France
51 D1 **Grenville, Cape** Austr.
134 B1 **Gresham** U.S.A.
100 C1 **Greven** Ger.
111 B2 **Grevena** Greece
100 C2 **Grevenbroich** Ger.
101 E1 **Grevesmühlen** Ger.
136 B2 **Greybull** U.S.A.
128 A1 **Grey Hunter Peak** Can.
131 E1 **Grey Islands** Can.
54 B2 **Greymouth** N.Z.
52 B1 **Grey Range** *hills* Austr.
97 C2 **Greystones** Ireland
143 D2 **Griffin** U.S.A.
53 C2 **Griffith** Austr.
101 F2 **Grimma** Ger.
102 C1 **Grimmen** Ger.
98 C2 **Grimsby** U.K.
128 C2 **Grimshaw** Can.
92 B2 **Grímsstaðir** Iceland
93 E4 **Grimstad** Norway
137 E2 **Grinnell** U.S.A.
123 C3 **Griqualand East** *reg.* S. Afr
122 B2 **Griqualand West** *reg.* S. Africa
127 F1 **Grise Fiord** Can.
96 C1 **Gritley** U.K.
123 C2 **Groblersdal** S. Africa
122 B2 **Groblershoop** S. Africa
Grodno Belarus *see* **Hrodr**
104 B2 **Groix, Île de** *i.* France
100 C1 **Gronau (Westfalen)** Ger.
92 F3 **Grong** Norway
100 C1 **Groningen** Neth.
122 B2 **Grootdrink** S. Africa
51 C1 **Groote Eylandt** *i.* Austr.
120 A2 **Grootfontein** Namibia
122 A2 **Groot Karas Berg** *plat.* Namibia
122 B3 **Groot Swartberge** *mts* S. A
123 C3 **Groot Winterberg** *mt.* S. A
101 D2 **Großenlüder** Ger.
102 C2 **Großer Rachel** *mt.* Ger.
103 C2 **Grosser Speikkogel** *mt.* Austria
108 B2 **Grosseto** Italy
101 D3 **Groß-Gerau** Ger.
102 C2 **Großglockner** *mt.* Austria
100 C1 **Groß-Hesepe** Ger.
101 E2 **Großlohra** Ger.
122 A1 **Gross Ums** Namibia
131 E1 **Groswater Bay** Can.
130 B2 **Groundhog** *r.* Can.
49 I4 **Groupe Actéon** *is* Fr. Poly
135 B3 **Grover Beach** U.S.A.
141 E2 **Groveton** U.S.A.
87 D4 **Groznyy** Rus. Fed.
109 C1 **Grubišno Polje** Croatia
103 D1 **Grudziądz** Pol.
122 A2 **Grünau** Namibia
92 A3 **Grundarfjörður** Iceland
89 E3 **Gryazi** Rus. Fed.
89 F2 **Gryazovets** Rus. Fed.
103 D1 **Gryfice** Pol.
102 C1 **Gryfino** Pol.
146 C2 **Guacanayabo, Golfo de** *b.* Cuba
144 B2 **Guadalajara** Mex.
106 C1 **Guadalajara** Spain
49 E3 **Guadalcanal** *i.* Solomon I
107 C1 **Guadalope** *r.* Spain
106 B2 **Guadalquivir** *r.* Spain
132 B4 **Guadalupe** *i.* Mex.
106 B2 **Guadalupe, Sierra de** *mts* Spain
138 C2 **Guadalupe Peak** U.S.A.
144 B2 **Guadalupe Victoria** Mex.
144 B2 **Guadalupe y Calvo** Mex.
106 C1 **Guadarrama, Sierra de** *m* Spain
147 D3 **Guadeloupe** *terr.* West Inc

B2 **Guadiana** *r.* Port./Spain
C2 **Guadix** Spain
B2 **Guaíra** Brazil
C3 **Guajira, Península de la** *pen.* Col.
A2 **Gualaceo** Ecuador
D2 **Guam** *terr.* N. Pacific Ocean
B2 **Guamúchil** Mex.
B2 **Guanacevi** Mex.
D3 **Guanambi** Brazil
B1 **Guanare** Venez.
B2 **Guane** Cuba
A2 **Guang'an** China
B3 **Guangchang** China
B3 **Guangdong** *prov.* China
A3 **Guangxi Zhuangzu Zizhiqu** *aut. reg.* China
A2 **Guangyuan** China
B3 **Guangzhou** China
D1 **Guanhães** Brazil
D4 **Guanipa** *r.* Venez.
A3 **Guanling** China
A1 **Guanshui** China
Guansuo China *see* **Guanling**
C2 **Guantánamo** Cuba
B3 **Guaporé** *r.* Bol./Brazil
B3 **Guarapuava** Brazil
C3 **Guaraqueçaba** Brazil
C2 **Guaratinguetá** Brazil
B1 **Guarda** Port.
C1 **Guarda Mor** Brazil
C1 **Guardo** Spain
C2 **Guarujá** Brazil
B2 **Guasave** Mex.
A3 **Guatemala** *country* Central America
A3 **Guatemala City** Guat.
B1 **Guaviare** *r.* Col.
C2 **Guaxupé** Brazil
A2 **Guayaquil** Ecuador
B3 **Guayaramerín** Bol.
A2 **Guaymas** Mex.
C2 **Guazhou** China
B3 **Guba** Eth.
E1 **Guba Dolgaya** Rus. Fed.
E3 **Gubkin** Rus. Fed.
C1 **Guelma** Alg.
A2 **Guelmine** Morocco
B2 **Guelph** Can.
C2 **Guémez** Mex.
C2 **Guéret** France
C4 **Guernsey** *terr.* Channel Is
A2 **Guerrero Negro** Mex.
D1 **Guers, Lac** *l.* Can.
B2 **Guider** Cameroon
B2 **Guidonia-Montecelio** Italy
A3 **Guigang** China
A3 **Guignicourt** France
D1 **Guija** Moz.
C3 **Guildford** U.K.
B3 **Guilin** China
C1 **Guillaume-Delisle, Lac** *l.* Can.
B1 **Guimarães** Port.
A3 **Guinea** *country* Africa
F6 **Guinea, Gulf of** Africa
A3 **Guinea-Bissau** *country* Africa
B2 **Guingamp** France
B2 **Guipavas** France
B1 **Guiratinga** Brazil
B1 **Güiria** Venez.
A3 **Guise** France
B1 **Guiuan** Phil.
A3 **Guiyang** China
A3 **Guizhou** *prov.* China
B1 **Gujranwala** Pak.
B1 **Gujrat** Pak.
91 D2 **Gukovo** Rus. Fed.
53 C2 **Gulargambone** Austr.
73 B3 **Gulbarga** India
88 C2 **Gulbene** Latvia
79 C2 **Gulf, The** Asia
111 B3 **Gulf of Corinth** *sea chan.* Greece
142 C2 **Gulfport** U.S.A.
69 E1 **Gulian** China
77 C2 **Guliston** Uzbek.
Gulja China *see* **Yining**
129 D2 **Gull Lake** Can.
111 C3 **Güllük** Turkey
119 D2 **Gulu** Uganda
120 B2 **Gumare** Botswana
76 B3 **Gumdag** Turkm.
75 C2 **Gumla** India
100 C2 **Gummersbach** Ger.
74 B2 **Guna** India
53 C3 **Gundagai** Austr.
111 C3 **Güney** Turkey
118 B3 **Gungu** Dem. Rep. Congo
129 E2 **Gunisao** *r.* Can.
53 D2 **Gunnedah** Austr.
136 B3 **Gunnison** *CO* U.S.A.
135 D3 **Gunnison** *UT* U.S.A.
136 B3 **Gunnison** *r.* U.S.A.
73 B3 **Guntakal** India
60 A1 **Gunungsitoli** Indon.
60 A1 **Gunungtua** Indon.
102 C2 **Günzburg** Ger.
102 C2 **Gunzenhausen** Ger.
70 B2 **Guojiaba** China
74 B2 **Gurgaon** India
151 D2 **Gurgueia** *r.* Brazil
150 B1 **Guri, Embalse de** *resr* Venez.
154 C1 **Gurinhatã** Brazil
151 D2 **Gurupi** *r.* Brazil
74 B2 **Guru Sikhar** *mt.* India
Gur'yev Kazakh. *see* **Atyrau**
115 C3 **Gusau** Nigeria
65 A2 **Gushan** China
70 B2 **Gushi** China
83 I3 **Gusinoozersk** Rus. Fed.
89 F2 **Gus'-Khrustal'nyy** Rus. Fed.
108 A3 **Guspini** *Sardegna* Italy
128 A2 **Gustavus** U.S.A.
101 F1 **Güstrow** Ger.
101 D2 **Gütersloh** Ger.
121 C2 **Gutu** Zimbabwe
75 D2 **Guwahati** India
150 C1 **Guyana** *country* S. America
Guyi China *see* **Sanjiang**
139 C1 **Guymon** U.S.A.
53 D2 **Guyra** Austr.
70 A2 **Guyuan** China
144 B1 **Guzmán** Mex.
74 A2 **Gwadar** Pak.
75 B2 **Gwalior** India
121 B3 **Gwanda** Zimbabwe
117 D3 **Gwardafuy, Gees** *c.* Somalia
97 B1 **Gweebarra Bay** Ireland
121 B2 **Gweru** Zimbabwe
115 D3 **Gwoza** Nigeria
53 D2 **Gwydir** *r.* Austr.
75 C2 **Gyangzê** China
75 C1 **Gyaring Co** *l.* China
68 C2 **Gyaring Hu** *l.* China
86 G1 **Gydan Peninsula** Rus. Fed.
Gydanskiy Poluostrov *pen.* Rus. Fed. *see* **Gydan Peninsula**
Gyêgu China *see* **Yushu**
68 C3 **Gyigang** China
51 E2 **Gympie** Austr.
103 D2 **Gyöngyös** Hungary
103 D2 **Győr** Hungary
129 E2 **Gypsumville** Can.
103 E2 **Gyula** Hungary
81 C1 **Gyumri** Armenia

H

88 B2 **Haapsalu** Estonia
100 B1 **Haarlem** Neth.
101 C2 **Haarstrang** *ridge* Ger.
54 A2 **Haast** N.Z.
78 B3 **Habbān** Yemen
81 C2 **Ḥabbānīyah, Hawr al** *l.* Iraq
67 C4 **Hachijō-jima** *i.* Japan
66 D2 **Hachinohe** Japan
121 C3 **Hacufera** Moz.
79 C2 **Ḥadd, Ra's al** *pt* Oman
96 C3 **Haddington** U.K.
115 D3 **Hadejia** Nigeria
93 E4 **Haderslev** Denmark
91 C1 **Hadyach** Ukr.
65 B2 **Haeju** N. Korea
65 B2 **Haeju-man** *b.* N. Korea
65 B3 **Haenam** S. Korea
78 B2 **Ḥafar al Bāṭin** Saudi Arabia
62 A1 **Haflong** India
92 A3 **Hafnarfjörður** Iceland
78 A3 **Hagar Nish Plateau** Eritrea/Sudan
48 D2 **Hagåtña** Guam
100 C2 **Hagen** Ger.
101 E1 **Hagenow** Ger.
128 B2 **Hagensborg** Can.
141 D3 **Hagerstown** U.S.A.
93 F3 **Hagfors** Sweden
67 B4 **Hagi** Japan
62 B1 **Ha Giang** Vietnam
97 B2 **Hag's Head** Ireland
104 B2 **Hague, Cap de la** *c.* France
119 D3 **Hai** Tanz.
62 B1 **Hai Dương** Vietnam
80 B2 **Haifa** Israel
71 B3 **Haifeng** China
71 B3 **Haikou** China
78 B2 **Ḥā'il** Saudi Arabia
92 H2 **Hailuoto** *i.* Fin.
69 D3 **Hainan** *i.* China
71 A4 **Hainan** *prov.* China
128 A2 **Haines** U.S.A.
128 A1 **Haines Junction** Can.
101 E2 **Hainich** *ridge* Ger.
101 E2 **Hainleite** *ridge* Ger.
62 B1 **Hai Phong** Vietnam
147 C3 **Haiti** *country* West Indies
116 B3 **Haiya** Sudan
103 E2 **Hajdúböszörmény** Hungary
78 B3 **Ḥajjah** Yemen
79 C2 **Ḥājjīābād** Iran
62 A1 **Haka** Myanmar
81 C2 **Hakkârı** Turkey
66 D2 **Hakodate** Japan
Ḥalab Syria *see* **Aleppo**
78 B2 **Halabān** Saudi Arabia
81 C2 **Ḥalabja** Iraq
116 B2 **Halaib** Sudan
78 A2 **Halaib Triangle** *terr.* Egypt/Sudan
79 C3 **Ḥalāniyāt, Juzur al** *is* Oman
78 A2 **Ḥālat 'Ammār** Saudi Arabia
101 E2 **Halberstadt** Ger.
64 B1 **Halcon, Mount** Phil.
93 F4 **Halden** Norway
101 E1 **Haldensleben** Ger.
75 B2 **Haldwani** India
79 C2 **Hāleh** Iran
54 A3 **Halfmoon Bay** N.Z.
131 D2 **Halifax** Can.

98 C2 **Halifax** U.K.
141 D3 **Halifax** U.S.A.
65 B3 **Halla-san** *mt.* S. Korea
127 F2 **Hall Beach** Can.
100 B2 **Halle** Belgium
101 E2 **Halle (Saale)** Ger.
102 C2 **Hallein** Austria
137 D1 **Hallock** U.S.A.
127 G2 **Hall Peninsula** Can.
50 B1 **Halls Creek** Austr.
59 C2 **Halmahera** *i.* Indon.
93 F4 **Halmstad** Sweden
62 B1 **Ha Long** Vietnam
67 B4 **Hamada** Japan
81 C2 **Hamadān** Iran
80 B2 **Ḩamāh** Syria
67 C4 **Hamamatsu** Japan
93 F3 **Hamar** Norway
116 B2 **Ḩamāţah, Jabal** *mt.* Egypt
73 C4 **Hambantota** Sri Lanka
101 D1 **Hamburg** Ger.
78 A2 **Ḩamḑ, Wādī al** *watercourse* Saudi Arabia
78 B3 **Ḩamḑah** Saudi Arabia
93 H3 **Hämeenlinna** Fin.
101 D1 **Hameln** Ger.
50 A2 **Hamersley Range** *mts* Austr.
65 B2 **Hamhŭng** N. Korea
68 C2 **Hami** China
116 B2 **Hamid** Sudan
52 B3 **Hamilton** Austr.
130 C2 **Hamilton** Can.
54 C1 **Hamilton** N.Z.
96 B3 **Hamilton** U.K.
142 C2 **Hamilton** *AL* U.S.A.
134 D1 **Hamilton** *MT* U.S.A.
140 C3 **Hamilton** *OH* U.S.A.
93 I3 **Hamina** Fin.
100 C2 **Hamm** Ger.
81 C2 **Ḩammār, Hawr al** *imp. l.* Iraq
101 D2 **Hammelburg** Ger.
92 G3 **Hammerdal** Sweden
92 H1 **Hammerfest** Norway
142 B2 **Hammond** U.S.A.
141 E3 **Hammonton** U.S.A.
115 D2 **Ḩamrā', Al Ḩamādah al** *plat.* Libya
78 A2 **Ḩanak** Saudi Arabia
66 D3 **Hanamaki** Japan
101 D2 **Hanau** Ger.
69 D2 **Hanbogd** Mongolia
70 B2 **Hancheng** China
140 B1 **Hancock** U.S.A.
70 B2 **Handan** China
135 C3 **Hanford** U.S.A.
68 C1 **Hangayn Nuruu** *mts* Mongolia
Hanggin Houqi China *see* **Xamba**
Hangö Fin. *see* **Hanko**
70 C2 **Hangzhou** China
70 C2 **Hangzhou Wan** *b.* China
Hanjia China *see* **Pengshui**
Hanjiang China *see* **Yangzhou**
93 H4 **Hanko** Fin.
135 D3 **Hanksville** U.S.A.
54 B2 **Hanmer Springs** N.Z.
129 C2 **Hanna** Can.
137 E3 **Hannibal** U.S.A.
101 D1 **Hannover** Ger.
101 D2 **Hannoversch Münden** Ger.
93 F4 **Hanöbukten** *b.* Sweden
62 B1 **Ha Nôi** Vietnam
Hanoi Vietnam *see* **Ha Nôi**
130 B2 **Hanover** Can.
122 B3 **Hanover** S. Africa
93 E4 **Hanstholm** Denmark
88 C3 **Hantsavichy** Belarus
75 C2 **Hanumana** India
74 B2 **Hanumangarh** India
70 A2 **Hanzhong** China
92 H2 **Haparanda** Sweden
100 B2 **Hapert** Neth.
131 D1 **Happy Valley-Goose Bay** Can.
78 A2 **Ḩaql** Saudi Arabia
79 B2 **Ḩaraḑh** Saudi Arabia
88 C2 **Haradok** Belarus
78 B3 **Ḩarajā** Saudi Arabia
121 C2 **Harare** Zimbabwe
79 C3 **Ḩarāsīs, Jiddat al** *des.* Oman
69 D1 **Har-Ayrag** Mongolia
69 E1 **Harbin** China
131 E2 **Harbour Breton** Can.
74 B2 **Harda** India
Hardangerfjorden *sea chan.* Norway
100 C1 **Hardenberg** Neth.
100 B1 **Harderwijk** Neth.
122 A3 **Hardeveld** *mts* S. Africa
134 E1 **Hardin** U.S.A.
128 C1 **Hardisty Lake** Can.
100 C1 **Haren (Ems)** Ger.
117 C4 **Hārer** Eth.
117 C4 **Hargeysa** Somalia
110 C1 **Harghita-Mădăraş, Vârful** *mt.* Romania
68 C2 **Har Hu** *l.* China
74 B1 **Haripur** Pak.
74 A1 **Hari Rūd** *r.* Afgh./Iran
100 B1 **Harlingen** Neth.
139 D3 **Harlingen** U.S.A.
99 D3 **Harlow** U.K.
134 E1 **Harlowton** U.S.A.
134 C2 **Harney Basin** U.S.A.
134 C2 **Harney Lake** U.S.A.
93 G3 **Härnösand** Sweden
69 E1 **Har Nur** China
68 C1 **Har Nuur** *l.* Mongolia
114 B4 **Harper** Liberia
101 D1 **Harpstedt** Ger.
130 C1 **Harricana, Rivière d'** *r.* Can.
53 D2 **Harrington** Austr.
131 E1 **Harrington Harbour** Can.
96 A2 **Harris, Sound of** *sea chan.* U.K.
140 B3 **Harrisburg** *IL* U.S.A.
141 D2 **Harrisburg** *PA* U.S.A.
123 C2 **Harrismith** S. Africa
142 B1 **Harrison** U.S.A.
131 E1 **Harrison, Cape** Can.
126 A2 **Harrison Bay** U.S.A.
141 D3 **Harrisonburg** U.S.A.
137 E3 **Harrisonville** U.S.A.
98 C2 **Harrogate** U.K.
110 C2 **Hârşova** Romania
92 G2 **Harstad** Norway
122 B2 **Hartbees** *watercourse* S. Africa
103 D2 **Hartberg** Austria
141 E2 **Hartford** U.S.A.
99 A3 **Hartland Point** U.K.
98 C1 **Hartlepool** U.K.
128 B2 **Hartley Bay** Can.
123 B2 **Harts** *r.* S. Africa
143 D2 **Hartwell Reservoir** U.S.A.
68 C1 **Har Us Nuur** *l.* Mongolia
136 C1 **Harvey** U.S.A.
99 D3 **Harwich** U.K.
101 E2 **Harz** *hills* Ger.
73 B3 **Hassan** India
100 B2 **Hasselt** Belgium
115 C1 **Hassi Messaoud** Alg.
93 F4 **Hässleholm** Sweden
100 B2 **Hastière-Lavaux** Belgium
53 C3 **Hastings** Austr.
54 C1 **Hastings** N.Z.
99 D3 **Hastings** U.K.
137 E2 **Hastings** *MN* U.S.A.
137 D2 **Hastings** *NE* U.S.A.
Hatay Turkey *see* **Antakya**
129 D2 **Hatchet Lake** Can.
52 B2 **Hatfield** Austr.
68 C1 **Hatgal** Mongolia
62 B2 **Ha Tinh** Vietnam
143 E1 **Hatteras, Cape** U.S.A.
142 C2 **Hattiesburg** U.S.A.
100 C2 **Hattingen** Ger.
63 B3 **Hat Yai** Thai.
117 C4 **Haud** *reg.* Eth.
93 E4 **Haugesund** Norway
93 E4 **Haukeligrend** Norway
92 I2 **Haukipudas** Fin.
54 C1 **Hauraki Gulf** N.Z.
114 B1 **Haut Atlas** *mts* Morocco
131 D2 **Hauterive** Can.
114 B1 **Hauts Plateaux** Alg.
146 B2 **Havana** Cuba
99 C3 **Havant** U.K.
101 E1 **Havel** *r.* Ger.
101 F1 **Havelberg** Ger.
54 B2 **Havelock** N.Z.
54 C1 **Havelock North** N.Z.
99 A3 **Haverfordwest** U.K.
103 D2 **Havlíčkův Brod** Czech Re
92 H1 **Havøysund** Norway
111 C3 **Havran** Turkey
134 E1 **Havre** U.S.A.
131 D2 **Havre-Aubert** Can.
131 D1 **Havre-St-Pierre** Can.
124 E5 **Hawai'i** *i.* U.S.A.
124 E5 **Hawai'ian Islands** N. Pac. Ocean
98 B2 **Hawarden** U.K.
54 A2 **Hawea, Lake** N.Z.
54 B1 **Hawera** N.Z.
98 B1 **Hawes** U.K.
96 C3 **Hawick** U.K.
54 C1 **Hawke Bay** N.Z.
52 A2 **Hawker** Austr.
52 B1 **Hawkers Gate** Austr.
135 C3 **Hawthorne** U.S.A.
52 B2 **Hay** Austr.
128 C1 **Hay** *r.* Can.
134 C1 **Hayden** U.S.A.
129 E2 **Hayes** *r. Man.* Can.
126 E2 **Hayes** *r. Nunavut* Can.
79 C3 **Haymā'** Oman
77 C2 **Hayotboshi tog'i** *mt.* Uzb
111 C2 **Hayrabolu** Turkey
128 C1 **Hay River** Can.
137 D3 **Hays** U.S.A.
78 B3 **Ḩays** Yemen
90 B2 **Haysyn** Ukr.
99 C3 **Haywards Heath** U.K.
81 D2 **Hazar** Turkm.
74 A1 **Hazarajat** *reg.* Afgh.
140 C3 **Hazard** U.S.A.
75 C2 **Hazaribagh** India
75 C2 **Hazaribagh Range** *mts* In
128 B2 **Hazelton** Can.
141 D2 **Hazleton** U.S.A.
53 C3 **Healesville** Austr.
130 B2 **Hearst** Can.
70 B2 **Hebei** *prov.* China
53 C1 **Hebel** Austr.
142 B1 **Heber Springs** U.S.A.
70 B2 **Hebi** China
131 D1 **Hebron** Can.
128 A2 **Hecate Strait** Can.
71 A3 **Hechi** China
93 F3 **Hede** Sweden
100 B1 **Heerenveen** Neth.

00 B1 **Heerhugowaard** Neth.
00 B2 **Heerlen** Neth.
Hefa Israel *see* **Haifa**
70 B2 **Hefei** China
70 B3 **Hefeng** China
59 E1 **Hegang** China
02 B1 **Heide** Ger.
22 A1 **Heide** Namibia
02 B2 **Heidelberg** Ger.
22 B3 **Heidelberg** S. Africa
02 B2 **Heilbronn** Ger.
59 E1 **Heilong Jiang** *r.* China
93 I3 **Heinola** Fin.
92 F3 **Helagsfjället** *mt.* Sweden
42 B2 **Helena** *AR* U.S.A.
34 D1 **Helena** *MT* U.S.A.
96 B2 **Helensburgh** U.K.
02 B1 **Helgoland** *i.* Ger.
02 B1 **Helgoländer Bucht** *g.* Ger.
Helixi China *see* **Ningguo**
92 A3 **Hella** Iceland
00 B2 **Hellevoetsluis** Neth.
07 C2 **Hellín** Spain
76 C3 **Helmand** *r.* Afgh.
01 E2 **Helmbrechts** Ger.
22 A2 **Helmeringhausen** Namibia
00 B2 **Helmond** Neth.
96 C1 **Helmsdale** U.K.
96 C1 **Helmsdale** *r.* U.K.
01 E1 **Helmstedt** Ger.
65 B1 **Helong** China
93 F4 **Helsingborg** Sweden
Helsingfors Fin. *see* **Helsinki**
93 F4 **Helsingør** Denmark
93 H3 **Helsinki** Fin.
97 C2 **Helvick Head** Ireland
99 C3 **Hemel Hempstead** U.K.
01 D1 **Hemmoor** Ger.
92 F2 **Hemnesberget** Norway
70 B2 **Henan** *prov.* China
40 B3 **Henderson** *KY* U.S.A.
43 E1 **Henderson** *NC* U.S.A.
35 D3 **Henderson** *NV* U.S.A.
39 E2 **Henderson** *TX* U.S.A.
43 D1 **Hendersonville** U.S.A.
99 C3 **Hendon** U.K.
62 A1 **Hengduan Shan** *mts* China
00 C1 **Hengelo** Neth.
Hengnan China *see* **Hengyang**
70 B2 **Hengshui** China
71 A3 **Hengxian** China
71 B3 **Hengyang** China
Hengzhou China *see* **Hengxian**
91 C2 **Heniches'k** Ukr.
00 C2 **Hennef (Sieg)** Ger.
30 B1 **Henrietta Maria, Cape** Can.
39 D1 **Henryetta** U.S.A.
27 G2 **Henry Kater, Cape** Can.
01 D1 **Henstedt-Ulzburg** Ger.
20 A3 **Hentiesbaai** Namibia
71 A3 **Hepu** China
76 C3 **Herāt** Afgh.
29 D2 **Herbert** Can.
01 D2 **Herbstein** Ger.
99 B2 **Hereford** U.K.
39 C2 **Hereford** U.S.A.
01 D1 **Herford** Ger.
00 C2 **Herkenbosch** Neth.
96 □ **Herma Ness** *hd* U.K.
22 A3 **Hermanus** S. Africa
53 C2 **Hermidale** Austr.
34 C1 **Hermiston** U.S.A.
59 D3 **Hermit Islands** P.N.G.
44 A2 **Hermosillo** Mex.
54 B3 **Hernandarias** Para.
00 C2 **Herne** Ger.

93 E4 **Herning** Denmark
99 C3 **Hertford** U.K.
123 C2 **Hertzogville** S. Africa
51 E2 **Hervey Bay** Austr.
101 F2 **Herzberg** Ger.
101 E3 **Herzogenaurach** Ger.
71 A3 **Heshan** China
128 A1 **Hess** *r.* Can.
101 D2 **Hessisch Lichtenau** Ger.
136 C1 **Hettinger** U.S.A.
101 E2 **Hettstedt** Ger.
98 B1 **Hexham** U.K.
71 B3 **Heyuan** China
52 B3 **Heywood** Austr.
70 B2 **Heze** China
71 B3 **Hezhou** China
137 D3 **Hiawatha** U.S.A.
137 E1 **Hibbing** U.S.A.
54 C1 **Hicks Bay** N.Z.
66 D2 **Hidaka-sanmyaku** *mts* Japan
145 C2 **Hidalgo** Mex.
144 B2 **Hidalgo del Parral** Mex.
154 C1 **Hidrolândia** Brazil
High Atlas *mts* Morocco *see* **Haut Atlas**
134 B2 **High Desert** U.S.A.
128 C2 **High Level** Can.
143 E1 **High Point** U.S.A.
128 C2 **High Prairie** Can.
128 C2 **High River** Can.
129 D2 **Highrock Lake** Can.
99 C3 **High Wycombe** U.K.
88 B2 **Hiiumaa** *i.* Estonia
78 A2 **Hijaz** *reg.* Saudi Arabia
54 C1 **Hikurangi** *mt.* N.Z.
101 E2 **Hildburghausen** Ger.
101 E2 **Hilders** Ger.
101 D1 **Hildesheim** Ger.
81 C2 **Hillah** Iraq
100 C2 **Hillesheim** Ger.
140 C3 **Hillsboro** *OH* U.S.A.
139 D2 **Hillsboro** *TX* U.S.A.
53 C2 **Hillston** Austr.
143 D2 **Hilton Head Island** U.S.A.
100 B1 **Hilversum** Neth.
68 B2 **Himalaya** *mts* Asia
67 B4 **Himeji** Japan
123 C2 **Himeville** S. Africa
51 D1 **Hinchinbrook Island** Austr.
74 A1 **Hindu Kush** *mts* Afgh./Pak.
143 D2 **Hinesville** U.S.A.
75 B2 **Hinganghat** India
81 C2 **Hınıs** Turkey
92 G2 **Hinnøya** *i.* Norway
106 B2 **Hinojosa del Duque** Spain
62 A2 **Hinthada** Myanmar
128 C2 **Hinton** Can.
75 C2 **Hirakud Reservoir** India
66 D2 **Hirosaki** Japan
67 B4 **Hiroshima** Japan
101 E3 **Hirschaid** Ger.
101 E2 **Hirschberg** Ger.
105 C2 **Hirson** France
93 E4 **Hirtshals** Denmark
74 B2 **Hisar** India
147 C2 **Hispaniola** *i.* Caribbean Sea
81 C2 **Hīt** Iraq
67 D3 **Hitachi** Japan
67 D3 **Hitachinaka** Japan
92 E3 **Hitra** *i.* Norway
49 I3 **Hiva Oa** *i.* Fr. Polynesia
93 G4 **Hjälmaren** *l.* Sweden
129 D1 **Hjalmar Lake** Can.
93 F4 **Hjørring** Denmark
123 D2 **Hlabisa** S. Africa
92 B2 **Hlíð** Iceland
91 C2 **Hlobyne** Ukr.

123 C2 **Hlohlowane** S. Africa
123 C2 **Hlotse** Lesotho
91 C1 **Hlukhiv** Ukr.
88 C2 **Hlybokaye** Belarus
114 C4 **Ho** Ghana
62 B2 **Hoa Binh** Vietnam
122 A1 **Hoachanas** Namibia
51 D4 **Hobart** Austr.
139 D1 **Hobart** U.S.A.
139 C2 **Hobbs** U.S.A.
93 E4 **Hobro** Denmark
117 C4 **Hobyo** Somalia
63 B2 **Ho Chi Minh City** Vietnam
114 B3 **Hôḍ** *reg.* Maur.
78 B3 **Hodeidah** Yemen
103 E2 **Hódmezővásárhely** Hungary
Hoek van Holland Neth. *see* **Hook of Holland**
65 B2 **Hoeyang** N. Korea
101 E2 **Hof** Ger.
101 E2 **Hofheim in Unterfranken** Ger.
92 B3 **Höfn** *Austurland* Iceland
92 A2 **Höfn** *Vestfirðir* Iceland
92 B3 **Hofsjökull** Iceland
67 B4 **Hōfu** Japan
115 C2 **Hoggar** *plat.* Alg.
93 G4 **Högsby** Sweden
101 D2 **Hohe Rhön** *mts* Ger.
100 C2 **Hohe Venn** *moorland* Belgium
70 B1 **Hohhot** China
75 C1 **Hoh Xil Shan** *mts* China
63 B2 **Hôi An** Vietnam
62 A1 **Hojai** India
54 B2 **Hokitika** N.Z.
66 D2 **Hokkaidō** *i.* Japan
128 B2 **Holberg** Can.
138 A2 **Holbrook** U.S.A.
137 D2 **Holdrege** U.S.A.
146 C2 **Holguín** Cuba
92 B2 **Hóll** Iceland
Holland *country* Europe *see* **Netherlands**
140 B2 **Holland** U.S.A.
100 B1 **Hollum** Neth.
142 C2 **Holly Springs** U.S.A.
134 C4 **Hollywood** U.S.A.
143 D3 **Hollywood** U.S.A.
92 F2 **Holm** Norway
92 H3 **Holmsund** Sweden
122 A2 **Holoog** Namibia
93 E4 **Holstebro** Denmark
143 D1 **Holston** *r.* U.S.A.
98 A2 **Holyhead** U.K.
98 C1 **Holy Island** *England* U.K.
98 A2 **Holy Island** *Wales* U.K.
136 C2 **Holyoke** U.S.A.
101 D2 **Holzminden** Ger.
62 A1 **Homalin** Myanmar
101 D2 **Homberg (Efze)** Ger.
114 B3 **Hombori** Mali
127 G2 **Home Bay** Can.
143 D3 **Homestead** U.S.A.
92 F3 **Hommelvik** Norway
80 B2 **Homs** Syria
89 D3 **Homyel'** Belarus
122 A3 **Hondeklipbaai** S. Africa
145 D3 **Hondo** *r.* Belize/Mex.
139 D3 **Hondo** U.S.A.
146 B3 **Honduras** *country* Central America
93 F3 **Hønefoss** Norway
135 B2 **Honey Lake** U.S.A.
104 C2 **Honfleur** France
70 B3 **Honghu** China
71 A3 **Hongjiang** China
69 D3 **Hong Kong** China

Hong Kong

71 B3 Hong Kong *aut. reg.* China
65 B1 Hongwŏn N. Korea
70 B2 Hongze Hu *l.* China
49 E3 Honiara Solomon Is
66 D3 Honjō Japan
92 I1 Honningsvåg Norway
67 B3 Honshū *i.* Japan
134 B1 Hood, Mount *vol.* U.S.A.
50 A3 Hood Point Austr.
134 B1 Hood River U.S.A.
100 C1 Hoogeveen Neth.
100 C1 Hoogezand-Sappemeer Neth.
100 C2 Hoog-Keppel Neth.
100 B2 Hook of Holland Neth.
128 A2 Hoonah U.S.A.
100 B1 Hoorn Neth.
128 B3 Hope Can.
142 B2 Hope U.S.A.
83 N2 Hope, Point U.S.A.
131 D1 Hopedale Can.
131 D1 Hope Mountains Can.
52 B3 Hopetoun Austr.
122 B2 Hopetown S. Africa
141 D3 Hopewell U.S.A.
130 C1 Hopewell Islands Can.
50 B2 Hopkins, Lake *imp. l.* Austr.
140 B3 Hopkinsville U.S.A.
134 B1 Hoquiam U.S.A.
81 C1 Horasan Turkey
93 F4 Hörby Sweden
89 D3 Horki Belarus
91 D2 Horlivka Ukr.
79 D2 Hormak Iran
79 C2 Hormuz, Strait of Iran/Oman
103 D2 Horn Austria
92 A2 Horn *c.* Iceland
153 B6 Horn, Cape Chile
141 D2 Hornell U.S.A.
130 B2 Hornepayne Can.
98 C2 Hornsea U.K.
90 B2 Horodenka Ukr.
91 C1 Horodnya Ukr.
90 B2 Horodok *Khmel'nyts'ka Oblast'* Ukr.
90 A2 Horodok *L'vivs'ka Oblast'* Ukr.
90 A1 Horokhiv Ukr.
        Horqin Youyi Qianqi China *see* Ulanhot
131 E1 Horse Islands Can.
52 B3 Horsham Austr.
126 C2 Horton *r.* Can.
117 B4 Hosa'ina Eth.
74 A2 Hoshab Pak.
74 B1 Hoshiarpur India
77 E3 Hotan China
122 B2 Hotazel S. Africa
142 B2 Hot Springs *AR* U.S.A.
136 C2 Hot Springs *SD* U.S.A.
128 C1 Hottah Lake Can.
62 B2 Houayxay Laos
100 B2 Houffalize Belgium
70 B2 Houma China
142 B3 Houma U.S.A.
128 B2 Houston Can.
139 D3 Houston U.S.A.
122 B3 Houwater S. Africa
68 C1 Hovd Mongolia
99 C3 Hove U.K.
68 C1 Hövsgöl Nuur *l.* Mongolia
116 A3 Howar, Wadi *watercourse* Sudan
53 C3 Howe, Cape Austr.
49 G2 Howland Island N. Pacific Ocean
53 C3 Howlong Austr.
101 D2 Höxter Ger.

96 C1 Hoy *i.* U.K.
93 E3 Høyanger Norway
102 C1 Hoyerswerda Ger.
62 A2 Hpapun Myanmar
103 D1 Hradec Králové Czech Rep.
109 C2 Hrasnica Bos.-Herz.
91 C1 Hrebinka Ukr.
88 B3 Hrodna Belarus
62 A1 Hsi-hseng Myanmar
71 C3 Hsinchu Taiwan
62 A1 Hsinying Taiwan
62 A1 Hsipaw Myanmar
70 A2 Huachi China
150 A3 Huacho Peru
69 D2 Huade China
65 B1 Huadian China
70 B2 Huai'an China
70 B2 Huaibei China
71 A3 Huaihua China
70 B2 Huainan China
70 B2 Huaiyang China
145 C3 Huajuápan de León Mex.
59 C3 Huaki Indon.
71 C3 Hualien Taiwan
150 A2 Huallaga *r.* Peru
120 A2 Huambo Angola
150 A3 Huancayo Peru
        Huangcaoba China *see* Xingyi
70 B2 Huangchuan China
        Huang Hai *sea* N. Pacific Ocean *see* Yellow Sea
        Huang He *r.* China *see* Yellow River
71 A4 Huangliu China
70 B3 Huangshan China
70 B2 Huangshi China
70 A2 Huangtu Gaoyuan *plat.* China
70 A2 Huangyan China
70 A2 Huanren China
150 A2 Huanuco Peru
152 B2 Huanuni Bol.
150 A2 Huaráz Peru
150 A3 Huarmey Peru
152 A3 Huasco Chile
152 A3 Huasco *r.* Chile
144 B2 Huatabampo Mex.
145 C3 Huatusco Mex.
71 A3 Huayuan China
70 B2 Hubei *prov.* China
73 B3 Hubli India
100 C2 Hückelhoven Ger.
98 C2 Hucknall U.K.
98 C2 Huddersfield U.K.
93 G3 Hudiksvall Sweden
141 E2 Hudson *r.* U.S.A.
129 D2 Hudson Bay Can.
127 F3 Hudson Bay *sea* Can.
128 B2 Hudson's Hope Can.
127 G2 Hudson Strait Can.
63 B2 Huê Vietnam
146 A3 Huehuetenango Guat.
144 B2 Huehueto, Cerro *mt.* Mex.
145 C2 Huejutla Mex.
106 B2 Huelva Spain
107 C2 Huércal-Overa Spain
107 C1 Huesca Spain
106 C2 Huéscar Spain
50 B3 Hughes (abandoned) Austr.
139 D2 Hugo U.S.A.
122 B2 Huib-Hoch Plateau Namibia
71 B3 Huichang China
65 B1 Huich'ŏn N. Korea
120 A2 Huíla, Planalto da Angola
71 B3 Huilai China

62 B1 Huili China
65 B1 Huinan China
93 H3 Huittinen Fin.
145 C3 Huixtla Mex.
        Huiyang China *see* Huizhou
62 B1 Huize China
71 B3 Huizhou China
78 B2 Hujr Saudi Arabia
122 B1 Hukuntsi Botswana
78 B2 Ḥulayfah Saudi Arabia
66 B1 Hulin China
130 C2 Hull Can.
        Hulun China *see* Hulun Buir
69 D1 Hulun Buir China
69 D1 Hulun Nur *l.* China
91 D2 Hulyaypole Ukr.
69 E1 Huma China
150 B2 Humaitá Brazil
122 B3 Humansdorp S. Africa
98 C2 Humber *est.* U.K.
126 D3 Humboldt Can.
142 C1 Humboldt U.S.A.
135 C2 Humboldt *r.* U.S.A.
103 E2 Humenné Slovakia
53 C3 Hume Reservoir Austr.
138 A1 Humphreys Peak U.S.A.
92 A2 Húnaflói *b.* Iceland
71 B3 Hunan *prov.* China
65 C1 Hunchun China
110 B1 Hunedoara Romania
101 D2 Hünfeld Ger.
103 D2 Hungary *country* Europe
52 B1 Hungerford Austr.
65 B2 Hŭngnam N. Korea
65 A1 Hun He *r.* China
99 D2 Hunstanton U.K.
101 D1 Hunte *r.* Ger.
51 D4 Hunter Islands Austr.
99 C2 Huntingdon U.K.
140 B2 Huntington *IN* U.S.A.
140 C3 Huntington *WV* U.S.A.
54 C1 Huntly N.Z.
96 C2 Huntly U.K.
130 C2 Huntsville Can.
142 C2 Huntsville *AL* U.S.A.
139 D2 Huntsville *TX* U.S.A.
59 D3 Huon Peninsula P.N.G.
70 B2 Huozhou China
137 D2 Huron U.S.A.
140 C2 Huron, Lake Can./U.S.A.
135 D3 Hurricane U.S.A.
92 B2 Húsavík Iceland
110 C1 Huşi Romania
126 A2 Huslia U.S.A.
78 B3 Ḥusn Āl 'Abr Yemen
102 B1 Husum Ger.
69 C1 Hutag-Öndör Mongolia
60 A1 Hutanopan Indon.
137 D3 Hutchinson U.S.A.
70 C2 Huzhou China
92 C3 Hvalnes Iceland
92 B3 Hvannadalshnúkur *vol.* Iceland
109 C2 Hvar *i.* Croatia
120 B2 Hwange Zimbabwe
136 C2 Hyannis U.S.A.
68 C1 Hyargas Nuur *salt l.* Mongolia
50 A3 Hyden Austr.
73 B3 Hyderabad India
74 A2 Hyderabad Pak.
105 D3 Hyères France
105 D3 Hyères, Îles d' *is* France
65 B1 Hyesan N. Korea
128 B2 Hyland Post Can.
67 B3 Hyōno-sen *mt.* Japan

9 D3 **Hythe** U.K.
3 H3 **Hyvinkää** Fin.

I

0 B2 **Iaco** *r.* Brazil
0 C2 **Ialomița** *r.* Romania
0 C1 **Ianca** Romania
0 C1 **Iași** Romania
4 A1 **Iba** Phil.
5 C4 **Ibadan** Nigeria
0 A1 **Ibagué** Col.
0 A1 **Ibarra** Ecuador
8 B3 **Ibb** Yemen
0 C1 **Ibbenbüren** Ger.
5 C4 **Ibi** Nigeria
5 C1 **Ibiá** Brazil
5 D1 **Ibiraçu** Brazil
7 D2 **Ibiza** Spain
7 D2 **Ibiza** *i.* Spain
1 D3 **Ibotirama** Brazil
9 C2 **Ibrā'** Oman
9 C2 **Ibrī** Oman
0 A3 **Ica** Peru
2 B2 **Iceland** *country* Europe
6 D3 **Ichinoseki** Japan
1 C1 **Ichnya** Ukr.
5 B2 **Ich'ŏn** N. Korea
9 E2 **Idabel** U.S.A.
4 D2 **Idaho** *state* U.S.A.
4 D2 **Idaho Falls** U.S.A.
0 C3 **Idar-Oberstein** Ger.
6 B2 **Idfū** Egypt
8 B3 **Idiofa** Dem. Rep. Congo
0 B2 **Idlib** Syria
4 B2 **Iepê** Brazil
0 A2 **Ieper** Belgium
9 D3 **Ifakara** Tanz.
1 D3 **Ifanadiana** Madag.
5 C4 **Ife** Nigeria
4 C3 **Ifôghas, Adrar des** *hills* Mali
1 C1 **Igan** *Sarawak* Malaysia
4 C2 **Igarapava** Brazil
2 G2 **Igarka** Rus. Fed.
4 B3 **Igatpuri** India
1 C2 **Iğdır** Turkey
8 A3 **Iglesias** *Sardegna* Italy
7 F2 **Igloolik** Can.
Igluligaarjuk Can. *see* **Chesterfield Inlet**
0 A2 **Ignace** Can.
8 C2 **Ignalina** Lith.
0 C2 **İğneada** Turkey
1 B3 **Igoumenitsa** Greece
6 E3 **Igra** Rus. Fed.
6 F2 **Igrim** Rus. Fed.
4 B3 **Iguaçu** *r.* Brazil
4 B3 **Iguaçu Falls** Arg./Brazil
5 C3 **Iguala** Mex.
7 D1 **Igualada** Spain
4 C2 **Iguape** Brazil
4 B2 **Iguatemi** Brazil
4 B2 **Iguatemi** *r.* Brazil
1 E2 **Iguatu** Brazil
8 A3 **Iguéla** Gabon
9 D3 **Igunga** Tanz.
1 D3 **Ihosy** Madag.
2 I3 **Iisalmi** Fin.
5 C4 **Ijebu-Ode** Nigeria
0 B1 **IJmuiden** Neth.
0 B1 **IJssel** *r.* Neth.
0 B1 **IJsselmeer** *l.* Neth.
3 C2 **Ikageng** S. Africa
1 C3 **Ikaria** *i.* Greece
8 C3 **Ikela** Dem. Rep. Congo
110 B2 **Ikhtiman** Bulg.
67 A4 **Iki-shima** *i.* Japan
121 D3 **Ikongo** Madag.
65 B2 **Iksan** S. Korea
64 B1 **Ilagan** Phil.
81 C2 **Īlām** Iran
75 C2 **Ilam** Nepal
103 D1 **Iława** Pol.
79 C2 **Ilazārān, Kūh-e** *mt.* Iran
129 D2 **Île-à-la-Crosse** Can.
129 D2 **Île-à-la-Crosse, Lac** *l.* Can.
118 C3 **Ilebo** Dem. Rep. Congo
124 H6 **Île Clipperton** *terr.* N. Pacific Ocean
119 D2 **Ileret** Kenya
113 K11 **Îles Crozet** *is* Indian Ocean
49 I3 **Îles du Désappointement** *is* Fr. Polynesia
49 I4 **Îles Gambier** *is* Fr. Polynesia
99 D3 **Ilford** U.K.
99 A3 **Ilfracombe** U.K.
155 D2 **Ilha Grande, Baía da** *b.* Brazil
154 B2 **Ilha Grande, Represa** *resr* Brazil
154 B2 **Ilha Solteíra, Represa** *resr* Brazil
106 B1 **Ílhavo** Port.
151 E3 **Ilhéus** Brazil
64 B2 **Iligan** Phil.
152 A4 **Illapel** Chile
90 C2 **Illichivs'k** Ukr.
140 A3 **Illinois** *r.* U.S.A.
140 B3 **Illinois** *state* U.S.A.
90 B2 **Illintsi** Ukr.
115 C2 **Illizi** Alg.
89 D2 **Il'men', Ozero** *l.* Rus. Fed.
101 E2 **Ilmenau** Ger.
150 A3 **Ilo** Peru
64 B1 **Iloilo** Phil.
92 J3 **Ilomantsi** Fin.
115 C4 **Ilorin** Nigeria
53 D1 **Iluka** Austr.
127 H2 **Ilulissat** Greenland
67 A4 **Imari** Japan
117 C4 **Īmī** Eth.
108 B2 **Imola** Italy
151 D2 **Imperatriz** Brazil
136 C2 **Imperial** U.S.A.
118 B2 **Impfondo** Congo
62 A1 **Imphal** India
111 C2 **İmroz** Turkey
150 B3 **Inambari** *r.* Peru
115 C2 **In Aménas** Alg.
59 C3 **Inanwatan** Indon.
92 I2 **Inari** Fin.
92 I2 **Inarijärvi** *l.* Fin.
67 D3 **Inawashiro-ko** *l.* Japan
80 B1 **İnce Burun** *pt* Turkey
65 B2 **Inch'ŏn** S. Korea
123 D2 **Incomati** *r.* Moz.
78 A3 **Inda Silasē** Eth.
144 B2 **Indé** Mex.
135 C3 **Independence** *CA* U.S.A.
137 E2 **Independence** *IA* U.S.A.
137 D3 **Independence** *KS* U.S.A.
137 E3 **Independence** *MO* U.S.A.
134 C2 **Independence Mountains** U.S.A.
76 B2 **Inderborskiy** Kazakh.
72 B2 **India** *country* Asia
141 D2 **Indiana** U.S.A.
140 B2 **Indiana** *state* U.S.A.
140 B3 **Indianapolis** U.S.A.
129 D2 **Indian Head** Can.
159 **Indian Ocean** World
137 E2 **Indianola** *IA* U.S.A.
142 B2 **Indianola** *MS* U.S.A.
135 C3 **Indian Springs** U.S.A.
86 D2 **Indiga** Rus. Fed.
83 K2 **Indigirka** *r.* Rus. Fed.
109 D1 **Inđija** Serbia
135 C4 **Indio** U.S.A.
58 B3 **Indonesia** *country* Asia
74 B2 **Indore** India
61 B2 **Indramayu, Tanjung** *pt* Indon.
104 C2 **Indre** *r.* France
74 A2 **Indus** *r.* China/Pak.
74 A2 **Indus, Mouths of the** Pak.
80 B1 **İnebolu** Turkey
111 C2 **İnegöl** Turkey
144 B3 **Infiernillo, Presa** *resr* Mex.
53 D1 **Inglewood** Austr.
102 C2 **Ingolstadt** Ger.
75 C2 **Ingraj Bazar** India
123 D2 **Inhaca** Moz.
121 C3 **Inhambane** Moz.
97 A2 **Inishbofin** *i.* Ireland
97 B2 **Inishmore** *i.* Ireland
97 C1 **Inishowen** *pen.* Ireland
54 B2 **Inland Kaikoura Range** *mts* N.Z.
102 C2 **Inn** *r.* Europe
127 G1 **Innaanganeq** *c.* Greenland
96 B2 **Inner Sound** *sea chan.* U.K.
51 D1 **Innisfail** Austr.
102 C2 **Innsbruck** Austria
154 B1 **Inocência** Brazil
118 B3 **Inongo** Dem. Rep. Congo
103 D1 **Inowrocław** Pol.
114 C2 **In Salah** Alg.
62 A2 **Insein** Myanmar
86 F2 **Inta** Rus. Fed.
137 E1 **International Falls** U.S.A.
130 C1 **Inukjuak** Can.
126 C2 **Inuvik** Can.
96 B2 **Inveraray** U.K.
54 A3 **Invercargill** N.Z.
53 D1 **Inverell** Austr.
96 B2 **Invergordon** U.K.
128 C2 **Invermere** Can.
131 D2 **Inverness** Can.
96 B2 **Inverness** U.K.
96 C2 **Inverurie** U.K.
52 A3 **Investigator Strait** Austr.
77 E1 **Inya** Rus. Fed.
119 D3 **Inyonga** Tanz.
87 D3 **Inza** Rus. Fed.
111 B3 **Ioannina** Greece
137 D3 **Iola** U.S.A.
96 A2 **Iona** *i.* U.K.
111 B3 **Ionian Islands** Greece
109 C3 **Ionian Sea** Greece/Italy
Ionioi Nisoi *is* Greece *see* **Ionian Islands**
111 C3 **Ios** *i.* Greece
137 E2 **Iowa** *state* U.S.A.
137 E2 **Iowa City** U.S.A.
154 C1 **Ipameri** Brazil
155 D1 **Ipatinga** Brazil
81 C1 **Ipatovo** Rus. Fed.
123 C2 **Ipelegeng** S. Africa
150 A1 **Ipiales** Col.
154 B3 **Ipiranga** Brazil
60 B1 **Ipoh** Malaysia
154 B1 **Iporá** Brazil
118 C2 **Ippy** C.A.R.
111 C2 **İpsala** Turkey
53 D1 **Ipswich** Austr.
99 D2 **Ipswich** U.K.
127 G2 **Iqaluit** Can.
152 A3 **Iquique** Chile
150 A2 **Iquitos** Peru
Irakleio Greece *see* **Iraklion**
111 C3 **Iraklion** Greece

76 B3 **Iran** *country* Asia
61 C1 **Iran, Pegunungan** *mts* Indon.
79 D2 **Īrānshahr** Iran
144 B2 **Irapuato** Mex.
81 C2 **Iraq** *country* Asia
154 B3 **Irati** Brazil
80 B2 **Irbid** Jordan
86 F3 **Irbit** Rus. Fed.
151 D3 **Irecê** Brazil
97 C2 **Ireland** *country* Europe
118 C3 **Irema** Dem. Rep. Congo
76 C2 **Irgiz** Kazakh.
114 B3 **Irîgui** *reg.* Mali/Maur.
119 D3 **Iringa** Tanz.
151 C2 **Iriri** *r.* Brazil
95 B3 **Irish Sea** Ireland/U.K.
69 C1 **Irkutsk** Rus. Fed.
52 A2 **Iron Knob** Austr.
140 B1 **Iron Mountain** U.S.A.
140 A1 **Ironwood** U.S.A.
64 B1 **Irosin** Phil.
67 C4 **Irō-zaki** *pt* Japan
90 C1 **Irpin'** Ukr.
62 A2 **Irrawaddy** *r.* Myanmar
63 A2 **Irrawaddy, Mouths of the** Myanmar
86 F2 **Irtysh** *r.* Kazakh./Rus. Fed.
107 C1 **Irun** Spain
96 B3 **Irvine** U.K.
64 B2 **Isabela** Phil.
146 B3 **Isabelia, Cordillera** *mts* Nic.
92 A2 **Ísafjörður** Iceland
67 B4 **Isahaya** Japan
105 E2 **Isar** *r.* Ger.
96 □ **Isbister** U.K.
108 B2 **Ischia, Isola d'** *i.* Italy
67 C4 **Ise** Japan
118 C2 **Isengi** Dem. Rep. Congo
100 C2 **Iserlohn** Ger.
101 D1 **Isernhagen** Ger.
67 C4 **Ise-wan** *b.* Japan
114 C4 **Iseyin** Nigeria
Isfahan Iran *see* **Eşfahān**
66 D2 **Ishikari-wan** *b.* Japan
77 D1 **Ishim** *r.* Kazakh./Rus. Fed.
66 D3 **Ishinomaki** Japan
67 D3 **Ishioka** Japan
140 B1 **Ishpeming** U.S.A.
111 C2 **Işıklar Dağı** *mts* Turkey
111 C3 **Işıklı** Turkey
123 D2 **Isipingo** S. Africa
119 C2 **Isiro** Dem. Rep. Congo
80 B2 **İskenderun** Turkey
82 G3 **Iskitim** Rus. Fed.
110 B2 **Iskŭr** *r.* Bulg.
128 A2 **Iskut** *r.* Can.
74 B1 **Islamabad** Pak.
52 A2 **Island Lagoon** *imp. l.* Austr.
129 E2 **Island Lake** Can.
54 B1 **Islands, Bay of** N.Z.
96 A3 **Islay** *i.* U.K.
98 A1 **Isle of Man** *i.* Irish Sea
77 D3 **Ismoili Somoní, Qullai** *mt.* Tajik.
109 C3 **Isola di Capo Rizzuto** Italy
110 C2 **Isperikh** Bulg.
80 B2 **Israel** *country* Asia
105 C2 **Issoire** France
111 C2 **İstanbul** Turkey
İstanbul Boğazı *str.* Turkey *see* **Bosporus**
111 B3 **Istiaia** Greece
105 C3 **Istres** France
108 B1 **Istria** *pen.* Croatia
151 D3 **Itaberaba** Brazil
155 D1 **Itabira** Brazil
155 D2 **Itabirito** Brazil
151 E3 **Itabuna** Brazil
150 C2 **Itacoatiara** Brazil
154 B2 **Itaguajé** Brazil
154 C2 **Itaí** Brazil
154 B3 **Itaipu, Represa de** *resr* Brazil
151 C2 **Itaituba** Brazil
152 D3 **Itajaí** Brazil
155 C2 **Itajubá** Brazil
108 B2 **Italy** *country* Europe
155 D1 **Itamarandiba** Brazil
155 D1 **Itambacuri** Brazil
155 D1 **Itambé, Pico de** *mt.* Brazil
62 A1 **Itanagar** India
154 C2 **Itanhaém** Brazil
155 D1 **Itanhém** Brazil
155 D1 **Itaobím** Brazil
154 C1 **Itapajipe** Brazil
155 E1 **Itapebi** Brazil
155 D2 **Itapemirim** Brazil
155 D2 **Itaperuna** Brazil
155 D1 **Itapetinga** Brazil
154 C2 **Itapetininga** Brazil
154 C2 **Itapeva** Brazil
151 E3 **Itapicuru** *r.* Brazil
151 D2 **Itapicuru Mirim** Brazil
154 C1 **Itapuranga** Brazil
154 C2 **Itararé** Brazil
75 B2 **Itarsi** India
154 B1 **Itarumã** Brazil
155 D2 **Itaúna** Brazil
71 C3 **Itbayat** *i.* Phil.
141 D2 **Ithaca** U.S.A.
101 D1 **Ith Hils** *ridge* Ger.
118 C2 **Itimbiri** *r.* Dem. Rep. Congo
155 D1 **Itinga** Brazil
154 B1 **Itiquira** Brazil
154 A1 **Itiquira** *r.* Brazil
67 C4 **Itō** Japan
154 C2 **Itu** Brazil
150 A2 **Ituí** *r.* Brazil
154 C1 **Ituiutaba** Brazil
119 C3 **Itula** Dem. Rep. Congo
154 C1 **Itumbiara** Brazil
154 B1 **Iturama** Brazil
101 D1 **Itzehoe** Ger.
83 N2 **Iul'tin** Rus. Fed.
154 B2 **Ivaí** *r.* Brazil
92 I2 **Ivalo** Fin.
88 C3 **Ivanava** Belarus
52 B2 **Ivanhoe** Austr.
90 B1 **Ivankiv** Ukr.
90 A2 **Ivano-Frankivs'k** Ukr.
89 F2 **Ivanovo** Rus. Fed.
88 C3 **Ivatsevichy** Belarus
111 C2 **Ivaylovgrad** Bulg.
86 F2 **Ivdel'** Rus. Fed.
154 B2 **Ivinheima** Brazil
154 B2 **Ivinheima** *r.* Brazil
127 H2 **Ivittuut** Greenland
Ivory Coast *country* Africa *see* **Côte d'Ivoire**
108 A1 **Ivrea** Italy
111 C3 **İvrindi** Turkey
127 F2 **Ivujivik** Can.
67 D3 **Iwaki** Japan
67 B4 **Iwakuni** Japan
66 D2 **Iwamizawa** Japan
66 D2 **Iwanai** Japan
88 C3 **Iwye** Belarus
123 D3 **Ixopo** S. Africa
144 B2 **Ixtlán** Mex.
145 D2 **Izamal** Mex.
81 C1 **Izberbash** Rus. Fed.
86 E3 **Izhevsk** Rus. Fed.
86 E2 **Izhma** Rus. Fed.
89 E3 **Izmalkovo** Rus. Fed.
90 B2 **Izmayil** Ukr.
111 C3 **İzmir** Turkey
111 C2 **İznik Gölü** *l.* Turkey
152 B2 **Izozog, Bañados del** *swamp* Bol.
67 B3 **Izumo** Japan
90 B1 **Izyaslav** Ukr.
91 D2 **Izyum** Ukr.

J

Jabal, Bahr el *r.* Sudan/Uganda *see* **White Nile**
106 C2 **Jabalón** *r.* Spain
75 B2 **Jabalpur** India
50 C1 **Jabiru** Austr.
109 C2 **Jablanica** Bos.-Herz.
151 E2 **Jaboatão dos Guararapes** Brazil
154 C2 **Jaboticabal** Brazil
107 C1 **Jaca** Spain
145 C2 **Jacala** Mex.
151 C2 **Jacareacanga** Brazil
155 C2 **Jacareí** Brazil
155 D1 **Jacinto** Brazil
141 E1 **Jackman** U.S.A.
142 C2 **Jackson** *AL* U.S.A.
140 C2 **Jackson** *MI* U.S.A.
142 B2 **Jackson** *MS* U.S.A.
142 C1 **Jackson** *TN* U.S.A.
136 A2 **Jackson** *WY* U.S.A.
54 A2 **Jackson Head** N.Z.
142 B2 **Jacksonville** *AR* U.S.A.
143 D2 **Jacksonville** *FL* U.S.A.
140 A3 **Jacksonville** *IL* U.S.A.
143 E2 **Jacksonville** *NC* U.S.A.
139 D2 **Jacksonville** *TX* U.S.A.
147 C3 **Jacmel** Haiti
74 A2 **Jacobabad** Pak.
151 D3 **Jacobina** Brazil
131 D2 **Jacques-Cartier, Mont** *mt.* Can.
151 D2 **Jacunda** Brazil
154 C2 **Jacupiranga** Brazil
109 C2 **Jadovnik** *mt.* Bos.-Herz.
150 A2 **Jaén** Peru
106 C2 **Jaén** Spain
52 A3 **Jaffa, Cape** Austr.
73 B4 **Jaffna** Sri Lanka
73 C3 **Jagdalpur** India
123 C2 **Jagersfontein** S. Africa
79 C2 **Jaghīn** Iran
154 C2 **Jaguariaíva** Brazil
79 C2 **Jahrom** Iran
74 B2 **Jaipur** India
74 B2 **Jaisalmer** India
75 C2 **Jajarkot** Nepal
109 C2 **Jajce** Bos.-Herz.
60 B2 **Jakarta** Indon.
128 A1 **Jakes Corner** Can.
92 G2 **Jäkkvik** Sweden
92 H3 **Jakobstad** Fin.
77 D3 **Jalālābād** Afgh.
77 D2 **Jalal-Abad** Kyrg.
74 B1 **Jalandhar** India
145 C3 **Jalapa** Mex.
154 B2 **Jales** Brazil
74 B2 **Jalgaon** India
115 D4 **Jalingo** Nigeria
74 B3 **Jalna** India
144 B2 **Jalpa** Mex.
75 C2 **Jalpaiguri** India
145 C2 **Jalpan** Mex.
115 E2 **Jālū** Libya
146 C3 **Jamaica** *country* West Indies

5 C3 **Jamaica Channel** Haiti/Jamaica
5 C2 **Jamalpur** Bangl.
0 B2 **Jambi** Indon.
7 D2 **James** *r. N. Dakota/S. Dakota* U.S.A.
4 D3 **James** *r. VA* U.S.A.
0 B1 **James Bay** Can.
2 A2 **Jamestown** Austr.
7 D1 **Jamestown** *ND* U.S.A.
4 D2 **Jamestown** *NY* U.S.A.
4 B1 **Jammu** India
4 B1 **Jammu and Kashmir** *terr.* Asia
4 B2 **Jamnagar** India
3 I3 **Jämsä** Fin.
5 C2 **Jamshedpur** India
5 C2 **Jamuna** *r.* Bangl.
5 C2 **Janakpur** Nepal
5 D1 **Janaúba** Brazil
1 D2 **Jandaq** Iran
0 B2 **Janesville** U.S.A.
4 F1 **Jan Mayen** *terr.* Arctic Ocean
1 D1 **Jaňňa** Turkm.
2 B3 **Jansenville** S. Africa
5 D1 **Januária** Brazil
4 B2 **Jaora** India
7 C3 **Japan** *country* Asia
5 C3 **Japan, Sea of** N. Pacific Ocean
0 B2 **Japurá** *r.* Brazil
4 C1 **Jaraguá** Brazil
4 B2 **Jaraguari** Brazil
2 C3 **Jardim** Brazil
3 D1 **Jarocin** Pol.
3 E1 **Jarosław** Pol.
2 F3 **Järpen** Sweden
0 A2 **Jartai** China
0 B3 **Jarú** Brazil
Jarud China *see* **Lubei**
9 H3 **Jarvis Island** S. Pacific Ocean
9 C2 **Jāsk** Iran
3 E2 **Jasło** Pol.
8 C2 **Jasper** Can.
0 B3 **Jasper** *IN* U.S.A.
9 E2 **Jasper** *TX* U.S.A.
3 D2 **Jastrzębie-Zdrój** Pol.
3 D2 **Jászberény** Hungary
4 B1 **Jataí** Brazil
4 A2 **Jati** Pak.
4 C2 **Jaú** Brazil
0 B2 **Jaú** *r.* Brazil
5 C2 **Jaumave** Mex.
5 C2 **Jaunpur** India
4 B1 **Jauru** Brazil
1 B2 **Java** *i.* Indon.
Java Sea Indon. *see* **Jawa, Laut**
Jawa *i.* Indon. *see* **Java**
9 D4 **Jawa, Laut** *sea* Indon.
7 C4 **Jawhar** Somalia
3 D1 **Jawor** Pol.
3 D1 **Jaworzno** Pol.
9 D3 **Jaya, Puncak** *mt.* Indon.
9 D3 **Jayapura** Indon.
9 C2 **Jaz Mūrīān, Hāmūn-e** *imp. l.* Iran
8 B1 **Jean Marie River** Can.
1 D1 **Jeannin, Lac** *l.* Can.
6 A3 **Jebel Abyad Plateau** Sudan
6 C3 **Jedburgh** U.K.
8 A2 **Jeddah** Saudi Arabia
1 E1 **Jeetze** *r.* Ger.
5 C3 **Jefferson, Mount** U.S.A.
7 E3 **Jefferson City** U.S.A.
8 C2 **Jēkabpils** Latvia
3 D1 **Jelenia Góra** Pol.
8 B2 **Jelgava** Latvia
1 C2 **Jember** Indon.
1 E2 **Jena** Ger.
Jengish Chokusu *mt.* China/Kyrg. *see* **Pobeda Peak**
80 B2 **Jenīn** West Bank
142 B2 **Jennings** U.S.A.
151 D3 **Jequié** Brazil
155 D1 **Jequitaí** Brazil
155 D1 **Jequitinhonha** Brazil
155 E1 **Jequitinhonha** *r.* Brazil
147 C3 **Jérémie** Haiti
144 B2 **Jerez** Mex.
106 B2 **Jerez de la Frontera** Spain
109 D3 **Jergucat** Albania
115 C1 **Jerid, Chott el** *salt l.* Tunisia
134 D2 **Jerome** U.S.A.
95 C4 **Jersey** *terr.* Channel Is
151 D2 **Jerumenha** Brazil
80 B2 **Jerusalem** Israel/West Bank
53 D3 **Jervis Bay Territory** *admin. div.* Austr.
108 B1 **Jesenice** Slovenia
108 B2 **Jesi** Italy
101 F2 **Jessen** Ger.
75 C2 **Jessore** Bangl.
143 D2 **Jesup** U.S.A.
145 C3 **Jesús Carranza** Mex.
74 B2 **Jhalawar** India
74 B1 **Jhang** Pak.
75 B2 **Jhansi** India
75 C2 **Jharsuguda** India
74 B1 **Jhelum** Pak.
70 C2 **Jiading** China
69 E1 **Jiamusi** China
71 B3 **Ji'an** *Jiangxi* China
65 B1 **Ji'an** *Jilin* China
62 A1 **Jianchuan** China
Jiandaoyu China *see* **Guojiaba**
70 B2 **Jiangsu** *prov.* China
71 B3 **Jiangxi** *prov.* China
70 A2 **Jiangyou** China
70 B3 **Jianli** China
70 B2 **Jianqiao** China
71 B3 **Jianyang** *Fujian* China
70 A2 **Jianyang** *Sichuan* China
70 C2 **Jiaozhou** China
70 B2 **Jiaozuo** China
70 C2 **Jiaxing** China
68 C2 **Jiayuguan** China
Jiddah Saudi Arabia *see* **Jeddah**
92 G2 **Jiehkkevárri** *mt.* Norway
70 B2 **Jiexiu** China
68 C2 **Jigzhi** China
103 D2 **Jihlava** Czech Rep.
117 C4 **Jijiga** Eth.
116 A2 **Jilf al Kabīr, Haḑabat al** *plat.* Egypt
117 C4 **Jilib** Somalia
69 E2 **Jilin** China
65 B1 **Jilin** *prov.* China
65 A1 **Jilin Hada Ling** *mts* China
117 B4 **Jīma** Eth.
144 B2 **Jiménez** *Chihuahua* Mex.
145 C2 **Jiménez** *Tamaulipas* Mex.
70 B2 **Jinan** China
70 B2 **Jincheng** China
53 C3 **Jindabyne** Austr.
103 D2 **Jindřichův Hradec** Czech Rep.
71 B3 **Jingdezhen** China
70 B2 **Jinghang Yunhe** *canal* China
62 B1 **Jinghong** China
70 B2 **Jingmen** China
70 A2 **Jingning** China
70 A2 **Jingtai** China
71 A3 **Jingxi** China
65 B1 **Jingyu** China
70 A2 **Jingyuan** China
70 B2 **Jingzhou** China
70 B2 **Jingzhou** China
71 B3 **Jinhua** China
70 B1 **Jining** *Nei Mongol* China
70 B2 **Jining** *Shandong* China
119 D2 **Jinja** Uganda
117 B4 **Jinka** Eth.
146 B3 **Jinotepe** Nic.
71 A3 **Jinping** China
Jinsha Jiang *r.* China *see* **Yangtze**
70 B3 **Jinshi** China
70 B2 **Jinzhong** China
70 C1 **Jinzhou** China
150 B2 **Jiparaná** *r.* Brazil
75 C1 **Jirang** China
79 C2 **Jīroft** Iran
71 A3 **Jishou** China
110 B2 **Jiu** *r.* Romania
70 A2 **Jiuding Shan** *mt.* China
70 B3 **Jiujiang** China
66 B1 **Jixi** China
78 B3 **Jīzān** Saudi Arabia
77 C2 **Jizzax** Uzbek.
151 E2 **João Pessoa** Brazil
155 C1 **João Pinheiro** Brazil
74 B2 **Jodhpur** India
92 I3 **Joensuu** Fin.
67 C3 **Jōetsu** Japan
121 C3 **Jofane** Moz.
88 C2 **Jõgeva** Estonia
123 C2 **Johannesburg** S. Africa
134 C2 **John Day** U.S.A.
134 B1 **John Day** *r.* U.S.A.
128 C2 **John D'Or Prairie** Can.
143 E1 **John H. Kerr Reservoir** U.S.A.
96 C1 **John o'Groats** U.K.
143 D1 **Johnson City** U.S.A.
128 A1 **Johnson's Crossing** Can.
49 H1 **Johnston Atoll** N. Pacific Ocean
96 B3 **Johnstone** U.K.
141 D2 **Johnstown** U.S.A.
60 B1 **Johor Bahru** Malaysia
88 C2 **Jõhvi** Estonia
154 C3 **Joinville** Brazil
105 D2 **Joinville** France
92 G2 **Jokkmokk** Sweden
92 B2 **Jökulsá á Fjöllum** *r.* Iceland
140 B2 **Joliet** U.S.A.
130 C2 **Joliette** Can.
64 B2 **Jolo** Phil.
64 B2 **Jolo** *i.* Phil.
61 C2 **Jombang** Indon.
75 C2 **Jomsom** Nepal
88 B2 **Jonava** Lith.
142 B1 **Jonesboro** *AR* U.S.A.
142 B2 **Jonesboro** *LA* U.S.A.
127 F1 **Jones Sound** *sea chan.* Can.
93 F4 **Jönköping** Sweden
131 C2 **Jonquière** Can.
145 C3 **Jonuta** Mex.
137 E3 **Joplin** U.S.A.
80 B2 **Jordan** *country* Asia
80 B2 **Jordan** *r.* Asia
136 B1 **Jordan** U.S.A.
134 C2 **Jordan Valley** U.S.A.
62 A1 **Jorhat** India
93 E4 **Jørpeland** Norway
115 C4 **Jos** Nigeria
145 C3 **José Cardel** Mex.
131 D1 **Joseph, Lac** *l.* Can.
50 B1 **Joseph Bonaparte Gulf** Austr.
115 C4 **Jos Plateau** Nigeria
93 E3 **Jotunheimen** *mts* Norway
122 B3 **Joubertina** S. Africa
123 C2 **Jouberton** S. Africa
93 I3 **Joutseno** Fin.

134 B1 **Juan de Fuca Strait** Can./U.S.A.
Juanshui China *see* **Tongcheng**
145 B2 **Juaréz** Mex.
151 D2 **Juazeiro** Brazil
151 E2 **Juazeiro do Norte** Brazil
117 B4 **Juba** Sudan
117 C5 **Jubba** *r.* Somalia
78 B2 **Jubbah** Saudi Arabia
145 C3 **Juchitán** Mex.
102 C2 **Judenburg** Austria
101 D2 **Jühnde** Ger.
146 B3 **Juigalpa** Nic.
100 C1 **Juist** *i.* Ger.
155 D2 **Juiz de Fora** Brazil
150 A3 **Juliaca** Peru
75 C2 **Jumla** Nepal
74 B2 **Junagadh** India
139 D2 **Junction** U.S.A.
137 D3 **Junction City** U.S.A.
154 C2 **Jundiaí** Brazil
128 A2 **Juneau** U.S.A.
53 C2 **Junee** Austr.
105 D2 **Jungfrau** *mt.* Switz.
141 D2 **Juniata** *r.* U.S.A.
92 G3 **Junsele** Sweden
134 C2 **Juntura** U.S.A.
154 C2 **Juquiá** Brazil
117 A4 **Jur** *r.* Sudan
105 D2 **Jura** *mts* France/Switz.
96 B2 **Jura** *i.* U.K.
96 B3 **Jura, Sound of** *sea chan.* U.K.
88 B2 **Jurbarkas** Lith.
88 B2 **Jūrmala** Latvia
150 B2 **Juruá** *r.* Brazil
150 C2 **Juruena** *r.* Brazil
150 B2 **Jutaí** *r.* Brazil
101 F2 **Jüterbog** Ger.
146 B2 **Juventud, Isla de la** *i.* Cuba
70 B2 **Juxian** China
79 C2 **Jūyom** Iran
122 B1 **Jwaneng** Botswana
93 I3 **Jyväskylä** Fin.

K

74 B1 **K2** *mt.* China/Pakistan
119 C3 **Kabalo** Dem. Rep. Congo
119 C3 **Kabare** Dem. Rep. Congo
130 B2 **Kabinakagami Lake** Can.
118 C3 **Kabinda** Dem. Rep. Congo
118 B2 **Kabo** C.A.R.
120 B2 **Kabompo** Zambia
119 C3 **Kabongo** Dem. Rep. Congo
77 C3 **Kābul** Afgh.
64 B2 **Kaburuang** *i.* Indon.
121 B2 **Kabwe** Zambia
74 A2 **Kachchh, Gulf of** India
74 B2 **Kachchh, Rann of** *marsh* India
83 I3 **Kachug** Rus. Fed.
81 C1 **Kaçkar Dağı** *mt.* Turkey
111 C2 **Kadıköy** Turkey
114 B3 **Kadiolo** Mali
73 B3 **Kadmat** *atoll* India
121 B2 **Kadoma** Zimbabwe
63 A2 **Kadonkani** Myanmar
117 A3 **Kadugli** Sudan
115 C3 **Kaduna** Nigeria
89 E2 **Kaduy** Rus. Fed.
86 E2 **Kadzherom** Rus. Fed.
114 A3 **Kaédi** Maur.
118 B1 **Kaélé** Cameroon
65 B2 **Kaesŏng** N. Korea
114 A3 **Kaffrine** Senegal
121 B2 **Kafue** Zambia
120 B2 **Kafue** *r.* Zambia
118 B2 **Kaga Bandoro** C.A.R.
91 E2 **Kagal'nitskaya** Rus. Fed.
67 B4 **Kagoshima** Japan
90 C2 **Kaharlyk** Ukr.
61 C2 **Kahayan** *r.* Indon.
118 B3 **Kahemba** Dem. Rep. Congo
101 E2 **Kahla** Ger.
79 C2 **Kahnūj** Iran
92 H2 **Kahperusvaarat** *mts* Fin.
80 B2 **Kahramanmaraş** Turkey
79 C2 **Kahūrak** Iran
59 C3 **Kai, Kepulauan** *is* Indon.
115 C4 **Kaiama** Nigeria
54 B2 **Kaiapoi** N.Z.
59 C3 **Kai Besar** *i.* Indon.
70 B2 **Kaifeng** China
Kaihua China *see* **Wenshan**
122 B2 **Kaiingveld** *reg.* S. Africa
59 C3 **Kai Kecil** *i.* Indon.
54 B2 **Kaikoura** N.Z.
114 A4 **Kailahun** Sierra Leone
71 A3 **Kaili** China
59 C3 **Kaimana** Indon.
54 C1 **Kaimanawa Mountains** N.Z.
67 C4 **Kainan** Japan
115 C3 **Kainji Reservoir** Nigeria
54 B1 **Kaipara Harbour** N.Z.
74 B2 **Kairana** India
115 D1 **Kairouan** Tunisia
54 B1 **Kaitaia** N.Z.
54 C1 **Kaitawa** N.Z.
Kaitong China *see* **Tongyu**
59 C3 **Kaiwatu** Indon.
65 A1 **Kaiyuan** *Liaoning* China
62 B1 **Kaiyuan** *Yunnan* China
92 I3 **Kajaani** Fin.
51 D2 **Kajabbi** Austr.
122 B2 **Kakamas** S. Africa
119 D2 **Kakamega** Kenya
91 C2 **Kakhovka** Ukr.
91 C2 **Kakhovs'ke Vodoskhovyshche** *resr* Ukr.
73 C3 **Kakinada** India
128 C1 **Kakisa** Can.
119 C3 **Kakoswa** Dem. Rep. Congo
126 B2 **Kaktovik** U.S.A.
Kalaallit Nunaat *terr.* N. America *see* **Greenland**
59 C3 **Kalabahi** Indon.
120 B2 **Kalabo** Zambia
91 E1 **Kalach** Rus. Fed.
119 D2 **Kalacha Dida** Kenya
62 A1 **Kaladan** *r.* India/Myanmar
120 B3 **Kalahari Desert** Africa
92 H3 **Kalajoki** Fin.
111 B2 **Kalamaria** Greece
111 B3 **Kalamata** Greece
140 B2 **Kalamazoo** U.S.A.
111 B3 **Kalampaka** Greece
91 C2 **Kalanchak** Ukr.
115 E1 **Kalanshiyū ar Ramlī al Kabīr, Sarīr** *des.* Libya
63 B2 **Kalasin** Thai.
74 A1 **Kalāt** Afgh.
79 C2 **Kalāt** Iran
74 A2 **Kalat** Pak.
50 A2 **Kalbarri** Austr.
111 C3 **Kale** Turkey
80 B1 **Kalecik** Turkey
118 C3 **Kalema** Dem. Rep. Congo
119 C3 **Kalemie** Dem. Rep. Congo
62 A1 **Kalemyo** Myanmar
Kalgan China *see* **Zhangjiakou**
50 B3 **Kalgoorlie** Austr.
109 C2 **Kali** Croatia
110 C2 **Kaliakra, Nos** *pt* Bulg.
119 C3 **Kalima** Dem. Rep. Congo
61 C2 **Kalimantan** *reg.* Indon.
88 B3 **Kaliningrad** Rus. Fed.
91 D2 **Kalininskaya** Rus. Fed.
88 C3 **Kalinkavichy** Belarus
134 D1 **Kalispell** U.S.A.
103 D1 **Kalisz** Pol.
91 E2 **Kalitva** *r.* Rus. Fed.
92 H2 **Kalix** Sweden
92 H2 **Kalixälven** *r.* Sweden
111 C3 **Kalkan** Turkey
120 A3 **Kalkfeld** Namibia
92 I3 **Kallavesi** *l.* Fin.
92 F3 **Kallsjön** *l.* Sweden
93 G4 **Kalmar** Sweden
93 G4 **Kalmarsund** *sea chan.* Sweden
120 B2 **Kalomo** Zambia
128 B2 **Kalone Peak** Can.
75 B1 **Kalpa** India
73 B3 **Kalpeni** *atoll* India
75 B2 **Kalpi** India
101 D1 **Kaltenkirchen** Ger.
89 E3 **Kaluga** Rus. Fed.
93 F4 **Kalundborg** Denmark
90 A2 **Kalush** Ukr.
73 B3 **Kalyan** India
89 E2 **Kalyazin** Rus. Fed.
111 C3 **Kalymnos** *i.* Greece
119 C3 **Kama** Dem. Rep. Congo
62 A2 **Kama** Myanmar
86 E3 **Kama** *r.* Rus. Fed.
66 D3 **Kamaishi** Japan
80 B2 **Kaman** Turkey
120 A2 **Kamanjab** Namibia
78 B3 **Kamarān** *i.* Yemen
74 A2 **Kamarod** Pak.
50 B3 **Kambalda** Austr.
119 C4 **Kambove** Dem. Rep. Cong[o]
183 L3 **Kamchatka Peninsula** Rus. Fed.
110 C2 **Kamchiya** *r.* Bulg.
110 B2 **Kamenitsa** *mt.* Bulg.
108 B2 **Kamenjak, Rt** *pt* Croatia
76 B1 **Kamenka** Kazakh.
91 D1 **Kamenka** Rus. Fed.
91 E2 **Kamenolomni** Rus. Fed.
83 M2 **Kamenskoye** Rus. Fed.
91 E2 **Kamensk-Shakhtinskiy** Rus. Fed.
86 F3 **Kamensk-Ural'skiy** Rus. Fe[d.]
122 A3 **Kamiesberge** *mts* S. Africa
122 A3 **Kamieskroon** S. Africa
129 D1 **Kamilukuak Lake** Can.
119 C3 **Kamina** Dem. Rep. Congo
129 E1 **Kaminak Lake** Can.
90 A1 **Kamin'-Kashyrs'kyy** Ukr.
128 B2 **Kamloops** Can.
118 C3 **Kamonia** Dem. Rep. Congo
119 D2 **Kampala** Uganda
60 B1 **Kampar** *r.* Indon.
60 B1 **Kampar** Malaysia
100 B1 **Kampen** Neth.
119 C3 **Kampene** Dem. Rep. Cong[o]
63 A2 **Kamphaeng Phet** Thai.
63 B2 **Kâmpóng Cham** Cambodi[a]
63 B2 **Kâmpóng Chhnăng** Cambodia
Kâmpóng Saôm Cambodia **Sihanoukville**
63 B2 **Kâmpóng Spœ** Cambodia
63 B2 **Kâmpôt** Cambodia
129 D2 **Kamsack** Can.
86 E3 **Kamskoye Vodokhranilishc[he]** *resr* Rus. Fed.
117 C4 **Kamsuuma** Somalia
90 B2 **Kam"yanets'-Podil's'kyy** U[kr.]

0 A1 **Kam"yanka-Buz'ka** Ukr.
8 B3 **Kamyanyets** Belarus
1 D2 **Kamyshevatskaya** Rus. Fed.
7 D3 **Kamyshin** Rus. Fed.
5 D3 **Kanab** U.S.A.
8 C3 **Kananga** Dem. Rep. Congo
7 D3 **Kanash** Rus. Fed.
0 C3 **Kanawha** *r.* U.S.A.
7 C3 **Kanazawa** Japan
2 A1 **Kanbalu** Myanmar
3 A2 **Kanchanaburi** Thai.
3 B3 **Kanchipuram** India
7 C3 **Kandahār** Afgh.
6 C2 **Kandalaksha** Rus. Fed.
1 C2 **Kandangan** Indon.
4 A2 **Kandh Kot** Pak.
4 C3 **Kandi** Benin
4 B2 **Kandla** India
3 C2 **Kandos** Austr.
1 D2 **Kandreho** Madag.
3 C4 **Kandy** Sri Lanka
6 B2 **Kandyagash** Kazakh.
7 G1 **Kane Bassin** *b.* Greenland
1 D2 **Kanevskaya** Rus. Fed.
2 B1 **Kang** Botswana
7 H2 **Kangaatsiaq** Greenland
4 B3 **Kangaba** Mali
0 B2 **Kangal** Turkey
9 C2 **Kangān** Iran
0 B1 **Kangar** Malaysia
2 A3 **Kangaroo Island** Austr.
5 C2 **Kangchenjunga** *mt.* India/Nepal
5 B2 **Kangdong** N. Korea
1 C2 **Kangean, Kepulauan** *is* Indon.
7 I2 **Kangeq** *c.* Greenland
7 H2 **Kangerlussuaq** *inlet* Greenland
7 I2 **Kangerlussuaq** *inlet* Greenland
7 H2 **Kangersuatsiaq** Greenland
5 B1 **Kanggye** N. Korea
1 D1 **Kangiqsualujjuaq** Can.
7 G2 **Kangiqsujuaq** Can.
7 G2 **Kangirsuk** Can.
5 C2 **Kangmar** China
5 B2 **Kangnŭng** S. Korea
5 A1 **Kangping** China
2 D2 **Kangto** *mt.* China/India
2 A1 **Kani** Myanmar
6 D2 **Kanin, Poluostrov** *pen.* Rus. Fed.
6 D2 **Kanin Nos** Rus. Fed.
1 C2 **Kaniv** Ukr.
3 H3 **Kankaanpää** Fin.
0 B2 **Kankakee** U.S.A.
4 B3 **Kankan** Guinea
5 C2 **Kanker** India
3 B3 **Kannur** India
5 C3 **Kano** Nigeria
2 B3 **Kanonpunt** *pt* S. Africa
7 B4 **Kanoya** Japan
5 C2 **Kanpur** India
6 C3 **Kansas** *r.* U.S.A.
7 D3 **Kansas** *state* U.S.A.
7 E3 **Kansas City** U.S.A.
3 H3 **Kansk** Rus. Fed.
4 C3 **Kantchari** Burkina
1 D2 **Kantemirovka** Rus. Fed.
7 B2 **Kanturk** Ireland
3 D2 **Kanyamazane** S. Africa
3 C1 **Kanye** Botswana
1 C3 **Kaohsiung** Taiwan
0 A2 **Kaokoveld** *plat.* Namibia
4 A3 **Kaolack** Senegal
0 B2 **Kaoma** Zambia
8 C3 **Kapanga** Dem. Rep. Congo
7 D2 **Kapchagay** Kazakh.
77 D2 **Kapchagayskoye Vodokhranilishche** *resr* Kazakh.
100 B2 **Kapellen** Belgium
121 B2 **Kapiri Mposhi** Zambia
127 H2 **Kapisillit** Greenland
130 B1 **Kapiskau** *r.* Can.
61 C1 **Kapit** *Sarawak* Malaysia
63 A3 **Kapoe** Thai.
117 B4 **Kapoeta** Sudan
103 D2 **Kaposvár** Hungary
61 B2 **Kapuas** *r.* Indon.
52 A2 **Kapunda** Austr.
130 B2 **Kapuskasing** Can.
103 D2 **Kapuvár** Hungary
88 C3 **Kapyl'** Belarus
114 C4 **Kara** Togo
111 C3 **Kara Ada** *i.* Turkey
76 C1 **Karabalyk** Kazakh.
80 B1 **Karabük** Turkey
76 C2 **Karabutak** Kazakh.
110 C2 **Karacaköy** Turkey
89 D3 **Karachev** Rus. Fed.
74 A2 **Karachi** Pak.
Kara Deniz *sea* Asia/Europe *see* **Black Sea**
77 D2 **Karaganda** Kazakh.
77 D2 **Karagayly** Kazakh.
83 L3 **Karaginskiy Zaliv** *b.* Rus. Fed.
81 D2 **Karaj** Iran
64 B2 **Karakelong** *i.* Indon.
77 D2 **Kara-Köl** Kyrg.
77 D2 **Karakol** Kyrg.
74 B1 **Karakoram Range** *mts* Asia
Karakum, Peski *des.* Kazakh. *see* **Karakum Desert**
76 B2 **Karakum Desert** Kazakh.
76 C3 **Karakum Desert** Turkm.
Karakumy, Peski *des.* Turkm. *see* **Karakum Desert**
80 B2 **Karaman** Turkey
77 E2 **Karamay** China
54 B2 **Karamea** N.Z.
54 B2 **Karamea Bight** *b.* N.Z.
80 B2 **Karapınar** Turkey
122 A2 **Karasburg** Namibia
86 F1 **Kara Sea** Rus. Fed.
92 I2 **Karasjok** Norway
82 G3 **Karasuk** Rus. Fed.
77 D2 **Karatau** Kazakh.
77 C2 **Karatau, Khrebet** *mts* Kazakh.
86 F2 **Karatayka** Rus. Fed.
67 A4 **Karatsu** Japan
60 B2 **Karawang** Indon.
81 C2 **Karbalā'** Iraq
103 E2 **Karcag** Hungary
111 B3 **Karditsa** Greece
88 B2 **Kärdla** Estonia
122 B3 **Kareeberge** *mts* S. Africa
75 B2 **Kareli** India
74 B1 **Kargil** India
121 B2 **Kariba** Zimbabwe
121 B2 **Kariba, Lake** *resr* Zambia/Zimbabwe
61 B2 **Karimata, Pulau-pulau** *is* Indon.
61 B2 **Karimata, Selat** *str.* Indon.
73 B3 **Karimnagar** India
61 C2 **Karimunjawa, Pulau-pulau** *is* Indon.
91 C2 **Karkinits'ka Zatoka** *g.* Ukr.
91 D2 **Karlivka** Ukr.
109 C1 **Karlovac** Croatia
102 C1 **Karlovy Vary** Czech Rep.
93 F4 **Karlshamn** Sweden
93 G4 **Karlskrona** Sweden
102 B2 **Karlsruhe** Ger.
93 F4 **Karlstad** Sweden
101 D3 **Karlstadt** Ger.
89 D3 **Karma** Belarus
93 E4 **Karmøy** *i.* Norway
75 D2 **Karnafuli Reservoir** Bangl.
74 B2 **Karnal** India
110 C2 **Karnobat** Bulg.
74 A2 **Karodi** Pak.
121 B2 **Karoi** Zimbabwe
121 C1 **Karonga** Malawi
116 B3 **Karora** Eritrea
111 C3 **Karpathos** *i.* Greece
111 B3 **Karpenisi** Greece
86 D2 **Karpogory** Rus. Fed.
50 A2 **Karratha** Austr.
81 C1 **Kars** Turkey
88 C2 **Kārsava** Latvia
86 E2 **Karskiye Vorota, Proliv** *str.* Rus. Fed.
Karskoye More *sea* Rus. Fed. *see* **Kara Sea**
101 E1 **Karstädt** Ger.
111 C2 **Kartal** Turkey
87 F3 **Kartaly** Rus. Fed.
73 B3 **Karwar** India
83 I3 **Karymskoye** Rus. Fed.
111 B3 **Karystos** Greece
80 A2 **Kaş** Turkey
130 B1 **Kasabonika Lake** Can.
118 C4 **Kasaji** Dem. Rep. Congo
121 C2 **Kasama** Zambia
120 B2 **Kasane** Botswana
118 B3 **Kasangulu** Dem. Rep. Congo
73 B3 **Kasaragod** India
129 D1 **Kasba Lake** Can.
120 B2 **Kasempa** Zambia
119 C4 **Kasenga** Dem. Rep. Congo
119 C3 **Kasese** Dem. Rep. Congo
119 D2 **Kasese** Uganda
81 D2 **Kāshān** Iran
Kashgar China *see* **Kashi**
77 D3 **Kashi** China
67 D3 **Kashima-nada** *b.* Japan
89 E2 **Kashin** Rus. Fed.
89 E3 **Kashira** Rus. Fed.
89 E3 **Kashirskoye** Rus. Fed.
67 C3 **Kashiwazaki** Japan
76 B3 **Kāshmar** Iran
74 A2 **Kashmore** Pak.
119 C3 **Kashyukulu** Dem. Rep. Congo
87 D3 **Kasimov** Rus. Fed.
93 H3 **Kaskinen** Fin.
119 C3 **Kasongo** Dem. Rep. Congo
118 B3 **Kasongo-Lunda** Dem. Rep. Congo
111 C3 **Kasos** *i.* Greece
Kaspiyskoye More *l.* Asia/Europe *see* **Caspian Sea**
116 B3 **Kassala** Sudan
101 D2 **Kassel** Ger.
80 B1 **Kastamonu** Turkey
111 B2 **Kastoria** Greece
89 D3 **Kastsyukovichy** Belarus
119 D3 **Kasulu** Tanz.
121 C2 **Kasungu** Malawi
141 F1 **Katahdin, Mount** U.S.A.
118 C3 **Katako-Kombe** Dem. Rep. Congo
50 A3 **Katanning** Austr.
63 A3 **Katchall** *i.* India
111 B2 **Katerini** Greece
128 A2 **Kate's Needle** *mt.* Can./U.S.A.
121 C2 **Katete** Zambia
62 A1 **Katha** Myanmar
50 C1 **Katherine** *r.* Austr.
74 B2 **Kathiawar** *pen.* India
75 C2 **Kathmandu** Nepal
122 B2 **Kathu** S. Africa

74 B1 **Kathua** India
114 B3 **Kati** Mali
75 C2 **Katihar** India
54 C1 **Katikati** N.Z.
123 C3 **Katikati** S. Africa
120 B2 **Katima Mulilo** Namibia
123 C2 **Katlehong** S. Africa
111 B3 **Kato Achaïa** Greece
53 D2 **Katoomba** Austr.
103 D1 **Katowice** Pol.
78 A2 **Kātrīnā, Jabal** *mt.* Egypt
93 G4 **Katrineholm** Sweden
115 C3 **Katsina** Nigeria
115 C4 **Katsina-Ala** Nigeria
77 C3 **Kattaqo'rg'on** Uzbek.
93 F4 **Kattegat** *str.* Denmark/Sweden
100 B1 **Katwijk aan Zee** Neth.
124 E5 **Kaua'i** *i.* U.S.A.
93 H3 **Kauhajoki** Fin.
88 B3 **Kaunas** Lith.
115 C3 **Kaura-Namoda** Nigeria
92 H2 **Kautokeino** Norway
111 B2 **Kavala** Greece
66 C2 **Kavalerovo** Rus. Fed.
73 C3 **Kavali** India
73 B3 **Kavaratti** *atoll* India
110 C2 **Kavarna** Bulg.
81 D2 **Kavīr, Dasht-e** *des.* Iran
67 C3 **Kawagoe** Japan
54 B1 **Kawakawa** N.Z.
67 C3 **Kawanishi** Japan
130 C2 **Kawartha Lakes** Can.
67 C3 **Kawasaki** Japan
54 C1 **Kawerau** N.Z.
63 A2 **Kawkareik** Myanmar
62 A1 **Kawlin** Myanmar
63 A2 **Kawmapyin** Myanmar
63 A2 **Kawthaung** Myanmar
77 D3 **Kaxgar He** *r.* China
114 B3 **Kaya** Burkina
61 C1 **Kayan** *r.* Indon.
136 B2 **Kaycee** U.S.A.
138 A1 **Kayenta** U.S.A.
114 A3 **Kayes** Mali
77 D2 **Kaynar** Kazakh.
80 B2 **Kayseri** Turkey
77 D1 **Kazakhskiy Melkosopochnik** *plain* Kazakh.
81 D1 **Kazakhskiy Zaliv** *b.* Kazakh.
76 C2 **Kazakhstan** *country* Asia
87 D3 **Kazan'** Rus. Fed.
80 A1 **Kazanlŭk** Bulg.
76 A2 **Kazbek** *mt.* Georgia/Rus. Fed.
81 D3 **Kāzerūn** Iran
103 E2 **Kazincbarcika** Hungary
86 F2 **Kazymskiy Mys** Rus. Fed.
111 B3 **Kea** *i.* Greece
97 C1 **Keady** U.K.
137 D2 **Kearney** U.S.A.
138 A2 **Kearny** U.S.A.
116 A3 **Kebkabiya** Sudan
92 G2 **Kebnekaise** *mt.* Sweden
117 C4 **K'ebrī Dehar** Eth.
61 B2 **Kebumen** Indon.
128 B2 **Kechika** *r.* Can.
103 D2 **Kecskemét** Hungary
88 B2 **Kėdainiai** Lith.
114 A3 **Kédougou** Senegal
103 D1 **Kędzierzyn-Koźle** Pol.
128 B1 **Keele** *r.* Can.
128 A1 **Keele Peak** Can.
Keelung Taiwan *see* **Chilung**
141 E2 **Keene** U.S.A.
122 A2 **Keetmanshoop** Namibia
129 E3 **Keewatin** Can.
Kefallonia *i.* Greece *see* **Cephalonia**
59 C3 **Kefamenanu** Indon.
92 A3 **Keflavík** Iceland
77 D2 **Kegen** Kazakh.
128 C2 **Keg River** Can.
62 A1 **Kehsi Mansam** Myanmar
98 C2 **Keighley** U.K.
88 B2 **Keila** Estonia
122 B2 **Keimoes** S. Africa
92 I3 **Keitele** *l.* Fin.
52 B3 **Keith** Austr.
103 E2 **Kékes** *mt.* Hungary
92 J2 **Keles-Uayv, Gora** *h.* Rus. Fed.
102 C2 **Kelheim** Ger.
80 B1 **Kelkit** *r.* Turkey
128 B1 **Keller Lake** Can.
134 C1 **Kellogg** U.S.A.
92 I2 **Kelloselkä** Fin.
97 C2 **Kells** Ireland
88 B2 **Kelmė** Lith.
115 D4 **Kélo** Chad
128 C3 **Kelowna** Can.
96 C3 **Kelso** U.K.
134 B1 **Kelso** U.S.A.
60 B1 **Keluang** Malaysia
129 D2 **Kelvington** Can.
86 C2 **Kem'** Rus. Fed.
128 B2 **Kemano (abandoned)** Can.
111 C3 **Kemer** Turkey
82 G3 **Kemerovo** Rus. Fed.
92 H2 **Kemi** Fin.
92 I2 **Kemijärvi** Fin.
92 I2 **Kemijoki** *r.* Fin.
136 A2 **Kemmerer** U.S.A.
92 I3 **Kempele** Fin.
53 D2 **Kempsey** Austr.
130 C2 **Kempt, Lac** *l.* Can.
102 C2 **Kempten (Allgäu)** Ger.
123 C2 **Kempton Park** S. Africa
61 C2 **Kemujan** *i.* Indon.
129 D2 **Kenaston** Can.
98 B1 **Kendal** U.K.
59 C3 **Kendari** Indon.
61 C2 **Kendawangan** Indon.
115 D3 **Kendégué** Chad
114 A4 **Kenema** Sierra Leone
118 B3 **Kenge** Dem. Rep. Congo
62 A1 **Kengtung** Myanmar
122 B2 **Kenhardt** S. Africa
114 B1 **Kenitra** Morocco
97 B3 **Kenmare** Ireland
136 C1 **Kenmare** U.S.A.
97 A3 **Kenmare River** *inlet* Ireland
100 C3 **Kenn** Ger.
137 E3 **Kennett** U.S.A.
134 C1 **Kennewick** U.S.A.
129 E3 **Kenora** Can.
140 B2 **Kenosha** U.S.A.
138 C2 **Kent** U.S.A.
77 C2 **Kentau** Kazakh.
140 B3 **Kentucky** *r.* U.S.A.
140 C3 **Kentucky** *state* U.S.A.
140 B3 **Kentucky Lake** U.S.A.
119 D2 **Kenya** *country* Africa
119 D3 **Kenya, Mount** Kenya
137 E2 **Keokuk** U.S.A.
75 C2 **Keonjhar** India
111 C3 **Kepsut** Turkey
52 B3 **Kerang** Austr.
91 D2 **Kerch** Ukr.
59 D3 **Kerema** P.N.G.
128 C3 **Keremeos** Can.
116 B3 **Keren** Eritrea
81 C2 **Kerend** Iran
159 C7 **Kerguelen Plateau** Indian Ocean
119 D3 **Kericho** Kenya
54 B1 **Kerikeri** N.Z.
60 B2 **Kerinci, Gunung** *vol.* Indon
111 A3 **Kerkyra** Greece
Kerkyra *i.* Greece *see* **Corfu**
116 B3 **Kerma** Sudan
49 G4 **Kermadec Islands** S. Pacifi Ocean
79 C1 **Kermān** Iran
81 C2 **Kermānshāh** Iran
139 C2 **Kermit** U.S.A.
135 C3 **Kern** *r.* U.S.A.
100 C2 **Kerpen** Ger.
129 D2 **Kerrobert** Can.
139 D2 **Kerrville** U.S.A.
Keryneia Cyprus *see* **Kyreni**
130 B1 **Kesagami Lake** Can.
111 C2 **Keşan** Turkey
66 D3 **Kesennuma** Japan
74 B2 **Keshod** India
100 C2 **Kessel** Neth.
98 B1 **Keswick** U.K.
103 D2 **Keszthely** Hungary
82 G3 **Ket'** *r.* Rus. Fed.
61 C2 **Ketapang** Indon.
128 A2 **Ketchikan** U.S.A.
134 D2 **Ketchum** U.S.A.
99 C2 **Kettering** U.K.
93 H3 **Keuruu** Fin.
100 C2 **Kevelaer** Ger.
140 B2 **Kewanee** U.S.A.
140 B1 **Keweenaw Bay** U.S.A.
140 B1 **Keweenaw Peninsula** U.S.A
143 D3 **Key Largo** U.S.A.
141 D3 **Keyser** U.S.A.
143 D4 **Key West** U.S.A.
123 C2 **Kgotsong** S. Africa
69 E1 **Khabarovsk** Rus. Fed.
80 B1 **Khadyzhensk** Rus. Fed.
62 A1 **Khagrachari** Bangl.
74 A2 **Khairpur** Pak.
122 B1 **Khakhea** Botswana
68 C1 **Khamar-Daban, Khrebet** *m* Rus. Fed.
74 B2 **Khambhat** India
73 B3 **Khambhat, Gulf of** India
74 B2 **Khamgaon** India
78 B3 **Khamir** Yemen
78 B3 **Khamis Mushayţ** Saudi Ara
77 C3 **Khānābād** Afgh.
74 B2 **Khandwa** India
83 K2 **Khandyga** Rus. Fed.
74 B1 **Khanewal** Pak.
66 B2 **Khanka, Lake** China/Rus. F
74 B2 **Khanpur** Pak.
77 D2 **Khantau** Kazakh.
83 H2 **Khantayskoye, Ozero** *l.* Rus. Fed.
86 F2 **Khanty-Mansiysk** Rus. Fed.
63 A3 **Khao Chum Thong** Thai.
63 A2 **Khao Laem, Ang Kep Nam** Thai.
87 D4 **Kharabali** Rus. Fed.
75 C2 **Kharagpur** India
79 C2 **Khārān** *r.* Iran
116 B2 **Khārijah, Wāḩāt al** *oasis* Eg
91 D2 **Kharkiv** Ukr.
Khar'kov Ukr. *see* **Kharkiv**
110 C2 **Kharmanli** Bulg.
86 D3 **Kharovsk** Rus. Fed.
116 B3 **Khartoum** Sudan
87 D4 **Khasavyurt** Rus. Fed.
79 D2 **Khāsh** Iran
78 A3 **Khashm el Girba** Sudan
78 A3 **Khashm el Girba Dam** Sud
74 D2 **Khasi Hills** India
110 C2 **Khaskovo** Bulg.
123 C3 **Khayamnandi** S. Africa
78 A2 **Khaybar** Saudi Arabia

A3 Khayelitsha S. Africa
B2 Khemis Miliana Alg.
B2 Khemmarat Thai.
C1 Khenchela Alg.
D3 Kherämeh Iran
D3 Kherson Ukr.
H2 Kheta r. Rus. Fed.
C3 Khilok Rus. Fed.
E2 Khimki Rus. Fed.
A2 Khipro Pak.
E3 Khlevnoye Rus. Fed.
B2 Khmel'nyts'kyy Ukr.
B1 Khobda Kazakh.
E3 Khokhol'skiy Rus. Fed.
B3 Khokhropar Pak.
B2 Kholm Rus. Fed.
D2 Kholm-Zhirkovskiy Rus. Fed.
C2 Khonj Iran
B2 Khon Kaen Thai.
A1 Khonsa India
C2 Khonuu Rus. Fed.
E2 Khoreyver Rus. Fed.
D1 Khorinsk Rus. Fed.
C2 Khorol Ukr.
C2 Khorramābād Iran
C2 Khorramshahr Iran
D3 Khorugh Tajik.
A1 Khóst Afgh.
A1 Khreum Myanmar
A1 Khromtau Ukr.
B2 Khrystynivka Ukr.
C2 Khŭjand Tajik.
B2 Khu Khan Thai.
A2 Khulays Saudi Arabia
A2 Khulna Bangl.
B2 Khunsar Iran
B2 Khurays Saudi Arabia
B3 Khushab Pak.
A2 Khust Ukr.
A2 Khutsong S. Africa
A2 Khuzdar Pak.
C2 Khvormūj Iran
C2 Khvoy Iran
D2 Khvoynaya Rus. Fed.
D2 Khyber Pass Afgh./Pak.
D2 Kiama Austr.
A1 Kiambi Dem. Rep. Congo
C3 Kibiti Tanz.
C3 Kičevo Macedonia
C3 Kidal Mali
B2 Kidderminster U.K.
A3 Kidira Senegal
C1 Kidnappers, Cape N.Z.
C1 Kiel Ger.
E1 Kielce Pol.
B1 Kielder Water U.K.
C1 Kiev Ukr.
A3 Kiffa Maur.
B3 Kigali Rwanda
B3 Kigoma Tanz.
B2 Kihnu i. Estonia
I2 Kiiminki Fin.
B4 Kii-suidō sea chan. Japan
D1 Kikinda Serbia
D3 Kikondja Dem. Rep. Congo
D3 Kikori P.N.G.
D3 Kikori r. P.N.G.
B3 Kikwit Dem. Rep. Congo
C1 Kilchu N. Korea
B3 Kilembe Dem. Rep. Congo
E2 Kilgore U.S.A.
C3 Kilimanjaro vol. Tanz.
B2 Kilis Turkey
D2 Kiliya Ukr.
B2 Kilkee Ireland
C2 Kilkeel U.K.
C2 Kilkenny Ireland

111 B2 Kilkis Greece
97 B1 Killala Bay Ireland
97 B1 Killaloe Ireland
129 C2 Killam Can.
97 B1 Killarney Ireland
139 D2 Killeen U.S.A.
96 B3 Killin U.K.
97 B1 Killybegs Ireland
96 B3 Kilmarnock U.K.
53 B3 Kilmore Austr.
119 D3 Kilosa Tanz.
97 B2 Kilrush Ireland
119 C3 Kilwa Dem. Rep. Congo
119 D3 Kilwa Masoko Tanz.
119 D3 Kimambi Tanz.
52 A2 Kimba Austr.
136 C2 Kimball U.S.A.
128 C3 Kimberley Can.
122 B2 Kimberley S. Africa
50 B1 Kimberley Plateau Austr.
65 B1 Kimch'aek N. Korea
65 B2 Kimch'ŏn S. Korea
127 G2 Kimmirut Can.
89 E3 Kimovsk Rus. Fed.
118 B3 Kimpese Dem. Rep. Congo
89 E2 Kimry Rus. Fed.
61 C1 Kinabalu, Gunung mt. Sabah
       Malaysia
128 C2 Kinbasket Lake Can.
130 B2 Kincardine Can.
62 A1 Kinchang Myanmar
119 C3 Kinda Dem. Rep. Congo
98 C2 Kinder Scout h. U.K.
129 D2 Kindersley Can.
114 A3 Kindia Guinea
119 C3 Kindu Dem. Rep. Congo
86 D3 Kineshma Rus. Fed.
51 E2 Kingaroy Austr.
135 B3 King City U.S.A.
130 C1 King George Islands Can.
88 C2 Kingisepp Rus. Fed.
51 D3 King Island Austr.
50 B1 King Leopold Ranges hills
       Austr.
138 A1 Kingman U.S.A.
135 B3 Kings r. U.S.A.
52 A3 Kingscote Austr.
99 D2 King's Lynn U.K.
48 F3 Kingsmill Group is Kiribati
50 B1 King Sound b. Austr.
134 D2 Kings Peak U.S.A.
143 D1 Kingsport U.S.A.
130 C2 Kingston Can.
146 C3 Kingston Jamaica
141 E2 Kingston U.S.A.
52 A3 Kingston South East Austr.
98 C2 Kingston upon Hull U.K.
147 D3 Kingstown St Vincent
139 D3 Kingsville U.S.A.
99 B3 Kingswood U.K.
96 B2 Kingussie U.K.
126 E2 King William Island Can.
123 C3 King William's Town S. Africa
67 D3 Kinka-san i. Japan
93 F4 Kinna Sweden
97 B3 Kinsale Ireland
118 B3 Kinshasa Dem. Rep. Congo
143 E1 Kinston U.S.A.
88 D3 Kintai Lith.
114 B4 Kintampo Ghana
96 B3 Kintyre pen. U.K.
62 A1 Kin-U Myanmar
130 C2 Kipawa, Lac l. Can.
83 J3 Kirensk Rus. Fed.
89 E3 Kireyevsk Rus. Fed.
       Kirghizia country Asia see
       Kyrgyzstan

49 G3 Kiribati country Pacific Ocean
80 B2 Kırıkkale Turkey
89 E2 Kirillov Rus. Fed.
       Kirin China see Jilin
       Kirinyaga mt. Kenya see
       Kenya, Mount
89 D2 Kirishi Rus. Fed.
49 H2 Kiritimati atoll Kiribati
111 C3 Kırkağaç Turkey
96 C2 Kirkcaldy U.K.
96 B3 Kirkcudbright U.K.
92 J2 Kirkenes Norway
130 B2 Kirkland Lake Can.
137 E2 Kirksville U.S.A.
91 C4 Kirkūk Iraq
96 C1 Kirkwall U.K.
89 D3 Kirov Kaluzhskaya Oblast'
       Rus. Fed.
86 D3 Kirov Rus. Fed.
       Kirovabad Azer. see Gäncä
86 E3 Kirovo-Chepetsk Rus. Fed.
91 C2 Kirovohrad Ukr.
86 C2 Kirovsk Rus. Fed.
91 D3 Kirovs'ke Ukr.
96 C2 Kirriemuir U.K.
86 E3 Kirs Rus. Fed.
74 A2 Kirthar Range mts Pak.
92 H2 Kiruna Sweden
67 C3 Kiryū Japan
89 E2 Kirzhach Rus. Fed.
119 C2 Kisangani Dem. Rep. Congo
118 B3 Kisantu Dem. Rep. Congo
60 A1 Kisaran Indon.
82 G3 Kiselevsk Rus. Fed.
75 C2 Kishanganj India
115 C4 Kishi Nigeria
       Kishinev Moldova see
       Chişinău
77 D1 Kishkenekol' Kazakh.
74 B1 Kishtwar India
119 D2 Kisii Kenya
103 D2 Kiskunfélegyháza Hungary
103 D2 Kiskunhalas Hungary
87 D4 Kislovodsk Rus. Fed.
117 C5 Kismaayo Somalia
93 I3 Kisoro Uganda
111 B3 Kissamos Greece
114 A4 Kissidougou Guinea
143 D3 Kissimmee U.S.A.
143 D3 Kissimmee, Lake U.S.A.
129 C2 Kississing Lake Can.
119 D2 Kisumu Kenya
114 B3 Kita Mali
66 D3 Kitakami Japan
66 D3 Kitakami-gawa r. Japan
67 B4 Kita-Kyūshū Japan
119 D2 Kitale Kenya
66 D2 Kitami Japan
130 B2 Kitchener Can.
93 J3 Kitee Fin.
119 D2 Kitgum Uganda
128 B2 Kitimat Can.
118 B3 Kitona Dem. Rep. Congo
119 D3 Kitunda Tanz.
128 B2 Kitwanga Can.
121 B2 Kitwe Zambia
101 E3 Kitzingen Ger.
92 I3 Kiuruvesi Fin.
119 C3 Kivu, Lake Dem. Rep.
       Congo/Rwanda
110 C2 Kıyıköy Turkey
86 E3 Kizel Rus. Fed.
111 C3 Kızılca Dağ mt. Turkey
87 D4 Kızılyar Rus. Fed.
92 I1 Kjøllefjord Norway
92 G2 Kjøpsvik Norway
102 C1 Kladno Czech Rep.

102 C2 **Klagenfurt** Austria
88 B2 **Klaipėda** Lith.
94 B1 **Klaksvík** Faroe Is
134 B2 **Klamath** *r.* U.S.A.
134 B2 **Klamath Falls** U.S.A.
134 B2 **Klamath Mountains** U.S.A.
60 B1 **Klang** Malaysia
102 C2 **Klatovy** Czech Rep.
122 A3 **Klawer** S. Africa
128 A2 **Klawock** U.S.A.
128 B2 **Kleena Kleene** Can.
122 B2 **Kleinbegin** S. Africa
122 A2 **Kleinsee** S. Africa
123 C2 **Klerksdorp** S. Africa
89 D3 **Kletnya** Rus. Fed.
100 C2 **Kleve** Ger.
89 D3 **Klimavichy** Belarus
89 D3 **Klimovo** Rus. Fed.
89 E2 **Klimovsk** Rus. Fed.
89 E2 **Klin** Rus. Fed.
101 F2 **Klínovec** *mt.* Czech Rep.
93 G4 **Klintehamn** Sweden
89 D3 **Klintsy** Rus. Fed.
109 C2 **Ključ** Bos.-Herz.
103 D1 **Kłodzko** Pol.
100 C1 **Kloosterhaar** Neth.
103 D2 **Klosterneuburg** Austria
101 E1 **Klötze (Altmark)** Ger.
103 D1 **Kluczbork** Pol.
128 A2 **Klukwan** U.S.A.
88 C3 **Klyetsk** Belarus
98 C1 **Knaresborough** U.K.
93 F3 **Knästen** *h.* Sweden
129 E2 **Knee Lake** Can.
101 E1 **Knesebeck** Ger.
101 E3 **Knetzgau** Ger.
109 C2 **Knin** Croatia
103 C2 **Knittelfeld** Austria
109 D2 **Knjaževac** Serbia
100 A2 **Knokke-Heist** Belgium
143 D1 **Knoxville** U.S.A.
122 B3 **Knysna** S. Africa
67 C4 **Kōbe** Japan
København Denmark *see* **Copenhagen**
100 C2 **Koblenz** Ger.
59 C3 **Kobroör** *i.* Indon.
88 B3 **Kobryn** Belarus
109 D2 **Kočani** Macedonia
111 C2 **Kocasu** *r.* Turkey
75 C2 **Koch Bihar** India
73 B4 **Kochi** India
67 B4 **Kōchi** Japan
87 D4 **Kochubey** Rus. Fed.
75 C2 **Kodarma** India
117 B4 **Kodok** Sudan
90 B2 **Kodyma** Ukr.
111 C2 **Kodzhaele** *mt.* Bulg./Greece
122 A2 **Koës** Namibia
122 C2 **Koffiefontein** S. Africa
114 B4 **Koforidua** Ghana
67 C3 **Kōfu** Japan
131 D1 **Kogaluk** *r.* Can.
74 B1 **Kohat** Pak.
62 A1 **Kohima** India
88 C2 **Kohtla-Järve** Estonia
92 H3 **Kokkola** Fin.
140 B2 **Kokomo** U.S.A.
77 E2 **Kokpekti** Kazakh.
77 C1 **Kokshetau** Kazakh.
131 D1 **Koksoak** *r.* Can.
123 C3 **Kokstad** S. Africa
Koktokay China *see* **Fuyun**
58 C3 **Kolaka** Indon.
86 C2 **Kola Peninsula** Rus. Fed.
92 H2 **Kolari** Fin.
114 A3 **Kolda** Senegal
93 E4 **Kolding** Denmark
107 D2 **Koléa** Alg.
86 D2 **Kolguyev, Ostrov** *i.* Rus. Fed.
73 B3 **Kolhapur** India
88 B2 **Kolkasrags** *pt* Latvia
75 C2 **Kolkata** India
73 B4 **Kollam** India
Köln Ger. *see* **Cologne**
103 D1 **Kołobrzeg** Pol.
114 B3 **Kolokani** Mali
89 E2 **Kolomna** Rus. Fed.
90 B2 **Kolomyya** Ukr.
122 B2 **Kolonkwaneng** Botswana
82 G3 **Kolpashevo** Rus. Fed.
89 E3 **Kolpny** Rus. Fed.
Kol'skiy Poluostrov *pen.* Rus. Fed. *see* **Kola Peninsula**
78 B3 **Koluli** Eritrea
119 C4 **Kolwezi** Dem. Rep. Congo
83 L2 **Kolyma** *r.* Rus. Fed.
83 L2 **Kolymskaya Nizmennost'** *lowland* Rus. Fed.
83 M2 **Kolymskiy, Khrebet** *mts* Rus. Fed.
67 C3 **Komaki** Japan
83 M3 **Komandorskiye Ostrova** *is* Rus. Fed.
103 D2 **Komárno** Slovakia
123 D2 **Komati** *r.* S. Africa/Swaziland
67 C3 **Komatsu** Japan
119 C3 **Kombe** Dem. Rep. Congo
90 C2 **Kominternivs'ke** Ukr.
109 C2 **Komiža** Croatia
103 D2 **Komló** Hungary
118 B3 **Komono** Congo
111 C2 **Komotini** Greece
122 B3 **Komsberg** *mts* S. Africa
83 H1 **Komsomolets, Ostrov** *i.* Rus. Fed.
89 F2 **Komsomol'sk** Rus. Fed.
91 C2 **Komsomol's'k** Ukr.
87 D4 **Komsomol'skiy** Rus. Fed.
69 E1 **Komsomol'sk-na-Amure** Rus. Fed.
89 E2 **Konakovo** Rus. Fed.
75 C3 **Kondagaon** India
86 F2 **Kondinskoye** Rus. Fed.
119 D3 **Kondoa** Tanz.
86 C2 **Kondopoga** Rus. Fed.
89 E3 **Kondrovo** Rus. Fed.
127 I2 **Kong Christian IX Land** *reg.* Greenland
127 I2 **Kong Frederik VI Kyst** *coastal area* Greenland
65 B2 **Kongju** S. Korea
119 C3 **Kongolo** Dem. Rep. Congo
93 E4 **Kongsberg** Norway
93 F3 **Kongsvinger** Norway
77 D3 **Kongur Shan** *mt.* China
100 C2 **Königswinter** Ger.
103 D1 **Konin** Pol.
109 C2 **Konjic** Bos.-Herz.
122 A2 **Konkiep** *watercourse* Namibia
91 C1 **Konotop** Ukr.
102 B2 **Konstanz** Ger.
115 C3 **Kontagora** Nigeria
63 B2 **Kon Tum** Vietnam
63 B2 **Kon Tum, Cao Nguyên** *plat.* Vietnam
80 B2 **Konya** Turkey
100 C3 **Konz** Ger.
86 E3 **Konzhakovskiy Kamen', Gora** *mt.* Rus. Fed.
134 C1 **Kooskia** U.S.A.
128 C3 **Kootenay Lake** Can.
122 B3 **Kootjieskolk** S. Africa
92 B2 **Kópasker** Iceland
108 B1 **Koper** Slovenia
93 G4 **Kopparberg** Sweden
109 C1 **Koprivnica** Croatia
89 F3 **Korablino** Rus. Fed.
73 C3 **Koraput** India
101 D2 **Korbach** Ger.
109 D2 **Korçë** Albania
109 C2 **Korčula** Croatia
109 C2 **Korčula** *i.* Croatia
70 C2 **Korea Bay** *g.* China/N. Ko
65 B1 **Korea, North** *country* Asia
65 B2 **Korea, South** *country* Asia
65 B3 **Korea Strait** Japan/S. Kore
91 D2 **Korenovsk** Rus. Fed.
90 B1 **Korets'** Ukr.
111 C2 **Körfez** Turkey
114 B4 **Korhogo** Côte d'Ivoire
Korinthos Greece *see* **Cori**
103 D2 **Kőris-hegy** *h.* Hungary
109 D2 **Koritnik** *mt.* Albania/Koso
67 D3 **Kōriyama** Japan
80 B2 **Korkuteli** Turkey
68 B2 **Korla** China
103 D2 **Körmend** Hungary
114 B3 **Koro** Mali
131 D1 **Koroc** *r.* Can.
91 D1 **Korocha** Rus. Fed.
119 D3 **Korogwe** Tanz.
59 C2 **Koror** Palau
90 B1 **Korosten'** Ukr.
90 B1 **Korostyshiv** Ukr.
115 D3 **Koro Toro** Chad
91 C2 **Korsun'-Shevchenkivs'kyy** Ukr.
103 E1 **Korsze** Pol.
100 A2 **Kortrijk** Belgium
83 L3 **Koryakskaya, Sopka** *vol.* Rus. Fed.
83 M2 **Koryakskoye Nagor'ye** *mts* Rus. Fed.
86 D2 **Koryazhma** Rus. Fed.
65 B2 **Koryŏng** S. Korea
91 C1 **Koryukivka** Ukr.
111 C3 **Kos** Greece
111 C3 **Kos** *i.* Greece
65 B2 **Kosan** N. Korea
103 D1 **Kościan** Pol.
53 C3 **Kosciuszko, Mount** Austr.
68 B1 **Kosh-Agach** Rus. Fed.
103 E2 **Košice** Slovakia
92 H2 **Koskullskulle** Sweden
65 B2 **Kosŏng** N. Korea
109 D2 **Kosovo** *country* Europe
Kosovska Mitrovica Kosov *see* **Mitrovicë**
48 E2 **Kosrae** *atoll* Micronesia
114 B4 **Kossou, Lac de** *l.* Côte d'Iv
76 C1 **Kostanay** Kazakh.
110 B2 **Kostenets** Bulg.
123 C2 **Koster** S. Africa
117 B3 **Kosti** Sudan
86 C2 **Kostomuksha** Rus. Fed.
90 B1 **Kostopil'** Ukr.
89 F2 **Kostroma** Rus. Fed.
89 F2 **Kostroma** *r.* Rus. Fed.
102 C1 **Kostrzyn** Pol.
103 D1 **Koszalin** Pol.
103 D2 **Kőszeg** Hungary
74 B2 **Kota** India
60 B2 **Kotaagung** Indon.
61 C2 **Kotabaru** Indon.
61 C1 **Kota Belud** *Sabah* Malaysi
60 B1 **Kota Bharu** Malaysia
60 B2 **Kotabumi** Indon.
61 C1 **Kota Kinabalu** *Sabah* Mala
61 C1 **Kota Samarahan** *Sarawak* Malaysia

D3 **Kotel'nich** Rus. Fed.
D4 **Kotel'nikovo** Rus. Fed.
K1 **Kotel'nyy, Ostrov** *i.* Rus. Fed.
E2 **Köthen (Anhalt)** Ger.
I3 **Kotka** Fin.
D2 **Kotlas** Rus. Fed.
C2 **Kotor Varoš** Bos.-Herz.
D3 **Kotovo** Rus. Fed.
E1 **Kotovsk** Rus. Fed.
B2 **Kotovs'k** Ukr.
H2 **Kotuy** *r.* Rus. Fed.
A2 **Koudekerke** Neth.
B3 **Koudougou** Burkina
B3 **Kougaberge** *mts* S. Africa
B3 **Koulamoutou** Gabon
B3 **Koulikoro** Mali
A3 **Koundâra** Guinea
C1 **Kourou** Fr. Guiana
B3 **Kouroussa** Guinea
D3 **Kousséri** Cameroon
B3 **Koutiala** Mali
I3 **Kouvola** Fin.
J2 **Kovdor** Rus. Fed.
A1 **Kovel'** Ukr.
F2 **Kovrov** Rus. Fed.
B2 **Kowhitirangi** N.Z.
C3 **Köyceğiz** Turkey
D2 **Koyda** Rus. Fed.
A2 **Koyukuk** *r.* U.S.A.
B2 **Kozani** Greece
C1 **Kozelets'** Ukr.
E3 **Kozel'sk** Rus. Fed.
B3 **Kozhikode** India
B2 **Kozyatyn** Ukr.
A3 **Krabi** Thai.
A2 **Kra Buri** Thai.
B2 **Krâchéh** Cambodia
E4 **Kragerø** Norway
B1 **Kraggenburg** Neth.
D2 **Kragujevac** Serbia
B2 **Krakatau** *i.* Indon.
D1 **Kraków** Pol.
D2 **Kramators'k** Ukr.
G3 **Kramfors** Sweden
B3 **Kranidi** Greece
E1 **Krasino** Rus. Fed.
C2 **Krāslava** Latvia
F2 **Kraslice** Czech Rep.
D3 **Krasnapollye** Belarus
D3 **Krasnaya Gora** Rus. Fed.
D3 **Krasnoarmeysk** Rus. Fed.
D2 **Krasnoarmiys'k** Ukr.
D2 **Krasnoborsk** Rus. Fed.
D2 **Krasnodar** Rus. Fed.
D2 **Krasnodon** Ukr.
C2 **Krasnogorodskoye** Rus. Fed.
D1 **Krasnogvardeyskoye** Rus. Fed.
D2 **Krasnohrad** Ukr.
C2 **Krasnohvardiys'ke** Ukr.
E3 **Krasnokamsk** Rus. Fed.
D2 **Krasnomayskiy** Rus. Fed.
C2 **Krasnoperekops'k** Ukr.
D3 **Krasnoslobodsk** Rus. Fed.
E3 **Krasnoufimsk** Rus. Fed.
H3 **Krasnoyarsk** Rus. Fed.
F2 **Krasnoye-na-Volge** Rus. Fed.
D3 **Krasnyy** Rus. Fed.
E2 **Krasnyy Kholm** Rus. Fed.
C4 **Krasnyy Luch** Ukr.
E2 **Krasnyy Sulin** Rus. Fed.
B2 **Krasyliv** Ukr.
C2 **Krefeld** Ger.
C2 **Kremenchuk** Ukr.
C2 **Kremenchuts'ke Vodoskhovyshche** *resr* Ukr.
D2 **Křemešník** *h.* Czech Rep.
D2 **Kreminna** Ukr.
103 D2 **Krems an der Donau** Austria
89 D2 **Kresttsy** Rus. Fed.
88 B2 **Kretinga** Lith.
100 C2 **Kreuzau** Ger.
100 C2 **Kreuztal** Ger.
118 A2 **Kribi** Cameroon
111 B3 **Krikellos** Greece
66 D1 **Kril'on, Mys** *c.* Rus. Fed.
73 C3 **Krishna** *r.* India
73 C3 **Krishna, Mouths of the** India
75 C2 **Krishnanagar** India
93 E4 **Kristiansand** Norway
93 F4 **Kristianstad** Sweden
92 E3 **Kristiansund** Norway
93 F4 **Kristinehamn** Sweden
Kriti *i.* Greece *see* **Crete**
111 C3 **Kritiko Pelagos** *sea* Greece
Krivoy Rog Ukr. *see* **Kryvyy Rih**
109 C1 **Križevci** Croatia
108 B1 **Krk** *i.* Croatia
92 F3 **Krokom** Sweden
91 C1 **Krolevets'** Ukr.
101 E2 **Kronach** Ger.
63 B2 **Krŏng Kaôh Kŏng** Cambodia
127 I2 **Kronprins Frederik Bjerge** *nunataks* Greenland
123 C2 **Kroonstad** S. Africa
87 D4 **Kropotkin** Rus. Fed.
103 E2 **Krosno** Pol.
103 D1 **Krotoszyn** Pol.
60 B2 **Krui** Indon.
109 C2 **Krujë** Albania
111 C2 **Krumovgrad** Bulg.
Krung Thep Thai. *see* **Bangkok**
88 C3 **Krupki** Belarus
109 D2 **Kruševac** Serbia
101 F2 **Krušné hory** *mts* Czech Rep.
128 A2 **Kruzof Island** U.S.A.
89 D3 **Krychaw** Belarus
91 D3 **Krymsk** Rus. Fed.
91 C2 **Kryvyy Rih** Ukr.
114 B2 **Ksabi** Alg.
107 D2 **Ksar el Boukhari** Alg.
114 B1 **Ksar el Kebir** Morocco
89 E3 **Kshenskiy** Rus. Fed.
78 B2 **Kū', Jabal al** *h.* Saudi Arabia
61 C1 **Kuala Belait** Brunei
60 B1 **Kuala Kerai** Malaysia
60 B1 **Kuala Lipis** Malaysia
60 B1 **Kuala Lumpur** Malaysia
61 C2 **Kualapembuang** Indon.
60 B1 **Kuala Terengganu** Malaysia
60 B2 **Kualatungal** Indon.
61 C1 **Kuamut** *Sabah* Malaysia
65 A1 **Kuandian** China
60 B1 **Kuantan** Malaysia
91 D2 **Kuban'** *r.* Rus. Fed.
89 E2 **Kubenskoye, Ozero** *l.* Rus. Fed.
110 C2 **Kubrat** Bulg.
61 C1 **Kubuang** Indon.
61 C1 **Kuching** *Sarawak* Malaysia
109 C2 **Kuçovë** Albania
61 C1 **Kudat** *Sabah* Malaysia
61 C2 **Kudus** Indon.
102 C2 **Kufstein** Austria
127 F2 **Kugaaruk** Can.
126 D2 **Kugluktuk** Can.
92 I3 **Kuhmo** Fin.
79 C2 **Kūhrān, Kūh-e** *mt.* Iran
Kuitin China *see* **Kuytun**
120 A2 **Kuito** Angola
92 I2 **Kuivaniemi** Fin.
65 B2 **Kujang** N. Korea
109 D2 **Kukës** Albania
111 C3 **Kula** Turkey
75 D2 **Kula Kangri** *mt.* Bhutan/China
76 B2 **Kulandy** Kazakh.
88 B2 **Kuldīga** Latvia
122 B1 **Kule** Botswana
101 E2 **Kulmbach** Ger.
77 C3 **Kŭlob** Tajik.
76 B2 **Kul'sary** Kazakh.
77 D1 **Kulunda** Rus. Fed.
127 I2 **Kulusuk** Greenland
67 C3 **Kumagaya** Japan
67 B4 **Kumamoto** Japan
109 D2 **Kumanovo** Macedonia
114 B4 **Kumasi** Ghana
118 A2 **Kumba** Cameroon
78 B2 **Kumdah** Saudi Arabia
87 E3 **Kumertau** Rus. Fed.
65 B2 **Kumi** S. Korea
93 G4 **Kumla** Sweden
115 D3 **Kumo** Nigeria
62 A1 **Kumon Range** *mts* Myanmar
62 B2 **Kumphawapi** Thai.
Kumul China *see* **Hami**
66 D2 **Kunashir, Ostrov** *i.* Rus. Fed.
120 A2 **Kunene** *r.* Angola/Namibia
77 D2 **Kungei Alatau** *mts* Kazakh./Kyrg.
93 F4 **Kungsbacka** Sweden
118 B2 **Kungu** Dem. Rep. Congo
86 E3 **Kungur** Rus. Fed.
62 A1 **Kunhing** Myanmar
77 D3 **Kunlun Shan** *mts* China
62 B1 **Kunming** China
65 B2 **Kunsan** S. Korea
50 B1 **Kununurra** Austr.
92 I3 **Kuopio** Fin.
109 C1 **Kupa** *r.* Croatia/Slovenia
59 C3 **Kupang** Indon.
88 B2 **Kupiškis** Lith.
111 C2 **Küplü** Turkey
128 A2 **Kupreanof Island** U.S.A.
91 D2 **Kup"yans'k** Ukr.
77 E2 **Kuqa** China
67 B4 **Kurashiki** Japan
67 B3 **Kurayoshi** Japan
89 E3 **Kurchatov** Rus. Fed.
110 C2 **Kŭrdzhali** Bulg.
67 B4 **Kure** Japan
88 B2 **Kuressaare** Estonia
86 F3 **Kurgan** Rus. Fed.
93 H3 **Kurikka** Fin.
156 C3 **Kuril Trench** N. Pacific Ocean
89 E3 **Kurkino** Rus. Fed.
117 B3 **Kurmuk** Sudan
73 B3 **Kurnool** India
67 D3 **Kuroiso** Japan
53 D2 **Kurri Kurri** Austr.
89 E3 **Kursk** Rus. Fed.
122 B2 **Kuruman** S. Africa
122 B2 **Kuruman** *watercourse* S. Africa
67 B4 **Kurume** Japan
83 I3 **Kurumkan** Rus. Fed.
73 C4 **Kurunegala** Sri Lanka
111 C3 **Kuşadası** Turkey
111 C3 **Kuşadası Körfezi** *b.* Turkey
111 C2 **Kuş Gölü** *l.* Turkey
91 D2 **Kushchevskaya** Rus. Fed.
66 D2 **Kushiro** Japan
76 C1 **Kushmurun** Kazakh.
75 C2 **Kushtia** Bangl.
66 D2 **Kussharo-ko** *l.* Japan
111 C3 **Kütahya** Turkey
81 C1 **K'ut'aisi** Georgia
109 C1 **Kutjevo** Croatia
103 D1 **Kutno** Pol.
118 B3 **Kutu** Dem. Rep. Congo
126 D2 **Kuujjua** *r.* Can.

131 D1 **Kuujjuaq** Can.
130 C1 **Kuujjuarapik** Can.
92 I2 **Kuusamo** Fin.
120 A2 **Kuvango** Angola
89 D2 **Kuvshinovo** Rus. Fed.
78 B2 **Kuwait** *country* Asia
79 B2 **Kuwait** Kuwait
Kuybyshev Rus. Fed. *see* **Samara**
91 D2 **Kuybysheve** Ukr.
87 D3 **Kuybyshevskoye Vodokhranilishche** *resr* Rus. Fed.
77 E2 **Kuytun** China
111 C3 **Kuyucak** Turkey
87 D3 **Kuznetsk** Rus. Fed.
90 B1 **Kuznetsovs'k** Ukr.
92 H1 **Kvalsund** Norway
123 D2 **KwaMashu** S. Africa
65 B2 **Kwangju** S. Korea
65 B1 **Kwanmo-bong** *mt.* N. Korea
123 C3 **Kwanobuhle** S. Africa
122 B3 **KwaNonzame** S. Africa
123 C3 **Kwatinidubu** S. Africa
123 C2 **KwaZamokuhle** S. Africa
123 D2 **KwaZulu-Natal** *prov.* S. Africa
121 B2 **Kwekwe** Zimbabwe
118 B3 **Kwenge** *r.* Dem. Rep. Congo
103 D1 **Kwidzyn** Pol.
118 B3 **Kwilu** *r.* Angola/Dem. Rep. Congo
59 C3 **Kwoka** *mt.* Indon.
53 C3 **Kyabram** Austr.
62 A2 **Kyaikto** Myanmar
69 D1 **Kyakhta** Rus. Fed.
52 A2 **Kyancutta** Austr.
62 A1 **Kyaukpadaung** Myanmar
62 A2 **Kyaukpyu** Myanmar
88 B3 **Kybartai** Lith.
62 A2 **Kyebogyi** Myanmar
62 A2 **Kyeintali** Myanmar
74 B1 **Kyelang** India
Kyiv Ukr. *see* **Kiev**
90 C1 **Kyivs'ke Vodoskhovyshche** *resr* Ukr.
Kyklades *is* Greece *see* **Cyclades**
129 D2 **Kyle** Can.
96 B2 **Kyle of Lochalsh** U.K.
100 C3 **Kyll** *r.* Ger.
111 B3 **Kyllini** *mt.* Greece
111 B3 **Kymi** Greece
52 B3 **Kyneton** Austr.
119 D2 **Kyoga, Lake** Uganda
53 D1 **Kyogle** Austr.
65 B2 **Kyŏnggi-man** *b.* S. Korea
65 B2 **Kyŏngju** S. Korea
67 C4 **Kyōto** Japan
111 B3 **Kyparissia** Greece
77 C1 **Kypshak, Ozero** *salt l.* Kazakh.
111 B3 **Kyra Panagia** *i.* Greece
80 B2 **Kyrenia** Cyprus
77 D2 **Kyrgyzstan** *country* Asia
101 F1 **Kyritz** Ger.
92 H3 **Kyrönjoki** *r.* Fin.
86 E2 **Kyrta** Rus. Fed.
86 D2 **Kyssa** Rus. Fed.
111 B3 **Kythira** *i.* Greece
111 B3 **Kythnos** *i.* Greece
128 B2 **Kyuquot** Can.
67 B4 **Kyūshū** *i.* Japan
110 B2 **Kyustendil** Bulg.
92 H3 **Kyyjärvi** Fin.
68 C1 **Kyzyl** Rus. Fed.
76 C2 **Kyzylkum Desert** Kazakh./Uzbek.
77 C2 **Kyzylorda** Kazakh.

L

145 C3 **La Angostura, Presa de** *resr* Mex.
117 C4 **Laascaanood** Somalia
150 B1 **La Asunción** Venez.
114 A2 **Laâyoune** Western Sahara
87 D4 **Laba** *r.* Rus. Fed.
144 B2 **La Babia** Mex.
146 B3 **La Bahía, Islas de** *is* Hond.
152 B3 **La Banda** Arg.
104 B2 **La Baule-Escoublac** France
114 A3 **Labé** Guinea
128 A1 **Laberge, Lake** Can.
129 C2 **La Biche, Lac** *l.* Can.
87 D4 **Labinsk** Rus. Fed.
64 B1 **Labo** Phil.
104 B3 **Labouheyre** France
131 D1 **Labrador** *reg.* Can.
131 D1 **Labrador City** Can.
158 C1 **Labrador Sea** Can./Greenland
150 B2 **Lábrea** Brazil
61 C1 **Labuan** Malaysia
60 B1 **Labuhanbilik** Indon.
59 C3 **Labuna** Indon.
63 A2 **Labutta** Myanmar
86 F2 **Labytnangi** Rus. Fed.
109 C2 **Laç** Albania
105 C2 **La Capelle** France
73 B3 **Laccadive Islands** India
129 E2 **Lac du Bonnet** Can.
146 B3 **La Ceiba** Hond.
53 B2 **Lachlan** *r.* Austr.
141 E1 **Lachute** Can.
105 D3 **La Ciotat** France
129 C2 **Lac La Biche** Can.
Lac la Martre Can. *see* **Whatî**
141 E1 **Lac-Mégantic** Can.
128 C2 **Lacombe** Can.
146 B4 **La Concepción** Panama
145 C3 **La Concordia** Mex.
108 A3 **Laconi** *Sardegna* Italy
141 E2 **Laconia** U.S.A.
128 C2 **La Crete** Can.
140 A2 **La Crosse** U.S.A.
144 B2 **La Cruz** Mex.
144 B2 **La Cuesta** Mex.
75 B1 **Ladakh Range** *mts* India/Pak.
122 B3 **Ladismith** S. Africa
79 D2 **Lādīz** Iran
86 C2 **Ladoga, Lake** Rus. Fed.
Ladozhskoye Ozero *l.* Rus. Fed. *see* **Ladoga, Lake**
128 B3 **Ladysmith** Can.
123 C2 **Ladysmith** S. Africa
59 D3 **Lae** P.N.G.
152 B3 **La Esmeralda** Bol.
93 F4 **Læsø** *i.* Denmark
143 C2 **La Fayette** U.S.A.
140 B2 **Lafayette** *IN* U.S.A.
142 B2 **Lafayette** *LA* U.S.A.
115 C4 **Lafia** Nigeria
104 B2 **La Flèche** France
143 D1 **La Follette** U.S.A.
131 C1 **Laforge** Can.
79 C2 **Lāft** Iran
108 A3 **La Galite** *i.* Tunisia
81 C1 **Lagan'** Rus. Fed.
118 B2 **Lagdo, Lac de** *l.* Cameroon
115 C1 **Laghouat** Alg.
155 D1 **Lagoa Santa** Brazil
114 A2 **La Gomera** *i.* Islas Canarias
114 C4 **Lagos** Nigeria
106 B2 **Lagos** Port.
134 C1 **La Grande** U.S.A.
130 C1 **La Grande 3, Réservoir** *re* Can.
131 C1 **La Grande 4, Réservoir** *re* Can.
50 B1 **La Grange** Austr.
143 C2 **La Grange** U.S.A.
150 B1 **La Gran Sabana** *plat.* Ven
152 D3 **Laguna** Brazil
144 A2 **Laguna, Picacho de la** *mt* Mex.
150 A2 **Lagunas** Peru
La Habana Cuba *see* **Hav**
61 C1 **Lahad Datu** *Sabah* Malay
60 B2 **Lahat** Indon.
78 B3 **Laḩij** Yemen
81 C2 **Lāhījān** Iran
100 C2 **Lahnstein** Ger.
74 B1 **Lahore** Pak.
74 A2 **Lahri** Pak.
93 I3 **Lahti** Fin.
115 D4 **Laï** Chad
53 D1 **Laidley** Austr.
104 C2 **L'Aigle** France
111 B3 **Laimos, Akrotirio** *pt* Gree
122 B3 **Laingsburg** S. Africa
92 H2 **Lainioälven** *r.* Sweden
96 B1 **Lairg** U.K.
108 B1 **Laives** Italy
70 B2 **Laiwu** China
70 C2 **Laiyang** China
70 B2 **Laizhou** China
70 B2 **Laizhou Wan** *b.* China
50 C1 **Lajamanu** Austr.
152 C3 **Lajes** Brazil
144 B2 **La Junta** Mex.
136 C3 **La Junta** U.S.A.
121 C2 **Lake Cabora Bassa** *resr* M
53 C2 **Lake Cargelligo** Austr.
53 D2 **Lake Cathie** Austr.
142 B2 **Lake Charles** U.S.A.
143 D2 **Lake City** *FL* U.S.A.
143 E2 **Lake City** *SC* U.S.A.
108 A1 **Lake Como** Italy
128 B3 **Lake Cowichan** Can.
108 B1 **Lake Garda** Italy
138 A2 **Lake Havasu City** U.S.A.
143 D3 **Lakeland** U.S.A.
128 C2 **Lake Louise** Can.
134 B1 **Lake Oswego** U.S.A.
54 A2 **Lake Paringa** N.Z.
142 B2 **Lake Providence** U.S.A.
54 B2 **Lake Pukaki** N.Z.
53 C3 **Lakes Entrance** Austr.
134 B2 **Lakeview** U.S.A.
136 B3 **Lakewood** *CO* U.S.A.
141 E2 **Lakewood** *NJ* U.S.A.
143 D3 **Lake Worth** U.S.A.
74 A2 **Lakhpat** India
74 B1 **Lakki Marwat** Pak.
111 B3 **Lakonikos Kolpos** *b.* Gree
92 H1 **Lakselv** Norway
107 C1 **L'Alcora** Spain
145 C3 **La Libertad** Guat.
106 B1 **Lalín** Spain
75 B2 **Lalitpur** India
129 D2 **La Loche** Can.
100 B2 **La Louvière** Belgium
108 A2 **La Maddalena** *Sardegna* I
61 C1 **Lamag** *Sabah* Malaysia
La Manche *str.* France/U. **English Channel**
136 C3 **Lamar** U.S.A.
79 C2 **Lamard** Iran
108 A3 **La Marmora, Punta** *mt.* *Sardegna* Italy
128 C1 **La Martre, Lac** *l.* Can.
118 B3 **Lambaréné** Gabon

2 A3 **Lambert's Bay** S. Africa
2 A2 **Lambeyri** Iceland
6 B1 **Lamego** Port.
0 A3 **La Merced** Peru
2 B3 **Lameroo** Austr.
9 C2 **Lamesa** U.S.A.
1 B3 **Lamia** Greece
7 E2 **Lamoni** U.S.A.
2 A2 **Lampang** Thai.
9 D2 **Lampasas** U.S.A.
5 B2 **Lampazos** Mex.
9 A2 **Lampeter** U.K.
2 A2 **Lamphun** Thai.
9 E3 **Lamu** Kenya
6 C3 **Lanark** U.K.
3 A2 **Lanbi Kyun** *i.* Myanmar
Lancang Jiang *r.* China *see* **Mekong**
8 B1 **Lancaster** U.K.
5 C4 **Lancaster** *CA* U.S.A.
0 C3 **Lancaster** *OH* U.S.A.
1 D2 **Lancaster** *PA* U.S.A.
3 D2 **Lancaster** *SC* U.S.A.
7 F2 **Lancaster Sound** *str.* Can.
Lanchow China *see* **Lanzhou**
2 C2 **Landeck** Austria
6 B2 **Lander** U.S.A.
9 A3 **Land's End** *pt* U.K.
2 C2 **Landshut** Ger.
3 F4 **Landskrona** Sweden
3 C2 **Lanett** U.S.A.
2 B2 **Langberg** *mts* S. Africa
7 D1 **Langdon** U.S.A.
3 F4 **Langeland** *i.* Denmark
1 D1 **Langen** Ger.
0 C1 **Langeoog** Ger.
0 C1 **Langeoog** *i.* Ger.
1 D2 **Langgöns** Ger.
2 A3 **Langjökull** Iceland
5 C3 **Langogne** France
4 B3 **Langon** France
5 D2 **Langres** France
0 A1 **Langsa** Indon.
2 B1 **Lang Sơn** Vietnam
1 D1 **Langwedel** Ger.
9 D2 **Lanigan** Can.
3 A4 **Lanín, Volcán** *vol.* Arg./Chile
1 C2 **Länkäran** Azer.
4 B2 **Lannion** France
0 C2 **Lansing** U.S.A.
1 B3 **Lanxi** China
7 B4 **Lanya** Sudan
4 A2 **Lanzarote** *i.* Islas Canarias
0 A2 **Lanzhou** China
4 B1 **Laoag** Phil.
2 B1 **Lao Cai** Vietnam
0 B2 **Laohekou** China
8 C2 **Laojunmiao** China
5 B1 **Laoling** China
5 B1 **Lao Ling** *mts* China
5 C2 **Laon** France
2 B2 **Laos** *country* Asia
5 B1 **Laotougou** China
4 C3 **Lapa** Brazil
4 A2 **La Palma** *i.* Islas Canarias
6 C4 **La Palma** Panama
0 B1 **La Paragua** Venez.
2 B2 **La Paz** Bol.
4 A2 **La Paz** Mex.
0 B2 **La Pedrera** Col.
6 D1 **La Pérouse Strait** Japan/Rus. Fed.
5 C2 **La Pesca** Mex.
4 B2 **La Piedad** Mex.
3 C4 **La Plata** Arg.
3 C4 **La Plata, Río de** *sea chan.* Arg./Uru.
93 I3 **Lappeenranta** Fin.
92 G2 **Lappland** *reg.* Europe
111 C2 **Lâpseki** Turkey
83 J1 **Laptev Sea** Rus. Fed.
Laptevykh, More *sea* Rus. Fed. *see* **Laptev Sea**
92 H3 **Lapua** Fin.
152 B3 **La Quiaca** Arg.
79 C2 **Lār** Iran
114 B1 **Larache** Morocco
136 B2 **Laramie** U.S.A.
136 B2 **Laramie Mountains** U.S.A.
154 B3 **Laranjeiras do Sul** Brazil
59 C3 **Larantuka** Indon.
59 C3 **Larat** *i.* Indon.
107 D2 **Larba** Alg.
106 C1 **Laredo** Spain
139 D3 **Laredo** U.S.A.
96 B3 **Largs** U.K.
152 B3 **La Rioja** Arg.
111 B3 **Larisa** Greece
74 A2 **Larkana** Pak.
80 B2 **Larnaca** Cyprus
97 D1 **Larne** U.K.
100 B2 **La Roche-en-Ardenne** Belgium
104 B2 **La Rochelle** France
104 B2 **La Roche-sur-Yon** France
107 C2 **La Roda** Spain
147 D3 **La Romana** Dom. Rep.
129 D2 **La Ronge** Can.
129 D2 **La Ronge, Lac** *l.* Can.
50 C1 **Larrimah** Austr.
55 P3 **Larsen Ice Shelf** Antarctica
93 F4 **Larvik** Norway
130 C2 **La Sarre** Can.
138 B2 **Las Cruces** U.S.A.
153 C4 **Las Flores** Arg.
153 B4 **Las Heras** Arg.
62 A1 **Lashio** Myanmar
74 A1 **Lashkar Gāh** Afgh.
109 C3 **La Sila** *reg.* Italy
152 B3 **Las Lomitas** Arg.
144 B2 **Las Nieves** Mex.
114 A2 **Las Palmas de Gran Canaria** Islas Canarias
108 A2 **La Spezia** Italy
153 B5 **Las Plumas** Arg.
129 D2 **Last Mountain Lake** Can.
152 B3 **Las Tórtolas, Cerro** *mt.* Arg./Chile
118 B3 **Lastoursville** Gabon
109 C2 **Lastovo** *i.* Croatia
144 A2 **Las Tres Vírgenes, Volcán** *vol.* Mex.
146 C2 **Las Tunas** Cuba
144 B2 **Las Varas** *Chihuahua* Mex.
144 B2 **Las Varas** *Nayarit* Mex.
138 B1 **Las Vegas** *NM* U.S.A.
135 C3 **Las Vegas** *NV* U.S.A.
131 E1 **La Tabatière** Can.
80 B2 **Latakia** Syria
104 B3 **La Teste-de-Buch** France
108 B2 **Latina** Italy
147 D3 **La Tortuga, Isla** *i.* Venez.
64 B1 **La Trinidad** Phil.
89 E2 **Latskoye** Rus. Fed.
131 C2 **La Tuque** Can.
88 B2 **Latvia** *country* Europe
102 C1 **Lauchhammer** Ger.
101 E3 **Lauf an der Pegnitz** Ger.
105 D2 **Laufen** Switz.
51 D4 **Launceston** Austr.
99 A3 **Launceston** U.K.
62 A1 **Launggyaung** Myanmar
51 D1 **Laura** Austr.
142 C2 **Laurel** *MS* U.S.A.
134 E1 **Laurel** *MT* U.S.A.
109 C2 **Lauria** Italy
143 E2 **Laurinburg** U.S.A.
105 D2 **Lausanne** Switz.
61 C2 **Laut** *i.* Indon.
61 C2 **Laut Bali** *sea* Indon.
101 D2 **Lautersbach (Hessen)** Ger.
61 C2 **Laut Kecil, Kepulauan** *is* Indon.
100 C1 **Lauwersmeer** *l.* Neth.
104 B2 **Laval** France
107 C2 **La Vall d'Uixó** Spain
50 B2 **Laverton** Austr.
155 D2 **Lavras** Brazil
123 D2 **Lavumisa** Swaziland
61 C1 **Lawas** *Sarawak* Malaysia
62 A1 **Lawksawk** Myanmar
114 B3 **Lawra** Ghana
137 D3 **Lawrence** U.S.A.
142 C1 **Lawrenceburg** U.S.A.
139 D2 **Lawton** U.S.A.
78 A2 **Lawz, Jabal al** *mt.* Saudi Arabia
93 F4 **Laxå** Sweden
74 B1 **Layyah** Pak.
109 D2 **Lazarevac** Serbia
144 A1 **Lázaro Cárdenas** *Baja California* Mex.
144 B3 **Lázaro Cárdenas** *Michoacán* Mex.
88 B3 **Lazdijai** Lith.
136 C2 **Lead** U.S.A.
129 D2 **Leader** Can.
136 B3 **Leadville** U.S.A.
Leaf Bay Can. *see* **Tasiujaq**
129 D2 **Leaf Rapids** Can.
97 B2 **Leane, Lough** *l.* Ireland
137 E3 **Leavenworth** U.S.A.
80 B2 **Lebanon** *country* Asia
137 E3 **Lebanon** *MO* U.S.A.
141 E2 **Lebanon** *NH* U.S.A.
134 B2 **Lebanon** *OR* U.S.A.
141 D2 **Lebanon** *PA* U.S.A.
89 E3 **Lebedyan'** Rus. Fed.
91 C1 **Lebedyn** Ukr.
104 C2 **Le Blanc** France
103 D1 **Lębork** Pol.
123 C1 **Lebowakgomo** S. Africa
106 B2 **Lebrija** Spain
153 A4 **Lebu** Chile
104 C3 **Le Bugue** France
109 C2 **Lecce** Italy
108 A1 **Lecco** Italy
102 C2 **Lech** *r.* Austria/Ger.
111 B3 **Lechaina** Greece
71 B3 **Lechang** China
102 B1 **Leck** Ger.
104 C3 **Lectoure** France
106 B1 **Ledesma** Spain
104 C2 **Le Dorat** France
128 C2 **Leduc** Can.
137 E1 **Leech Lake** U.S.A.
98 C2 **Leeds** U.K.
98 B2 **Leek** U.K.
100 C1 **Leer (Ostfriesland)** Ger.
143 D3 **Leesburg** U.S.A.
142 B2 **Leesville** U.S.A.
53 C2 **Leeton** Austr.
122 B3 **Leeu-Gamka** S. Africa
100 B1 **Leeuwarden** Neth.
50 A3 **Leeuwin, Cape** Austr.
147 D3 **Leeward Islands** Caribbean Sea
111 B3 **Lefkada** Greece
111 B3 **Lefkada** *i.* Greece
Lefkosia Cyprus *see* **Nicosia**
64 B1 **Legaspi** Phil.
108 B1 **Legnago** Italy

103 D1 **Legnica** Pol.
75 B1 **Leh** India
104 C2 **Le Havre** France
122 B1 **Lehututu** Botswana
103 D2 **Leibnitz** Austria
99 C2 **Leicester** U.K.
51 C1 **Leichhardt** *r.* Austr.
100 B1 **Leiden** Neth.
100 A2 **Leie** *r.* Belgium
52 A2 **Leigh Creek** Austr.
93 E3 **Leikanger** Norway
101 D1 **Leine** *r.* Ger.
97 C2 **Leinster** *reg.* Ireland
101 F2 **Leipzig** Ger.
92 F2 **Leiranger** Norway
106 B2 **Leiria** Port.
93 E4 **Leirvik** Norway
97 C2 **Leixlip** Ireland
71 B3 **Leiyang** China
71 B3 **Leizhou** China
71 A3 **Leizhou Bandao** *pen.* China
118 B3 **Lékana** Congo
100 B1 **Lelystad** Neth.
153 B6 **Le Maire, Estrecho de** *sea chan.* Arg.
Léman, Lac *l.* France/Switz. *see* **Geneva, Lake**
104 C2 **Le Mans** France
137 D2 **Le Mars** U.S.A.
154 C2 **Leme** Brazil
Lemesos Cyprus *see* **Limassol**
101 D1 **Lemförde** Ger.
127 G2 **Lemieux Islands** Can.
136 C1 **Lemmon** U.S.A.
135 C3 **Lemoore** U.S.A.
131 D1 **Le Moyne, Lac** *l.* Can.
62 A1 **Lemro** *r.* Myanmar
109 C2 **Le Murge** *hills* Italy
83 J2 **Lena** *r.* Rus. Fed.
100 C1 **Lengerich** Ger.
71 B3 **Lengshuijiang** China
71 B3 **Lengshuitan** China
91 D2 **Lenine** Ukr.
Leningrad Rus. Fed. *see* **St Petersburg**
91 D2 **Leningradskaya** Rus. Fed.
77 D3 **Lenin Peak** Kyrg./Tajik.
Leninsk Kazakh. *see* **Baykonyr**
89 E3 **Leninskiy** Rus. Fed.
100 A2 **Lens** Belgium
104 C1 **Lens** France
83 I2 **Lensk** Rus. Fed.
103 D2 **Lenti** Hungary
109 C3 **Lentini** *Sicilia* Italy
114 B3 **Léo** Burkina
103 D2 **Leoben** Austria
99 B2 **Leominster** U.K.
144 B2 **León** Mex.
146 B3 **León** Nic.
106 B1 **León** Spain
122 A1 **Leonardville** Namibia
50 B2 **Leonora** Austr.
155 D2 **Leopoldina** Brazil
123 C1 **Lephalale** S. Africa
123 C1 **Lephepe** Botswana
123 C3 **Lephoi** S. Africa
71 B3 **Leping** China
105 C2 **Le Puy-en-Velay** France
150 A2 **Lérida** Col.
106 C1 **Lerma** Spain
111 C3 **Leros** *i.* Greece
130 C1 **Le Roy, Lac** *l.* Can.
93 F4 **Lerum** Sweden
96 □ **Lerwick** U.K.
111 C3 **Lesbos** *i.* Greece
147 C3 **Les Cayes** Haiti
69 C3 **Leshan** China
86 D2 **Leshukonskoye** Rus. Fed.
109 D2 **Leskovac** Serbia
104 B2 **Lesneven** France
89 E2 **Lesnoye** Rus. Fed.
83 H3 **Lesosibirsk** Rus. Fed.
123 C2 **Lesotho** *country* Africa
66 B1 **Lesozavodsk** Rus. Fed.
104 B2 **Les Sables-d'Olonne** France
147 D3 **Lesser Antilles** *is* Caribbean Sea
81 C1 **Lesser Caucasus** *mts* Asia
128 C2 **Lesser Slave Lake** Can.
58 B3 **Lesser Sunda Islands** *is* Indon.
105 C3 **Les Vans** France
Lesvos *i.* Greece *see* **Lesbos**
103 D1 **Leszno** Pol.
99 C3 **Letchworth Garden City** U.K.
128 C3 **Lethbridge** Can.
150 C1 **Lethem** Guyana
59 C3 **Leti, Kepulauan** *is* Indon.
150 B2 **Leticia** Col.
123 C1 **Letlhakeng** Botswana
104 C1 **Le Touquet-Paris-Plage** France
99 D3 **Le Tréport** France
63 A2 **Letsok-aw Kyun** *i.* Myanmar
123 C2 **Letsopa** S. Africa
97 C1 **Letterkenny** Ireland
105 C3 **Leucate, Étang de** *l.* France
60 A1 **Leuser, Gunung** *mt.* Indon.
100 B2 **Leuven** Belgium
92 F3 **Levanger** Norway
139 C2 **Levelland** U.S.A.
50 B1 **Lévêque, Cape** Austr.
100 C2 **Leverkusen** Ger.
103 D2 **Levice** Slovakia
54 C2 **Levin** N.Z.
131 C2 **Lévis** Can.
89 E3 **Lev Tolstoy** Rus. Fed.
99 D3 **Lewes** U.K.
96 A1 **Lewis, Isle of** *i.* U.K.
140 C3 **Lewisburg** U.S.A.
134 D1 **Lewis Range** *mts* U.S.A.
134 C1 **Lewiston** *ID* U.S.A.
141 E2 **Lewiston** *ME* U.S.A.
134 E1 **Lewistown** U.S.A.
140 C3 **Lexington** *KY* U.S.A.
136 D2 **Lexington** *NE* U.S.A.
141 D3 **Lexington** *VA* U.S.A.
64 B1 **Leyte** *i.* Phil.
109 C2 **Lezhë** Albania
89 F2 **Lezhnevo** Rus. Fed.
89 E3 **L'gov** Rus. Fed.
75 C2 **Lhagoi Kangri** *mt.* China
68 C2 **Lharigarbo** China
75 D2 **Lhasa** China
75 C2 **Lhazê** China
60 A1 **Lhokseumawe** Indon.
111 B3 **Liakoura** *mt.* Greece
67 B3 **Liancourt Rocks** *i.* N. Pacific Ocean
71 B3 **Lianhua** China
71 B3 **Lianjiang** China
70 C1 **Lianshan** China
70 B2 **Lianyungang** China
71 B3 **Lianzhou** China
70 B2 **Liaocheng** China
70 C1 **Liaodong Bandao** *pen.* China
70 C1 **Liaodong Wan** *b.* China
65 A1 **Liao He** *r.* China
70 C1 **Liaoning** *prov.* China
65 A1 **Liaoyang** China
65 B1 **Liaoyuan** China
128 B1 **Liard** *r.* Can.
134 C1 **Libby** U.S.A.
118 B2 **Libenge** Dem. Rep. Congo
136 C3 **Liberal** U.S.A.
103 D1 **Liberec** Czech Rep.
114 B4 **Liberia** *country* Africa
146 B3 **Liberia** Costa Rica
150 B1 **Libertad** Venez.
100 B3 **Libin** Belgium
104 B3 **Libourne** France
118 A2 **Libreville** Gabon
115 D2 **Libya** *country* Africa
115 E2 **Libyan Desert** Egypt/Libya
116 A1 **Libyan Plateau** Egypt/Liby
108 B3 **Licata** *Sicilia* Italy
Licheng China *see* **Lipu**
121 C2 **Lichinga** Moz.
101 E2 **Lichte** Ger.
123 C2 **Lichtenburg** S. Africa
101 E2 **Lichtenfels** Ger.
88 C3 **Lida** Belarus
93 F4 **Lidköping** Sweden
50 C2 **Liebig, Mount** Austr.
105 D2 **Liechtenstein** *country* Euro
100 B2 **Liège** Belgium
92 J3 **Lieksa** Fin.
119 C2 **Lienart** Dem. Rep. Congo
63 B2 **Liên Nghia** Vietnam
102 C2 **Lienz** Austria
88 B2 **Liepāja** Latvia
102 C2 **Liezen** Austria
97 C2 **Liffey** *r.* Ireland
97 C1 **Lifford** Ireland
53 C1 **Lightning Ridge** Austr.
121 C2 **Ligonha** *r.* Moz.
105 D3 **Ligurian Sea** France/Italy
119 C4 **Likasi** Dem. Rep. Congo
128 B2 **Likely** Can.
89 E2 **Likhoslavl'** Rus. Fed.
61 B1 **Liku** Indon.
105 D3 **L'Île-Rousse** *Corse* France
71 B3 **Liling** China
93 F4 **Lilla Edet** Sweden
100 B2 **Lille** Belgium
105 C1 **Lille** France
Lille Bælt *sea chan.* Denma *see* **Little Belt**
93 F3 **Lillehammer** Norway
93 F4 **Lillestrøm** Norway
128 B2 **Lillooet** Can.
121 C2 **Lilongwe** Malawi
64 B2 **Liloy** Phil.
150 A3 **Lima** Peru
140 C2 **Lima** U.S.A.
80 B2 **Limassol** Cyprus
97 C1 **Limavady** U.K.
153 B4 **Limay** *r.* Arg.
101 F2 **Limbach-Oberfrohna** Ger.
88 B2 **Limbaži** Latvia
118 A2 **Limbe** Cameroon
100 D2 **Limburg an der Lahn** Ger.
122 B2 **Lime Acres** S. Africa
154 C2 **Limeira** Brazil
97 B2 **Limerick** Ireland
93 E4 **Limfjorden** *sea chan.* Denr
111 C3 **Limnos** *i.* Greece
104 C2 **Limoges** France
136 C3 **Limon** U.S.A.
104 C3 **Limoux** France
123 C1 **Limpopo** *prov.* S. Africa
121 C3 **Limpopo** *r.* S. Africa/Zimbabwe
64 A1 **Linapacan** *i.* Phil.
153 A4 **Linares** Chile
145 C2 **Linares** Mex.
106 C2 **Linares** Spain
62 B1 **Lincang** China
Linchuan *Jiangxi* China *see* **Fuzhou**
98 C2 **Lincoln** U.K.

B2 **Lincoln** *IL* U.S.A.
F1 **Lincoln** *ME* U.S.A.
D2 **Lincoln** *NE* U.S.A.
C1 **Linden** Guyana
C1 **Linden** U.S.A.
C2 **Lindi** *r.* Dem. Rep. Congo
D3 **Lindi** Tanz.
Lindisfarne *i.* U.K. *see* **Holy Island**
A2 **Lindos** Greece
D2 **Lindsay** Can.
H2 **Line Islands** Kiribati
B2 **Linfen** China
B1 **Lingayen** Phil.
B2 **Lingbao** China
C3 **Lingelethu** S. Africa
C3 **Lingelihle** S. Africa
C1 **Lingen (Ems)** Ger.
B2 **Lingga, Kepulauan** *is* Indon.
A3 **Lingshan** China
A4 **Lingshui** China
A3 **Linguère** Senegal
D1 **Linhares** Brazil
A1 **Linhe** China
G4 **Linköping** Sweden
B1 **Linkou** China
B2 **Linqing** China
C2 **Lins** Brazil
C1 **Linton** U.S.A.
D2 **Linxi** China
C2 **Linxia** China
B2 **Linyi** *Shandong* China
B2 **Linyi** *Shandong* China
B2 **Linying** China
C2 **Linz** Austria
C3 **Lion, Golfe du** *g.* France
B3 **Lipari** Italy
B3 **Lipari, Isole** *is* Italy
E3 **Lipetsk** Rus. Fed.
B1 **Lipova** Romania
D2 **Lippstadt** Ger.
B3 **Lipu** China
C1 **Lisakovsk** Kazakh.
C2 **Lisala** Dem. Rep. Congo
Lisboa Port. *see* **Lisbon**
B2 **Lisbon** Port.
C1 **Lisburn** U.K.
B2 **Liscannor Bay** Ireland
C2 **Lisieux** France
A3 **Liskeard** U.K.
E3 **Liski** Rus. Fed.
D1 **Lismore** Austr.
C1 **Lisnaskea** U.K.
B2 **Listowel** Ireland
A3 **Litang** *Guangxi* China
C2 **Litang** *Sichuan* China
B3 **Litchfield** *IL* U.S.A.
E1 **Litchfield** *MN* U.S.A.
D2 **Lithgow** Austr.
B3 **Lithino, Akrotirio** *pt* Greece
B2 **Lithuania** *country* Europe
C1 **Litoměřice** Czech Rep.
C2 **Little Abaco** *i.* Bahamas
D3 **Little Andaman** *i.* India
E4 **Little Belt** *sea chan.* Denmark
E1 **Little Falls** U.S.A.
C2 **Littlefield** U.S.A.
C3 **Littlehampton** U.K.
A2 **Little Karas Berg** *plat.* Namibia
B3 **Little Karoo** *plat.* S. Africa
A2 **Little Minch** *sea chan.* U.K.
C1 **Little Missouri** *r.* U.S.A.
A3 **Little Nicobar** *i.* India
B2 **Little Rock** U.S.A.
E2 **Littleton** U.S.A.
B2 **Liujiachang** China

71 A3 **Liuzhou** China
111 B3 **Livadeia** Greece
88 C2 **Līvāni** Latvia
50 B1 **Liveringa** Austr.
138 C2 **Livermore, Mount** U.S.A.
131 D2 **Liverpool** Can.
98 B2 **Liverpool** U.K.
127 F2 **Liverpool, Cape** Can.
53 C2 **Liverpool Range** *mts* Austr.
134 D1 **Livingston** *MT* U.S.A.
139 E2 **Livingston** *TX* U.S.A.
139 D2 **Livingston, Lake** U.S.A.
120 B2 **Livingstone** Zambia
109 C2 **Livno** Bos.-Herz.
89 E3 **Livny** Rus. Fed.
140 C2 **Livonia** U.S.A.
108 B2 **Livorno** Italy
119 D3 **Liwale** Tanz.
70 B2 **Liyang** China
99 A4 **Lizard Point** U.K.
108 B1 **Ljubljana** Slovenia
93 G3 **Ljungan** *r.* Sweden
93 F4 **Ljungby** Sweden
93 G3 **Ljusdal** Sweden
93 G3 **Ljusnan** *r.* Sweden
99 B3 **Llandeilo** U.K.
99 B3 **Llandovery** U.K.
99 B2 **Llandrindod Wells** U.K.
98 B2 **Llandudno** U.K.
99 A3 **Llanelli** U.K.
98 A2 **Llangefni** U.K.
139 C2 **Llano Estacado** *plain* U.S.A.
150 B1 **Llanos** *plain* Col./Venez.
107 D1 **Lleida** Spain
99 A2 **Lleyn Peninsula** U.K.
107 C2 **Llíria** Spain
106 C1 **Llodio** Spain
128 B2 **Lloyd George, Mount** Can.
129 D2 **Lloyd Lake** Can.
129 C2 **Lloydminster** Can.
152 B3 **Llullaillaco, Volcán** *vol.* Chile
123 C2 **Lobatse** Botswana
120 A2 **Lobito** Angola
101 F1 **Loburg** Ger.
96 B2 **Lochaber** *reg.* U.K.
104 C2 **Loches** France
96 B2 **Lochgilphead** U.K.
96 B1 **Lochinver** U.K.
96 A2 **Lochmaddy** U.K.
96 C2 **Lochnagar** *mt.* U.K.
52 A2 **Lock** Austr.
96 C3 **Lockerbie** U.K.
139 D3 **Lockhart** U.S.A.
141 D2 **Lock Haven** U.S.A.
141 D2 **Lockport** U.S.A.
63 B2 **Lôc Ninh** Vietnam
105 C3 **Lodève** France
86 C2 **Lodeynoye Pole** Rus. Fed.
92 F2 **Løding** Norway
119 D2 **Lodwar** Kenya
103 D1 **Łódź** Pol.
62 B2 **Loei** Thai.
122 A3 **Loeriesfontein** S. Africa
92 F2 **Lofoten** *is* Norway
134 D2 **Logan** U.S.A.
126 B2 **Logan, Mount** Can.
140 B2 **Logansport** U.S.A.
108 B1 **Logatec** Slovenia
106 C1 **Logroño** Spain
101 D1 **Löhne** Ger.
101 D1 **Lohne (Oldenburg)** Ger.
62 A2 **Loikaw** Myanmar
62 A2 **Loi Lan** *mt.* Myanmar/Thai.
104 B2 **Loire** *r.* France
150 A2 **Loja** Ecuador
106 C2 **Loja** Spain
92 I2 **Lokan tekojärvi** *resr* Fin.

100 B2 **Lokeren** Belgium
122 B1 **Lokgwabe** Botswana
119 D2 **Lokichar** Kenya
119 D2 **Lokichokio** Kenya
89 D2 **Loknya** Rus. Fed.
115 C4 **Lokoja** Nigeria
89 D3 **Lokot'** Rus. Fed.
88 C2 **Loksa** Estonia
127 G2 **Loks Land** *i.* Can.
93 F4 **Lolland** *i.* Denmark
119 D3 **Lollondo** Tanz.
122 B2 **Lolwane** S. Africa
110 B2 **Lom** Bulg.
93 E3 **Lom** Norway
119 C2 **Lomami** *r.* Dem. Rep. Congo
153 C4 **Lomas de Zamora** Arg.
61 C2 **Lombok** *i.* Indon.
61 C2 **Lombok, Selat** *sea chan.* Indon.
114 C4 **Lomé** Togo
118 C3 **Lomela** *r.* Dem. Rep. Congo
100 B2 **Lommel** Belgium
96 B2 **Lomond, Loch** *l.* U.K.
88 C2 **Lomonosov** Rus. Fed.
135 B4 **Lompoc** U.S.A.
63 B2 **Lom Sak** Thai.
103 E1 **Łomża** Pol.
130 B2 **London** Can.
99 C3 **London** U.K.
140 C3 **London** U.S.A.
97 C1 **Londonderry** U.K.
50 B1 **Londonderry, Cape** Austr.
154 B2 **Londrina** Brazil
83 M2 **Longa, Proliv** *sea chan.* Rus. Fed.
61 C1 **Long Akah** *Sarawak* Malaysia
143 E2 **Long Bay** U.S.A.
135 C4 **Long Beach** U.S.A.
97 C2 **Longford** Ireland
61 C2 **Longiram** Indon.
147 C2 **Long Island** Bahamas
130 C1 **Long Island** Can.
59 D3 **Long Island** P.N.G.
141 E2 **Long Island** U.S.A.
130 B2 **Longlac** Can.
130 B2 **Long Lake** Can.
136 B2 **Longmont** U.S.A.
70 A2 **Longnan** China
140 C2 **Long Point** Can.
71 B3 **Longquan** China
131 E2 **Long Range Mountains** Can.
51 D2 **Longreach** Austr.
99 D2 **Long Stratton** U.K.
98 B1 **Longtown** U.K.
105 D2 **Longuyon** France
139 E2 **Longview** *TX* U.S.A.
134 B1 **Longview** *WA* U.S.A.
70 A2 **Longxi** China
71 B3 **Longxi Shan** *mt.* China
63 B2 **Long Xuyên** Vietnam
71 B3 **Longyan** China
82 C1 **Longyearbyen** Svalbard
102 B2 **Lons-le-Saunier** France
143 E2 **Lookout, Cape** U.S.A.
97 B2 **Loop Head** Ireland
63 B2 **Lop Buri** Thai.
64 B1 **Lopez** Phil.
68 C2 **Lop Nur** *salt flat* China
118 B2 **Lopori** *r.* Dem. Rep. Congo
74 A2 **Lora, Hamun-i-** *dry lake* Afgh./Pak.
106 B2 **Lora del Río** Spain
140 C2 **Lorain** U.S.A.
74 A1 **Loralai** Pak.
107 C2 **Lorca** Spain
48 E5 **Lord Howe Island** Austr.
138 B2 **Lordsburg** U.S.A.

155 C2 **Lorena** Brazil
152 B2 **Loreto** Bol.
144 A2 **Loreto** Mex.
104 B2 **Lorient** France
96 B2 **Lorn, Firth of** *est.* U.K.
52 B3 **Lorne** Austr.
138 B1 **Los Alamos** U.S.A.
139 D3 **Los Aldamas** Mex.
153 A4 **Los Ángeles** Chile
135 C4 **Los Angeles** U.S.A.
135 B3 **Los Banos** U.S.A.
152 B3 **Los Blancos** Arg.
91 E1 **Losevo** Rus. Fed.
108 B2 **Lošinj** *i.* Croatia
144 B2 **Los Mochis** Mex.
118 B2 **Losombo** Dem. Rep. Congo
147 D3 **Los Roques, Islas** *is* Venez.
96 C2 **Lossiemouth** U.K.
150 B1 **Los Teques** Venez.
152 A4 **Los Vilos** Chile
104 C3 **Lot** *r.* France
96 C1 **Loth** U.K.
119 D2 **Lotikipi Plain** Kenya/Sudan
118 C3 **Loto** Dem. Rep. Congo
89 E2 **Lotoshino** Rus. Fed.
62 B1 **Louangnamtha** Laos
62 B2 **Louangphabang** Laos
118 B3 **Loubomo** Congo
104 B2 **Loudéac** France
71 B3 **Loudi** China
118 B3 **Loudima** Congo
114 A3 **Louga** Senegal
99 C2 **Loughborough** U.K.
97 B2 **Loughrea** Ireland
105 D2 **Louhans** France
97 B2 **Louisburgh** Ireland
142 B2 **Louisiana** *state* U.S.A.
123 C1 **Louis Trichardt** S. Africa
140 B3 **Louisville** *KY* U.S.A.
142 C2 **Louisville** *MS* U.S.A.
86 C2 **Loukhi** Rus. Fed.
130 C1 **Loups Marins, Lacs des** *lakes* Can.
104 B3 **Lourdes** France
151 C1 **Lourenço** Brazil
106 B1 **Lousã** Port.
53 C2 **Louth** Austr.
98 C2 **Louth** U.K.
Louvain Belgium *see* **Leuven**
89 D2 **Lovat'** *r.* Rus. Fed.
110 B2 **Lovech** Bulg.
136 B2 **Loveland** U.S.A.
135 C2 **Lovelock** U.S.A.
139 C2 **Lovington** U.S.A.
119 C3 **Lowa** Dem. Rep. Congo
141 E2 **Lowell** U.S.A.
128 C3 **Lower Arrow Lake** Can.
54 B2 **Lower Hutt** N.Z.
97 C1 **Lower Lough Erne** *l.* U.K.
128 B2 **Lower Post** Can.
99 D2 **Lowestoft** U.K.
103 D1 **Łowicz** Pol.
141 D2 **Lowville** U.S.A.
52 B2 **Loxton** Austr.
Loyang China *see* **Luoyang**
48 F4 **Loyauté, Îles** *is* New Caledonia
89 D3 **Loyew** Belarus
92 F2 **Løypskardtinden** *mt.* Norway
109 C2 **Loznica** Serbia
91 D2 **Lozova** Ukr.
120 B2 **Luacano** Angola
70 B2 **Lu'an** China
120 A1 **Luanda** Angola
121 C2 **Luangwa** *r.* Zambia
121 B2 **Luanshya** Zambia
106 B1 **Luarca** Spain
120 B2 **Luau** Angola
103 E1 **Lubaczów** Pol.
120 A2 **Lubango** Angola
119 C3 **Lubao** Dem. Rep. Congo
103 E1 **Lubartów** Pol.
101 D1 **Lübbecke** Ger.
139 C2 **Lubbock** U.S.A.
101 E1 **Lübeck** Ger.
69 E2 **Lubei** China
87 E3 **Lubenka** Kazakh.
103 D1 **Lubin** Pol.
103 E1 **Lublin** Pol.
91 C1 **Lubny** Ukr.
61 C1 **Lubok Antu** *Sarawak* Malaysia
101 E1 **Lübow** Ger.
101 E1 **Lübtheen** Ger.
119 C3 **Lubudi** Dem. Rep. Congo
60 B2 **Lubuklinggau** Indon.
119 C4 **Lubumbashi** Dem. Rep. Congo
120 B2 **Lubungu** Zambia
119 C3 **Lubutu** Dem. Rep. Congo
120 A1 **Lucala** Angola
97 C2 **Lucan** Ireland
120 B1 **Lucapa** Angola
96 B3 **Luce Bay** U.K.
154 B2 **Lucélia** Brazil
64 B1 **Lucena** Phil.
106 C2 **Lucena** Spain
103 D2 **Lučenec** Slovakia
109 C2 **Lucera** Italy
105 D2 **Lucerne** Switz.
101 E1 **Lüchow** Ger.
120 A2 **Lucira** Angola
101 F1 **Luckenwalde** Ger.
122 B2 **Luckhoff** S. Africa
75 C2 **Lucknow** India
120 B2 **Lucusse** Angola
Lüda China *see* **Dalian**
100 C2 **Lüdenscheid** Ger.
101 E1 **Lüder** Ger.
120 A3 **Lüderitz** Namibia
74 B1 **Ludhiana** India
140 B2 **Ludington** U.S.A.
99 B2 **Ludlow** U.K.
135 C4 **Ludlow** U.S.A.
110 C2 **Ludogorie** *reg.* Bulg.
93 G3 **Ludvika** Sweden
102 B2 **Ludwigsburg** Ger.
101 F1 **Ludwigsfelde** Ger.
101 D3 **Ludwigshafen am Rhein** Ger.
101 E1 **Ludwigslust** Ger.
88 C2 **Ludza** Latvia
118 C3 **Luebo** Dem. Rep. Congo
120 A2 **Luena** Angola
70 A2 **Lüeyang** China
71 B3 **Lufeng** China
139 E2 **Lufkin** U.S.A.
88 C2 **Luga** Rus. Fed.
88 C2 **Luga** *r.* Rus. Fed.
105 D2 **Lugano** Switz.
121 C2 **Lugenda** *r.* Moz.
97 C2 **Lugnaquilla** *h.* Ireland
106 B1 **Lugo** Spain
110 B1 **Lugoj** Romania
91 D2 **Luhans'k** Ukr.
119 D3 **Luhombero** Tanz.
90 B1 **Luhyny** Ukr.
120 B2 **Luiana** Angola
118 C3 **Luilaka** *r.* Dem. Rep. Congo
105 D2 **Luino** Italy
92 I2 **Luiro** *r.* Fin.
118 C3 **Luiza** Dem. Rep. Congo
70 B2 **Lujiang** China
109 C2 **Lukavac** Bos.-Herz.
118 B3 **Lukenie** *r.* Dem. Rep. Congo
138 A2 **Lukeville** U.S.A.
89 E3 **Lukhovitsy** Rus. Fed.
103 E1 **Łuków** Pol.
120 B2 **Lukulu** Zambia
92 H2 **Luleå** Sweden
92 H2 **Luleälven** *r.* Sweden
110 C2 **Lüleburgaz** Turkey
70 B2 **Lüliang Shan** *mts* China
61 C2 **Lumajang** Indon.
75 C1 **Lumajangdong Co** *salt l.* China
120 B2 **Lumbala Kaquengue** Ango
120 B2 **Lumbala N'guimbo** Angol
143 E2 **Lumberton** U.S.A.
61 C1 **Lumbis** Indon.
106 B1 **Lumbrales** Spain
63 B2 **Lumphăt** Cambodia
129 D2 **Lumsden** Can.
54 A3 **Lumsden** N.Z.
93 F4 **Lund** Sweden
121 C2 **Lundazi** Zambia
99 A3 **Lundy** *i.* U.K.
101 E1 **Lüneburg** Ger.
101 E1 **Lüneburger Heide** *reg.* Ge
100 C2 **Lünen** Ger.
105 D2 **Lunéville** France
120 B2 **Lunga** *r.* Zambia
114 A4 **Lungi** Sierra Leone
62 A1 **Lunglei** India
120 B2 **Lungwebungu** *r.* Zambia
74 B2 **Luni** *r.* India
88 C3 **Luninyets** Belarus
114 A4 **Lunsar** Sierra Leone
77 E2 **Luntai** China
71 A3 **Luodian** China
71 B3 **Luoding** China
70 B2 **Luohe** China
70 B2 **Luoyang** China
121 B2 **Lupane** Zimbabwe
71 A3 **Lupanshui** China
110 B1 **Lupeni** Romania
121 C2 **Lupilichi** Moz.
101 F2 **Luppa** Ger.
121 D2 **Lúrio** Moz.
121 D2 **Lurio** *r.* Moz.
121 B2 **Lusaka** Zambia
118 C3 **Lusambo** Dem. Rep. Cong
109 C2 **Lushnjë** Albania
136 C2 **Lusk** U.S.A.
76 B3 **Lut, Dasht-e** *des.* Iran
99 C3 **Luton** U.K.
61 C1 **Lutong** *Sarawak* Malaysia
129 C1 **Łutselk'e** Can.
90 B1 **Luts'k** Ukr.
122 B2 **Lutzputs** S. Africa
122 A3 **Lutzville** S. Africa
117 C4 **Luuq** Somalia
137 D2 **Luverne** U.S.A.
119 C3 **Luvua** *r.* Dem. Rep. Congo
123 D1 **Luvuvhu** *r.* S. Africa
119 D2 **Luwero** Uganda
59 C3 **Luwuk** Indon.
100 C3 **Luxembourg** *country* Euro
100 C3 **Luxembourg** Lux.
105 D2 **Luxeuil-les-Bains** France
123 C3 **Luxolweni** S. Africa
116 B2 **Luxor** Egypt
100 B2 **Luyksgestel** Neth.
86 D2 **Luza** Rus. Fed.
Luzern Switz. *see* **Lucerne**
71 A3 **Luzhou** China
154 C1 **Luziânia** Brazil
151 D2 **Luzilândia** Brazil
64 B1 **Luzon** *i.* Phil.
71 C3 **Luzon Strait** Phil./Taiwan
90 A2 **L'viv** Ukr.
L'vov Ukr. *see* **L'viv**
88 C3 **Lyakhavichy** Belarus

92 G3 **Lycksele** Sweden
88 C3 **Lyel'chytsy** Belarus
88 C3 **Lyepyel'** Belarus
99 B3 **Lyme Bay** U.K.
41 D3 **Lynchburg** U.S.A.
29 D2 **Lynn Lake** Can.
29 D1 **Lynx Lake** Can.
05 C2 **Lyon** France
89 D2 **Lyozna** Belarus
86 E3 **Lys'va** Rus. Fed.
91 D2 **Lysychans'k** Ukr.
98 B2 **Lytham St Anne's** U.K.
88 C3 **Lyuban'** Belarus
89 E2 **Lyubertsy** Rus. Fed.
90 B1 **Lyubeshiv** Ukr.
89 F2 **Lyubim** Rus. Fed.
91 D2 **Lyubotyn** Ukr.
89 D2 **Lyubytino** Rus. Fed.
89 D3 **Lyudinovo** Rus. Fed.

M

80 B2 **Ma'ān** Jordan
88 C2 **Maardu** Estonia
00 B2 **Maas** *r.* Neth.
00 B2 **Maaseik** Belgium
64 B1 **Maasin** Phil.
00 B2 **Maastricht** Neth.
21 C3 **Mabalane** Moz.
50 C1 **Mabaruma** Guyana
21 C3 **Mabote** Moz.
22 B2 **Mabule** Botswana
22 B1 **Mabutsane** Botswana
55 D2 **Macaé** Brazil
21 C2 **Macaloge** Moz.
26 E2 **MacAlpine Lake** Can.
71 B3 **Macao** *aut. reg.* China
51 C1 **Macapá** Brazil
50 A2 **Macará** Ecuador
55 D1 **Macarani** Brazil
51 E2 **Macau** Brazil
23 D1 **Maccaretane** Moz.
98 B2 **Macclesfield** U.K.
50 B2 **Macdonald, Lake** *imp. l.* Austr.
50 C2 **Macdonnell Ranges** *mts* Austr.
30 A1 **MacDowell Lake** Can.
06 B1 **Macedo de Cavaleiros** Port.
52 B3 **Macedon** *mt.* Austr.
09 D2 **Macedonia** *country* Europe
51 E2 **Maceió** Brazil
08 B2 **Macerata** Italy
52 A2 **Macfarlane, Lake** *imp. l.* Austr.
97 B3 **Macgillycuddy's Reeks** *mts* Ireland
74 A2 **Mach** Pak.
55 C2 **Machado** Brazil
21 C3 **Machaila** Moz.
19 D3 **Machakos** Kenya
50 A2 **Machala** Ecuador
21 C3 **Machanga** Moz.
70 B2 **Macheng** China
41 F2 **Machias** U.S.A.
50 A1 **Machiques** Venez.
50 A3 **Machu Picchu** *tourist site* Peru
23 D2 **Macia** Moz.
10 C1 **Măcin** Romania
14 B3 **Macina** Mali
53 D1 **Macintyre** *r.* Austr.
51 D2 **Mackay** Austr.
50 B2 **Mackay, Lake** *imp. l.* Austr.
29 C1 **MacKay Lake** Can.
28 B2 **Mackenzie** Can.
28 A1 **Mackenzie** *r.* Can.
26 B2 **Mackenzie Bay** Can.
26 D1 **Mackenzie King Island** Can.
128 A1 **Mackenzie Mountains** Can.
129 D2 **Macklin** Can.
53 D2 **Macksville** Austr.
53 D1 **Maclean** Austr.
50 A2 **MacLeod, Lake** *dry lake* Austr.
140 A2 **Macomb** U.S.A.
108 A2 **Macomer** *Sardegna* Italy
105 C2 **Mâcon** France
143 D2 **Macon** *GA* U.S.A.
137 E3 **Macon** *MO* U.S.A.
53 C2 **Macquarie** *r.* Austr.
48 E6 **Macquarie Island** S. Pacific Ocean
53 C2 **Macquarie Marshes** Austr.
97 B3 **Macroom** Ireland
52 A1 **Macumba** *watercourse* Austr.
145 C3 **Macuspana** Mex.
144 B2 **Macuzari, Presa** *resr* Mex.
123 D2 **Madadeni** S. Africa
121 D3 **Madagascar** *country* Africa
115 D2 **Madama** Niger
111 B2 **Madan** Bulg.
59 D3 **Madang** P.N.G.
150 C2 **Madeira** *r.* Brazil
114 A1 **Madeira** *terr.* N. Atlantic Ocean
131 D2 **Madeleine, Îles de la** *is* Can.
144 B2 **Madera** Mex.
135 B3 **Madera** U.S.A.
73 B3 **Madgaon** India
118 B3 **Madingou** Congo
140 B3 **Madison** *IN* U.S.A.
137 D2 **Madison** *SD* U.S.A.
140 B2 **Madison** *WI* U.S.A.
140 C3 **Madison** *WV* U.S.A.
134 D1 **Madison** *r.* U.S.A.
140 B3 **Madisonville** U.S.A.
61 C2 **Madiun** Indon.
119 D2 **Mado Gashi** Kenya
68 C2 **Madoi** China
88 C2 **Madona** Latvia
78 A2 **Madrakah** Saudi Arabia
Madras India *see* **Chennai**
134 B2 **Madras** U.S.A.
145 C2 **Madre, Laguna** *lag.* Mex.
145 B3 **Madre del Sur, Sierra** *mts* Mex.
144 B2 **Madre Occidental, Sierra** *mts* Mex.
145 B2 **Madre Oriental, Sierra** *mts* Mex.
106 C1 **Madrid** Spain
106 C2 **Madridejos** Spain
61 C2 **Madura** *i.* Indon.
61 C2 **Madura, Selat** *sea chan.* Indon.
73 B4 **Madurai** India
67 C3 **Maebashi** Japan
62 A2 **Mae Hong Son** Thai.
62 A1 **Mae Sai** Thai.
62 A2 **Mae Sariang** Thai.
62 A2 **Mae Suai** Thai.
123 C2 **Mafeteng** Lesotho
119 D3 **Mafia Island** Tanz.
123 C2 **Mafikeng** S. Africa
119 D3 **Mafinga** Tanz.
154 C3 **Mafra** Brazil
83 L3 **Magadan** Rus. Fed.
147 C4 **Magangue** Col.
144 A1 **Magdalena** Mex.
138 B2 **Magdalena** U.S.A.
144 A2 **Magdalena, Bahía** *b.* Mex.
101 E1 **Magdeburg** Ger.
153 A6 **Magellan, Strait of** Chile
97 C1 **Magherafelt** U.K.
87 E3 **Magnitogorsk** Rus. Fed.
142 B2 **Magnolia** U.S.A.
131 D1 **Magpie, Lac** *l.* Can.
114 A3 **Magṭa' Laḥjar** Maur.
151 D2 **Maguarinho, Cabo** *c.* Brazil
123 D2 **Magude** Moz.
62 A1 **Magwe** Myanmar
81 C2 **Mahābād** Iran
74 B2 **Mahajan** India
121 D2 **Mahajanga** Madag.
61 C2 **Mahakam** *r.* Indon.
123 C1 **Mahalapye** Botswana
121 D2 **Mahalevona** Madag.
75 C2 **Mahanadi** *r.* India
121 D2 **Mahanoro** Madag.
63 B2 **Maha Sarakham** Thai.
121 D2 **Mahavavy** *r.* Madag.
78 B2 **Mahd adh Dhahab** Saudi Arabia
150 C1 **Mahdia** Guyana
113 K7 **Mahé** *i.* Seychelles
74 B2 **Mahesana** India
74 B2 **Mahi** *r.* India
54 C1 **Mahia Peninsula** N.Z.
89 D3 **Mahilyow** Belarus
107 D2 **Mahón** Spain
74 B2 **Mahuva** India
110 C2 **Mahya Dağı** *mt.* Turkey
74 A1 **Maīdān Shahr** Afgh.
129 D2 **Maidstone** Can.
99 D3 **Maidstone** U.K.
115 D3 **Maiduguri** Nigeria
75 C2 **Mailani** India
101 D2 **Main** *r.* Ger.
118 B3 **Mai-Ndombe, Lac** *l.* Dem. Rep. Congo
101 E3 **Main-Donau-Kanal** *canal* Ger.
141 F1 **Maine** *state* U.S.A.
62 A1 **Maingkwan** Myanmar
96 C1 **Mainland** *i. Scotland* U.K.
96 □ **Mainland** *i. Scotland* U.K.
121 D2 **Maintirano** Madag.
101 D2 **Mainz** Ger.
150 B1 **Maiquetía** Venez.
53 D2 **Maitland** *N.S.W.* Austr.
52 A2 **Maitland** *S.A.* Austr.
146 B3 **Maíz, Islas del** *is* Nic.
67 C3 **Maizuru** Japan
109 C2 **Maja Jezercë** *mt.* Albania
61 C2 **Majene** Indon.
107 D2 **Majorca** *i.* Spain
48 F2 **Majuro** *atoll* Marshall Is
123 C2 **Majwemasweu** S. Africa
118 B3 **Makabana** Congo
58 B3 **Makale** Indon.
77 E2 **Makanchi** Kazakh.
109 C2 **Makarska** Croatia
58 B3 **Makassar** Indon.
61 C2 **Makassar, Selat** *str.* Indon.
Makassar Strait Indon. *see* **Makassar, Selat**
76 B2 **Makat** Kazakh.
123 D2 **Makatini Flats** *lowland* S. Africa
114 A4 **Makeni** Sierra Leone
120 B3 **Makgadikgadi** *depr.* Botswana
87 D4 **Makhachkala** Rus. Fed.
76 B2 **Makhambet** Kazakh.
119 D3 **Makindu** Kenya
77 D1 **Makinsk** Kazakh.
91 D2 **Makiyivka** Ukr.
Makkah Saudi Arabia *see* **Mecca**
131 E1 **Makkovik** Can.
103 E2 **Makó** Hungary
118 B2 **Makokou** Gabon
119 D3 **Makongolosi** Tanz.
122 B2 **Makopong** Botswana
79 D2 **Makran** *reg.* Iran/Pak.
74 A2 **Makran Coast Range** *mts* Pak.

89 E2 **Maksatikha** Rus. Fed.
81 C2 **Mākū** Iran
62 A1 **Makum** India
67 B4 **Makurazaki** Japan
115 C4 **Makurdi** Nigeria
92 G2 **Malå** Sweden
146 B4 **Mala, Punta** *pt* Panama
118 A2 **Malabo** Equat. Guinea
60 A1 **Malacca, Strait of** Indon./Malaysia
134 D2 **Malad City** U.S.A.
88 C3 **Maladzyechna** Belarus
106 C2 **Málaga** Spain
97 B1 **Málainn Mhóir** Ireland
48 E3 **Malaita** *i.* Solomon Is
117 B4 **Malakal** Sudan
48 F4 **Malakula** *i.* Vanuatu
61 C2 **Malang** Indon.
120 A1 **Malanje** Angola
93 G4 **Mälaren** *l.* Sweden
153 B4 **Malargüe** Arg.
80 B2 **Malatya** Turkey
121 C2 **Malawi** *country* Africa
Malawi, Lake Africa *see* **Nyasa, Lake**
89 D2 **Malaya Vishera** Rus. Fed.
64 B2 **Malaybalay** Phil.
81 C2 **Malāyer** Iran
60 B1 **Malaysia** *country* Asia
81 C2 **Malazgirt** Turkey
103 D1 **Malbork** Pol.
101 F1 **Malchin** Ger.
100 A2 **Maldegem** Belgium
49 H3 **Malden Island** Kiribati
56 G6 **Maldives** *country* Indian Ocean
153 C4 **Maldonado** Uru.
56 G6 **Male** Maldives
111 B3 **Maleas, Akrotirio** *pt* Greece
103 D2 **Malé Karpaty** *hills* Slovakia
134 C2 **Malheur Lake** U.S.A.
114 B3 **Mali** *country* Africa
114 A3 **Mali** Guinea
58 C3 **Malili** Indon.
119 E3 **Malindi** Kenya
97 C1 **Malin Head** Ireland
111 C2 **Malkara** Turkey
88 C3 **Mal'kavichy** Belarus
110 C2 **Malko Tŭrnovo** Bulg.
53 C3 **Mallacoota** Austr.
53 C3 **Mallacoota Inlet** *b.* Austr.
96 B2 **Mallaig** U.K.
129 E1 **Mallery Lake** Can.
Mallorca *i.* Spain *see* **Majorca**
97 B2 **Mallow** Ireland
92 H2 **Malmberget** Sweden
100 C2 **Malmédy** Belgium
122 A3 **Malmesbury** S. Africa
93 F4 **Malmö** Sweden
62 B1 **Malong** China
118 C4 **Malonga** Dem. Rep. Congo
93 E3 **Måløy** Norway
89 E2 **Maloyaroslavets** Rus. Fed.
89 E2 **Maloye Borisovo** Rus. Fed.
85 H5 **Malta** *country* Europe
88 C2 **Malta** Latvia
134 E1 **Malta** U.S.A.
122 A1 **Maltahöhe** Namibia
98 C1 **Malton** U.K.
Maluku *is* Indon. *see* **Moluccas**
59 C3 **Maluku, Laut** *sea* Indon.
93 F3 **Malung** Sweden
123 C2 **Maluti Mountains** Lesotho
73 B3 **Malvan** India
142 B2 **Malvern** U.S.A.
90 B1 **Malyn** Ukr.
83 L2 **Malyy Anyuy** *r.* Rus. Fed.
83 K2 **Malyy Lyakhovskiy, Ostrov** *i.* Rus. Fed.
123 C2 **Mamafubedu** S. Africa
119 C2 **Mambasa** Dem. Rep. Congo
118 B2 **Mambéré** *r.* C.A.R.
123 C2 **Mamelodi** S. Africa
150 B3 **Mamoré** *r.* Bol./Brazil
114 A3 **Mamou** Guinea
61 C2 **Mamuju** Indon.
114 B4 **Man** Côte d'Ivoire
98 A1 **Man, Isle of** *i.* Irish Sea
150 B2 **Manacapuru** Brazil
107 D2 **Manacor** Spain
59 C2 **Manado** Indon.
146 B3 **Managua** Nic.
121 D3 **Manakara** Madag.
78 B3 **Manākhah** Yemen
79 C2 **Manama** Bahrain
59 D3 **Manam Island** P.N.G.
121 D3 **Mananara** *r.* Madag.
121 D2 **Mananara Avaratra** Madag.
121 D3 **Mananjary** Madag.
114 A3 **Manantali, Lac de** *l.* Mali
77 E2 **Manas Hu** *l.* China
59 C3 **Manatuto** East Timor
62 A2 **Man-aung Kyun** *i.* Myanmar
150 B2 **Manaus** Brazil
80 B2 **Manavgat** Turkey
98 B2 **Manchester** U.K.
141 E2 **Manchester** U.S.A.
121 D3 **Mandabe** Madag.
93 E4 **Mandal** Norway
59 D3 **Mandala, Puncak** *mt.* Indon.
62 A1 **Mandalay** Myanmar
69 D1 **Mandalgovĭ** Mongolia
136 C1 **Mandan** U.S.A.
118 B1 **Mandara Mountains** Cameroon/Nigeria
108 A3 **Mandas** *Sardegna* Italy
100 C2 **Manderscheid** Ger.
74 B1 **Mandi** India
114 B3 **Mandiana** Guinea
75 C2 **Mandla** India
121 D2 **Mandritsara** Madag.
74 B2 **Mandsaur** India
50 A3 **Mandurah** Austr.
73 B3 **Mandya** India
108 B1 **Manerbio** Italy
90 B1 **Manevychi** Ukr.
109 C2 **Manfredonia** Italy
114 B3 **Manga** Burkina
118 B3 **Mangai** Dem. Rep. Congo
54 C1 **Mangakino** N.Z.
110 C2 **Mangalia** Romania
73 B3 **Mangalore** India
123 C2 **Mangaung** S. Africa
61 B2 **Manggar** Indon.
76 B2 **Mangistau** Kazakh.
68 C2 **Mangnai** China
121 C2 **Mangochi** Malawi
59 C3 **Mangole** *i.* Indon.
154 B3 **Mangueirinha** Brazil
69 E1 **Mangui** China
137 D3 **Manhattan** U.S.A.
121 C3 **Manhica** Moz.
155 D2 **Manhuaçu** Brazil
121 D2 **Mania** *r.* Madag.
108 B1 **Maniago** Italy
150 B2 **Manicoré** Brazil
131 D2 **Manicouagan** *r.* Can.
131 D1 **Manicouagan, Petit Lac** *l.* Can.
131 D1 **Manicouagan, Réservoir** *resr* Can.
79 B2 **Manīfah** Saudi Arabia
64 B1 **Manila** Phil.
53 D2 **Manilla** Austr.
111 C3 **Manisa** Turkey
140 B2 **Manistee** U.S.A.
129 E2 **Manitoba** *prov.* Can.
129 E2 **Manitoba, Lake** Can.
140 B1 **Manitou Islands** U.S.A.
130 B2 **Manitoulin Island** Can.
140 B2 **Manitowoc** U.S.A.
130 C2 **Maniwaki** Can.
150 A1 **Manizales** Col.
137 E2 **Mankato** U.S.A.
114 B4 **Mankono** Côte d'Ivoire
129 D3 **Mankota** Can.
73 C4 **Mankulam** Sri Lanka
74 B2 **Manmad** India
73 B4 **Mannar, Gulf of** India/Sri Lanka
101 D3 **Mannheim** Ger.
128 C2 **Manning** Can.
52 A2 **Mannum** Austr.
129 C2 **Mannville** Can.
59 C3 **Manokwari** Indon.
119 C3 **Manono** Dem. Rep. Congo
63 A2 **Manoron** Myanmar
105 D3 **Manosque** France
131 C1 **Manouane, Lac** *l.* Can.
107 D1 **Manresa** Spain
121 B2 **Mansa** Zambia
127 F2 **Mansel Island** Can.
92 I2 **Mansel'kya** *ridge* Fin./Rus.
53 C3 **Mansfield** Austr.
98 C2 **Mansfield** U.K.
142 B2 **Mansfield** *LA* U.S.A.
140 C2 **Mansfield** *OH* U.S.A.
141 D2 **Mansfield** *PA* U.S.A.
150 A2 **Manta** Ecuador
143 E1 **Manteo** U.S.A.
104 C2 **Mantes-la-Jolie** France
155 C2 **Mantiqueira, Serra da** *mts* Brazil
Mantova Italy *see* **Mantua**
108 B1 **Mantua** Italy
151 C2 **Manuelzinho** Brazil
59 C3 **Manui** *i.* Indon.
54 B1 **Manukau** N.Z.
142 B2 **Many** U.S.A.
87 D4 **Manych-Gudilo, Ozero** *l.* Rus. Fed.
119 D3 **Manyoni** Tanz.
106 C2 **Manzanares** Spain
144 B3 **Manzanillo** Mex.
69 D1 **Manzhouli** China
123 D2 **Manzini** Swaziland
115 D3 **Mao** Chad
59 D3 **Maoke, Pegunungan** *mts* Indon.
123 C2 **Maokeng** S. Africa
65 A1 **Maokui Shan** *mt.* China
71 B3 **Maoming** China
121 C3 **Mapai** Moz.
75 C1 **Mapam Yumco** *l.* China
145 C3 **Mapastepec** Mex.
144 B2 **Mapimí** Mex.
121 C3 **Mapinhane** Moz.
129 D3 **Maple Creek** Can.
121 C3 **Maputo** Moz.
123 D2 **Maputo** *r.* Moz./S. Africa
75 C2 **Maquan He** *r.* China
120 A1 **Maquela do Zombo** Angola
153 B5 **Maquinchao** Arg.
137 E2 **Maquoketa** U.S.A.
150 B2 **Maraã** Brazil
151 D2 **Marabá** Brazil
151 C1 **Maracá, Ilha de** *i.* Brazil
150 A1 **Maracaibo** Venez.
150 A1 **Maracaibo, Lake** Venez.
152 C3 **Maracaju, Serra de** *hills* Bra
154 A2 **Maracaju, Serra de** *hills* Bra
150 B1 **Maracay** Venez.

45 D2 Marādah Libya
45 C3 Maradi Niger
59 B2 Marāgheh Iran
81 C2 Marajó, Baía de est. Brazil
81 C2 Marajó, Ilha de i. Brazil
79 C2 Maraki Iran
49 D2 Maralal Kenya
93 C2 Maralinga Austr.
81 C2 Marand Iran
60 A2 Marañón r. Peru
30 B2 Marathon Can.
43 D4 Marathon U.S.A.
06 C2 Marbella Spain
50 A2 Marble Bar Austr.
23 C1 Marble Hall S. Africa
24 D3 Marburg S. Africa
01 D2 Marburg an der Lahn Ger.
90 B2 March U.K.
00 B2 Marche-en-Famenne Belgium
66 B2 Marchena Spain
62 B4 Mar Chiquita, Laguna l. Arg.
41 E2 Marcy, Mount U.S.A.
74 E1 Mardan Pak.
62 A1 Mar del Plata Arg.
81 C2 Mardın Turkey
48 B2 Maree, Loch l. U.K.
48 B3 Marettimo, Isola i. Sicilia Italy
43 D3 Marevo Rus. Fed.
48 C2 Marfa U.S.A.
50 A3 Margaret River Austr.
47 D3 Margarita, Isla de i. Venez.
23 D3 Margate S. Africa
99 D3 Margate U.K.
19 C2 Margherita Peak Dem. Rep. Congo/Uganda
76 C3 Mārgow, Dasht-e des. Afgh.
43 E2 Marhanets' Ukr.
62 B2 Mari Myanmar
62 A2 María Elena Chile
56 C5 Mariana Trench N. Pacific Ocean
42 B2 Marianna AR U.S.A.
42 C2 Marianna FL U.S.A.
02 C2 Mariánské Lázně Czech Rep.
45 C2 Marías, Islas is Mex.
78 B3 Ma'rib Yemen
09 C1 Maribor Slovenia
17 A4 Maridi watercourse Sudan
55 M2 Marie Byrd Land reg. Antarctica
47 D3 Marie-Galante i. Guadeloupe
93 G3 Mariehamn Fin.
92 A1 Mariental Namibia
93 F4 Mariestad Sweden
42 C2 Marietta GA U.S.A.
40 C2 Marietta OH U.S.A.
05 D3 Marignane France
83 K3 Marii, Mys pt Rus. Fed.
03 E3 Marijampolė Lith.
54 E2 Marília Brazil
06 B1 Marín Spain
08 B3 Marina di Gioiosa Ionica Italy
88 C3 Mar"ina Horka Belarus
04 B2 Marinette U.S.A.
54 B2 Maringá Brazil
06 B2 Marinha Grande Port.
40 B2 Marion IN U.S.A.
40 C2 Marion OH U.S.A.
43 D2 Marion SC U.S.A.
40 C3 Marion VA U.S.A.
42 D2 Marion, Lake U.S.A.
52 A3 Marion Bay Austr.
52 B3 Mariscal José Félix Estigarribia Para.
10 D2 Maritsa r. Bulg.

91 D2 Mariupol' Ukr.
17 C4 Marka Somalia
23 C1 Marken S. Africa
00 B1 Markermeer l. Neth.
83 I2 Markha r. Rus. Fed.
91 D2 Markivka Ukr.
42 B2 Marksville U.S.A.
01 E2 Marktheidenfeld Ger.
01 F2 Marktredwitz Ger.
00 C2 Marl Ger.
00 A3 Marle France
39 D2 Marlin U.S.A.
04 C3 Marmande France
11 C2 Marmara, Sea of g. Turkey
11 C2 Marmara Denizi g. Turkey see Marmara, Sea of
11 C3 Marmaris Turkey
04 C2 Marne-la-Vallée France
21 D2 Maroantsetra Madag.
01 E2 Maroldsweisach Ger.
21 D2 Maromokotro mt. Madag.
21 C2 Marondera Zimbabwe
51 C1 Maroni r. Fr. Guiana
18 B1 Maroua Cameroon
21 D2 Marovoay Madag.
49 I3 Marquesas Islands is Fr. Polynesia
40 B1 Marquette U.S.A.
17 A3 Marra, Jebel mt. Sudan
17 A3 Marra, Jebel plat. Sudan
23 D2 Marracuene Moz.
14 B1 Marrakech Morocco
52 A1 Marree Austr.
86 F2 Marresale Rus. Fed.
21 C2 Marromeu Moz.
21 C2 Marrupa Moz.
16 B2 Marsá al 'Alam Egypt
15 D1 Marsa al Burayqah Libya
19 D2 Marsabit Kenya
08 B3 Marsala Sicilia Italy
16 A1 Marsá Maţrūh Egypt
01 D2 Marsberg Ger.
08 B2 Marsciano Italy
53 C2 Marsden Austr.
05 D3 Marseille France
37 D2 Marshall MN U.S.A.
37 E3 Marshall MO U.S.A.
48 F2 Marshall TX U.S.A.
39 E3 Marshall Islands country N. Pacific Ocean
37 E2 Marshalltown U.S.A.
40 A2 Marshfield U.S.A.
43 E3 Marsh Harbour Bahamas
42 B3 Marsh Island U.S.A.
88 A2 Märsta Sweden
61 C2 Martapura Kalimantan Selatan Indon.
60 B2 Martapura Sumatera Selatan Indon.
41 E2 Martha's Vineyard i. U.S.A.
05 D2 Martigny Switz.
03 D2 Martin Slovakia
36 C2 Martin U.S.A.
45 C2 Martínez Mex.
47 D3 Martinique terr. West Indies
40 D3 Martinsburg U.S.A.
40 C3 Martinsville U.S.A.
54 C2 Marton N.Z.
07 D1 Martorell Spain
06 C2 Martos Spain
76 B1 Martuk Kazakh.
05 C3 Marvejols France
76 C3 Mary Turkm.
51 E2 Maryborough Austr.
22 B2 Marydale S. Africa
41 D3 Maryland state U.S.A.
37 D3 Marysville U.S.A.

37 E2 Maryville MO U.S.A.
43 D1 Maryville TN U.S.A.
19 D3 Masai Steppe plain Tanz.
19 D3 Masaka Uganda
65 B2 Masan S. Korea
19 D3 Masasi Tanz.
64 B1 Masbate Phil.
64 B1 Masbate i. Phil.
23 C2 Maseru Lesotho
76 B3 Mashhad Iran
23 D2 Mashishing S. Africa
74 A2 Mashkel, Hamun-i- salt flat Pak.
23 C3 Masibambane S. Africa
79 C3 Masilah, Wādī al watercourse Yemen
23 C2 Masilo S. Africa
19 D2 Masindi Uganda
79 C2 Maşīrah, Jazīrat i. Oman
79 C3 Maşīrah, Khalīj b. Oman
81 C2 Masjed Soleymān Iran
97 B2 Mask, Lough l. Ireland
21 E2 Masoala, Tanjona c. Madag.
37 D2 Mason City U.S.A.
79 C2 Masqaţ Oman see Muscat
08 B2 Massa Italy
41 E2 Massachusetts state U.S.A.
41 E2 Massachusetts Bay U.S.A.
21 C3 Massangena Moz.
20 A1 Massango Angola
16 B3 Massawa Eritrea
41 E2 Massena U.S.A.
28 A2 Masset Can.
05 C2 Massif Central mts France
40 C2 Massillon U.S.A.
21 C3 Massinga Moz.
23 D1 Massingir Moz.
78 A2 Mastābah Saudi Arabia
54 C2 Masterton N.Z.
74 A2 Mastung Pak.
78 A2 Mastürah Saudi Arabia
88 B3 Masty Belarus
67 B4 Masuda Japan
Masuku Gabon see Franceville
21 C3 Masvingo Zimbabwe
69 D1 Matad Mongolia
18 B3 Matadi Dem. Rep. Congo
46 B3 Matagalpa Nic.
30 C2 Matagami Can.
30 C2 Matagami, Lac l. Can.
39 D3 Matagorda Island U.S.A.
20 A2 Matala Angola
14 A3 Matam Senegal
44 B2 Matamoros Coahuila Mex.
45 C2 Matamoros Tamaulipas Mex.
19 D3 Matandu r. Tanz.
31 D2 Matane Can.
46 B2 Matanzas Cuba
73 C4 Matara Sri Lanka
61 C2 Mataram Indon.
50 C1 Mataranka Austr.
07 D1 Mataró Spain
23 C3 Matatiele S. Africa
54 A3 Mataura N.Z.
54 A3 Mataura r. N.Z.
49 G3 Matā'utu Wallis and Futuna Is
54 C1 Matawai N.Z.
52 B2 Mategua Bol.
45 B2 Matehuala Mex.
09 C2 Matera Italy
39 D3 Mathis U.S.A.
75 B2 Mathura India
64 B2 Mati Phil.
98 C2 Matlock U.K.
50 C3 Mato Grosso Brazil
23 D2 Matola Moz.
Matou China see Pingguo
67 B3 Matsue Japan

66 D2 **Matsumae** Japan
67 C4 **Matsusaka** Japan
71 C3 **Matsu Tao** *i.* Taiwan
67 B4 **Matsuyama** Japan
130 B1 **Mattagami** *r.* Can.
105 D2 **Matterhorn** *mt.* Italy/Switz.
134 C2 **Matterhorn** *mt.* U.S.A.
140 B3 **Mattoon** U.S.A.
150 B1 **Maturín** Venez.
123 C2 **Matwabeng** S. Africa
100 A2 **Maubeuge** France
104 C3 **Maubourguet** France
124 E5 **Maui** *i.* U.S.A.
140 C2 **Maumee** *r.* U.S.A.
120 B2 **Maun** Botswana
62 A1 **Maungdaw** Myanmar
50 C2 **Maurice, Lake** *imp. l.* Austr.
114 A3 **Mauritania** *country* Africa
113 K9 **Mauritius** *country* Indian Ocean
78 B2 **Māwān, Khashm** *mt.* Saudi Arabia
118 B3 **Mawanga** Dem. Rep. Congo
71 B3 **Mawei** China
62 A1 **Mawkmai** Myanmar
62 A1 **Mawlaik** Myanmar
63 A2 **Mawlamyaing** Myanmar
78 B2 **Mawqaq** Saudi Arabia
78 B3 **Mawza** Yemen
108 A3 **Maxia, Punta** *mt. Sardegna* Italy
83 J2 **Maya** *r.* Rus. Fed.
147 C2 **Mayaguana** *i.* Bahamas
96 B3 **Maybole** U.K.
104 B2 **Mayenne** France
104 B2 **Mayenne** *r.* France
128 C2 **Mayerthorpe** Can.
140 B3 **Mayfield** U.S.A.
87 D4 **Maykop** Rus. Fed.
76 C3 **Maymanah** Afgh.
126 B2 **Mayo** Can.
118 B3 **Mayoko** Congo
121 D2 **Mayotte** *terr.* Africa
83 J3 **Mayskiy** Rus. Fed.
140 C3 **Maysville** U.S.A.
118 B3 **Mayumba** Gabon
137 D1 **Mayville** U.S.A.
151 C2 **Mazagão** Brazil
104 C3 **Mazamet** France
77 D3 **Mazar** China
108 B3 **Mazara del Vallo** *Sicilia* Italy
77 C3 **Mazār-e Sharīf** Afgh.
144 A2 **Mazatán** Mex.
146 A3 **Mazatenango** Guat.
144 B2 **Mazatlán** Mex.
88 B2 **Mažeikiai** Lith.
88 B2 **Mazirbe** Latvia
121 B3 **Mazunga** Zimbabwe
88 C3 **Mazyr** Belarus
123 D2 **Mbabane** Swaziland
118 B2 **Mbaïki** C.A.R.
121 C1 **Mbala** Zambia
119 D2 **Mbale** Uganda
118 B2 **Mbalmayo** Cameroon
118 B3 **Mbandaka** Dem. Rep. Congo
118 A2 **Mbanga** Cameroon
120 A1 **M'banza Congo** Angola
119 D3 **Mbeya** Tanz.
119 D4 **Mbinga** Tanz.
118 B2 **Mbomo** Congo
118 B2 **Mbouda** Cameroon
114 A3 **Mbour** Senegal
114 A3 **Mbout** Maur.
118 C3 **Mbuji-Mayi** Dem. Rep. Congo
119 D3 **Mbuyuni** Tanz.
139 D2 **McAlester** U.S.A.
139 D3 **McAllen** U.S.A.
128 B2 **McBride** Can.
134 C2 **McCall** U.S.A.
126 E2 **McClintock Channel** Can.
126 D2 **McClure Strait** Can.
142 B2 **McComb** U.S.A.
136 C2 **McConaughy, Lake** U.S.A.
136 C2 **McCook** U.S.A.
134 C2 **McDermitt** U.S.A.
134 D1 **McDonald Peak** U.S.A.
134 D1 **McGuire, Mount** U.S.A.
128 C2 **McLennan** Can.
128 B2 **McLeod Lake** Can.
134 B1 **McMinnville** *OR* U.S.A.
142 C1 **McMinnville** *TN* U.S.A.
137 D3 **McPherson** U.S.A.
123 C3 **Mdantsane** S. Africa
135 D3 **Mead, Lake** *resr* U.S.A.
129 D2 **Meadow Lake** Can.
140 C2 **Meadville** U.S.A.
66 D2 **Meaken-dake** *vol.* Japan
106 B1 **Mealhada** Port.
131 E1 **Mealy Mountains** Can.
128 C2 **Meander River** Can.
78 A2 **Mecca** Saudi Arabia
100 B2 **Mechelen** Belgium
100 B2 **Mechelen** Neth.
100 C2 **Mechernich** Ger.
100 C2 **Meckenheim** Ger.
106 B1 **Meda** Port.
60 A1 **Medan** Indon.
153 B5 **Medanosa, Punta** *pt* Arg.
73 C4 **Medawachchiya** Sri Lanka
107 D2 **Médéa** Alg.
150 A1 **Medellín** Col.
115 D1 **Medenine** Tunisia
134 B2 **Medford** U.S.A.
110 C2 **Medgidia** Romania
110 B1 **Mediaş** Romania
136 B2 **Medicine Bow Mountains** U.S.A.
136 B2 **Medicine Bow Peak** U.S.A.
129 C2 **Medicine Hat** Can.
137 D3 **Medicine Lodge** U.S.A.
155 D1 **Medina** Brazil
78 A2 **Medina** Saudi Arabia
106 C1 **Medinaceli** Spain
106 C1 **Medina del Campo** Spain
106 B1 **Medina de Rioseco** Spain
84 G5 **Mediterranean Sea**
129 C2 **Medley** Can.
87 E3 **Mednogorsk** Rus. Fed.
83 L2 **Medvezh'i, Ostrova** *is* Rus. Fed.
86 C2 **Medvezh'yegorsk** Rus. Fed.
50 A2 **Meekatharra** Austr.
136 B2 **Meeker** U.S.A.
75 B2 **Meerut** India
100 A2 **Meetkerke** Belgium
111 B3 **Megalopoli** Greece
75 C2 **Meghasani** *mt.* India
80 A2 **Megisti** *i.* Greece
92 I1 **Mehamn** Norway
50 A2 **Meharry, Mount** Austr.
79 C2 **Mehrān** *watercourse* Iran
74 B1 **Mehtar Lām** Afgh.
154 C1 **Meia Ponte** *r.* Brazil
118 B2 **Meiganga** Cameroon
65 B1 **Meihekou** China
Meijiang China *see* **Ningdu**
62 A1 **Meiktila** Myanmar
101 E2 **Meiningen** Ger.
102 C1 **Meißen** Ger.
71 B3 **Meizhou** China
152 B3 **Mejicana** *mt.* Arg.
152 A3 **Mejillones** Chile
117 B3 **Mek'elē** Eth.
114 C2 **Mekerrhane, Sebkha** *salt p* Alg.
114 B1 **Meknès** Morocco
63 B2 **Mekong** *r.* Asia
63 B3 **Mekong, Mouths of the** Vietnam
60 B1 **Melaka** Malaysia
53 B3 **Melbourne** Austr.
143 D3 **Melbourne** U.S.A.
108 A2 **Mele, Capo** *c.* Italy
131 C1 **Mélèzes, Rivière aux** *r.* Can.
115 D3 **Melfi** Chad
109 C2 **Melfi** Italy
129 D2 **Melfort** Can.
92 F3 **Melhus** Norway
106 B1 **Melide** Spain
114 B1 **Melilla** N. Africa
91 D2 **Melitopol'** Ukr.
101 D1 **Melle** Ger.
93 F4 **Mellerud** Sweden
101 E2 **Mellrichstadt** Ger.
100 D1 **Mellum** *i.* Ger.
152 C4 **Melo** Uru.
115 C1 **Melrhir, Chott** *salt l.* Alg.
99 C2 **Melton Mowbray** U.K.
104 C2 **Melun** France
129 D2 **Melville** Can.
51 D1 **Melville, Cape** Austr.
131 E1 **Melville, Lake** Can.
50 C1 **Melville Island** Austr.
126 D1 **Melville Island** Can.
127 F2 **Melville Peninsula** Can.
102 C2 **Memmingen** Ger.
61 B1 **Mempawah** Indon.
80 B3 **Memphis** *tourist site* Egypt
142 B1 **Memphis** *TN* U.S.A.
139 C2 **Memphis** *TX* U.S.A.
91 C1 **Mena** Ukr.
142 B2 **Mena** U.S.A.
114 C3 **Ménaka** Mali
Mènam Khong *r.* Laos/Thai *see* **Mekong**
105 C3 **Mende** France
116 B3 **Mendefera** Eritrea
145 C2 **Méndez** Mex.
119 D2 **Mendī** Eth.
59 D3 **Mendi** P.N.G.
99 B3 **Mendip Hills** U.K.
153 B4 **Mendoza** Arg.
111 C3 **Menemen** Turkey
60 B2 **Menggala** Indon.
62 B1 **Mengzi** China
131 D1 **Menihek** Can.
52 B2 **Menindee** Austr.
52 B2 **Menindee Lake** Austr.
52 A3 **Meningie** Austr.
104 C2 **Mennecy** France
140 B1 **Menominee** U.S.A.
120 A2 **Menongue** Angola
Menorca *i.* Spain *see* **Minor**
60 A2 **Mentawai, Kepulauan** *is* Indon.
60 B2 **Mentok** Indon.
50 B2 **Menzies** Austr.
100 C1 **Meppel** Neth.
100 C1 **Meppen** Ger.
123 D1 **Mepuze** Moz.
123 C2 **Meqheleng** S. Africa
108 B1 **Merano** Italy
59 D3 **Merauke** Indon.
52 B2 **Merbein** Austr.
135 B3 **Merced** U.S.A.
152 C3 **Mercedes** Arg.
127 G2 **Mercy, Cape** Can.
139 C1 **Meredith, Lake** U.S.A.
91 D2 **Merefa** Ukr.
116 A3 **Merga Oasis** Sudan

3 A2	Mergui Archipelago is Myanmar	
0 C2	Meriç r. Greece/Turkey	
5 D2	Mérida Mex.	
6 B2	Mérida Spain	
0 A1	Mérida Venez.	
3 C3	Meridian U.S.A.	
2 B3	Merimbula Austr.	
6 C3	Merowe Sudan	
0 C2	Merredin Austr.	
6 B3	Merrick h. U.K.	
0 B1	Merrill U.S.A.	
3 B3	Merrillville U.S.A.	
3 C2	Merritt Can.	
2 B3	Merrygoen Austr.	
6 C3	Mersa Fatma Eritrea	
6 B2	Mersch Lux.	
1 E2	Merseburg (Saale) Ger.	
8 B2	Mersey r. U.K.	
9 C2	Mersin Turkey	
0 B1	Mersing Malaysia	
5 B2	Mers-les-Bains France	
4 B2	Merta India	
9 B3	Merthyr Tydfil U.K.	
6 B2	Mértola Port.	
6 B2	Mertvyy Kultuk, Sor dry lake Kazakh.	
9 D3	Meru vol. Tanz.	
2 F3	Merzig Ger.	
8 A2	Mesa U.S.A.	
9 C2	Mesagne Italy	
9 E3	Meschede Ger.	
1 E2	Meshchovsk Rus. Fed.	
1 E2	Meshkovskaya Rus. Fed.	
9 B3	Mesimeri Greece	
1 B3	Mesolongi Greece	
9 C3	Messalo r. Moz.	
9 C3	Messina Sicilia Italy	
9 C3	Messina, Strait of Italy	
1 B3	Messiniakos Kolpos g. Greece	
0 B2	Mesta r. Bulg.	
1 B2	Meta r. Col./Venez.	
7 G2	Meta Incognita Peninsula Can.	
3 B2	Metán Arg.	
1 B3	Methoni Greece	
9 C2	Metković Croatia	
9 C2	Metro Indon.	
7 B4	Metu Eth.	
5 D2	Metz France	
9 B2	Meuse r. Belgium/France	
9 D2	Mexia U.S.A.	
4 A1	Mexicali Mex.	
4 B2	Mexico country Central America	
7 E3	Mexico U.S.A.	
5 I5	Mexico, Gulf of Mex./U.S.A.	
4 C3	Mexico City Mex.	
1 F1	Meyenburg Ger.	
6 D2	Mezen' Rus. Fed.	
6 D2	Mezen' r. Rus. Fed.	
6 E1	Mezhdusharskiy, Ostrov i. Rus. Fed.	
3 E2	Mezőtúr Hungary	
4 B2	Mezquitic Mex.	
1 C2	Mežvidi Latvia	
9 D2	Mfuwe Zambia	
3 D2	Mhlume Swaziland	
4 B3	Mhow India	
5 C2	Miahuatlán Mex.	
5 B2	Miajadas Spain	
3 D3	Miami FL U.S.A.	
1 E1	Miami OK U.S.A.	
3 D3	Miami Beach U.S.A.	
1 C2	Miāndowāb Iran	
1 C2	Miāneh Iran	
74 B1	Mianwali Pak.	
70 A2	Mianyang China	
121 D2	Miarinarivo Madag.	
87 F3	Miass Rus. Fed.	
128 C2	Mica Creek Can.	
103 E2	Michalovce Slovakia	
140 B1	Michigan state U.S.A.	
140 B2	Michigan, Lake U.S.A.	
140 B2	Michigan City U.S.A.	
130 B2	Michipicoten Island Can.	
130 B2	Michipicoten River Can.	
89 F3	Michurinsk Rus. Fed.	
48 D2	Micronesia, Federated States of country N. Pacific Ocean	
100 A2	Middelburg Neth.	
123 C3	Middelburg E. Cape S. Africa	
123 C2	Middelburg Mpumalanga S. Africa	
100 B2	Middelharnis Neth.	
134 B2	Middle Alkali Lake U.S.A.	
73 D3	Middle Andaman i. India	
136 D2	Middle Loup r. U.S.A.	
140 C3	Middlesboro U.S.A.	
98 C1	Middlesbrough U.K.	
141 E2	Middletown NY U.S.A.	
140 C3	Middletown OH U.S.A.	
78 B3	Midi Yemen	
137 D3	Midland Can.	
140 C2	Midland MI U.S.A.	
139 C2	Midland TX U.S.A.	
97 B3	Midleton Ireland	
94 B1	Miðvágur Faroe Is	
69 D2	Midzhur mt. Bulg./S.M.	
103 E1	Mielec Pol.	
110 C1	Miercurea-Ciuc Romania	
106 B3	Mieres Spain	
101 E1	Mieste Ger.	
75 D1	Migriggyangzham Co l. China	
145 C3	Miguel Alemán, Presa resr Mex.	
144 B2	Miguel Auza Mex.	
145 C2	Miguel Hidalgo, Presa resr Mex.	
63 A2	Migyaunglaung Myanmar	
89 E3	Mikhaylov Rus. Fed.	
	Mikhaylovgrad Bulg. see Montana	
66 B2	Mikhaylovka Rus. Fed.	
77 D1	Mikhaylovskiy Rus. Fed.	
93 I3	Mikkeli Fin.	
86 E2	Mikun' Rus. Fed.	
67 C3	Mikuni-sanmyaku mts Japan	
108 A1	Milan Italy	
	Milano Italy see Milan	
121 C2	Milange Moz.	
111 C3	Milas Turkey	
137 D1	Milbank U.S.A.	
99 D2	Mildenhall U.K.	
52 B2	Mildura Austr.	
62 B1	Mile China	
136 B1	Miles City U.S.A.	
141 D3	Milford DE U.S.A.	
135 D3	Milford UT U.S.A.	
99 A3	Milford Haven U.K.	
54 A2	Milford Sound N.Z.	
107 D2	Miliana Alg.	
116 B3	Milk, Wadi el watercourse Sudan	
83 L3	Mil'kovo Rus. Fed.	
129 C3	Milk River Can.	
105 C3	Millau France	
143 D2	Milledgeville U.S.A.	
137 E1	Mille Lacs lakes U.S.A.	
130 A2	Mille Lacs, Lac des l. Can.	
137 D2	Miller U.S.A.	
91 E2	Millerovo Rus. Fed.	
52 A2	Millers Creek Austr.	
52 B3	Millicent Austr.	
141 F1	Millinocket U.S.A.	
53 D1	Millmerran Austr.	
98 B1	Millom U.K.	
128 C1	Mills Lake Can.	
111 B3	Milos i. Greece	
89 E3	Miloslavskoye Rus. Fed.	
91 E2	Milove Ukr.	
52 B1	Milparinka Austr.	
53 A3	Milton N.Z.	
99 C2	Milton Keynes U.K.	
140 B2	Milwaukee U.S.A.	
104 B3	Mimizan France	
118 B3	Mimongo Gabon	
79 C2	Mīnāb Iran	
58 C2	Minahasa, Semenanjung pen. Indon.	
79 C2	Mina Jebel Ali U.A.E.	
60 B1	Minas Indon.	
153 C4	Minas Uru.	
155 D1	Minas Novas Brazil	
145 C3	Minatitlán Mex.	
62 A1	Minbu Myanmar	
64 B2	Mindanao i. Phil.	
101 D1	Minden Ger.	
142 B2	Minden LA U.S.A.	
137 D2	Minden NE U.S.A.	
64 B1	Mindoro i. Phil.	
64 A1	Mindoro Strait Phil.	
118 B3	Mindouli Congo	
99 B3	Minehead U.K.	
154 B1	Mineiros Brazil	
139 D2	Mineral Wells U.S.A.	
77 E3	Minfeng China	
119 C4	Minga Dem. Rep. Congo	
81 C1	Mingāçevir Azer.	
131 D1	Mingan Can.	
52 B2	Mingary Austr.	
70 B2	Mingguang China	
62 A1	Mingin Myanmar	
107 C2	Minglanilla Spain	
119 D4	Mingoyo Tanz.	
69 E1	Mingshui China	
71 B3	Mingxi China	
73 B4	Minicoy atoll India	
50 A2	Minilya Austr.	
131 D1	Minipi Lake Can.	
130 A1	Miniss Lake Can.	
115 C4	Minna Nigeria	
137 E2	Minneapolis U.S.A.	
129 E2	Minnedosa Can.	
137 E2	Minnesota r. U.S.A.	
137 E1	Minnesota state U.S.A.	
106 B1	Miño r. Port./Spain	
107 D1	Minorca i. Spain	
136 C1	Minot U.S.A.	
88 C3	Minsk Belarus	
103 E1	Mińsk Mazowiecki Pol.	
131 D2	Minto Can.	
130 C1	Minto, Lac l. Can.	
70 A2	Minxian China	
155 D1	Mirabela Brazil	
155 C3	Miralta Brazil	
131 D2	Miramichi N.B. Can.	
111 C3	Mirampellou, Kolpos b. Greece	
152 C3	Miranda Brazil	
152 C3	Miranda r. Brazil	
106 C1	Miranda de Ebro Spain	
106 B1	Mirandela Port.	
154 B2	Mirandópolis Brazil	
79 C3	Mirbāt Oman	
61 C1	Miri Sarawak Malaysia	
153 C4	Mirim, Lagoa l. Brazil/Uru.	
79 D2	Mīrjāveh Iran	
83 I2	Mirnyy Rus. Fed.	
101 F1	Mirow Ger.	

74 A2 **Mirpur Khas** Pak.
111 B3 **Mirtoö Pelagos** *sea* Greece
65 B2 **Miryang** S. Korea
75 C2 **Mirzapur** India
66 B1 **Mishan** China
146 B3 **Miskitos, Cayos** *is* Nic.
103 E2 **Miskolc** Hungary
59 C3 **Misoöl** *i.* Indon.
115 D1 **Mişrātah** Libya
130 B1 **Missinaibi** *r.* Can.
130 B2 **Missinaibi Lake** Can.
128 B3 **Mission** Can.
130 B1 **Missisa Lake** Can.
142 C3 **Mississippi** *r.* U.S.A.
142 C2 **Mississippi** *state* U.S.A.
142 C3 **Mississippi Delta** U.S.A.
134 D1 **Missoula** U.S.A.
137 E3 **Missouri** *r.* U.S.A.
137 E3 **Missouri** *state* U.S.A.
131 C2 **Mistassibi** *r.* Can.
130 C1 **Mistassini, Lac** *l.* Can.
131 D1 **Mistastin Lake** Can.
103 D2 **Mistelbach** Austria
131 D1 **Mistinibi, Lac** *l.* Can.
130 C1 **Mistissini** Can.
51 D2 **Mitchell** Austr.
51 D1 **Mitchell** *r.* Austr.
137 D2 **Mitchell** U.S.A.
97 B2 **Mitchelstown** Ireland
74 A2 **Mithi** Pak.
67 D3 **Mito** Japan
119 D3 **Mitole** Tanz.
109 D2 **Mitrovicë** Kosovo
53 D2 **Mittagong** Austr.
101 E2 **Mittelhausen** Ger.
101 D1 **Mittellandkanal** *canal* Ger.
101 F3 **Mitterteich** Ger.
150 A1 **Mitú** Col.
119 C4 **Mitumba, Chaîne des** *mts* Dem. Rep. Congo
119 C3 **Mitumba, Monts** *mts* Dem. Rep. Congo
118 B2 **Mitzic** Gabon
78 B2 **Miyah, Wādī al** *watercourse* Saudi Arabia
67 C4 **Miyake-jima** *i.* Japan
66 D3 **Miyako** Japan
67 B4 **Miyakonojō** Japan
76 B2 **Miyaly** Kazakh.
Miyang China *see* **Mile**
67 B4 **Miyazaki** Japan
115 D1 **Mizdah** Libya
97 B3 **Mizen Head** Ireland
90 A2 **Mizhhirr"ya** Ukr.
93 G4 **Mjölby** Sweden
93 F3 **Mjøsa** *l.* Norway
119 D3 **Mkomazi** Tanz.
103 C1 **Mladá Boleslav** Czech Rep.
109 D2 **Mladenovac** Serbia
103 E1 **Mława** Pol.
123 C3 **Mlungisi** S. Africa
90 B1 **Mlyniv** Ukr.
123 C2 **Mmabatho** S. Africa
123 C2 **Mmathethe** Botswana
135 E3 **Moab** U.S.A.
123 D2 **Moamba** Moz.
119 C3 **Moba** Dem. Rep. Congo
118 C2 **Mobayi-Mbongo** Dem. Rep. Congo
137 E3 **Moberly** U.S.A.
142 C2 **Mobile** U.S.A.
142 C2 **Mobile Bay** U.S.A.
136 C1 **Mobridge** U.S.A.
121 D2 **Moçambique** Moz.
62 B1 **Môc Châu** Vietnam
78 B3 **Mocha** Yemen
123 C1 **Mochudi** Botswana
121 D2 **Mocimboa da Praia** Moz.
150 A1 **Mocoa** Col.
154 C2 **Mococa** Brazil
144 B2 **Mocorito** Mex.
144 B1 **Moctezuma** *Chihuahua* Mex.
145 B2 **Moctezuma** *San Luis Potosí* Mex.
144 B2 **Moctezuma** *Sonora* Mex.
121 C2 **Mocuba** Moz.
105 D2 **Modane** France
122 B2 **Modder** *r.* S. Africa
108 B2 **Modena** Italy
135 B3 **Modesto** U.S.A.
123 C1 **Modimolle** S. Africa
53 C3 **Moe** Austr.
100 C2 **Moers** Ger.
96 C3 **Moffat** U.K.
117 C4 **Mogadishu** Somalia
123 C1 **Mogalakwena** *r.* S. Africa
62 A1 **Mogaung** Myanmar
Mogilev Belarus *see* **Mahilyow**
154 C2 **Mogi-Mirim** Brazil
83 I3 **Mogocha** Rus. Fed.
62 A1 **Mogok** Myanmar
103 D2 **Mohács** Hungary
123 C3 **Mohale's Hoek** Lesotho
107 D2 **Mohammadia** Alg.
141 E2 **Mohawk** *r.* U.S.A.
119 D3 **Mohoro** Tanz.
90 B2 **Mohyliv-Podil's'kyy** Ukr.
110 C1 **Moinești** Romania
92 F2 **Mo i Rana** Norway
104 C3 **Moissac** France
135 C3 **Mojave** U.S.A.
135 C3 **Mojave Desert** U.S.A.
62 B1 **Mojiang** China
155 C2 **Moji das Cruzes** Brazil
154 C2 **Moji-Guaçu** *r.* Brazil
54 B1 **Mokau** N.Z.
123 C2 **Mokhotlong** Lesotho
123 C1 **Mokopane** S. Africa
65 B3 **Mokp'o** S. Korea
145 C2 **Molango** Mex.
Moldavia *country* Europe *see* **Moldova**
92 E3 **Molde** Norway
90 B2 **Moldova** *country* Europe
110 B1 **Moldoveanu, Vârful** *mt.* Romania
90 B2 **Moldovei Centrale, Podișul** *plat.* Moldova
123 C1 **Molepolole** Botswana
88 C2 **Molėtai** Lith.
109 C2 **Molfetta** Italy
107 C1 **Molina de Aragón** Spain
150 A3 **Mollendo** Peru
53 C2 **Molong** Austr.
122 B2 **Molopo** *watercourse* Botswana/S. Africa
118 B2 **Moloundou** Cameroon
59 C3 **Moluccas** *is* Indon.
Molucca Sea Indon. *see* **Maluku, Laut**
52 B2 **Momba** Austr.
119 D3 **Mombasa** Kenya
154 B1 **Mombuca, Serra da** *hills* Brazil
93 F4 **Møn** *i.* Denmark
105 D3 **Monaco** *country* Europe
96 B2 **Monadhliath Mountains** U.K.
97 C1 **Monaghan** Ireland
89 D3 **Monastyrshchina** Rus. Fed.
90 B2 **Monastyryshche** Ukr.
66 D2 **Monbetsu** Japan
108 A1 **Moncalieri** Italy
86 C2 **Monchegorsk** Rus. Fed.
100 C2 **Mönchengladbach** Ger.
144 B2 **Monclova** Mex.
131 D2 **Moncton** Can.
106 B1 **Mondego** *r.* Port.
123 D2 **Mondlo** S. Africa
108 A2 **Mondovì** Italy
111 B3 **Monemvasia** Greece
66 D1 **Moneron, Ostrov** *i.* Rus. Fe
137 E3 **Monett** U.S.A.
108 B1 **Monfalcone** Italy
106 B1 **Monforte de Lemos** Spain
62 B1 **Mông Cai** Vietnam
62 B1 **Mong Lin** Myanmar
68 C1 **Mongolia** *country* Asia
62 A1 **Mong Pawk** Myanmar
62 A1 **Mong Ping** Myanmar
120 B2 **Mongu** Zambia
135 C3 **Monitor Range** *mts* U.S.A.
114 C4 **Mono** *r.* Benin/Togo
135 C3 **Mono Lake** U.S.A.
109 C2 **Monopoli** Italy
107 C1 **Monreal del Campo** Spain
142 B2 **Monroe** *LA* U.S.A.
140 B2 **Monroe** *WI* U.S.A.
142 C2 **Monroeville** U.S.A.
114 A4 **Monrovia** Liberia
100 A2 **Mons** Belgium
122 B3 **Montagu** S. Africa
109 C3 **Montalto** *mt.* Italy
110 B2 **Montana** Bulg.
134 E1 **Montana** *state* U.S.A.
104 C2 **Montargis** France
104 C3 **Montauban** France
141 E2 **Montauk Point** U.S.A.
123 C2 **Mont-aux-Sources** *mt.* Lesotho
105 C2 **Montbard** France
105 C2 **Montbrison** France
100 B3 **Montcornet** France
104 B3 **Mont-de-Marsan** France
104 C2 **Montdidier** France
151 C2 **Monte Alegre** Brazil
105 D3 **Monte-Carlo** Monaco
152 C4 **Monte Caseros** Arg.
146 C3 **Montego Bay** Jamaica
105 C3 **Montélimar** France
109 C2 **Montella** Italy
145 C2 **Montemorelos** Mex.
104 B2 **Montendre** France
109 C2 **Montenegro** *country* Europe
121 C2 **Montepuez** Moz.
108 B2 **Montepulciano** Italy
135 B3 **Monterey** U.S.A.
135 B3 **Monterey Bay** U.S.A.
150 A1 **Montería** Col.
152 B2 **Montero** Bol.
145 B2 **Monterrey** Mex.
109 C2 **Montesano sulla Marcellar** Italy
109 C2 **Monte Sant'Angelo** Italy
151 E3 **Monte Santo** Brazil
108 A2 **Monte Santu, Capo di** *c.* *Sardegna* Italy
155 D1 **Montes Claros** Brazil
153 C4 **Montevideo** Uru.
137 D2 **Montevideo** U.S.A.
136 B3 **Monte Vista** U.S.A.
142 C2 **Montgomery** U.S.A.
105 D2 **Monthey** Switz.
142 B2 **Monticello** *AR* U.S.A.
135 E3 **Monticello** *UT* U.S.A.
104 C2 **Montignac** France
105 D2 **Montigny-le-Roi** France
106 C2 **Montilla** Spain
131 D2 **Mont-Joli** Can.
130 C2 **Mont-Laurier** Can.
104 C2 **Montluçon** France
131 C2 **Montmagny** Can.
104 C2 **Montmorillon** France

1 E2 **Monto** Austr.
4 D2 **Montpelier** *ID* U.S.A.
5 C3 **Montpelier** *VT* U.S.A.
5 C3 **Montpellier** France
9 D2 **Montréal** Can.
9 D2 **Montreal Lake** Can.
9 D2 **Montreal Lake** Can.
9 D3 **Montreuil** France
6 B3 **Montreux** Switz.
6 B3 **Montrose** U.K.
6 B3 **Montrose** U.S.A.
7 **Montserrat** *terr.* West Indies
2 A1 **Monywa** Myanmar
8 A1 **Monza** Italy
2 A1 **Monzón** Spain
3 C3 **Mookane** Botswana
3 D1 **Moonie** Austr.
3 D1 **Moonie** *r.* Austr.
2 A2 **Moonta** Austr.
3 **Moore, Lake** *imp. l.* Austr.
7 D1 **Moorhead** U.S.A.
2 B3 **Mooroopna** Austr.
2 A3 **Moorreesburg** S. Africa
0 B1 **Moose** *r.* Can.
1 B1 **Moose Factory** Can.
1 F1 **Moosehead Lake** U.S.A.
9 D2 **Moose Jaw** Can.
0 B1 **Moose Lake** U.S.A.
9 D2 **Moosomin** Can.
0 B1 **Moosonee** Can.
2 B2 **Mootwingee** Austr.
3 C1 **Mopane** S. Africa
8 A3 **Mopti** Mali
0 A3 **Moquegua** Peru
2 B3 **Mora** Sweden
1 **Mora** U.S.A.
7 E1 **Mora** U.S.A.
5 F3 **Moradabad** India
1 D2 **Moramanga** Madag.
6 **Morava** *r.* Europe
6 C2 **Moray Firth** U.K.
5 G3 **Morbach** Ger.
4 B3 **Morbi** India
4 B3 **Morcenx** France
9 E1 **Mordaga** China
6 C3 **Morden** Can.
7 E1 **Mordovo** Rus. Fed.
8 B1 **Morecambe** U.K.
8 B1 **Morecambe Bay** U.K.
3 C1 **Moree** Austr.
3 D2 **Morehead** P.N.G.
0 C2 **Morehead** U.S.A.
3 D2 **Morehead City** U.S.A.
5 B3 **Morelia** Mex.
2 D2 **Morella** Spain
4 **Morena, Sierra** *mts* Spain
0 C2 **Moreni** Romania
8 A2 **Moresby, Mount** Can.
8 A2 **Moresby Island** Can.
2 B3 **Morgan City** U.S.A.
3 D2 **Morganton** U.S.A.
Morgantown U.S.A.
6 C3 **Morges** Switz.
5 **Morghāb** Afgh.
7 C3 **Morghāb** *r.* Afgh.
3 C3 **Mori** Japan
8 B2 **Morice Lake** Can.
3 D2 **Morioka** Japan
3 D2 **Morisset** Austr.
4 B2 **Morlaix** France
1 C1 **Mornington Island** Austr.
3 D2 **Morobe** P.N.G.
8 **Morocco** *country* Africa
8 B1 **Morogoro** Tanz.
8 **Moro Gulf** Phil.
8 A3 **Morokweng** S. Africa
1 D2 **Morombe** Madag.
8 **Mörön** Mongolia

121 D3 **Morondava** Madag.
88 **Moroni** Comoros
59 C2 **Morotai** *i.* Indon.
98 C1 **Moroto** Uganda
98 C1 **Morpeth** U.K.
154 C1 **Morrinhos** Brazil
129 E3 **Morris** Can.
131 **Morris** U.S.A.
143 D1 **Morristown** U.S.A.
87 D3 **Morshanka** Rus. Fed.
154 B1 **Mortes, Rio das** *r.* Brazil
52 B3 **Mortlake** Austr.
53 D3 **Moruya** Austr.
96 B2 **Morvern** *reg.* U.K.
53 C3 **Morwell** Austr.
102 B2 **Mosbach** Ger.
89 E2 **Moscow** Rus. Fed.
134 C1 **Moscow** U.S.A.
105 D2 **Mosel** *r.* Ger.
105 D2 **Moselle** *r.* France
77 D2 **Mosfellsbær** Iceland
92 A3 **Mosgiel** N.Z.
89 D2 **Moshenskoye** Rus. Fed.
119 D3 **Moshi** Tanz.
92 F2 **Mosjøen** Norway
103 D2 **Moskva** *r. Rus. Fed.* see **Moscow**
103 D2 **Mosonmagyaróvár** Hungary
146 B4 **Mosquitos, Golfo de los** *b.* Panama
93 F4 **Moss** Norway
122 B3 **Mossel Bay** Zimbabwe
122 B3 **Mossel Bay** S. Africa
118 B3 **Mossendjo** Congo
52 B2 **Mossgiel** Austr.
51 D1 **Mossman** Austr.
151 E2 **Mossoró** Brazil
53 C3 **Moss Vale** Austr.
102 C1 **Most** Czech Rep.
114 C1 **Mostaganem** Alg.
109 C2 **Mostar** Bos.-Herz.
152 C4 **Mostardas** Brazil
81 C2 **Mosul** Iraq
93 G4 **Motala** Sweden
96 C3 **Motherwell** U.K.
107 C2 **Motilla del Palancar** Spain
122 B1 **Motokwe** Botswana
106 C2 **Motril** Spain
110 B2 **Motru** Romania
63 A2 **Mottama, Gulf of** Myanmar
59 D3 **Motul** Mex.
111 C3 **Moudros** Greece
118 B3 **Mouila** Gabon
52 B3 **Moulamein** Austr.
105 C2 **Moulins** France
143 D2 **Moultrie** U.S.A.
143 D2 **Moultrie, Lake** U.S.A.
115 D4 **Moundou** Chad
140 B3 **Mound City** U.S.A.
140 **Mountain Grove** U.S.A.
142 B1 **Mountain Home** *AR* U.S.A.
134 C2 **Mountain Home** *ID* U.S.A.
143 D2 **Mount Airy** U.S.A.
52 A3 **Mount Barker** Austr.
53 C3 **Mount Beauty** Austr.
121 C2 **Mount Darwin** Zimbabwe
141 F2 **Mount Desert Island** U.S.A.
123 C3 **Mount Fletcher** S. Africa
123 C3 **Mount Frere** S. Africa
52 A3 **Mount Gambier** Austr.
59 D3 **Mount Hagen** P.N.G.
52 B2 **Mount Hope** Austr.
51 C2 **Mount Isa** Austr.
50 A2 **Mount Magnet** Austr.
52 B2 **Mount Manara** Austr.
54 C1 **Mount Maunganui** N.Z.
111 B2 **Mount Olympus** Greece

137 E2 **Mount Pleasant** *IA* U.S.A.
140 C2 **Mount Pleasant** *MI* U.S.A.
139 E2 **Mount Pleasant** *TX* U.S.A.
99 A3 **Mount's Bay** U.K.
134 B3 **Mount Shasta** U.S.A.
140 C3 **Mount Vernon** *IL* U.S.A.
140 C2 **Mount Vernon** *OH* U.S.A.
134 B1 **Mount Vernon** *WA* U.S.A.
51 D2 **Moura** Austr.
115 E3 **Mourdi, Dépression du** *depr.* Chad
97 C1 **Mourne Mountains** *hills* U.K.
100 A2 **Mouscron** Belgium
115 D3 **Moussoro** Chad
62 B1 **Moutong** Indon.
115 C2 **Mouydir, Monts du** *plat.* Alg.
100 B3 **Mouzon** France
97 C1 **Moy** *r.* Ireland
117 B4 **Moyale** Eth.
123 C3 **Moyeni** Lesotho
76 B2 **Mo'ynoq** Uzbek.
77 D2 **Moyynty** Kazakh.
121 C3 **Mozambique** *country* Africa
113 I9 **Mozambique Channel** Africa
89 F2 **Mozhaysk** Rus. Fed.
119 D3 **Mpanda** Tanz.
121 C2 **Mpika** Tanz.
121 C2 **Mporokoso** Zambia
123 C2 **Mpumalanga** *prov.* S. Africa
62 A1 **Mrauk-U** Myanmar
88 **Mshinskaya** Rus. Fed.
107 D2 **M'Sila** Alg.
89 D2 **Msta** *r.* Rus. Fed.
89 D2 **Mstinskiy Most** Rus. Fed.
89 D3 **Mstsislaw** Belarus
89 E3 **Mtsensk** Rus. Fed.
119 E4 **Mtwara** Tanz.
118 B3 **Muanda** Dem. Rep. Congo
63 B2 **Muang Không** Laos
62 B1 **Muang Ngoy** Laos
62 B2 **Muang Pakbeng** Laos
62 B1 **Muang Sing** Laos
62 B2 **Muang Vangviang** Laos
60 B1 **Muar** Malaysia
60 B2 **Muarabungo** Indon.
60 B2 **Muaradua** Indon.
60 C2 **Muaralaung** Indon.
60 A2 **Muarasiberut** Indon.
61 C2 **Muaratembesi** Indon.
61 C2 **Muarateweh** Indon.
119 D2 **Mubende** Uganda
115 D3 **Mubi** Nigeria
120 B2 **Muconda** Angola
155 E1 **Mucuri** Brazil
155 E1 **Mucuri** *r.* Brazil
66 A2 **Mudanjiang** China
66 A1 **Mudan Jiang** *r.* China
111 C2 **Mudanya** Turkey
101 E1 **Müden (Örtze)** Ger.
53 C2 **Mudgee** Austr.
62 A2 **Mudon** Myanmar
80 B1 **Mudurnu** Turkey
121 C3 **Mueda** Moz.
121 B2 **Mufulira** Zambia
120 B2 **Mufumbwe** Zambia
111 C3 **Muğla** Turkey
116 B3 **Muhammad Qol** Sudan
101 F2 **Mühlberg** Ger.
101 E2 **Mühlhausen (Thüringen)** Ger.
119 D3 **Muite** Moz.
65 B2 **Muju** S. Korea
90 A1 **Mukacheve** Ukr.
61 C1 **Mukah** *Sarawak* Malaysia
78 B3 **Mukalla** Yemen
79 B3 **Mukdahan** Thai.
50 A3 **Mukinbudin** Austr.
60 B2 **Mukomuko** Indon.

121 C2 **Mulanje, Mount** Malawi
101 F2 **Mulde** *r.* Ger.
144 A2 **Mulegé** Mex.
139 C2 **Muleshoe** U.S.A.
106 C2 **Mulhacén** *mt.* Spain
100 C2 **Mülheim an der Ruhr** Ger.
105 D2 **Mulhouse** France
66 B2 **Muling** China
66 B1 **Muling He** *r.* China
96 B2 **Mull** *i.* U.K.
53 C2 **Mullaley** Austr.
136 C2 **Mullen** U.S.A.
61 C1 **Muller, Pegunungan** *mts* Indon.
50 A2 **Mullewa** Austr.
97 C2 **Mullingar** Ireland
96 B3 **Mull of Galloway** *c.* U.K.
96 B3 **Mull of Kintyre** *hd* U.K.
96 A3 **Mull of Oa** *hd* U.K.
120 B2 **Mulobezi** Zambia
74 B1 **Multan** Pak.
73 B3 **Mumbai** India
120 B2 **Mumbwa** Zambia
145 D2 **Muna** Mex.
101 E2 **Münchberg** Ger.
München Ger. *see* **Munich**
140 B2 **Muncie** U.S.A.
50 B3 **Mundrabilla** Austr.
119 C2 **Mungbere** Dem. Rep. Congo
75 C2 **Munger** India
52 A1 **Mungeranie** Austr.
53 C1 **Mungindi** Austr.
102 C2 **Munich** Ger.
155 D2 **Muniz Freire** Brazil
101 E1 **Münster** *Niedersachsen* Ger.
100 C2 **Münster** *Nordrhein-Westfalen* Ger.
97 B2 **Munster** *reg.* Ireland
100 C2 **Münsterland** *reg.* Ger.
62 B1 **Mường Nhe** Vietnam
92 H2 **Muonio** Fin.
92 H2 **Muonioälven** *r.* Fin./Sweden
Muqdisho Somalia *see* **Mogadishu**
103 D2 **Mur** *r.* Austria
119 C3 **Muramvya** Burundi
119 D3 **Murang'a** Kenya
81 B2 **Murat** *r.* Turkey
111 C2 **Muratlı** Turkey
50 A2 **Murchison** *watercourse* Austr.
107 C2 **Murcia** Spain
111 C2 **Mürefte** Turkey
110 B1 **Mureşul** *r.* Romania
104 C3 **Muret** France
142 C1 **Murfreesboro** U.S.A.
77 D3 **Murghob** Tajik.
155 D2 **Muriaé** Brazil
120 B1 **Muriege** Angola
101 F1 **Müritz** *l.* Ger.
86 C2 **Murmansk** Rus. Fed.
87 D3 **Murom** Rus. Fed.
66 D2 **Muroran** Japan
106 B1 **Muros** Spain
67 B4 **Muroto** Japan
67 B4 **Muroto-zaki** *pt* Japan
143 D1 **Murphy** U.S.A.
53 C1 **Murra Murra** Austr.
52 A3 **Murray** *r.* Austr.
128 B2 **Murray** *r.* Can.
140 B3 **Murray** U.S.A.
143 D2 **Murray, Lake** U.S.A.
52 A3 **Murray Bridge** Austr.
122 B3 **Murraysburg** S. Africa
52 B3 **Murrayville** Austr.
52 B2 **Murrumbidgee** *r.* Austr.
121 C2 **Murrupula** Moz.
53 D2 **Murrurundi** Austr.
109 C1 **Murska Sobota** Slovenia
54 C1 **Murupara** N.Z.
49 I4 **Mururoa** *atoll* Fr. Polynesia
75 C2 **Murwara** India
53 D1 **Murwillumbah** Austr.
115 D2 **Murzūq** Libya
115 D2 **Murzūq, Idhān** *des.* Libya
81 C2 **Muş** Turkey
110 B2 **Musala** *mt.* Bulg.
65 B1 **Musan** N. Korea
78 B3 **Musaymir** Yemen
79 C2 **Muscat** Oman
137 E2 **Muscatine** U.S.A.
50 C2 **Musgrave Ranges** *mts* Austr.
118 B3 **Mushie** Dem. Rep. Congo
60 B2 **Musi** *r.* Indon.
123 D1 **Musina** S. Africa
140 B2 **Muskegon** U.S.A.
139 D1 **Muskogee** U.S.A.
128 B2 **Muskwa** *r.* Can.
74 A1 **Muslimbagh** Pak.
78 A3 **Musmar** Sudan
119 D3 **Musoma** Tanz.
96 C3 **Musselburgh** U.K.
88 B2 **Mustjala** Estonia
53 D2 **Muswellbrook** Austr.
116 A2 **Mūţ** Egypt
121 C2 **Mutare** Zimbabwe
66 D2 **Mutsu** Japan
121 C2 **Mutuali** Moz.
92 I2 **Muurola** Fin.
70 A2 **Mu Us Shamo** *des.* China
120 A1 **Muxaluando** Angola
86 C2 **Muyezerskiy** Rus. Fed.
119 D3 **Muyinga** Burundi
74 B1 **Muzaffargarh** Pak.
75 C2 **Muzaffarpur** India
144 B2 **Múzquiz** Mex.
75 C1 **Muztag** *mt.* China
119 C3 **Mwanza** Dem. Rep. Congo
119 D3 **Mwanza** Tanz.
118 C3 **Mweka** Dem. Rep. Congo
121 B2 **Mwenda** Zambia
118 C3 **Mwene-Ditu** Dem. Rep. Congo
121 C3 **Mwenezi** Zimbabwe
119 C3 **Mweru, Lake** Dem. Rep. Congo/Zambia
118 C3 **Mwimba** Dem. Rep. Congo
120 B2 **Mwinilunga** Zambia
88 C3 **Myadzyel** Belarus
62 A2 **Myanaung** Myanmar
62 A1 **Myanmar** *country* Asia
63 A2 **Myaungmya** Myanmar
63 A2 **Myeik** Myanmar
Myeik Kyunzu *is* Myanmar *see* **Mergui Archipelago**
62 A1 **Myingyan** Myanmar
62 A1 **Myitkyina** Myanmar
91 C2 **Mykolayiv** Ukr.
111 C3 **Mykonos** Greece
111 C3 **Mykonos** *i.* Greece
86 E2 **Myla** Rus. Fed.
75 D2 **Mymensingh** Bangl.
65 B1 **Myŏnggan** N. Korea
88 C2 **Myory** Belarus
92 B3 **Mýrdalsjökull** Iceland
91 C2 **Myrhorod** Ukr.
90 C2 **Myronivka** Ukr.
143 E2 **Myrtle Beach** U.S.A.
53 C3 **Myrtleford** Austr.
134 B2 **Myrtle Point** U.S.A.
89 E2 **Myshkin** Rus. Fed.
103 C1 **Myślibórz** Pol.
73 B3 **Mysore** India
83 N2 **Mys Shmidta** Rus. Fed.
63 B2 **My Tho** Vietnam
111 C3 **Mytilini** Greece
89 E3 **Mytishchi** Rus. Fed.
123 C3 **Mzamomhle** S. Africa
121 C2 **Mzimba** Malawi
121 C2 **Mzuzu** Malawi

N

97 C2 **Naas** Ireland
122 A2 **Nababeep** S. Africa
87 E3 **Naberezhnyye Chelny** Rus. Fed.
59 D3 **Nabire** Indon.
80 B2 **Nāblus** West Bank
123 C1 **Naboomspruit** S. Africa
121 D2 **Nacala** Moz.
63 A2 **Nachuge** India
139 E2 **Nacogdoches** U.S.A.
144 B1 **Nacozari de García** Mex.
74 B2 **Nadiad** India
90 A2 **Nadvirna** Ukr.
86 C2 **Nadvoitsy** Rus. Fed.
86 G2 **Nadym** Rus. Fed.
93 F4 **Næstved** Denmark
111 B3 **Nafpaktos** Greece
111 B3 **Nafplio** Greece
115 D1 **Nafūsah, Jabal** *hills* Libya
78 B2 **Nafy** Saudi Arabia
64 B1 **Naga** Phil.
130 B1 **Nagagami** *r.* Can.
67 C3 **Nagano** Japan
67 C3 **Nagaoka** Japan
75 D2 **Nagaon** India
74 B1 **Nagar** India
74 B2 **Nagar Parkar** Pak.
67 A4 **Nagasaki** Japan
67 B4 **Nagato** Japan
74 B2 **Nagaur** India
73 B4 **Nagercoil** India
74 A2 **Nagha Kalat** Pak.
75 B2 **Nagina** India
67 C3 **Nagoya** Japan
75 B2 **Nagpur** India
68 C2 **Nagqu** China
103 D2 **Nagyatád** Hungary
103 D2 **Nagykanizsa** Hungary
128 B1 **Nahanni Butte** Can.
76 A3 **Nahāvand** Iran
101 E1 **Nahrendorf** Ger.
153 A5 **Nahuel Huapí, Lago** *l.* Arg.
131 D1 **Nain** Can.
81 D2 **Nā'īn** Iran
96 C2 **Nairn** U.K.
119 D3 **Nairobi** Kenya
119 D3 **Naivasha** Kenya
81 D2 **Najafābād** Iran
78 B2 **Najd** *reg.* Saudi Arabia
106 C1 **Nájera** Spain
65 C1 **Najin** N. Korea
78 B3 **Najrān** Saudi Arabia
Nakambé *r.* Burkina/Ghana **White Volta**
67 C3 **Nakatsugawa** Japan
78 A3 **Nakfa** Eritrea
66 B2 **Nakhodka** Rus. Fed.
63 B2 **Nakhon Pathom** Thai.
63 B2 **Nakhon Ratchasima** Thai.
63 B2 **Nakhon Sawan** Thai.
63 A3 **Nakhon Si Thammarat** Th
130 B1 **Nakina** Can.
121 C1 **Nakonde** Zambia
93 F4 **Nakskov** Denmark
119 D3 **Nakuru** Kenya
128 C2 **Nakusp** Can.
75 D2 **Nalbari** India

D4 **Nal'chik** Rus. Fed.
D1 **Nālūt** Libya
C2 **Namahadi** S. Africa
D2 **Namangan** Uzbek.
A2 **Namaqualand** *reg.* S. Africa
E2 **Nambour** Austr.
D2 **Nambucca Heads** Austr.
D1 **Nam Co** *salt l.* China
B1 **Nam Định** Vietnam
A3 **Namib Desert** Namibia
A2 **Namibe** Angola
A3 **Namibia** *country* Africa
D2 **Namjagbarwa Feng** *mt.* China
C3 **Namlea** Indon.
C2 **Namoi** *r.* Austr.
C2 **Nampa** U.S.A.
B3 **Nampala** Mali
B2 **Namp'o** N. Korea
C2 **Nampula** Moz.
A1 **Namrup** India
A1 **Namsang** Myanmar
F3 **Namsos** Norway
A2 **Nam Tok** Thai.
J2 **Namtsy** Rus. Fed.
A1 **Namtu** Myanmar
B2 **Namur** Belgium
B2 **Namwala** Zambia
B2 **Namwŏn** S. Korea
A1 **Namya Ra** Myanmar
B2 **Nan** Thai.
B3 **Nanaimo** Can.
B3 **Nan'an** China
A1 **Nananib Plateau** Namibia
C3 **Nanao** Japan
B3 **Nanchang** *Jiangxi* China
B3 **Nanchang** *Jiangxi* China
A2 **Nanchong** China
A3 **Nancowry** *i.* India
D2 **Nancy** France
C1 **Nanda Devi** *mt.* India
A3 **Nandan** China
B3 **Nanded** India
B2 **Nandurbar** India
B3 **Nandyal** India
B3 **Nanfeng** China
B2 **Nanga Eboko** Cameroon
C2 **Nangahpinoh** Indon.
B1 **Nanga Parbat** *mt.* Pak.
C2 **Nangatayap** Indon.
B2 **Nangong** China
D3 **Nangulangwa** Tanz.
C2 **Nanhui** China
B2 **Nanjing** China
Nanking China *see* **Nanjing**
A2 **Nankova** Angola
B3 **Nan Ling** *mts* China
A3 **Nanning** China
H2 **Nanortalik** Greenland
A3 **Nanpan Jiang** *r.* China
C2 **Nanpara** India
B3 **Nanping** China
Nansei-shotō *is* Japan *see* **Ryukyu Islands**
B2 **Nantes** France
C2 **Nantong** China
F2 **Nantucket Island** U.S.A.
D1 **Nanuque** Brazil
B2 **Nanusa, Kepulauan** *is* Indon.
B3 **Nanxiong** China
B2 **Nanyang** China
B2 **Nanzhang** China
D2 **Nao, Cabo de la** *c.* Spain
C1 **Naococane, Lac** *l.* Can.
B3 **Napa** U.S.A.
D2 **Napaktulik Lake** Can.
H2 **Napasoq** Greenland
C1 **Napier** N.Z.
108 B2 **Naples** Italy
143 D3 **Naples** U.S.A.
150 A2 **Napo** *r.* Ecuador/Peru
Napoli Italy *see* **Naples**
114 B3 **Nara** Mali
93 I4 **Narach** Belarus
52 B3 **Naracoorte** Austr.
145 C2 **Naranjos** Mex.
63 B3 **Narathiwat** Thai.
105 C3 **Narbonne** France
63 A2 **Narcondam Island** India
127 G1 **Nares Strait** Can./Greenland
122 A1 **Narib** Namibia
87 D4 **Narimanov** Rus. Fed.
67 D3 **Narita** Japan
74 B2 **Narmada** *r.* India
74 B2 **Narnaul** India
108 B2 **Narni** Italy
90 B1 **Narodychi** Ukr.
89 E2 **Naro-Fominsk** Rus. Fed.
53 D3 **Narooma** Austr.
88 C3 **Narowlya** Belarus
53 C2 **Narrabri** Austr.
53 C2 **Narrandera** Austr.
53 C2 **Narromine** Austr.
88 C2 **Narva** Estonia
88 C2 **Narva Bay** Estonia/Rus. Fed.
92 G2 **Narvik** Norway
88 C2 **Narvskoye Vodokhranilishche** *resr* Estonia/Rus. Fed.
86 E2 **Nar'yan-Mar** Rus. Fed.
77 D2 **Naryn** Kyrg.
74 B2 **Nashik** India
141 E2 **Nashua** U.S.A.
142 C1 **Nashville** U.S.A.
117 B4 **Nasir** Sudan
128 B2 **Nass** *r.* Can.
146 C2 **Nassau** Bahamas
116 B2 **Nasser, Lake** *resr* Egypt
93 F4 **Nässjö** Sweden
130 C1 **Nastapoca** *r.* Can.
130 C1 **Nastapoka Islands** Can.
120 B3 **Nata** Botswana
151 E2 **Natal** Brazil
131 D1 **Natashquan** Can.
131 D1 **Natashquan** *r.* Can.
142 B2 **Natchez** U.S.A.
142 B2 **Natchitoches** U.S.A.
53 C3 **Nathalia** Austr.
107 D1 **Nati, Punta** *pt* Spain
114 C3 **Natitingou** Benin
151 D3 **Natividade** Brazil
67 D3 **Natori** Japan
131 D1 **Natuashish** Can.
61 B1 **Natuna, Kepulauan** *is* Indon.
61 B1 **Natuna Besar** *i.* Indon.
120 A3 **Nauchas** Namibia
101 F1 **Nauen** Ger.
88 B2 **Naujoji Akmenė** Lith.
74 A2 **Naukot** Pak.
101 E2 **Naumburg (Saale)** Ger.
48 F3 **Nauru** *country* S. Pacific Ocean
145 C2 **Nautla** Mex.
88 C3 **Navahrudak** Belarus
106 B2 **Navalmoral de la Mata** Spain
106 B2 **Navalvillar de Pela** Spain
97 C2 **Navan** Ireland
88 C2 **Navapolatsk** Belarus
83 M2 **Navarin, Mys** *c.* Rus. Fed.
153 B6 **Navarino, Isla** *i.* Chile
96 B1 **Naver** *r.* U.K.
73 B3 **Navi Mumbai** India
89 D3 **Navlya** Rus. Fed.
110 C2 **Năvodari** Romania
77 C2 **Navoiy** Uzbek.
144 B2 **Navojoa** Mex.
144 B2 **Navolato** Mex.
74 A2 **Nawabshah** Pak.
62 A1 **Nawnghkio** Myanmar
62 A1 **Nawngleng** Myanmar
81 C2 **Naxçıvan** Azer.
111 C3 **Naxos** *i.* Greece
144 B2 **Nayar** Mex.
66 D2 **Nayoro** Japan
144 B2 **Nazas** Mex.
144 B2 **Nazas** *r.* Mex.
150 A3 **Nazca** Peru
80 B2 **Nazerat** Israel
111 C3 **Nazilli** Turkey
117 B4 **Nazrēt** Eth.
79 C2 **Nazwá** Oman
121 B1 **Nchelenge** Zambia
122 B1 **Ncojane** Botswana
120 A1 **N'dalatando** Angola
118 C2 **Ndélé** C.A.R.
118 B3 **Ndendé** Gabon
115 D3 **Ndjamena** Chad
121 B2 **Ndola** Zambia
97 C1 **Neagh, Lough** *l.* U.K.
50 C2 **Neale, Lake** *imp. l.* Austr.
111 B2 **Nea Roda** Greece
99 B3 **Neath** U.K.
53 C1 **Nebine Creek** *r.* Austr.
150 B1 **Neblina, Pico da** *mt.* Brazil
89 D2 **Nebolchi** Rus. Fed.
136 C2 **Nebraska** *state* U.S.A.
137 D2 **Nebraska City** U.S.A.
108 B3 **Nebrodi, Monti** *mts Sicilia* Italy
153 C4 **Necochea** Arg.
131 C1 **Nedlouc, Lac** *l.* Can.
135 D4 **Needles** U.S.A.
74 B2 **Neemuch** India
129 E2 **Neepawa** Can.
87 E3 **Neftekamsk** Rus. Fed.
82 F2 **Nefteyugansk** Rus. Fed.
120 A1 **Negage** Angola
117 B4 **Negēlē** Eth.
150 A2 **Negra, Punta** *pt* Peru
63 A2 **Negrais, Cape** Myanmar
153 B5 **Negro** *r.* Arg.
150 C2 **Negro** *r.* S. America
152 C4 **Negro** *r.* Uru.
106 B2 **Negro, Cabo** *c.* Morocco
64 B2 **Negros** *i.* Phil.
69 E1 **Nehe** China
70 A3 **Neijiang** China
129 D2 **Neilburg** Can.
150 A1 **Neiva** Col.
129 E2 **Nejanilini Lake** Can.
117 B4 **Nek'emtē** Eth.
89 F2 **Nekrasovskoye** Rus. Fed.
89 D2 **Nelidovo** Rus. Fed.
73 B3 **Nellore** India
128 C3 **Nelson** Can.
129 E2 **Nelson** *r.* Can.
54 B2 **Nelson** N.Z.
52 B3 **Nelson, Cape** Austr.
53 D2 **Nelson Bay** Austr.
129 E2 **Nelson House** Can.
134 E1 **Nelson Reservoir** U.S.A.
123 D2 **Nelspruit** S. Africa
114 B3 **Néma** Maur.
88 B2 **Neman** Rus. Fed.
104 C2 **Nemours** France
66 D2 **Nemuro** Japan
90 B2 **Nemyriv** Ukr.
97 B2 **Nenagh** Ireland
99 D2 **Nene** *r.* U.K.
69 E1 **Nenjiang** China
137 E3 **Neosho** U.S.A.
75 C2 **Nepal** *country* Asia
75 C2 **Nepalganj** Nepal
135 D3 **Nephi** U.S.A.

97 B1 **Nephin** *h.* Ireland
97 B1 **Nephin Beg Range** *hills* Ireland
131 D2 **Nepisiguit** *r.* Can.
119 C2 **Nepoko** *r.* Dem. Rep. Congo
104 C3 **Nérac** France
53 D1 **Nerang** Austr.
69 D1 **Nerchinsk** Rus. Fed.
89 F2 **Nerekhta** Rus. Fed.
109 C2 **Neretva** *r.* Bos.-Herz./Croatia
120 B2 **Neriquinha** Angola
88 B3 **Neris** *r.* Lith.
89 E2 **Nerl'** *r.* Rus. Fed.
86 F2 **Nerokhi** Rus. Fed.
154 C1 **Nerópolis** Brazil
83 J3 **Neryungri** Rus. Fed.
92 C2 **Neskaupstaður** Iceland
96 B2 **Ness, Loch** *l.* U.K.
136 D3 **Ness City** U.S.A.
111 B2 **Nestos** *r.* Greece
100 B1 **Netherlands** *country* Europe
147 D3 **Netherlands Antilles** *terr.* West Indies
127 G2 **Nettilling Lake** Can.
101 F1 **Neubrandenburg** Ger.
105 D2 **Neuchâtel** Switz.
100 C2 **Neuerburg** Ger.
100 B3 **Neufchâteau** Belgium
105 D2 **Neufchâteau** France
104 C2 **Neufchâtel-en-Bray** France
101 D2 **Neuhof** Ger.
102 B1 **Neumünster** Ger.
102 B2 **Neunkirchen** Ger.
153 B4 **Neuquén** Arg.
153 B4 **Neuquén** *r.* Arg.
101 F1 **Neuruppin** Ger.
100 C2 **Neuss** Ger.
101 D1 **Neustadt am Rübenberge** Ger.
101 E3 **Neustadt an der Aisch** Ger.
101 F1 **Neustrelitz** Ger.
100 C2 **Neuwied** Ger.
137 E3 **Nevada** U.S.A.
135 C3 **Nevada** *state* U.S.A.
106 C2 **Nevada, Sierra** *mts* Spain
135 B2 **Nevada, Sierra** *mts* U.S.A.
88 C2 **Nevel'** Rus. Fed.
105 C2 **Nevers** France
53 C2 **Nevertire** Austr.
109 C2 **Nevesinje** Bos.-Herz.
87 D4 **Nevinnomyssk** Rus. Fed.
128 B2 **New Aiyansh** Can.
140 B3 **New Albany** U.S.A.
151 C1 **New Amsterdam** Guyana
141 E2 **Newark** *NJ* U.S.A.
140 C2 **Newark** *OH* U.S.A.
98 C2 **Newark-on-Trent** U.K.
141 E2 **New Bedford** U.S.A.
143 E1 **New Bern** U.S.A.
143 D2 **Newberry** U.S.A.
139 E2 **New Boston** U.S.A.
139 D3 **New Braunfels** U.S.A.
97 C2 **Newbridge** Ireland
48 E3 **New Britain** *i.* P.N.G.
131 D2 **New Brunswick** *prov.* Can.
99 C3 **Newbury** U.K.
48 E4 **New Caledonia** *terr.* S. Pacific Ocean
53 D2 **Newcastle** Austr.
123 C2 **Newcastle** S. Africa
97 D1 **Newcastle** U.K.
140 C2 **New Castle** U.S.A.
136 C2 **Newcastle** U.S.A.
98 B2 **Newcastle-under-Lyme** U.K.
98 C1 **Newcastle upon Tyne** U.K.
97 B2 **Newcastle West** Ireland
74 B2 **New Delhi** India
128 C3 **New Denver** Can.
53 D2 **New England Range** *mts* Austr.
131 E2 **Newfoundland** *i.* Can.
131 E1 **Newfoundland and Labrador** *prov.* Can.
131 D2 **New Glasgow** Can.
59 D3 **New Guinea** *i.* Indon./P.N.G.
141 E2 **New Hampshire** *state* U.S.A.
141 E2 **New Haven** U.S.A.
128 B2 **New Hazelton** Can.
New Hebrides *country* S. Pacific Ocean *see* **Vanuatu**
142 B2 **New Iberia** U.S.A.
48 E3 **New Ireland** *i.* P.N.G.
141 E3 **New Jersey** *state* U.S.A.
130 C2 **New Liskeard** Can.
50 A2 **Newman** Austr.
138 B2 **New Mexico** *state* U.S.A.
142 B3 **New Orleans** U.S.A.
140 C2 **New Philadelphia** U.S.A.
54 B1 **New Plymouth** N.Z.
99 C3 **Newport** *England* U.K.
99 B3 **Newport** *Wales* U.K.
142 B1 **Newport** *AR* U.S.A.
134 B2 **Newport** *OR* U.S.A.
141 E2 **Newport** *RI* U.S.A.
141 E2 **Newport** *VT* U.S.A.
134 C1 **Newport** *WA* U.S.A.
141 D3 **Newport News** U.S.A.
143 E3 **New Providence** *i.* Bahamas
99 A3 **Newquay** U.K.
142 B2 **New Roads** U.S.A.
97 C2 **New Ross** Ireland
97 C1 **Newry** U.K.
83 K1 **New Siberia Islands** Rus. Fed.
52 B2 **New South Wales** *state* Austr.
137 E2 **Newton** *IA* U.S.A.
137 D3 **Newton** *KS* U.S.A.
99 B3 **Newton Abbot** U.K.
96 B3 **Newton Stewart** U.K.
97 B2 **Newtown** Ireland
99 B2 **Newtown** U.K.
136 C1 **New Town** U.S.A.
97 D1 **Newtownabbey** U.K.
97 D1 **Newtownards** U.K.
96 C3 **Newtown St Boswells** U.K.
97 C1 **Newtownstewart** U.K.
137 E2 **New Ulm** U.S.A.
141 E2 **New York** U.S.A.
141 D2 **New York** *state* U.S.A.
54 B2 **New Zealand** *country* Oceania
79 C2 **Neyrīz** Iran
76 B3 **Neyshābūr** Iran
145 C3 **Nezahualcóyotl** Mex.
145 C3 **Nezahualcóyotl, Presa** *resr* Mex.
61 B1 **Ngabang** Indon.
75 C2 **Ngamring** China
75 C1 **Ngangla Ringco** *salt l.* China
75 C1 **Nganglong Kangri** *mts* China
75 C1 **Ngangzê Co** *salt l.* China
62 A2 **Ngao** Thai.
118 B2 **Ngaoundéré** Cameroon
54 C1 **Ngaruawahia** N.Z.
62 A2 **Ngathainggyaung** Myanmar
118 B3 **Ngo** Congo
63 B2 **Ngok Linh** *mt.* Vietnam
115 D4 **Ngol Bembo** Nigeria
68 C2 **Ngoring Hu** *l.* China
115 D3 **Ngourti** Niger
115 D3 **Nguigmi** Niger
59 D2 **Ngulu** *atoll* Micronesia
115 D3 **Nguru** Nigeria
123 D2 **Ngwelezana** S. Africa
121 C2 **Nhamalabué** Moz.
63 B2 **Nha Trang** Vietnam
52 B3 **Nhill** Austr.
123 D2 **Nhlangano** Swaziland
51 C1 **Nhulunbuy** Austr.
141 D2 **Niagara Falls** Can.
114 C3 **Niamey** Niger
119 C2 **Niangara** Dem. Rep. Cong
114 B3 **Niangay, Lac** *l.* Mali
60 A1 **Nias** *i.* Indon.
146 B3 **Nicaragua** *country* Central America
146 B3 **Nicaragua, Lake** Nic.
105 D3 **Nice** France
73 D4 **Nicobar Islands** India
80 B2 **Nicosia** Cyprus
146 B4 **Nicoya, Golfo de** *b.* Costa
88 B2 **Nida** Lith.
103 E1 **Nidzica** Pol.
102 B1 **Niebüll** Ger.
101 D2 **Niederaula** Ger.
118 B2 **Niefang** Equat. Guinea
101 F1 **Niemegk** Ger.
101 D1 **Nienburg (Weser)** Ger.
100 B1 **Nieuwe-Niedorp** Neth.
151 C1 **Nieuw Nickerie** Suriname
122 A3 **Nieuwoudtville** S. Africa
100 A2 **Nieuwpoort** Belgium
80 B2 **Niğde** Turkey
115 C3 **Niger** *country* Africa
115 C4 **Niger** *r.* Africa
115 C4 **Niger, Mouths of the** Nigeria
115 C4 **Nigeria** *country* Africa
130 B2 **Nighthawk Lake** Can.
111 B2 **Nigrita** Greece
67 C3 **Niigata** Japan
67 B4 **Niihama** Japan
67 C4 **Nii-jima** *i.* Japan
67 C3 **Niitsu** Japan
100 B2 **Nijmegen** Neth.
100 C1 **Nijverdal** Neth.
92 J2 **Nikel'** Rus. Fed.
83 M3 **Nikol'skoye** Rus. Fed.
91 C2 **Nikopol'** Ukr.
80 B1 **Niksar** Turkey
79 D2 **Nīkshahr** Iran
109 C2 **Nikšić** Montenegro
116 B1 **Nile** *r.* Africa
140 B2 **Niles** U.S.A.
74 A1 **Nīlī** Afgh.
105 C3 **Nîmes** France
53 C3 **Nimmitabel** Austr.
117 B4 **Nimule** Sudan
53 C1 **Nindigully** Austr.
73 B4 **Nine Degree Channel** Ind
53 C3 **Ninety Mile Beach** Austr.
54 B1 **Ninety Mile Beach** N.Z.
70 C3 **Ningbo** China
71 B3 **Ningde** China
71 B3 **Ningdu** China
70 B2 **Ningguo** China
71 C3 **Ninghai** China
Ningjiang China *see* **Songyuan**
68 C2 **Ningjing Shan** *mts* China
70 A2 **Ningxia Huizu Zizhiqu** *au reg.* China
70 B2 **Ningyang** China
62 B1 **Ninh Binh** Vietnam
63 B2 **Ninh Hoa** Vietnam
66 D2 **Ninohe** Japan
137 D2 **Niobrara** *r.* U.S.A.
114 B3 **Niono** Mali
114 B3 **Nioro** Mali
104 B2 **Niort** France
129 D2 **Nipawin** Can.
130 B2 **Nipigon** Can.
130 B2 **Nipigon, Lake** Can.
131 D1 **Nipishish Lake** Can.

C2 **Nipissing, Lake** Can.
C3 **Nipton** U.S.A.
D3 **Niquelândia** Brazil
B3 **Nirmal** India
D2 **Niš** Serbia
D2 **Nišava** *r.* Serbia
B3 **Niscemi** *Sicilia* Italy
B4 **Nishino-omote** Japan
D2 **Niterói** Brazil
C3 **Nith** *r.* U.K.
D2 **Nitra** Slovakia
G4 **Niue** *terr.* S. Pacific Ocean
H3 **Nivala** Fin.
B2 **Nivelles** Belgium
B3 **Nizamabad** India
E3 **Nizhnekamsk** Rus. Fed.
H3 **Nizhneudinsk** Rus. Fed.
G2 **Nizhnevartovsk** Rus. Fed.
F3 **Nizhniy Kislyay** Rus. Fed.
D3 **Nizhniy Lomov** Rus. Fed.
D3 **Nizhniy Novgorod** Rus. Fed.
E2 **Nizhniy Odes** Rus. Fed.
E3 **Nizhniy Tagil** Rus. Fed.
G2 **Nizhnyaya Tunguska** *r.* Rus. Fed.
C1 **Nizhyn** Ukr.
D2 **Njazidja** *i.* Comoros
D3 **Njinjo** Tanz.
D3 **Njombe** Tanz.
C2 **Nkhotakota** Malawi
A2 **Nkongsamba** Cameroon
C3 **Nkululeko** S. Africa
C3 **Nkwenkwezi** S. Africa
B4 **Nobeoka** Japan
B1 **Noccundra** Austr.
A1 **Nogales** Mex.
A2 **Nogales** U.S.A.
C2 **Nogent-le-Rotrou** France
E2 **Noginsk** Rus. Fed.
B2 **Nohar** India
C3 **Nohfelden** Ger.
B2 **Noirmoutier, Île de** *i.* France
B2 **Noirmoutier-en-l'Île** France
C4 **Nojima-zaki** *c.* Japan
B2 **Nokha** India
H3 **Nokia** Fin.
A2 **Nok Kundi** Pak.
B2 **Nola** C.A.R.
D3 **Nolinsk** Rus. Fed.
C3 **Nomonde** S. Africa
D2 **Nondweni** S. Africa
B2 **Nong Khai** Thai.
A2 **Nonning** Austr.
B2 **Nonoava** Mex.
B2 **Nonsan** S. Korea
B2 **Nonthaburi** Thai.
B3 **Nonzwakazi** S. Africa
C3 **Norak** Tajik.
C1 **Nordaustlandet** *i.* Svalbard
C2 **Nordegg** Can.
C1 **Norden** Ger.
H1 **Nordenshel'da, Arkhipelag** *is* Rus. Fed.
C1 **Norderney** Ger.
C1 **Norderney** *i.* Ger.
E1 **Norderstedt** Ger.
E3 **Nordfjordeid** Norway
E2 **Nordhausen** Ger.
D1 **Nordholz** Ger.
C1 **Nordhorn** Ger.
Nordkapp *c.* Norway *see* **North Cape**
F3 **Nordli** Norway
C2 **Nördlingen** Ger.
G3 **Nordmaling** Sweden
B1 **Norðoyar** *is* Faroe Is
C2 **Nore** *r.* Ireland
137 D2 **Norfolk** *NE* U.S.A.
141 D3 **Norfolk** *VA* U.S.A.
48 F4 **Norfolk Island** *terr.* S. Pacific Ocean
93 E3 **Norheimsund** Norway
82 G2 **Noril'sk** Rus. Fed.
75 C2 **Norkyung** China
139 D1 **Norman** U.S.A.
Normandes, Îles *is* English Chan. *see* **Channel Islands**
51 D1 **Normanton** Austr.
93 G4 **Norrköping** Sweden
93 G4 **Norrtälje** Sweden
50 B3 **Norseman** Austr.
92 G3 **Norsjö** Sweden
98 C1 **Northallerton** U.K.
50 A2 **Northampton** Austr.
99 C2 **Northampton** U.K.
73 D3 **North Andaman** *i.* India
129 D2 **North Battleford** Can.
130 C2 **North Bay** Can.
130 C1 **North Belcher Islands** Can.
96 C2 **North Berwick** U.K.
92 I1 **North Cape** Norway
54 B1 **North Cape** N.Z.
130 A1 **North Caribou Lake** Can.
143 E1 **North Carolina** *state* U.S.A.
130 B2 **North Channel** *lake channel* Can.
96 A3 **North Channel** U.K.
128 B3 **North Cowichan** Can.
136 C1 **North Dakota** *state* U.S.A.
99 C3 **North Downs** *hills* U.K.
143 E3 **Northeast Providence Channel** Bahamas
101 D2 **Northeim** Ger.
122 A2 **Northern Cape** *prov.* S. Africa
129 E2 **Northern Indian Lake** Can.
97 C1 **Northern Ireland** *prov.* U.K.
48 D1 **Northern Mariana Islands** *terr.* N. Pacific Ocean
50 C1 **Northern Territory** *admin. div.* Austr.
96 C2 **North Esk** *r.* U.K.
137 E2 **Northfield** U.S.A.
99 D3 **North Foreland** *c.* U.K.
54 B1 **North Island** N.Z.
129 E2 **North Knife Lake** Can.
65 B1 **North Korea** *country* Asia
62 A1 **North Lakhimpur** India
128 B1 **North Nahanni** *r.* Can.
136 C2 **North Platte** U.S.A.
136 C2 **North Platte** *r.* U.S.A.
96 C1 **North Ronaldsay** *i.* U.K.
94 D2 **North Sea** Europe
130 A1 **North Spirit Lake** Can.
53 D1 **North Stradbroke Island** Austr.
54 B1 **North Taranaki Bight** *b.* N.Z.
130 C1 **North Twin Island** Can.
98 B1 **North Tyne** *r.* U.K.
96 A2 **North Uist** *i.* U.K.
131 D2 **Northumberland Strait** Can.
122 C2 **North West** *prov.* S. Africa
50 A2 **North West Cape** Austr.
143 E3 **Northwest Providence Channel** Bahamas
131 E1 **North West River** Can.
128 B1 **Northwest Territories** *admin. div.* Can.
98 C1 **North York Moors** *moorland* U.K.
140 C3 **Norton** U.S.A.
121 C2 **Norton** Zimbabwe
140 C2 **Norwalk** U.S.A.
93 F3 **Norway** *country* Europe
129 E2 **Norway House** Can.
160 A3 **Norwegian Sea** N. Atlantic Ocean
99 D2 **Norwich** U.K.
141 E2 **Norwich** *CT* U.S.A.
141 D2 **Norwich** *NY* U.S.A.
66 D2 **Noshiro** Japan
91 C1 **Nosivka** Ukr.
122 B2 **Nosop** *watercourse* Africa
86 E2 **Nosovaya** Rus. Fed.
79 C2 **Noşratābād** Iran
Nossob *watercourse* Africa *see* **Nosop**
103 D1 **Noteć** *r.* Pol.
93 E4 **Notodden** Norway
67 C3 **Noto-hantō** *pen.* Japan
131 D2 **Notre-Dame, Monts** *mts* Can.
131 E2 **Notre Dame Bay** Can.
130 C1 **Nottaway** *r.* Can.
99 C2 **Nottingham** U.K.
114 A2 **Nouâdhibou** Maur.
114 A3 **Nouakchott** Maur.
114 A3 **Nouâmghâr** Maur.
48 F4 **Nouméa** New Caledonia
114 B3 **Nouna** Burkina
154 B2 **Nova Esperança** Brazil
155 D2 **Nova Friburgo** Brazil
109 C1 **Nova Gradiška** Croatia
154 C2 **Nova Granada** Brazil
155 D2 **Nova Iguaçu** Brazil
91 C2 **Nova Kakhovka** Ukr.
155 D1 **Nova Lima** Brazil
154 B2 **Nova Londrina** Brazil
91 C2 **Nova Odesa** Ukr.
150 B1 **Nova Paraiso** Brazil
131 D2 **Nova Scotia** *prov.* Can.
155 D1 **Nova Venécia** Brazil
83 K1 **Novaya Sibir', Ostrov** *i.* Rus. Fed.
86 E1 **Novaya Zemlya** *is* Rus. Fed.
103 D2 **Nové Zámky** Slovakia
91 C1 **Novhorod-Sivers'kyy** Ukr.
110 B2 **Novi Iskŭr** Bulg.
108 A2 **Novi Ligure** Italy
109 D2 **Novi Pazar** Serbia
109 C1 **Novi Sad** Serbia
87 D3 **Novoanninskiy** Rus. Fed.
150 B2 **Novo Aripuanã** Brazil
91 D2 **Novoazovs'k** Ukr.
91 E2 **Novocherkassk** Rus. Fed.
86 D2 **Novodvinsk** Rus. Fed.
152 C3 **Novo Hamburgo** Brazil
154 C2 **Novo Horizonte** Brazil
90 B1 **Novohrad-Volyns'kyy** Ukr.
103 D2 **Novo Mesto** Slovenia
91 D3 **Novomikhaylovskiy** Rus. Fed.
89 E3 **Novomoskovsk** Rus. Fed.
91 D2 **Novomoskovs'k** Ukr.
91 C2 **Novomyrhorod** Ukr.
91 C2 **Novooleksiyivka** Ukr.
91 D2 **Novopskov** Ukr.
91 D3 **Novorossiysk** Rus. Fed.
88 C2 **Novorzhev** Rus. Fed.
87 E3 **Novosergiyevka** Rus. Fed.
91 D2 **Novoshakhtinsk** Rus. Fed.
82 G3 **Novosibirsk** Rus. Fed.
Novosibirskiye Ostrova *is* Rus. Fed. *see* **New Siberia Islands**
89 E3 **Novosil'** Rus. Fed.
89 D2 **Novosokol'niki** Rus. Fed.
91 C2 **Novotroyits'ke** Ukr.
91 C2 **Novoukrayinka** Ukr.
90 A1 **Novovolyns'k** Ukr.
89 D3 **Novozybkov** Rus. Fed.
103 D2 **Nový Jičín** Czech Rep.
86 E2 **Novyy Bor** Rus. Fed.
91 D1 **Novyy Oskol** Rus. Fed.

86 G2 Novyy Port Rus. Fed.
82 G2 Novyy Urengoy Rus. Fed.
69 E1 Novyy Urgal Rus. Fed.
103 D1 Nowogard Pol.
53 D2 Nowra Austr.
81 D2 Nowshahr Iran
74 B1 Nowshera Pak.
103 E2 Nowy Sącz Pol.
103 E2 Nowy Targ Pol.
87 G2 Noyabr'sk Rus. Fed.
105 C2 Noyon France
68 C2 Noyon Mongolia
121 C2 Nsanje Malawi
118 B3 Ntandembele Dem. Rep. Congo
111 B3 Ntoro, Kavo pt Greece
119 D3 Ntungamo Uganda
79 C3 Nu'aym reg. Oman
116 B2 Nubian Desert Sudan
150 A3 Nudo Coropuna mt. Peru
129 E1 Nueltin Lake Can.
153 A5 Nueva Lubecka Arg.
145 B2 Nueva Rosita Mex.
144 B1 Nuevo Casas Grandes Mex.
144 B2 Nuevo Ideal Mex.
145 C2 Nuevo Laredo Mex.
117 C4 Nugaal watercourse Somalia
105 C2 Nuits-St-Georges France
    Nu Jiang r. China/Myanmar see Salween
49 G4 Nuku'alofa Tonga
49 I3 Nuku Hiva i. Fr. Polynesia
76 B2 Nukus Uzbek.
50 B2 Nullagine Austr.
50 B3 Nullarbor Plain Austr.
115 D4 Numan Nigeria
67 C3 Numazu Japan
93 E3 Numedal val. Norway
59 C3 Numfoor i. Indon.
53 C3 Numurkah Austr.
    Nunap Isua c. Greenland see Farewell, Cape
127 G3 Nunavik reg. Can.
129 E1 Nunavut admin. div. Can.
99 C2 Nuneaton U.K.
106 B1 Nuñomoral Spain
108 A2 Nuoro Sardegna Italy
78 B2 Nuqrah Saudi Arabia
101 E3 Nuremberg Ger.
74 B1 Nūrestān Afgh.
52 A2 Nuriootpa Austr.
92 I3 Nurmes Fin.
    Nürnberg Ger. see Nuremberg
62 A1 Nu Shan mts China
74 A2 Nushki Pak.
127 H2 Nuuk Greenland
127 H2 Nuussuaq Greenland
127 H2 Nuussuaq pen. Greenland
78 A2 Nuwaybi' al Muzayyinah Egypt
122 B3 Nuweveldberge mts S. Africa
86 F2 Nyagan' Rus. Fed.
75 D1 Nyainqêntanglha Feng mt. China
75 D2 Nyainqêntanglha Shan mts China
117 A3 Nyala Sudan
86 D2 Nyandoma Rus. Fed.
118 B3 Nyanga r. Gabon
121 C2 Nyanga Zimbabwe
121 C1 Nyasa, Lake Africa
93 F4 Nyborg Denmark
92 I1 Nyborg Norway
93 G4 Nybro Sweden
119 D3 Nyeri Kenya
75 C1 Nyima China
68 C3 Nyingchi China

103 E2 Nyíregyháza Hungary
93 F4 Nykøbing Denmark
93 G4 Nyköping Sweden
53 C2 Nymagee Austr.
93 G4 Nynäshamn Sweden
53 C2 Nyngan Austr.
88 B3 Nyoman r. Belarus/Lith.
105 D3 Nyons France
86 F2 Nyrob Rus. Fed.
134 C2 Nyssa U.S.A.
119 C3 Nyunzu Dem. Rep. Congo
91 C2 Nyzhn'ohirs'kyy Ukr.
119 D3 Nzega Tanz.
114 B4 Nzérékoré Guinea
120 A1 N'zeto Angola

O

136 C2 Oahe, Lake U.S.A.
124 E5 O'ahu i. U.S.A.
52 B2 Oakbank Austr.
142 B2 Oakdale U.S.A.
53 D1 Oakey Austr.
134 B1 Oak Harbor U.S.A.
140 C3 Oak Hill U.S.A.
135 B3 Oakland U.S.A.
50 B2 Oakover r. Austr.
134 B2 Oakridge U.S.A.
143 D1 Oak Ridge U.S.A.
54 B3 Oamaru N.Z.
64 B1 Oas Phil.
145 C3 Oaxaca Mex.
86 F2 Ob' r. Rus. Fed.
118 B3 Obala Cameroon
96 B2 Oban U.K.
106 B1 O Barco Spain
53 C2 Oberon Austr.
101 F3 Oberpfälzer Wald mts Ger.
101 F3 Oberviechtach Ger.
59 C3 Obi i. Indon.
151 D2 Óbidos Brazil
70 D2 Obihiro Japan
69 E1 Obluch'ye Rus. Fed.
89 E2 Obninsk Rus. Fed.
119 C2 Obo C.A.R.
117 C3 Obock Djibouti
118 B3 Obouya Congo
89 E3 Oboyan' Rus. Fed.
144 B2 Obregón, Presa resr Mex.
109 D2 Obrenovac Serbia
87 E3 Obshchiy Syrt hills Kazakh./Rus. Fed.
86 G2 Obskaya Guba sea chan. Rus. Fed.
114 B4 Obuasi Ghana
90 C1 Obukhiv Ukr.
86 D2 Ob'yachevo Rus. Fed.
143 D3 Ocala U.S.A.
141 B3 Ocampo Mex.
144 B2 Ocampo Mex.
107 C2 Ocaña Spain
150 A1 Occidental, Cordillera mts Col.
150 A3 Occidental, Cordillera mts Peru
141 D3 Ocean City U.S.A.
128 B2 Ocean Falls Can.
135 C4 Oceanside U.S.A.
91 C2 Ochakiv Ukr.
86 E3 Ocher Rus. Fed.
101 E3 Ochsenfurt Ger.
143 D2 Oconee r. U.S.A.
55 B3 Ocosingo Mex.
58 C3 Ocussi enclave East Timor
66 D2 Ōdate Japan

67 C3 Odawara Japan
93 E3 Odda Norway
106 B2 Odemira Port.
111 C3 Ödemiş Turkey
93 F4 Odense Denmark
101 D3 Odenwald reg. Ger.
102 C1 Oderbucht b. Ger.
    Odesa Ukr. see Odessa
90 C2 Odessa Ukr.
139 C2 Odessa U.S.A.
114 B4 Odienné Côte d'Ivoire
103 D2 Odra r. Ger./Pol.
151 D2 Oeiras Brazil
100 D2 Oelde Ger.
136 C2 Oelrichs U.S.A.
101 F2 Oelsnitz Ger.
100 B1 Oenkerk Neth.
109 C2 Ofanto r. Italy
101 D2 Offenbach am Main Ger.
102 B2 Offenburg Ger.
117 C4 Ogadēn reg. Eth.
66 C3 Oga-hantō pen. Japan
67 C3 Ōgaki Japan
136 C2 Ogallala U.S.A.
115 C4 Ogbomosho Nigeria
134 D2 Ogden U.S.A.
141 D2 Ogdensburg U.S.A.
126 B2 Ogilvie r. Can.
126 B2 Ogilvie Mountains Can.
143 D2 Oglethorpe, Mount U.S.A.
130 B1 Ogoki r. Can.
130 B1 Ogoki Reservoir Can.
88 B2 Ogre Latvia
109 C1 Ogulin Croatia
140 B3 Ohio r. U.S.A.
140 C2 Ohio state U.S.A.
101 E2 Ohrdruf Ger.
109 D2 Ohrid Macedonia
151 C1 Oiapoque Brazil
100 A3 Oise r. France
67 B4 Ōita Japan
144 B2 Ojinaga Mex.
152 B3 Ojos del Salado, Nevado Arg./Chile
89 F2 Oka r. Rus. Fed.
120 A3 Okahandja Namibia
120 A3 Okakarara Namibia
128 C3 Okanagan Falls Can.
128 C3 Okanagan Lake Can.
134 C1 Okanogan U.S.A.
134 C1 Okanogan r. U.S.A.
74 B1 Okara Pak.
120 B2 Okavango r. Africa
120 B2 Okavango Delta swamp Botswana
67 C3 Okaya Japan
67 C4 Okayama Japan
67 C4 Okazaki Japan
143 D3 Okeechobee, Lake U.S.A.
143 D2 Okefenokee Swamp U.S.A.
99 A3 Okehampton U.K.
74 A2 Okha India
83 K3 Okha Rus. Fed.
75 C2 Okhaldhunga Nepal
83 K3 Okhotka r. Rus. Fed.
83 K3 Okhotsk Rus. Fed.
156 C2 Okhotsk, Sea of Japan/Rus. Fed.
91 C1 Okhtyrka Ukr.
69 E3 Okinawa i. Japan
67 B3 Oki-shotō is Japan
139 D1 Oklahoma state U.S.A.
139 D1 Oklahoma City U.S.A.
67 C3 Okmulgee U.S.A.
78 A2 Oko, Wadi watercourse Su
118 B3 Okondja Gabon

C2 **Okotoks** Can.
D3 **Okovskiy Les** *for.* Rus. Fed.
B3 **Okoyo** Congo
H1 **Øksfjord** Norway
A2 **Oktwin** Myanmar
D2 **Oktyabr'skiy** *Arkhangel'skaya Oblast'* Rus. Fed.
L3 **Oktyabr'skiy** *Kamchatskiy Kray* Rus. Fed.
E3 **Oktyabr'skiy** *Respublika Bashkortostan* Rus. Fed.
F2 **Oktyabr'skoye** Rus. Fed.
H1 **Oktyabr'skoy Revolyutsii, Ostrov** *i.* Rus. Fed.
D2 **Okulovka** Rus. Fed.
C2 **Okushiri-tō** *i.* Japan
A3 **Ólafsvík** Iceland
G4 **Öland** *i.* Sweden
B2 **Olary** Austr.
B4 **Olavarría** Arg.
D1 **Oława** Pol.
A2 **Olbia** *Sardegna* Italy
B2 **Old Crow** Can.
D1 **Oldenburg** Ger.
C1 **Oldenburg in Holstein** Ger.
C1 **Oldenzaal** Neth.
B3 **Old Head of Kinsale** Ireland
C2 **Olds** Can.
D2 **Old Wives Lake** Can.
D2 **Olean** U.S.A.
E1 **Olecko** Pol.
J2 **Olekminsk** Rus. Fed.
C2 **Oleksandriya** Ukr.
C2 **Olenegorsk** Rus. Fed.
I2 **Olenek** Rus. Fed.
I2 **Olenek** *r.* Rus. Fed.
D2 **Olenino** Rus. Fed.
B1 **Olevs'k** Ukr.
B2 **Olhão** Port.
A2 **Olifants** *watercourse* Namibia
D1 **Olifants** S. Africa
D1 **Olifants** *r. Northern* S. Africa
A3 **Olifants** *r. W. Cape* S. Africa
B2 **Olifantshoek** S. Africa
C2 **Olímpia** Brazil
E2 **Olinda** Brazil
C1 **Oliphants Drift** Botswana
C2 **Oliva** Spain
D2 **Oliveira** Brazil
B2 **Olivenza** Spain
B3 **Ollagüe** Chile
A2 **Olmos** Peru
B3 **Olney** U.S.A.
D2 **Olomouc** Czech Rep.
B1 **Olongapo** Phil.
B3 **Oloron-Ste-Marie** France
D1 **Olot** Spain
D1 **Olovyannaya** Rus. Fed.
L2 **Oloy** *r.* Rus. Fed.
C2 **Olpe** Ger.
E1 **Olsztyn** Pol.
B2 **Olt** *r.* Romania
C1 **Oltu** Turkey
B3 **Olympia** *tourist site* Greece
B1 **Olympia** U.S.A.
B1 **Olympus, Mount** U.S.A.
M3 **Olyutorskiy, Mys** *c.* Rus. Fed.
C1 **Omagh** U.K.
D2 **Omaha** U.S.A.
C2 **Oman** *country* Asia
C2 **Oman, Gulf of** Asia
A3 **Omaruru** Namibia
B2 **Omatako** *watercourse* Namibia
B3 **Omdurman** Sudan
C3 **Omeo** Austr.
C3 **Ometepec** Mex.

78 A3 **Om Hajēr** Eritrea
128 B2 **Omineca Mountains** Can.
100 C1 **Ommen** Neth.
83 L2 **Omolon** *r.* Rus. Fed.
100 B3 **Omont** France
82 F3 **Omsk** Rus. Fed.
83 L2 **Omsukchan** Rus. Fed.
110 C1 **Omu, Vârful** *mt.* Romania
67 A4 **Ōmura** Japan
141 D3 **Onancock** U.S.A.
140 C1 **Onaping Lake** Can.
131 C2 **Onatchiway, Lac** *l.* Can.
120 A2 **Oncócua** Angola
122 B3 **Onderstedorings** S. Africa
120 A2 **Ondjiva** Angola
86 C2 **Onega** Rus. Fed.
86 C2 **Onega** *r.* Rus. Fed.
Onega, Lake *l.* Rus. Fed. *see* **Onezhskoye Ozero**
141 D2 **Oneida Lake** U.S.A.
137 D2 **O'Neill** U.S.A.
141 D2 **Oneonta** U.S.A.
110 C1 **Onești** Romania
86 C2 **Onezhskoye Ozero** *l.* Rus. Fed.
122 B2 **Ongers** *watercourse* S. Africa
65 B2 **Ongjin** N. Korea
73 C3 **Ongole** India
121 D3 **Onilahy** *r.* Madag.
115 C4 **Onitsha** Nigeria
122 A2 **Onseepkans** S. Africa
50 A2 **Onslow** Austr.
143 E2 **Onslow Bay** U.S.A.
130 A1 **Ontario** *prov.* Can.
134 C2 **Ontario** U.S.A.
141 D2 **Ontario, Lake** Can./U.S.A.
51 C2 **Oodnadatta** Austr.
Oostende Belgium *see* **Ostend**
100 B2 **Oosterhout** Neth.
100 A2 **Oosterschelde** *est.* Neth.
100 B1 **Oost-Vlieland** Neth.
128 B2 **Ootsa Lake** Can.
128 B2 **Ootsa Lake** *l.* Can.
118 C3 **Opala** Dem. Rep. Congo
130 C1 **Opataca, Lac** *l.* Can.
103 D2 **Opava** Czech Rep.
143 C2 **Opelika** U.S.A.
142 B2 **Opelousas** U.S.A.
130 C1 **Opinaca, Réservoir** *resr* Can.
131 D1 **Opiscotéo, Lac** *l.* Can.
88 C2 **Opochka** Rus. Fed.
144 A2 **Opodepe** Mex.
103 D1 **Opole** Pol.
106 B1 **Oporto** Port.
54 C1 **Opotiki** N.Z.
93 E3 **Oppdal** Norway
54 B1 **Opunake** N.Z.
120 A2 **Opuwo** Namibia
110 B1 **Oradea** Romania
Orahovac Kosovo *see* **Rahovec**
114 B1 **Oran** Alg.
152 B3 **Orán** Arg.
65 B1 **Ŏrang** N. Korea
53 C2 **Orange** Austr.
105 C3 **Orange** France
122 A2 **Orange** *r.* Namibia/S. Africa
139 E2 **Orange** U.S.A.
143 D2 **Orangeburg** U.S.A.
140 C2 **Orangeville** Can.
101 F1 **Oranienburg** Ger.
122 A2 **Oranjemund** Namibia
120 B3 **Orapa** Botswana
110 B1 **Orăștie** Romania
108 B2 **Orbetello** Italy
53 C3 **Orbost** Austr.
50 B1 **Ord, Mount** *h.* Austr.

106 B1 **Ordes** Spain
70 B2 **Ordos** China
80 B1 **Ordu** Turkey
Ordzhonikidze Rus. Fed. *see* **Vladikavkaz**
91 C2 **Ordzhonikidze** Ukr.
93 G4 **Örebro** Sweden
134 B2 **Oregon** *state* U.S.A.
134 B1 **Oregon City** U.S.A.
87 C3 **Orekhovo-Zuyevo** Rus. Fed.
89 E3 **Orel** Rus. Fed.
83 K3 **Orel', Ozero** *l.* Rus. Fed.
135 D2 **Orem** U.S.A.
111 C3 **Ören** Turkey
87 E3 **Orenburg** Rus. Fed.
54 A3 **Orepuki** N.Z.
93 F4 **Öresund** *str.* Denmark/Sweden
99 D2 **Orford Ness** *hd* U.K.
111 C3 **Orhaneli** Turkey
111 C2 **Orhangazi** Turkey
83 I3 **Orhon Gol** *r.* Mongolia
152 B2 **Oriental, Cordillera** *mts* Bol.
150 A1 **Oriental, Cordillera** *mts* Col.
150 A3 **Oriental, Cordillera** *mts* Peru
107 C2 **Orihuela** Spain
91 D2 **Orikhiv** Ukr.
130 C2 **Orillia** Can.
150 B1 **Orinoco** *r.* Col./Venez.
150 B1 **Orinoco Delta** Venez.
93 H4 **Orissaare** Estonia
108 A3 **Oristano** *Sardegna* Italy
93 I3 **Orivesi** *l.* Fin.
151 C2 **Oriximiná** Brazil
145 C3 **Orizaba** Mex.
145 C3 **Orizaba, Pico de** *vol.* Mex.
92 E3 **Orkanger** Norway
93 F4 **Örkelljunga** Sweden
92 E3 **Orkla** *r.* Norway
96 C1 **Orkney Islands** U.K.
154 C2 **Orlândia** Brazil
143 D3 **Orlando** U.S.A.
104 C2 **Orléans** France
74 A2 **Ormara** Pak.
64 B1 **Ormoc** Phil.
98 B2 **Ormskirk** U.K.
92 G3 **Örnsköldsvik** Sweden
114 B3 **Orodara** Burkina
134 C1 **Orofino** U.S.A.
Oroqen Zizhiqi China *see* **Alihe**
64 B2 **Oroquieta** Phil.
108 A2 **Orosei** *Sardegna* Italy
108 A2 **Orosei, Golfo di** *b. Sardegna* Italy
103 E2 **Orosháza** Hungary
135 B3 **Oroville** U.S.A.
52 A2 **Orroroo** Austr.
89 D3 **Orsha** Belarus
87 E3 **Orsk** Rus. Fed.
93 E3 **Ørsta** Norway
106 B1 **Ortegal, Cabo** *c.* Spain
104 B3 **Orthez** France
106 B1 **Ortigueira** Spain
137 D1 **Ortonville** U.S.A.
83 J2 **Orulgan, Khrebet** *mts* Rus. Fed.
Orūmīyeh, Daryācheh-ye *salt l.* Iran *see* **Urmia, Lake**
152 B2 **Oruro** Bol.
108 B2 **Orvieto** Italy
146 B4 **Osa, Península de** *pen.* Costa Rica
137 E3 **Osage** *r.* U.S.A.
67 C4 **Ōsaka** Japan
101 E1 **Oschersleben (Bode)** Ger.
108 A2 **Oschiri** *Sardegna* Italy

89 E3 **Osetr** *r.* Rus. Fed.
77 D2 **Osh** Kyrg.
120 A2 **Oshakati** Namibia
130 C2 **Oshawa** Can.
66 C2 **Ō-shima** *i.* Japan
67 C4 **Ō-shima** *i.* Japan
140 B2 **Oshkosh** U.S.A.
81 C2 **Oshnovīyeh** Iran
115 C4 **Oshogbo** Nigeria
118 B3 **Oshwe** Dem. Rep. Congo
109 C1 **Osijek** Croatia
128 B2 **Osilinka** *r.* Can.
108 B2 **Osimo** Italy
123 D2 **Osizweni** S. Africa
137 E2 **Oskaloosa** U.S.A.
93 G4 **Oskarshamn** Sweden
89 E3 **Oskol** *r.* Rus. Fed.
93 F4 **Oslo** Norway
93 F4 **Oslofjorden** *sea chan.* Norway
80 B1 **Osmancık** Turkey
111 C2 **Osmaneli** Turkey
80 B2 **Osmaniye** Turkey
88 C2 **Os'mino** Rus. Fed.
100 D1 **Osnabrück** Ger.
153 A5 **Osorno** Chile
106 C1 **Osorno** Spain
128 C3 **Osoyoos** Can.
100 B2 **Oss** Neth.
51 D4 **Ossa, Mount** Austr.
83 L3 **Ossora** Rus. Fed.
89 D2 **Ostashkov** Rus. Fed.
101 D1 **Oste** *r.* Ger.
100 A2 **Ostend** Belgium
101 E1 **Osterburg (Altmark)** Ger.
93 F3 **Österdalälven** *r.* Sweden
101 D1 **Osterholz-Scharmbeck** Ger.
101 E2 **Osterode am Harz** Ger.
92 F3 **Östersund** Sweden
Ostfriesische Inseln *is* Ger. *see* **East Frisian Islands**
100 C1 **Ostfriesland** *reg.* Ger.
93 G3 **Östhammar** Sweden
103 D2 **Ostrava** Czech Rep.
103 D1 **Ostróda** Pol.
89 E3 **Ostrogozhsk** Rus. Fed.
103 E1 **Ostrołęka** Pol.
101 F2 **Ostrov** Czech Rep.
88 C2 **Ostrov** Rus. Fed.
103 E1 **Ostrowiec Świętokrzyski** Pol.
103 E1 **Ostrów Mazowiecka** Pol.
103 D1 **Ostrów Wielkopolski** Pol.
110 B2 **Osŭm** *r.* Bulg.
67 B4 **Ōsumi-kaikyō** *sea chan.* Japan
67 B4 **Ōsumi-shotō** *is* Japan
106 B2 **Osuna** Spain
141 D2 **Oswego** U.S.A.
99 B2 **Oswestry** U.K.
67 C3 **Ōta** Japan
54 B3 **Otago Peninsula** N.Z.
54 C2 **Otaki** N.Z.
66 D2 **Otaru** Japan
120 A2 **Otavi** Namibia
134 C1 **Othello** U.S.A.
120 A3 **Otjiwarongo** Namibia
117 B3 **Otoro, Jebel** *mt.* Sudan
93 E4 **Otra** *r.* Norway
109 C2 **Otranto, Strait of** Albania/Italy
67 C3 **Ōtsu** Japan
93 E3 **Otta** Norway
130 C2 **Ottawa** Can.
130 C2 **Ottawa** *r.* Can.
140 B2 **Ottawa** *IL* U.S.A.
137 D3 **Ottawa** *KS* U.S.A.
130 B1 **Otter Rapids** Can.
100 B2 **Ottignies** Belgium
137 E2 **Ottumwa** U.S.A.
150 A2 **Otuzco** Peru
52 B3 **Otway, Cape** Austr.
142 B2 **Ouachita** *r.* U.S.A.
142 B2 **Ouachita, Lake** U.S.A.
142 B2 **Ouachita Mountains** U.S.A.
118 C2 **Ouadda** C.A.R.
115 D3 **Ouaddaï** *reg.* Chad
114 B3 **Ouagadougou** Burkina
114 B3 **Ouahigouya** Burkina
114 B3 **Oualâta** Maur.
118 C2 **Ouanda-Djailé** C.A.R.
114 B2 **Ouarâne** *reg.* Maur.
115 C1 **Ouargla** Alg.
114 B1 **Ouarzazate** Morocco
100 A2 **Oudenaarde** Belgium
122 B3 **Oudtshoorn** S. Africa
107 C2 **Oued Tlélat** Alg.
104 A2 **Ouessant, Île d'** *i.* France
118 B2 **Ouesso** Congo
114 B1 **Oujda** Morocco
107 D2 **Ouled Farès** Alg.
92 I2 **Oulu** Fin.
92 I3 **Oulujärvi** *l.* Fin.
108 A1 **Oulx** Italy
115 E3 **Oum-Chalouba** Chad
115 D3 **Oum-Hadjer** Chad
115 E3 **Ounianga Kébir** Chad
100 B2 **Oupeye** Belgium
106 B1 **Ourense** Spain
154 C2 **Ourinhos** Brazil
155 D2 **Ouro Preto** Brazil
100 B2 **Ourthe** *r.* Belgium
98 C2 **Ouse** *r.* U.K.
131 D2 **Outardes, Rivière aux** *r.* Can.
131 D1 **Outardes Quatre, Réservoir** *resr* Can.
96 A2 **Outer Hebrides** *is* U.K.
120 A3 **Outjo** Namibia
129 D2 **Outlook** Can.
92 I3 **Outokumpu** Fin.
52 B3 **Ouyen** Austr.
106 B1 **Ovar** Port.
92 H2 **Överkalix** Sweden
135 D3 **Overton** U.S.A.
92 H2 **Övertorneå** Sweden
106 B1 **Oviedo** Spain
93 E3 **Øvre Årdal** Norway
93 F3 **Øvre Rendal** Norway
90 B1 **Ovruch** Ukr.
118 B3 **Owando** Congo
67 C4 **Owase** Japan
137 E2 **Owatonna** U.S.A.
140 B3 **Owensboro** U.S.A.
135 C3 **Owens Lake** U.S.A.
130 B2 **Owen Sound** Can.
115 C4 **Owerri** Nigeria
140 C2 **Owosso** U.S.A.
134 C2 **Owyhee** U.S.A.
134 C2 **Owyhee** *r.* U.S.A.
54 B2 **Oxford** N.Z.
99 C3 **Oxford** U.K.
142 C2 **Oxford** U.S.A.
129 E2 **Oxford Lake** Can.
52 B2 **Oxley** Austr.
97 B1 **Ox Mountains** *hills* Ireland
135 C4 **Oxnard** U.S.A.
67 C3 **Oyama** Japan
118 B2 **Oyem** Gabon
129 C2 **Oyen** Can.
105 D2 **Oyonnax** France
64 B2 **Ozamiz** Phil.
142 C2 **Ozark** U.S.A.
137 E3 **Ozark Plateau** U.S.A.
137 E3 **Ozarks, Lake of the** U.S.A.
83 L3 **Ozernovskiy** Rus. Fed.
88 B3 **Ozersk** Rus. Fed.
89 E3 **Ozery** Rus. Fed.
87 D3 **Ozinki** Rus. Fed.

P

127 H2 **Paamiut** Greenland
122 A3 **Paarl** S. Africa
103 D1 **Pabianice** Pol.
75 C2 **Pabna** Bangl.
74 A2 **Pab Range** *mts* Pak.
109 C3 **Pachino** *Sicilia* Italy
145 C2 **Pachuca** Mex.
156 **Pacific Ocean**
103 D1 **Paczków** Pol.
60 B2 **Padang** Indon.
60 B1 **Padang Endau** Malaysia
60 B2 **Padangpanjang** Indon.
60 A1 **Padangsidimpuan** Indon.
101 D2 **Paderborn** Ger.
Padova Italy *see* **Padua**
139 D3 **Padre Island** U.S.A.
52 B3 **Padthaway** Austr.
108 B1 **Padua** Italy
140 B3 **Paducah** *KY* U.S.A.
139 C2 **Paducah** *TX* U.S.A.
65 B1 **Paegam** N. Korea
65 A2 **Paengnyŏng-do** *i.* S. Kore
54 C1 **Paeroa** N.Z.
Pafos Cyprus *see* **Paphos**
109 C2 **Pag** Croatia
64 B2 **Pagadian** Phil.
60 B2 **Pagai Selatan** *i.* Indon.
60 B2 **Pagai Utara** *i.* Indon.
59 D1 **Pagan** *i.* N. Mariana Is
61 C2 **Pagatan** Indon.
138 A1 **Page** U.S.A.
88 B2 **Pagėgiai** Lith.
136 B3 **Pagosa Springs** U.S.A.
88 C2 **Paide** Estonia
93 I3 **Päijänne** *l.* Fin.
75 C2 **Paikü Co** *l.* China
138 A1 **Painted Desert** U.S.A.
96 B3 **Paisley** U.K.
92 H2 **Pajala** Sweden
150 B1 **Pakaraima Mountains** S. America
150 C1 **Pakaraima Mountains** S. America
74 A2 **Pakistan** *country* Asia
62 A1 **Pakokku** Myanmar
88 B2 **Pakruojis** Lith.
103 D2 **Paks** Hungary
130 A1 **Pakwash Lake** Can.
62 B2 **Pakxan** Laos
63 B2 **Pakxé** Laos
115 D4 **Pala** Chad
60 B2 **Palabuhanratu, Teluk** *b.* Indon.
111 C3 **Palaikastro** Greece
111 B3 **Palaiochora** Greece
122 B1 **Palamakoloi** Botswana
107 D1 **Palamós** Spain
83 L3 **Palana** Rus. Fed.
64 B1 **Palanan** Phil.
61 C2 **Palangkaraya** Indon.
74 B2 **Palanpur** India
120 B3 **Palapye** Botswana
83 L2 **Palatka** Rus. Fed.
143 D3 **Palatka** U.S.A.
59 C2 **Palau** *country* N. Pacific O
63 A2 **Palaw** Myanmar
64 A2 **Palawan** *i.* Phil.
93 H4 **Paldiski** Estonia
60 B2 **Palembang** Indon.
106 C1 **Palencia** Spain

5 C3 **Palenque** Mex.
3 B3 **Palermo** *Sicilia* Italy
D2 **Palestine** U.S.A.
2 A1 **Paletwa** Myanmar
4 B2 **Pali** India
3 E2 **Palikir** Micronesia
C2 **Palinuro, Capo** *c.* Italy
1 B3 **Paliouri, Akrotirio** *pt* Greece
B3 **Paliseul** Belgium
2 I3 **Paljakka** *h.* Fin.
3 C2 **Palkino** Rus. Fed.
3 B4 **Palk Strait** India/Sri Lanka
4 C2 **Palliser, Cape** N.Z.
9 I3 **Palliser, Îles** *is* Fr. Polynesia
5 B2 **Palma del Río** Spain
7 D2 **Palma de Mallorca** Spain
4 B3 **Palmas** Brazil
1 D3 **Palmas** Brazil
4 B4 **Palmas, Cape** Liberia
4 C3 **Palmeira** Brazil
1 D2 **Palmeirais** Brazil
5 P2 **Palmer Land** *reg.* Antarctica
4 C2 **Palmerston North** N.Z.
C3 **Palmi** Italy
5 C2 **Palmillas** Mex.
A1 **Palmira** Col.
5 C4 **Palm Springs** U.S.A.
H2 **Palmyra Atoll** N. Pacific Ocean
7 B3 **Paloich** Sudan
5 C3 **Palomares** Mex.
7 C2 **Palos, Cabo de** *c.* Spain
2 I3 **Paltamo** Fin.
3 B3 **Palu** Indon.
3 M2 **Palyavaam** *r.* Rus. Fed.
4 C3 **Pamiers** France
7 D3 **Pamir** *mts* Asia
3 E1 **Pamlico Sound** *sea chan.* U.S.A.
2 B2 **Pampa Grande** Bol.
3 B4 **Pampas** *reg.* Arg.
A1 **Pamplona** Col.
C1 **Pamplona** Spain
1 D2 **Pamukova** Turkey
0 B2 **Panaitan** *i.* Indon.
3 B3 **Panaji** India
6 B4 **Panama** *country* Central America
5 C4 **Panamá, Canal de** Panama
5 C4 **Panama, Gulf of** Panama
5 C4 **Panama City** Panama
2 C2 **Panama City** U.S.A.
5 C3 **Panamint Range** *mts* U.S.A.
1 B1 **Panarik** Indon.
4 B1 **Panay** *i.* Phil.
9 D2 **Pančevo** Serbia
4 B1 **Pandan** Phil.
5 C2 **Pandaria** India
3 B3 **Pandharpur** India
8 B2 **Panevėžys** Lith.
1 C2 **Pangkalanbuun** Indon.
0 A1 **Pangkalansusu** Indon.
0 B2 **Pangkalpinang** Indon.
7 G2 **Pangnirtung** Can.
6 G2 **Pangody** Rus. Fed.
9 F3 **Panino** Rus. Fed.
4 B2 **Panipat** India
4 A2 **Panjgur** Pak.
5 C1 **Pan Ling** *mts* China
5 C2 **Panna** India
A2 **Pannawonica** Austr.
4 B2 **Panorama** Brazil
5 B1 **Panshi** China
5 C2 **Pánuco** Mex.
1 A3 **Panxian** China
2 B1 **Panzhihua** China
9 C3 **Paola** Italy
63 B2 **Paôy Pêt** Cambodia
103 D2 **Pápa** Hungary
54 B1 **Papakura** N.Z.
145 C2 **Papantla** Mex.
49 I4 **Papeete** Fr. Polynesia
100 C1 **Papenburg** Ger.
80 B2 **Paphos** Cyprus
59 D3 **Papua, Gulf of** P.N.G.
59 D3 **Papua New Guinea** *country* Oceania
50 A2 **Paraburdoo** Austr.
154 C1 **Paracatu** Brazil
155 C1 **Paracatu** *r.* Brazil
52 A2 **Parachilna** Austr.
109 D2 **Paraćin** Serbia
155 D1 **Pará de Minas** Brazil
135 B3 **Paradise** U.S.A.
142 B1 **Paragould** U.S.A.
151 C3 **Paraguai** *r.* Brazil
152 C3 **Paraguay** *r.* Arg./Para.
152 C3 **Paraguay** *country* S. America
155 D2 **Paraíba do Sul** *r.* Brazil
154 B1 **Paraíso** Brazil
145 C3 **Paraíso** Mex.
114 C4 **Parakou** Benin
151 C1 **Paramaribo** Suriname
83 L3 **Paramushir, Ostrov** *i.* Rus. Fed.
152 B4 **Paraná** Arg.
154 A3 **Paraná** *r.* S. America
154 C3 **Paranaguá** Brazil
154 B1 **Paranaíba** Brazil
154 B2 **Paranaíba** *r.* Brazil
154 B2 **Paranapanema** *r.* Brazil
154 B2 **Paranapiacaba, Serra** *mts* Brazil
154 B2 **Paranavaí** Brazil
54 B2 **Paraparaumu** N.Z.
155 D2 **Parati** Brazil
154 B1 **Paraúna** Brazil
105 C2 **Paray-le-Monial** France
73 B3 **Parbhani** India
101 E1 **Parchim** Ger.
155 E1 **Pardo** *r. Bahia* Brazil
154 B2 **Pardo** *r. Mato Grosso do Sul* Brazil
154 C2 **Pardo** *r. São Paulo* Brazil
103 D1 **Pardubice** Czech Rep.
150 B3 **Parecis, Serra dos** *hills* Brazil
130 C2 **Parent, Lac** *l.* Can.
58 B3 **Parepare** Indon.
89 D2 **Parfino** Rus. Fed.
111 B3 **Parga** Greece
109 C3 **Parghelia** Italy
147 D3 **Paria, Gulf of** Trin. and Tob./Venez.
150 B1 **Parima, Serra** *mts* Brazil
151 C2 **Parintins** Brazil
104 C2 **Paris** France
142 C1 **Paris** *TN* U.S.A.
139 D2 **Paris** *TX* U.S.A.
93 H3 **Parkano** Fin.
138 A2 **Parker** U.S.A.
140 C3 **Parkersburg** U.S.A.
53 C2 **Parkes** Austr.
140 A1 **Park Falls** U.S.A.
137 D1 **Park Rapids** U.S.A.
108 B2 **Parma** Italy
151 D2 **Parnaíba** Brazil
151 D2 **Parnaíba** *r.* Brazil
54 B2 **Parnassus** N.Z.
111 B3 **Parnonas** *mts* Greece
88 B2 **Pärnu** Estonia
65 B2 **P'aro-ho** *l.* S. Korea
52 B2 **Paroo** *watercourse* Austr.
111 C3 **Paros** *i.* Greece
144 B2 **Parras** Mex.
126 C2 **Parry, Cape** Can.
126 D1 **Parry Islands** Can.
130 B2 **Parry Sound** Can.
137 D3 **Parsons** U.S.A.
101 D2 **Partenstein** Ger.
104 B2 **Parthenay** France
97 B2 **Partry Mountains** *hills* Ireland
151 C2 **Paru** *r.* Brazil
135 C4 **Pasadena** U.S.A.
62 A2 **Pasawng** Myanmar
142 C2 **Pascagoula** U.S.A.
110 C1 **Paşcani** Romania
134 C1 **Pasco** U.S.A.
102 C1 **Pasewalk** Ger.
129 D2 **Pasfield Lake** Can.
60 B1 **Pasir Putih** Malaysia
74 A2 **Pasni** Pak.
153 A5 **Paso Río Mayo** Arg.
135 B3 **Paso Robles** U.S.A.
155 D2 **Passa Tempo** Brazil
102 C2 **Passau** Ger.
152 C3 **Passo Fundo** Brazil
155 C2 **Passos** Brazil
88 C2 **Pastavy** Belarus
150 A2 **Pastaza** *r.* Peru
150 A1 **Pasto** Col.
61 C2 **Pasuruan** Indon.
88 B2 **Pasvalys** Lith.
153 A6 **Patagonia** *reg.* Arg.
75 C2 **Patan** Nepal
54 B1 **Patea** N.Z.
141 E2 **Paterson** U.S.A.
Pathein Myanmar *see* **Bassein**
136 B2 **Pathfinder Reservoir** U.S.A.
61 C2 **Pati** Indon.
62 A1 **Patkai Bum** *mts* India/Myanmar
111 C3 **Patmos** *i.* Greece
75 C2 **Patna** India
81 C2 **Patnos** Turkey
154 B3 **Pato Branco** Brazil
152 C4 **Patos, Lagoa dos** *l.* Brazil
155 C1 **Patos de Minas** Brazil
152 B4 **Patquía** Arg.
111 B3 **Patras** Greece
75 C2 **Patratu** India
154 C1 **Patrocínio** Brazil
63 B3 **Pattani** Thai.
63 B2 **Pattaya** Thai.
128 B2 **Pattullo, Mount** Can.
129 D2 **Patuanak** Can.
144 B3 **Pátzcuaro** Mex.
104 B3 **Pau** France
104 B2 **Pauillac** France
62 A1 **Pauk** Myanmar
151 D2 **Paulistana** Brazil
151 E2 **Paulo Afonso** Brazil
123 D2 **Paulpietersburg** S. Africa
139 D2 **Pauls Valley** U.S.A.
62 A2 **Paungde** Myanmar
155 D1 **Pavão** Brazil
108 A1 **Pavia** Italy
88 B2 **Pāvilosta** Latvia
110 C2 **Pavlikeni** Bulg.
77 D1 **Pavlodar** Kazakh.
91 D2 **Pavlohrad** Ukr.
91 E1 **Pavlovsk** Rus. Fed.
91 D2 **Pavlovskaya** Rus. Fed.
60 B2 **Payakumbuh** Indon.
134 C2 **Payette** U.S.A.
134 C2 **Payette** *r.* U.S.A.
86 F2 **Pay-Khoy, Khrebet** *hills* Rus. Fed.
152 C4 **Paysandú** Uru.
81 C1 **Pazar** Turkey
110 B2 **Pazardzhik** Bulg.
111 C3 **Pazarköy** Turkey

108 B1 **Pazin** Croatia
63 A2 **Pe** Myanmar
128 C2 **Peace** *r.* Can.
128 C2 **Peace River** Can.
135 E3 **Peale, Mount** U.S.A.
142 C2 **Pearl** *r.* U.S.A.
139 D3 **Pearsall** U.S.A.
121 C2 **Pebane** Moz.
Peć Kosovo *see* **Pejë**
155 D1 **Peçanha** Brazil
86 E2 **Pechora** Rus. Fed.
86 E2 **Pechora** *r.* Rus. Fed.
88 C2 **Pechory** Rus. Fed.
139 C2 **Pecos** U.S.A.
139 C3 **Pecos** *r.* U.S.A.
103 D2 **Pécs** Hungary
155 D1 **Pedra Azul** Brazil
154 C2 **Pedregulho** Brazil
151 D2 **Pedreiras** Brazil
73 C4 **Pedro, Point** Sri Lanka
151 D2 **Pedro Afonso** Brazil
154 B1 **Pedro Gomes** Brazil
152 C3 **Pedro Juan Caballero** Para.
96 C3 **Peebles** U.K.
143 E2 **Pee Dee** *r.* U.S.A.
126 C2 **Peel** *r.* Can.
98 A1 **Peel** Isle of Man
128 C2 **Peerless Lake** Can.
54 B2 **Pegasus Bay** N.Z.
101 E3 **Pegnitz** Ger.
62 A2 **Pegu** Myanmar
62 A2 **Pegu Yoma** *mts* Myanmar
153 B4 **Pehuajó** Arg.
101 E1 **Peine** Ger.
88 C2 **Peipus, Lake** Estonia/Rus. Fed.
154 B2 **Peixe** *r.* Brazil
109 D2 **Pejë** Kosovo
61 B2 **Pekalongan** Indon.
60 B1 **Pekan** Malaysia
60 B1 **Pekanbaru** Indon.
Peking China *see* **Beijing**
130 B2 **Pelee Island** Can.
59 C3 **Peleng** *i.* Indon.
92 I2 **Pelkosenniemi** Fin.
122 A2 **Pella** S. Africa
59 D3 **Pelleluhu Islands** P.N.G.
92 H2 **Pello** Fin.
128 A1 **Pelly** *r.* Can.
128 A1 **Pelly Mountains** Can.
152 C4 **Pelotas** Brazil
152 C3 **Pelotas, Rio das** *r.* Brazil
141 F1 **Pemadumcook Lake** U.S.A.
61 B1 **Pemangkat** Indon.
60 A1 **Pematangsiantar** Indon.
121 D2 **Pemba** Moz.
120 B2 **Pemba** Zambia
119 D3 **Pemba Island** Tanz.
128 B2 **Pemberton** Can.
137 D1 **Pembina** *r.* Can./U.S.A.
130 C2 **Pembroke** Can.
99 A3 **Pembroke** U.K.
145 C2 **Peña Nevada, Cerro** *mt.* Mex.
154 B2 **Penápolis** Brazil
106 B1 **Peñaranda de Bracamonte** Spain
107 C1 **Peñarroya** *mt.* Spain
106 B2 **Peñarroya-Pueblonuevo** Spain
106 B1 **Peñas, Cabo de** *c.* Spain
153 A5 **Penas, Golfo de** *g.* Chile
134 C1 **Pendleton** U.S.A.
128 B2 **Pendleton Bay** Can.
134 C1 **Pend Oreille Lake** U.S.A.
74 B3 **Penganga** *r.* India
123 D1 **Penge** S. Africa
70 C2 **Penglai** China
71 A3 **Pengshui** China
106 B2 **Peniche** Port.
98 B1 **Penicuik** U.K.
108 B2 **Penne** Italy
98 B1 **Pennines** *hills* U.K.
141 D2 **Pennsylvania** *state* U.S.A.
127 G2 **Penny Icecap** Can.
141 F2 **Penobscot** *r.* U.S.A.
52 B3 **Penola** Austr.
50 C3 **Penong** Austr.
49 H3 **Penrhyn** *atoll* Cook Is
98 B1 **Penrith** U.K.
142 C2 **Pensacola** U.S.A.
55 Q1 **Pensacola Mountains** Antarctica
61 C1 **Pensiangan** *Sabah* Malaysia
128 C3 **Penticton** Can.
96 C1 **Pentland Firth** *sea chan.* U.K.
99 B2 **Penygadair** *h.* U.K.
87 D3 **Penza** Rus. Fed.
99 A3 **Penzance** U.K.
140 B2 **Peoria** U.S.A.
107 C1 **Perales del Alfambra** Spain
51 E2 **Percy Isles** Austr.
86 F2 **Peregrebnoye** Rus. Fed.
150 A1 **Pereira** Col.
154 B2 **Pereira Barreto** Brazil
90 A2 **Peremyshlyany** Ukr.
89 E2 **Pereslavl'-Zalesskiy** Rus. Fed.
91 C1 **Pereyaslav-Khmel'nyts'kyy** Ukr.
153 B4 **Pergamino** Arg.
92 H3 **Perhonjoki** *r.* Fin.
131 C1 **Péribonka, Lac** *l.* Can.
152 B3 **Perico** Arg.
144 B2 **Pericos** Mex.
104 C2 **Périgueux** France
147 C4 **Perija, Sierra de** *mts* Venez.
153 A5 **Perito Moreno** Arg.
101 E1 **Perleberg** Ger.
86 E3 **Perm'** Rus. Fed.
52 A2 **Pernatty Lagoon** *imp. l.* Austr.
105 C2 **Péronne** France
145 C3 **Perote** Mex.
104 C3 **Perpignan** France
99 A3 **Perranporth** U.K.
143 D2 **Perry** *FL* U.S.A.
143 D2 **Perry** *GA* U.S.A.
137 E2 **Perry** *IA* U.S.A.
139 C1 **Perryton** U.S.A.
137 F3 **Perryville** U.S.A.
99 B2 **Pershore** U.K.
91 D2 **Pershotravens'k** Ukr.
Persian Gulf Asia *see* **The Gulf**
50 A3 **Perth** Austr.
96 C2 **Perth** U.K.
105 D3 **Pertuis** France
108 A2 **Pertusato, Capo** *c. Corse* France
150 A2 **Peru** *country* S. America
157 H4 **Peru-Chile Trench** S. Pacific Ocean
108 B2 **Perugia** Italy
154 C2 **Peruíbe** Brazil
100 A2 **Péruwelz** Belgium
90 C2 **Pervomays'k** Ukr.
91 C2 **Pervomays'ke** Ukr.
89 F3 **Pervomayskiy** Rus. Fed.
91 D2 **Pervomays'kyy** Ukr.
108 B2 **Pesaro** Italy
108 B2 **Pescara** Italy
108 B2 **Pescara** *r.* Italy
74 B1 **Peshawar** Pak.
109 D2 **Peshkopi** Albania
109 C1 **Pesnica** Slovenia
89 E2 **Pestovo** Rus. Fed.
144 B3 **Petatlán** Mex.
140 B2 **Petenwell Lake** U.S.A.
52 A2 **Peterborough** Austr.
130 C2 **Peterborough** Can.
99 C2 **Peterborough** U.K.
96 D2 **Peterhead** U.K.
50 B2 **Petermann Ranges** *mts* Au
129 D2 **Peter Pond Lake** Can.
128 A2 **Petersburg** *AK* U.S.A.
141 D3 **Petersburg** *VA* U.S.A.
101 D1 **Petershagen** Ger.
131 E1 **Petit Mécatina** *r.* Can.
145 D2 **Peto** Mex.
140 C1 **Petoskey** U.S.A.
80 B2 **Petra** *tourist site* Jordan
66 B2 **Petra Velikogo, Zaliv** *b.* Rus.
111 B2 **Petrich** Bulg.
151 D2 **Petrolina** Brazil
77 C1 **Petropavlovsk** Kazakh.
83 L3 **Petropavlovsk-Kamchatsk** Rus. Fed.
110 B1 **Petroșani** Romania
89 F3 **Petrovskoye** Rus. Fed.
86 C2 **Petrozavodsk** Rus. Fed.
123 C2 **Petrusburg** S. Africa
123 C2 **Petrus Steyn** S. Africa
122 B3 **Petrusville** S. Africa
89 E2 **Petushki** Rus. Fed.
60 A1 **Peureula** Indon.
83 M2 **Pevek** Rus. Fed.
102 B2 **Pforzheim** Ger.
102 C2 **Pfunds** Austria
101 D3 **Pfungstadt** Ger.
123 C2 **Phahameng** S. Africa
123 D1 **Phalaborwa** S. Africa
74 B2 **Phalodi** India
63 B2 **Phang Hoei, San Khao** *mt* Thai.
63 A3 **Phangnga** Thai.
62 B1 **Phăng Xi Păng** *mt.* Vietna
63 B2 **Phan Rang-Thap Cham** Vietnam
63 B2 **Phan Thiêt** Vietnam
63 B3 **Phatthalung** Thai.
62 A2 **Phayao** Thai.
129 D2 **Phelps Lake** Can.
143 C2 **Phenix City** U.S.A.
63 A2 **Phet Buri** Thai.
63 B2 **Phichit** Thai.
141 D3 **Philadelphia** U.S.A.
136 C2 **Philip** U.S.A.
100 B2 **Philippeville** Belgium
100 A2 **Philippine** Neth.
64 B1 **Philippines** *country* Asia
64 B1 **Philippine Sea** N. Pacific Ocean
126 B2 **Philip Smith Mountains** U.S.A.
122 B3 **Philipstown** S. Africa
53 C3 **Phillip Island** Austr.
137 D3 **Phillipsburg** U.S.A.
123 C2 **Phiritona** S. Africa
63 B2 **Phitsanulok** Thai.
63 B2 **Phnom Penh** Cambodia
Phnum Penh Cambodia *se* **Phnom Penh**
138 A2 **Phoenix** U.S.A.
49 G3 **Phoenix Islands** Kiribati
63 B2 **Phon** Thai.
62 B1 **Phôngsali** Laos
62 B2 **Phônsavan** Laos
62 B2 **Phrae** Thai.
63 A3 **Phuket** Thai.
62 A2 **Phumiphon, Khuan** Thai.
63 B2 **Phumĭ Sâmraông** Camboc
123 C2 **Phuthaditjhaba** S. Africa
62 A2 **Phyu** Myanmar
108 A1 **Piacenza** Italy
110 C1 **Piatra Neamț** Romania
151 D2 **Piauí** *r.* Brazil

98 B1 **Piave** *r.* Italy
17 B4 **Pibor** *r.* Sudan
17 B4 **Pibor Post** Sudan
42 C2 **Picayune** U.S.A.
52 B3 **Pichanal** Arg.
44 A2 **Pichilingue** Mex.
98 C1 **Pickering** U.K.
30 A1 **Pickle Lake** Can.
51 D2 **Picos** Brazil
53 B5 **Pico Truncado** Arg.
53 D2 **Picton** Austr.
50 B3 **Piedras, Río de las** *r.* Peru
45 C3 **Piedras Negras** Guat.
45 B2 **Piedras Negras** Mex.
93 I3 **Pieksämäki** Fin.
92 I3 **Pielinen** *l.* Fin.
36 C2 **Pierre** U.S.A.
05 C3 **Pierrelatte** France
23 D2 **Pietermaritzburg** S. Africa
10 B1 **Pietrosa** *mt.* Romania
28 C2 **Pigeon Lake** Can.
53 B4 **Pigüé** Arg.
92 I3 **Pihtipudas** Fin.
45 C3 **Pijijiapan** Mex.
36 C3 **Pikes Peak** U.S.A.
22 A3 **Piketberg** S. Africa
40 C3 **Pikeville** U.S.A.
03 D1 **Piła** Pol.
53 C4 **Pilar** Arg.
52 C3 **Pilar** Para.
53 C2 **Pilliga** Austr.
54 C1 **Pilões, Serra dos** *mts* Brazil
50 B3 **Pimenta Bueno** Brazil
53 C4 **Pinamar** Arg.
80 B2 **Pınarbaşı** Turkey
46 B2 **Pinar del Río** Cuba
03 E1 **Pińczów** Pol.
51 D2 **Pindaré** *r.* Brazil
Pindos *mts* Greece *see* **Pindus Mountains**
11 B2 **Pindus Mountains** Greece
42 B2 **Pine Bluff** U.S.A.
50 C1 **Pine Creek** Austr.
36 B2 **Pinedale** U.S.A.
86 D2 **Pinega** Rus. Fed.
29 D2 **Pinehouse Lake** Can.
11 B3 **Pineios** *r.* Greece
28 C1 **Pine Point (abandoned)** Can.
36 C2 **Pine Ridge** U.S.A.
23 D2 **Pinetown** S. Africa
70 B2 **Pingdingshan** China
71 A3 **Pingguo** China
71 B3 **Pingjiang** China
70 A2 **Pingliang** China
71 C3 **P'ingtung** Taiwan
71 A3 **Pingxiang** *Guangxi* China
71 B3 **Pingxiang** *Jiangxi* China
70 B2 **Pingyin** China
51 D2 **Pinheiro** Brazil
01 D1 **Pinneberg** Ger.
45 C3 **Pinotepa Nacional** Mex.
88 C3 **Pinsk** Belarus
35 D3 **Pioche** U.S.A.
19 C3 **Piodi** Dem. Rep. Congo
03 E1 **Pionki** Pol.
03 D1 **Piotrków Trybunalski** Pol.
37 D2 **Pipestone** U.S.A.
31 C2 **Pipmuacan, Réservoir** *resr* Can.
54 B2 **Piquiri** *r.* Brazil
54 C1 **Piracanjuba** Brazil
54 C2 **Piracicaba** Brazil
55 D1 **Piracicaba** *r.* Brazil
54 C2 **Piraçununga** Brazil
11 B3 **Piraeus** Greece
54 C2 **Piraí do Sul** Brazil
54 C2 **Pirajuí** Brazil
154 B1 **Piranhas** Brazil
151 E2 **Piranhas** *r.* Brazil
155 D1 **Pirapora** Brazil
154 C1 **Pires do Rio** Brazil
151 D2 **Piripiri** Brazil
59 C3 **Piru** Indon.
108 B2 **Pisa** Italy
152 A2 **Pisagua** Chile
150 A3 **Pisco** Peru
102 C2 **Písek** Czech Rep.
79 D2 **Pīshīn** Iran
145 D2 **Pisté** Mex.
109 C2 **Pisticci** Italy
108 B2 **Pistoia** Italy
106 C1 **Pisuerga** *r.* Spain
134 B2 **Pit** *r.* U.S.A.
154 B2 **Pitanga** Brazil
155 D1 **Pitangui** Brazil
49 J4 **Pitcairn Island** *i.* Pitcairn Is
92 H2 **Piteå** Sweden
92 H2 **Piteälven** *r.* Sweden
110 B2 **Pitești** Romania
75 C2 **Pithoragarh** India
96 C2 **Pitlochry** U.K.
128 B2 **Pitt Island** Can.
137 E3 **Pittsburg** U.S.A.
141 D2 **Pittsburgh** U.S.A.
141 E2 **Pittsfield** U.S.A.
53 D1 **Pittsworth** Austr.
155 C2 **Piumhí** Brazil
150 A2 **Piura** Peru
90 C2 **Pivdennyy Buh** *r.* Ukr.
131 E2 **Placentia** Can.
135 B3 **Placerville** U.S.A.
146 C2 **Placetas** Cuba
139 C2 **Plainview** U.S.A.
154 C1 **Planaltina** Brazil
142 B2 **Plaquemine** U.S.A.
106 B1 **Plasencia** Spain
147 C4 **Plato** Col.
137 D2 **Platte** *r.* U.S.A.
141 E2 **Plattsburgh** U.S.A.
101 F1 **Plau** Ger.
101 F2 **Plauen** Ger.
101 F1 **Plauer See** *l.* Ger.
89 E3 **Plavsk** Rus. Fed.
129 E2 **Playgreen Lake** Can.
63 B2 **Plây Ku** Vietnam
153 B4 **Plaza Huincul** Arg.
139 D3 **Pleasanton** U.S.A.
54 B2 **Pleasant Point** N.Z.
104 C2 **Pleaux** France
130 B1 **Pledger Lake** Can.
54 C1 **Plenty, Bay of** *g.* N.Z.
136 C1 **Plentywood** U.S.A.
86 D2 **Plesetsk** Rus. Fed.
131 C1 **Plétipi, Lac** *l.* Can.
100 C2 **Plettenberg** Ger.
122 B3 **Plettenberg Bay** S. Africa
110 B2 **Pleven** Bulg.
109 C2 **Pljevlja** Montenegro
109 C2 **Ploče** Croatia
103 D1 **Płock** Pol.
109 C2 **Pločno** *mt.* Bos.-Herz.
104 B2 **Ploemeur** France
110 C2 **Ploiești** Romania
89 F2 **Ploskoye** Rus. Fed.
104 B2 **Plouzané** France
110 B2 **Plovdiv** Bulg.
88 B2 **Plungė** Lith.
88 C3 **Plyeshchanitsy** Belarus
99 A3 **Plymouth** U.K.
140 B2 **Plymouth** U.S.A.
147 D3 **Plymouth (abandoned)** Montserrat
88 C2 **Plyussa** Rus. Fed.
102 C2 **Plzeň** Czech Rep.
114 B3 **Pô** Burkina
108 B1 **Po** *r.* Italy
77 E2 **Pobeda Peak** China/Kyrg.
142 B1 **Pocahontas** U.S.A.
134 D2 **Pocatello** U.S.A.
90 B1 **Pochayiv** Ukr.
89 D3 **Pochep** Rus. Fed.
89 D3 **Pochinok** Rus. Fed.
145 C3 **Pochutla** Mex.
141 D3 **Pocomoke City** U.S.A.
155 C2 **Poços de Caldas** Brazil
89 D2 **Poddor'ye** Rus. Fed.
91 D1 **Podgorenskiy** Rus. Fed.
109 C2 **Podgorica** Montenegro
82 G3 **Podgornoye** Rus. Fed.
83 H2 **Podkamennaya Tunguska** *r.* Rus. Fed.
89 E2 **Podol'sk** Rus. Fed.
109 D2 **Podujevë** Kosovo
Podujevo Kosovo *see* **Podujevë**
122 A2 **Pofadder** S. Africa
89 D3 **Pogar** Rus. Fed.
109 D2 **Pogradec** Albania
65 B2 **P'ohang** S. Korea
48 E2 **Pohnpei** *atoll* Micronesia
110 B2 **Poiana Mare** Romania
118 C3 **Poie** Dem. Rep. Congo
118 B3 **Pointe-Noire** Congo
126 D2 **Point Lake** Can.
140 C3 **Point Pleasant** U.S.A.
104 C2 **Poitiers** France
74 B2 **Pokaran** India
75 C2 **Pokhara** Nepal
83 J2 **Pokrovsk** Rus. Fed.
91 D2 **Pokrovskoye** Rus. Fed.
138 A1 **Polacca** U.S.A.
106 B1 **Pola de Lena** Spain
103 D1 **Poland** *country* Europe
88 C2 **Polatsk** Belarus
77 C3 **Pol-e Khomrī** Afgh.
61 C2 **Polewali** Indon.
118 B2 **Poli** Cameroon
102 C1 **Police** Pol.
109 C2 **Policoro** Italy
105 D2 **Poligny** France
64 B1 **Polillo Islands** Phil.
90 B1 **Polis'ke** Ukr.
103 D1 **Polkowice** Pol.
109 C3 **Pollino, Monte** *mt.* Italy
91 D2 **Polohy** Ukr.
123 C1 **Polokwane** S. Africa
90 B1 **Polonne** Ukr.
134 D1 **Polson** U.S.A.
91 C2 **Poltava** Ukr.
66 B2 **Poltavka** Rus. Fed.
91 D2 **Poltavskaya** Rus. Fed.
88 C2 **Põlva** Estonia
111 B2 **Polygyros** Greece
106 B2 **Pombal** Port.
102 C1 **Pomeranian Bay** Ger./Pol.
108 B2 **Pomezia** Italy
92 I2 **Pomokaira** *reg.* Fin.
110 C2 **Pomorie** Bulg.
Pomorska, Zatoka *b.* Ger./Pol. *see* **Pomeranian Bay**
155 D1 **Pompéu** Brazil
139 D1 **Ponca City** U.S.A.
147 D3 **Ponce** Puerto Rico
Pondicherry India *see* **Puducherry**
127 F2 **Pond Inlet** Can.
106 B1 **Ponferrada** Spain
117 A4 **Pongo** *watercourse* Sudan
123 D2 **Pongola** *r.* S. Africa
128 C2 **Ponoka** Can.
84 D5 **Ponta Delgada** Arquipélago dos Açores

154 B3 **Ponta Grossa** Brazil
154 C1 **Pontalina** Brazil
105 D2 **Pont-à-Mousson** France
105 D2 **Pontarlier** France
102 B2 **Pontcharra** France
142 B2 **Pontchartrain, Lake** U.S.A.
106 B2 **Ponte de Sor** Port.
129 D3 **Ponteix** Can.
150 C3 **Pontes-e-Lacerda** Brazil
106 B1 **Pontevedra** Spain
140 B2 **Pontiac** *IL* U.S.A.
140 C2 **Pontiac** *MI* U.S.A.
61 B2 **Pontianak** Indon.
104 B2 **Pontivy** France
151 C1 **Pontoetoe** Suriname
129 E2 **Ponton** Can.
99 B3 **Pontypool** U.K.
108 B2 **Ponziane, Isole** *is* Italy
99 C3 **Poole** U.K.
Poona India *see* **Pune**
52 B2 **Pooncarie** Austr.
152 B2 **Poopó, Lago de** *l.* Bol.
150 A1 **Popayán** Col.
83 I2 **Popigay** *r.* Rus. Fed.
52 B2 **Popiltah** Austr.
129 E2 **Poplar** *r.* Can.
137 E3 **Poplar Bluff** U.S.A.
118 B3 **Popokabaka** Dem. Rep. Congo
110 C2 **Popovo** Bulg.
103 E2 **Poprad** Slovakia
151 D3 **Porangatu** Brazil
74 A2 **Porbandar** India
126 B2 **Porcupine** *r.* Can./U.S.A.
108 B1 **Poreč** Croatia
54 B2 **Porirua** N.Z.
88 C2 **Porkhov** Rus. Fed.
104 B2 **Pornic** France
83 K3 **Poronaysk** Rus. Fed.
111 B3 **Poros** Greece
93 E4 **Porsgrunn** Norway
97 C1 **Portadown** U.K.
97 D1 **Portaferry** U.K.
140 B2 **Portage** U.S.A.
129 E3 **Portage la Prairie** Can.
128 B3 **Port Alberni** Can.
106 B2 **Portalegre** Port.
139 C2 **Portales** U.S.A.
128 A2 **Port Alexander** U.S.A.
128 B2 **Port Alice** Can.
134 B1 **Port Angeles** U.S.A.
51 D4 **Port Arthur** Austr.
139 E3 **Port Arthur** U.S.A.
96 A3 **Port Askaig** U.K.
52 A2 **Port Augusta** Austr.
147 C3 **Port-au-Prince** Haiti
131 E1 **Port aux Choix** Can.
73 D3 **Port Blair** India
52 B3 **Port Campbell** Austr.
54 B3 **Port Chalmers** N.Z.
143 D3 **Port Charlotte** U.S.A.
147 C3 **Port-de-Paix** Haiti
128 A2 **Port Edward** Can.
155 D1 **Porteirinha** Brazil
151 C2 **Portel** Brazil
130 B2 **Port Elgin** Can.
123 C3 **Port Elizabeth** S. Africa
96 A3 **Port Ellen** U.K.
98 A1 **Port Erin** Isle of Man
122 A3 **Porterville** S. Africa
135 C3 **Porterville** U.S.A.
52 B3 **Port Fairy** Austr.
54 C1 **Port Fitzroy** N.Z.
118 A3 **Port-Gentil** Gabon
115 C4 **Port Harcourt** Nigeria
128 B2 **Port Hardy** Can.
Port Harrison Can. *see* **Inukjuak**
131 D2 **Port Hawkesbury** Can.
50 A2 **Port Hedland** Austr.
99 A2 **Porthmadog** U.K.
131 E1 **Port Hope Simpson** Can.
140 C2 **Port Huron** U.S.A.
106 B2 **Portimão** Port.
53 C2 **Portland** *N.S.W.* Austr.
52 B3 **Portland** *Vic.* Austr.
141 E2 **Portland** *ME* U.S.A.
134 B1 **Portland** *OR* U.S.A.
128 A2 **Portland Canal** *inlet* Can.
97 C2 **Portlaoise** Ireland
139 D3 **Port Lavaca** U.S.A.
52 A2 **Port Lincoln** Austr.
114 A4 **Port Loko** Sierra Leone
113 K9 **Port Louis** Mauritius
53 D2 **Port Macquarie** Austr.
128 B2 **Port McNeill** Can.
131 D2 **Port-Menier** Can.
59 D3 **Port Moresby** P.N.G.
122 A2 **Port Nolloth** S. Africa
Port-Nouveau-Québec Can. *see* **Kangiqsualujjuaq**
Porto Port. *see* **Oporto**
150 B2 **Porto Acre** Brazil
152 C4 **Porto Alegre** Brazil
151 C3 **Porto Artur** Brazil
151 C3 **Porto dos Gaúchos Óbidos** Brazil
150 C3 **Porto Esperidião** Brazil
108 B2 **Portoferraio** Italy
96 A1 **Port of Ness** U.K.
151 D2 **Porto Franco** Brazil
147 D3 **Port of Spain** Trin. and Tob.
108 B1 **Portogruaro** Italy
108 B2 **Portomaggiore** Italy
154 B2 **Porto Mendes** Brazil
152 C3 **Porto Murtinho** Brazil
151 D3 **Porto Nacional** Brazil
114 C4 **Porto-Novo** Benin
154 B2 **Porto Primavera, Represa** *resr* Brazil
151 C2 **Porto Santana** Brazil
155 E1 **Porto Seguro** Brazil
108 B2 **Porto Tolle** Italy
108 A2 **Porto Torres** *Sardegna* Italy
105 D3 **Porto-Vecchio** *Corse* France
150 B2 **Porto Velho** Brazil
150 A2 **Portoviejo** Ecuador
52 B3 **Port Phillip Bay** Austr.
52 A2 **Port Pirie** Austr.
96 A2 **Portree** U.K.
128 B3 **Port Renfrew** Can.
97 C1 **Portrush** U.K.
116 B1 **Port Said** Egypt
143 C3 **Port St Joe** U.S.A.
123 C3 **Port St Johns** S. Africa
123 D3 **Port Shepstone** S. Africa
99 C3 **Portsmouth** U.K.
141 E2 **Portsmouth** *NH* U.S.A.
140 C3 **Portsmouth** *OH* U.S.A.
141 D3 **Portsmouth** *VA* U.S.A.
97 C1 **Portstewart** U.K.
116 B3 **Port Sudan** Sudan
142 C3 **Port Sulphur** U.S.A.
99 B3 **Port Talbot** U.K.
106 B2 **Portugal** *country* Europe
97 B2 **Portumna** Ireland
105 C3 **Port-Vendres** France
48 F4 **Port Vila** Vanuatu
93 I3 **Porvoo** Fin.
65 B2 **Poryŏng** S. Korea
152 C3 **Posadas** Arg.
89 E2 **Poshekhon'ye** Rus. Fed.
92 I2 **Posio** Fin.
58 C3 **Poso** Indon.
151 D3 **Posse** Brazil
101 E2 **Pößneck** Ger.
139 C2 **Post** U.S.A.
Poste-de-la-Baleine Can. *se* **Kuujjuarapik**
122 B2 **Postmasburg** S. Africa
109 C2 **Posušje** Bos.-Herz.
139 E1 **Poteau** U.S.A.
109 C2 **Potenza** Italy
151 D2 **Poti** *r.* Brazil
81 C1 **P'ot'i** Georgia
115 D3 **Potiskum** Nigeria
141 D3 **Potomac, South Branch** *r.* U.
152 B2 **Potosí** Bol.
64 B1 **Pototan** Phil.
138 C3 **Potrero del Llano** Mex.
101 F1 **Potsdam** Ger.
141 E2 **Potsdam** U.S.A.
141 D2 **Pottstown** U.S.A.
141 D2 **Pottsville** U.S.A.
131 E2 **Pouch Cove** Can.
141 E2 **Poughkeepsie** U.S.A.
98 B2 **Poulton-le-Fylde** U.K.
155 C2 **Pouso Alegre** Brazil
63 B2 **Poŭthĭsăt** Cambodia
103 D2 **Považská Bystrica** Slovakia
109 C2 **Povlen** *mt.* Serbia
106 B1 **Póvoa de Varzim** Port.
136 B2 **Powell** U.S.A.
135 D3 **Powell, Lake** *resr* U.S.A.
128 B3 **Powell River** Can.
154 B1 **Poxoréu** Brazil
71 B3 **Poyang** China
71 B3 **Poyang Hu** *l.* China
109 D2 **Požarevac** Serbia
145 C2 **Poza Rica** Mex.
109 C1 **Požega** Croatia
109 D2 **Požega** Serbia
79 D2 **Pozm Tīāb** Iran
103 D1 **Poznań** Pol.
106 C2 **Pozoblanco** Spain
108 B2 **Pozzuoli** Italy
60 B2 **Prabumulih** Indon.
102 C2 **Prachatice** Czech Rep.
63 A2 **Prachuap Khiri Khan** Thai.
155 E1 **Prado** Brazil
102 C1 **Prague** Czech Rep.
Praha Czech Rep. *see* **Pragu**
112 C5 **Praia** Cape Verde
139 C2 **Prairie Dog Town Fork** *r.* U.S.A.
140 A2 **Prairie du Chien** U.S.A.
60 A1 **Prapat** Indon.
154 C1 **Prata** Brazil
105 E3 **Prato** Italy
137 D3 **Pratt** U.S.A.
61 C2 **Praya** Indon.
63 B2 **Preăh Vihéar** Cambodia
89 F2 **Prechistoye** Rus. Fed.
129 D2 **Preeceville** Can.
88 C2 **Preiļi** Latvia
53 C2 **Premer** Austr.
105 C2 **Prémery** France
101 F1 **Premnitz** Ger.
102 C1 **Prenzlau** Ger.
63 A2 **Preparis Island** Cocos Is
63 A2 **Preparis North Channel** Cocos Is
63 A2 **Preparis South Channel** Cocos Is
103 D2 **Přerov** Czech Rep.
138 A2 **Prescott** U.S.A.
109 D2 **Preševo** Serbia
152 B3 **Presidencia Roque Sáenz Peña** Arg.
151 D2 **Presidente Dutra** Brazil
154 B2 **Presidente Epitácio** Brazil
154 B2 **Presidente Prudente** Brazil

38 C3 **Presidio** U.S.A.
3 E2 **Prešov** Slovakia
1 F1 **Presque Isle** U.S.A.
1 F2 **Pressel** Ger.
8 B2 **Preston** U.K.
4 D2 **Preston** U.S.A.
6 B3 **Prestwick** U.K.
5 C1 **Preto** *r.* Brazil
3 C2 **Pretoria** S. Africa
1 B3 **Preveza** Greece
3 B2 **Prey Vêng** Cambodia
9 C2 **Priboj** Serbia
5 D3 **Price** U.S.A.
38 B3 **Prienai** Lith.
2 B2 **Prieska** S. Africa
3 D2 **Prievidza** Slovakia
9 C2 **Prijedor** Bos.-Herz.
Prikaspiyskaya Nizmennost' *lowland* Kazakh./Rus. Fed. *see* **Caspian Lowland**
9 D2 **Prilep** Macedonia
1 D2 **Primorsko-Akhtarsk** Rus. Fed.
9 D2 **Primrose Lake** Can.
9 D2 **Prince Albert** Can.
2 B3 **Prince Albert** S. Africa
6 D2 **Prince Albert Peninsula** Can.
2 B3 **Prince Albert Road** S. Africa
6 C2 **Prince Alfred, Cape** Can.
2 A3 **Prince Alfred Hamlet** S. Africa
7 F2 **Prince Charles Island** Can.
5 E2 **Prince Charles Mountains** Antarctica
1 D2 **Prince Edward Island** *prov.* Can.
3 I11 **Prince Edward Islands** Indian Ocean
8 B2 **Prince George** Can.
6 E2 **Prince of Wales Island** Can.
8 A2 **Prince of Wales Island** U.S.A.
6 D2 **Prince of Wales Strait** Can.
6 D1 **Prince Patrick Island** Can.
6 E2 **Prince Regent Inlet** *sea chan.* Can.
8 A2 **Prince Rupert** Can.
1 D1 **Princess Charlotte Bay** Austr.
8 B2 **Princess Royal Island** Can.
8 B3 **Princeton** Can.
4 B2 **Prineville** U.S.A.
0 B1 **Pripet** *r.* Belarus/Ukr.
0 A1 **Pripet Marshes** Belarus/Ukr.
9 D2 **Prishtinë** Kosovo
Priština Kosovo *see* **Prishtinë**
1 F1 **Pritzwalk** Ger.
9 C2 **Privlaka** Croatia
9 F2 **Privolzhsk** Rus. Fed.
9 D2 **Prizren** Kosovo
1 C1 **Professor van Blommestein Meer** *resr* Suriname
5 D2 **Progreso** Mex.
1 C1 **Prokhladnyy** Rus. Fed.
9 D2 **Prokuplje** Serbia
6 C3 **Prophet** *r.* Can.
8 B2 **Prophet River** Can.
1 D2 **Proserpine** Austr.
9 E3 **Protvino** Rus. Fed.
0 C2 **Provadiya** Bulg.
1 E2 **Providence** U.S.A.
6 B3 **Providencia, Isla de** *i.* Caribbean Sea
3 N2 **Provideniya** Rus. Fed.
5 D2 **Provo** U.S.A.
9 C2 **Provost** Can.
4 B3 **Prudentópolis** Brazil
6 B2 **Prudhoe Bay** U.S.A.
0 C2 **Prüm** Ger.
5 D3 **Prunelli-di-Fiumorbo** *Corse* France
103 E1 **Pruszków** Pol.
110 C1 **Prut** *r.* Europe
91 C1 **Pryluky** Ukr.
91 D2 **Prymors'k** Ukr.
139 D1 **Pryor** U.S.A.
Prypyats' *r.* Belarus *see* **Pripet**
103 E2 **Przemyśl** Pol.
111 C3 **Psara** *i.* Greece
81 C1 **Psebay** Rus. Fed.
91 D3 **Pshekha** *r.* Rus. Fed.
88 C2 **Pskov** Rus. Fed.
88 C2 **Pskov, Lake** Estonia/Rus. Fed.
111 B2 **Ptolemaïda** Greece
109 C1 **Ptuj** Slovenia
150 A2 **Pucallpa** Peru
71 B3 **Pucheng** China
65 B2 **Puch'ŏn** S. Korea
103 D1 **Puck** Pol.
92 I2 **Pudasjärvi** Fin.
86 C2 **Pudozh** Rus. Fed.
73 B3 **Puducherry** India
145 C3 **Puebla** Mex.
136 C3 **Pueblo** U.S.A.
153 B4 **Puelén** Arg.
106 C2 **Puente-Genil** Spain
153 A5 **Puerto Aisén** Chile
152 B2 **Puerto Alegre** Bol.
145 C3 **Puerto Ángel** Mex.
146 B4 **Puerto Armuelles** Panama
150 B1 **Puerto Ayacucho** Venez.
146 B3 **Puerto Cabezas** Nic.
150 B1 **Puerto Carreño** Col.
153 A5 **Puerto Cisnes** Chile
144 A2 **Puerto Cortés** Mex.
145 C3 **Puerto Escondido** Mex.
152 B2 **Puerto Frey** Bol.
150 B1 **Puerto Inírida** Col.
152 C2 **Puerto Isabel** Bol.
150 A2 **Puerto Leguizamo** Col.
144 A2 **Puerto Libertad** Mex.
146 B3 **Puerto Limón** Costa Rica
106 C2 **Puertollano** Spain
153 B5 **Puerto Madryn** Arg.
150 B3 **Puerto Maldonado** Peru
153 A5 **Puerto Montt** Chile
153 A6 **Puerto Natales** Chile
150 B1 **Puerto Nuevo** Col.
144 A1 **Puerto Peñasco** Mex.
152 C3 **Puerto Pinasco** Para.
147 C3 **Puerto Plata** Dom. Rep.
150 A2 **Puerto Portillo** Peru
64 A2 **Puerto Princesa** Phil.
147 D3 **Puerto Rico** *terr.* West Indies
158 B3 **Puerto Rico Trench** Caribbean Sea
146 A3 **Puerto San José** Guat.
153 B6 **Puerto Santa Cruz** Arg.
144 B2 **Puerto Vallarta** Mex.
87 D3 **Pugachev** Rus. Fed.
74 B2 **Pugal** India
54 B2 **Pukaki, Lake** N.Z.
129 D2 **Pukatawagan** Can.
65 B1 **Pukchin** N. Korea
65 B1 **Pukch'ŏng** N. Korea
54 B1 **Pukekohe** N.Z.
65 B1 **Puksubaek-san** *mt.* N. Korea
108 B2 **Pula** Croatia
108 A3 **Pula** *Sardegna* Italy
152 B3 **Pulacayo** Bol.
92 I3 **Pulkkila** Fin.
134 C1 **Pullman** U.S.A.
64 B1 **Pulog, Mount** Phil.
150 A2 **Puná, Isla** *i.* Ecuador
54 B2 **Punakaiki** N.Z.
123 D1 **Punda Maria** S. Africa
73 B3 **Pune** India
65 B1 **P'ungsan** N. Korea
121 C2 **Púnguè** *r.* Moz.
153 B4 **Punta Alta** Arg.
153 A6 **Punta Arenas** Chile
146 B3 **Puntarenas** Costa Rica
150 A1 **Punto Fijo** Venez.
92 I3 **Puolanka** Fin.
82 G2 **Pur** *r.* Rus. Fed.
75 C3 **Puri** India
100 B1 **Purmerend** Neth.
75 C2 **Purnia** India
75 C2 **Puruliya** India
150 B2 **Purus** *r.* Brazil/Peru
61 B2 **Purwakarta** Indon.
65 B1 **Puryŏng** N. Korea
65 B2 **Pusan** S. Korea
88 C2 **Pushkinskiye Gory** Rus. Fed.
88 C2 **Pustoshka** Rus. Fed.
62 A1 **Putao** Myanmar
71 B3 **Putian** China
Puting China *see* **De'an**
61 C2 **Puting, Tanjung** *pt* Indon.
101 F1 **Putlitz** Ger.
58 A2 **Putrajaya** Malaysia
102 C1 **Puttgarden** Ger.
150 A2 **Putumayo** *r.* Col.
61 C1 **Putusibau** Indon.
91 C1 **Putyvl'** Ukr.
127 F2 **Puvirnituq** Can.
70 B2 **Puyang** China
104 C3 **Puylaurens** France
99 A2 **Pwllheli** U.K.
63 A2 **Pyapon** Myanmar
82 G2 **Pyasina** *r.* Rus. Fed.
87 D4 **Pyatigorsk** Rus. Fed.
91 C2 **P"yatykhatky** Ukr.
62 A2 **Pyè** Myanmar
88 C3 **Pyetrykaw** Belarus
93 H3 **Pyhäjärvi** *l.* Fin.
92 H3 **Pyhäjoki** *r.* Fin.
92 I3 **Pyhäsalmi** Fin.
62 A2 **Pyinmana** Myanmar
65 B2 **Pyŏksŏng** N. Korea
65 B2 **P'yŏnggang** N. Korea
65 B2 **P'yŏngsan** N. Korea
65 B2 **P'yŏngyang** N. Korea
135 C2 **Pyramid Lake** U.S.A.
80 B3 **Pyramids of Giza** *tourist site* Egypt
107 D1 **Pyrenees** *mts* Europe
111 B3 **Pyrgos** Greece
91 C1 **Pyryatyn** Ukr.
103 C1 **Pyrzyce** Pol.
88 C2 **Pytalovo** Rus. Fed.
111 B3 **Pyxaria** *mt.* Greece

Q

Qaanaaq Greenland *see* **Thule**
123 C3 **Qacha's Nek** Lesotho
69 D2 **Qagan Nur** China
68 C2 **Qaidam Pendi** *basin* China
78 B2 **Qal'at Bīshah** Saudi Arabia
129 E1 **Qamanirjuaq Lake** Can.
Qamanittuaq Can. *see* **Baker Lake**
79 C3 **Qamar, Ghubbat al** *b.* Yemen
78 B3 **Qam Hadīl** Saudi Arabia
77 C3 **Qarshi** Uzbek.
78 B2 **Qaryat al Ulyā** Saudi Arabia
127 H2 **Qasigiannguit** Greenland
79 D2 **Qaşr-e Qand** Iran
81 C2 **Qaşr-e Shīrīn** Iran
127 H2 **Qassimiut** Greenland
78 B3 **Qa'tabah** Yemen
79 C2 **Qatar** *country* Asia

116 A2 **Qattara Depression** Egypt
81 C1 **Qazax** Azer.
81 C1 **Qazımämmäd** Azer.
81 C2 **Qazvīn** Iran
127 H2 **Qeqertarsuaq** *i.* Greenland
127 H2 **Qeqertarsuatsiaat** Greenland
127 H2 **Qeqertarsuup Tunua** *b.* Greenland
79 C2 **Qeshm** Iran
70 A3 **Qianjiang** *Chongqing* China
70 B2 **Qianjiang** *Hubei* China
65 A1 **Qian Shan** *mts* China
70 C2 **Qidong** China
68 B2 **Qiemo** China
71 A3 **Qijiang** China
68 C2 **Qijiaojing** China
127 G2 **Qikiqtarjuaq** Can.
74 A2 **Qila Ladgasht** Pak.
68 C2 **Qilian Shan** *mts* China
127 I2 **Qillak** *i.* Greenland
70 B3 **Qimen** China
127 G1 **Qimusseriarsuaq** *b.* Greenland
116 B2 **Qinā** Egypt
70 C2 **Qingdao** China
68 C2 **Qinghai Hu** *salt l.* China
68 C2 **Qinghai Nanshan** *mts* China
70 A2 **Qingyang** *Gansu* China
71 B3 **Qingyuan** *Guangdong* China
65 A1 **Qingyuan** *Liaoning* China
Qingzang Gaoyuan *plat.* China *see* **Tibet, Plateau of**
70 B2 **Qingzhou** China
70 B2 **Qinhuangdao** China
70 A2 **Qin Ling** *mts* China
Qinting China *see* **Lianhua**
70 B2 **Qinyang** China
71 A3 **Qinzhou** China
71 B4 **Qionghai** China
68 C2 **Qionglai Shan** *mts* China
71 B4 **Qiongshan** China
69 E1 **Qiqihar** China
79 C2 **Qīr** Iran
66 B1 **Qitaihe** China
70 B2 **Qixian** China
Qogir Feng *mt.* China/Pakistan *see* **K2**
81 D2 **Qom** Iran
Qomolangma Feng *mt.* China/Nepal *see* **Everest, Mount**
76 B2 **Qo'ng'irot** Uzbek.
Qoqek China *see* **Tacheng**
77 D2 **Qo'qon** Uzbek.
76 B2 **Qoraqalpog'iston** Uzbek.
100 C1 **Quakenbrück** Ger.
63 B2 **Quang Ngai** Vietnam
63 B2 **Quang Tri** Vietnam
71 B3 **Quanzhou** *Fujian* China
71 B3 **Quanzhou** *Guangxi* China
108 A3 **Quartu Sant'Elena** *Sardegna* Italy
138 A2 **Quartzsite** U.S.A.
81 C1 **Quba** Azer.
53 C3 **Queanbeyan** Austr.
131 C2 **Québec** Can.
130 C1 **Québec** *prov.* Can.
101 E2 **Quedlinburg** Ger.
128 A2 **Queen Charlotte** Can.
128 A2 **Queen Charlotte Islands** Can.
128 B2 **Queen Charlotte Sound** *sea chan.* Can.
128 B2 **Queen Charlotte Strait** Can.
126 D1 **Queen Elizabeth Islands** Can.
126 E2 **Queen Maud Gulf** Can.
55 B2 **Queen Maud Land** *reg.* Antarctica
55 N1 **Queen Maud Mountains** Antarctica
52 B1 **Queensland** *state* Austr.
51 D4 **Queenstown** Austr.
54 A3 **Queenstown** N.Z.
123 C3 **Queenstown** S. Africa
121 C2 **Quelimane** Moz.
138 B2 **Quemado** U.S.A.
154 B2 **Querência do Norte** Brazil
145 B2 **Querétaro** Mex.
101 E2 **Querfurt** Ger.
128 B2 **Quesnel** Can.
128 B2 **Quesnel Lake** Can.
74 A1 **Quetta** Pak.
64 A2 **Quezon** Phil.
64 B1 **Quezon City** Phil.
120 A2 **Quibala** Angola
150 A1 **Quibdó** Col.
104 B2 **Quiberon** France
104 C3 **Quillan** France
153 C4 **Quilmes** Arg.
Quilon India *see* **Kollam**
51 D2 **Quilpie** Austr.
153 A4 **Quilpué** Chile
120 A1 **Quimbele** Angola
152 B3 **Quimilí** Arg.
104 B2 **Quimper** France
104 B2 **Quimperlé** France
137 E3 **Quincy** *IL* U.S.A.
141 E2 **Quincy** *MA* U.S.A.
107 C1 **Quinto** Spain
121 D2 **Quionga** Moz.
53 D2 **Quirindi** Austr.
121 C3 **Quissico** Moz.
120 A2 **Quitapa** Angola
150 A2 **Quito** Ecuador
151 E2 **Quixadá** Brazil
71 A3 **Qujing** China
52 A2 **Quorn** Austr.
79 C2 **Qurayat** Oman
77 C3 **Qŭrghonteppa** Tajik.
63 B2 **Quy Nhơn** Vietnam
71 B3 **Quzhou** China

R

103 D2 **Raab** *r.* Austria
92 H3 **Raahe** Fin.
100 C1 **Raalte** Neth.
61 C2 **Raas** *i.* Indon.
61 C2 **Raba** Indon.
114 B1 **Rabat** Morocco
48 E3 **Rabaul** P.N.G.
78 A2 **Rābigh** Saudi Arabia
131 E2 **Race, Cape** Can.
142 B3 **Raceland** U.S.A.
63 B3 **Rach Gia** Vietnam
140 B2 **Racine** U.S.A.
78 B3 **Radā'** Yemen
110 C1 **Rădăuți** Romania
140 B3 **Radcliff** U.S.A.
74 B2 **Radhanpur** India
130 C1 **Radisson** Can.
103 E1 **Radom** Pol.
103 D1 **Radomsko** Pol.
90 B1 **Radomyshl'** Ukr.
109 D2 **Radoviš** Macedonia
88 B2 **Radviliškis** Lith.
78 A2 **Raḍwá, Jabal** *mt.* Saudi Arabia
90 B1 **Radyvyliv** Ukr.
75 C2 **Rae Bareli** India
100 C2 **Raeren** Belgium
54 C1 **Raetihi** N.Z.
152 B4 **Rafaela** Arg.
118 C2 **Rafaï** C.A.R.
78 B2 **Rafḩā'** Saudi Arabia
79 C1 **Rafsanjān** Iran
64 B2 **Ragang, Mount** *vol.* Phil.
109 B3 **Ragusa** *Sicilia* Italy
59 C3 **Raha** Indon.
88 D3 **Rahachow** Belarus
74 B2 **Rahimyar Khan** Pak.
109 D2 **Rahovec** Kosovo
73 B3 **Raichur** India
75 C2 **Raigarh** India
128 C2 **Rainbow Lake** Can.
134 B1 **Rainier, Mount** *vol.* U.S.A.
130 A2 **Rainy Lake** Can./U.S.A.
129 E3 **Rainy River** Can.
75 C2 **Raipur** India
93 H3 **Raisio** Fin.
73 C3 **Rajahmundry** India
61 C1 **Rajang** *r. Sarawak* Malaysia
74 B2 **Rajanpur** Pak.
73 B4 **Rajapalaiyam** India
74 B2 **Rajasthan Canal** India
74 B2 **Rajgarh** India
74 B2 **Rajkot** India
74 B2 **Rajpur** India
75 C2 **Rajshahi** Bangl.
54 B2 **Rakaia** *r.* N.Z.
90 A2 **Rakhiv** Ukr.
91 D1 **Rakitnoye** Rus. Fed.
88 C2 **Rakke** Estonia
88 C2 **Rakvere** Estonia
143 E1 **Raleigh** U.S.A.
48 F2 **Ralik Chain** *is* Marshall Is
74 B2 **Ramgarh** India
81 C2 **Rāmhormoz** Iran
Ramlat Rabyānah *des.* Libya *see* **Rebiana Sand Sea**
110 C1 **Râmnicu Sărat** Romania
110 B1 **Râmnicu Vâlcea** Romania
89 E3 **Ramon'** Rus. Fed.
123 C1 **Ramotswa** Botswana
75 B2 **Rampur** India
62 A2 **Ramree Island** Myanmar
98 A1 **Ramsey** Isle of Man
99 D3 **Ramsgate** U.K.
75 C2 **Ranaghat** India
61 C1 **Ranau** *Sabah* Malaysia
153 A4 **Rancagua** Chile
75 C2 **Ranchi** India
93 F4 **Randers** Denmark
54 B2 **Rangiora** N.Z.
54 C1 **Rangitaiki** *r.* N.Z.
62 A2 **Rangoon** Myanmar
75 C2 **Rangpur** Bangl.
129 E1 **Rankin Inlet** Can.
53 C2 **Rankin's Springs** Austr.
96 B2 **Rannoch Moor** *moorland* U.
63 A3 **Ranong** Thai.
59 C3 **Ransiki** Indon.
61 C2 **Rantaupanjang** Indon.
60 A1 **Rantauprapat** Indon.
92 I2 **Ranua** Fin.
78 B2 **Ranyah, Wādī** *watercourse* Saudi Arabia
49 I4 **Rapa** *i.* Fr. Polynesia
136 C2 **Rapid City** U.S.A.
88 B2 **Rapla** Estonia
74 A2 **Rapur** India
49 H4 **Rarotonga** *i.* Cook Is
153 B5 **Rasa, Punta** *pt* Arg.
79 C2 **Ra's al Khaymah** U.A.E.
117 B3 **Ras Dejen** *mt.* Eth.
88 B2 **Raseiniai** Lith.
81 C2 **Rasht** Iran
74 A2 **Ras Koh** *mt.* Pak.
88 C2 **Rasony** Belarus
87 D3 **Rasskazovo** Rus. Fed.
79 C2 **Ras Tannūrah** Saudi Arabia

1 D1 **Rastede** Ger.
3 F3 **Rätan** Sweden
4 B2 **Ratangarh** India
3 A2 **Rat Buri** Thai.
2 A1 **Rathedaung** Myanmar
1 F1 **Rathenow** Ger.
7 C1 **Rathlin Island** U.K.
4 B2 **Ratlam** India
3 B3 **Ratnagiri** India
3 C4 **Ratnapura** Sri Lanka
0 A1 **Ratne** Ukr.
3 C1 **Raton** U.S.A.
6 D2 **Rattray Head** U.K.
1 E1 **Ratzeburg** Ger.
2 B2 **Raufarhöfn** Iceland
4 C1 **Raukumara Range** *mts* N.Z.
3 H3 **Rauma** Fin.
1 C2 **Raung, Gunung** *vol.* Indon.
5 C2 **Raurkela** India
4 D1 **Ravalli** U.S.A.
1 C2 **Ravānsar** Iran
3 B2 **Ravenna** Italy
2 B2 **Ravensburg** Ger.
4 B1 **Ravi** *r.* Pak.
4 B1 **Rawalpindi** Pak.
3 D1 **Rawicz** Pol.
0 B3 **Rawlinna** Austr.
5 B2 **Rawlins** U.S.A.
3 B5 **Rawson** Arg.
3 C3 **Rayagada** India
9 E1 **Raychikhinsk** Rus. Fed.
8 B3 **Raydah** Yemen
7 E3 **Rayevskiy** Rus. Fed.
4 B1 **Raymond** U.S.A.
3 D2 **Raymond Terrace** Austr.
9 D3 **Raymondville** U.S.A.
5 C2 **Rayón** Mex.
3 B2 **Rayong** Thai.
3 A2 **Rayyis** Saudi Arabia
4 B2 **Raz, Pointe du** *pt* France
1 C2 **Razāzah, Buḩayrat ar** *l.* Iraq
0 C2 **Razgrad** Bulg.
0 C2 **Razim, Lacul** *lag.* Romania
0 B2 **Razlog** Bulg.
4 B2 **Ré, Île de** *i.* France
9 C3 **Reading** U.K.
1 D2 **Reading** U.S.A.
5 E2 **Rebiana Sand Sea** *des.* Libya
6 D1 **Rebun-tō** *i.* Japan
0 B3 **Recherche, Archipelago of the** *is* Austr.
9 D3 **Rechytsa** Belarus
1 E2 **Recife** Brazil
3 C3 **Recife, Cape** S. Africa
0 C2 **Recklinghausen** Ger.
2 C3 **Reconquista** Arg.
2 B2 **Red** *r.* U.S.A.
1 E1 **Red Bay** Can.
5 B2 **Red Bluff** U.S.A.
3 C1 **Redcar** U.K.
9 C2 **Redcliff** Can.
2 B2 **Red Cliffs** Austr.
3 C2 **Red Deer** Can.
5 D3 **Red Deer** *r.* Can.
9 D2 **Red Deer Lake** Can.
4 B2 **Redding** U.S.A.
9 C2 **Redditch** U.K.
7 D2 **Redfield** U.S.A.
0 A1 **Red Lake** Can.
7 E1 **Red Lakes** U.S.A.
4 E1 **Red Lodge** U.S.A.
4 B2 **Redmond** U.S.A.
7 D2 **Red Oak** U.S.A.
5 B2 **Redondo** Port.
9 B2 **Red Sea** Africa/Asia
3 B1 **Redstone** *r.* Can.
0 B1 **Reduzum** Neth.

137 E2 **Red Wing** U.S.A.
137 D2 **Redwood Falls** U.S.A.
97 C2 **Ree, Lough** *l.* Ireland
134 B2 **Reedsport** U.S.A.
54 B2 **Reefton** N.Z.
102 C2 **Regen** Ger.
155 E1 **Regência** Brazil
102 C2 **Regensburg** Ger.
114 C2 **Reggane** Alg.
109 C3 **Reggio di Calabria** Italy
108 B2 **Reggio nell'Emilia** Italy
110 B1 **Reghin** Romania
129 D2 **Regina** Can.
122 A1 **Rehoboth** Namibia
101 F2 **Reichenbach** Ger.
143 E1 **Reidsville** U.S.A.
99 C3 **Reigate** U.K.
105 C2 **Reims** France
101 E1 **Reinbek** Ger.
129 D2 **Reindeer** *r.* Can.
129 E2 **Reindeer Island** Can.
129 D2 **Reindeer Lake** Can.
92 F2 **Reine** Norway
100 C3 **Reinsfeld** Ger.
123 C2 **Reitz** S. Africa
122 B2 **Reivilo** S. Africa
129 D1 **Reliance** Can.
107 D2 **Relizane** Alg.
79 C2 **Remeshk** Iran
105 D2 **Remiremont** France
100 C2 **Remscheid** Ger.
102 B1 **Rendsburg** Ger.
141 D1 **Renfrew** Can.
60 B2 **Rengat** Indon.
90 B2 **Reni** Ukr.
52 B2 **Renmark** Austr.
100 D2 **Rennerod** Ger.
104 B2 **Rennes** France
129 D1 **Rennie Lake** Can.
108 B2 **Reno** *r.* Italy
135 C3 **Reno** U.S.A.
70 A3 **Renshou** China
140 B2 **Rensselaer** U.S.A.
75 C2 **Renukut** India
54 B2 **Renwick** N.Z.
58 C3 **Reo** Indon.
136 D3 **Republican** *r.* U.S.A.
127 F2 **Repulse Bay** Can.
150 A2 **Requena** Peru
107 C2 **Requena** Spain
154 B2 **Reserva** Brazil
152 C3 **Resistencia** Arg.
110 B1 **Reşiţa** Romania
126 E2 **Resolute** Can.
127 G2 **Resolution Island** Can.
105 C2 **Rethel** France
111 B3 **Rethymno** Greece
113 K9 **Réunion** *terr.* Indian Ocean
107 D1 **Reus** Spain
102 B2 **Reutlingen** Ger.
128 C2 **Revelstoke** Can.
144 A3 **Revillagigedo, Islas** *is* Mex.
128 A2 **Revillagigedo Island** U.S.A.
75 C2 **Rewa** India
134 D2 **Rexburg** U.S.A.
92 A3 **Reykjanestá** *pt* Iceland
92 A3 **Reykjavík** Iceland
145 C2 **Reynosa** Mex.
88 C2 **Rēzekne** Latvia
Rhein *r.* Ger. *see* **Rhine**
100 C1 **Rheine** Ger.
101 F1 **Rheinsberg** Ger.
Rhin *r.* France *see* **Rhine**
100 C2 **Rhine** *r.* Europe
140 B1 **Rhinelander** U.S.A.
101 F1 **Rhinluch** *marsh* Ger.
101 F1 **Rhinow** Ger.

141 E2 **Rhode Island** *state* U.S.A.
111 C3 **Rhodes** Greece
111 C3 **Rhodes** *i.* Greece
110 B2 **Rhodope Mountains** Bulg./Greece
105 C3 **Rhône** *r.* France/Switz.
Rhuthun U.K. *see* **Ruthin**
98 B2 **Rhyl** U.K.
154 C1 **Rianópolis** Brazil
60 B1 **Riau, Kepulauan** *is* Indon.
106 B1 **Ribadeo** Spain
106 B1 **Ribadesella** Spain
154 B2 **Ribas do Rio Pardo** Brazil
121 C2 **Ribáuè** Moz.
98 B2 **Ribble** *r.* U.K.
154 C2 **Ribeira** *r.* Brazil
154 C2 **Ribeirão Preto** Brazil
104 C2 **Ribérac** France
152 B2 **Riberalta** Bol.
90 B2 **Rîbniţa** Moldova
102 C1 **Ribnitz-Damgarten** Ger.
140 A1 **Rice Lake** U.S.A.
123 D2 **Richards Bay** S. Africa
126 B2 **Richardson Mountains** Can.
135 D3 **Richfield** U.S.A.
134 C1 **Richland** U.S.A.
140 A2 **Richland Center** U.S.A.
53 D2 **Richmond** *N.S.W.* Austr.
51 D2 **Richmond** *Qld* Austr.
54 B2 **Richmond** N.Z.
122 B3 **Richmond** S. Africa
98 C1 **Richmond** U.K.
140 C3 **Richmond** *IN* U.S.A.
140 C3 **Richmond** *KY* U.S.A.
141 D3 **Richmond** *VA* U.S.A.
130 C2 **Rideau Lakes** Can.
135 C3 **Ridgecrest** U.S.A.
102 C1 **Riesa** Ger.
100 D1 **Rieste** Ger.
123 B2 **Riet** *r.* S. Africa
101 D2 **Rietberg** Ger.
108 B2 **Rieti** Italy
136 B3 **Rifle** U.S.A.
88 B2 **Rīga** Latvia
88 B2 **Riga, Gulf of** Estonia/Latvia
79 C2 **Rīgān** Iran
134 D2 **Rigby** U.S.A.
131 E1 **Rigolet** Can.
93 H3 **Riihimäki** Fin.
108 B1 **Rijeka** Croatia
134 C2 **Riley** U.S.A.
78 B2 **Rimah, Wādī al** *watercourse* Saudi Arabia
103 E2 **Rimavská Sobota** Slovakia
128 C2 **Rimbey** Can.
108 B2 **Rimini** Italy
131 D2 **Rimouski** Can.
93 F3 **Ringebu** Norway
93 E4 **Ringkøbing** Denmark
92 G2 **Ringvassøya** *i.* Norway
101 D1 **Rinteln** Ger.
150 A2 **Riobamba** Ecuador
150 B3 **Rio Branco** Brazil
154 C3 **Rio Branco do Sul** Brazil
154 B2 **Rio Brilhante** Brazil
154 C2 **Rio Claro** Brazil
153 B4 **Río Colorado** Arg.
153 B4 **Río Cuarto** Arg.
155 D2 **Rio de Janeiro** Brazil
153 B6 **Río Gallegos** Arg.
153 B6 **Río Grande** Arg.
152 C4 **Rio Grande** Brazil
144 B2 **Río Grande** Mex.
139 D3 **Rio Grande** *r.* Mex./U.S.A.
139 D3 **Rio Grande City** U.S.A.
150 A1 **Ríohacha** Col.
150 A2 **Rioja** Peru

145 D2 **Río Lagartos** Mex.
105 C2 **Riom** France
152 B2 **Río Mulatos** Bol.
154 C3 **Rio Negro** Brazil
155 D1 **Rio Pardo de Minas** Brazil
138 B1 **Rio Rancho** U.S.A.
150 A2 **Río Tigre** Ecuador
154 B1 **Rio Verde** Brazil
145 C2 **Río Verde** Mex.
154 B1 **Rio Verde de Mato Grosso** Brazil
90 C1 **Ripky** Ukr.
98 C2 **Ripley** U.K.
107 D1 **Ripoll** Spain
98 C1 **Ripon** U.K.
66 D1 **Rishiri-tō** *i.* Japan
93 E4 **Risør** Norway
122 B2 **Ritchie** S. Africa
63 A2 **Ritchie's Archipelago** *is* India
134 C1 **Ritzville** U.S.A.
152 B3 **Rivadavia** Arg.
108 B1 **Riva del Garda** Italy
146 B3 **Rivas** Nic.
152 C4 **Rivera** Uru.
129 D2 **Riverhurst** Can.
52 B2 **Riverina** *reg.* Austr.
122 B3 **Riversdale** S. Africa
135 C4 **Riverside** U.S.A.
136 B2 **Riverton** U.S.A.
131 D2 **Riverview** Can.
104 C3 **Rivesaltes** France
131 D2 **Rivière-du-Loup** Can.
90 B1 **Rivne** Ukr.
54 B2 **Riwaka** N.Z.
78 B2 **Riyadh** Saudi Arabia
81 C1 **Rize** Turkey
70 B2 **Rizhao** China
105 C2 **Roanne** France
141 D3 **Roanoke** U.S.A.
143 E1 **Roanoke** *r.* U.S.A.
143 E1 **Roanoke Rapids** U.S.A.
52 A3 **Robe** Austr.
101 F1 **Röbel** Ger.
130 C1 **Robert-Bourassa, Réservoir** *resr* Can.
92 H3 **Robertsfors** Sweden
122 A3 **Robertson** S. Africa
114 A4 **Robertsport** Liberia
131 C2 **Roberval** Can.
50 A2 **Robinson Range** *hills* Austr.
52 B2 **Robinvale** Austr.
129 D2 **Roblin** Can.
128 C2 **Robson, Mount** Can.
108 B3 **Rocca Busambra** *mt. Sicilia* Italy
153 C4 **Rocha** Uru.
98 B2 **Rochdale** U.K.
154 B1 **Rochedo** Brazil
100 B2 **Rochefort** Belgium
104 B2 **Rochefort** France
137 E2 **Rochester** *MN* U.S.A.
141 E2 **Rochester** *NH* U.S.A.
141 D2 **Rochester** *NY* U.S.A.
140 B2 **Rockford** U.S.A.
51 E2 **Rockhampton** Austr.
143 D2 **Rock Hill** U.S.A.
50 A3 **Rockingham** Austr.
140 A2 **Rock Island** U.S.A.
136 B1 **Rock Springs** *MT* U.S.A.
139 C3 **Rocksprings** U.S.A.
136 B2 **Rock Springs** *WY* U.S.A.
136 C3 **Rocky Ford** U.S.A.
143 E1 **Rocky Mount** U.S.A.
128 C2 **Rocky Mountain House** Can.
124 G3 **Rocky Mountains** Can./U.S.A.
100 B3 **Rocroi** France
102 C1 **Rødbyhavn** Denmark
131 E1 **Roddickton** Can.
104 C3 **Rodez** France
89 F2 **Rodniki** Rus. Fed.
Rodos Greece *see* **Rhodes**
Rodos *i.* Greece *see* **Rhodes**
50 A2 **Roebourne** Austr.
50 B1 **Roebuck Bay** Austr.
123 C1 **Roedtan** S. Africa
100 B2 **Roermond** Neth.
100 A2 **Roeselare** Belgium
127 F2 **Roes Welcome Sound** *sea chan.* Can.
142 B1 **Rogers** U.S.A.
122 B3 **Roggeveldberge** *esc.* S. Africa
92 G2 **Rognan** Norway
134 B2 **Rogue** *r.* U.S.A.
88 B2 **Roja** Latvia
60 B1 **Rokan** *r.* Indon.
88 C2 **Rokiškis** Lith.
90 B1 **Rokytne** Ukr.
154 B2 **Rolândia** Brazil
137 E3 **Rolla** U.S.A.
51 D2 **Roma** Austr.
Roma Italy *see* **Rome**
123 C2 **Roma** Lesotho
139 D3 **Roma** U.S.A.
143 E2 **Romain, Cape** U.S.A.
110 C1 **Roman** Romania
59 C3 **Romang, Pulau** *i.* Indon.
110 B1 **Romania** *country* Europe
91 C3 **Roman-Kosh** *mt.* Ukr.
69 D1 **Romanovka** Rus. Fed.
105 D2 **Rombas** France
64 B1 **Romblon** Phil.
108 B2 **Rome** Italy
143 C2 **Rome** *GA* U.S.A.
141 D2 **Rome** *NY* U.S.A.
99 D3 **Romford** U.K.
105 C2 **Romilly-sur-Seine** France
91 C1 **Romny** Ukr.
104 C2 **Romorantin-Lanthenay** France
99 C3 **Romsey** U.K.
96 □ **Ronas Hill** U.K.
151 C3 **Roncador, Serra do** *hills* Brazil
106 B2 **Ronda** Spain
154 B2 **Rondon** Brazil
154 B1 **Rondonópolis** Brazil
74 B1 **Rondu** Pak.
71 A3 **Rong'an** China
71 A3 **Rongjiang** China
62 A1 **Rongklang Range** *mts* Myanmar
Rongmei China *see* **Hefeng**
93 F4 **Rønne** Denmark
55 P2 **Ronne Ice Shelf** Antarctica
101 D1 **Ronnenberg** Ger.
100 A2 **Ronse** Belgium
75 B2 **Roorkee** India
100 B2 **Roosendaal** Neth.
135 E2 **Roosevelt** U.S.A.
128 B2 **Roosevelt, Mount** Can.
55 K2 **Roosevelt Island** Antarctica
104 B3 **Roquefort** France
150 B1 **Roraima, Mount** Guyana
93 F3 **Røros** Norway
153 B4 **Rosario** Arg.
144 A1 **Rosario** *Baja California* Mex.
144 B2 **Rosario** *Sinaloa* Mex.
144 B2 **Rosario** *Sonora* Mex.
151 C3 **Rosário Oeste** Brazil
144 A2 **Rosarito** Mex.
109 C3 **Rosarno** Italy
104 B2 **Roscoff** France
97 B2 **Roscommon** Ireland
97 C2 **Roscrea** Ireland
147 D3 **Roseau** Dominica
137 D1 **Roseau** U.S.A.
134 B2 **Roseburg** U.S.A.
139 D3 **Rosenberg** U.S.A.
101 D1 **Rosengarten** Ger.
102 C2 **Rosenheim** Ger.
129 D2 **Rosetown** Can.
122 A2 **Rosh Pinah** Namibia
110 C2 **Roșiori de Vede** Romania
93 F4 **Roskilde** Denmark
89 D3 **Roslavl'** Rus. Fed.
109 C3 **Rossano** Italy
97 B1 **Rossan Point** Ireland
55 K1 **Ross Ice Shelf** Antarctica
131 D2 **Rossignol, Lake** Can.
128 C3 **Rossland** Can.
97 C2 **Rosslare** Ireland
114 A3 **Rosso** Maur.
105 D3 **Rosso, Capo** *c. Corse* Franc
99 B3 **Ross-on-Wye** U.K.
91 D1 **Rossosh'** Rus. Fed.
128 A1 **Ross River** Can.
55 K2 **Ross Sea** Antarctica
92 F2 **Røssvatnet** *l.* Norway
79 C2 **Rostāq** Iran
129 D2 **Rosthern** Can.
102 C1 **Rostock** Ger.
89 E2 **Rostov** Rus. Fed.
91 D2 **Rostov-na-Donu** Rus. Fed.
92 H2 **Rosvik** Sweden
138 C2 **Roswell** U.S.A.
59 D2 **Rota** *i.* N. Mariana Is
59 C3 **Rote** *i.* Indon.
101 D1 **Rotenburg (Wümme)** Ger.
102 C2 **Roth** Ger.
98 C1 **Rothbury** U.K.
98 C2 **Rotherham** U.K.
96 B3 **Rothesay** U.K.
53 C2 **Roto** Austr.
105 D3 **Rotondo, Monte** *mt. Corse* France
54 C1 **Rotorua** N.Z.
54 C1 **Rotorua, Lake** N.Z.
101 E2 **Rottenbach** Ger.
102 C2 **Rottenmann** Austria
100 B2 **Rotterdam** Neth.
102 B2 **Rottweil** Ger.
49 F3 **Rotuma** *i.* Fiji
105 C1 **Roubaix** France
104 C2 **Rouen** France
Roulers Belgium *see* **Roeselare**
53 D2 **Round Mountain** Austr.
131 E2 **Round Pond** *l.* Can.
139 D2 **Round Rock** U.S.A.
134 E1 **Roundup** U.S.A.
96 C1 **Rousay** *i.* U.K.
130 C2 **Rouyn-Noranda** Can.
92 I2 **Rovaniemi** Fin.
91 D2 **Roven'ki** Rus. Fed.
91 D2 **Roven'ky** Ukr.
108 B1 **Rovereto** Italy
63 B2 **Rôviěng Tbong** Cambodia
108 B1 **Rovigo** Italy
108 B1 **Rovinj** Croatia
53 C1 **Rowena** Austr.
64 B1 **Roxas** *Capiz* Phil.
64 B1 **Roxas** *Oriental Mindoro* Ph
64 A1 **Roxas** *Palawan* Phil.
64 B2 **Roxas** *Zamboanga del Nort* Phil.
52 A2 **Roxby Downs** Austr.
138 C1 **Roy** U.S.A.
140 B1 **Royale, Isle** *i.* U.S.A.
104 B2 **Royan** France
99 C2 **Royston** U.K.
90 C2 **Rozdil'na** Ukr.
91 C2 **Rozdol'ne** Ukr.

00 B3 **Rozoy-sur-Serre** France
87 D3 **Rtishchevo** Rus. Fed.
54 C1 **Ruapehu, Mount** *vol.* N.Z.
54 A3 **Ruapuke Island** N.Z.
78 B3 **Rub' al Khālī** *des.* Saudi Arabia
91 D2 **Rubizhne** Ukr.
77 E1 **Rubtsovsk** Rus. Fed.
35 C2 **Ruby Mountains** U.S.A.
66 C2 **Rudnaya Pristan'** Rus. Fed.
89 D3 **Rudnya** Rus. Fed.
76 C1 **Rudnyy** Kazakh.
82 E1 **Rudol'fa, Ostrov** *i.* Rus. Fed.
01 E2 **Rudolstadt** Ger.
19 D3 **Rufiji** *r.* Tanz.
53 B4 **Rufino** Arg.
21 B2 **Rufunsa** Zambia
70 C2 **Rugao** China
99 C2 **Rugby** U.K.
36 C1 **Rugby** U.S.A.
02 C1 **Rügen** *i.* Ger.
01 E2 **Ruhla** Ger.
88 B2 **Ruhnu** *i.* Estonia
00 C2 **Ruhr** *r.* Ger.
71 C3 **Rui'an** China
38 B2 **Ruidoso** U.S.A.
44 B2 **Ruiz** Mex.
19 D3 **Rukwa, Lake** Tanz.
96 A2 **Rum** *i.* U.K.
09 C1 **Ruma** Serbia
78 B2 **Rumāh** Saudi Arabia
17 A4 **Rumbek** Sudan
05 D2 **Rumilly** France
50 C1 **Rum Jungle** Austr.
54 B2 **Runanga** N.Z.
98 B2 **Runcorn** U.K.
20 A2 **Rundu** Namibia
68 B2 **Ruoqiang** China
30 C1 **Rupert** *r.* Can.
30 C1 **Rupert Bay** Can.
21 C2 **Rusape** Zimbabwe
10 C2 **Ruse** Bulg.
77 D3 **Rushon** Tajik.
36 C2 **Rushville** U.S.A.
53 C3 **Rushworth** Austr.
29 D2 **Russell** Can.
54 B1 **Russell** N.Z.
42 C2 **Russellville** *AL* U.S.A.
42 B1 **Russellville** *AR* U.S.A.
40 B3 **Russellville** *KY* U.S.A.
01 D2 **Rüsselsheim** Ger.
82 F2 **Russian Federation** *country* Asia/Europe
23 C2 **Rustenburg** S. Africa
42 B2 **Ruston** U.S.A.
98 B2 **Ruthin** U.K.
41 E2 **Rutland** U.S.A.
19 E4 **Ruvuma** *r.* Moz./Tanz.
79 C2 **Ruweis** U.A.E.
77 C1 **Ruzayevka** Kazakh.
87 D3 **Ruzayevka** Rus. Fed.
19 C3 **Rwanda** *country* Africa
89 E3 **Ryazan'** Rus. Fed.
89 F3 **Ryazhsk** Rus. Fed.
86 C2 **Rybachiy, Poluostrov** *pen.* Rus. Fed.
89 E2 **Rybinsk** Rus. Fed.
89 E2 **Rybinskoye Vodokhranilishche** *resr* Rus. Fed.
03 D1 **Rybnik** Pol.
89 E3 **Rybnoye** Rus. Fed.
99 D3 **Rye** U.K.
89 D3 **Ryl'sk** Rus. Fed.
67 C3 **Ryōtsu** Japan
69 E3 **Ryukyu Islands** Japan
03 E1 **Rzeszów** Pol.
89 D2 **Rzhev** Rus. Fed.

S

79 C2 **Sa'ādatābād** Iran
101 E2 **Saale** *r.* Ger.
101 E2 **Saalfeld** Ger.
102 B2 **Saarbrücken** Ger.
88 B2 **Saaremaa** *i.* Estonia
92 I2 **Saarenkylä** Fin.
93 I3 **Saarijärvi** Fin.
102 B2 **Saarlouis** Ger.
80 B2 **Sab' Ābār** Syria
107 D1 **Sabadell** Spain
61 C1 **Sabah** *state* Malaysia
61 C2 **Sabalana** *i.* Indon.
155 D1 **Sabará** Brazil
108 B2 **Sabaudia** Italy
115 D2 **Sabhā** Libya
123 D2 **Sabie** *r.* Moz./S. Africa
145 B2 **Sabinas** Mex.
145 B2 **Sabinas Hidalgo** Mex.
131 D2 **Sable, Cape** Can.
143 D3 **Sable, Cape** U.S.A.
131 E2 **Sable Island** Can.
106 B1 **Sabugal** Port.
78 B3 **Şabyā** Saudi Arabia
76 B3 **Sabzevār** Iran
120 A2 **Sachanga** Angola
130 A1 **Sachigo Lake** Can.
65 B3 **Sach'on** S. Korea
126 C2 **Sachs Harbour** Can.
135 B3 **Sacramento** U.S.A.
138 B2 **Sacramento Mountains** U.S.A.
135 B2 **Sacramento Valley** U.S.A.
123 C3 **Sada** S. Africa
107 C1 **Sádaba** Spain
78 B3 **Şa'dah** Yemen
62 A1 **Sadiya** India
67 C3 **Sadoga-shima** *i.* Japan
107 D2 **Sa Dragonera** *i.* Spain
93 F4 **Säffle** Sweden
138 B2 **Safford** U.S.A.
99 D2 **Saffron Walden** U.K.
114 B1 **Safi** Morocco
76 C3 **Safid Kūh** *mts* Afgh.
86 D2 **Safonovo** *Arkhangel'skaya Oblast'* Rus. Fed.
89 D2 **Safonovo** *Smolenskaya Oblast'* Rus. Fed.
78 B2 **Safrā' as Sark** *esc.* Saudi Arabia
75 C2 **Saga** China
67 B4 **Saga** Japan
62 A1 **Sagaing** Myanmar
67 C3 **Sagamihara** Japan
75 B2 **Sagar** India
140 C2 **Saginaw** U.S.A.
140 C2 **Saginaw Bay** U.S.A.
106 B2 **Sagres** Port.
146 B2 **Sagua la Grande** Cuba
141 F1 **Saguenay** *r.* Can.
107 C2 **Sagunto** Spain
76 B2 **Sagyndyk, Mys** *pt* Kazakh.
106 B1 **Sahagún** Spain
114 C3 **Sahara** *des.* Africa
Saharan Atlas *mts* Alg. *see* **Atlas Saharien**
75 B2 **Saharanpur** India
75 C2 **Saharsa** India
114 B3 **Sahel** *reg.* Africa
144 B2 **Sahuayo** Mex.
78 B2 **Şāḩūq** *reg.* Saudi Arabia
Saïda Lebanon *see* **Sidon**
75 C2 **Saidpur** Bangl.
Saigon Vietnam *see* **Ho Chi Minh City**
62 A1 **Saiha** India
69 D2 **Saihan Tal** China
67 B4 **Saiki** Japan
93 I3 **Saimaa** *l.* Fin.
144 B2 **Sain Alto** Mex.
96 C3 **St Abb's Head** U.K.
99 C3 **St Albans** U.K.
99 B3 **St Aldhelm's Head** U.K.
96 C2 **St Andrews** U.K.
131 E1 **St Anthony** Can.
134 D2 **St Anthony** U.S.A.
52 B3 **St Arnaud** Austr.
131 E1 **St-Augustin** Can.
131 E1 **St Augustin** *r.* Can.
143 D3 **St Augustine** U.S.A.
99 A3 **St Austell** U.K.
104 C2 **St-Avertin** France
98 B1 **St Bees Head** U.K.
105 D3 **St-Bonnet-en-Champsaur** France
99 A3 **St Bride's Bay** U.K.
104 B2 **St-Brieuc** France
130 C2 **St Catharines** Can.
99 C3 **St Catherine's Point** U.K.
137 E3 **St Charles** U.S.A.
140 C2 **St Clair, Lake** Can./U.S.A.
105 D2 **St-Claude** France
137 E1 **St Cloud** U.S.A.
140 A1 **St Croix** *r.* U.S.A.
147 D3 **St Croix** *i.* Virgin Is (U.S.A.)
105 C2 **St-Dizier** France
131 D2 **Ste-Anne-des-Monts** Can.
105 D2 **St-Égrève** France
126 B2 **St Elias Mountains** Can.
131 D1 **Ste-Marguerite** *r.* Can.
129 E2 **Sainte Rose du Lac** Can.
104 B2 **Saintes** France
105 C2 **St-Étienne** France
108 A2 **St-Florent** *Corse* France
105 C2 **St-Flour** France
136 C3 **St Francis** U.S.A.
104 C3 **St-Gaudens** France
53 C1 **St George** Austr.
135 D3 **St George** U.S.A.
143 D3 **St George Island** U.S.A.
131 C2 **St-Georges** Can.
147 D3 **St George's** Grenada
97 C3 **St George's Channel** Ireland/U.K.
105 D2 **St Gotthard Pass** Switz.
113 E8 **St Helena** *terr.* S. Atlantic Ocean
122 A3 **St Helena Bay** S. Africa
122 A3 **St Helena Bay** S. Africa
98 B2 **St Helens** U.K.
134 B1 **St Helens, Mount** *vol.* U.S.A.
95 C4 **St Helier** Channel Is
100 B2 **St-Hubert** Belgium
141 E1 **St-Hyacinthe** Can.
140 C1 **St Ignace** U.S.A.
130 B2 **St Ignace Island** Can.
99 A3 **St Ives** U.K.
128 A2 **St James, Cape** Can.
131 C2 **St-Jean, Lac** *l.* Can.
104 B2 **St-Jean-d'Angély** France
104 B2 **St-Jean-de-Monts** France
130 C2 **St-Jean-sur-Richelieu** Can.
141 E1 **St-Jérôme** Can.
134 C1 **St Joe** *r.* U.S.A.
131 D2 **Saint John** Can.
141 F1 **St John** *r.* U.S.A.
147 D3 **St John's** Antigua
131 E2 **St John's** Can.
138 B2 **St Johns** U.S.A.
141 E2 **St Johnsbury** U.S.A.
137 E3 **St Joseph** U.S.A.
130 A1 **St Joseph, Lake** Can.
130 B2 **St Joseph Island** Can.

104 C2 **St-Junien** France
94 B2 **St Kilda** *is* U.K.
147 D3 **St Kitts and Nevis** *country* West Indies
St-Laurent, Golfe du *g.* Can. *see* **St Lawrence, Gulf of**
151 C1 **St-Laurent-du-Maroni** Fr. Guiana
131 D2 **St Lawrence** *inlet* Can.
131 D2 **St Lawrence, Gulf of** Can.
83 N2 **St Lawrence Island** U.S.A.
104 B2 **St-Lô** France
114 A3 **St-Louis** Senegal
137 E3 **St Louis** U.S.A.
137 E1 **St Louis** *r.* U.S.A.
147 D3 **St Lucia** *country* West Indies
123 D2 **St Lucia Estuary** S. Africa
104 B2 **St-Malo** France
104 B2 **St-Malo, Golfe de** *g.* France
122 A3 **St Martin, Cape** S. Africa
141 D2 **St Marys** U.S.A.
130 C2 **St-Maurice** *r.* Can.
104 B2 **St-Nazaire** France
104 C1 **St-Omer** France
129 C2 **St Paul** Can.
137 E2 **St Paul** U.S.A.
137 E2 **St Peter** U.S.A.
95 C4 **St Peter Port** Channel Is
89 D2 **St Petersburg** Rus. Fed.
143 D3 **St Petersburg** U.S.A.
131 E2 **St-Pierre** St Pierre and Miquelon
131 E2 **St Pierre and Miquelon** *terr.* N. America
104 B2 **St-Pierre-d'Oléron** France
105 C2 **St-Pourçain-sur-Sioule** France
131 D2 **St Quentin** Can.
105 C2 **St-Quentin** France
131 D2 **St-Siméon** Can.
129 E2 **St Theresa Point** Can.
130 B2 **St Thomas** Can.
105 D3 **St-Tropez** France
105 D3 **St-Tropez, Cap de** *c.* France
52 A3 **St Vincent, Gulf** Austr.
147 D3 **St Vincent and the Grenadines** *country* West Indies
100 C2 **St-Vith** Belgium
129 D2 **St Walburg** Can.
104 C2 **St-Yrieix-la-Perche** France
59 D1 **Saipan** *i.* N. Mariana Is
67 C3 **Saitama** Japan
152 B2 **Sajama, Nevado** *mt.* Bol.
122 B2 **Sak** *watercourse* S. Africa
67 C4 **Sakai** Japan
67 B4 **Sakaide** Japan
78 B2 **Sakākah** Saudi Arabia
136 C1 **Sakakawea, Lake** U.S.A.
111 D2 **Sakarya** *r.* Turkey
66 C3 **Sakata** Japan
65 B1 **Sakchu** N. Korea
83 K3 **Sakhalin** *i.* Rus. Fed.
123 C2 **Sakhile** S. Africa
81 C1 **Şäki** Azer.
88 B3 **Šakiai** Lith.
69 E3 **Sakishima-shotō** *is* Japan
62 B2 **Sakon Nakhon** Thai.
122 B3 **Sakrivier** S. Africa
67 D3 **Sakura** Japan
91 C2 **Saky** Ukr.
93 G4 **Sala** Sweden
130 C2 **Salaberry-de-Valleyfield** Can.
88 B2 **Salacgrīva** Latvia
109 C2 **Sala Consilina** Italy
135 C4 **Salada, Laguna** *salt l.* Mex.
152 B4 **Salado** *r.* Arg.
145 C2 **Salado** *r.* Mex.
114 B4 **Salaga** Ghana
122 B1 **Salajwe** Botswana
115 D3 **Salal** Chad
78 A2 **Salâla** Sudan
79 C3 **Şalālah** Oman
145 B2 **Salamanca** Mex.
106 B1 **Salamanca** Spain
106 B1 **Salas** Spain
63 B2 **Salavan** Laos
59 C3 **Salawati** *i.* Indon.
58 C3 **Salayar** *i.* Indon.
104 C2 **Salbris** France
88 C3 **Šalčininkai** Lith.
106 C1 **Saldaña** Spain
122 A3 **Saldanha** S. Africa
88 B2 **Saldus** Latvia
53 C3 **Sale** Austr.
86 F2 **Salekhard** Rus. Fed.
73 B3 **Salem** India
137 E3 **Salem** *MO* U.S.A.
134 B2 **Salem** *OR* U.S.A.
96 B2 **Salen** U.K.
109 B2 **Salerno** Italy
98 B2 **Salford** U.K.
151 E2 **Salgado** *r.* Brazil
103 D2 **Salgótarján** Hungary
151 E2 **Salgueiro** Brazil
136 B3 **Salida** U.S.A.
111 C3 **Salihli** Turkey
88 C3 **Salihorsk** Belarus
121 C2 **Salima** Malawi
121 C2 **Salimo** Moz.
137 D3 **Salina** U.S.A.
108 B3 **Salina, Isola** *i.* Italy
145 C3 **Salina Cruz** Mex.
155 D1 **Salinas** Brazil
144 B2 **Salinas** Mex.
135 B3 **Salinas** U.S.A.
107 D2 **Salines, Cap de ses** *c.* Spain
151 D2 **Salinópolis** Brazil
99 C3 **Salisbury** U.K.
141 D3 **Salisbury** *MD* U.S.A.
143 D1 **Salisbury** *NC* U.S.A.
99 B3 **Salisbury Plain** U.K.
151 D2 **Salitre** *r.* Brazil
92 I2 **Salla** Fin.
127 F2 **Salluit** Can.
75 C2 **Sallyana** Nepal
81 C2 **Salmās** Iran
134 D1 **Salmon** U.S.A.
134 C1 **Salmon** *r.* U.S.A.
128 C2 **Salmon Arm** Can.
134 C2 **Salmon River Mountains** U.S.A.
100 C3 **Salmtal** Ger.
93 H3 **Salo** Fin.
87 D4 **Sal'sk** Rus. Fed.
122 B3 **Salt** *watercourse* S. Africa
138 A2 **Salt** *r.* U.S.A.
152 B3 **Salta** Arg.
145 B2 **Saltillo** Mex.
134 D2 **Salt Lake City** U.S.A.
154 C2 **Salto** Brazil
152 C4 **Salto** Uru.
155 E1 **Salto da Divisa** Brazil
154 B2 **Salto del Guairá** Para.
135 C4 **Salton Sea** *salt l.* U.S.A.
143 D2 **Saluda** U.S.A.
108 A2 **Saluzzo** Italy
151 E3 **Salvador** Brazil
79 C2 **Salwah** Saudi Arabia
62 A1 **Salween** *r.* China/Myanmar
81 C2 **Salyan** Azer.
102 C2 **Salzburg** Austria
101 E1 **Salzgitter** Ger.
101 D2 **Salzkotten** Ger.
101 E1 **Salzwedel** Ger.
144 B1 **Samalayuca** Mex.
66 D2 **Samani** Japan
64 B1 **Samar** *i.* Phil.
87 E3 **Samara** Rus. Fed.
61 C2 **Samarinda** Indon.
77 C3 **Samarqand** Uzbek.
81 C2 **Sāmarrā'** Iraq
81 C1 **Şamaxı** Azer.
119 C3 **Samba** Dem. Rep. Congo
61 C1 **Sambaliung** *mts* Indon.
75 C2 **Sambalpur** India
61 C2 **Sambar, Tanjung** *pt* Indon.
61 B1 **Sambas** Indon.
121 E2 **Sambava** Madag.
90 A2 **Sambir** Ukr.
153 C4 **Samborombón, Bahía** *b.* Arg.
65 B2 **Samch'ŏk** S. Korea
81 C2 **Samdi Dag** *mt.* Turkey
119 D3 **Same** Tanz.
78 B2 **Samīrah** Saudi Arabia
65 B1 **Samjiyŏn** N. Korea
49 G3 **Samoa** *country* S. Pacific Ocean
109 C1 **Samobor** Croatia
111 C3 **Samos** *i.* Greece
111 C2 **Samothraki** Greece
111 C2 **Samothraki** *i.* Greece
61 C2 **Sampit** Indon.
119 C3 **Sampwe** Dem. Rep. Congo
139 E2 **Sam Rayburn Reservoir** U.S.A.
80 B1 **Samsun** Turkey
81 C1 **Samtredia** Georgia
63 B3 **Samui, Ko** *i.* Thai.
63 B2 **Samut Songkhram** Thai.
114 B3 **San** Mali
78 B3 **Şan'ā'** Yemen
118 A2 **Sanaga** *r.* Cameroon
81 C2 **Sanandaj** Iran
146 B3 **San Andrés, Isla de** *i.* Caribbean Sea
138 B2 **San Andres Mountains** U.S.A.
145 C3 **San Andrés Tuxtla** Mex.
139 C2 **San Angelo** U.S.A.
139 D3 **San Antonio** U.S.A.
135 C4 **San Antonio, Mount** U.S.A.
152 B3 **San Antonio de los Cobres** Arg.
153 B5 **San Antonio Oeste** Arg.
108 B2 **San Benedetto del Tronto** Italy
144 A3 **San Benedicto, Isla** *i.* Mex.
135 C4 **San Bernardino** U.S.A.
135 C4 **San Bernardino Mountains** U.S.A.
143 C3 **San Blas, Cape** U.S.A.
152 B2 **San Borja** Bol.
144 B2 **San Buenaventura** Mex.
64 B1 **San Carlos** Phil.
147 D4 **San Carlos** Venez.
153 A5 **San Carlos de Bariloche** Arg.
147 C4 **San Carlos del Zulia** Venez.
135 C4 **San Clemente Island** U.S.A.
104 C2 **Sancoins** France
150 A1 **San Cristóbal** Venez.
145 C3 **San Cristóbal de las Casas** Mex.
146 C2 **Sancti Spíritus** Cuba
123 D1 **Sand** *r.* S. Africa
61 C1 **Sandakan** *Sabah* Malaysia
93 E3 **Sandane** Norway
111 B2 **Sandanski** Bulg.
96 C1 **Sanday** *i.* U.K.
139 C2 **Sanderson** U.S.A.
150 B3 **Sandia** Peru
135 C4 **San Diego** U.S.A.
80 B2 **Sandıklı** Turkey
93 E4 **Sandnes** Norway

F2 Sandnessjøen Norway	134 B1 San Juan Islands U.S.A.	145 C3 Santa Cruz Barillas Guat.
C3 Sandoa Dem. Rep. Congo	144 B2 San Juanito Mex.	155 E1 Santa Cruz Cabrália Brazil
E1 Sandomierz Pol.	136 B3 San Juan Mountains U.S.A.	107 C3 Santa Cruz de Moya Spain
E2 Sandovo Rus. Fed.	153 B5 San Julián Arg.	114 A2 Santa Cruz de Tenerife Islas
B1 Sandoy i. Faroe Is	75 C2 Sankh r. India	Canarias
C1 Sandpoint U.S.A.	105 D2 Sankt Gallen Switz.	135 C3 Santa Cruz Island U.S.A.
C3 Sandu China	105 D2 Sankt Moritz Switz.	48 F3 Santa Cruz Islands
B1 Sandur Faroe Is	Sankt-Peterburg Rus. Fed. see	Solomon Is
C2 Sandusky U.S.A.	St Petersburg	152 B4 Santa Fé Arg.
B3 Sandveld mts S. Africa	102 C2 Sankt Veit an der Glan Austria	138 B1 Santa Fe U.S.A.
F3 Sandvika Norway	100 C3 Sankt Wendel Ger.	154 B1 Santa Helena de Goiás Brazil
G3 Sandviken Sweden	80 B2 Şanlıurfa Turkey	153 B4 Santa Isabel Arg.
B3 Sandwich Bay Can.	138 B3 San Lorenzo Mex.	154 B1 Santa Luisa, Serra de hills
D2 Sandy Bay Can.	106 B2 Sanlúcar de Barrameda Spain	Brazil
A1 Sandy Cape Austr.	144 B2 San Lucas Mex.	152 C3 Santa Maria Brazil
A1 Sandy Lake Can.	153 B4 San Luis Arg.	144 B1 Santa María r. Mex.
B1 Sandy Lake Can.	145 B2 San Luis de la Paz Mex.	135 B4 Santa Maria U.S.A.
A1 San Felipe Baja California	138 A2 San Luisito Mex.	123 D2 Santa Maria, Cabo c. Moz.
Mex.	135 B3 San Luis Obispo U.S.A.	106 B2 Santa Maria, Cabo de c. Port.
B2 San Felipe Guanajuato Mex.	145 B2 San Luis Potosí Mex.	151 D2 Santa Maria das Barreiras
B1 San Felipe Venez.	141 A1 San Luis Río Colorado Mex.	Brazil
B1 San Fernando Baja California	139 D3 San Marcos U.S.A.	109 C3 Santa Maria di Leuca, Capo c.
Mex.	108 B2 San Marino country Europe	Italy
C2 San Fernando Tamaulipas	108 B2 San Marino San Marino	150 A1 Santa Marta Col.
Mex.	144 B2 San Martín de Bolaños Mex.	135 C4 Santa Monica U.S.A.
B1 San Fernando La Union Phil.	153 A5 San Martín de los Andes Arg.	152 B3 Santana Brazil
B1 San Fernando Pampanga Phil.	153 B5 San Matías, Golfo g. Arg.	106 C1 Santander Spain
B2 San Fernando Spain	70 B2 Sanmenxia China	108 A3 Sant'Antioco Sardegna Italy
D3 San Fernando Trin. and Tob.	146 B3 San Miguel El Salvador	108 A3 Sant'Antioco, Isola di i.
B1 San Fernando de Apure	152 B3 San Miguel de Tucumán Arg.	Sardegna Italy
Venez.	144 B2 San Miguel Sola de Vega	107 D2 Sant Antoni de Portmany
D3 Sanford FL U.S.A.	Mex.	Spain
F2 Sanford ME U.S.A.	71 B3 Sanming China	151 C2 Santarém Brazil
B2 San Francisco Arg.	153 B4 San Nicolás de los Arroyos	106 B2 Santarém Port.
E3 San Francisco U.S.A.	Arg.	154 B1 Santa Rita do Araguaia Brazil
D2 San Francisco Javier Spain	135 C4 San Nicolas Island U.S.A.	153 B4 Santa Rosa Arg.
J2 Sangar Rus. Fed.	123 C2 Sannieshof S. Africa	152 C3 Santa Rosa Brazil
A3 San Gavino Monreale	103 E2 Sanok Pol.	135 B3 Santa Rosa CA U.S.A.
Sardegna Italy	64 B1 San Pablo Phil.	138 C2 Santa Rosa NM U.S.A.
E2 Sangerhausen Ger.	144 B2 San Pablo Balleza Mex.	146 B3 Santa Rosa de Copán Hond.
C1 Sanggau Indon.	152 B3 San Pedro Bol.	135 B4 Santa Rosa Island U.S.A.
C3 Sangha r. Congo	152 B2 San Pedro Bol.	144 A2 Santa Rosalía Mex.
C3 San Giovanni in Fiore Italy	114 B4 San-Pédro Côte d'Ivoire	152 B3 Santiago Brazil
E1 Sangir i. Indon.	138 A2 San Pedro Mex.	153 A4 Santiago Chile
B2 Sangir, Kepulauan is Indon.	106 B2 San Pedro watercourse U.S.A.	147 C3 Santiago Dom. Rep.
E1 Sangju S. Korea	106 B2 San Pedro, Sierra de mts	144 B2 Santiago Mex.
C1 Sangkulirang Indon.	Spain	146 C4 Santiago Panama
C3 Sangli India	144 B2 San Pedro de las Colonias	64 B1 Santiago Phil.
B2 Sangmélima Cameroon	Mex.	106 B1 Santiago de Compostela
C3 Sango Zimbabwe	146 B3 San Pedro Sula Hond.	Spain
B3 Sangre de Cristo Range mts	108 A3 San Pietro, Isola di i. Sardegna	144 B2 Santiago Ixcuintla Mex.
U.S.A.	Italy	144 B2 Santiago Papasquiaro Mex.
C2 Sangsang China	144 A1 San Quintín, Cabo c. Mex.	107 C2 Sant Joan de Labritja Spain
A2 San Hipólito, Punta pt Mex.	153 B4 San Rafael Arg.	107 D1 Sant Jordi, Golf de g. Spain
C2 San Ignacio Mex.	108 A2 San Remo Italy	155 D2 Santo Amaro de Campos
C1 Sanikiluaq Can.	146 B3 San Salvador El Salvador	Brazil
C3 Sanjiang China	152 B3 San Salvador de Jujuy Arg.	155 D2 Santo André Brazil
B3 San Joaquin r. U.S.A.	109 C2 San Severo Italy	152 C3 Santo Ângelo Brazil
B3 San Jorge, Golfo de g. Arg.	152 B2 Sanski Most Bos.-Herz.	154 B3 Santo Antônio da Platina
B4 San Jose Costa Rica	152 B2 Santa Ana Bol.	Brazil
B4 San Jose Nueva Ecija Phil.	146 B3 Santa Ana El Salvador	151 E3 Santo Antônio de Jesus
B1 San Jose Occidental Mindoro	144 A1 Santa Ana Mex.	Brazil
Phil.	135 C4 Santa Ana U.S.A.	150 B2 Santo Antônio do Içá Brazil
B3 San Jose U.S.A.	144 B2 Santa Bárbara Mex.	155 C2 Santo Antônio do Monte
A2 San José, Isla i. Mex.	135 C4 Santa Barbara U.S.A.	Brazil
B2 San José de Bavicora Mex.	154 B3 Santa Bárbara, Serra de hills	147 D3 Santo Domingo Dom. Rep.
B1 San Jose de Buenavista Phil.	Brazil	138 B1 Santo Domingo Pueblo
B2 San José de Comondú Mex.	152 B3 Santa Catalina Chile	U.S.A.
B2 San José del Cabo Mex.	150 B3 Santa Clara Col.	111 C3 Santorini i. Greece
A1 San José del Guaviare Col.	146 C2 Santa Clara Cuba	155 C2 Santos Brazil
A1 San Juan Arg.	135 C4 Santa Clarita U.S.A.	152 C3 Santo Tomé Arg.
B6 San Juan r. Costa Rica/Nic.	109 C3 Santa Croce, Capo c. Sicilia	153 A5 San Valentín, Cerro mt. Chile
D3 San Juan Puerto Rico	Italy	146 B3 San Vicente El Salvador
C3 San Juan r. U.S.A.	153 B6 Santa Cruz r. Arg.	150 A3 San Vicente de Cañete Peru
B1 San Juan Bautista Tuxtepec	152 B2 Santa Cruz Bol.	108 A2 San Vincenzo Italy
Mex.	64 B1 Santa Cruz Phil.	108 B3 San Vito, Capo c. Sicilia Italy
	135 B3 Santa Cruz U.S.A.	

71 A4 **Sanya** China
155 C2 **São Bernardo do Campo** Brazil
152 C3 **São Borja** Brazil
154 C2 **São Carlos** Brazil
151 C3 **São Félix** *Mato Grosso* Brazil
151 C2 **São Félix** *Pará* Brazil
155 D2 **São Fidélis** Brazil
155 D1 **São Francisco** Brazil
151 E3 **São Francisco** *r.* Brazil
154 C3 **São Francisco, Ilha de** *i.* Brazil
154 C3 **São Francisco do Sul** Brazil
152 C4 **São Gabriel** Brazil
155 D2 **São Gonçalo** Brazil
155 C1 **São Gotardo** Brazil
155 D2 **São João da Barra** Brazil
155 C2 **São João da Boa Vista** Brazil
106 B1 **São João da Madeira** Port.
155 D1 **São João do Paraíso** Brazil
155 D2 **São João Nepomuceno** Brazil
154 C2 **São Joaquim da Barra** Brazil
154 C2 **São José do Rio Preto** Brazil
155 C2 **São José dos Campos** Brazil
154 C3 **São José dos Pinhais** Brazil
155 C2 **São Lourenço** Brazil
151 D2 **São Luís** Brazil
154 C2 **São Manuel** Brazil
154 C1 **São Marcos** *r.* Brazil
151 D2 **São Marcos, Baía de** *b.* Brazil
155 E1 **São Mateus** Brazil
155 C2 **São Paulo** Brazil
151 D2 **São Raimundo Nonato** Brazil
155 C1 **São Romão** Brazil
155 C2 **São Sebastião, Ilha do** *i.* Brazil
154 C2 **São Sebastião do Paraíso** Brazil
154 B1 **São Simão** Brazil
154 B1 **São Simão, Barragem de** *resr* Brazil
59 C2 **Sao-Siu** Indon.
113 F6 **São Tomé** São Tomé and Príncipe
155 D2 **São Tomé, Cabo de** *c.* Brazil
113 F6 **São Tomé and Príncipe** *country* Africa
155 C2 **São Vicente** Brazil
106 B2 **São Vicente, Cabo de** *c.* Port.
59 C3 **Saparua** Indon.
89 F3 **Sapozhok** Rus. Fed.
66 D2 **Sapporo** Japan
109 C2 **Sapri** Italy
81 C2 **Saqqez** Iran
81 C2 **Sarāb** Iran
63 B2 **Sara Buri** Thai.
109 C2 **Sarajevo** Bos.-Herz.
76 B1 **Saraktash** Rus. Fed.
141 E2 **Saranac Lake** U.S.A.
109 D3 **Sarandë** Albania
64 B2 **Sarangani Islands** Phil.
87 D3 **Saransk** Rus. Fed.
87 E3 **Sarapul** Rus. Fed.
143 D3 **Sarasota** U.S.A.
90 B2 **Sarata** Ukr.
136 B2 **Saratoga** U.S.A.
141 E2 **Saratoga Springs** U.S.A.
61 C1 **Saratok** *Sarawak* Malaysia
87 D3 **Saratov** Rus. Fed.
79 D2 **Saravan** Iran
61 C1 **Sarawak** *state* Malaysia
110 C2 **Saray** Turkey
111 C3 **Sarayköy** Turkey
79 D2 **Sarbāz** Iran
74 B2 **Sardarshahr** India
Sardegna *i.* Italy *see* **Sardinia**
108 A2 **Sardinia** *i.* Italy
92 G2 **Sarektjåkkå** *mt.* Sweden
77 C3 **Sar-e Pol** Afgh.
158 B3 **Sargasso Sea** N. Atlantic Ocean
74 B1 **Sargodha** Pak.
115 D4 **Sarh** Chad
79 D2 **Sarhad** *reg.* Iran
81 D2 **Sārī** Iran
111 C3 **Sarıgöl** Turkey
81 C1 **Sarıkamış** Turkey
61 C1 **Sarikei** *Sarawak* Malaysia
51 D2 **Sarina** Austr.
115 D2 **Sarīr Tibesti** *des.* Libya
65 B2 **Sariwŏn** N. Korea
111 C2 **Sarıyer** Turkey
77 D2 **Sarkand** Kazakh.
111 C2 **Şarköy** Turkey
59 D3 **Sarmi** Indon.
140 C2 **Sarnia** Can.
90 B1 **Sarny** Ukr.
60 B2 **Sarolangun** Indon.
111 B3 **Saronikos Kolpos** *g.* Greece
111 C2 **Saros Körfezi** *b.* Turkey
87 D3 **Sarova** Rus. Fed.
105 D2 **Sarrebourg** France
106 B1 **Sarria** Spain
107 C1 **Sarrión** Spain
105 D3 **Sartène** *Corse* France
103 D2 **Sárvár** Hungary
76 B2 **Sarykamyshskoye Ozero** *salt l.* Turkm./Uzbek.
77 D2 **Saryozek** Kazakh.
77 D2 **Saryshagan** Kazakh.
82 F3 **Sarysu** *watercourse* Kazakh.
77 D3 **Sary-Tash** Kyrg.
75 C2 **Sasaram** India
67 A4 **Sasebo** Japan
129 D2 **Saskatchewan** *prov.* Can.
129 D2 **Saskatchewan** *r.* Can.
129 D2 **Saskatoon** Can.
83 I2 **Saskylakh** Rus. Fed.
123 C2 **Sasolburg** S. Africa
87 D3 **Sasovo** Rus. Fed.
114 B4 **Sassandra** Côte d'Ivoire
108 A2 **Sassari** *Sardegna* Italy
102 C1 **Sassnitz** Ger.
114 A3 **Satadougou** Mali
123 D1 **Satara** S. Africa
75 C2 **Satna** India
74 B2 **Satpura Range** *mts* India
63 B2 **Sattahip** Thai.
110 B1 **Satu Mare** Romania
63 B3 **Satun** Thai.
144 B2 **Saucillo** Mex.
93 E4 **Sauda** Norway
92 B2 **Sauðárkrókur** Iceland
78 B2 **Saudi Arabia** *country* Asia
105 C3 **Saugues** France
105 C2 **Saulieu** France
130 B2 **Sault Sainte Marie** Can.
140 C1 **Sault Sainte Marie** U.S.A.
77 C1 **Saumalkol'** Kazakh.
59 C3 **Saumlakki** Indon.
104 B2 **Saumur** France
120 B1 **Saurimo** Angola
109 D2 **Sava** *r.* Europe
49 G3 **Savai'i** *i.* Samoa
91 E1 **Savala** *r.* Rus. Fed.
143 D2 **Savannah** *GA* U.S.A.
142 C1 **Savannah** *TN* U.S.A.
143 D2 **Savannah** *r.* U.S.A.
63 B2 **Savannakhét** Laos
130 A1 **Savant Lake** Can.
111 C3 **Savaştepe** Turkey
89 F2 **Savino** Rus. Fed.
86 D2 **Savinskiy** Rus. Fed.
108 A2 **Savona** Italy
93 I3 **Savonlinna** Fin.
92 I2 **Savukoski** Fin.
Savu Sea Indon. *see* **Sawu, Laut**
74 B2 **Sawai Madhopur** India
62 A2 **Sawankhalok** Thai.
136 B3 **Sawatch Range** *mts* U.S.A.
53 D2 **Sawtell** Austr.
59 C3 **Sawu, Laut** *sea* Indon.
79 C3 **Sayḩūt** Yemen
69 D2 **Saynshand** Mongolia
141 D2 **Sayre** U.S.A.
144 B3 **Sayula** *Jalisco* Mex.
145 C3 **Sayula** *Veracruz* Mex.
128 B2 **Sayward** Can.
89 E2 **Sazonovo** Rus. Fed.
114 B2 **Sbaa** Alg.
98 B1 **Scafell Pike** *h.* U.K.
109 C3 **Scalea** Italy
96 C1 **Scapa Flow** *inlet* U.K.
130 C2 **Scarborough** Can.
147 D3 **Scarborough** Trin. and Tob
98 C1 **Scarborough** U.K.
64 A1 **Scarborough Shoal** *sea fea* S. China Sea
96 A2 **Scarinish** U.K.
Scarpanto *i.* Greece *see* **Karpathos**
105 D2 **Schaffhausen** Switz.
100 B1 **Schagen** Neth.
102 C2 **Schärding** Austria
100 A2 **Scharendijke** Neth.
101 D1 **Scharhörn** *i.* Ger.
101 D1 **Scheeßel** Ger.
131 D1 **Schefferville** Can.
135 D3 **Schell Creek Range** *mts* U.
141 E2 **Schenectady** U.S.A.
101 E3 **Scheßlitz** Ger.
100 C1 **Schiermonnikoog** *i.* Neth.
108 B1 **Schio** Italy
101 F2 **Schkeuditz** Ger.
101 E1 **Schladen** Ger.
101 E2 **Schleiz** Ger.
102 B1 **Schleswig** Ger.
101 D2 **Schloss Holte-Stukenbroc** Ger.
101 D2 **Schlüchtern** Ger.
101 E3 **Schlüsselfeld** Ger.
101 D2 **Schmallenberg** Ger.
101 D1 **Schneverdingen** Ger.
101 E1 **Schönebeck (Elbe)** Ger.
101 E1 **Schöningen** Ger.
100 B2 **Schoonhoven** Neth.
59 D3 **Schouten Islands** P.N.G.
102 B2 **Schwäbische Alb** *mts* Ger.
102 C2 **Schwandorf** Ger.
61 C2 **Schwaner, Pegunungan** *mt* Indon.
101 E1 **Schwarzenbek** Ger.
101 F2 **Schwarzenberg** Ger.
122 A2 **Schwarzrand** *mts* Namibia
Schwarzwald *mts* Ger. *see* **Black Forest**
102 C2 **Schwaz** Austria
102 C1 **Schwedt an der Oder** Ger.
101 E2 **Schweinfurt** Ger.
101 E1 **Schwerin** Ger.
101 E1 **Schweriner See** *l.* Ger.
105 D2 **Schwyz** Switz.
108 B3 **Sciacca** *Sicilia* Italy
95 B4 **Scilly, Isles of** U.K.
140 C3 **Scioto** *r.* U.S.A.
136 B1 **Scobey** U.S.A.
53 D2 **Scone** Austr.
55 R3 **Scotia Ridge** S. Atlantic Oc
158 C8 **Scotia Sea** S. Atlantic Ocea
96 C2 **Scotland** *admin. div.* U.K.
128 B2 **Scott, Cape** Can.
123 D3 **Scottburgh** S. Africa

6 C3 **Scott City** U.S.A.
5 C2 **Scottsbluff** U.S.A.
2 C2 **Scottsboro** U.S.A.
5 B1 **Scourie** U.K.
1 D2 **Scranton** U.S.A.
8 C2 **Scunthorpe** U.K.
5 E2 **Scuol** Switz.
9 E2 **Seal** *r.* Can.
2 B3 **Seal, Cape** S. Africa
2 B3 **Sea Lake** Austr.
9 D3 **Sealy** U.S.A.
2 B1 **Searcy** U.S.A.
3 B1 **Seascale** U.K.
4 B1 **Seattle** U.S.A.
1 E2 **Sebago Lake** U.S.A.
4 A2 **Sebastián Vizcaíno, Bahía** *b.* Mex.
0 B1 **Sebeş** Romania
0 B2 **Sebesi** *i.* Indon.
3 C2 **Sebezh** Rus. Fed.
0 B1 **Şebinkarahisar** Turkey
3 D3 **Sebring** U.S.A.
3 B3 **Sechelt** Can.
0 A2 **Sechura** Peru
3 B3 **Secunderabad** India
7 E3 **Sedalia** U.S.A.
5 C2 **Sedan** France
4 B2 **Seddon** N.Z.
3 A2 **Sedona** U.S.A.
1 E2 **Seeburg** Ger.
1 E1 **Seehausen (Altmark)** Ger.
2 A2 **Seeheim** Namibia
4 C2 **Sées** France
1 E2 **Seesen** Ger.
1 E1 **Seevetal** Ger.
4 A4 **Sefadu** Sierra Leone
3 C1 **Sefare** Botswana
0 B1 **Segamat** Malaysia
5 C2 **Segezha** Rus. Fed.
4 B3 **Ségou** Mali
5 C1 **Segovia** Spain
5 D2 **Séguédine** Niger
4 B4 **Séguéla** Côte d'Ivoire
9 D3 **Seguin** U.S.A.
7 C2 **Segura** *r.* Spain
5 C2 **Segura, Sierra de** *mts* Spain
0 B3 **Sehithwa** Botswana
3 H3 **Seinäjoki** Fin.
4 C2 **Seine** *r.* France
4 B2 **Seine, Baie de** *b.* France
3 E1 **Sejny** Pol.
0 B2 **Sekayu** Indon.
4 B4 **Sekondi** Ghana
9 C3 **Selaru** *i.* Indon.
1 C2 **Selatan, Tanjung** *pt* Indon.
5 A2 **Selawik** U.S.A.
3 C2 **Selby** U.K.
0 B3 **Selebi-Phikwe** Botswana
5 D2 **Sélestat** France
2 A3 **Selfoss** Iceland
4 A3 **Sélibabi** Maur.
3 A1 **Seligman** U.S.A.
5 A2 **Selîma Oasis** Sudan
1 C3 **Selimiye** Turkey
4 B3 **Sélingué, Lac de** *l.* Mali
9 D2 **Selizharovo** Rus. Fed.
3 E4 **Seljord** Norway
9 E2 **Selkirk** Can.
5 C3 **Selkirk** U.K.
3 C2 **Selkirk Mountains** Can.
2 C2 **Selma** *AL* U.S.A.
5 C3 **Selma** *CA* U.S.A.
9 D3 **Sel'tso** Rus. Fed.
0 A2 **Selvas** *reg.* Brazil
4 C1 **Selway** *r.* U.S.A.
9 D1 **Selwyn Lake** Can.
3 A1 **Selwyn Mountains** Can.

51 C2 **Selwyn Range** *hills* Austr.
60 B2 **Semangka, Teluk** *b.* Indon.
61 C2 **Semarang** Indon.
61 B1 **Sematan** *Sarawak* Malaysia
118 B2 **Sembé** Congo
81 C2 **Şemdinli** Turkey
91 C1 **Semenivka** Ukr.
86 D3 **Semenov** Rus. Fed.
61 C2 **Semeru, Gunung** *vol.* Indon.
89 E3 **Semiluki** Rus. Fed.
136 B2 **Seminoe Reservoir** U.S.A.
139 C2 **Seminole** U.S.A.
143 D2 **Seminole, Lake** U.S.A.
77 E1 **Semipalatinsk** Kazakh.
61 C1 **Semitau** Indon.
81 D2 **Semnān** Iran
61 C1 **Semporna** *Sabah* Malaysia
105 C2 **Semur-en-Auxois** France
150 B2 **Sena Madureira** Brazil
120 B2 **Senanga** Zambia
67 B4 **Sendai** *Kagoshima* Japan
67 D3 **Sendai** *Miyagi* Japan
114 A3 **Senegal** *country* Africa
114 A3 **Sénégal** *r.* Maur./Senegal
102 C1 **Senftenberg** Ger.
119 D3 **Sengerema** Tanz.
151 D3 **Senhor do Bonfim** Brazil
108 B2 **Senigallia** Italy
109 B2 **Senj** Croatia
92 G2 **Senja** *i.* Norway
122 B2 **Senlac** S. Africa
104 C2 **Senlis** France
63 B2 **Senmonorom** Cambodia
117 B3 **Sennar** Sudan
130 C2 **Senneterre** Can.
123 C3 **Senqu** *r.* Lesotho
105 C2 **Sens** France
109 D1 **Senta** Serbia
128 B2 **Sentinel Peak** Can.
123 C1 **Senwabarwana** S. Africa
75 B2 **Seoni** India
65 B2 **Seoul** S. Korea
155 D2 **Sepetiba, Baía de** *b.* Brazil
59 D3 **Sepik** *r.* P.N.G.
61 C1 **Sepinang** Indon.
131 D1 **Sept-Îles** Can.
59 C3 **Seram** *i.* Indon.
59 C3 **Seram, Laut** *sea* Indon.
60 B2 **Serang** Indon.
109 D2 **Serbia** *country* Europe
76 B3 **Serdar** Turkm.
89 E3 **Serebryanyye Prudy** Rus. Fed.
60 B1 **Seremban** Malaysia
119 D3 **Serengeti Plain** Tanz.
87 D3 **Sergach** Rus. Fed.
89 E2 **Sergiyev Posad** Rus. Fed.
74 A1 **Serhetabat** Turkm.
61 C1 **Seria** Brunei
61 C1 **Serian** *Sarawak* Malaysia
111 B3 **Serifos** *i.* Greece
80 B2 **Serik** Turkey
59 C3 **Sermata, Kepulauan** *is* Indon.
86 F3 **Serov** Rus. Fed.
120 B3 **Serowe** Botswana
106 B2 **Serpa** Port.
89 E3 **Serpukhov** Rus. Fed.
151 D3 **Serra da Mesa, Represa** *resr* Brazil
154 B1 **Serranópolis** Brazil
100 A3 **Serre** *r.* France
111 B2 **Serres** Greece
151 E3 **Serrinha** Brazil
155 D1 **Sêrro** Brazil
154 C2 **Sertãozinho** Brazil
61 C2 **Seruyan** *r.* Indon.
68 C2 **Sêrxü** China
120 A2 **Sesfontein** Namibia

108 B2 **Sessa Aurunca** Italy
108 A2 **Sestri Levante** Italy
105 C3 **Sète** France
155 D1 **Sete Lagoas** Brazil
92 G2 **Setermoen** Norway
93 E4 **Setesdal** *val.* Norway
115 C1 **Sétif** Alg.
67 B4 **Seto-naikai** *sea* Japan
114 B1 **Settat** Morocco
98 B1 **Settle** U.K.
106 B2 **Setúbal** Port.
106 B2 **Setúbal, Baía de** *b.* Port.
130 A1 **Seul, Lac** *l.* Can.
76 A2 **Sevan, Lake** Armenia
Sevana Lich *l.* Armenia *see* **Sevan, Lake**
91 C3 **Sevastopol'** Ukr.
105 C3 **Sévérac-le-Château** France
130 B1 **Severn** *r.* Can.
122 B2 **Severn** S. Africa
99 B3 **Severn** *r.* U.K.
86 D2 **Severnaya Dvina** *r.* Rus. Fed.
83 H1 **Severnaya Zemlya** *is* Rus. Fed.
86 D2 **Severnyy** *Nenetskiy Avtonomnyy Okrug* Rus. Fed.
86 F2 **Severnyy** *Respublika Komi* Rus. Fed.
86 C2 **Severodvinsk** Rus. Fed.
86 C2 **Severomorsk** Rus. Fed.
91 D3 **Severskaya** Rus. Fed.
135 D3 **Sevier** *r.* U.S.A.
135 D3 **Sevier Lake** U.S.A.
Sevilla Spain *see* **Seville**
106 B2 **Seville** Spain
128 A2 **Sewell Inlet** Can.
128 C2 **Sexsmith** Can.
144 B2 **Sextín** *r.* Mex.
86 G1 **Seyakha** Rus. Fed.
113 J7 **Seychelles** *country* Indian Ocean
92 C2 **Seyðisfjörður** Iceland
91 C1 **Seym** *r.* Rus. Fed./Ukr.
83 L2 **Seymchan** Rus. Fed.
53 C3 **Seymour** Austr.
140 B3 **Seymour** *IN* U.S.A.
139 D2 **Seymour** *TX* U.S.A.
105 C2 **Sézanne** France
110 C1 **Sfântu Gheorghe** Romania
115 D1 **Sfax** Tunisia
's-Gravenhage Neth. *see* **The Hague**
96 A2 **Sgurr Alasdair** *h.* U.K.
70 A2 **Shaanxi** *prov.* China
91 D2 **Shabel'sk** Rus. Fed.
77 D3 **Shache** China
55 R1 **Shackleton Range** *mts* Antarctica
99 B3 **Shaftesbury** U.K.
75 C2 **Shahdol** India
77 C3 **Shah Fuladi** *mt.* Afgh.
75 B2 **Shahjahanpur** India
81 D2 **Shahr-e Kord** Iran
81 D2 **Shāhrezā** Iran
77 C3 **Shahrisabz** Uzbek.
89 E2 **Shakhovskaya** Rus. Fed.
91 E2 **Shakhty** Rus. Fed.
86 D3 **Shakhun'ya** Rus. Fed.
66 D2 **Shakotan-misaki** *c.* Japan
76 B2 **Shalkar** Kazakh.
68 C2 **Shaluli Shan** *mts* China
129 E2 **Shamattawa** Can.
139 C1 **Shamrock** U.S.A.
68 C2 **Shandan** China
70 B2 **Shandong** *prov.* China
70 C2 **Shandong Bandao** *pen.* China
121 B2 **Shangani** *r.* Zimbabwe
70 C2 **Shanghai** China

70 C2 **Shanghai** *mun.* China
71 B3 **Shanghang** China
70 A2 **Shangluo** China
71 B3 **Shangrao** China
70 B2 **Shangshui** China
70 C2 **Shangyu** China
69 E1 **Shangzhi** China
97 B2 **Shannon** *r.* Ireland
97 B2 **Shannon, Mouth of the** Ireland
71 B3 **Shantou** China
70 B2 **Shanxi** *prov.* China
71 B3 **Shaoguan** China
71 B3 **Shaowu** China
70 C2 **Shaoxing** China
71 B3 **Shaoyang** China
116 C2 **Shaqrā'** Saudi Arabia
74 A1 **Sharan** Afgh.
90 B2 **Sharhorod** Ukr.
79 C2 **Sharjah** U.A.E.
88 C2 **Sharkawshchyna** Belarus
50 A2 **Shark Bay** Austr.
78 A2 **Sharm ash Shaykh** Egypt
140 C2 **Sharon** U.S.A.
86 D3 **Shar'ya** Rus. Fed.
121 B3 **Shashe** *r.* Botswana/Zimbabwe
117 B4 **Shashemenē** Eth.
134 B2 **Shasta, Mount** *vol.* U.S.A.
134 B2 **Shasta Lake** U.S.A.
89 E2 **Shatura** Rus. Fed.
129 D3 **Shaunavon** Can.
140 B2 **Shawano** U.S.A.
131 C2 **Shawinigan** Can.
139 D1 **Shawnee** U.S.A.
50 B2 **Shay Gap (abandoned)** Austr.
89 E3 **Shchekino** Rus. Fed.
89 E2 **Shchelkovo** Rus. Fed.
89 E3 **Shchigry** Rus. Fed.
91 C1 **Shchors** Ukr.
88 B3 **Shchuchyn** Belarus
91 D1 **Shebekino** Rus. Fed.
117 C4 **Shebelē Wenz, Wabē** *r.* Ethiopia/Somalia
77 C3 **Sheberghān** Afgh.
140 B2 **Sheboygan** U.S.A.
91 D3 **Shebsh** *r.* Rus. Fed.
97 C2 **Sheelin, Lough** *l.* Ireland
98 C2 **Sheffield** U.K.
89 E2 **Sheksna** Rus. Fed.
89 E2 **Sheksninskoye Vodokhranilishche** *resr* Rus. Fed.
83 M2 **Shelagskiy, Mys** *pt* Rus. Fed.
131 D2 **Shelburne** Can.
134 D1 **Shelby** U.S.A.
140 B3 **Shelbyville** *IN* U.S.A.
142 C1 **Shelbyville** *TN* U.S.A.
83 L2 **Shelikhova, Zaliv** *g.* Rus. Fed.
129 D2 **Shellbrook** Can.
134 B1 **Shelton** U.S.A.
137 D2 **Shenandoah** U.S.A.
141 D3 **Shenandoah** *r.* U.S.A.
141 D3 **Shenandoah Mountains** U.S.A.
118 A2 **Shendam** Nigeria
86 D2 **Shenkursk** Rus. Fed.
65 A1 **Shenyang** China
71 B3 **Shenzhen** China
90 B1 **Shepetivka** Ukr.
53 C3 **Shepparton** Austr.
99 D3 **Sheppey, Isle of** *i.* U.K.
131 D2 **Sherbrooke** *N.S.* Can.
131 C2 **Sherbrooke** *Que.* Can.
116 B3 **Shereiq** Sudan
136 B2 **Sheridan** U.S.A.
139 D2 **Sherman** U.S.A.
100 B2 **'s-Hertogenbosch** Neth.
96 □ **Shetland Islands** U.K.
76 B2 **Shetpe** Kazakh.
Shevchenko Kazakh. *see* **Aktau**
137 D1 **Sheyenne** *r.* U.S.A.
79 B3 **Shibām** Yemen
66 D2 **Shibetsu** Japan
71 B3 **Shicheng** China
96 B2 **Shiel, Loch** *l.* U.K.
77 E2 **Shihezi** China
Shijiao China *see* **Fogang**
70 B2 **Shijiazhuang** China
74 A2 **Shikarpur** Pak.
67 B4 **Shikoku** *i.* Japan
66 D2 **Shikotsu-ko** *l.* Japan
86 D2 **Shilega** Rus. Fed.
75 C2 **Shiliguri** India
75 D2 **Shillong** India
89 F3 **Shilovo** Rus. Fed.
117 C3 **Shimbiris** *mt.* Somalia
67 C3 **Shimizu** Japan
73 B3 **Shimoga** India
67 B4 **Shimonoseki** Japan
96 B1 **Shin, Loch** *l.* U.K.
67 C4 **Shingū** Japan
123 D1 **Shingwedzi** S. Africa
123 D1 **Shingwedzi** *r.* S. Africa
119 D3 **Shinyanga** Tanz.
67 C4 **Shiono-misaki** *c.* Japan
138 B1 **Shiprock** U.S.A.
71 A3 **Shiqian** China
70 A2 **Shiquan** China
Shiquanhe China *see* **Gar**
Shiquan He *r.* China/Pak. *see* **Indus**
67 C3 **Shirane-san** *mt.* Japan
81 D3 **Shīrāz** Iran
66 D2 **Shiretoko-misaki** *c.* Japan
66 D2 **Shiriya-zaki** *c.* Japan
74 B2 **Shiv** India
75 B2 **Shivpuri** India
70 B2 **Shiyan** China
70 A2 **Shizuishan** China
67 C4 **Shizuoka** Japan
89 D3 **Shklow** Belarus
109 C2 **Shkodër** Albania
83 H1 **Shmidta, Ostrov** *i.* Rus. Fed.
135 C3 **Shoshone** U.S.A.
135 C3 **Shoshone Mountains** U.S.A.
123 C1 **Shoshong** Botswana
91 C1 **Shostka** Ukr.
70 B2 **Shouxian** China
138 A2 **Show Low** U.S.A.
91 C2 **Shpola** Ukr.
142 B2 **Shreveport** U.S.A.
99 B2 **Shrewsbury** U.K.
62 A1 **Shuangjiang** China
87 E4 **Shubarkuduk** Kazakh.
116 B1 **Shubrā al Khaymah** Egypt
89 D2 **Shugozero** Rus. Fed.
120 B2 **Shumba** Zimbabwe
110 C2 **Shumen** Bulg.
88 C2 **Shumilina** Belarus
89 D3 **Shumyachi** Rus. Fed.
126 A2 **Shungnak** U.S.A.
78 B3 **Shuqrah** Yemen
89 F2 **Shushkodom** Rus. Fed.
81 C2 **Shushtar** Iran
128 C2 **Shuswap Lake** Can.
89 F2 **Shuya** Rus. Fed.
89 F2 **Shuyskoye** Rus. Fed.
62 A1 **Shwebo** Myanmar
62 A1 **Shwedwin** Myanmar
62 A2 **Shwegyin** Myanmar
77 C2 **Shymkent** Kazakh.
91 C2 **Shyroke** Ukr.
59 C3 **Sia** Indon.
74 A2 **Siahan Range** *mts* Pak.
74 B1 **Sialkot** Pak.
64 B2 **Siargao** *i.* Phil.
88 B2 **Šiauliai** Lith.
109 C2 **Šibenik** Croatia
83 I2 **Siberia** *reg.* Rus. Fed.
60 A2 **Siberut** *i.* Indon.
74 A2 **Sibi** Pak.
110 B1 **Sibiu** Romania
60 A1 **Sibolga** Indon.
62 A1 **Sibsagar** India
61 C1 **Sibu** *Sarawak* Malaysia
118 B2 **Sibut** C.A.R.
64 B1 **Sibuyan** *i.* Phil.
64 B1 **Sibuyan Sea** Phil.
128 C2 **Sicamous** Can.
63 A3 **Sichon** Thai.
70 A2 **Sichuan** *prov.* China
70 A3 **Sichuan Pendi** *basin* Chin
105 D3 **Sicié, Cap** *c.* France
Sicilia *i.* Italy *see* **Sicily**
108 B3 **Sicilian Channel** Italy/Tur
108 B3 **Sicily** *i.* Italy
150 A3 **Sicuani** Peru
111 C3 **Sideros, Akrotirio** *pt* Gree
74 B2 **Sidhpur** India
107 D2 **Sidi Aïssa** Alg.
107 D2 **Sidi Ali** Alg.
114 B1 **Sidi Bel Abbès** Alg.
114 A2 **Sidi Ifni** Morocco
60 A1 **Sidikalang** Indon.
96 C2 **Sidlaw Hills** U.K.
99 B3 **Sidmouth** U.K.
134 B1 **Sidney** Can.
136 C1 **Sidney** *MT* U.S.A.
136 C2 **Sidney** *NE* U.S.A.
140 C2 **Sidney** *OH* U.S.A.
143 D2 **Sidney Lanier, Lake** U.S.A
80 B2 **Sidon** Lebanon
154 B2 **Sidrolândia** Brazil
103 E1 **Siedlce** Pol.
100 C2 **Sieg** *r.* Ger.
100 D2 **Siegen** Ger.
63 B2 **Siĕmréab** Cambodia
108 B2 **Siena** Italy
103 D1 **Sieradz** Pol.
153 B5 **Sierra Grande** Arg.
114 A4 **Sierra Leone** *country* Afric
144 B2 **Sierra Mojada** Mex.
138 A2 **Sierra Vista** U.S.A.
105 D2 **Sierre** Switz.
111 B3 **Sifnos** *i.* Greece
107 C2 **Sig** Alg.
127 H2 **Sigguup Nunaa** *pen.* Greenland
103 E2 **Sighetu Marmației** Roma
110 B1 **Sighișoara** Romania
60 A1 **Sigli** Indon.
92 B2 **Siglufjörður** Iceland
102 B2 **Sigmaringen** Ger.
100 B3 **Signy-l'Abbaye** France
106 C1 **Sigüenza** Spain
114 B3 **Siguiri** Guinea
88 B2 **Sigulda** Latvia
63 B2 **Sihanoukville** Cambodia
92 I3 **Siilinjärvi** Fin.
81 C2 **Siirt** Turkey
60 B2 **Sijunjung** Indon.
74 B2 **Sikar** India
114 B3 **Sikasso** Mali
137 F3 **Sikeston** U.S.A.
66 B2 **Sikhote-Alin'** *mts* Rus. Fed
111 C3 **Sikinos** *i.* Greece
144 B2 **Silao** Mex.
75 D2 **Silchar** India
77 D1 **Siletiteniz, Ozero** *salt l.* Kazakh.
75 C2 **Silgarhi** Nepal

0 B2 Silifke Turkey
5 C1 Siling Co *salt l.* China
0 C2 Silistra Bulg.
0 A1 Silivri Turkey
3 F3 Siljan *l.* Sweden
3 E4 Silkeborg Denmark
8 C2 Sillamäe Estonia
2 B1 Siloam Springs U.S.A.
3 D2 Silobela S. Africa
8 B2 Šilutė Lith.
1 C2 Silvan Turkey
8 B2 Silver City U.S.A.
6 B3 Silverton U.S.A.
2 B1 Simao China
0 C2 Simard, Lac *l.* Can.
1 C3 Simav Turkey
1 C3 Simav Dağları *mts* Turkey
8 C2 Simba Dem. Rep. Congo
1 D2 Simcoe, Lake Can.
0 A1 Simeulue *i.* Indon.
1 C3 Simferopol' Ukr.
0 B1 Şimleu Silvaniei Romania
0 C3 Simmern (Hunsrück) Ger.
9 D2 Simonhouse Can.
1 C2 Simpson Desert Austr.
3 F4 Simrishamn Sweden
0 A1 Sinabang Indon.
6 B2 Sinai *pen.* Egypt
1 A3 Sinan China
5 B2 Sinanju N. Korea
2 A1 Sinbo Myanmar
0 A1 Sincelejo Col.
1 C3 Sındırgı Turkey
6 E2 Sindor Rus. Fed.
1 C2 Sinekçi Turkey
6 B2 Sines Port.
6 B2 Sines, Cabo de *c.* Port.
5 C2 Singahi India
0 B1 Singapore *country* Asia
1 C2 Singaraja Indon.
9 D3 Singida Tanz.
2 A1 Singkaling Hkamti Myanmar
1 B1 Singkawang Indon.
0 A1 Singkil Indon.
3 D2 Singleton Austr.
2 A1 Singu Myanmar
8 A2 Siniscola *Sardegna* Italy
9 C2 Sinj Croatia
6 B3 Sinkat Sudan
Sinkiang Uighur Autonomous Region *aut. reg.* China *see* Xinjiang Uygur Zizhiqu
0 B1 Sinop Turkey
5 B1 Sinp'o N. Korea
1 C1 Sintang Indon.
0 B2 Sint Anthonis Neth.
0 A2 Sint-Laureins Belgium
7 D3 Sint Maarten *i.* Neth. Antilles
0 B2 Sint-Niklaas Belgium
9 D3 Sinton U.S.A.
5 A1 Sinŭiju N. Korea
3 D2 Siófok Hungary
5 D2 Sion Switz.
7 D2 Sioux Center U.S.A.
7 D2 Sioux City U.S.A.
7 D2 Sioux Falls U.S.A.
0 A1 Sioux Lookout Can.
5 A1 Siping China
9 E2 Sipiwesk Lake Can.
0 A2 Sipura *i.* Indon.
3 E4 Sira *r.* Norway
Siracusa Italy *see* Syracuse
1 C1 Sir Edward Pellew Group *is* Austr.
6 B1 Sirhān, Wādī an *watercourse* Saudi Arabia
9 C2 Sīrīk Iran
62 B2 Siri Kit, Khuan Thai.
128 B1 Sir James MacBrien, Mount Can.
79 C2 Sīrjān Iran
81 C2 Şırnak Turkey
74 B2 Sirohi India
74 B2 Sirsa India
115 D1 Sirte Libya
115 D1 Sirte, Gulf of Libya
88 B2 Širvintos Lith.
145 C2 Sisal Mex.
122 B2 Sishen S. Africa
81 C2 Sisian Armenia
129 D2 Sisipuk Lake Can.
63 B2 Sisŏphŏn Cambodia
105 D3 Sisteron France
75 C2 Sitapur India
123 D2 Siteki Swaziland
128 A2 Sitka U.S.A.
100 B2 Sittard Neth.
62 A2 Sittaung *r.* Myanmar
62 A1 Sittwe Myanmar
61 C2 Situbondo Indon.
80 B2 Sivas Turkey
111 C3 Sivaslı Turkey
80 B2 Siverek Turkey
80 B2 Sivrihisar Turkey
116 A2 Sīwah Egypt
74 B1 Siwalik Range *mts* India/Nepal
105 D3 Six-Fours-les-Plages France
70 B2 Sixian China
123 C2 Siyabuswa S. Africa
109 D2 Sjenica Serbia
92 G2 Sjøvegan Norway
91 C2 Skadovs'k Ukr.
93 F4 Skagen Denmark
93 E4 Skagerrak *str.* Denmark/Norway
134 B1 Skagit *r.* U.S.A.
128 A2 Skagway U.S.A.
74 B1 Skardu Pak.
103 E1 Skarżysko-Kamienna Pol.
103 D2 Skawina Pol.
128 B2 Skeena *r.* Can.
128 B2 Skeena Mountains Can.
98 D2 Skegness U.K.
92 H3 Skellefteå Sweden
92 H3 Skellefteälven *r.* Sweden
97 C2 Skerries Ireland
111 B3 Skiathos *i.* Greece
97 B3 Skibbereen Ireland
92 B2 Skíðadals-jökull *glacier* Iceland
98 B1 Skiddaw *h.* U.K.
93 E4 Skien Norway
103 E1 Skierniewice Pol.
115 C1 Skikda Alg.
52 B3 Skipton Austr.
98 B2 Skipton U.K.
93 E4 Skive Denmark
92 H1 Skjervøy Norway
111 B3 Skopelos *i.* Greece
89 E3 Skopin Rus. Fed.
109 D2 Skopje Macedonia
93 F4 Skövde Sweden
141 F2 Skowhegan U.S.A.
88 B2 Skrunda Latvia
128 A1 Skukum, Mount Can.
123 D1 Skukuza S. Africa
88 B2 Skuodas Lith.
96 A2 Skye *i.* U.K.
111 B3 Skyros Greece
111 B3 Skyros *i.* Greece
93 F4 Slagelse Denmark
97 C2 Slaney *r.* Ireland
88 C2 Slantsy Rus. Fed.
109 C1 Slatina Croatia
110 B2 Slatina Romania
129 C1 Slave *r.* Can.
114 C4 Slave Coast Africa
128 C2 Slave Lake Can.
82 G3 Slavgorod Rus. Fed.
109 C1 Slavonski Brod Croatia
90 B1 Slavuta Ukr.
90 C1 Slavutych Ukr.
91 D2 Slavyansk-na-Kubani Rus. Fed.
89 D3 Slawharad Belarus
103 D1 Sławno Pol.
97 A2 Slea Head Ireland
130 C1 Sleeper Islands Can.
97 D1 Slieve Donard *h.* U.K.
Slieve Gamph *hills* Ireland *see* Ox Mountains
97 B1 Sligo Ireland
97 B1 Sligo Bay Ireland
93 G4 Slite Sweden
110 C2 Sliven Bulg.
110 C2 Slobozia Romania
128 C3 Slocan Can.
88 C3 Slonim Belarus
100 B1 Sloten Neth.
99 C3 Slough U.K.
103 D2 Slovakia *country* Europe
108 B1 Slovenia *country* Europe
91 D2 Slov"yans'k Ukr.
90 B1 Sluch *r.* Ukr.
103 D1 Słupsk Pol.
88 C3 Slutsk Belarus
97 A2 Slyne Head Ireland
131 D1 Smallwood Reservoir Can.
88 C3 Smalyavichy Belarus
88 C3 Smarhon' Belarus
129 D2 Smeaton Can.
109 D2 Smederevo Serbia
109 D2 Smederevska Palanka Serbia
91 C2 Smila Ukr.
88 C2 Smiltene Latvia
128 B2 Smithers Can.
143 E1 Smithfield U.S.A.
141 D3 Smith Mountain Lake U.S.A.
130 C2 Smiths Falls Can.
137 D3 Smoky Hills U.S.A.
92 E3 Smøla *i.* Norway
89 D3 Smolensk Rus. Fed.
110 B2 Smolyan Bulg.
130 B2 Smooth Rock Falls Can.
Smyrna Turkey *see* İzmir
92 B3 Snæfell *mt.* Iceland
98 A1 Snaefell *h.* Isle of Man
132 B2 Snake *r.* U.S.A.
134 D2 Snake River Plain U.S.A.
100 B1 Sneek Neth.
97 B3 Sneem Ireland
122 B3 Sneeuberge *mts* S. Africa
108 B1 Snežnik *mt.* Slovenia
91 C2 Snihurivka Ukr.
93 E3 Snøhetta *mt.* Norway
129 D1 Snowbird Lake Can.
98 A2 Snowdon *mt.* U.K.
Snowdrift Can. *see* Łutselk'e
129 C1 Snowdrift *r.* Can.
138 A2 Snowflake U.S.A.
129 D2 Snow Lake Can.
52 A2 Snowtown Austr.
53 C3 Snowy *r.* Austr.
53 C3 Snowy Mountains Austr.
139 C2 Snyder U.S.A.
121 D2 Soalala Madag.
117 B4 Sobat *r.* Sudan
89 F2 Sobinka Rus. Fed.
151 D3 Sobradinho, Barragem de *resr* Brazil
151 D2 Sobral Brazil

87	C4	Sochi Rus. Fed.
65	B2	Sŏch'ŏn S. Korea
49	H4	Society Islands Fr. Polynesia
150	A1	Socorro Col.
138	B2	Socorro U.S.A.
144	A3	Socorro, Isla i. Mex.
56	F6	Socotra i. Yemen
63	B3	Soc Trăng Vietnam
106	C2	Socuéllamos Spain
92	I2	Sodankylä Fin.
134	D2	Soda Springs U.S.A.
93	G3	Söderhamn Sweden
93	G4	Södertälje Sweden
116	A3	Sodiri Sudan
117	B4	Sodo Eth.
93	G3	Södra Kvarken str. Fin./Sweden
100	D2	Soest Ger.
110	B2	Sofia Bulg.
		Sofiya Bulg. see Sofia
68	C2	Sog China
93	E3	Sognefjorden inlet Norway
111	D2	Söğüt Turkey
100	B2	Soignies Belgium
105	C2	Soissons France
90	A1	Sokal' Ukr.
111	C3	Söke Turkey
81	C1	Sokhumi Georgia
114	C4	Sokodé Togo
89	F2	Sokol Rus. Fed.
101	F2	Sokolov Czech Rep.
115	C3	Sokoto Nigeria
115	C3	Sokoto r. Nigeria
90	B2	Sokyryany Ukr.
73	B3	Solapur India
135	B3	Soledad U.S.A.
89	F2	Soligalich Rus. Fed.
99	C2	Solihull U.K.
86	E3	Solikamsk Rus. Fed.
87	E3	Sol'-Iletsk Rus. Fed.
100	C2	Solingen Ger.
92	G3	Sollefteå Sweden
93	G4	Sollentuna Sweden
101	D2	Solling hills Ger.
89	E2	Solnechnogorsk Rus. Fed.
60	B2	Solok Indon.
48	E3	Solomon Islands country S. Pacific Ocean
48	E3	Solomon Sea S. Pacific Ocean
105	D2	Solothurn Switz.
101	D1	Soltau Ger.
89	D2	Sol'tsy Rus. Fed.
96	C3	Solway Firth est. U.K.
120	B2	Solwezi Zambia
111	C3	Soma Turkey
117	C4	Somalia country Africa
120	B1	Sombo Angola
109	C1	Sombor Serbia
144	B2	Sombrerete Mex.
140	C3	Somerset U.S.A.
123	C3	Somerset East S. Africa
126	E2	Somerset Island Can.
122	A3	Somerset West S. Africa
101	E2	Sömmerda Ger.
75	C2	Son r. India
65	C1	Sŏnbong N. Korea
93	E4	Sønderborg Denmark
101	E2	Sondershausen Ger.
		Søndre Strømfjord inlet Greenland see Kangerlussuaq
62	B1	Sông Đa, Hô resr Vietnam
119	D4	Songea Tanz.
65	B1	Sŏnggan N. Korea
65	B1	Songhua Hu resr China
		Sŏngjin N. Korea see Kimch'aek
63	B3	Songkhla Thai.
65	B2	Sŏngnam S. Korea
65	B2	Songnim N. Korea
120	A1	Songo Angola
121	C2	Songo Moz.
69	E1	Songyuan China
		Sonid Youqi China see Saihan Tal
89	E2	Sonkovo Rus. Fed.
62	B1	Son La Vietnam
74	A2	Sonmiani Pak.
101	E2	Sonneberg Ger.
138	A2	Sonoita Mex.
144	A2	Sonora r. Mex.
135	B3	Sonora CA U.S.A.
139	C2	Sonora TX U.S.A.
117	A4	Sopo watercourse Sudan
103	D2	Sopron Hungary
108	B2	Sora Italy
130	C2	Sorel Can.
51	D4	Sorell Austr.
106	C1	Soria Spain
90	B2	Soroca Moldova
154	C2	Sorocaba Brazil
87	E3	Sorochinsk Rus. Fed.
59	D2	Sorol atoll Micronesia
59	C3	Sorong Indon.
119	D2	Soroti Uganda
92	H1	Sørøya i. Norway
92	G2	Sorsele Sweden
64	B1	Sorsogon Phil.
86	C2	Sortavala Rus. Fed.
92	G2	Sortland Norway
65	B2	Sŏsan S. Korea
123	C2	Soshanguve S. Africa
89	E3	Sosna r. Rus. Fed.
153	B4	Sosneado mt. Arg.
86	E2	Sosnogorsk Rus. Fed.
86	D2	Sosnovka Rus. Fed.
88	C2	Sosnovyy Bor Rus. Fed.
103	D1	Sosnowiec Pol.
91	D2	Sosyka r. Rus. Fed.
145	C2	Soto la Marina Mex.
118	B2	Souanké Congo
104	C3	Souillac France
		Sŏul S. Korea see Seoul
104	B2	Soulac-sur-Mer France
104	B3	Soulom France
		Soûr Lebanon see Tyre
107	D2	Sour el Ghozlane Alg.
129	D3	Souris Man. Can.
131	D2	Souris P.E.I. Can.
129	E3	Souris r. Can.
151	E2	Sousa Brazil
115	D1	Sousse Tunisia
104	B3	Soustons France
122	B3	South Africa, Republic of country Africa
99	C3	Southampton U.K.
127	F2	Southampton Island Can.
73	D3	South Andaman i. India
52	A1	South Australia state Austr.
130	B2	South Baymouth Can.
140	B2	South Bend U.S.A.
143	D2	South Carolina state U.S.A.
156	B4	South China Sea N. Pacific Ocean
136	C2	South Dakota state U.S.A.
99	C3	South Downs hills U.K.
129	D2	Southend Can.
99	D3	Southend-on-Sea U.K.
54	B2	Southern Alps mts N.Z.
50	A3	Southern Cross Austr.
129	E2	Southern Indian Lake Can.
159		Southern Ocean
143	E1	Southern Pines U.S.A.
96	B3	Southern Uplands hills U.K.
149	F6	South Georgia and the South Sandwich Islands terr. S. Atlantic Ocean
96	A2	South Harris pen. U.K.
129	E1	South Henik Lake Can.
54	B2	South Island N.Z.
65	B2	South Korea country Asia
135	B3	South Lake Tahoe U.S.A.
55	Q4	South Orkney Islands S. Atlantic Ocean
136	C2	South Platte r. U.S.A.
98	B2	Southport U.K.
143	E2	Southport U.S.A.
96	C1	South Ronaldsay i. U.K.
123	D3	South Sand Bluff pt S. Afri
129	D2	South Saskatchewan r. Can
129	E2	South Seal r. Can.
55	T3	South Shetland Islands Antarctica
98	C1	South Shields U.K.
54	B1	South Taranaki Bight b. N.
130	C1	South Twin Island Can.
96	A2	South Uist i. U.K.
53	D2	South West Rocks Austr.
99	D2	Southwold U.K.
109	C3	Soverato Italy
88	B2	Sovetsk Rus. Fed.
66	F2	Sovetskiy Rus. Fed.
91	C2	Sovyets'kyy Ukr.
123	C2	Soweto S. Africa
66	D1	Sōya-misaki c. Japan
90	C1	Sozh r. Belarus
110	C2	Sozopol Bulg.
106	C1	Spain country Europe
99	C2	Spalding U.K.
135	D2	Spanish Fork U.S.A.
97	B2	Spanish Point Ireland
108	B3	Sparagio, Monte mt. Sicilia Italy
135	C3	Sparks U.S.A.
140	A2	Sparta U.S.A.
143	D2	Spartanburg U.S.A.
111	B3	Sparti Greece
109	C3	Spartivento, Capo c. Italy
89	D3	Spas-Demensk Rus. Fed.
89	F2	Spas-Klepiki Rus. Fed.
66	B2	Spassk-Dal'niy Rus. Fed.
89	F3	Spassk-Ryazanskiy Rus. Fe
111	B3	Spatha, Akrotirio pt Greece
136	C2	Spearfish U.S.A.
139	C1	Spearman U.S.A.
137	D2	Spencer U.S.A.
52	A2	Spencer Gulf est. Austr.
98	C1	Spennymoor U.K.
54	B2	Spenser Mountains N.Z.
101	D3	Spessart reg. Ger.
96	C2	Spey r. U.K.
100	C2	Speyer Ger.
100	C1	Spiekeroog i. Ger.
100	B2	Spijkenisse Neth.
128	C2	Spirit River Can.
103	E2	Spišská Nová Ves Slovakia
82	C1	Spitsbergen i. Svalbard
102	C2	Spittal an der Drau Austria
109	C2	Split Croatia
129	E2	Split Lake Can.
129	E2	Split Lake Can.
134	C1	Spokane U.S.A.
140	A1	Spooner U.S.A.
102	C1	Spree r. Ger.
122	A2	Springbok S. Africa
131	E2	Springdale Can.
138	B1	Springdale U.S.A.
101	D1	Springe Ger.
138	C1	Springer U.S.A.
138	B2	Springerville U.S.A.
136	C3	Springfield CO U.S.A.

0 B3 **Springfield** *IL* U.S.A.
1 E2 **Springfield** *MA* U.S.A.
7 E3 **Springfield** *MO* U.S.A.
0 C3 **Springfield** *OH* U.S.A.
4 B2 **Springfield** *OR* U.S.A.
3 C3 **Springfontein** S. Africa
1 D2 **Springhill** Can.
D3 **Spring Hill** U.S.A.
4 B2 **Springs Junction** N.Z.
8 D2 **Spurn Head** U.K.
8 B3 **Squamish** Can.
9 C3 **Squillace, Golfo di** *g.* Italy
Srbija *country* Europe *see* **Serbia**
9 C2 **Srebrenica** Bos.-Herz.
0 C2 **Sredets** Bulg.
3 L3 **Sredinnyy Khrebet** *mts* Rus. Fed.
3 L2 **Srednekolymsk** Rus. Fed.
Sredne-Russkaya Vozvyshennost' *hills* Rus. Fed. *see* **Central Russian Upland**
Sredne-Sibirskoye Ploskogor'ye *plat.* Rus. Fed. *see* **Central Siberian Plateau**
0 B2 **Srednogorie** Bulg.
9 D1 **Sretensk** Rus. Fed.
1 C1 **Sri Aman** *Sarawak* Malaysia
3 B4 **Sri Jayewardenepura Kotte** Sri Lanka
3 C3 **Srikakulam** India
3 C4 **Sri Lanka** *country* Asia
8 A2 **Srinagar** India
4 B1 **Srinagar** India
3 B3 **Srivardhan** India
1 D1 **Stade** Ger.
1 E1 **Stadensen** Ger.
0 C1 **Stadskanaal** Neth.
1 D2 **Stadtallendorf** Ger.
1 D1 **Stadthagen** Ger.
1 E2 **Staffelstein** Ger.
9 B2 **Stafford** U.K.
9 C3 **Staines** U.K.
1 D2 **Stakhanov** Ukr.
Stalingrad Rus. Fed. *see* **Volgograd**
3 E1 **Stalowa Wola** Pol.
9 C2 **Stamford** U.K.
1 E2 **Stamford** *CT* U.S.A.
9 D2 **Stamford** *TX* U.S.A.
2 A1 **Stampriet** Namibia
2 F2 **Stamsund** Norway
3 C2 **Standerton** S. Africa
0 C2 **Standish** U.S.A.
3 D2 **Stanger** S. Africa
3 C6 **Stanley** Falkland Is
6 C1 **Stanley** U.S.A.
3 I3 **Stanovoye Nagor'ye** *mts* Rus. Fed.
3 J3 **Stanovoy Khrebet** *mts* Rus. Fed.
3 D1 **Stanthorpe** Austr.
3 E1 **Starachowice** Pol.
Stara Planina *mts* Bulg./Serbia *see* **Balkan Mountains**
9 D2 **Staraya Russa** Rus. Fed.
9 D2 **Staraya Toropa** Rus. Fed.
0 C2 **Stara Zagora** Bulg.
3 D1 **Stargard Szczeciński** Pol.
2 C2 **Starkville** U.S.A.
1 D2 **Starobil's'k** Ukr.
9 D3 **Starodub** Rus. Fed.
3 D1 **Starogard Gdański** Pol.
0 B2 **Starokostyantyniv** Ukr.
1 D2 **Starominskaya** Rus. Fed.
1 D2 **Staroshcherbinovskaya** Rus. Fed.
1 D2 **Starotitarovskaya** Rus. Fed.
89 F3 **Staroyur'yevo** Rus. Fed.
99 B3 **Start Point** U.K.
88 C3 **Staryya Darohi** Belarus
89 E3 **Staryy Oskol** Rus. Fed.
101 E2 **Staßfurt** Ger.
141 D2 **State College** U.S.A.
143 D2 **Statesboro** U.S.A.
143 D1 **Statesville** U.S.A.
93 E4 **Stavanger** Norway
87 D4 **Stavropol'** Rus. Fed.
87 D4 **Stavropol'skaya Vozvyshennost'** *hills* Rus. Fed.
52 B3 **Stawell** Austr.
123 C2 **Steadville** S. Africa
136 B2 **Steamboat Springs** U.S.A.
101 E2 **Stedten** Ger.
128 C2 **Steen River** Can.
134 C2 **Steens Mountain** U.S.A.
100 C1 **Steenwijk** Neth.
126 D2 **Stefansson Island** Can.
101 E3 **Steigerwald** *mts* Ger.
129 E3 **Steinbach** Can.
100 C1 **Steinfurt** Ger.
120 A3 **Steinhausen** Namibia
92 F3 **Steinkjer** Norway
122 A2 **Steinkopf** S. Africa
122 B2 **Stella** S. Africa
105 D2 **Stenay** France
101 E1 **Stendal** Ger.
Stepanakert Azer. *see* **Xankändi**
131 E2 **Stephenville** Can.
139 D2 **Stephenville** U.S.A.
122 B3 **Sterling** S. Africa
136 C2 **Sterling** *CO* U.S.A.
140 B2 **Sterling** *IL* U.S.A.
87 E3 **Sterlitamak** Rus. Fed.
101 E1 **Sternberg** Ger.
128 C2 **Stettler** Can.
140 C2 **Steubenville** U.S.A.
99 C3 **Stevenage** U.K.
129 E2 **Stevenson Lake** Can.
126 B2 **Stevens Village** U.S.A.
128 B2 **Stewart** Can.
126 B2 **Stewart** *r.* Can.
54 A3 **Stewart Island** N.Z.
127 F2 **Stewart Lake** Can.
102 C2 **Steyr** Austria
122 B3 **Steytlerville** S. Africa
128 A2 **Stikine** *r.* Can.
128 A2 **Stikine Plateau** Can.
122 B3 **Stilbaai** S. Africa
139 D1 **Stillwater** U.S.A.
109 D2 **Štip** Macedonia
96 C2 **Stirling** U.K.
92 F3 **Stjørdalshalsen** Norway
103 D2 **Stockerau** Austria
93 G4 **Stockholm** Sweden
98 B2 **Stockport** U.K.
135 B3 **Stockton** U.S.A.
98 C1 **Stockton-on-Tees** U.K.
63 B2 **Stœng Trêng** Cambodia
96 B1 **Stoer, Point of** U.K.
98 B2 **Stoke-on-Trent** U.K.
109 D2 **Stol** *mt.* Serbia
109 C2 **Stolac** Bos.-Herz.
100 C2 **Stolberg (Rheinland)** Ger.
88 C3 **Stolin** Belarus
101 F2 **Stollberg** Ger.
101 D1 **Stolzenau** Ger.
96 C2 **Stonehaven** U.K.
129 E2 **Stonewall** Can.
129 D2 **Stony Rapids** Can.
92 G2 **Storavan** *l.* Sweden
Store Bælt *sea chan.* Denmark *see* **Great Belt**
92 F3 **Støren** Norway
92 F2 **Storforshei** Norway
126 D2 **Storkerson Peninsula** Can.
137 D2 **Storm Lake** U.S.A.
93 E3 **Stornosa** *mt.* Norway
96 A1 **Stornoway** U.K.
86 E2 **Storozhevsk** Rus. Fed.
90 B2 **Storozhynets'** Ukr.
92 F3 **Storsjön** *l.* Sweden
92 H2 **Storslett** Norway
92 G2 **Storuman** Sweden
99 C2 **Stour** *r. England* U.K.
99 C3 **Stour** *r. England* U.K.
130 A1 **Stout Lake** Can.
88 C3 **Stowbtsy** Belarus
97 C1 **Strabane** U.K.
102 C2 **Strakonice** Czech Rep.
102 C1 **Stralsund** Ger.
122 A3 **Strand** S. Africa
93 E3 **Stranda** Norway
97 D1 **Strangford Lough** *inlet* U.K.
96 B3 **Stranraer** U.K.
105 D2 **Strasbourg** France
140 C2 **Stratford** Can.
54 B1 **Stratford** N.Z.
139 C1 **Stratford** U.S.A.
99 C2 **Stratford-upon-Avon** U.K.
128 C2 **Strathmore** Can.
96 C2 **Strathspey** *val.* U.K.
102 C2 **Straubing** Ger.
51 C3 **Streaky Bay** Austr.
140 B2 **Streator** U.S.A.
110 B2 **Strehaia** Romania
153 B5 **Stroeder** Arg.
101 D1 **Ströhen** Ger.
109 C3 **Stromboli, Isola** *i.* Italy
96 C1 **Stromness** U.K.
92 G3 **Strömsund** Sweden
96 C1 **Stronsay** *i.* U.K.
53 D2 **Stroud** Austr.
99 B3 **Stroud** U.K.
100 C1 **Strücklingen (Saterland)** Ger.
109 D2 **Struga** Macedonia
88 C2 **Strugi-Krasnyye** Rus. Fed.
122 B3 **Struis Bay** S. Africa
109 D2 **Strumica** Macedonia
122 B2 **Strydenburg** S. Africa
111 B2 **Strymonas** *r.* Greece
90 A2 **Stryy** Ukr.
128 B2 **Stuart Lake** Can.
130 A1 **Stull Lake** Can.
89 E3 **Stupino** Rus. Fed.
140 B2 **Sturgeon Bay** U.S.A.
130 C2 **Sturgeon Falls** Can.
130 A2 **Sturgeon Lake** Can.
140 B2 **Sturgis** *MI* U.S.A.
136 C2 **Sturgis** *SD* U.S.A.
50 B1 **Sturt Creek** *watercourse* Austr.
52 B1 **Sturt Stony Desert** Austr.
123 C3 **Stutterheim** S. Africa
102 B2 **Stuttgart** Ger.
142 B2 **Stuttgart** U.S.A.
92 A2 **Stykkishólmur** Iceland
90 B1 **Styr** *r.* Belarus/Ukr.
155 D1 **Suaçuí Grande** *r.* Brazil
116 B3 **Suakin** Sudan
78 A3 **Suara** Eritrea
109 C1 **Subotica** Serbia
110 C1 **Suceava** Romania
97 B2 **Suck** *r.* Ireland
152 B2 **Sucre** Bol.
154 B2 **Sucuriú** *r.* Brazil
89 E2 **Suda** Rus. Fed.
91 C3 **Sudak** Ukr.
117 A3 **Sudan** *country* Africa
130 B2 **Sudbury** Can.
117 A4 **Sudd** *swamp* Sudan
89 F2 **Sudislavl'** Rus. Fed.

89 F2 **Sudogda** Rus. Fed.
94 B1 **Suðuroy** *i.* Faroe Is
107 C2 **Sueca** Spain
116 B2 **Suez** Egypt
116 B2 **Suez, Gulf of** Egypt
80 B2 **Suez Canal** Egypt
141 D3 **Suffolk** U.S.A.
116 B2 **Sūhāj** Egypt
79 C2 **Şuḩār** Oman
69 D1 **Sühbaatar** Mongolia
101 E2 **Suhl** Ger.
109 C1 **Suhopolje** Croatia
70 B2 **Suide** China
66 B2 **Suifenhe** China
69 E1 **Suihua** China
70 A2 **Suining** China
70 B2 **Suiping** China
70 B2 **Suiyang** China
70 B2 **Suizhou** China
74 B2 **Sujangarh** India
74 B1 **Sujanpur** India
74 A2 **Sujawal** Pak.
60 B2 **Sukabumi** Indon.
61 B2 **Sukadana** Indon.
61 C2 **Sukaraja** Indon.
89 E3 **Sukhinichi** Rus. Fed.
89 F2 **Sukhona** *r.* Rus. Fed.
62 A2 **Sukhothai** Thai.
74 A2 **Sukkur** Pak.
89 E2 **Sukromny** Rus. Fed.
59 C3 **Sula, Kepulauan** *is* Indon.
74 A1 **Sulaiman Range** *mts* Pak.
Sulawesi *i.* Indon. *see* **Celebes**
150 A2 **Sullana** Peru
137 E3 **Sullivan** U.S.A.
139 D2 **Sulphur Springs** U.S.A.
64 B2 **Sulu Archipelago** *is* Phil.
64 A2 **Sulu Sea** N. Pacific Ocean
101 E3 **Sulzbach-Rosenberg** Ger.
79 C2 **Sumāil** Oman
Sumatera *i.* Indon. *see* **Sumatra**
60 A1 **Sumatra** *i.* Indon.
58 C3 **Sumba** *i.* Indon.
61 C2 **Sumbawa** *i.* Indon.
61 C2 **Sumbawabesar** Indon.
119 D3 **Sumbawanga** Tanz.
120 A2 **Sumbe** Angola
96 □ **Sumburgh** U.K.
96 □ **Sumburgh Head** U.K.
61 C2 **Sumenep** Indon.
67 D4 **Sumisu-jima** *i.* Japan
131 D2 **Summerside** Can.
140 C3 **Summersville** U.S.A.
128 B2 **Summit Lake** Can.
103 D2 **Šumperk** Czech Rep.
81 C1 **Sumqayıt** Azer.
143 D2 **Sumter** U.S.A.
91 C1 **Sumy** Ukr.
75 D2 **Sunamganj** Bangl.
65 B2 **Sunan** N. Korea
79 C2 **Şunaynah** Oman
52 B3 **Sunbury** Austr.
141 D2 **Sunbury** U.S.A.
65 B2 **Sunch'ŏn** N. Korea
65 B3 **Sunch'ŏn** S. Korea
123 C2 **Sun City** S. Africa
60 B2 **Sunda, Selat** *str.* Indon.
136 C2 **Sundance** U.S.A.
75 C2 **Sundarbans** *coastal area* Bangl./India
98 C1 **Sunderland** U.K.
128 C2 **Sundre** Can.
93 G3 **Sundsvall** Sweden
123 D2 **Sundumbili** S. Africa
60 B2 **Sungailiat** Indon.
60 B2 **Sungaipenuh** Indon.
60 B1 **Sungai Petani** Malaysia
80 B1 **Sungurlu** Turkey
93 E3 **Sunndalsøra** Norway
134 C1 **Sunnyside** U.S.A.
135 B3 **Sunnyvale** U.S.A.
83 I2 **Suntar** Rus. Fed.
74 A2 **Suntsar** Pak.
114 B4 **Sunyani** Ghana
82 D2 **Suoyarvi** Rus. Fed.
138 A2 **Superior** *AZ* U.S.A.
137 D2 **Superior** *NE* U.S.A.
140 A1 **Superior** *WI* U.S.A.
140 B1 **Superior, Lake** Can./U.S.A.
89 D3 **Suponevo** Rus. Fed.
81 C2 **Sūq ash Shuyūkh** Iraq
70 B2 **Suqian** China
78 A2 **Sūq Suwayq** Saudi Arabia
79 C2 **Şūr** Oman
74 A2 **Surab** Pak.
61 C2 **Surabaya** Indon.
61 C2 **Surakarta** Indon.
74 B2 **Surat** India
74 B2 **Suratgarh** India
63 A3 **Surat Thani** Thai.
89 D3 **Surazh** Rus. Fed.
109 D2 **Surdulica** Serbia
74 B2 **Surendranagar** India
82 F2 **Surgut** Rus. Fed.
64 B2 **Surigao** Phil.
63 B2 **Surin** Thai.
151 C1 **Suriname** *country* S. America
Surt Libya *see* **Sirte**
Surt, Khalīj *g.* Libya *see* **Sirte, Gulf of**
60 B2 **Surulangun** Indon.
89 F2 **Susanino** Rus. Fed.
135 B2 **Susanville** U.S.A.
80 B1 **Suşehri** Turkey
131 D2 **Sussex** Can.
101 D1 **Süstedt** Ger.
100 C1 **Sustrum** Ger.
83 K2 **Susuman** Rus. Fed.
111 C3 **Susurluk** Turkey
75 B1 **Sutak** India
122 B3 **Sutherland** S. Africa
99 C2 **Sutton Coldfield** U.K.
66 D2 **Suttsu** Japan
49 F4 **Suva** Fiji
89 E3 **Suvorov** Rus. Fed.
103 E1 **Suwałki** Pol.
63 B2 **Suwannaphum** Thai.
143 D3 **Suwannee** *r.* U.S.A.
Suweis, Qanâ el *canal* Egypt *see* **Suez Canal**
65 B2 **Suwŏn** S. Korea
79 C2 **Sūzā** Iran
89 F2 **Suzdal'** Rus. Fed.
70 B2 **Suzhou** *Anhui* China
70 C2 **Suzhou** *Jiangsu* China
67 C3 **Suzu** Japan
67 C3 **Suzu-misaki** *pt* Japan
82 B1 **Svalbard** *terr.* Arctic Ocean
91 D2 **Svatove** Ukr.
63 B2 **Svay Riĕng** Cambodia
93 F3 **Sveg** Sweden
88 C2 **Švenčionys** Lith.
93 F4 **Svendborg** Denmark
Sverdlovsk Rus. Fed. *see* **Yekaterinburg**
109 D2 **Sveti Nikole** Macedonia
88 B3 **Svetlogorsk** Rus. Fed.
88 B3 **Svetlyy** Rus. Fed.
93 I3 **Svetogorsk** Rus. Fed.
110 C2 **Svilengrad** Bulg.
110 B2 **Svinecea Mare, Vârful** *mt.* Romania
110 C2 **Svishtov** Bulg.
103 D2 **Svitavy** Czech Rep.
91 C2 **Svitlovods'k** Ukr.
69 E1 **Svobodnyy** Rus. Fed.
92 F2 **Svolvær** Norway
88 C3 **Svyetlahorsk** Belarus
143 D2 **Swainsboro** U.S.A.
120 A3 **Swakopmund** Namibia
52 B3 **Swan Hill** Austr.
128 C2 **Swan Hills** Can.
129 D2 **Swan Lake** Can.
129 D2 **Swan River** Can.
53 D2 **Swansea** Austr.
99 B3 **Swansea** U.K.
123 C2 **Swartruggens** S. Africa
Swatow China *see* **Shantou**
123 D2 **Swaziland** *country* Africa
93 G3 **Sweden** *country* Europe
139 C2 **Sweetwater** U.S.A.
136 B2 **Sweetwater** *r.* U.S.A.
122 B3 **Swellendam** S. Africa
103 D1 **Świdnica** Pol.
103 D1 **Świdwin** Pol.
103 D1 **Świebodzin** Pol.
103 D1 **Świecie** Pol.
129 D2 **Swift Current** Can.
97 C1 **Swilly, Lough** *inlet* Ireland
99 C3 **Swindon** U.K.
102 C1 **Świnoujście** Pol.
105 D2 **Switzerland** *country* Europe
97 C2 **Swords** Ireland
88 C3 **Syanno** Belarus
89 D2 **Sychevka** Rus. Fed.
53 D2 **Sydney** Austr.
131 D2 **Sydney** Can.
131 D2 **Sydney Mines** Can.
91 D2 **Syeverodonets'k** Ukr.
86 E2 **Syktyvkar** Rus. Fed.
142 C2 **Sylacauga** U.S.A.
75 D2 **Sylhet** Bangl.
102 B1 **Sylt** *i.* Ger.
111 C3 **Symi** *i.* Greece
91 D2 **Synel'nykove** Ukr.
109 C3 **Syracuse** *Sicilia* Italy
136 C3 **Syracuse** *KS* U.S.A.
141 D2 **Syracuse** *NY* U.S.A.
77 C2 **Syrdar'ya** *r.* Asia
80 B2 **Syria** *country* Asia
80 B2 **Syrian Desert** Asia
111 B3 **Syros** *i.* Greece
87 D3 **Syzran'** Rus. Fed.
102 C1 **Szczecin** Pol.
103 D1 **Szczecinek** Pol.
103 E1 **Szczytno** Pol.
103 E2 **Szeged** Hungary
103 D2 **Székesfehérvár** Hungary
103 D2 **Szekszárd** Hungary
103 E2 **Szentes** Hungary
103 D2 **Szentgotthárd** Hungary
103 D2 **Szigetvár** Hungary
103 E2 **Szolnok** Hungary
103 D2 **Szombathely** Hungary

T

78 B2 **Tābah** Saudi Arabia
76 B3 **Ţabas** Iran
81 D3 **Tābask, Kūh-e** *mt.* Iran
150 B2 **Tabatinga** Brazil
114 B2 **Tabelbala** Alg.
129 C3 **Taber** Can.
102 C2 **Tábor** Czech Rep.
119 D3 **Tabora** Tanz.
114 B4 **Tabou** Côte d'Ivoire
81 C2 **Tabrīz** Iran
78 A2 **Tabūk** Saudi Arabia

7 E2 **Tacheng** China
2 C2 **Tachov** Czech Rep.
4 B1 **Tacloban** Phil.
0 A3 **Tacna** Peru
4 B1 **Tacoma** U.S.A.
2 C4 **Tacuarembó** Uru.
8 B3 **Tacupeto** Mex.
7 C3 **Tadjourah** Djibouti
0 B2 **Tadmur** Syria
9 E2 **Tadoule Lake** Can.
5 B2 **Taegu** S. Korea
5 B2 **Taejŏn** S. Korea
5 B3 **Taejŏng** S. Korea
5 B2 **T'aepaek** S. Korea
9 E1 **Ta'erqi** China
7 C1 **Tafalla** Spain
2 B3 **Tafi Viejo** Arg.
9 D2 **Taftān, Kūh-e** *mt.* Iran
1 D2 **Taganrog** Rus. Fed.
1 D2 **Taganrog, Gulf of** Rus. Fed./Ukr.
2 A1 **Tagaung** Myanmar
4 B1 **Tagaytay City** Phil.
4 B2 **Tagbilaran** Phil.
4 B1 **Tagudin** Phil.
4 B2 **Tagum** Phil.
6 B2 **Tagus** *r.* Port./Spain
0 B1 **Tahan, Gunung** *mt.* Malaysia
5 C2 **Tahat, Mont** *mt.* Alg.
9 E1 **Tahe** China
9 I4 **Tahiti** *i.* Fr. Polynesia
9 E1 **Tahlequah** U.S.A.
5 B3 **Tahoe, Lake** U.S.A.
5 B3 **Tahoe City** U.S.A.
6 D2 **Tahoe Lake** Can.
5 C3 **Tahoua** Niger
9 C2 **Tahrūd** Iran
8 B3 **Tahsis** Can.
0 B2 **Tai'an** China
Taibus Qi China *see* **Baochang**
1 C3 **T'aichung** Taiwan
4 C1 **Taihape** N.Z.
0 C2 **Tai Hu** *l.* China
2 A3 **Tailem Bend** Austr.
1 C3 **T'ainan** Taiwan
5 D1 **Taiobeiras** Brazil
1 C3 **T'aipei** Taiwan
0 B1 **Taiping** Malaysia
1 B3 **Taishan** China
3 A5 **Taitao, Península de** *pen.* Chile
1 C3 **T'aitung** Taiwan
2 I2 **Taivalkoski** Fin.
2 H2 **Taivaskero** *h.* Fin.
1 C3 **Taiwan** *country* Asia
1 B3 **Taiwan Strait** China/Taiwan
0 B2 **Taiyuan** China
0 B2 **Taizhou** *Jiangsu* China
1 C3 **Taizhou** *Zhejiang* China
8 B3 **Ta'izz** Yemen
7 D3 **Tajikistan** *country* Asia
5 B2 **Taj Mahal** *tourist site* India
Tajo *r.* Port. *see* **Tagus**
8 A1 **Tak** Thai.
4 B2 **Takaka** N.Z.
7 B4 **Takamatsu** Japan
7 C3 **Takaoka** Japan
4 B1 **Takapuna** N.Z.
7 C3 **Takasaki** Japan
2 B1 **Takatokwane** Botswana
7 C3 **Takayama** Japan
7 C3 **Takefu** Japan
0 A1 **Takengon** Indon.
3 B2 **Takêv** Cambodia
3 B2 **Ta Khmau** Cambodia
6 D2 **Takikawa** Japan
8 B2 **Takla Lake** Can.
8 B2 **Takla Landing** Can.
77 E3 **Taklimakan Desert** China
Taklimakan Shamo *des.* China *see* **Taklimakan Desert**
128 A2 **Taku** *r.* Can./U.S.A.
63 A3 **Takua Pa** Thai.
115 C4 **Takum** Nigeria
88 C3 **Talachyn** Belarus
74 B1 **Talagang** Pak.
150 A2 **Talara** Peru
59 C2 **Talaud, Kepulauan** *is* Indon.
106 C2 **Talavera de la Reina** Spain
153 A4 **Talca** Chile
153 A4 **Talcahuano** Chile
89 E2 **Taldom** Rus. Fed.
77 D2 **Taldykorgan** Kazakh.
59 C3 **Taliabu** *i.* Indon.
64 B1 **Talisay** Phil.
61 C2 **Taliwang** Indon.
81 C2 **Tall 'Afar** Iraq
143 D2 **Tallahassee** U.S.A.
88 B2 **Tallinn** Estonia
142 B2 **Tallulah** U.S.A.
104 B2 **Talmont-St-Hilaire** France
90 C2 **Tal'ne** Ukr.
117 B3 **Talodi** Sudan
91 E1 **Talovaya** Rus. Fed.
126 E2 **Taloyoak** Can.
88 B2 **Talsi** Latvia
152 A3 **Taltal** Chile
129 C1 **Taltson** *r.* Can.
60 A1 **Talu** Indon.
53 C1 **Talwood** Austr.
114 B4 **Tamale** Ghana
115 C2 **Tamanrasset** Alg.
99 A3 **Tamar** *r.* U.K.
145 C2 **Tamazunchale** Mex.
114 A3 **Tambacounda** Senegal
61 B1 **Tambelan, Kepulauan** *is* Indon.
91 E1 **Tambov** Rus. Fed.
145 C2 **Tamiahua, Laguna de** *lag.* Mex.
143 D3 **Tampa** U.S.A.
143 D3 **Tampa Bay** U.S.A.
93 H3 **Tampere** Fin.
145 C2 **Tampico** Mex.
69 D1 **Tamsagbulag** Mongolia
102 C2 **Tamsweg** Austria
53 D2 **Tamworth** Austr.
99 C2 **Tamworth** U.K.
119 E3 **Tana** *r.* Kenya
117 B3 **Tana, Lake** Eth.
67 C4 **Tanabe** Japan
92 I1 **Tana Bru** Norway
61 C2 **Tanahgrogot** Indon.
58 C3 **Tanahjampea** *i.* Indon.
50 C1 **Tanami Desert** Austr.
126 A2 **Tanana** U.S.A.
108 A1 **Tanaro** *r.* Italy
65 B1 **Tanch'ŏn** N. Korea
64 B2 **Tandag** Phil.
110 C2 **Țăndărei** Romania
153 C4 **Tandil** Arg.
74 A2 **Tando Adam** Pak.
74 A2 **Tando Muhammad Khan** Pak.
114 B2 **Tanezrouft** *reg.* Alg./Mali
119 D3 **Tanga** Tanz.
119 C3 **Tanganyika, Lake** Africa
Tanger Morocco *see* **Tangier**
101 E1 **Tangermünde** Ger.
75 C1 **Tanggula Shan** *mts* China
114 B1 **Tangier** Morocco
75 C1 **Tangra Yumco** *salt l.* China
70 B2 **Tangshan** China
68 C2 **Taniantaweng Shan** *mts* China
59 C3 **Tanimbar, Kepulauan** *is* Indon.
64 B2 **Tanjay** Phil.
60 A1 **Tanjungbalai** Indon.
61 B2 **Tanjungpandan** Indon.
60 B1 **Tanjungpinang** Indon.
61 C1 **Tanjungredeb** Indon.
61 C1 **Tanjungselor** Indon.
74 B1 **Tank** Pak.
115 C3 **Tanout** Niger
75 C2 **Tansen** Nepal
116 B1 **Ţanţā** Egypt
119 D3 **Tanzania** *country* Africa
69 E1 **Taonan** China
138 B1 **Taos** U.S.A.
114 B2 **Taoudenni** Mali
88 C2 **Tapa** Estonia
145 C3 **Tapachula** Mex.
151 C2 **Tapajós** *r.* Brazil
60 A1 **Tapaktuan** Indon.
145 C3 **Tapanatepec** Mex.
150 B2 **Tapauá** Brazil
114 B4 **Tapeta** Liberia
74 B2 **Tapi** *r.* India
141 D3 **Tappahannock** U.S.A.
150 B2 **Tapurucuara** Brazil
154 A1 **Taquarí** *r.* Brazil
154 B1 **Taquari, Serra do** *hills* Brazil
154 C2 **Taquaritinga** Brazil
115 D4 **Taraba** *r.* Nigeria
Ţarābulus Libya *see* **Tripoli**
61 C1 **Tarakan** Indon.
88 A3 **Taran, Mys** *pt* Rus. Fed.
54 B1 **Taranaki, Mount** *vol.* N.Z.
106 C1 **Tarancón** Spain
109 C2 **Taranto** Italy
109 C2 **Taranto, Golfo di** *g.* Italy
150 A2 **Tarapoto** Peru
91 E2 **Tarasovskiy** Rus. Fed.
150 A2 **Tarauacá** Brazil
150 B2 **Tarauacá** *r.* Brazil
48 F2 **Tarawa** *atoll* Kiribati
77 D2 **Taraz** Kazakh.
107 C1 **Tarazona** Spain
77 E2 **Tarbagatay, Khrebet** *mts* Kazakh.
96 A2 **Tarbert** *Scotland* U.K.
96 B3 **Tarbert** *Scotland* U.K.
104 C3 **Tarbes** France
96 B2 **Tarbet** U.K.
51 C3 **Tarcoola** Austr.
53 D2 **Taree** Austr.
110 C2 **Târgovişte** Romania
110 B1 **Târgu Jiu** Romania
110 B1 **Târgu Mureş** Romania
110 C1 **Târgu Neamţ** Romania
79 C2 **Tarif** U.A.E.
152 B3 **Tarija** Bol.
79 B3 **Tarīm** Yemen
77 E3 **Tarim Basin** China
77 E2 **Tarim He** *r.* China
Tarim Pendi *basin* China *see* **Tarim Basin**
59 D3 **Taritatu** *r.* Indon.
82 G2 **Tarko-Sale** Rus. Fed.
114 B4 **Tarkwa** Ghana
64 B1 **Tarlac** Phil.
92 G2 **Tärnaby** Sweden
77 C3 **Tarnak** *r.* Afgh.
110 B1 **Târnăveni** Romania
103 E1 **Tarnobrzeg** Pol.
103 E1 **Tarnów** Pol.
114 B1 **Taroudannt** Morocco
108 B2 **Tarquinia** Italy
107 D1 **Tarragona** Spain
107 D1 **Tàrrega** Spain
80 B2 **Tarsus** Turkey
152 B3 **Tartagal** Arg.
104 B3 **Tartas** France

88 C2 **Tartu** Estonia
80 B2 **Ţarţūs** Syria
155 D1 **Tarumirim** Brazil
89 E3 **Tarusa** Rus. Fed.
108 B1 **Tarvisio** Italy
81 D3 **Tashk, Daryācheh-ye** *l.* Iran
Tashkent Uzbek. *see* **Toshkent**
131 D1 **Tasiujaq** Can.
77 E2 **Taskesken** Kazakh.
54 B2 **Tasman Bay** N.Z.
51 D4 **Tasmania** *state* Austr.
54 B2 **Tasman Mountains** N.Z.
156 D8 **Tasman Sea** S. Pacific Ocean
115 C2 **Tassili du Hoggar** *plat.* Alg.
115 C2 **Tassili n'Ajjer** *plat.* Alg.
103 D2 **Tatabánya** Hungary
90 B2 **Tatarbunary** Ukr.
83 K3 **Tatarskiy Proliv** *str.* Rus. Fed.
67 C4 **Tateyama** Japan
128 C1 **Tathlina Lake** Can.
78 B3 **Tathlīth** Saudi Arabia
78 B2 **Tathlīth, Wādī** *watercourse* Saudi Arabia
53 C3 **Tathra** Austr.
62 A1 **Tatkon** Myanmar
128 B2 **Tatla Lake** Can.
103 D2 **Tatra Mountains** *mts* Pol./Slovakia
Tatry *mts* Pol./Slovakia *see* **Tatra Mountains**
154 C2 **Tatuí** Brazil
139 C2 **Tatum** U.S.A.
81 C2 **Tatvan** Turkey
151 D2 **Taua** Brazil
155 C2 **Taubaté** Brazil
101 D3 **Tauberbischofsheim** Ger.
54 C1 **Taumarunui** N.Z.
62 A1 **Taunggyi** Myanmar
62 A2 **Taung-ngu** Myanmar
62 A2 **Taungup** Myanmar
99 B3 **Taunton** U.K.
100 C2 **Taunus** *hills* Ger.
54 C1 **Taupo** N.Z.
54 C1 **Taupo, Lake** N.Z.
88 B2 **Tauragė** Lith.
54 C1 **Tauranga** N.Z.
80 B2 **Taurus Mountains** Turkey
111 C3 **Tavas** Turkey
86 F3 **Tavda** Rus. Fed.
106 B2 **Tavira** Port.
99 A3 **Tavistock** U.K.
63 A2 **Tavoy** Myanmar
111 C3 **Tavşanlı** Turkey
99 A3 **Taw** *r.* U.K.
140 C2 **Tawas City** U.S.A.
61 C1 **Tawau** *Sabah* Malaysia
64 A2 **Tawi-Tawi** *i.* Phil.
145 C3 **Taxco** Mex.
76 B2 **Taxiatosh** Uzbek.
77 D3 **Taxkorgan** China
96 C2 **Tay** *r.* U.K.
96 C2 **Tay, Firth of** *est.* U.K.
96 B2 **Tay, Loch** *l.* U.K.
128 B2 **Taylor** Can.
139 D2 **Taylor** U.S.A.
140 B3 **Taylorville** U.S.A.
78 A2 **Taymā'** Saudi Arabia
83 H2 **Taymura** *r.* Rus. Fed.
83 H2 **Taymyr, Ozero** *l.* Rus. Fed.
Taymyr, Poluostrov *pen.* Rus. Fed. *see* **Taymyr Peninsula**
83 G2 **Taymyr Peninsula** Rus. Fed.
63 B2 **Tây Ninh** Vietnam
64 A1 **Taytay** Phil.
82 G2 **Taz** *r.* Rus. Fed.
114 B1 **Taza** Morocco
129 D2 **Tazin Lake** Can.
86 G2 **Tazovskaya Guba** *sea chan.* Rus. Fed.
81 C1 **T'bilisi** Georgia
91 E2 **Tbilisskaya** Rus. Fed.
118 B3 **Tchibanga** Gabon
118 B2 **Tcholliré** Cameroon
103 D1 **Tczew** Pol.
144 B2 **Teacapán** Mex.
54 A3 **Te Anau** N.Z.
54 A3 **Te Anau, Lake** N.Z.
145 C3 **Teapa** Mex.
54 C1 **Te Awamutu** N.Z.
115 C1 **Tébessa** Alg.
60 B2 **Tebingtinggi** *Sumatera Selatan* Indon.
60 A1 **Tebingtinggi** *Sumatera Utara* Indon.
114 B4 **Techiman** Ghana
144 B3 **Tecomán** Mex.
144 B2 **Tecoripa** Mex.
145 B3 **Técpan** Mex.
144 B2 **Tecuala** Mex.
110 C1 **Tecuci** Romania
68 C1 **Teeli** Rus. Fed.
98 C1 **Tees** *r.* U.K.
111 C3 **Tefenni** Turkey
61 B2 **Tegal** Indon.
146 B3 **Tegucigalpa** Hond.
115 C3 **Teguidda-n-Tessoumt** Niger
114 B4 **Téhini** Côte d'Ivoire
81 D2 **Tehrān** Iran
145 C3 **Tehuacán** Mex.
145 C3 **Tehuantepec, Gulf of** Mex.
145 C3 **Tehuantepec, Istmo de** *isth.* Mex.
99 A2 **Teifi** *r.* U.K.
76 C3 **Tejen** Turkm.
76 C3 **Tejen** *r.* Turkm.
Tejo *r.* Spain *see* **Tagus**
145 B3 **Tejupilco** Mex.
54 B2 **Tekapo, Lake** N.Z.
145 D2 **Tekax** Mex.
116 B3 **Tekezē Wenz** *r.* Eritrea/Eth.
111 C2 **Tekirdağ** Turkey
54 C1 **Te Kuiti** N.Z.
75 C2 **Tel** *r.* India
81 C1 **T'elavi** Georgia
80 B2 **Tel Aviv-Yafo** Israel
145 D2 **Telchac Puerto** Mex.
128 A2 **Telegraph Creek** Can.
154 B2 **Telêmaco Borba** Brazil
99 B2 **Telford** U.K.
60 A2 **Telo** Indon.
86 E2 **Telpoziz, Gora** *mt.* Rus. Fed.
88 B2 **Telšiai** Lith.
61 B2 **Telukbatang** Indon.
60 A1 **Telukdalam** Indon.
60 B1 **Teluk Intan** Malaysia
130 C2 **Temagami Lake** Can.
61 C2 **Temanggung** Indon.
123 C2 **Temba** S. Africa
60 B2 **Tembilahan** Indon.
120 A1 **Tembo Aluma** Angola
99 B2 **Teme** *r.* U.K.
60 B1 **Temerluh** Malaysia
77 D1 **Temirtau** Kazakh.
53 C2 **Temora** Austr.
139 D2 **Temple** U.S.A.
97 C2 **Templemore** Ireland
145 C2 **Tempoal** Mex.
91 D2 **Temryuk** Rus. Fed.
153 A4 **Temuco** Chile
54 B2 **Temuka** N.Z.
145 C2 **Tenabo** Mex.
73 C3 **Tenali** India
63 A2 **Tenasserim** Myanmar
99 A3 **Tenby** U.K.
117 C3 **Tendaho** Eth.
105 D3 **Tende** France
108 A2 **Tende, Col de** *pass* France/Italy
73 D4 **Ten Degree Channel** India
67 D3 **Tendō** Japan
114 B3 **Ténenkou** Mali
115 D3 **Ténéré, Erg du** *des.* Niger
115 D2 **Ténéré du Tafassâsset** *des.* Niger
114 A2 **Tenerife** *i.* Islas Canarias
107 D2 **Ténès** Alg.
61 C2 **Tengah, Kepulauan** *is* Indo
62 A1 **Tengchong** China
61 C2 **Tenggarong** Indon.
70 A2 **Tengger Shamo** *des.* China
71 B3 **Tengxian** China
119 C4 **Tenke** Dem. Rep. Congo
114 B3 **Tenkodogo** Burkina
51 C1 **Tennant Creek** Austr.
142 C1 **Tennessee** *r.* U.S.A.
142 C1 **Tennessee** *state* U.S.A.
145 C3 **Tenosique** Mex.
53 D1 **Tenterfield** Austr.
154 B2 **Teodoro Sampaio** Brazil
155 D1 **Teófilo Otôni** Brazil
145 C3 **Teopisca** Mex.
144 B2 **Tepache** Mex.
54 B1 **Te Paki** N.Z.
144 B3 **Tepalcatepec** Mex.
144 B2 **Tepatitlán** Mex.
144 B2 **Tepehuanes** Mex.
109 D2 **Tepelenë** Albania
144 B2 **Tepic** Mex.
102 C1 **Teplice** Czech Rep.
89 E3 **Teploye** Rus. Fed.
144 B2 **Tequila** Mex.
108 B2 **Teramo** Italy
89 E3 **Terbuny** Rus. Fed.
90 B2 **Terebovlya** Ukr.
87 D4 **Terek** *r.* Rus. Fed.
151 D2 **Teresina** Brazil
155 D2 **Teresópolis** Brazil
63 A3 **Teressa Island** India
80 B1 **Terme** Turkey
108 B3 **Termini Imerese** *Sicilia* Ita
145 C3 **Términos, Laguna de** *lag.* M
77 C3 **Termiz** Uzbek.
109 B2 **Termoli** Italy
59 C2 **Ternate** Indon.
100 A2 **Terneuzen** Neth.
108 B2 **Terni** Italy
90 B2 **Ternopil'** Ukr.
128 B2 **Terrace** Can.
130 B2 **Terrace Bay** Can.
122 B2 **Terra Firma** S. Africa
140 B3 **Terre Haute** U.S.A.
131 E2 **Terrenceville** Can.
100 B1 **Terschelling** *i.* Neth.
108 A3 **Tertenia** *Sardegna* Italy
107 C1 **Teruel** Spain
92 H2 **Tervola** Fin.
109 C2 **Tešanj** Bos.-Herz.
116 B3 **Teseney** Eritrea
66 D2 **Teshio-gawa** *r.* Japan
128 A1 **Teslin** Can.
128 A1 **Teslin Lake** Can.
154 B1 **Tesouro** Brazil
115 C3 **Tessaoua** Niger
121 C2 **Tete** Moz.
90 C1 **Teteriv** *r.* Ukr.
101 F1 **Teterow** Ger.
90 B2 **Tetiyiv** Ukr.
114 B1 **Tétouan** Morocco
109 D2 **Tetovo** Macedonia
152 B3 **Teuco** *r.* Arg.

4 B2 **Teul de González Ortega** Mex.
1 D1 **Teutoburger Wald** *hills* Ger.
Tevere *r.* Italy *see* **Tiber**
4 A3 **Teviot** N.Z.
1 E2 **Tewantin** Austr.
4 C2 **Te Wharau** N.Z.
9 E2 **Texarkana** U.S.A.
3 D1 **Texas** Austr.
9 D2 **Texas** *state* U.S.A.
9 E3 **Texas City** U.S.A.
0 B1 **Texel** *i.* Neth.
9 D2 **Texoma, Lake** U.S.A.
3 C2 **Teyateyaneng** Lesotho
9 F2 **Teykovo** Rus. Fed.
9 F2 **Teza** *r.* Rus. Fed.
5 D2 **Tezpur** India
2 A1 **Tezu** India
9 E1 **Tha-anne** *r.* Can.
3 C2 **Thabana-Ntlenyana** *mt.* Lesotho
3 C2 **Thaba Putsoa** *mt.* Lesotho
3 C1 **Thabazimbi** S. Africa
3 C2 **Thabong** S. Africa
3 A2 **Thagyettaw** Myanmar
2 B1 **Thai Binh** Vietnam
3 B2 **Thailand** *country* Asia
3 B2 **Thailand, Gulf of** Asia
2 B1 **Thai Nguyên** Vietnam
2 B2 **Thakèk** Laos
3 A3 **Thalang** Thai.
4 B1 **Thal Desert** Pak.
1 E2 **Thale (Harz)** Ger.
2 B2 **Tha Li** Thai.
3 C1 **Thamaga** Botswana
6 C3 **Thamar, Jabal** *mt.* Yemen
9 C3 **Thamarīt** Oman
0 B2 **Thames** *r.* Can.
4 C1 **Thames** N.Z.
9 D3 **Thames** *est.* U.K.
9 D3 **Thames** *r.* U.K.
3 A2 **Thanbyuzayat** Myanmar
2 A2 **Thandwè** Myanmar
2 B2 **Thanh Hoa** Vietnam
3 B3 **Thanjavur** India
3 A2 **Thanlyin** Myanmar
4 A2 **Thano Bula Khan** Pak.
2 B1 **Than Uyên** Vietnam
4 A2 **Thar Desert** India/Pak.
2 B1 **Thargomindah** Austr.
1 C2 **Tharthār, Buḩayrat ath** *l.* Iraq
1 B2 **Thasos** *i.* Greece
2 B1 **Thât Khê** Vietnam
2 A2 **Thaton** Myanmar
4 A2 **Thatta** Pak.
2 A1 **Thaungdut** Myanmar
2 A2 **Thayawadi** Myanmar
2 A2 **Thayetmyo** Myanmar
2 A1 **Thazi** Myanmar
6 C2 **The Bahamas** *country* West Indies
8 B1 **The Cheviot** *h.* U.K.
4 B1 **The Dalles** U.S.A.
9 C2 **The Fens** *reg.* U.K.
4 A3 **The Gambia** *country* Africa
The Great Oasis Egypt *see* **Khārijah, Wāḩāt al**
9 C2 **The Gulf** Asia
0 B1 **The Hague** Neth.
9 E1 **Thelon** *r.* Can.
1 E2 **Themar** Ger.
6 A1 **The Minch** *sea chan.* U.K.
0 B2 **Theodore Roosevelt** *r.* Brazil
9 D2 **The Pas** Can.
1 B2 **Thermaïkos Kolpos** *g.* Greece
6 B2 **Thermopolis** U.S.A.
3 C3 **The Rock** Austr.
0 B2 **Thessalon** Can.
111 B2 **Thessaloniki** Greece
99 D2 **Thetford** U.K.
131 C2 **Thetford Mines** Can.
62 A1 **The Triangle** *mts* Myanmar
131 D1 **Thévenet, Lac** *l.* Can.
99 D2 **The Wash** *b.* U.K.
139 D2 **The Woodlands** U.S.A.
142 B3 **Thibodaux** U.S.A.
129 E2 **Thicket Portage** Can.
137 D1 **Thief River Falls** U.S.A.
105 C2 **Thiers** France
119 D3 **Thika** Kenya
73 B4 **Thiladhunmathi Atoll** Maldives
75 C2 **Thimphu** Bhutan
105 D2 **Thionville** France
Thira *i.* Greece *see* **Santorini**
98 C1 **Thirsk** U.K.
73 B4 **Thiruvananthapuram** India
93 E4 **Thisted** Denmark
129 E1 **Thlewiaza** *r.* Can.
62 A2 **Thoen** Thai.
123 D1 **Thohoyandou** S. Africa
101 E1 **Thomasburg** Ger.
97 C2 **Thomastown** Ireland
143 D2 **Thomasville** U.S.A.
100 C2 **Thommen** Belgium
129 E2 **Thompson** Can.
128 E3 **Thompson** *r.* U.S.A.
134 C1 **Thompson Falls** U.S.A.
128 B2 **Thompson Sound** Can.
96 C3 **Thornhill** U.K.
55 C2 **Thorshavnheiane** *reg.* Antarctica
104 B2 **Thouars** France
128 C2 **Three Hills** Can.
63 A2 **Three Pagodas Pass** Myanmar/Thai.
114 B4 **Three Points, Cape** Ghana
73 B3 **Thrissur** India
63 B2 **Thu Dâu Môt** Vietnam
100 B2 **Thuin** Belgium
127 G1 **Thule** Greenland
121 B3 **Thuli** Zimbabwe
130 B2 **Thunder Bay** Can.
63 A3 **Thung Song** Thai.
101 E2 **Thüringer Becken** *reg.* Ger.
101 E2 **Thüringer Wald** *mts* Ger.
102 C1 **Thüringer Wald** *mts* Ger.
97 C2 **Thurles** Ireland
96 C1 **Thurso** U.K.
96 C1 **Thurso** *r.* U.K.
151 D2 **Tianguá** Brazil
70 B2 **Tianjin** China
70 B2 **Tianjin** *mun.* China
71 A3 **Tianlin** China
70 B2 **Tianmen** China
70 A2 **Tianshui** China
154 B2 **Tibagi** *r.* Brazil
118 B2 **Tibati** Cameroon
108 B2 **Tiber** *r.* Italy
Tiberias, Lake Israel *see* **Galilee, Sea of**
115 D2 **Tibesti** *mts* Chad
Tibet *aut. reg.* China *see* **Xizang Zizhiqu**
68 B2 **Tibet, Plateau of** China
Tibet Autonomous Region *aut. reg.* China *see* **Xizang Zizhiqu**
52 B1 **Tibooburra** Austr.
144 A2 **Tiburón, Isla** *i.* Mex.
114 B3 **Tîchît** Maur.
114 A2 **Tichla** Western Sahara
145 D2 **Ticul** Mex.
114 A3 **Tidjikja** Maur.
100 B2 **Tiel** Neth.
65 A1 **Tieling** China
100 A2 **Tielt** Belgium
100 B2 **Tienen** Belgium
68 B2 **Tien Shan** *mts* China/Kyrg.
Tientsin China *see* **Tianjin**
93 G3 **Tierp** Sweden
145 C3 **Tierra Blanca** Mex.
145 C3 **Tierra Colorada** Mex.
153 B6 **Tierra del Fuego, Isla Grande de** *i.* Arg./Chile
154 C2 **Tietê** Brazil
Tiflis Georgia *see* **T'bilisi**
143 D2 **Tifton** U.S.A.
90 B2 **Tighina** Moldova
131 D2 **Tignish** Can.
150 A2 **Tigre** *r.* Ecuador/Peru
81 C2 **Tigris** *r.* Asia
145 C2 **Tihuatlán** Mex.
144 A1 **Tijuana** Mex.
91 E2 **Tikhoretsk** Rus. Fed.
89 D2 **Tikhvin** Rus. Fed.
89 D2 **Tikhvinskaya Gryada** *ridge* Rus. Fed.
54 C1 **Tikokino** N.Z.
81 C2 **Tikrīt** Iraq
83 J2 **Tiksi** Rus. Fed.
100 B2 **Tilburg** Neth.
152 B3 **Tilcara** Arg.
52 B1 **Tilcha (abandoned)** Austr.
114 C3 **Tillabéri** Niger
134 B1 **Tillamook** U.S.A.
63 A3 **Tillanchong Island** India
111 C3 **Tilos** *i.* Greece
52 B2 **Tilpa** Austr.
86 F2 **Til'tim** Rus. Fed.
89 E3 **Tim** Rus. Fed.
86 D2 **Timanskiy Kryazh** *ridge* Rus. Fed.
54 B2 **Timaru** N.Z.
91 D2 **Timashevsk** Rus. Fed.
114 B3 **Timbedgha** Maur.
50 C1 **Timber Creek** Austr.
114 B3 **Timbuktu** Mali
114 C2 **Timimoun** Alg.
111 B2 **Timiou Prodromou, Akrotirio** *pt* Greece
110 B1 **Timiș** *r.* Romania
110 B1 **Timișoara** Romania
130 B2 **Timmins** Can.
89 E2 **Timokhino** Rus. Fed.
151 D2 **Timon** Brazil
59 C3 **Timor** *i.* East Timor/Indonesia
58 C3 **Timor Sea** Austr./Indon.
93 G3 **Timrå** Sweden
114 B2 **Tindouf** Alg.
75 C2 **Tingri** China
93 F4 **Tingsryd** Sweden
59 D2 **Tinian** *i.* N. Mariana Is
152 B3 **Tinogasta** Arg.
111 C3 **Tinos** Greece
111 C3 **Tinos** *i.* Greece
115 C2 **Tinrhert, Hamada de** Alg.
62 A1 **Tinsukia** India
107 D2 **Tipasa** Alg.
97 B2 **Tipperary** Ireland
109 C2 **Tirana** Albania
Tiranë Albania *see* **Tirana**
108 B1 **Tirano** Italy
90 B2 **Tiraspol** Moldova
111 C3 **Tire** Turkey
96 A2 **Tiree** *i.* U.K.
74 B1 **Tirich Mir** *mt.* Pak.
73 B3 **Tiruchchirappalli** India
73 B4 **Tirunelveli** India
73 B3 **Tirupati** India
73 B3 **Tiruppattur** India
73 B3 **Tiruppur** India

109 D1 **Tisa** *r.* Serbia
129 D2 **Tisdale** Can.
107 D2 **Tissemsilt** Alg.
152 B2 **Titicaca, Lake** Bol./Peru
75 C2 **Titlagarh** India
110 C2 **Titu** Romania
143 D3 **Titusville** U.S.A.
99 B3 **Tiverton** U.K.
108 B2 **Tivoli** Italy
79 C2 **Ṭīwī** Oman
145 D2 **Tizimín** Mex.
107 D2 **Tizi Ouzou** Alg.
114 B2 **Tiznit** Morocco
145 C3 **Tlacotalpán** Mex.
144 B2 **Tlahualilo** Mex.
145 C3 **Tlapa** Mex.
145 C3 **Tlaxcala** Mex.
145 C3 **Tlaxiaco** Mex.
114 B1 **Tlemcen** Alg.
123 C1 **Tlokweng** Botswana
128 B2 **Toad River** Can.
121 D2 **Toamasina** Madag.
60 A1 **Toba, Danau** *l.* Indon.
74 A1 **Toba and Kakar Ranges** *mts* Pak.
147 D3 **Tobago** *i.* Trin. and Tob.
59 C2 **Tobelo** Indon.
130 B2 **Tobermory** Can.
96 A2 **Tobermory** U.K.
129 D2 **Tobin Lake** Can.
60 B2 **Toboali** Indon.
76 C1 **Tobol** *r.* Kazakh./Rus. Fed.
86 F3 **Tobol'sk** Rus. Fed.
151 D2 **Tocantinópolis** Brazil
151 D2 **Tocantins** *r.* Brazil
143 D2 **Toccoa** U.S.A.
108 A1 **Toce** *r.* Italy
152 A3 **Tocopilla** Chile
53 C3 **Tocumwal** Austr.
144 A2 **Todos Santos** Mex.
128 B3 **Tofino** Can.
96 □ **Toft** U.K.
49 G4 **Tofua** *i.* Tonga
59 C3 **Togian, Kepulauan** *is* Indon.
114 C4 **Togo** *country* Africa
74 B2 **Tohana** India
126 B2 **Tok** U.S.A.
116 B3 **Tokar** Sudan
69 E3 **Tokara-rettō** *is* Japan
91 E1 **Tokarevka** Rus. Fed.
49 G3 **Tokelau** *terr.* S. Pacific Ocean
91 D2 **Tokmak** Ukr.
77 D2 **Tokmok** Kyrg.
54 C1 **Tokoroa** N.Z.
68 B2 **Toksun** China
67 B4 **Tokushima** Japan
67 C3 **Tōkyō** Japan
121 D3 **Tôlañaro** Madag.
154 B2 **Toledo** Brazil
106 C2 **Toledo** Spain
140 C2 **Toledo** U.S.A.
106 C2 **Toledo, Montes de** *mts* Spain
142 B2 **Toledo Bend Reservoir** U.S.A.
121 D3 **Toliara** Madag.
58 C2 **Tolitoli** Indon.
108 B1 **Tolmezzo** Italy
104 B3 **Tolosa** Spain
145 C3 **Toluca** Mex.
87 D3 **Tol'yatti** Rus. Fed.
140 A2 **Tomah** U.S.A.
66 D2 **Tomakomai** Japan
106 B2 **Tomar** Port.
103 E1 **Tomaszów Lubelski** Pol.
103 E1 **Tomaszów Mazowiecki** Pol.
144 B3 **Tomatlán** Mex.
142 C2 **Tombigbee** *r.* U.S.A.
155 D2 **Tombos** Brazil
Tombouctou Mali *see* **Timbuktu**
120 A2 **Tombua** Angola
123 C1 **Tom Burke** S. Africa
53 C2 **Tomingley** Austr.
58 C3 **Tomini, Teluk** *g.* Indon.
109 C2 **Tomislavgrad** Bos.-Herz.
50 A2 **Tom Price** Austr.
82 G3 **Tomsk** Rus. Fed.
93 F4 **Tomtabacken** *h.* Sweden
145 C3 **Tonalá** Mex.
150 B2 **Tonantins** Brazil
59 C2 **Tondano** Indon.
49 G4 **Tonga** *country* S. Pacific Ocean
49 G4 **Tongatapu Group** *is* Tonga
71 B3 **Tongcheng** China
70 A2 **Tongchuan** China
71 A3 **Tongdao** China
65 B2 **Tongduch'ŏn** S. Korea
100 B2 **Tongeren** Belgium
65 B2 **Tonghae** S. Korea
62 B1 **Tonghai** China
65 B1 **Tonghua** China
65 B2 **Tongjosŏn-man** *b.* N. Korea
62 B1 **Tongking, Gulf of** China/Vietnam
69 E2 **Tongliao** China
70 B2 **Tongling** China
52 B2 **Tongo** Austr.
71 A3 **Tongren** China
Tongshan China *see* **Xuzhou**
Tongtian He *r.* China *see* **Yangtze**
96 B1 **Tongue** U.K.
65 B3 **T'ongyŏng** S. Korea
69 E2 **Tongyu** China
65 A1 **Tongyuanpu** China
74 B2 **Tonk** India
63 B2 **Tonle Sap** *l.* Cambodia
135 C3 **Tonopah** U.S.A.
93 F4 **Tønsberg** Norway
135 D2 **Tooele** U.S.A.
52 B3 **Tooleybuc** Austr.
53 D1 **Toowoomba** Austr.
137 D3 **Topeka** U.S.A.
144 B2 **Topia** Mex.
144 B2 **Topolobampo** Mex.
86 C2 **Topozero, Ozero** *l.* Rus. Fed.
134 B1 **Toppenish** U.S.A.
111 C3 **Torbalı** Turkey
76 B3 **Torbat-e Heydarīyeh** Iran
76 C3 **Torbat-e Jām** Iran
106 C1 **Tordesillas** Spain
107 C1 **Tordesilos** Spain
107 D1 **Torelló** Spain
101 F2 **Torgau** Ger.
100 A2 **Torhout** Belgium
Torino Italy *see* **Turin**
154 B1 **Torixoréu** Brazil
106 B1 **Tormes** *r.* Spain
92 H2 **Torneälven** *r.* Sweden
127 G3 **Torngat Mountains** Can.
92 H2 **Tornio** Fin.
106 B1 **Toro** Spain
130 C2 **Toronto** Can.
119 D2 **Tororo** Uganda
Toros Dağları *mts* Turkey *see* **Taurus Mountains**
99 B3 **Torquay** U.K.
106 B2 **Torrão** Port.
106 B1 **Torre** *mt.* Port.
107 D1 **Torreblanca** Spain
106 C1 **Torrecerredo** *mt.* Spain
106 B1 **Torre de Moncorvo** Port.
106 C1 **Torrelavega** Spain
106 C2 **Torremolinos** Spain
52 A2 **Torrens, Lake** *imp. l.* Austr.
107 C2 **Torrent** Spain
144 B2 **Torreón** Mex.
106 B2 **Torres Novas** Port.
106 B2 **Torres Vedras** Port.
107 C2 **Torrevieja** Spain
96 B2 **Torridon** U.K.
106 C2 **Torrijos** Spain
141 E2 **Torrington** *CT* U.S.A.
136 C2 **Torrington** *WY* U.S.A.
107 D1 **Torroella de Montgrí** Spain
94 B1 **Tórshavn** Faroe Is
108 A3 **Tortolì** *Sardegna* Italy
107 D1 **Tortosa** Spain
103 D1 **Toruń** Pol.
97 B1 **Tory Island** Ireland
89 D2 **Torzhok** Rus. Fed.
122 B2 **Tosca** S. Africa
108 B2 **Toscano, Arcipelago** *is* Italy
77 C2 **Toshkent** Uzbek.
89 D2 **Tosno** Rus. Fed.
152 B3 **Tostado** Arg.
101 D1 **Tostedt** Ger.
80 B1 **Tosya** Turkey
86 D3 **Tot'ma** Rus. Fed.
67 B3 **Tottori** Japan
114 B4 **Touba** Côte d'Ivoire
114 B1 **Toubkal, Jbel** *mt.* Morocco
114 B3 **Tougan** Burkina
115 C1 **Touggourt** Alg.
105 D2 **Toul** France
71 C3 **Touliu** Taiwan
105 D3 **Toulon** France
104 C3 **Toulouse** France
100 A2 **Tournai** Belgium
105 C2 **Tournus** France
151 E2 **Touros** Brazil
104 C2 **Tours** France
115 D2 **Tousside, Pic** *mt.* Chad
122 B3 **Touwsrivier** S. Africa
66 D2 **Towada** Japan
134 D1 **Townsend** U.S.A.
51 D1 **Townsville** Austr.
77 E2 **Toxkan He** *r.* China
66 D2 **Tōya-ko** *l.* Japan
67 C3 **Toyama** Japan
67 C3 **Toyota** Japan
115 C1 **Tozeur** Tunisia
81 C1 **Tqvarch'eli** Georgia
Trâblous Lebanon *see* **Tripo**
80 B1 **Trabzon** Turkey
106 B2 **Trafalgar, Cabo** *c.* Spain
128 C3 **Trail** Can.
88 B3 **Trakai** Lith.
97 B2 **Tralee** Ireland
97 C2 **Tramore** Ireland
63 A3 **Trang** Thai.
59 C3 **Trangan** *i.* Indon.
55 I2 **Transantarctic Mountains** Antarctica
110 B1 **Transylvanian Alps** *mts* Romania
108 B3 **Trapani** *Sicilia* Italy
53 C3 **Traralgon** Austr.
63 B2 **Trat** Thai.
102 C2 **Traunstein** Ger.
140 B2 **Traverse City** U.S.A.
103 D2 **Třebíč** Czech Rep.
109 C2 **Trebinje** Bos.-Herz.
103 E2 **Trebišov** Slovakia
109 C1 **Trebnje** Slovenia
153 C4 **Treinta y Tres** Uru.
153 B5 **Trelew** Arg.
93 F4 **Trelleborg** Sweden
130 C2 **Tremblant, Mont** *h.* Can.
109 C2 **Tremiti, Isole** *is* Italy
134 D2 **Tremonton** U.S.A.
107 D1 **Tremp** Spain

3 D2 **Trenčín** Slovakia
3 B4 **Trenque Lauquén** Arg.
8 C2 **Trent** *r.* U.K.
8 B1 **Trento** Italy
1 D2 **Trenton** Can.
7 E2 **Trenton** *MO* U.S.A.
1 E2 **Trenton** *NJ* U.S.A.
1 E2 **Trepassey** Can.
3 B4 **Tres Arroyos** Arg.
5 C2 **Três Corações** Brazil
4 B2 **Três Lagoas** Brazil
3 A5 **Tres Lagos** Arg.
5 C1 **Três Marias, Represa** *resr* Brazil
5 C2 **Três Pontas** Brazil
3 B5 **Tres Puntas, Cabo** *c.* Arg.
5 D2 **Três Rios** Brazil
1 F1 **Treuenbrietzen** Ger.
8 A1 **Treviglio** Italy
8 B1 **Treviso** Italy
9 A3 **Trevose Head** U.K.
9 C3 **Tricase** Italy
3 C2 **Trida** Austr.
0 C3 **Trier** Ger.
8 B1 **Trieste** Italy
8 B1 **Triglav** *mt.* Slovenia
9 D3 **Trikora, Puncak** *mt.* Indon.
7 C2 **Trim** Ireland
3 C4 **Trincomalee** Sri Lanka
4 C1 **Trindade** Brazil
2 B2 **Trinidad** Bol.
7 D3 **Trinidad** *i.* Trin. and Tob.
6 C3 **Trinidad** U.S.A.
7 D3 **Trinidad and Tobago** *country* West Indies
31 E2 **Trinity Bay** Can.
1 B3 **Tripoli** Greece
30 B2 **Tripoli** Lebanon
15 D1 **Tripoli** Libya
3 D10 **Tristan da Cunha** *i.* S. Atlantic Ocean
Trivandrum India *see* **Thiruvananthapuram**
8 B2 **Trivento** Italy
3 D2 **Trnava** Slovakia
9 C2 **Trogir** Croatia
9 C2 **Troia** Italy
00 C2 **Troisdorf** Ger.
31 C2 **Trois-Rivières** Can.
36 E2 **Troitsko-Pechorsk** Rus. Fed.
1 C2 **Trombetas** *r.* Brazil
23 C3 **Trompsburg** S. Africa
92 G2 **Tromsø** Norway
92 F3 **Trondheim** Norway
8 C2 **Trout Lake** Can.
28 B1 **Trout Lake** *N.W.T.* Can.
30 A1 **Trout Lake** *Ont.* Can.
99 B3 **Trowbridge** U.K.
42 C2 **Troy** *AL* U.S.A.
41 E2 **Troy** *NY* U.S.A.
05 C2 **Troyes** France
09 D2 **Trstenik** Serbia
39 D3 **Trubchevsk** Rus. Fed.
06 B1 **Truchas** Spain
79 C2 **Trucial Coast** U.A.E.
46 B3 **Trujillo** Hond.
50 A2 **Trujillo** Peru
06 B2 **Trujillo** Spain
47 C4 **Trujillo** Venez.
42 B1 **Trumann** U.S.A.
31 D2 **Truro** Can.
99 A3 **Truro** U.K.
38 B2 **Truth or Consequences** U.S.A.
03 D1 **Trutnov** Czech Rep.
93 F3 **Trysil** Norway
03 D1 **Trzebiatów** Pol.
68 B1 **Tsagaannuur** Mongolia

121 D2 **Tsaratanana, Massif du** *mts* Madag.
110 C2 **Tsarevo** Bulg.
122 A2 **Tses** Namibia
122 B1 **Tsetseng** Botswana
68 C1 **Tsetserleg** Mongolia
68 C1 **Tsetserleg** Mongolia
122 B2 **Tshabong** Botswana
122 B1 **Tshane** Botswana
91 D2 **Tshchikskoye Vodokhranilishche** *resr* Rus. Fed.
118 B3 **Tshela** Dem. Rep. Congo
118 C3 **Tshikapa** Dem. Rep. Congo
118 C3 **Tshikapa** *r.* Dem. Rep. Congo
123 D1 **Tshipise** S. Africa
118 C3 **Tshitanzu** Dem. Rep. Congo
118 C3 **Tshuapa** *r.* Dem. Rep. Congo
Tshwane S. Africa *see* **Pretoria**
87 D4 **Tsimlyanskoye Vodokhranilishche** *resr* Rus. Fed.
Tsingtao China *see* **Qingdao**
Tsining China *see* **Jining**
121 D2 **Tsiroanomandidy** Madag.
123 C3 **Tsomo** S. Africa
67 C4 **Tsu** Japan
67 D3 **Tsuchiura** Japan
66 D2 **Tsugarū-kaikyō** *str.* Japan
120 A2 **Tsumeb** Namibia
122 A1 **Tsumis Park** Namibia
120 B2 **Tsumkwe** Namibia
67 C3 **Tsuruga** Japan
66 C3 **Tsuruoka** Japan
67 A4 **Tsushima** *is* Japan
Tsushima-kaikyō *str.* Japan/S. Korea *see* **Korea Strait**
67 B3 **Tsuyama** Japan
123 C2 **Tswelelang** S. Africa
91 C2 **Tsyurupyns'k** Ukr.
Tthenaagoo Can. *see* **Nahanni Butte**
59 C3 **Tual** Indon.
97 B2 **Tuam** Ireland
91 D3 **Tuapse** Rus. Fed.
54 A3 **Tuatapere** N.Z.
96 A1 **Tuath, Loch a'** *b.* U.K.
138 A1 **Tuba City** U.S.A.
61 C2 **Tuban** Indon.
152 D3 **Tubarão** Brazil
102 B2 **Tübingen** Ger.
115 E1 **Tubruq** Libya
49 I4 **Tubuai** *i.* Fr. Polynesia
49 H4 **Tubuai** *is* Fr. Polynesia
144 A1 **Tubutama** Mex.
152 C2 **Tucavaca** Bol.
128 B1 **Tuchitua** Can.
138 A2 **Tucson** U.S.A.
139 C1 **Tucumcari** U.S.A.
150 B1 **Tucupita** Venez.
151 D2 **Tucuruí** Brazil
151 D2 **Tucuruí, Represa** *resr* Brazil
107 C1 **Tudela** Spain
106 B1 **Tuela** *r.* Port.
62 A1 **Tuensang** India
123 D2 **Tugela** *r.* S. Africa
64 B1 **Tuguegarao** Phil.
106 B1 **Tui** Spain
59 C3 **Tukangbesi, Kepulauan** *is* Indon.
126 C2 **Tuktoyaktuk** Can.
88 B2 **Tukums** Latvia
145 C2 **Tula** Mex.
89 E3 **Tula** Rus. Fed.
145 C2 **Tulancingo** Mex.
135 C3 **Tulare** U.S.A.
138 B2 **Tularosa** U.S.A.

110 C1 **Tulcea** Romania
90 B2 **Tul'chyn** Ukr.
129 E1 **Tulemalu Lake** Can.
139 C2 **Tulia** U.S.A.
142 C1 **Tullahoma** U.S.A.
97 C2 **Tullamore** Ireland
104 C2 **Tulle** France
51 D1 **Tully** Austr.
139 D1 **Tulsa** U.S.A.
150 A1 **Tumaco** Col.
123 C2 **Tumahole** S. Africa
93 G4 **Tumba** Sweden
118 B3 **Tumba, Lac** *l.* Dem. Rep. Congo
53 C3 **Tumbarumba** Austr.
150 A2 **Tumbes** Peru
128 B2 **Tumbler Ridge** Can.
52 A2 **Tumby Bay** Austr.
65 B1 **Tumen** China
150 B1 **Tumereng** Guyana
64 A2 **Tumindao** *i.* Phil.
74 A2 **Tump** Pak.
151 C1 **Tumucumaque, Serra** *hills* Brazil
53 C3 **Tumut** Austr.
99 D3 **Tunbridge Wells, Royal** U.K.
80 B2 **Tunceli** Turkey
53 D2 **Tuncurry** Austr.
119 D4 **Tunduru** Tanz.
110 C2 **Tundzha** *r.* Bulg.
128 B1 **Tungsten (abandoned)** Can.
115 D1 **Tunis** Tunisia
115 C1 **Tunisia** *country* Africa
150 A1 **Tunja** Col.
92 F3 **Tunnsjøen** *l.* Norway
Tunxi China *see* **Huangshan**
154 B2 **Tupã** Brazil
154 C1 **Tupaciguara** Brazil
142 C2 **Tupelo** U.S.A.
152 B3 **Tupiza** Bol.
83 H2 **Tura** Rus. Fed.
86 F3 **Tura** *r.* Rus. Fed.
78 B2 **Turabah** Saudi Arabia
83 J3 **Turana, Khrebet** *mts* Rus. Fed.
54 C1 **Turangi** N.Z.
76 B2 **Turan Lowland** Asia
78 A1 **Ţurayf** Saudi Arabia
88 B2 **Turba** Estonia
74 A2 **Turbat** Pak.
150 A1 **Turbo** Col.
110 B1 **Turda** Romania
Turfan China *see* **Turpan**
76 C2 **Turgay** Kazakh.
111 C3 **Turgutlu** Turkey
80 B1 **Turhal** Turkey
107 C2 **Turia** *r.* Spain
108 A1 **Turin** Italy
86 F3 **Turinsk** Rus. Fed.
90 A1 **Turiys'k** Ukr.
119 D2 **Turkana, Lake** *salt l.* Eth./Kenya
77 C2 **Turkestan** Kazakh.
80 B2 **Turkey** *country* Asia/Europe
76 C3 **Türkmenabat** Turkm.
76 B2 **Türkmenbaşy** Turkm.
76 B2 **Turkmenistan** *country* Asia
147 C2 **Turks and Caicos Islands** *terr.* West Indies
93 H3 **Turku** Fin.
135 B3 **Turlock** U.S.A.
54 C2 **Turnagain, Cape** N.Z.
100 B2 **Turnhout** Belgium
129 D2 **Turnor Lake** Can.
110 B2 **Turnu Măgurele** Romania
68 B2 **Turpan** China
77 D2 **Turugart Pass** China/Kyrg.
142 C2 **Tuscaloosa** U.S.A.

142 C2 **Tuskegee** U.S.A.
73 B4 **Tuticorin** India
120 B3 **Tutume** Botswana
49 F3 **Tuvalu** *country* S. Pacific Ocean
78 B2 **Tuwayq, Jabal** *hills* Saudi Arabia
78 B2 **Tuwayq, Jabal** *mts* Saudi Arabia
78 A2 **Tuwwal** Saudi Arabia
144 B2 **Tuxpan** *Nayarit* Mex.
145 C2 **Tuxpan** *Veracruz* Mex.
145 C3 **Tuxtla Gutiérrez** Mex.
62 B1 **Tuyên Quang** Vietnam
63 B2 **Tuy Hoa** Vietnam
80 B2 **Tuz, Lake** *salt l.* Turkey
Tuz Gölü *salt l.* Turkey *see* **Tuz, Lake**
81 C2 **Tuz Khurmātū** Iraq
109 C2 **Tuzla** Bos.-Herz.
91 E2 **Tuzlov** *r.* Rus. Fed.
89 E2 **Tver'** Rus. Fed.
98 B1 **Tweed** *r.* U.K.
122 A2 **Twee Rivier** Namibia
135 C4 **Twentynine Palms** U.S.A.
131 E2 **Twillingate** Can.
134 D2 **Twin Falls** U.S.A.
137 E1 **Two Harbors** U.S.A.
129 C2 **Two Hills** Can.
139 D2 **Tyler** U.S.A.
83 J3 **Tynda** Rus. Fed.
93 F3 **Tynset** Norway
80 B2 **Tyre** Lebanon
111 B3 **Tyrnavos** Greece
52 B3 **Tyrrell, Lake** *dry lake* Austr.
108 B2 **Tyrrhenian Sea** France/Italy
76 B2 **Tyub-Karagan, Mys** *pt* Kazakh.
87 E3 **Tyul'gan** Rus. Fed.
86 F3 **Tyumen'** Rus. Fed.
83 J2 **Tyung** *r.* Rus. Fed.
99 A3 **Tywi** *r.* U.K.
123 D1 **Tzaneen** S. Africa

U

120 B2 **Uamanda** Angola
150 B2 **Uaupés** Brazil
155 D2 **Ubá** Brazil
155 D1 **Ubaí** Brazil
151 E3 **Ubaitaba** Brazil
118 B3 **Ubangi** *r.* C.A.R./Dem. Rep. Congo
67 B4 **Ube** Japan
106 C2 **Úbeda** Spain
154 C1 **Uberaba** Brazil
154 C1 **Uberlândia** Brazil
106 B1 **Ubiña, Peña** *mt.* Spain
123 D2 **Ubombo** S. Africa
63 B2 **Ubon Ratchathani** Thai.
119 C3 **Ubundu** Dem. Rep. Congo
150 A2 **Ucayali** *r.* Peru
74 B2 **Uch** Pak.
77 E2 **Ucharal** Kazakh.
66 D2 **Uchiura-wan** *b.* Japan
83 J3 **Uchur** *r.* Rus. Fed.
128 B3 **Ucluelet** Can.
74 B2 **Udaipur** India
91 C1 **Uday** *r.* Ukr.
93 F4 **Uddevalla** Sweden
92 G2 **Uddjaure** *l.* Sweden
100 B2 **Uden** Neth.
74 B1 **Udhampur** India
108 B1 **Udine** Italy
89 E2 **Udomlya** Rus. Fed.
62 B2 **Udon Thani** Thai.
73 B3 **Udupi** India
83 K3 **Udyl', Ozero** *l.* Rus. Fed.
67 C3 **Ueda** Japan
58 C3 **Uekuli** Indon.
118 C2 **Uele** *r.* Dem. Rep. Congo
101 E1 **Uelzen** Ger.
119 C2 **Uere** *r.* Dem. Rep. Congo
87 E3 **Ufa** Rus. Fed.
119 D3 **Ugalla** *r.* Tanz.
119 D2 **Uganda** *country* Africa
89 E2 **Uglich** Rus. Fed.
89 D2 **Uglovka** Rus. Fed.
89 D3 **Ugra** Rus. Fed.
103 D2 **Uherské Hradiště** Czech Rep.
101 E2 **Uichteritz** Ger.
96 A2 **Uig** U.K.
120 A1 **Uíge** Angola
65 B2 **Ŭijŏngbu** S. Korea
135 D2 **Uinta Mountains** U.S.A.
120 A3 **Uis Mine** Namibia
65 B2 **Ŭisŏng** S. Korea
123 C3 **Uitenhage** S. Africa
100 C1 **Uithuizen** Neth.
74 B2 **Ujjain** India
89 F3 **Ukholovo** Rus. Fed.
62 A1 **Ukhrul** India
86 E2 **Ukhta** Rus. Fed.
135 B3 **Ukiah** U.S.A.
127 H2 **Ukkusissat** Greenland
88 B2 **Ukmergė** Lith.
90 C2 **Ukraine** *country* Europe
Ulaanbaatar Mongolia *see* **Ulan Bator**
68 C1 **Ulaangom** Mongolia
69 D1 **Ulan Bator** Mongolia
Ulanhad China *see* **Chifeng**
69 E1 **Ulanhot** China
87 D4 **Ulan-Khol** Rus. Fed.
69 D1 **Ulan-Ude** Rus. Fed.
75 D1 **Ulan Ul Hu** *l.* China
65 B2 **Ulchin** S. Korea
Uleåborg Fin. *see* **Oulu**
88 C2 **Ülenurme** Estonia
69 D1 **Uliastai** China
68 C1 **Uliastay** Mongolia
59 D2 **Ulithi** *atoll* Micronesia
53 D3 **Ulladulla** Austr.
96 B2 **Ullapool** U.K.
98 B1 **Ullswater** *l.* U.K.
65 C2 **Ullŭng-do** *i.* S. Korea
102 B2 **Ulm** Ger.
65 B2 **Ulsan** S. Korea
96 □ **Ulsta** U.K.
97 C1 **Ulster** *reg.* Ireland/U.K.
52 B3 **Ultima** Austr.
111 C3 **Ulubey** Turkey
111 C2 **Uludağ** *mt.* Turkey
126 D2 **Ulukhaktok** Can.
123 D2 **Ulundi** S. Africa
77 E2 **Ulungur Hu** *l.* China
50 C2 **Uluru** *h.* Austr.
98 B1 **Ulverston** U.K.
87 D3 **Ul'yanovsk** Rus. Fed.
136 C3 **Ulysses** U.S.A.
90 C2 **Uman'** Ukr.
86 C2 **Umba** Rus. Fed.
59 D3 **Umboi** *i.* P.N.G.
92 H3 **Umeå** Sweden
92 H3 **Umeälven** *r.* Sweden
127 I2 **Umiiviip Kangertiva** *inlet* Greenland
126 D2 **Umingmaktok (abandoned)** Can.
123 D2 **Umlazi** S. Africa
117 A3 **Umm Keddada** Sudan
78 A2 **Umm Lajj** Saudi Arabia
117 B3 **Umm Ruwaba** Sudan
115 E1 **Umm Sa'ad** Libya
134 B2 **Umpqua** *r.* U.S.A.
120 A2 **Umpulo** Angola
123 C3 **Umtata** S. Africa
154 B2 **Umuarama** Brazil
109 C1 **Una** *r.* Bos.-Herz./Croatia
155 E1 **Una** Brazil
154 C1 **Unaí** Brazil
78 B2 **'Unayzah** Saudi Arabia
136 C1 **Underwood** U.S.A.
89 D3 **Unecha** Rus. Fed.
53 C2 **Ungarie** Austr.
52 A2 **Ungarra** Austr.
127 G2 **Ungava, Péninsule d'** *pen.* Can.
127 G3 **Ungava Bay** Can.
90 B2 **Ungheni** Moldova
Unguja *i.* Tanz. *see* **Zanzibar Island**
154 B3 **União da Vitória** Brazil
150 B2 **Unini** *r.* Brazil
142 C1 **Union City** U.S.A.
122 B3 **Uniondale** S. Africa
141 D3 **Uniontown** U.S.A.
79 C2 **United Arab Emirates** *count* Asia
95 C3 **United Kingdom** *country* Europe
132 D3 **United States of America** *country* N. America
129 D2 **Unity** Can.
96 □ **Unst** *i.* U.K.
101 E2 **Unstrut** *r.* Ger.
89 E3 **Upa** *r.* Rus. Fed.
119 C3 **Upemba, Lac** *l.* Dem. Rep. Congo
122 B2 **Upington** S. Africa
134 B2 **Upper Alkali Lake** U.S.A.
128 C2 **Upper Arrow Lake** Can.
134 B2 **Upper Klamath Lake** U.S.A.
128 B1 **Upper Liard** Can.
97 C1 **Upper Lough Erne** *l.* U.K.
93 G4 **Uppsala** Sweden
78 B2 **'Uqlat aş Şuqūr** Saudi Arabi
Urad Qianqi China *see* **Xishanzui**
76 B2 **Ural** *r.* Kazakh./Rus. Fed.
53 D2 **Uralla** Austr.
87 E3 **Ural Mountains** Rus. Fed.
76 B1 **Ural'sk** Kazakh.
Ural'skiy Khrebet *mts* Rus. Fed. *see* **Ural Mountain**
119 D3 **Urambo** Tanz.
53 C3 **Urana** Austr.
129 D2 **Uranium City** Can.
86 F2 **Uray** Rus. Fed.
98 C1 **Ure** *r.* U.K.
86 D3 **Uren'** Rus. Fed.
144 A2 **Ures** Mex.
76 C2 **Urganch** Uzbek.
100 B1 **Urk** Neth.
111 C3 **Urla** Turkey
81 C2 **Urmia, Lake** *salt l.* Iran
Uroševac Kosovo *see* **Ferizaj**
144 B2 **Uruáchic** Mex.
151 D3 **Uruaçu** Brazil
144 B3 **Uruapan** Mex.
150 A3 **Urubamba** *r.* Peru
151 C2 **Urucara** Brazil
151 D2 **Uruçuí** Brazil
151 C2 **Urucurituba** Brazil
152 C3 **Uruguaiana** Brazil
153 C4 **Uruguay** *country* S. America
Urumchi China *see* **Ürümqi**
68 B2 **Ürümqi** China
53 D2 **Urunga** Austr.

10 C2 **Urziceni** Romania
57 B4 **Usa** Japan
32 E2 **Usa** *r.* Rus. Fed.
11 C3 **Uşak** Turkey
32 G1 **Ushakova, Ostrov** *i.* Rus. Fed.
77 D2 **Ushtobe** Kazakh.
53 B6 **Ushuaia** Arg.
36 E2 **Usinsk** Rus. Fed.
38 C3 **Uskhodni** Belarus
39 E3 **Usman'** Rus. Fed.
36 D2 **Usogorsk** Rus. Fed.
04 C2 **Ussel** France
56 B2 **Ussuriysk** Rus. Fed.
08 B3 **Ustica, Isola di** *i. Sicilia* Italy
33 H3 **Ust'-Ilimsk** Rus. Fed.
36 E2 **Ust'-Ilych** Rus. Fed.
03 D1 **Ustka** Pol.
33 L3 **Ust'-Kamchatsk** Rus. Fed.
77 E2 **Ust'-Kamenogorsk** Kazakh.
36 F2 **Ust'-Kara** Rus. Fed.
36 E2 **Ust'-Kulom** Rus. Fed.
33 I3 **Ust'-Kut** Rus. Fed.
91 D2 **Ust'-Labinsk** Rus. Fed.
88 C2 **Ust'-Luga** Rus. Fed.
36 E2 **Ust'-Nem** Rus. Fed.
83 K2 **Ust'-Nera** Rus. Fed.
83 K2 **Ust'-Omchug** Rus. Fed.
83 H3 **Ust'-Ordynskiy** Rus. Fed.
36 E2 **Ust'-Tsil'ma** Rus. Fed.
36 D2 **Ust'-Ura** Rus. Fed.
76 B2 **Ustyurt Plateau** Kazakh./Uzbek.
89 E2 **Ustyuzhna** Rus. Fed.
89 D2 **Usvyaty** Rus. Fed.
35 D3 **Utah** *state* U.S.A.
35 D2 **Utah Lake** U.S.A.
93 I4 **Utena** Lith.
41 D2 **Utica** U.S.A.
07 C2 **Utiel** Spain
28 C2 **Utikuma Lake** Can.
00 B1 **Utrecht** Neth.
06 B2 **Utrera** Spain
92 I2 **Utsjoki** Fin.
67 C3 **Utsunomiya** Japan
87 D4 **Utta** Rus. Fed.
62 B2 **Uttaradit** Thai.
Uummannaq Greenland *see* **Dundas**
27 H2 **Uummannaq Fjord** *inlet* Greenland
93 H3 **Uusikaupunki** Fin.
39 D3 **Uvalde** U.S.A.
19 D3 **Uvinza** Tanz.
68 C1 **Uvs Nuur** *salt l.* Mongolia
67 B4 **Uwajima** Japan
78 A2 **'Uwayriḍ, Ḥarrat al** *lava field* Saudi Arabia
16 A2 **Uweinat, Jebel** *mt.* Sudan
83 H3 **Uyar** Rus. Fed.
15 C4 **Uyo** Nigeria
52 B3 **Uyuni, Salar de** *salt flat* Bol.
76 C2 **Uzbekistan** *country* Asia
04 C2 **Uzerche** France
05 C3 **Uzès** France
90 C1 **Uzh** *r.* Ukr.
90 A2 **Uzhhorod** Ukr.
09 C2 **Užice** Serbia
89 E3 **Uzlovaya** Rus. Fed.
11 C3 **Üzümlü** Turkey
11 C2 **Uzunköprü** Turkey

V

23 B2 **Vaal** *r.* S. Africa
23 C2 **Vaal Dam** S. Africa
123 C1 **Vaalwater** S. Africa
92 H3 **Vaasa** Fin.
103 D2 **Vác** Hungary
152 C3 **Vacaria** Brazil
154 B2 **Vacaria, Serra** *hills* Brazil
135 B3 **Vacaville** U.S.A.
74 B2 **Vadodara** India
92 I1 **Vadsø** Norway
105 D2 **Vaduz** Liechtenstein
94 B1 **Vágar** *i.* Faroe Is
94 B1 **Vágur** Faroe Is
103 D2 **Váh** *r.* Slovakia
49 F3 **Vaiaku** Tuvalu
88 B2 **Vaida** Estonia
136 B3 **Vail** U.S.A.
79 C2 **Vakīlābād** Iran
108 B1 **Valdagno** Italy
89 D2 **Valday** Rus. Fed.
89 D2 **Valdayskaya Vozvyshennost'** *hills* Rus. Fed.
106 B2 **Valdecañas, Embalse de** *resr* Spain
93 G4 **Valdemarsvik** Sweden
106 C2 **Valdepeñas** Spain
153 B5 **Valdés, Península** *pen.* Arg.
153 A4 **Valdivia** Chile
130 C2 **Val-d'Or** Can.
143 D2 **Valdosta** U.S.A.
128 C2 **Valemount** Can.
105 C3 **Valence** France
107 C2 **Valencia** Spain
150 B1 **Valencia** Venez.
107 D2 **Valencia, Golfo de** *g.* Spain
100 A2 **Valenciennes** France
136 C2 **Valentine** U.S.A.
64 B1 **Valenzuela** Phil.
150 A1 **Valera** Venez.
109 C2 **Valjevo** Serbia
88 C2 **Valka** Latvia
93 H3 **Valkeakoski** Fin.
100 B2 **Valkenswaard** Neth.
91 D2 **Valky** Ukr.
55 D2 **Valkyrie Dome** Antarctica
145 D2 **Valladolid** Mex.
106 C1 **Valladolid** Spain
93 E4 **Valle** Norway
145 C2 **Vallecillos** Mex.
150 B1 **Valle de la Pascua** Venez.
150 A1 **Valledupar** Col.
145 C2 **Valle Hermoso** Mex.
135 B3 **Vallejo** U.S.A.
152 A3 **Vallenar** Chile
85 H5 **Valletta** Malta
137 D1 **Valley City** U.S.A.
134 B2 **Valley Falls** U.S.A.
128 C2 **Valleyview** Can.
107 D1 **Valls** Spain
129 D3 **Val Marie** Can.
88 C2 **Valmiera** Latvia
88 C3 **Valozhyn** Belarus
154 B2 **Valparaíso** Brazil
153 A4 **Valparaíso** Chile
105 C3 **Valréas** France
59 D3 **Vals, Tanjung** *c.* Indon.
74 B2 **Valsad** India
122 B2 **Valspan** S. Africa
91 D1 **Valuyki** Rus. Fed.
106 B2 **Valverde del Camino** Spain
81 C2 **Van** Turkey
81 C2 **Van, Lake** *salt l.* Turkey
141 F1 **Van Buren** U.S.A.
128 B3 **Vancouver** Can.
134 B1 **Vancouver** U.S.A.
128 B3 **Vancouver Island** Can.
140 B3 **Vandalia** U.S.A.
123 C2 **Vanderbijlpark** S. Africa
128 B2 **Vanderhoof** Can.
88 C2 **Vändra** Estonia
93 F4 **Vänern** *l.* Sweden
93 F4 **Vänersborg** Sweden
121 D3 **Vangaindrano** Madag.
Van Gölü *salt l.* Turkey *see* **Van, Lake**
138 C2 **Van Horn** U.S.A.
59 D3 **Vanimo** P.N.G.
83 K3 **Vanino** Rus. Fed.
104 B2 **Vannes** France
59 D3 **Van Rees, Pegunungan** *mts* Indon.
122 A3 **Vanrhynsdorp** S. Africa
93 H3 **Vantaa** Fin.
49 F4 **Vanua Levu** *i.* Fiji
48 E3 **Vanuatu** *country* S. Pacific Ocean
140 C2 **Van Wert** U.S.A.
122 B3 **Vanwyksvlei** S. Africa
122 B2 **Van Zylsrus** S. Africa
75 C2 **Varanasi** India
92 I1 **Varangerfjorden** *sea chan.* Norway
92 I1 **Varangerhalvøya** *pen.* Norway
109 C1 **Varaždin** Croatia
93 F4 **Varberg** Sweden
109 D2 **Vardar** *r.* Macedonia
93 E4 **Varde** Denmark
92 J1 **Vardø** Norway
100 D1 **Varel** Ger.
88 B3 **Varėna** Lith.
108 A1 **Varese** Italy
155 C2 **Varginha** Brazil
93 I3 **Varkaus** Fin.
110 C2 **Varna** Bulg.
93 F4 **Värnamo** Sweden
155 D1 **Várzea da Palma** Brazil
86 C2 **Varzino** Rus. Fed.
Vasa Fin. *see* **Vaasa**
88 C2 **Vasknarva** Estonia
110 C1 **Vaslui** Romania
93 G4 **Västerås** Sweden
93 G3 **Västerdalälven** *r.* Sweden
88 A2 **Västerhaninge** Sweden
93 G4 **Västervik** Sweden
108 B2 **Vasto** Italy
90 C1 **Vasyl'kiv** Ukr.
104 C2 **Vatan** France
108 B2 **Vatican City** Europe
92 B3 **Vatnajökull** Iceland
110 C1 **Vatra Dornei** Romania
93 F4 **Vättern** *l.* Sweden
138 B2 **Vaughn** U.S.A.
105 C3 **Vauvert** France
49 G4 **Vava'u Group** *is* Tonga
88 B3 **Vawkavysk** Belarus
93 F4 **Växjö** Sweden
86 E1 **Vaygach, Ostrov** *i.* Rus. Fed.
101 D1 **Vechta** Ger.
110 C2 **Vedea** *r.* Romania
100 C1 **Veendam** Neth.
100 B1 **Veenendaal** Neth.
129 C2 **Vegreville** Can.
106 B2 **Vejer de la Frontera** Spain
93 E4 **Vejle** Denmark
109 D2 **Velbŭzhdki Prokhod** *pass* Bulg./Macedonia
100 B2 **Veldhoven** Neth.
109 B2 **Velebit** *mts* Croatia
100 C2 **Velen** Ger.
109 C1 **Velenje** Slovenia
109 D2 **Veles** Macedonia
106 C2 **Vélez-Málaga** Spain
155 D1 **Velhas** *r.* Brazil
109 D2 **Velika Plana** Serbia
88 C2 **Velikaya** *r.* Rus. Fed.
89 D2 **Velikiye Luki** Rus. Fed.

89 D2 **Velikiy Novgorod** Rus. Fed.
86 D2 **Velikiy Ustyug** Rus. Fed.
110 C2 **Veliko Tŭrnovo** Bulg.
108 B2 **Veli Lošinj** Croatia
89 D2 **Velizh** Rus. Fed.
86 D2 **Vel'sk** Rus. Fed.
101 F1 **Velten** Ger.
91 D1 **Velykyy Burluk** Ukr.
108 B2 **Venafro** Italy
154 C2 **Venceslau Bráz** Brazil
104 C2 **Vendôme** France
89 E3 **Venev** Rus. Fed.
Venezia Italy *see* **Venice**
150 B1 **Venezuela** *country* S. America
150 A1 **Venezuela, Golfo de** *g.* Venez.
108 B1 **Venice** Italy
143 D3 **Venice** U.S.A.
108 B1 **Venice, Gulf of** Europe
100 C2 **Venlo** Neth.
100 B2 **Venray** Neth.
88 B2 **Venta** *r.* Latvia/Lith.
88 B2 **Venta** Lith.
123 C3 **Venterstad** S. Africa
99 C3 **Ventnor** U.K.
88 B2 **Ventspils** Latvia
135 C4 **Ventura** U.S.A.
139 C3 **Venustiano Carranza, Presa** *resr* Mex.
107 C2 **Vera** Spain
145 C3 **Veracruz** Mex.
74 B2 **Veraval** India
108 A1 **Verbania** Italy
108 A1 **Vercelli** Italy
105 D3 **Vercors** *reg.* France
92 F3 **Verdalsøra** Norway
154 B1 **Verde** *r. Goiás* Brazil
154 B2 **Verde** *r. Mato Grosso do Sul* Brazil
144 B2 **Verde** *r.* Mex.
138 A2 **Verde** *r.* U.S.A.
155 D1 **Verde Grande** *r.* Brazil
101 D1 **Verden (Aller)** Ger.
154 B1 **Verdinho, Serra do** *mts* Brazil
108 A2 **Verdon** *r.* France
105 D2 **Verdun** France
123 C2 **Vereeniging** S. Africa
106 B1 **Verín** Spain
91 D3 **Verkhnebakanskiy** Rus. Fed.
92 J2 **Verkhnetulomskiy** Rus. Fed.
91 E1 **Verkhniy Mamon** Rus. Fed.
89 E3 **Verkhov'ye** Rus. Fed.
90 A2 **Verkhovyna** Ukr.
83 J2 **Verkhoyanskiy Khrebet** *mts* Rus. Fed.
129 C2 **Vermilion** Can.
137 D2 **Vermillion** U.S.A.
130 A2 **Vermillion Bay** Can.
141 E2 **Vermont** *state* U.S.A.
135 E2 **Vernal** U.S.A.
128 C2 **Vernon** Can.
139 D2 **Vernon** U.S.A.
143 D3 **Vero Beach** U.S.A.
111 B2 **Veroia** Greece
108 B1 **Verona** Italy
104 C2 **Versailles** France
104 B2 **Vertou** France
123 D2 **Verulam** S. Africa
100 B2 **Verviers** Belgium
105 C2 **Vervins** France
105 D3 **Vescovato** *Corse* France
87 E3 **Veselaya, Gora** *mt.* Rus. Fed.
91 C2 **Vesele** Ukr.
105 D2 **Vesoul** France
92 F2 **Vesterålen** *is* Norway
92 F2 **Vestfjorden** *sea chan.* Norway
94 B1 **Vestmanna** Faroe Is
93 E3 **Vestnes** Norway
108 B2 **Vesuvius** *vol.* Italy
89 E2 **Ves'yegonsk** Rus. Fed.
93 G4 **Vetlanda** Sweden
86 D3 **Vetluga** Rus. Fed.
100 A2 **Veurne** Belgium
105 D2 **Vevey** Switz.
91 D1 **Veydelevka** Rus. Fed.
80 B1 **Vezirköprü** Turkey
151 D2 **Viana** Brazil
106 B1 **Viana do Castelo** Port.
Viangchan Laos *see* **Vientiane**
62 B1 **Viangphoukha** Laos
111 C3 **Viannos** Greece
154 C1 **Vianópolis** Brazil
108 B2 **Viareggio** Italy
93 E4 **Viborg** Denmark
109 C3 **Vibo Valentia** Italy
107 D1 **Vic** Spain
144 A1 **Vicente Guerrero** Mex.
108 B1 **Vicenza** Italy
105 C2 **Vichy** France
142 B2 **Vicksburg** U.S.A.
155 D2 **Viçosa** Brazil
52 A3 **Victor Harbor** Austr.
50 C1 **Victoria** *r.* Austr.
52 B3 **Victoria** *state* Austr.
128 B3 **Victoria** Can.
153 A4 **Victoria** Chile
113 K7 **Victoria** Seychelles
139 D3 **Victoria** U.S.A.
119 D3 **Victoria, Lake** Africa
52 B2 **Victoria, Lake** Austr.
62 A1 **Victoria, Mount** Myanmar
59 D3 **Victoria, Mount** P.N.G.
120 B2 **Victoria Falls** Zambia/Zimbabwe
126 D2 **Victoria Island** Can.
50 C1 **Victoria River Downs** Austr.
122 B3 **Victoria West** S. Africa
135 C4 **Victorville** U.S.A.
110 C2 **Videle** Romania
92 A2 **Víðidalsá** Iceland
153 B5 **Viedma** Arg.
153 A5 **Viedma, Lago** *l.* Arg.
100 B2 **Vielsalm** Belgium
101 E2 **Vienenburg** Ger.
103 D2 **Vienna** Austria
105 C2 **Vienne** France
104 C2 **Vienne** *r.* France
62 B2 **Vientiane** Laos
100 C2 **Viersen** Ger.
104 C2 **Vierzon** France
144 B2 **Viesca** Mex.
109 C2 **Vieste** Italy
62 B2 **Vietnam** *country* Asia
62 B1 **Việt Tri** Vietnam
64 B1 **Vigan** Phil.
108 A1 **Vigevano** Italy
106 B1 **Vigo** Spain
73 C3 **Vijayawada** India
92 B3 **Vík** Iceland
129 C2 **Viking** Can.
106 B2 **Vila Franca de Xira** Port.
106 B1 **Vilagarcía de Arousa** Spain
106 B1 **Vilalba** Spain
106 B1 **Vila Nova de Gaia** Port.
107 D1 **Vilanova i la Geltrú** Spain
106 B1 **Vila Real** Port.
106 B1 **Vilar Formoso** Port.
155 D2 **Vila Velha** Brazil
150 A3 **Vilcabamba, Cordillera** *mts* Peru
92 G3 **Vilhelmina** Sweden
150 B3 **Vilhena** Brazil
88 C2 **Viljandi** Estonia
88 B3 **Vilkaviškis** Lith.
83 H1 **Vil'kitskogo, Proliv** *str.* Rus. Fed.
144 B1 **Villa Ahumada** Mex.
106 B1 **Villablino** Spain
102 C2 **Villach** Austria
144 B2 **Villa de Cos** Mex.
152 B4 **Villa Dolores** Arg.
145 C3 **Villa Flores** Mex.
145 C2 **Villagrán** Mex.
145 C3 **Villahermosa** Mex.
144 A2 **Villa Insurgentes** Mex.
152 B4 **Villa María** Arg.
152 B3 **Villa Montes** Bol.
144 B2 **Villanueva** Mex.
106 B2 **Villanueva de la Serena** Spa
106 C2 **Villanueva de los Infantes** Spain
152 C3 **Villa Ocampo** Arg.
108 A3 **Villaputzu** *Sardegna* Italy
152 C3 **Villarrica** Para.
106 C2 **Villarrobledo** Spain
152 B3 **Villa Unión** Arg.
144 B2 **Villa Unión** *Durango* Mex.
144 B2 **Villa Unión** *Sinaloa* Mex.
150 A1 **Villavicencio** Col.
152 B3 **Villazon** Bol.
107 C2 **Villena** Spain
104 C3 **Villeneuve-sur-Lot** France
142 B2 **Ville Platte** U.S.A.
105 C2 **Villeurbanne** France
102 B2 **Villingen** Ger.
88 C3 **Vilnius** Lith.
91 C2 **Vil'nohirs'k** Ukr.
91 D2 **Vil'nyans'k** Ukr.
100 B2 **Vilvoorde** Belgium
88 C3 **Vilyeyka** Belarus
83 J2 **Vilyuy** *r.* Rus. Fed.
93 G4 **Vimmerby** Sweden
153 A4 **Viña del Mar** Chile
107 D1 **Vinaròs** Spain
140 B3 **Vincennes** U.S.A.
55 G3 **Vincennes Bay** Antarctica
141 D3 **Vineland** U.S.A.
62 B2 **Vinh** Vietnam
63 B2 **Vinh Long** Vietnam
139 D1 **Vinita** U.S.A.
90 B2 **Vinnytsya** Ukr.
55 O2 **Vinson Massif** *mt.* Antarctic
93 E3 **Vinstra** Norway
108 B1 **Vipiteno** Italy
64 B1 **Virac** Phil.
129 D3 **Virden** Can.
104 B2 **Vire** France
120 A2 **Virei** Angola
155 D1 **Virgem da Lapa** Brazil
138 A1 **Virgin** *r.* U.S.A.
123 C2 **Virginia** S. Africa
137 E1 **Virginia** U.S.A.
141 D3 **Virginia** *state* U.S.A.
141 D3 **Virginia Beach** U.S.A.
135 C3 **Virginia City** U.S.A.
147 D3 **Virgin Islands (U.K.)** *terr.* West Indies
147 D3 **Virgin Islands (U.S.A.)** *terr.* West Indies
63 B2 **Virôchey** Cambodia
109 C1 **Virovitica** Croatia
100 B3 **Virton** Belgium
88 B2 **Virtsu** Estonia
109 C2 **Vis** *i.* Croatia
88 C2 **Visaginas** Lith.
135 C3 **Visalia** U.S.A.
74 B2 **Visavadar** India
64 B1 **Visayan Sea** Phil.
93 G4 **Visby** Sweden
126 D2 **Viscount Melville Sound** *sea chan.* Can.

1 D2 **Viseu** Brazil
6 B1 **Viseu** Port.
3 C3 **Vishakhapatnam** India
8 C2 **Višķi** Latvia
9 C2 **Visoko** Bos.-Herz.
3 D1 **Vistula** *r.* Pol.
8 B2 **Viterbo** Italy
9 F4 **Viti Levu** *i.* Fiji
3 I3 **Vitim** *r.* Rus. Fed.
5 D2 **Vitória** Brazil
1 D3 **Vitória da Conquista** Brazil
6 C1 **Vitoria-Gasteiz** Spain
4 B2 **Vitré** France
5 C2 **Vitry-le-François** France
9 D2 **Vitsyebsk** Belarus
5 D2 **Vittel** France
8 B3 **Vittoria** *Sicilia* Italy
8 B1 **Vittorio Veneto** Italy
6 B1 **Viveiro** Spain
4 A2 **Vizcaíno, Sierra** *mts* Mex.
0 C2 **Vize** Turkey
3 C3 **Vizianagaram** India
0 B2 **Vlaardingen** Neth.
7 D4 **Vladikavkaz** Rus. Fed.
9 F2 **Vladimir** Rus. Fed.
6 B2 **Vladivostok** Rus. Fed.
9 D2 **Vlasotince** Serbia
0 B1 **Vlieland** *i.* Neth.
0 A2 **Vlissingen** Neth.
9 C2 **Vlorë** Albania
2 C2 **Vöcklabruck** Austria
1 D2 **Vogelsberg** *hills* Ger.
9 D3 **Voi** Kenya
5 D2 **Voiron** France
1 D1 **Voisey's Bay** Can.
9 C1 **Vojvodina** *prov.* Serbia
2 J3 **Voknavolok** Rus. Fed.
Volcano Bay Japan *see* **Uchiura-wan**
9 E2 **Volga** Rus. Fed.
9 F2 **Volga** *r.* Rus. Fed.
7 D4 **Volgodonsk** Rus. Fed.
7 D4 **Volgograd** Rus. Fed.
9 D2 **Volkhov** Rus. Fed.
9 D1 **Volkhov** *r.* Rus. Fed.
1 E2 **Volkstedt** Ger.
1 D2 **Volnovakha** Ukr.
0 B2 **Volochys'k** Ukr.
1 D2 **Volodars'ke** Ukr.
0 B1 **Volodars'k-Volyns'kyy** Ukr.
0 B1 **Volodymyrets'** Ukr.
0 A1 **Volodymyr-Volyns'kyy** Ukr.
9 E2 **Vologda** Rus. Fed.
9 E2 **Volokolamsk** Rus. Fed.
1 D1 **Volokonovka** Rus. Fed.
1 B3 **Volos** Greece
8 C2 **Volosovo** Rus. Fed.
9 D2 **Volot** Rus. Fed.
9 E3 **Volovo** Rus. Fed.
7 D3 **Vol'sk** Rus. Fed.
4 C4 **Volta, Lake** *resr* Ghana
5 D2 **Volta Redonda** Brazil
7 D4 **Volzhskiy** Rus. Fed.
2 C2 **Vopnafjörður** Iceland
8 C3 **Voranava** Belarus
6 F2 **Vorkuta** Rus. Fed.
8 B2 **Vormsi** *i.* Estonia
9 E3 **Voronezh** Rus. Fed.
9 E3 **Voronezh** *r.* Rus. Fed.
1 E1 **Vorontsovka** Rus. Fed.
1 C2 **Vorskla** *r.* Rus. Fed.
8 C2 **Võrtsjärv** *l.* Estonia
8 C2 **Võru** Estonia
22 B3 **Vosburg** S. Africa
5 D2 **Vosges** *mts* France
89 E2 **Voskresensk** Rus. Fed.
93 E3 **Voss** Norway
83 H3 **Vostochnyy Sayan** *mts* Rus. Fed.
86 E3 **Votkinsk** Rus. Fed.
154 C2 **Votuporanga** Brazil
100 B3 **Vouziers** France
92 J2 **Voynitsa** Rus. Fed.
91 C2 **Voznesens'k** Ukr.
93 E4 **Vrådal** Norway
66 B2 **Vrangel'** Rus. Fed.
Vrangelya, Ostrov *i.* Rus. Fed. *see* **Wrangel Island**
109 D2 **Vranje** Serbia
110 C2 **Vratnik** *pass* Bulg.
110 B2 **Vratsa** Bulg.
109 C1 **Vrbas** *r.* Bos.-Herz.
109 C1 **Vrbas** Serbia
122 A3 **Vredenburg** S. Africa
122 A3 **Vredendal** S. Africa
100 B3 **Vresse** Belgium
109 D1 **Vršac** Serbia
122 B2 **Vryburg** S. Africa
123 D2 **Vryheid** S. Africa
89 D1 **Vsevolozhsk** Rus. Fed.
Vučitrn Kosovo *see* **Vushtrri**
109 C1 **Vukovar** Croatia
86 E2 **Vuktyl'** Rus. Fed.
123 C2 **Vukuzakhe** S. Africa
109 B3 **Vulcano, Isola** *i.* Italy
63 B2 **Vung Tau** Vietnam
109 D2 **Vushtrri** Kosovo
74 B2 **Vyara** India
Vyatka Rus. Fed. *see* **Kirov**
89 D2 **Vyaz'ma** Rus. Fed.
93 I3 **Vyborg** Rus. Fed.
88 C2 **Vyerkhnyadzvinsk** Belarus
87 D3 **Vyksa** Rus. Fed.
90 B2 **Vylkove** Ukr.
90 A2 **Vynohradiv** Ukr.
89 D2 **Vypolzovo** Rus. Fed.
89 D2 **Vyritsa** Rus. Fed.
91 D2 **Vyselki** Rus. Fed.
90 C1 **Vyshhorod** Ukr.
89 D2 **Vyshniy-Volochek** Rus. Fed.
103 D2 **Vyškov** Czech Rep.
86 C2 **Vytegra** Rus. Fed.

W

114 B3 **Wa** Ghana
100 B2 **Waal** *r.* Neth.
100 B2 **Waalwijk** Neth.
128 C2 **Wabasca** *r.* Can.
128 C2 **Wabasca-Desmarais** Can.
140 B3 **Wabash** *r.* U.S.A.
129 E2 **Wabowden** Can.
143 D3 **Waccasassa Bay** U.S.A.
101 D2 **Wächtersbach** Ger.
139 D2 **Waco** U.S.A.
115 D2 **Waddān** Libya
Waddeneilanden *is* Neth. *see* **West Frisian Islands**
100 B1 **Waddenzee** *sea chan.* Neth.
128 B2 **Waddington, Mount** Can.
100 B1 **Waddinxveen** Neth.
129 D2 **Wadena** Can.
137 D1 **Wadena** U.S.A.
74 A2 **Wadh** Pak.
116 B2 **Wadi Halfa** Sudan
116 B3 **Wad Medani** Sudan
70 C2 **Wafangdian** China
100 B2 **Wageningen** Neth.
127 F2 **Wager Bay** Can.
53 C3 **Wagga Wagga** Austr.
137 D2 **Wahoo** U.S.A.
137 D1 **Wahpeton** U.S.A.
54 B2 **Waiau** *r.* N.Z.
59 C3 **Waigeo** *i.* Indon.
58 B3 **Waikabubak** Indon.
52 A2 **Waikerie** Austr.
54 B2 **Waimate** N.Z.
75 B3 **Wainganga** *r.* India
58 C3 **Waingapu** Indon.
129 C2 **Wainwright** Can.
54 C1 **Waiouru** N.Z.
54 B2 **Waipara** N.Z.
54 C1 **Waipawa** N.Z.
54 B2 **Wairau** *r.* N.Z.
54 C1 **Wairoa** N.Z.
54 B2 **Waitaki** *r.* N.Z.
54 B1 **Waitara** N.Z.
54 B1 **Waiuku** N.Z.
119 E2 **Wajir** Kenya
67 C3 **Wakasa-wan** *b.* Japan
54 A3 **Wakatipu, Lake** N.Z.
129 D2 **Wakaw** Can.
67 C4 **Wakayama** Japan
136 D3 **WaKeeney** U.S.A.
54 B2 **Wakefield** N.Z.
98 C2 **Wakefield** U.K.
48 F1 **Wake Island** N. Pacific Ocean
66 D1 **Wakkanai** Japan
123 D2 **Wakkerstroom** S. Africa
103 D1 **Wałbrzych** Pol.
53 D2 **Walcha** Austr.
100 C1 **Walchum** Ger.
103 D1 **Wałcz** Pol.
99 B2 **Wales** *admin. div.* U.K.
53 C2 **Walgett** Austr.
119 C3 **Walikale** Dem. Rep. Congo
135 C3 **Walker Lake** U.S.A.
52 A2 **Wallaroo** Austr.
98 B2 **Wallasey** U.K.
134 C1 **Walla Walla** U.S.A.
101 D3 **Walldürn** Ger.
53 C2 **Wallendbeen** Austr.
49 G3 **Wallis and Futuna Islands** *terr.* S. Pacific Ocean
96 □ **Walls** U.K.
98 B1 **Walney, Isle of** *i.* U.K.
99 C2 **Walsall** U.K.
136 C3 **Walsenburg** U.S.A.
101 D1 **Walsrode** Ger.
143 D2 **Walterboro** U.S.A.
120 A3 **Walvis Bay** Namibia
119 C2 **Wamba** Dem. Rep. Congo
52 B1 **Wanaaring** Austr.
54 A2 **Wanaka** N.Z.
54 A2 **Wanaka, Lake** N.Z.
130 B2 **Wanapitei Lake** Can.
154 B3 **Wanda** Arg.
66 B1 **Wanda Shan** *mts* China
62 A1 **Wanding** China
54 C1 **Wanganui** N.Z.
53 C3 **Wangaratta** Austr.
65 B1 **Wangqing** China
62 A1 **Wan Hsa-la** Myanmar
71 B4 **Wanning** China
100 B2 **Wanroij** Neth.
99 C3 **Wantage** U.K.
70 A2 **Wanyuan** China
70 A2 **Wanzhou** China
73 B3 **Warangal** India
101 D2 **Warburg** Ger.
50 B2 **Warburton** Austr.
52 A1 **Warburton** *watercourse* Austr.
75 B2 **Wardha** India
96 C1 **Ward Hill** U.K.
128 B2 **Ware** Can.
101 F1 **Waren** Ger.
100 C2 **Warendorf** Ger.
53 D1 **Warialda** Austr.
122 A2 **Warmbad** Namibia

135 C3 **Warm Springs** U.S.A.
134 C2 **Warner Lakes** U.S.A.
143 D2 **Warner Robins** U.S.A.
152 B2 **Warnes** Bol.
52 B3 **Warracknabeal** Austr.
53 C2 **Warrego** *r.* Austr.
53 C2 **Warren** Austr.
142 B2 **Warren** *AR* U.S.A.
140 C2 **Warren** *OH* U.S.A.
141 D2 **Warren** *PA* U.S.A.
97 C1 **Warrenpoint** U.K.
137 E3 **Warrensburg** U.S.A.
122 B2 **Warrenton** S. Africa
115 C4 **Warri** Nigeria
98 B2 **Warrington** U.K.
52 B3 **Warrnambool** Austr.
103 E1 **Warsaw** Pol.
Warszawa Pol. *see* **Warsaw**
103 C1 **Warta** *r.* Pol.
53 D1 **Warwick** Austr.
99 C2 **Warwick** U.K.
135 C3 **Wasco** U.S.A.
136 C1 **Washburn** U.S.A.
141 D3 **Washington** *DC* U.S.A.
137 E2 **Washington** *IA* U.S.A.
140 B3 **Washington** *IN* U.S.A.
137 E3 **Washington** *MO* U.S.A.
143 E1 **Washington** *NC* U.S.A.
140 C2 **Washington** *PA* U.S.A.
134 B1 **Washington** *state* U.S.A.
141 E2 **Washington, Mount** U.S.A.
140 C3 **Washington Court House** U.S.A.
74 A2 **Washuk** Pak.
130 C1 **Waskaganish** Can.
129 E2 **Waskaiowaka Lake** Can.
122 A2 **Wasser** Namibia
130 C2 **Waswanipi, Lac** *l.* Can.
58 C3 **Watampone** Indon.
141 E2 **Waterbury** U.S.A.
129 D2 **Waterbury Lake** Can.
97 C2 **Waterford** Ireland
97 C2 **Waterford Harbour** Ireland
137 E2 **Waterloo** U.S.A.
123 C1 **Waterpoort** S. Africa
141 D2 **Watertown** *NY* U.S.A.
137 D2 **Watertown** *SD* U.S.A.
140 B2 **Watertown** *WI* U.S.A.
141 F2 **Waterville** U.S.A.
99 C3 **Watford** U.K.
136 C1 **Watford City** U.S.A.
129 D2 **Wathaman** *r.* Can.
139 D1 **Watonga** U.S.A.
129 D2 **Watrous** Can.
119 C2 **Watsa** Dem. Rep. Congo
140 B2 **Watseka** U.S.A.
118 C3 **Watsi Kengo** Dem. Rep. Congo
128 B1 **Watson Lake** Can.
135 B3 **Watsonville** U.S.A.
59 C3 **Watubela, Kepulauan** *is* Indon.
59 D3 **Wau** P.N.G.
117 A4 **Wau** Sudan
53 D2 **Wauchope** Austr.
140 B2 **Waukegan** U.S.A.
139 D2 **Waurika** U.S.A.
140 B2 **Wausau** U.S.A.
99 D2 **Waveney** *r.* U.K.
137 E2 **Waverly** U.S.A.
143 D2 **Waycross** U.S.A.
137 D2 **Wayne** U.S.A.
143 D2 **Waynesboro** *GA* U.S.A.
141 D3 **Waynesboro** *VA* U.S.A.
143 D1 **Waynesville** U.S.A.
74 B1 **Wazirabad** Pak.
98 C1 **Wear** *r.* U.K.
139 D2 **Weatherford** U.S.A.
134 B2 **Weaverville** U.S.A.
130 B1 **Webequie** Can.
137 D1 **Webster** U.S.A.
137 E2 **Webster City** U.S.A.
55 Q2 **Weddell Sea** Antarctica
100 B2 **Weert** Neth.
53 C2 **Wee Waa** Austr.
100 C2 **Wegberg** Ger.
103 E1 **Węgorzewo** Pol.
101 F3 **Weiden in der Oberpfalz** Ger.
70 B2 **Weifang** China
70 C2 **Weihai** China
53 C1 **Weilmoringle** Austr.
101 E2 **Weimar** Ger.
70 A2 **Weinan** China
51 D1 **Weipa** Austr.
53 C1 **Weir** *r.* Austr.
140 C2 **Weirton** U.S.A.
62 B1 **Weishan** China
101 E2 **Weißenfels** Ger.
102 C2 **Weißkugel** *mt.* Austria/Italy
103 D1 **Wejherowo** Pol.
128 C1 **Wekweêtì** Can.
140 C3 **Welch** U.S.A.
117 B3 **Weldiya** Eth.
123 C2 **Welkom** S. Africa
99 C2 **Welland** *r.* U.K.
51 C1 **Wellesley Islands** Austr.
53 C2 **Wellington** Austr.
54 B2 **Wellington** N.Z.
122 A3 **Wellington** S. Africa
137 D3 **Wellington** U.S.A.
153 A5 **Wellington, Isla** *i.* Chile
53 C3 **Wellington, Lake** Austr.
128 B2 **Wells** Can.
99 B3 **Wells** U.K.
134 D2 **Wells** U.S.A.
50 B2 **Wells, Lake** *imp. l.* Austr.
54 B1 **Wellsford** N.Z.
98 D2 **Wells-next-the-Sea** U.K.
102 C2 **Wels** Austria
99 B2 **Welshpool** U.K.
123 C2 **Wembesi** S. Africa
130 C1 **Wemindji** Can.
134 B1 **Wenatchee** U.S.A.
71 B4 **Wenchang** China
114 B4 **Wenchi** Ghana
70 C2 **Wendeng** China
101 E1 **Wendisch Evern** Ger.
117 B4 **Wendo** Eth.
134 D2 **Wendover** U.S.A.
71 B3 **Wengyuan** China
71 C3 **Wenling** China
71 A3 **Wenshan** China
52 B2 **Wentworth** Austr.
71 C3 **Wenzhou** China
123 C2 **Wepener** S. Africa
122 B2 **Werda** Botswana
101 F2 **Werdau** Ger.
101 F1 **Werder** Ger.
101 F3 **Wernberg-Köblitz** Ger.
101 E2 **Wernigerode** Ger.
101 D2 **Werra** *r.* Ger.
53 D2 **Werris Creek** Austr.
101 D3 **Wertheim** Ger.
100 C2 **Wesel** Ger.
101 E1 **Wesendorf** Ger.
101 D1 **Weser** *r.* Ger.
101 D1 **Weser** *sea chan.* Ger.
51 C1 **Wessel, Cape** Austr.
51 C1 **Wessel Islands** Austr.
123 C2 **Wesselton** S. Africa
80 B2 **West Bank** *terr.* Asia
140 B2 **West Bend** U.S.A.
99 C2 **West Bromwich** U.K.
100 C2 **Westerburg** Ger.
100 C1 **Westerholt** Ger.
50 B2 **Western Australia** *state* Aus
122 B3 **Western Cape** *prov.* S. Afric
116 A2 **Western Desert** Egypt
73 B3 **Western Ghats** *mts* India
114 A2 **Western Sahara** *terr.* Africa
100 A2 **Westerschelde** *est.* Neth.
100 C1 **Westerstede** Ger.
100 C2 **Westerwald** *hills* Ger.
153 B6 **West Falkland** *i.* Falkland Is
140 B3 **West Frankfort** U.S.A.
100 B1 **West Frisian Islands** *is* Net
147 D2 **West Indies** *is* Caribbean Se
96 A1 **West Loch Roag** *b.* U.K.
128 C2 **Westlock** Can.
100 B2 **Westmalle** Belgium
142 B1 **West Memphis** U.S.A.
140 C3 **Weston** U.S.A.
99 B3 **Weston-super-Mare** U.K.
143 D3 **West Palm Beach** U.S.A.
137 E3 **West Plains** U.S.A.
137 D2 **West Point** U.S.A.
54 B2 **Westport** N.Z.
97 B2 **Westport** Ireland
129 D2 **Westray** Can.
96 C1 **Westray** *i.* U.K.
100 B1 **West-Terschelling** Neth.
140 C3 **West Virginia** *state* U.S.A.
53 C2 **West Wyalong** Austr.
134 D2 **West Yellowstone** U.S.A.
59 C3 **Wetar** *i.* Indon.
128 C2 **Wetaskiwin** Can.
101 D2 **Wetzlar** Ger.
59 D3 **Wewak** P.N.G.
97 C2 **Wexford** Ireland
129 D2 **Weyakwin** Can.
129 D3 **Weyburn** Can.
101 D1 **Weyhe** Ger.
99 B3 **Weymouth** U.K.
54 C1 **Whakatane** N.Z.
129 E1 **Whale Cove** Can.
96 □ **Whalsay** *i.* U.K.
54 B1 **Whangarei** N.Z.
98 C2 **Wharfe** *r.* U.K.
139 D3 **Wharton** U.S.A.
128 C1 **Whatî** Can.
136 B2 **Wheatland** U.S.A.
138 B1 **Wheeler Peak** *NM* U.S.A.
135 D3 **Wheeler Peak** *NV* U.S.A.
140 C2 **Wheeling** U.S.A.
98 B1 **Whernside** *h.* U.K.
128 B2 **Whistler** Can.
98 C1 **Whitby** U.K.
142 B2 **White** *r.* U.S.A.
50 B2 **White, Lake** *imp. l.* Austr.
131 E2 **White Bay** Can.
136 C1 **White Butte** *mt.* U.S.A.
52 B2 **White Cliffs** Austr.
128 C2 **Whitecourt** Can.
134 D1 **Whitefish** U.S.A.
98 B1 **Whitehaven** U.K.
97 D1 **Whitehead** U.K.
128 A1 **Whitehorse** Can.
142 B3 **White Lake** U.S.A.
135 C3 **White Mountain Peak** U.S.A
116 B3 **White Nile** *r.* Sudan/Uganda
86 C2 **White Sea** Rus. Fed.
134 D1 **White Sulphur Springs** U.S.
143 E2 **Whiteville** U.S.A.
114 B3 **White Volta** *r.* Burkina/Ghan
138 B2 **Whitewater Baldy** *mt.* U.S.A.
130 B1 **Whitewater Lake** Can.
129 D2 **Whitewood** Can.
96 B3 **Whithorn** U.K.
54 C1 **Whitianga** N.Z.
135 C3 **Whitney, Mount** U.S.A.
51 D2 **Whitsunday Island** Austr.
52 A2 **Whyalla** Austr.

0 A2 **Wichelen** Belgium
7 D3 **Wichita** U.S.A.
9 D2 **Wichita Falls** U.S.A.
6 C1 **Wick** U.K.
8 A2 **Wickenburg** U.S.A.
97 C2 **Wicklow** Ireland
97 D2 **Wicklow Head** Ireland
97 C2 **Wicklow Mountains** Ireland
98 B2 **Widnes** U.K.
1 D1 **Wiehengebirge** *hills* Ger.
0 C2 **Wiehl** Ger.
3 D1 **Wieluń** Pol.
Wien Austria *see* **Vienna**
3 D2 **Wiener Neustadt** Austria
0 B1 **Wieringerwerf** Neth.
0 D2 **Wiesbaden** Ger.
0 C1 **Wiesmoor** Ger.
3 D1 **Wieżyca** *h.* Pol.
99 C3 **Wight, Isle of** *i.* U.K.
96 B3 **Wigtown** U.K.
0 B2 **Wijchen** Neth.
52 B2 **Wilcannia** Austr.
23 C3 **Wild Coast** S. Africa
23 C2 **Wilge** *r.* S. Africa
0 D1 **Wilhelmshaven** Ger.
1 D2 **Wilkes-Barre** U.S.A.
55 H3 **Wilkes Land** *reg.* Antarctica
29 D2 **Wilkie** Can.
38 B2 **Willcox** U.S.A.
0 B2 **Willebroek** Belgium
47 D3 **Willemstad** Neth. Antilles
52 B3 **William, Mount** Austr.
52 A1 **William Creek** Austr.
38 A1 **Williams** U.S.A.
41 D3 **Williamsburg** U.S.A.
28 B2 **Williams Lake** Can.
40 C3 **Williamson** U.S.A.
41 D2 **Williamsport** U.S.A.
43 E1 **Williamston** U.S.A.
22 B3 **Williston** S. Africa
36 C1 **Williston** U.S.A.
28 B2 **Williston Lake** Can.
35 B3 **Willits** U.S.A.
37 D1 **Willmar** U.S.A.
22 B3 **Willowmore** S. Africa
23 C3 **Willowvale** S. Africa
50 B2 **Wills, Lake** *imp. l.* Austr.
52 A3 **Willunga** Austr.
52 A2 **Wilmington** Austr.
41 D3 **Wilmington** *DE* U.S.A.
43 E2 **Wilmington** *NC* U.S.A.
0 D2 **Wilnsdorf** Ger.
43 E1 **Wilson** U.S.A.
53 C3 **Wilson's Promontory** *pen.* Austr.
0 B3 **Wiltz** Lux.
50 B2 **Wiluna** Austr.
99 C3 **Winchester** U.K.
40 C3 **Winchester** *KY* U.S.A.
41 D3 **Winchester** *VA* U.S.A.
98 B1 **Windermere** *l.* U.K.
20 A3 **Windhoek** Namibia
37 D2 **Windom** U.S.A.
51 D2 **Windorah** Austr.
36 B2 **Wind River Range** *mts* U.S.A.
53 D2 **Windsor** Austr.
30 B2 **Windsor** Can.
47 D3 **Windward Islands** Caribbean Sea
47 C3 **Windward Passage** Cuba/Haiti
37 D3 **Winfield** U.S.A.
0 A2 **Wingene** Belgium
53 D2 **Wingham** Austr.
30 B1 **Winisk** *r.* Can.
30 B1 **Winisk (abandoned)** Can.
30 B1 **Winisk Lake** Can.
63 A2 **Winkana** Myanmar
129 E3 **Winkler** Can.
114 B4 **Winneba** Ghana
140 B2 **Winnebago, Lake** U.S.A.
134 C2 **Winnemucca** U.S.A.
136 C2 **Winner** U.S.A.
142 B2 **Winnfield** U.S.A.
137 E1 **Winnibigoshish, Lake** U.S.A.
129 E3 **Winnipeg** Can.
129 E2 **Winnipeg** *r.* Can.
129 E2 **Winnipeg, Lake** Can.
129 D2 **Winnipegosis, Lake** Can.
141 E2 **Winnipesaukee, Lake** U.S.A.
142 B2 **Winnsboro** U.S.A.
137 E2 **Winona** *MN* U.S.A.
142 C2 **Winona** *MS* U.S.A.
100 C1 **Winschoten** Neth.
101 D1 **Winsen (Aller)** Ger.
101 E1 **Winsen (Luhe)** Ger.
138 A1 **Winslow** U.S.A.
143 D1 **Winston-Salem** U.S.A.
101 D2 **Winterberg** Ger.
143 D3 **Winter Haven** U.S.A.
100 C2 **Winterswijk** Neth.
105 D2 **Winterthur** Switz.
51 D2 **Winton** Austr.
54 A3 **Winton** N.Z.
52 A2 **Wirrabara** Austr.
99 D2 **Wisbech** U.K.
140 A2 **Wisconsin** *r.* U.S.A.
140 B2 **Wisconsin** *state* U.S.A.
140 B2 **Wisconsin Rapids** U.S.A.
Wisła *r.* Pol. *see* **Vistula**
101 E1 **Wismar** Ger.
123 C2 **Witbank** S. Africa
98 D2 **Withernsea** U.K.
100 B1 **Witmarsum** Neth.
99 C3 **Witney** U.K.
123 D2 **Witrivier** S. Africa
101 F2 **Wittenberg, Lutherstadt** Ger.
101 E1 **Wittenberge** Ger.
101 E1 **Wittenburg** Ger.
101 E1 **Wittingen** Ger.
100 C3 **Wittlich** Ger.
100 C1 **Wittmund** Ger.
101 F1 **Wittstock** Ger.
120 A3 **Witvlei** Namibia
101 D2 **Witzenhausen** Ger.
103 D1 **Władysławowo** Pol.
103 D1 **Włocławek** Pol.
53 C3 **Wodonga** Austr.
59 C3 **Wokam** *i.* Indon.
99 C3 **Woking** U.K.
101 F2 **Wolfen** Ger.
101 E1 **Wolfenbüttel** Ger.
101 D2 **Wolfhagen** Ger.
136 B1 **Wolf Point** U.S.A.
101 E1 **Wolfsburg** Ger.
100 C3 **Wolfstein** Ger.
131 D2 **Wolfville** Can.
102 C1 **Wolgast** Ger.
102 C1 **Wolin** Pol.
129 D2 **Wollaston Lake** Can.
129 D2 **Wollaston Lake** Can.
126 D2 **Wollaston Peninsula** Can.
53 D2 **Wollongong** Austr.
101 E2 **Wolmirsleben** Ger.
101 E1 **Wolmirstedt** Ger.
100 C1 **Wolvega** Neth.
99 B2 **Wolverhampton** U.K.
65 B2 **Wŏnju** S. Korea
128 B2 **Wonowon** Can.
65 B2 **Wŏnsan** N. Korea
53 C3 **Wonthaggi** Austr.
52 A2 **Woocalla** Austr.
51 C1 **Woodah, Isle** *i.* Austr.
99 D2 **Woodbridge** U.K.
136 B3 **Woodland Park** U.S.A.
50 C2 **Woodroffe, Mount** Austr.
51 C1 **Woods, Lake** *imp. l.* Austr.
129 E3 **Woods, Lake of the** Can./U.S.A.
53 C3 **Woods Point** Austr.
131 D2 **Woodstock** *N.B.* Can.
140 C2 **Woodstock** *Ont.* Can.
54 C2 **Woodville** N.Z.
139 D1 **Woodward** U.S.A.
53 D2 **Woolgoolga** Austr.
52 A2 **Woomera** Austr.
140 C2 **Wooster** U.S.A.
122 A3 **Worcester** S. Africa
99 B2 **Worcester** U.K.
141 E2 **Worcester** U.S.A.
102 C2 **Wörgl** Austria
98 B1 **Workington** U.K.
98 C2 **Worksop** U.K.
136 B2 **Worland** U.S.A.
101 D3 **Worms** Ger.
99 C3 **Worthing** U.K.
137 D2 **Worthington** U.S.A.
58 C3 **Wotu** Indon.
59 C3 **Wowoni** *i.* Indon.
83 N2 **Wrangel Island** Rus. Fed.
128 A2 **Wrangell** U.S.A.
96 B1 **Wrath, Cape** U.K.
136 C2 **Wray** U.S.A.
122 A2 **Wreck Point** S. Africa
98 B2 **Wrexham** U.K.
136 B2 **Wright** U.S.A.
63 A2 **Wrightmyo** India
128 B1 **Wrigley** Can.
103 D1 **Wrocław** Pol.
103 D1 **Września** Pol.
70 B2 **Wu'an** China
70 A2 **Wuhai** China
70 B2 **Wuhan** China
70 B2 **Wuhu** China
Wujin China *see* **Changzhou**
115 C4 **Wukari** Nigeria
62 B1 **Wuliang Shan** *mts* China
59 C3 **Wuliaru** *i.* Indon.
71 A3 **Wumeng Shan** *mts* China
130 B1 **Wunnummin Lake** Can.
101 F2 **Wunsiedel** Ger.
101 D1 **Wunstorf** Ger.
62 A1 **Wuntho** Myanmar
100 C2 **Wuppertal** Ger.
122 A3 **Wuppertal** S. Africa
101 E2 **Wurzbach** Ger.
101 D3 **Würzburg** Ger.
101 F2 **Wurzen** Ger.
68 C2 **Wuwei** China
70 A2 **Wuxi** *Chongqing* China
70 C2 **Wuxi** *Jiangsu* China
Wuxing China *see* **Huzhou**
71 A3 **Wuxuan** China
Wuyang China *see* **Zhenyuan**
69 E1 **Wuyiling** China
71 B3 **Wuyishan** China
71 B3 **Wuyi Shan** *mts* China
70 A1 **Wuyuan** China
71 A4 **Wuzhishan** China
70 A2 **Wuzhong** China
71 B3 **Wuzhou** China
53 C2 **Wyangala Reservoir** Austr.
52 B3 **Wycheproof** Austr.
99 B3 **Wye** *r.* U.K.
50 B1 **Wyndham** Austr.
142 B1 **Wynne** U.S.A.
129 D2 **Wynyard** Can.
136 B2 **Wyoming** *state* U.S.A.
103 E1 **Wyszków** Pol.
140 C3 **Wytheville** U.S.A.

X

117 D3 **Xaafuun** Somalia
62 B2 **Xaignabouli** Laos
121 C3 **Xai-Xai** Moz.
70 A1 **Xamba** China
62 B1 **Xam Nua** Laos
120 A2 **Xangongo** Angola
81 C2 **Xankändi** Azer.
111 B2 **Xanthi** Greece
150 B3 **Xapuri** Brazil
107 C2 **Xàtiva** Spain
Xiaguan China *see* **Dali**
71 B3 **Xiamen** China
70 A2 **Xi'an** China
70 A3 **Xianfeng** China
70 B2 **Xiangfan** China
62 A1 **Xianggelila** China
Xiangjiang China *see* **Huichang**
71 B3 **Xiangtan** China
Xiangyang China *see* **Xiangfan**
70 B2 **Xiantao** China
70 A2 **Xianyang** China
70 B2 **Xiaogan** China
69 E1 **Xiao Hinggan Ling** *mts* China
70 C2 **Xiaoshan** China
62 B1 **Xichang** China
145 C2 **Xicohténcatl** Mex.
71 A3 **Xifeng** *Guizhou* China
75 C2 **Xigazê** China
83 I4 **Xilinhot** China
70 B2 **Xincai** China
68 C2 **Xinghai** China
70 B2 **Xinghua** China
71 B3 **Xingning** China
70 A2 **Xingping** China
70 B2 **Xingtai** China
151 C2 **Xingu** *r.* Brazil
71 A3 **Xingyi** China
71 B3 **Xinhua** China
68 C2 **Xining** China
Xinjiang Uygur Autonomous Region *aut. reg.* China *see* **Xinjiang Uygur Zizhiqu**
75 C1 **Xinjiang Uygur Zizhiqu** *aut. reg.* China
Xinjing China *see* **Jingxi**
65 A1 **Xinmin** China
71 B3 **Xinning** China
70 B2 **Xintai** China
70 B2 **Xinxiang** China
70 B2 **Xinyang** China
70 B2 **Xinyi** China
71 B3 **Xinyu** China
69 D2 **Xinzhou** *Shanxi* China
70 B2 **Xinzhou** *Shanxi* China
106 B1 **Xinzo de Limia** Spain
Xiongshan China *see* **Zhenghe**
68 C2 **Xiqing Shan** *mts* China
151 D3 **Xique Xique** Brazil
70 A1 **Xishanzui** China
71 A3 **Xiushan** China
71 B3 **Xiuying** China
70 B2 **Xixia** China
68 B2 **Xizang Zizhiqu** *aut. reg.* China
76 B2 **Xo'jayli** Uzbek.
70 B2 **Xuancheng** China
71 A3 **Xuanwei** China
70 B2 **Xuchang** China
Xucheng China *see* **Xuwen**
117 C4 **Xuddur** Somalia
Xujiang China *see* **Guangchang**
71 B3 **Xun Jiang** *r.* China
71 B3 **Xunwu** China
107 C2 **Xúquer, Riu** *r.* Spain
71 B3 **Xuwen** China
71 A3 **Xuyong** China
70 B2 **Xuzhou** China

Y

117 B4 **Yabēlo** Eth.
69 D1 **Yablonovyy Khrebet** *mts* Rus. Fed.
143 D1 **Yadkin** *r.* U.S.A.
75 C2 **Yadong** China
89 E2 **Yagnitsa** Rus. Fed.
118 B1 **Yagoua** Cameroon
128 C3 **Yahk** Can.
144 B2 **Yahualica** Mex.
80 B2 **Yahyalı** Turkey
67 C4 **Yaizu** Japan
134 B1 **Yakima** U.S.A.
114 B3 **Yako** Burkina
66 D2 **Yakumo** Japan
126 B3 **Yakutat** U.S.A.
83 J2 **Yakutsk** Rus. Fed.
91 D2 **Yakymivka** Ukr.
63 B3 **Yala** Thai.
53 C3 **Yallourn** Austr.
111 C2 **Yalova** Turkey
91 C3 **Yalta** Ukr.
65 A1 **Yalu Jiang** *r.* China/N. Korea
67 D3 **Yamagata** Japan
67 B4 **Yamaguchi** Japan
Yamal, Poluostrov *pen.* Rus. Fed. *see* **Yamal Peninsula**
86 F1 **Yamal Peninsula** Rus. Fed.
53 D1 **Yamba** Austr.
117 A4 **Yambio** Sudan
110 C2 **Yambol** Bulg.
86 G2 **Yamburg** Rus. Fed.
62 A1 **Yamethin** Myanmar
114 B4 **Yamoussoukro** Côte d'Ivoire
90 B2 **Yampil'** Ukr.
75 C2 **Yamuna** *r.* India
75 D2 **Yamzho Yumco** *l.* China
83 K2 **Yana** *r.* Rus. Fed.
70 A2 **Yan'an** China
150 A3 **Yanaoca** Peru
78 A2 **Yanbu' al Baḩr** Saudi Arabia
70 C2 **Yancheng** China
50 A3 **Yanchep** Austr.
70 B2 **Yangcheng** China
71 B3 **Yangchun** China
65 B2 **Yangdok** N. Korea
71 B3 **Yangjiang** China
Yangôn Myanmar *see* **Rangoon**
70 B2 **Yangquan** China
71 B3 **Yangshuo** China
70 C3 **Yangtze** *r.* China
69 E2 **Yangtze, Mouth of the** China
70 B2 **Yangzhou** China
65 B1 **Yanji** China
137 D2 **Yankton** U.S.A.
83 K2 **Yano-Indigirskaya Nizmennost'** *lowland* Rus. Fed.
83 K2 **Yanskiy Zaliv** *g.* Rus. Fed.
53 C1 **Yantabulla** Austr.
70 C2 **Yantai** China
118 B2 **Yaoundé** Cameroon
59 D2 **Yap** *i.* Micronesia
59 D3 **Yapen** *i.* Indon.
59 D3 **Yapen, Selat** *sea chan.* Indon.
144 A2 **Yaqui** *r.* Mex.
51 D2 **Yaraka** Austr.
86 D3 **Yaransk** Rus. Fed.
48 F2 **Yaren** Nauru
78 B3 **Yarīm** Yemen
77 D3 **Yarkant He** *r.* China
75 D2 **Yarlung Zangbo** *r.* China
131 D2 **Yarmouth** Can.
86 F2 **Yarongo** Rus. Fed.
89 E2 **Yaroslavl'** Rus. Fed.
66 B2 **Yaroslavskiy** Rus. Fed.
53 C3 **Yarram** Austr.
89 D2 **Yartsevo** Rus. Fed.
89 E3 **Yasnogorsk** Rus. Fed.
63 B2 **Yasothon** Thai.
53 C2 **Yass** Austr.
111 C3 **Yatağan** Turkey
129 E1 **Yathkyed Lake** Can.
67 B4 **Yatsushiro** Japan
150 B2 **Yavari** *r.* Brazil/Peru
75 B2 **Yavatmal** India
90 A2 **Yavoriv** Ukr.
67 B4 **Yawatahama** Japan
81 D2 **Yazd** Iran
142 B2 **Yazoo City** U.S.A.
111 B3 **Ydra** *i.* Greece
63 A2 **Ye** Myanmar
77 D3 **Yecheng** China
144 B2 **Yécora** Mex.
89 E3 **Yefremov** Rus. Fed.
89 E2 **Yegor'yevsk** Rus. Fed.
117 B4 **Yei** Sudan
86 F3 **Yekaterinburg** Rus. Fed.
89 E3 **Yelets** Rus. Fed.
114 A3 **Yélimané** Mali
96 □ **Yell** *i.* U.K.
128 C1 **Yellowknife** Can.
70 B2 **Yellow River** *r.* China
69 E2 **Yellow Sea** N. Pacific Ocean
136 C1 **Yellowstone** *r.* U.S.A.
136 A2 **Yellowstone Lake** U.S.A.
88 C3 **Yel'sk** Belarus
78 B3 **Yemen** *country* Asia
86 E2 **Yemva** Rus. Fed.
91 D2 **Yenakiyeve** Ukr.
62 A1 **Yenangyaung** Myanmar
62 B1 **Yên Bai** Vietnam
114 B4 **Yendi** Ghana
111 C3 **Yenice** Turkey
111 C3 **Yenifoça** Turkey
68 C1 **Yenisey** *r.* Rus. Fed.
53 C2 **Yeoval** Austr.
99 B3 **Yeovil** U.K.
51 E2 **Yeppoon** Austr.
83 I2 **Yerbogachen** Rus. Fed.
81 C1 **Yerevan** Armenia
77 D1 **Yereymentau** Kazakh.
87 D3 **Yershov** Rus. Fed.
65 B2 **Yesan** S. Korea
77 C1 **Yesil'** Kazakh.
111 C3 **Yeşilova** Turkey
99 A3 **Yes Tor** *h.* U.K.
53 D1 **Yetman** Austr.
62 A1 **Ye-U** Myanmar
104 B2 **Yeu, Île d'** *i.* France
91 C2 **Yevpatoriya** Ukr.
91 D2 **Yeya** *r.* Rus. Fed.
91 D2 **Yeysk** Rus. Fed.
88 C2 **Yezyaryshcha** Belarus
71 A3 **Yibin** China
70 B2 **Yichang** China
69 E1 **Yichun** *Heilong.* China
71 B3 **Yichun** *Jiangxi* China
110 C2 **Yıldız Dağları** *mts* Turkey
80 B2 **Yıldızeli** Turkey
70 A2 **Yinchuan** China
65 B1 **Yingchengzi** China
71 B3 **Yingde** China
70 C1 **Yingkou** China
70 B2 **Yingshan** *Hubei* China
70 A2 **Yingshan** *Sichuan* China

1 B3 **Yingtan** China
7 E2 **Yining** China
7 B4 **Yirga Alem** Eth.
0 B2 **Yishui** China
8 C2 **Yiwu** China
1 B3 **Yiyang** China
1 A3 **Yizhou** China
2 I2 **Yli-Kitka** *l.* Fin.
2 H2 **Ylitornio** Fin.
2 H3 **Ylivieska** Fin.
1 C2 **Yogyakarta** Indon.
8 B2 **Yoko** Cameroon
7 C3 **Yokohama** Japan
5 D4 **Yola** Nigeria
7 D3 **Yonezawa** Japan
1 B3 **Yong'an** China
1 B3 **Yongchun** China
0 A2 **Yongdeng** China
5 B2 **Yŏngdŏk** S. Korea
1 C3 **Yongkang** China
2 B1 **Yongsheng** China
1 B3 **Yongzhou** China
0 A1 **Yopal** Col.
0 A3 **York** Austr.
8 C2 **York** U.K.
7 D2 **York** *NE* U.S.A.
1 D3 **York** *PA* U.S.A.
1 D1 **York, Cape** Austr.
2 A3 **Yorke Peninsula** Austr.
2 A3 **Yorketown** Austr.
8 C2 **Yorkshire Wolds** *hills* U.K.
9 D2 **Yorkton** Can.
7 D3 **Yoshkar-Ola** Rus. Fed.
7 C3 **Youghal** Ireland
3 C2 **Young** Austr.
2 A3 **Younghusband Peninsula** Austr.
0 C2 **Youngstown** U.S.A.
4 B3 **Youvarou** Mali
7 E2 **Youyi Feng** *mt.* China/Rus. Fed.
0 B2 **Yozgat** Turkey
4 B2 **Yreka** U.S.A.
Yr Wyddfa *mt.* U.K. *see* **Snowdon**
5 C2 **Yssingeaux** France
3 F4 **Ystad** Sweden
Ysyk-Köl Kyrg. *see* **Balykchy**
7 D2 **Ysyk-Köl** *salt l.* Kyrg.
2 A3 **Ytri-Rangá** *r.* Iceland
2 B1 **Yuanjiang** China
2 B1 **Yuan Jiang** *r.* China
2 B1 **Yuanmou** China
5 B3 **Yuba City** U.S.A.
6 D2 **Yūbari** Japan
5 C3 **Yucatán** *pen.* Mex.
6 B2 **Yucatan Channel** Cuba/Mex.
0 C2 **Yuendumu** Austr.
1 B3 **Yueyang** China
6 F2 **Yugorsk** Rus. Fed.
Yugoslavia Europe *see* **Bosnia-Herzegovina, Croatia, Kosovo, Macedonia, Montenegro, Serbia, Slovenia**
3 L2 **Yukagirskoye Ploskogor'ye** *plat.* Rus. Fed.
6 A2 **Yukon** *r.* Can./U.S.A.
8 A1 **Yukon Territory** *admin. div.* Can.
1 B3 **Yulin** *Guangxi* China
0 A2 **Yulin** *Shaanxi* China
2 B1 **Yulong Xueshan** *mt.* China
8 A2 **Yuma** *AZ* U.S.A.
6 C2 **Yuma** *CO* U.S.A.
Yumen China *see* **Laojunmiao**
0 B2 **Yunak** Turkey
0 B2 **Yuncheng** China
1 B3 **Yunfu** China
62 B1 **Yunnan** *prov.* China
52 A2 **Yunta** Austr.
70 B2 **Yunyang** China
150 A2 **Yurimaguas** Peru
77 E3 **Yurungkax He** *r.* China
71 C3 **Yü Shan** *mt.* Taiwan
68 C2 **Yushu** China
Yushuwan China *see* **Huaihua**
81 C1 **Yusufeli** Turkey
77 E3 **Yutian** China
62 B1 **Yuxi** China
66 D2 **Yuzhno-Kuril'sk** Rus. Fed.
83 K3 **Yuzhno-Sakhalinsk** Rus. Fed.
91 C2 **Yuzhnoukrayins'k** Ukr.
69 D2 **Yuzhou** China
104 C2 **Yvetot** France

Z

100 B1 **Zaandam** Neth.
69 D1 **Zabaykal'sk** Rus. Fed.
78 B3 **Zabīd** Yemen
76 C3 **Zābol** Iran
79 D2 **Zābolī** Iran
144 B3 **Zacapu** Mex.
144 B2 **Zacatecas** Mex.
145 C3 **Zacatepec** Mex.
145 C3 **Zacatlán** Mex.
111 B3 **Zacharo** Greece
144 B2 **Zacoalco** Mex.
145 C2 **Zacualtipán** Mex.
109 C2 **Zadar** Croatia
63 A3 **Zadetkyi Kyun** *i.* Myanmar
89 E3 **Zadonsk** Rus. Fed.
106 B2 **Zafra** Spain
109 C1 **Zagreb** Croatia
Zagros, Kūhhā-ye *mts* Iran *see* **Zagros Mountains**
81 C2 **Zagros Mountains** Iran
79 D2 **Zāhedān** Iran
80 B2 **Zahlé** Lebanon
78 B3 **Ẓahrān** Saudi Arabia
Zaire *country* Africa *see* **Congo, Democratic Republic of the**
109 D2 **Zaječar** Serbia
89 E3 **Zakharovo** Rus. Fed.
81 C2 **Zākhō** Iraq
111 B3 **Zakynthos** Greece
111 B3 **Zakynthos** *i.* Greece
103 D2 **Zalaegerszeg** Hungary
110 B1 **Zalău** Romania
78 B2 **Ẓalim** Saudi Arabia
117 A3 **Zalingei** Sudan
78 A2 **Ẓalmā, Jabal aẓ** *mt.* Saudi Arabia
128 C2 **Zama City** Can.
120 C2 **Zambeze** *r.* Moz.
Zambeze *r.* Moz. *see* **Zambeze**
120 C2 **Zambezi** *r.* Africa
120 B2 **Zambezi** Zambia
120 B2 **Zambia** *country* Africa
64 B2 **Zamboanga** Phil.
64 B2 **Zamboanga Peninsula** Phil.
106 B1 **Zamora** Spain
144 B3 **Zamora de Hidalgo** Mex.
103 E1 **Zamość** Pol.
75 B1 **Zanda** China
100 B2 **Zandvliet** Belgium
140 C3 **Zanesville** U.S.A.
81 C2 **Zanjān** Iran
75 B1 **Zanskar Mountains** India
Zante *i.* Greece *see* **Zakynthos**
119 D3 **Zanzibar** Tanz.
119 D3 **Zanzibar Island** Tanz.
89 E3 **Zaokskiy** Rus. Fed.
115 C2 **Zaouatallaz** Alg.
70 B2 **Zaozhuang** China
89 D2 **Zapadnaya Dvina** *r.* Europe
89 D2 **Zapadnaya Dvina** Rus. Fed.
68 B1 **Zapadnyy Sayan** *reg.* Rus. Fed.
139 D3 **Zapata** U.S.A.
92 J2 **Zapolyarnyy** Rus. Fed.
91 D2 **Zaporizhzhya** Ukr.
101 E2 **Zappendorf** Ger.
80 B2 **Zara** Turkey
145 B2 **Zaragoza** Mex.
107 C1 **Zaragoza** Spain
76 B3 **Zarand** Iran
76 C3 **Zaranj** Afgh.
88 C2 **Zarasai** Lith.
89 E3 **Zaraysk** Rus. Fed.
150 B1 **Zaraza** Venez.
115 C3 **Zaria** Nigeria
90 B1 **Zarichne** Ukr.
81 D3 **Zarqān** Iran
66 B2 **Zarubino** Rus. Fed.
103 D1 **Żary** Pol.
115 D1 **Zarzis** Tunisia
123 C3 **Zastron** S. Africa
69 E1 **Zavitinsk** Rus. Fed.
103 D1 **Zawiercie** Pol.
77 E2 **Zaysan, Lake** Kazakh.
Zaysan, Ozero *l.* Kazakh. *see* **Zaysan, Lake**
90 B1 **Zdolbuniv** Ukr.
93 F4 **Zealand** *i.* Denmark
Zealand *i.* Denmark *see* **Zealand**
100 A2 **Zeebrugge** Belgium
123 C2 **Zeerust** S. Africa
50 C2 **Zeil, Mount** Austr.
101 F2 **Zeitz** Ger.
88 B3 **Zelenogradsk** Rus. Fed.
82 E1 **Zemlya Aleksandry** *i.* Rus. Fed.
82 F1 **Zemlya Vil'cheka** *i.* Rus. Fed.
107 D2 **Zemmora** Alg.
145 C3 **Zempoaltépetl, Nudo de** *mt.* Mex.
65 B1 **Zengfeng Shan** *mt.* China
105 D2 **Zermatt** Switz.
91 E2 **Zernograd** Rus. Fed.
101 E2 **Zeulenroda** Ger.
101 D1 **Zeven** Ger.
100 C2 **Zevenaar** Neth.
83 J3 **Zeya** Rus. Fed.
79 C2 **Zeydābād** Iran
83 J3 **Zeyskoye Vodokhranilishche** *resr* Rus. Fed.
103 D1 **Zgierz** Pol.
88 B3 **Zhabinka** Belarus
76 A2 **Zhalpaktal** Kazakh.
77 C1 **Zhaltyr** Kazakh.
76 B2 **Zhanaozen** Kazakh.
Zhangde China *see* **Anyang**
71 B3 **Zhangjiajie** China
70 B1 **Zhangjiakou** China
71 B3 **Zhangping** China
71 B3 **Zhangshu** China
68 C2 **Zhangye** China
71 B3 **Zhangzhou** China
87 D4 **Zhanibek** Kazakh.
71 B3 **Zhanjiang** China
71 B3 **Zhao'an** China
71 B3 **Zhaoqing** China
71 A3 **Zhaotong** China
75 C1 **Zhari Namco** *salt l.* China
77 E2 **Zharkent** Kazakh.
89 D2 **Zharkovskiy** Rus. Fed.
77 E2 **Zharma** Kazakh.
90 C2 **Zhashkiv** Ukr.
71 C3 **Zhejiang** *prov.* China
82 F1 **Zhelaniya, Mys** *c.* Rus. Fed.

89 E3 **Zheleznogorsk** Rus. Fed.
70 A2 **Zhenba** China
71 A3 **Zheng'an** China
71 B3 **Zhenghe** China
70 B2 **Zhengzhou** China
70 B2 **Zhenjiang** China
71 A3 **Zhenyuan** China
91 E1 **Zherdevka** Rus. Fed.
86 D2 **Zheshart** Rus. Fed.
77 C2 **Zhezkazgan** *Karagandinskaya Oblast'* Kazakh.
77 C2 **Zhezkazgan** *Karagandinskaya Oblast'* Kazakh.
83 J2 **Zhigansk** Rus. Fed.
Zhi Qu *r.* China *see* **Yangtze**
76 C1 **Zhitikara** Kazakh.
88 D3 **Zhlobin** Belarus
90 B2 **Zhmerynka** Ukr.
74 A1 **Zhob** Pak.
83 L1 **Zhokhova, Ostrov** *i.* Rus. Fed.
75 C2 **Zhongba** China
Zhonghe China *see* **Xiushan**
70 A2 **Zhongning** China
71 B3 **Zhongshan** China
Zhongshan China *see* **Lupanshui**
70 A2 **Zhongwei** China
Zhongxin China *see* **Xianggelila**
70 B2 **Zhoukou** China
70 C2 **Zhoushan** China
91 C2 **Zhovti Vody** Ukr.
65 A2 **Zhuanghe** China
70 B2 **Zhucheng** China
89 D3 **Zhukovka** Rus. Fed.
89 E2 **Zhukovskiy** Rus. Fed.
70 B2 **Zhumadian** China
Zhuoyang China *see* **Suiping**
71 B3 **Zhuzhou** *Hunan* China
71 B3 **Zhuzhou** *Hunan* China
90 A2 **Zhydachiv** Ukr.
88 C3 **Zhytkavichy** Belarus
90 B1 **Zhytomyr** Ukr.
103 D2 **Žiar nad Hronom** Slovakia
70 B2 **Zibo** China
103 D1 **Zielona Góra** Pol.
62 A1 **Zigaing** Myanmar
71 A3 **Zigong** China
114 A3 **Ziguinchor** Senegal
144 B3 **Zihuatanejo** Mex.
103 D2 **Žilina** Slovakia
83 H3 **Zima** Rus. Fed.
145 C2 **Zimapán** Mex.
121 B2 **Zimbabwe** *country* Africa
114 A4 **Zimmi** Sierra Leone
110 C2 **Zimnicea** Romania
115 C3 **Zinder** Niger
78 B3 **Zinjibār** Yemen
103 D2 **Zirc** Hungary
62 A1 **Ziro** India
79 C2 **Zīr Rūd** Iran
103 D2 **Zistersdorf** Austria
145 B3 **Zitácuaro** Mex.
103 C1 **Zittau** Ger.
87 E3 **Zlatoust** Rus. Fed.
103 D2 **Zlín** Czech Rep.
89 D3 **Zlynka** Rus. Fed.
89 E3 **Zmiyevka** Rus. Fed.
91 D2 **Zmiyiv** Ukr.
89 E3 **Znamenka** *Orlovskaya Oblast'* Rus. Fed.
91 E1 **Znamenka** *Tambovskaya Oblast'* Rus. Fed.
91 C2 **Znam"yanka** Ukr.
103 D2 **Znojmo** Czech Rep.
91 D1 **Zolochiv** *Kharkivs'ka Oblas* Ukr.
90 A2 **Zolochiv** *L'vivs'ka Oblast'* U
91 C2 **Zolotonosha** Ukr.
89 E3 **Zolotukhino** Rus. Fed.
121 C2 **Zomba** Malawi
80 B1 **Zonguldak** Turkey
105 D3 **Zonza** *Corse* France
114 B4 **Zorzor** Liberia
115 D2 **Zouar** Chad
114 A2 **Zouérat** Maur.
109 D1 **Zrenjanin** Serbia
89 D2 **Zubtsov** Rus. Fed.
105 D2 **Zug** Switz.
81 C1 **Zugdidi** Georgia
106 B2 **Zújar** *r.* Spain
100 C2 **Zülpich** Ger.
121 C2 **Zumbo** Moz.
145 C3 **Zumpango** Mex.
138 B1 **Zuni Mountains** U.S.A.
71 A3 **Zunyi** China
109 C1 **Županja** Croatia
105 D2 **Zürich** Switz.
100 C1 **Zutphen** Neth.
115 D1 **Zuwārah** Libya
90 C2 **Zvenyhorodka** Ukr.
121 C3 **Zvishavane** Zimbabwe
103 D2 **Zvolen** Slovakia
109 C2 **Zvornik** Bos.-Herz.
114 B4 **Zwedru** Liberia
123 C3 **Zwelitsha** S. Africa
103 D2 **Zwettl** Austria
101 F2 **Zwickau** Ger.
100 C1 **Zwolle** Neth.
83 L2 **Zyryanka** Rus. Fed.

Acknowledgements

pages 36–37

Land Cover map data courtesy of
Center for Remote Sensing, Boston University, USA

pages 38–39

Population map data:
Gridded Population of the World (GPW), Version 3.
Palisades, NY: CIESN, Columbia University. Available at
http://sedac.ciesin.columbia.edu/plue/gpw